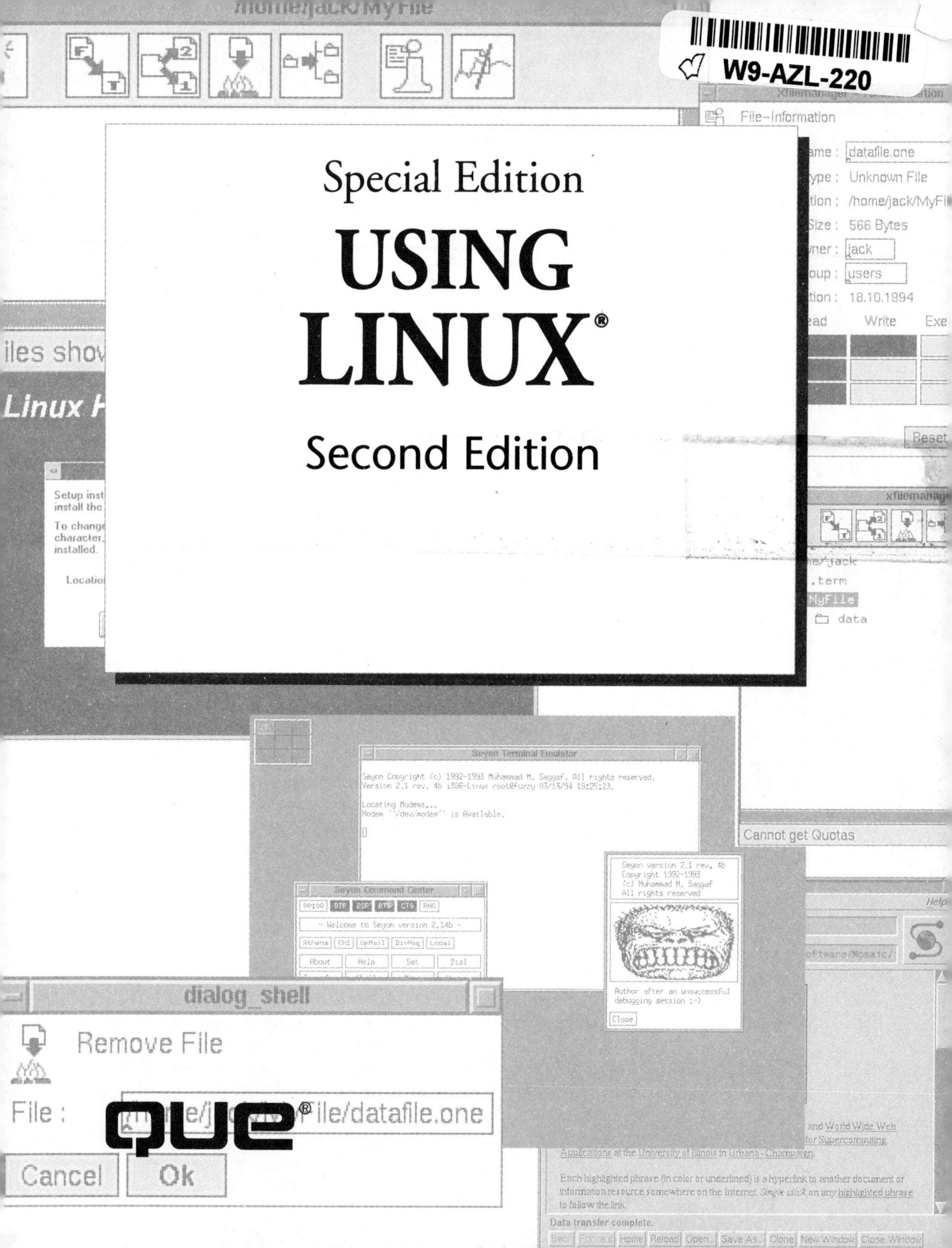
W9-AZL-220
Special Edition
USING
LINUX®
Second Edition
dialog_shell
Remove File
Cancel
Ok
que®

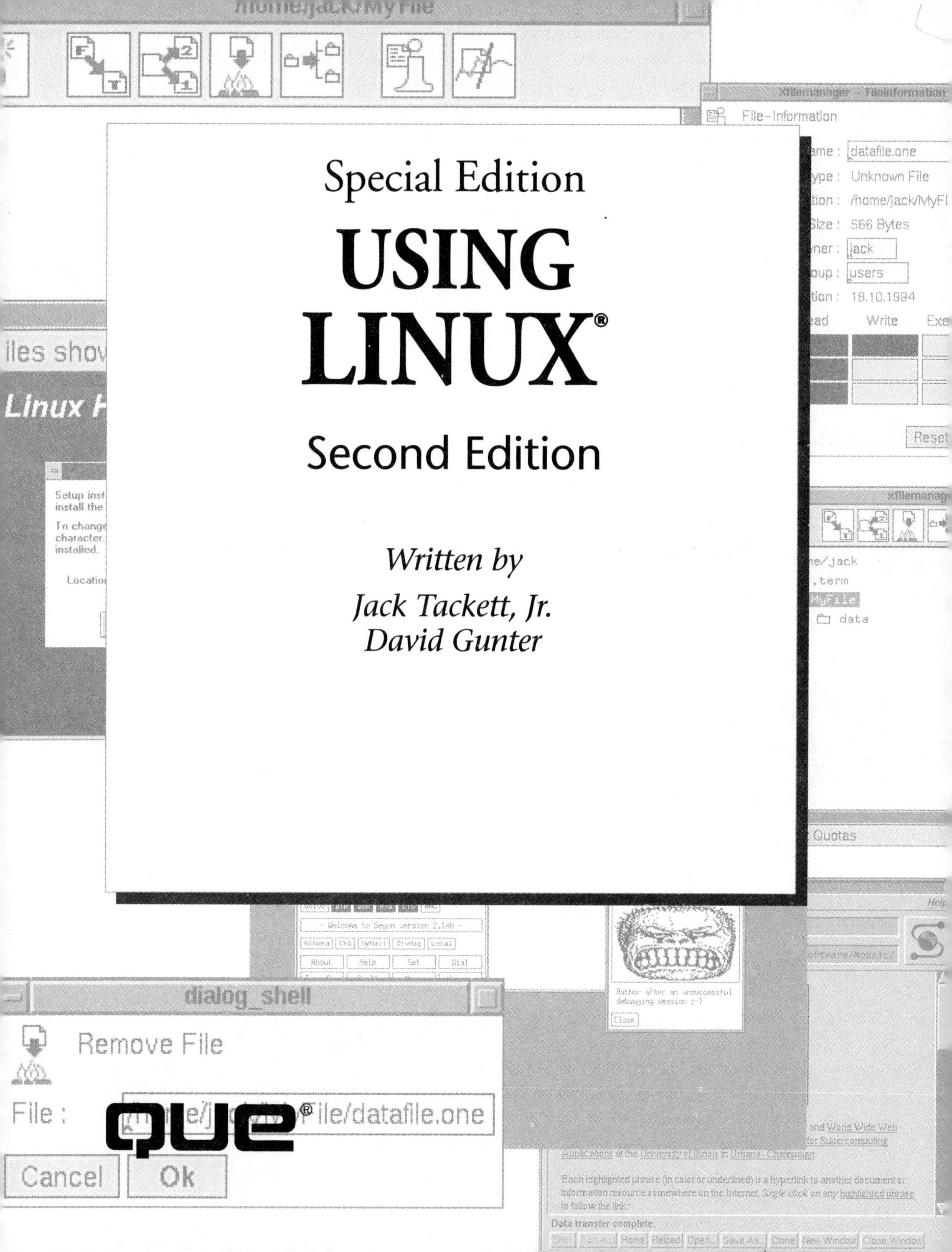
Special Edition
USING
LINUX®
Second Edition
Written by
Jack Tackett, Jr.
David Gunter
que®

Special Edition Using Linux, Second Edition

Library of Congress Catalog No.: 95-73291

ISBN: 0-7897-0742-X

98 97 96 6 5 4 3 2 1

Interpretation of the printing code: the rightmost double-digit number is the year of the book's printing; the rightmost single-digit number, the number of the book's printing. For example, a printing code of 96-1 shows that the first printing of the book occurred in 1996.

Screen reproductions in this book were created using Collage Plus from Inner Media, Inc., Hollis, NH.

Composed in *Stone Serif* and *MCPdigital* by Que Corporation.

Credits

President
Roland Elgey

Publisher
Joseph B. Wikert

Editorial Services Director
Elizabeth Keaffaber

Managing Editor
Sandy Doell

Director of Marketing
Lynn E. Zingraf

Senior Series Editor
Chris Nelson

Title Manager
Bryan Gambrel

Acquisitions Editor
Fred Slone

Product Director
Nancy D. Price

Production Editor
Susan Ross Moore

Editors
Kelli M. Brooks
Thomas C. Cirtin
C. Kazim Haidri

Assistant Product Marketing Manager
Kim Margolius

Technical Editor
Gary King

Acquisitions Coordinator
Angela C. Kozlowski

Operations Coordinator
Patricia J. Brooks

Freelance Coordinator
Michelle R. Newcomb

Editorial Assistant
Andrea Duvall

Technical Specialist
Nadeem Muhammed

Book Designer
Kim Scott

Cover Designer
Dan Armstrong

Production Team
Brian Buschkill
Jason Carr
Chad Dressler
DiMonique Ford
Jason Hand
Sonja Hart
Damon Jordan
Clint Lahnen
Bob LaRoche
Glenn Larsen
Stephanie Layton
Laura Robbins
Bobbi Satterfield
Todd Wente
Jody York

Indexer
Craig Small

To my beloved wife, Margaret Anne (Peggy) Tackett.

Jack Tackett, Jr.

To Lola: Without your support, I would not have been able to write this book. I love you.

David Gunter

About the Authors

Jack Tackett, Jr., is a computer consultant in Research Triangle Park, NC, specializing in C/C++ development on a variety of platforms. He currently does work for KMERL, a division of Panasonic, working on client/server and cross-platform TCP/IP applications.

During his spare time, Jack enjoys traveling, writing, reading, spending time with his friends, family, and his family's two dogs and two cats in his new home in Cary, NC.

David Gunter is a consultant and computer author based in Cary, NC. His areas of interest include UNIX systems management, and network and systems programming. David holds a Masters degree in computer science from the University of Tennessee. During his free time, David enjoys traveling, reading, and spending as much time as possible with his wonderful wife.

Acknowledgments

First, I want to thank all the readers of the first edition for their patronage and for their helpful and insightful comments. Your comments are important and make a difference; you have made this a better project!

I want to say thank you for the tremendous efforts put forth by the Linux developers scattered across the globe! I also want to acknowledge the fine contributions begun by Linus Torvalds and continued by so many others around the world—thanks for creating Linux and breathing life into such a monumentous effort! Also, thanks to Matt Welsh, et al for their work on the Linux Documentation project and to Patrick Volkerding for the Slackware distribution. Also a big thanks to the fine folks at InfoMagic for putting together such a great Linux CD combination and offer for our readers.

Next I want to express my regards for the people at the Que Continuum—never have I seen such professionalism in the publishing industry—their efforts all revolve around one goal—creating a quality product through team effort. I especially want to thank Joe Wikert, Fred Slone, and Nancy Price for their help in getting this project off the ground and finished. I also want to thank Susan Moore, Angela, Kelli, Gary King, and Bryan Gambrel for all their help.

To David V. Gunter, my partner in crime :-). Did you ever think we'd do a book after spending all those years just talking about writing? Did you think we'd do a second edition? Thanks for everything, dude. Also to Lance Brown for all his help in preparing this book! And thanks to Paul Barrett for his initial help with the research that eventually led to this book.

To my friends Paul Barrett, Keith E. Bugg, Gregg and Beckie Field, Lola Gunter, Tom Jennings, Shankar Lakshman, Kell Wilson, and Joe Williams. Thanks for the memories! Thanks to my combined family—the Tacketts and the Martins, for their support in all my endeavors. Also, a big thank you to the best cousins in the world—Bill and Hope Tackett, Jr.

I'd like to thank two of my best instructors, Dr. Joe Daugherty of the University of North Carolina-Asheville, and Myrtice Trent of the Blue Ridge Technical Community College. Thanks for the help and encouragement you both provided.

Finally, to my wife Peggy, who has yet again put up with me spending endless hours at the computer writing yet another computer book. Thanks, sweetheart, and I love you!

We'd Like To Hear From You!

As part of our continuing effort to produce books of the highest possible quality, Que would like to hear your comments. To stay competitive, we *really* want you, as a computer book reader and user, to let us know what you like or dislike most about *Special Edition Using Linux,* Second Edition or other Que products.

You can mail comments, ideas, or suggestions to the address below, or send us a fax at (317) 581-4663. For the online inclined, Macmillan Computer Publishing has a forum on CompuServe (type **GO QUEBOOKS** at any prompt) through which our staff and authors are available for questions and comments. The address of our Internet site is **http://www.mcp.com** (World Wide Web).

In addition to exploring our forum, please feel free to contact me personally on CompuServe at 75767,2543 to discuss your opinions of this book. You can also reach me on the Internet at **nprice@que.mcp.com**.

Thanks in advance—your comments will help us to continue publishing the best books available on computer topics in today's market.

Nancy D. Price
Product Development Specialist
Que Corporation
201 W. 103rd Street
Indianapolis, Indiana 46290
USA

Contents at a Glance

Contents

VIII Appendixes 695

A Sources of Information 697

B Applications for Linux 703

Introduction

Linux is a unique animal in the computer (r)evolution—it is not a commercial product backed by a huge corporation; rather, it is an operating system born of frustration and built by a rag-tag team of computer enthusiasts around the world. This team used the resources of the Internet to communicate and build the operating system named Linux.

Linus Torvalds, then a 23-year-old college student, began a personal project to expand the Minix operating system into a full-fledged clone of the UNIX operating system so popular on college campuses. The project is not complete—Linux is continuously updated and expanded by literally hundreds of people spread around the world.

Since its inception, almost the entire GNU library of utilities has been ported to Linux, and the X Windows GUI system—so popular on UNIX-type workstations—has also been ported. *GNU* (an acronym for *GNU's not UNIX*) is a project started by one man to make software available to anyone who wishes access. The GNU.TXT file describes the philosophy under which Linux and many other fine software packages are distributed. Many of these packages are provided on the CD-ROM that accompanies this book.

This book provides you with enough information to use and enjoy Linux. This book covers Linux version 1.1.18 and higher. The Linux distribution on the enclosed CD-ROM contains a version of Slackware, version 3.0, and should be compatible with later versions of Linux and Slackware.

Note

Probably the first order of business is to help you pronounce Linux. The proper pronunciation is *LEN*.nucks.

Who Should Use This Book?

Anyone interested in the Linux phenomenon can use this book as a guide to installing, configuring, and using Linux. Linux is often called a UNIX clone, but it is actually a POSIX-compliant multi-user, multitasking operating system for Intel 386 and later processors. *POSIX* is an international standard for operating systems and software detailing interoperability standards. Linux does not require MS-DOS or Windows to operate; in fact, Linux can replace those programs on your computer.

Since Linux is still evolving, it is imperative to understand the possibility of losing existing data on your system—do not install Linux without first backing up your system. It might be necessary to repartition your hard drive in order to make room for this new operating system, although it is possible to install Linux on top of MS-DOS, or to repartition your hard drive without losing data. This book and task are not for the novice user. With the proper precautions, however, anyone can install and enjoy Linux.

Note

The most current version of Linux is always available on the Internet, from sources that are listed in Appendix A of this book. The enclosed CD-ROM contains the latest possible version of Linux, but due to the rapid development of this popular operating system, and the chaotic process in which it is developed, it is impossible to provide the latest and greatest on such a CD-ROM. In fact, while all efforts are made to keep the book and CD-ROM in synch, that also is nearly impossible. Unlike commercial software, which changes infrequently and under controlled conditions, Linux and related software are perpetually dynamic.

Since Linux is very close to UNIX, many of the operations and procedures necessary for using Linux also apply to many UNIX systems. By learning to use Linux, you also learn how to use most UNIX systems.

UNIX has evolved over the years to become the premiere operating system used by hundreds of thousands of people throughout the world. This is not an accident. Earlier versions of UNIX were harder to manipulate than other operating systems, but in spite of this, UNIX managed to amass a distinguished following in academic and scientific circles. These professionals realized not only what a powerful, flexible, and manageable operating system UNIX was, but also its potential to be the best operating system ever. Their efforts have culminated in the UNIX of today, with its marvelous utilities, bundled with the newest communications capabilities and graphical user interfaces (GUIs).

The UNIX of today promises to once again revolutionize the personal computer industry, and perhaps redirect the industry's growth. UNIX has evolved from a minicomputer operating system to one that crosses all hardware configuration lines. There is no reason to think that this evolution will stop. UNIX may well become the standard for what most users dream of—eventual, complete standardization and compatibility of all computer systems, regardless of size or power.

UNIX comes in several flavors from a variety of vendors, including versions for the Intel PC platforms, but most of these versions cost big bucks. Linux provides a relatively inexpensive (free if you have access to the Internet) solution to learning about UNIX-type procedures and commands, the X Windows GUI, and accessing the Internet via Linux.

Who Should *Not* Use This Book?

If you are a Linux kernel hacker, or a UNIX guru, then this book may not be your cup of tea. This book is a great resource for someone wanting to know more about Linux and UNIX who has never been involved with either system. However, if you do know how to install Linux and maneuver around in UNIX, you may still find this book of use, particularly if you are only a UNIX user and have never had the chance to do system administration tasks. Several sections of the book explain the fine points of system administration and how to maintain a Linux/UNIX system. This typically is something a normal UNIX user is never allowed to perform, but with Linux you become king of the hill and ruler of the system, free to do whatever you want to do!

Now, if you don't have a clue what MS-DOS is, or what a floppy disk looks like, then you might want to brush up on some computer basics before tackling Linux. Linux is not for the faint of heart! You must have some understanding of how a computer works. If the thought of repartitioning or reformatting your hard drive sends shivers down your spine, then you probably should put off learning Linux for a while.

Hardware Needed to Use This Book

Since Linux is not a commercial software product, it has not gone through the rigorous quality assurance tests that most commercial software products endure. Also, most of Linux has been written across the Internet by computer *hackers* (not *crackers*, but people who truly enjoy writing software that accomplishes something), and thus, the hardware supported by Linux is the hardware owned by the various hackers. Table I.1 is a brief list of the supported hardware. If you do not have the correct hardware, it is unlikely that you will be able to boot Linux and productively use the system—forewarned is forearmed! Appendix C, "Linux Hardware Compatibility HOWTO," provides a more in-depth listing of Linux-supported hardware.

Table I.1 A Brief List of Hardware Supported by Linux

Item	Description
CPU	Intel 386 and later (and compatibles).
BUS	ISA, EISA, VESA local bus, and PCI; the MicroChannel bus is not supported.
RAM	Minimum of 2M of RAM; 4M recommended.

(continues)

Table I.1 Continued

Item	Description
HD controller	AT standard hard drive controller; Linux supports MFM, RLL, ESDI, and IDE controllers; Linux also supports several popular SCSI drive and CD-ROM drive controllers.
Disk space	Minimum of 20M; 80M recommended.
Monitor	Linux supports Hercules, CGA, EGA, VGA, and SVGA video cards and systems, with the exception of Diamond Speedstar video cards; X Windows has other requirements detailed in Chapter 6, "The X Windows System."
Mouse	Any standard serial mouse—for example, from Logitech, Microsoft, or Mouse Systems—or busmouse from Microsoft, Logitech, or ATIXL.
CD-ROM drive	Any CD-ROM drive works that uses a true SCSI interface; some proprietary CD-ROM drives such as the SoundBlaster series are also supported; CD-ROM drives known to work with Linux include: NEC CDR-74, Sony CDU-45, Sony CDU-31a, Mistsumi CD-ROMs, and Texel DM-3042.
Tape drive	Any SCSI tape drive works; other drives hosted from a floppy controller may also be supported; currently, the Colorado Jumbo 120 and 250 using the QIC 80 format are supported.
Printer	If you can access your parallel printer from MS-DOS, you should be able to access it from Linux; some fancy features might not be accessible.
Ethernet card	If you have access to an Ethernet network, Linux supports several standard Ethernet cards for accessing your network; cards supported include 3Com's 3C503 and 3C503/16, Novell's NE1000 and NE2000, and Western Digital's WD8003 and WD8013.

How to Use This Book

You may prefer to read this book from cover to cover. The information progresses from simple to complex as you read through the various sections and their chapters. Because the information is separated into seven parts and four appendixes, each with its own particular emphasis, you can choose to read only those parts that appeal to your immediate needs. Don't, however, let your immediate needs deter you from eventually giving attention to each chapter. Whenever you have the time, you can find a wealth of information in them all!

Part I, "Introduction to Linux," provides a detailed overview of the Linux system and the GNU concept of software development and distribution.

Chapter 1, "Understanding Linux," introduces the Linux operating system.

Chapter 2, "Overview of Features," provides a general overview of the various components that make up the Linux system.

Chapter 3, "Understanding the Linux Distributions," gives examples of the various distributions of Linux available, tells how to get the distributions, and describes their contents.

Part II, "Installing Linux," provides detailed information on what you need and what you ought to do to get Linux up and running.

Chapter 4, "Installing Linux," gives detailed instructions for installing the version of Slackware provided on the accompanying CD-ROM.

Chapter 5, "Running Linux Applications," provides a basic introduction to the process of setting up your Linux system.

Chapter 6, "Installing and Configuring the X Windows System," provides you with the necessary information to get the X Windows system up and running under Linux. Under Linux, the X Windows system is called XFree86 and is similar to other GUIs, such as Microsoft Windows or the OS/2 Workplace Shell.

Part III, "System Administration," provides basic information on configuring and managing a typical Linux installation.

Chapter 7, "Understanding System Administration," provides a brief background of the processes and procedures needed to configure and maintain a Linux system.

Chapter 8, "Booting and Shutting Down," details the various actions that happen when you boot up or shut down a Linux system, and explains why you cannot simply switch off the power supply.

Chapter 9, "Managing User Accounts," shows you how to add, delete, and manage user accounts on your machine.

Chapter 10, "Backing Up Data," explains the necessity of backing up your data, as well as the procedures needed to back up your Linux system.

Chapter 11, "Improving System Security," gives you a brief overview of system security on Linux systems and then explains the procedures needed to maintain a reasonably secure system.

Chapter 12, "Upgrading and Installing Software," provides you with the information needed to install new software from the Internet, and also tells you how to patch existing programs.

Part IV, "Network Administration," provides a greater understanding of the procedures and processes necessary to administer a robust Linux system.

Chapter 13, "Understanding the TCP/IP Protocol Suite," provides an overview of the most common network transport protocol suite in use today on the Internet.

Chapter 14, "Configuring a TCP/IP Network," shows you how to set up and configure TCP/IP on Linux.

Chapter 15, "Configuring Domain Name Service," provides you with the necessary information to get your system up and running with Domain Name Service (DNS).

Chapter 16, "Using SLIP and PPP," illustrates how to configure and use Serial Line Internet Protocol (SLIP) and Point-to-Point Protocol (PPP) lines to connect with the Internet.

Part V, "Managing the File System," provides detailed knowledge of how to be more productive with various Linux features. Everything you learn here can be transferred easily to other UNIX-type systems.

Chapter 17, "Managing File Systems," provides an overview of creating, mounting, and using a file system under Linux.

Chapter 18, "Understanding the File and Directory System," looks at subtle nuances of Linux command syntax, execution from the command prompt, parsing, command interpretation, and command feedback.

Chapter 19, "Managing Files and Directories," details the Linux file-system structure and organization, file-naming conventions, and directory hierarchy, and teaches you how to successfully navigate the Linux file system.

Part VI, "Working with Linux," increases your skill at working with the Linux command line tools and utilities.

Chapter 20, "Understanding Linux Shells," introduces you to the magical world of Linux shells, the powerful capabilities that exist through the use of shell scripting, and the different shells you may encounter with different versions of Linux.

Chapter 21, "Managing Multiple Processes," explores the capabilities of Linux when you run more than one process at a time. You learn how to initiate and manage multiple processes, as well as how to control and stop them.

Chapter 22, "Using the `vi` Editor," instructs you how to use UNIX's visual editor. While `vi` is not the most productive editor in the world, every Linux/UNIX system has it, and sometimes it is the only editor available for use.

Chapter 23, "Using the `emacs` Editor," teaches you how to use the ubiquitous UNIX editor written by GNU patriarch Richard Stallman.

Chapter 24, "Printing," covers all the printing basics, from issuing print commands and checking printer status to canceling print jobs and dealing with common printing problems.

Chapter 25, "Command-Line Reference," provides a brief description of many commands used by Linux, including their parameters and options.

Chapter 26, "Using X Windows," provides you with information necessary to use the X Windows system under Linux.

Part VII, "Using the Internet," provides a basic overview of the Internet.

Chapter 27, "Understanding the Internet," explains this network of networks that has become the information superhighway.

Chapter 28, "Accessing the Network with `telnet`, `ftp`, and the `r-` Commands," provides you with information on how to use various programs such as `telnet` and `ftp` to access information around the world.

Chapter 29, "Surfing the Internet," gives you an overview of using various Linux utilities to search for and retrieve information from the Internet. Topics include such items as Archie, Gopher, and the World Wide Web.

Chapter 30, "Using Electronic Mail," gives you an overview of electronic mail (e-mail) and how to use it on Linux.

Chapter 31, "Surviving USENET News," provides you with an explanation of USENET newsgroups, and then provides you with instructions for accessing the global community of newsgroups.

Chapter 32, "Using the World Wide Web," describes ways of navigating the World Wide Web under Linux.

Chapter 33, "Creating Web Documents with HTML," tells you how to create home pages for the World Wide Web using HTML for your Linux system.

Appendix A, "Sources of Information," provides you with a detailed listing of books, magazines, USENET newsgroups, and FTP sites dealing with Linux. Also, you get a brief glimpse of the myriad sources available to you as a Linux user.

Appendix B, "Applications for Linux," describes several of the major Linux and GNU programs available from various archive sites and CD-ROM vendors.

Appendix C, "The Linux Hardware Compatibility HOWTO," provides important details on the hardware supported by this distribution of Linux.

Appendix D, "The Linux CD-ROM HOWTO," provides information on how to get Linux to cooperate with a variety of CD-ROM drives.

Appendix E, "The GNU GENERAL PUBLIC LICENSE," is the verbatin license for using GNU applications. It describes your responsibilities in using GNU.

Appendix F, "The Red Hat Commercial Linux Distribution," describes the second CD-ROM accompanying this book. This CD-ROM contains the entire Red Hat 2.1 distribution of LInux. This second distribution is included in case you have problems installing Slackware.

Conventions Used in This Book

This book uses several special conventions that you need to become familiar with. These conventions are listed here for your reference.

Linux is a case-sensitive operating system; that means that when this book instructs you to type something at a command or shell prompt, you must type exactly what appears in the book, exactly as it is capitalized. This book uses a `special typeface` for Linux commands and file names to set them off from standard text. If you are instructed to type something, what you are to type appears in **`bold`**. For example, let's say the book instructs you to do the following:

> Type **`cat`** and press <Return>.

You must press the letters <c>, <a>, and <t>, then press the Return key.

At times, you are instructed to press a key such as <Return>, <Tab>, or <Spacebar>. Angle brackets surround the name of the key to distinguish it from a command you may have to type. When you press the key whose name appears in angle brackets, do not type the angle brackets.

Keys are sometimes pressed in combination; when this is the case, the keys are presented like this: <Ctrl-h>. This example implies that you must press and hold the <Ctrl> key, press the <h> key, and then release both keys.

> **Note**
>
> This book uses a convention for key names that may differ from what you are accustomed to. To avoid confusion in the case-sensitive UNIX environment, this book uses lowercase letters to refer to keys when uppercase letters may be the norm. For example, this book uses the form <Ctrl-c> instead of the form Ctrl-C (the latter form may make some readers wonder whether they should press <Ctrl> and <Shift> and <c>).

Some example listings show a portion of the screen after you type a specific command. These listings show the command prompt or shell prompt—usually a dollar sign ($)—followed by what you type in bold. Do not type the dollar sign when you follow the example on your own system. Consider this example:

```
$ lp report.txt &<Return>
 3146
$
```

You should type only what appears in bold on the first line (that is, type **`lp report.txt &`** and then press Return). The remainder of the listing shows Linux's response to the command.

When discussing the syntax of a Linux command, this book uses some special formatting to distinguish between the required portions and the variable portions. Consider the following example:

```
lp filename
```

In this syntax, the *filename* portion of the command is variable; that is, it changes depending on what file you actually want the `lp` command to work with. The `lp` is required, because it is the actual command name. Variable information is presented in *italic*; information that must be typed exactly is not in italic.

In some cases, command information is optional; that is, it is not required for the command to work. Square brackets ([ ]) surround parts of the command syntax that are optional. Consider the following example:

```
lp filename [device1] [abc]
```

Here, `lp` is the command name and is neither optional nor variable. The *device1* parameter is both variable and optional (it is in italic and surrounded by square brackets); this means that you can type any device name in place of *device1*, or type nothing at all for that parameter. The `abc` parameter is optional (you don't have to use it if you don't want to), but it is not variable—if you use it, you must type it exactly as it appears in the book.

Tips, notes, and cautions appear throughout the book in special formats to make the information they contain easy to locate. Longer discussions not integral to the flow of the chapter are set aside as sidebars (shaded blocks of text with their own heading).

The book also contains many cross references to appropriate topics throughout the book. A typical cross reference appears as:

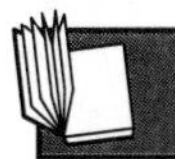

▶▶ See "What is X Windows?" p. 138

The arrow indicates whether the topics occurs in a later chapter (a right-pointing arrow) or a previous chapter (a left-pointing arrow).

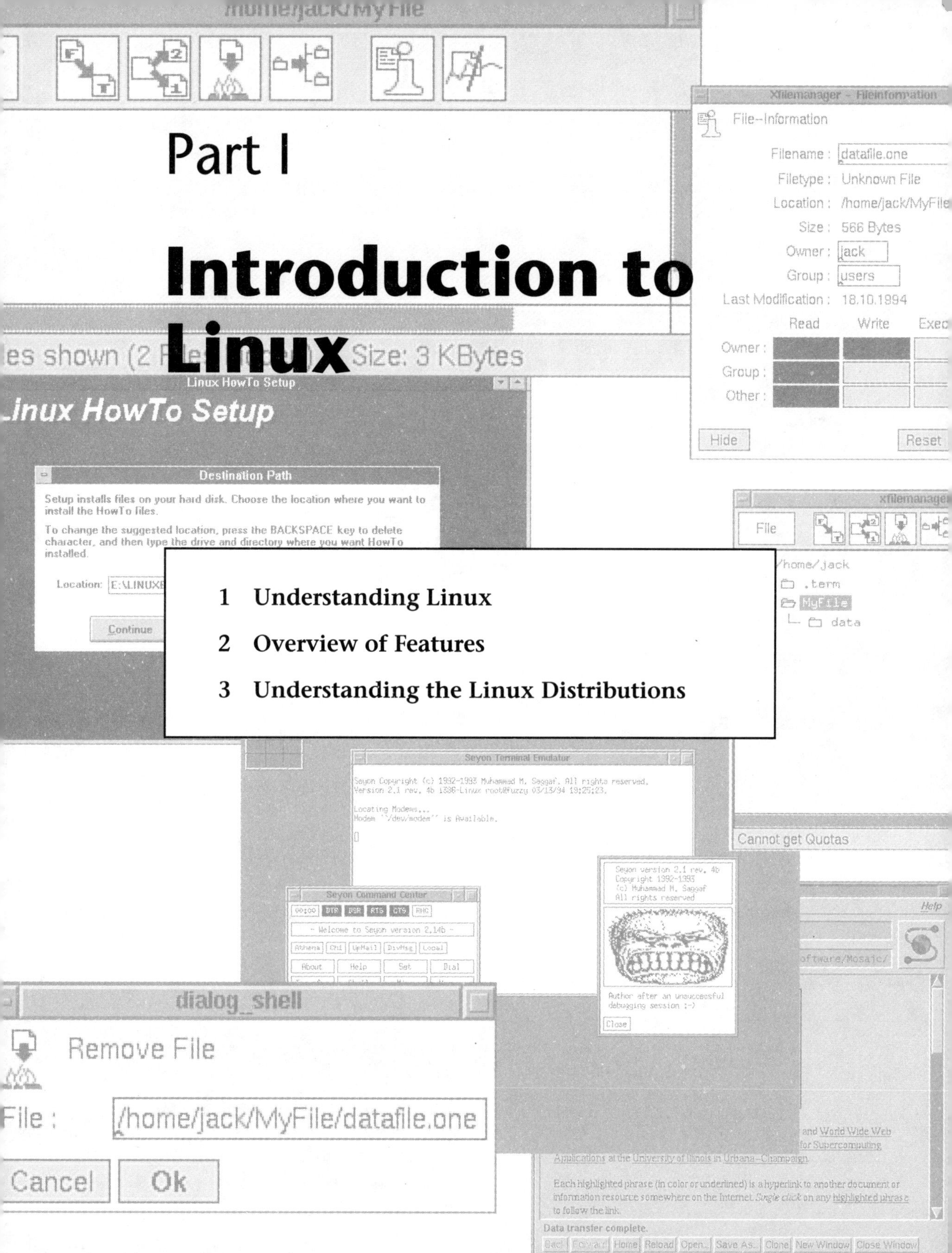

Part I

Introduction to Linux

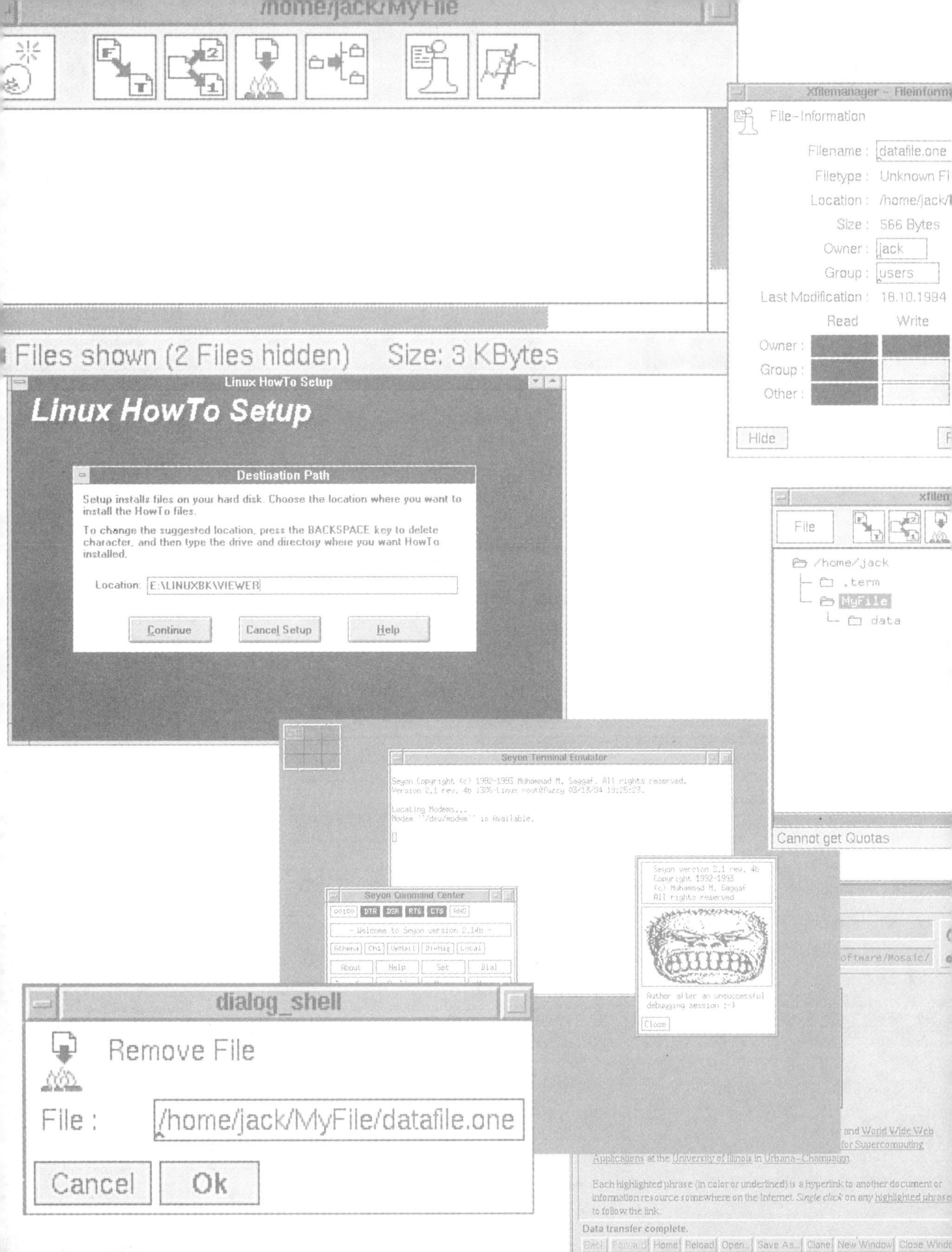

/home/jack/MyFile
Files shown (2 Files hidden)
Size: 3 KBytes
Xfilemanager – Fileinforma
File–Information
Filename : datafile.one
Filetype : Unknown Fi
Location : /home/jack/
Size : 566 Bytes
Owner : jack
Group : users
Last Modification : 18.10.1994
Read
Write
Owner :
Group :
Other :
Hide
Linux HowTo Setup
Linux HowTo Setup
Destination Path
Setup installs files on your hard disk. Choose the location where you want to install the HowTo files.
To change the suggested location, press the BACKSPACE key to delete character, and then type the drive and directory where you want HowTo installed.
Location: E:\LINUXBK\VIEWER
Continue
Cancel Setup
Help
File
/home/jack
.term
MyFile
data
Cannot get Quotas
Seyon Terminal Emulator
Seyon Command Center
Close
dialog_shell
Remove File
File :
/home/jack/MyFile/datafile.one
Cancel
Ok
Data transfer complete.
Home
Reload
Save As...
Clone
New Window

CHAPTER 1

Understanding Linux

To understand Linux, you must first understand the question, "What is UNIX?" The reason is that Linux is a project initiated to create a working version of UNIX on Intel-based machines, more commonly referred to as IBM PC-compatible computers that most people are familiar with.

UNIX is arguably the most versatile and popular operating system found today on scientific and high-end workstations. This chapter explains why you may want to select the UNIX-like Linux instead of one of the other operating systems available, such as MS-DOS, Windows 95, or OS/2.

This chapter covers the following:

- What is Linux?
- Why use Linux?
- What are the different versions of UNIX?
- What are the features of Linux/UNIX?
- Who owns Linux?

What Is Linux?

Linux is an operating system for Intel-based PCs. The system has been designed and built by hundreds of programmers scattered around the world. The goal has been to create a UNIX clone, free of any commercially copyrighted software, that the entire world can use. Actually, Linux started out as a hobby of Linus Torvalds while he was a student at the University of Helsinki in Finland. His goal was to create a replacement for the Minix operating system, a UNIX-like operating system available for Intel-based PCs. If some of these terms are unfamiliar to you, don't worry. Many of the terms are explained within this chapter.

Why Use Linux?

If you have a computer, you must have an operating system. An *operating system* is a complex set of computer codes that provides the operating process *protocols*, or laws of behavior. Without an operating system, your computer sits idly, unable to interpret and act on your input commands or run a simple program. Most operating systems are commercial programs supported by major software companies. If you buy an operating system, you must be content with what that vendor offers. Since the program is a proprietary program, you cannot modify or experiment with the system.

Application programs are software packages you purchase to perform certain activities, such as word processing. Each package is written for a specific operating system and machine. Again, you have little control on how modifications are made to the application program and when or if updates are ever performed.

You will want to use Linux because it is the only operating system today that is freely available to provide multitasking, multiprocessing capabilities for multiple users on IBM PC-compatible hardware platforms. No other operating system gives you these same features with the power that Linux enjoys. Linux also separates you from the marketing whims of the various commercial providers. You are not locked into upgrading every few years and paying outrageous sums to update all your applications. Many applications for Linux are freely available on the Internet, just as the source code to Linux itself is available on the Internet. Thus, you have access to the source code to modify and expand the operating system to your needs—something you cannot do with commercial operating systems like Windows 95, MS-DOS, or OS/2.

This feature, freedom from commercial vendors, is also a potential downside to using Linux. Because no one commercial vendor supports Linux, getting help is not just a phone call away. Linux can be finicky and may or may not run properly on a wide range of hardware. You can also damage or delete data files currently residing on your system. Linux is not a toy; it is a system designed to give users the feeling of tinkering with a new project, just like in the beginning of the PC revolution.

However, Linux is relatively stable on many systems and thus provides you an inexpensive opportunity to learn and use one of the most popular operating systems in the world today—UNIX. Linux is an alternative to other UNIX systems and can be used in place of those, sometimes expensive, systems. Thus, if you program on UNIX systems during the day, you can have a UNIX-like system at home. Are you a systems administrator of a UNIX system at work? Well, you can perform some of your duties from home using Linux. Don't have a clue as to what UNIX is? Well then, Linux provides a low-cost introduction to one of the most popular operating systems in the world—UNIX.

Linux also provides you with easy access to the Internet and the rest of the information superhighway!

UNIX Versions

The name *UNIX* can mean many things. It is one of the most context-specific terms used in the computer industry today. To better understand what is meant when someone uses the word *UNIX*, you must know which version of the operating system is being referred to.

Although versions of UNIX are offered by many different vendors, these versions fall into one of two major categories: UNIX System V and Berkeley Software Distribution (BSD). UNIX System V is the version developed by the creators of UNIX, AT&T Bell Laboratories. BSD UNIX was associated with the version of UNIX that was developed and proliferated by the University of California at Berkeley. The most popular version of BSD UNIX was sold by Sun Microsystems for its powerful workstations.

With UNIX System V Release 4, AT&T and Sun Microsystems merged their two versions of UNIX into UNIX System V. Because of this merger and the rallying of the industry around the UNIX System V standard, UNIX System V is now considered the standard UNIX system.

Undoubtedly, the best thing to happen to the UNIX operating system was the development of System V, Release 4.2 (SVR4.2). Created and introduced by UNIX System Laboratories (USL, now owned by Novell, Inc.), SVR4.2 combines the power and capabilities of UNIX with a "user-affectionate" graphical user interface (GUI). The result is an operating system that can be easily navigated by computer novices or radically customized by system administrators and other experts. SVR4.2 is sold by Novell as UnixWare.

Before the release of SVR4.2, UNIX users saw only a command-line prompt (a simple dollar sign) after logging onto the system. With no on-screen guidance evident, inexperienced users frequently were intimidated into forsaking UNIX in favor of other, better-known operating systems. No doubt this contributed to the UNIX reputation as an unfriendly operating system throughout its early years. Although experience and word of mouth dispelled some user reluctance, it was a reputation dying a slow death—until now.

An Overview of UNIX/Linux Features

The benefits derived from using the UNIX operating system, and hence Linux, stem from its power and flexibility. These are the result of the many features built into the system, ready for you to use as soon as you turn the system on. The following sections examine these features more closely.

Multitasking

The word *multitasking* describes the ability to seemingly execute multiple programs at the same time without hindering each application from running. This is called *preemptive multitasking* because each program is guaranteed a chance to run, each program executes until the operating system preempts it to allow another program to run. This type of multitasking is exactly what Linux does. MS-DOS and Windows 3.1 do not support preemptive multitasking; they do support a form of multitasking called *cooperative multitasking*. Under cooperative multitasking, programs run until they either voluntarily allow another program to run or have nothing else to do for the time being. To better understand the multitasking capability of Linux, examine it from another view. The microprocessor in your computer can do only one thing at a time, but it is capable of completing those individual tasks in periods of time so short they are difficult to comprehend. For example, typical microprocessors today operate at clock speeds of 25 to 90 MHz (megahertz) and faster. What this means is that they are capable of *transferring* from 25 to 90 and more *million bits per second*. When *processing* a complete set of instructions, the speeds are much faster, typically 30 nanoseconds (*billionths* of a second). The human mind cannot detect the difference between so short a delay and something occurring simultaneously. In short, it *appears* that tasks are performed at the same time.

Using a real-world example may further explain multitasking. Suppose that, while working in a spreadsheet application, you discover that the current month's information has not yet been merged from the database to the spreadsheet application. Typically, this takes some minutes to accomplish, so you start the process. Then you switch to another terminal window in Linux to work on a report you are preparing.

Before you finish the report, you switch back to the original Linux virtual terminal to check on the progress of your spreadsheet-merge process. Seeing that it is not yet complete, you switch back to the report terminal, only to realize that some of the information you want to include is located in a letter you wrote some time ago. So you open yet another window, select the file containing your letter, extract the information you need by using a copy utility, and return to the report, where you paste the copied information in place—all the while using the same word processor. Linux informs you that your merge process is now complete, so you close your word processing windows and return to the original spreadsheet window to finish your work there.

You can readily see the benefits of having preemptive multitasking capabilities. In addition to reducing dead time (time where you can't continue working on an application because a process has not yet finished), the flexibility of not having to close application windows before opening and working in others is infinitely more convenient.

Linux and other preemptive multitasking operating systems accomplish the preemptive processing by monitoring processes waiting to run as well as those currently running. The system then schedules each process to have equal access to the microprocessor. The result is that open applications appear to be running concurrently (in reality, there are delays of only billionths of a second between when the processor executes a set of instructions from one application and when it is scheduled by Linux to devote time to that process again). It is the ability to allocate time to running applications from within a freely available operating system that sets Linux apart from other operating systems and environments available today, like Windows 3.1 and Windows 95, MS-DOS, and commercial versions of UNIX. The other big feature of

Linux is that you have access to the source code for the operating system. Thus, if you want to change how the system works, and you have the necessary skills to implement the change, you can modify the Linux operating system to your heart's content. Commercial vendors will never allow you access to their source code to modify their wares.

Multiuser

The concept of many users accessing applications or processing power from a single PC was only dreamed of a few short years ago. UNIX and Windows NT helped develop that dream into reality. Linux's capability of allocating microprocessor time to many applications at once naturally lent itself to serving many people at once, each running one or more applications. The truly remarkable feature of Linux and its multiuser, multitasking features is that more than one person can work in the same version of the same application at the same time, from the same or separate terminals. Don't confuse this with multiple users updating the same *file* simultaneously, a feature that is potentially confusing, potentially hazardous, and positively undesirable.

Again, a real-world scenario helps further your understanding of this feature. Imagine a company whose personnel are networked to a Linux system. While one employee places the finishing touches on outgoing correspondence, another produces a company roster. Still another uses the same word processing package to ready a viewgraph presentation by importing pictures from a graphics package while the boss extracts information from a database for a report they are preparing, using (you guessed it) the *same* word processing application.

Down the hall in accounting, three data-entry clerks are updating files in the same accounting database; in the mailroom, the supervisor updates the shipping file that simultaneously updates the accounting database. At the same time, the system administrator sets up an account for a new employee and inactivates a second system account for an employee who is away on an extended leave of absence.

Although it may be difficult to imagine this scenario, it is being repeated thousands of times each day in offices throughout the world that utilize the UNIX operating system. Linux is a freely available UNIX clone and many systems are configured for scores of people to access; others are set up with only a few user accounts.

Programmable Shells

The *programmable shell* is another feature that makes UNIX, and hence Linux, what it is: the most flexible operating system available. Within the shell's framework is a whole new world available to those adventurous enough to master Linux's command syntax nuances.

Although you shouldn't be discouraged from attempting exciting forays into the Bourne, C, or bash shells, you should understand that, without proper guidance and preparation, shell programming can be a difficult lesson in frustration. Make sure that you have a reliable reference manual at hand (like the one you're reading now) and that you have the phone number of a good system administrator or other Linux expert in case you get bogged down.

▶▶ See " Understanding Shell Scripts," p. 386

For those who anticipate the rewarding experience of directing a powerful operating system like Linux, the importance of command syntax in Linux cannot be overstated. (*Syntax* is nothing more than the order and form of a command line.) The Linux shell scans each command line to determine whether the formation and spelling are consistent with its protocols.

The shell's scan process is termed *parsing*: the commands are broken down into more easily processed components. Each component is interpreted and executed—in-cluding those special characters that convey additional meaning to the shell. These special characters are further expanded into their proper command processes and executed.

Although many UNIX and Linux versions include more than one type of shell, they all function in essentially the same way. A shell works as the interpreter between the user and the *kernel* (the heart, or brain, of the Linux operating system). The primary difference among the three available shells lies in command-line syntax. Although it's not a severe limitation, you will encounter difficulties if you try to use C shell commands or syntax in the Bourne or `bash` shells.

Perhaps the simplest of scenarios to help further your understanding of UNIX and Linux shell programming is that of *background processing*. For example, you should back up all or parts of your system files at one time or another for protection against accidental erasure or hardware problems. If those files and their associated directories are of substantial size, the backup process can take a considerable amount of time.

With a simple shell program consisting of a line or two of command arguments, a backup process can run concurrently with other operations you may want to do (or *need* to do since the backup process can take quite some time). After programming the shell and starting the backup process, you can simply open a different window to access the desired application and begin your work there. When the background processing is completed, UNIX signals that the job is finished.

Linux shell programming serves as many different functions as there are people willing to attempt it. Many use this feature to personalize their system and make it more user friendly. Others find it helpful in streamlining many of the applications they run by enabling them to perform a number of processes in the background so that they are free to work in others.

Some users go even further by devising programs that link processes or applications so that they can reduce their work load to perhaps a single session of data entry and have the system update numerous software packages at once. Only the user's imagination limits what can be done with Linux shell programming.

Device Independence Under UNIX

At first glance, whether your computer system's peripherals can operate on a standalone, or independent, basis, may not seem important. When you view it from a multiuser UNIX environment, however, it becomes fundamental to a productive workplace. To understand the importance of device independence, you must first understand how other systems view attached peripherals and how UNIX views them.

Until recently, computer systems could generally support peripherals such as printers, terminals, disk drives, and modems. The technology explosion has added other devices too numerous to list to this list. Difficulties are encountered when the user cannot utilize a peripheral because an operating system cannot access the device. This inability can be the result of incompatible system architecture, operating-system addressing limitations, and so on.

UNIX sidesteps the problem of adding new devices by viewing each peripheral as a separate file. As new devices are required, the system administrator adds the required link to the kernel. This link, also known as the *device driver*, ensures that the kernel and the device merge in the same fashion each time the device is called on for service.

As new and better peripherals are developed and delivered to the user, the UNIX operating system allows immediate, unrestricted access to their services once the devices are linked to the kernel. The key to device independence lies in the adaptability of the kernel. Other operating systems allow only a certain number or a certain kind of device. UNIX can accommodate any number of any kind of device because each device is viewed independently through its dedicated link with the kernel.

Device Independence Under Linux

Linux shares many of the same benefits of device independence as does UNIX. Unfortunately, one of Linux's best features is also one of its biggest liabilities, freedom from a commercial entity. Linux has been developed over the last few years by a variety of programmers from around the world. These programmers do not have access to all the equipment created for the IBM PC and compatibles. In fact, Linux cannot run on some IBM PCs—those supporting the MicroChannel bus. Linux does support a wide variety of PC hardware, as illustrated in Chapter 3, "Understanding the Linux Distributions," and in Appendix C, "The Linux Hardware HOWTO."

However, because Linux is a UNIX clone, it too has an adaptable kernel; as more programmers join the Linux project, more hardware devices are added to the various Linux kernels and distributions. As a last resort, because you have the source code to the kernel, you, or someone you hire, can modify the kernel to work with new devices.

Communications and Networking

UNIX's superiority over other operating systems is equally evident in its communications and networking utilities. Linux is no exception. No other operating system includes such tightly coupled networking capabilities, and no other operating system has the built-in flexibility of these same features. Whether you need to talk with another user through a mail utility or download large files from another system across the nation, Linux provides the means to do so.

Accessing the Internet is a hot topic today, and people are spending hundreds of dollars on software to enable their PCs to hitch a ride on the information superhighway. With Linux, you get all that for free! The Internet was created and thrives in the UNIX world and thus Linux is quite at home there. With Linux you will be able to communicate almost instantly with the rest of the world.

Next, you can accomplish internal messaging or file transfer through a number of Linux commands, including `write`, `call`, `mail`, and `mailx`, as well as `cu` and `uucp`. These commands are examined more closely in later chapters. As an aid to understanding these capabilities, it is helpful to understand that information exchange *by users on the same system* (also called *internal* communications) is accomplished by terminal-to-terminal communication, e-mail, and an automatic calendar that serves as a scheduler/information manager.

An extension of Linux communications is found in the `cu` and `uucp` commands (used for *external* communications). Not only does Linux allow for file and program transfer, it gives system administrators and technicians a window of access to another system. Through this remote-access capability, one technician can effectively service many systems, even when those systems are located across great distances.

Networking in UNIX needs little explanation. The communications capabilities inherent in the operating system were designed to support many tasks and many users over many miles. UNIX quite naturally evolved in the professional marketplace as the operating system of choice, thanks to the same characteristics that gave it premier status in the scientific community and academia. Linux is set to follow that same route as a unique replacement for commercial UNIX systems.

Open Systems Portability

In the never-ending quest for standardization, many organizations have taken a renewed interest in the direction in which operating systems are developing. UNIX has not gone unnoticed. The drive to standardize UNIX stems from the many UNIX variants currently available. You learn more about how those variants were developed in the following section.

Efforts have been made to combine, collate, and otherwise absorb all versions of UNIX into a single, all-encompassing version of the operating system. Initially, the effort met with guarded enthusiasm and some effort was expended on coming to terms with blending the different versions. As with many noble efforts, this one was doomed to failure because developers were not willing to sacrifice part of what they had already invested into their particular version. (Sad to say, many developers still feel that way.)

However, the continued existence of varieties of UNIX is not necessarily cause for alarm. In spite of the different varieties, all are still inherently superior to all other operating systems available today because each contains the same elements described in the preceding pages.

Portability is merely the ability to transport an operating system from one platform to another so that it still performs the way it should. UNIX is indeed a portable operating system. Initially, UNIX could operate on only one specific platform, the DEC PDP-7 minicomputer. Today, the many variants of UNIX can operate in any environment and on any platform, from laptops to mainframes.

Portability provides the means for different computer platforms running UNIX to accurately and effectively communicate with any of the others without the addition of special, high price, after-market communications interfaces. No other operating system in existence can make this claim.

A Brief History of Linux

The history of Linux is tied to the history of UNIX and to a lesser extent a program called Minix. Minix was an operating system tutorial written by the well-known and respected computer scientist Andrew Tannebaum. This operating system became popular on several PC platforms, including MS-DOS-based PCs. More on Minix later. First, a brief history of UNIX.

When Novell, Inc. purchased UNIX System Laboratories from American Telephone and Telegraph Corporation (AT&T) in 1993, they gained the ownership of the registered trademark recognized as UNIX and, therefore, control the rights to who can use it for advertising or other commercial purposes. That is why you cannot call Linux UNIX.

Although AT&T was the creator of the UNIX operating system, many other companies and individuals have attempted to improve the basic idea over the years. The following sections examine a few of the leading variants in use today.

AT&T

Ken Thompson, a computer programmer for AT&T Bell Laboratories, and a group of people working under Ken's direction developed an operating system that was flexible and completely compatible with programmers' varied needs. Legend tells how Ken, who had been using the MULTICS operating system, dubbed this new product *UNIX* as he joked with others on his development team. He was lampooning the MULTICS multiuser operating system—UNIX was derived from *uni*, meaning *one* or *single*, followed by the homophone X. Perhaps the greater joke in this bit of folklore lies in the fact that MULTICS is remembered by few users today as a viable multiuser operating system, while UNIX has become the *de facto* industry standard for multiuser, multitasking operating systems.

BSD

Berkeley Software Distribution (BSD), University of California at Berkeley, released their first version of UNIX, based on AT&T's Version 7, in 1978. BSD UNIX, as it is known throughout the industry, contained enhancements developed by the academic community at Berkeley designed to make UNIX more user-friendly.

The user-friendly "improvements" in BSD UNIX were an attempt to make UNIX appeal to casual users as well as to advanced programmers who liked its flexibility in conforming to their changing demands. In spite of being less than 100 percent compatible with AT&T's original UNIX, BSD did accomplish its goals: the added features enticed casual users to use UNIX. BSD has become the academic standard. The original creators of BSD have since released a version for the Intel platform called, appropriately enough, BSD. This version too has a limited distribution on the Internet and via CD-ROM vendors. The authors also wrote several articles a few years ago in the computer magazine *Dr. Dobb's Journal* detailing the design and implementation of BSD386.

USL

UNIX System Laboratories (USL), was a spin-off company from the AT&T organization that had been developing the UNIX operating system since the early 1980s. Before Novell purchased it in 1993, USL produced the source code for all UNIX System V derivatives in the industry. However, USL itself did not sell a shrink-wrapped product at that time.

USL's last release of UNIX was UNIX System V Release 4.2 (SVR4.2). SVR4.2 marked USL's first entry into the off-the-shelf UNIX marketplace. In a joint venture with Novell, which temporarily created a company called Univel, USL produced a shrink-wrapped version of SVR4.2 called UnixWare. With Novell's purchase of USL, Novell had shifted the focus of USL from source-code producer to UnixWare producer. Novell has now sold their version of UNIX to the Santa Cruz Operation (SCO).

XENIX, SunOS, and AIX

Microsoft developed their UNIX version, called XENIX, in the late 1970s and early 1980s, during the peak of the PC revolution. Processing power available in PCs began to rival that of existing minicomputers. With the advent of Intel's 80386 microprocessor, it soon became evident that XENIX, which had been developed specifically for PCs, was no longer necessary. Microsoft and AT&T merged XENIX and UNIX into a single operating system called System V/386 Release 3.2, which can operate on practically any common hardware configuration. XENIX is still available today from Santa Cruz Operation (SCO), a co-developer with Microsoft, whose efforts to promote XENIX in the PC market have made this version of UNIX one of the most successful commercially. SCO also produced a version of UNIX, called SCO UNIX.

Sun Microsystems has contributed greatly to UNIX marketability by promoting the SunOS and their associated workstations. Sun's work with UNIX produced a version based on BSD. Interestingly enough, AT&T's SVR4 is compatible with BSD, too—no doubt an offshoot of AT&T and Sun Microsystems' collaboration in UNIX System V Release 4.0.

IBM's venture into the world of UNIX yielded a product called AIX (Advanced Interactive Executive). Although AIX is not as well known as some other UNIX versions, AIX performs well and has no problem holding its share of the operating-system market. It is perhaps the old mindset that any UNIX version is an unfriendly, unforgiving operating system that has kept AIX from a better market reception.

Linux

Linux is the brain child of a then 23-year-old computer science student named Linus Torvalds. Linux began life as a hobby project for Linus. He hoped to create a more robust version of UNIX for Minix users. Minix, as stated earlier, is a program developed by computer science professor Dr. Andrew Tannebaum.

The Minix system was written to demonstrate several computer science concepts found in operating systems. He incorporated these concepts into a standalone system that mimics UNIX. The program was widely available to computer science students all over the world and soon generated a wide following, including its own USENET newsgroups. Linus Torvalds set out to provide a better platform for his fellow Minix users that could run on the widely available IBM PC. Linus targeted the emerging 386-based computers because of the task-switching properties of the 80386 protected-mode interface.

Below are some of the announcements Linus made when announcing his Linux program.

> **Note**
>
> These announcements are from the "Linux Installation and Getting Started Guide," by Matt Welsh. (Copyright 1992-94 by Matt Welsh, 205 Gray Street NE, Wilson, NC 27893, **mdw@sunsite.unc.edu**.)
>
> They are used subject to section 3 of Matt's copyright. The complete "Linux Installation and Getting Started Guide," can be obtained from the Linux Documentation Project's various archives sites. You can find this book on **sunsite.unc.edu** in the directory **/pub/Linux/docs/LDP/install-guide**. For information on how to access archives and download files, refer to Chapter 28, "Accessing the Network with `telnet`, `ftp`, and the `r-` Commands."

"After that it was plain sailing: hairy coding still, but I had some devices, and debugging was easier. I started using C at this stage, and it certainly speeds up development. This is also when I started to get serious about my megalomaniac ideas to make 'a better Minix than Minix.' I was hoping I'd be able to recompile `gcc` under Linux some day....

"Two months for basic setup, but then only slightly longer until I had a disk-driver (seriously buggy, but it happened to work on my machine) and a small filesystem. That was about when I made 0.01 available [around late August of 1991]: it wasn't pretty, it had no floppy driver, and it couldn't do much [of] anything. I don't think anybody ever compiled that version. But by then I was hooked, and didn't want to stop until I could chuck out Minix."

In a later announcement, made in **comp.os.minix** on October 5th, 1991, Linus introduced to the world Linux version 0.02, the first official version of Linux.

"Do you pine for the nice days of Minix 1.1, when men were men and wrote their own device drivers? Are you without a nice project and just dying to cut your teeth on an OS you can try to modify for your needs? Are you finding it frustrating when everything works on Minix? No more all-nighters to get a nifty program working? Then this post might be just for you."

"As I mentioned a month ago, I'm working on a free version of a Minix lookalike for AT-386 computers. It has finally reached the stage where it's even usable (though may not be depending on what you want), and I am willing to put out the sources for wider distribution. It is just version 0.02, but I've successfully run `bash`, `gcc`, `gnu-make`, `gnu-sed`, `compress`, and so forth under it."

Who Owns Linux?

IBM owns the rights to OS/2, Microsoft owns the rights to MS-DOS and MS Windows, but who owns the rights to Linux? First and foremost, Linux is *not* public domain software; various components of Linux are copyrighted by many people. Linus Torvalds holds the copyright to the basic Linux kernel. Paul Volkerding holds the copyright to the Slackware Distribution. Many Linux utilities are under the GNU General Public License (GPL). In fact, Linus and most Linux contributors have placed their work under the protection of the GNU GPL. A copy of this license can be found on the enclosed CD-ROM in the file `copying` in the root directory.

This license is sometimes referred to as the GNU *Copyleft,* a play on the word copyright. This license covers all the software produced by GNU (itself a play on words—**G**NU's **N**ot **U**NIX) and the Free Software Foundation. The license allows programmers to create software for everyone. The basic premise behind GNU is that software should be available to everyone, and that if someone wants to modify the program to his or her own ends, that should be possible. The only caveat is that the modified code cannot be restricted—others have the right to the new code.

The GNU Copyleft, or GPL, allows the creators of a program to keep their legal copyright, but allows others to take and modify *and* sell the resulting new program. However, in doing so they cannot restrict any of these same rights from the ones buying the software. If you sell the program as is, or in a modified form, then you *must* provide the source code. That is why Linux comes with the complete source code.

From Here...

Linux is a viable alternative to UNIX on the desktop. Linux's freely available source code and applications make Linux a reasonable alternative to other operating systems for PC compatibles. For more information check out the following:

- Chapter 4, "Installing Linux," provides information on putting Linux on your computer.
- Chapter 5, "Running Linux Applications," explains how to use some of the applications that come on the enclosed CD-ROM.

CHAPTER 2

Overview of Features

Linux represents a chance for you to explore a new world, the world of UNIX. Linux also provides superior performance when compared to other operating systems. Linux provides a multiuser, multitasking, network-ready operating system that you can use today. There are thousands of applications available for Linux from all over the world. Finally, Linux presents you with an inexpensive learning tool for a variety of subjects, from UNIX to software development. In this chapter, you learn the following:

- The basic features Linux provides
- Advantages of using Linux
- Disadvantages of using Linux

Basic Features

Linux is a UNIX clone, which means that with Linux you get many of the advantages of UNIX. Linux multitasking is fully preemptive, which means you can run multiple programs at the same time and each program still seemingly continues to run. Other systems, such as Microsoft Windows 3.1, allow you to run multiple programs, but when you switch from one program to another, the first program typically stops running. Microsoft's Windows 95 and Windows NT are more like Linux since they allow pre-emptive multitasking. Linux allows you to start a file transfer, print a document, copy a floppy, and play a CD or game all at the same time.

Linux is fully multiuser, which means more than one person can log on to and use the system. While this feature may not be very useful at home, in a corporate or university setting this allows many people access to the same resources at the same time, without duplicating expensive machines. Even at home, you will find the ability to log on to separate accounts on what are called virtual terminals very useful. For a full discussion of virtual terminals, check out Chapter 5, "Running Linux Applications." Also from home you could provide your own personal online service by using Linux and several modems.

Linux is free—or nearly so. In fact, for the price of this book you have received a fully functioning copy of Linux on the enclosed CD-ROM. Everything you need to get Linux up and running is provided on the CD-ROM, including hundreds of applications.

Linux provides a learning opportunity unparalleled in today's society. Here you have a complete, working operating system, including source code, in which to play and learn what makes it tick. Learning what makes Linux tick is something you are not able to do in a typical UNIX environment and definitely something you can't do with a commercial operating system because no vendor is willing to just give away the source code.

Finally, Linux gives you a chance to re-live or perhaps experience for the first time the chaos of the early PC revolution. In the mid-seventies, computers were the province of large organizations, such as the government, big business, and universities. The ordinary person had no access to these marvels. However, with the introduction of the microprocessor and the first personal computers, things changed. At first, PCs were the province of the hackers, dedicated computer enthusiasts, who hacked the early systems because those systems could do very little in the way of productive work. But as the hackers experimented and became entrepreneurs, and the capabilities of PCs increased, PCs became commonplace. The same is true of system software (that is, operating systems) today. Linux represents a break away from a system controlled by large organizations that stifle creativity and enhancements in the name of market share. Although Linux is still the province of hackers, this is changing as Linux hackers become entrepreneurs to bring Linux to the masses.

Advantages of Using Linux

There are many advantages to using Linux. Of the many operating systems available today, Linux is the most popular free system that's widely available. For the IBM PC, Linux provides a complete system with built-in multiuser and multitasking capabilities that take advantage of the entire processing power of your 386 and higher computer systems. Linux comes with a complete implementation of the TCP/IP networking protocol. With Linux, you can connect to the Internet and the vast wealth of information it contains. With Linux you have a complete e-mail system to send messages back and forth through cyberspace. There is also a complete graphical user interface (GUI) for Linux, called XFree86, that is based on the popular X Windows system. XFree86 is a complete implementation of the X Windows system that can be distributed free with Linux. XFree86 provides the common GUI elements you find on other commercial GUI platforms like Windows and OS/2. All this is available for Linux, today, and basically for free. All you have to pay for is acquiring the programs, either from the Internet or via mail order from several different vendors. Of course, because you've purchased this book, you already have the entire Linux system on the enclosed CD-ROM.

Applications

Using an operating system, while sometimes fun in and of itself, is not the reason most people use a computer. Most people need to do productive work with their computer. Linux has literally thousands of applications available today. These applications include programs for spreadsheets, databases, word processing, application development with a variety of computer languages, and telecommunications packages to get you online. Linux also comes with a wide range of games, both text and graphics based. When you need a break from the drudgery of the daily grind, Linux can provide a few minutes (or hours) of relaxation.

Advantages for Computer Professionals

If you are a computer professional, Linux provides a wealth of tools for program development. There are compilers for many of the top computer programming languages today such as C, C++, and SmallTalk. If you don't like these languages, Linux provides you with the tools to build your own computer languages. Tools such as Flex and Bison are available. These tools come with the enclosed CD-ROM; their commercial counterparts can cost several hundred dollars each. If you want to learn one of the aforementioned languages but don't want to spend the hundreds of dollars for another compiler, Linux and its development tools are for you.

Linux also provides you with the ability to communicate with your company's office systems. And if you're a UNIX system administrator, Linux can help you perform your duties from home. While working from home is just in its infancy, perhaps some day you can use Linux to do your job at home, and then only occasionally visit the office for personal meetings.

Two of the industry's buzzwords are *open systems* and *interoperability*. These terms refer to many different systems being able to communicate with each other. Most open-systems specifications require POSIX compliance, which means some form of UNIX. Linux meets those standards today. In fact, Linux was designed for source-code portability, so if you have a corporate program running on one version of UNIX, you should be able to port that system relatively quickly to a system running Linux. Corporations are insisting on these types of open systems so that they are not locked into any single vendor. Remember the old adage, "Don't put all your eggs in one basket?" Corporations today are becoming leery of systems controlled by single companies because those in control can dictate how the software behaves and what hardware systems the software supports. If that company chooses a direction that's not good for your corporation, tough luck. You are stuck with their decision whether you like it or not. With UNIX/Linux and open systems, however, you are in control of your own destiny. If the operating system doesn't have a feature you need, there are plenty of consultants available who can make the necessary changes. Especially given that, at least with Linux, you have the source code to your operating system.

Education

If you are a student, Linux provides you with editors to write your assignments and spell checkers to proof those assignments. With Linux, you should be able to log on to your school's computer network. And, of course, with access to the Internet, you have an instant tap into the limitless wealth of information there. You also have access to thousands of experts in a wide variety of subjects who can answer your questions. Linux can be useful even if your major is not computer science.

How does Linux provide such advantages for so little? This is because of the spirit and philosophy of the community that built and continues to build Linux. Linux is a great experiment that took on a life of its own. Literally hundreds of computer hackers from around the world contributed to its development. Linus Torvalds first developed what became Linux for himself and later released his brain child to the world under the GNU copyleft.

Hackers

At the basic level, Linux is a system built by and for hackers. Currently, the popular definition of hacker has a negative connotation in today's society, but computer hackers are not criminals by their definition of the word. Their definition deals with how one approaches any activity in life and not just when dealing with computers. Hackers feel a certain depth of commitment and an enhanced level of excitement at hacking a system. *Hacking* basically means learning all there is to know about a system, becoming immersed to the point of distraction in the system, and being able to fix the system if it breaks. Hackers basically want to know how a system they find interesting works. They are not interested in such activities as making money or seeking revenge, although certain hackers do cross that line to become what the hacker community calls *crackers*. Computer hackers become outraged when they are compared with these vandals and criminals the popular media currently calls hackers (instead of crackers). Hopefully, Linux gives you a feeling of what it is like to be a hacker, and ideally, you shun becoming a cracker.

If you are simply the curious type and want to learn more about UNIX, Linux is for you. Here is a fully functional version of UNIX to which you have free, unrestricted access. This is something you seldom find in the real world. Most UNIX users are given accounts on UNIX machines that grant them only limited rights and privileges. There are some UNIX/Linux commands that a normal user cannot use or experiment with. This is not conducive to learning all about UNIX. With Linux, however, you have complete run of the place and can do what you want whenever you want. Of course, with this great power comes great responsibility; you must learn how to manage a real UNIX system, which can be fun in and of itself.

Disadvantages of Using Linux

Perhaps the biggest disadvantage of using Linux is the fact that no single corporate entity is in charge of its development. If something goes wrong or you have a problem, there are no toll-free technical support numbers to call to ask for help. But do those numbers provide real support for current commercial systems? How often are you referred elsewhere, providing you get through to tech support, to have your question answered? How many times are you asked to post a question on an online service to get help? Well, with Linux, even though there is no tech support number, there are literally thousands of users in the online communities to help answer your questions.

Lack of Technical Support

Having no source of technical support can be a problem with Linux, no doubt about it. The same goes for Linux applications; while there are a few commercial programs for Linux, most are developed by small groups and then posted to the world. Many developers, however, help out with questions.

Hardware Problems

Another disadvantage is that Linux can be hard to install and does not work on all hardware platforms. Unlike a commercial program development operation where a cohesive group spends months building and testing a program against a variety of conditions and hardware, Linux developers are scattered across the globe. There is no formal quality assurance program. Developers release their programs when they feel like releasing them. Also, the hardware supported by Linux depends on the hardware each developer owns while writing that portion of the code. Thus, Linux doesn't work with all the hardware available for PCs today.

> **Caution**
>
> If your system does not have the hardware supported by Linux, you will have problems installing and running the system. Chapter 4, "Installing Linux," details the hardware you need to use Linux as does Appendix C, "The Linux Hardware Compatibility HOWTO."

If you have the hardware that is supported, chances are you will have no problem installing and using Linux. If you don't have the necessary hardware, well, Linux developers expect you to fix it; after all, this is a hacker's system.

Inability To Use Current Software

Another disadvantage is that your current applications for such operating systems as DOS and OS/2 more than likely will not work under Linux. Fortunately, those other systems can co-exist with Linux; thus, while you cannot use both operating systems at the same time, you can leave Linux and boot the other system to use your applications there.

> **Note**
>
> Work is in progress on emulators that run both DOS and Windows programs. While the DOS project is much further along than the Windows project, both are in an early phase and not quite ready for prime time. But some day in the near future, Linux will be able to run your DOS and Windows applications.

To install Linux, you are going to have to repartition your hard drive. *Repartitioning* means that you have to erase part of your drive, thus wiping out your programs and data on that drive. There is no safe way of currently installing Linux without repartitioning. If you plan to install Linux, you should back up your disk. Also, you might not have enough hard-disk space to install Linux and keep your other software on the same disk, in which case you have to decide what goes and what stays. No matter what, you have to back up your system, repartition the drive, restore your old software, and then install Linux, which can be time consuming and error prone.

> **Note**
>
> There are alternatives to repartitioning your hard drive. You can share space with Linux and DOS, or you can use a program that repartitions your drive without erasing files. These alternatives do work, but you still face the possibility of losing data while installing the system. Also, by repartitioning, you gain improved performance and better control over the amount of disk space used for Linux.
>
> The amount of disk space you need to run Linux depends on what you plan to install. Chapter 3, "Understanding the Linux Distributions," provides some insight into the amount of disk space you need. However, you should have at least 120M free on the drive that you want to install Linux on, in addition to the programs and data you want to keep from your other operating systems. If you have 200M free, you should have more than enough space for a full installation of Linux.

Lack of Experience

Finally, unless you are already a UNIX guru, you must learn how to manage a Linux system. Linux and UNIX, unlike DOS, Windows, and OS/2, need to be managed. The manager is usually called the *system administrator*, and this person is responsible for maintaining the system and for performing such duties as adding and deleting user accounts, backing up the system on a regular basis, installing new software, configuring the system, and fixing things when they go wrong, which happens even on commercial versions of UNIX in use every day. Since UNIX does not run perfectly 100 percent of the time, the system administrator must maintain the system. This presents a great opportunity for you to learn how to be a system administrator on a UNIX system.

▶▶ See "Understanding Centralized-Processing Systems," p. 160

Overcoming the Disadvantages

At first it may sound as if using Linux puts you all alone in the world, having to survive by yourself. Part of this is true since Linux started life as a hacker's system, and hackers like to tinker and fix systems themselves. But today, as the popularity of Linux has grown, many sources of help are available.

There are thousands of pages of documentation provided with most distributions of Linux. On the enclosed CD-ROM, you can find this information in the /DOCS directory. There are magazines devoted to Linux, and there are plenty of online sources of information and online users willing to help with your questions. If you are a commercial entity and need a professional contractor, these too are available. Once you have installed Linux, you will also find a wealth of online help providing information on almost every Linux command and program available. Check out Appendix A, "Sources of Information," to see you are not alone.

From Here...

This chapter gave you an overview of the Linux system and the amount of software available. For more information see the following chapters:

- Part II, "Installing Linux," provides you with the details necessary to get your Linux system up and running.
- Chapter 5, "Running Linux Applications," provides you with information on using various Linux applications and utilities. You learn how to maneuver your way around UNIX/Linux.
- Chapter 6, "The X Windows System," provides you with information on using X Windows.
- Appendix B, "Applications for Linux," provides you with a brief list of the many available programs you can use with Linux.

CHAPTER 3

Understanding Linux Distributions

Linus Torvalds created Linux and distributed early versions across the Internet for the enjoyment of many hard-core hackers. (Don't confuse the term *hacker*, which means someone very skilled in computer problem solving, with the law-breaking *cracker*.) Today, Linux is distributed any number of ways, including on CD-ROMs, on tapes, over the networks, and even (if you can put up with shuffling up to 50 high-density 3 1/2-inch disks) on floppies. The CD-ROM accompanying this book contains a complete Linux system along with the X Windows clone XFree86 and many megabytes of Linux and GNU material. Linux is actually the operating system kernel, requiring specific hardware to run. A Linux distribution also has the utilities and other programs you expect in a UNIX system. The distribution selected for *Special Edition Using Linux* is called Slackware and is the one most recommended for users new to Linux because it is easy to install and frequently updated. The Linux Documentation Project, headed by Matt Welsh at `sunsite.unc.edu`, maintains a list describing each Linux distribution and how to retrieve it. You can find this list on the CD-ROM in the file `\howto\distrib`.

- An introduction to the CD-ROM that accompanies *Special Edition Using Linux, Second Edition*
- The packages available on the CD-ROM

Above all, even though the enclosed CD-ROM contains the latest possible version of Slackware available at production time, remember Linux is a growing system and a newer version may be available by the time you purchase this book. After you have this version of Linux up and running, you might want to check out the FTP site `ftp.cdrom.com` and the `/pub/linux/slackware` directory. This archive also contains the MS-DOS floppy-disk images already created and ready for downloading. You can use these disk images to install Linux if you do not have a CD-ROM drive.

In this chapter you will learn the following:

- What hardware is needed to run Linux
- How to find information on installing, configuring, and using Linux
- What constitutes a Linux distribution
- What files are included on the distribution residing on the enclosed CD-ROM

Note

If you do not understand some of the preceding terms, such as FTP, `/pub/linux/slackware`, or downloading, don't fret. This book provides the answers to all your questions.

Choosing the Right Hardware for Linux

Choosing the right level of hardware for your Linux system depends on such factors as the number of users to be supported and the types of applications to be run. All this translates into requirements for working memory, hard-disk storage space, the types of terminals needed, and so forth.

The majority of Linux systems today consist of PCs. These Linux installations are often for only a single user, although they may also be tied into larger Linux or UNIX systems.

Caution

Linux is a constantly evolving system and hardware support is sporadically updated. The Slackware distribution contained on the accompanying CD-ROM is relatively stable, but new hardware support may have been provided by the time this book sees print and the CD-ROM is created. While many hardware components have clones or compatible replacements, not all may work with Linux. If you do have the following hardware, the odds are excellent that Linux installs, boots, and operates properly. If you do not have the equipment listed, Linux may or may not operate properly, but the odds are against your getting a system up and running.

If you are using a version of Linux in a single-user configuration (the most likely configuration), you are the system administrator. It's your responsibility to understand the system well enough to do the administrative duties required to keep it operating at an optimum level. These duties include keeping enough space on the hard drive, backing up regularly, making sure that all devices attached to the system have the proper software drivers, installing and configuring software, and so forth.

Choosing the level of hardware you need depends heavily on the hardware used by the myriad people who programmed the Linux system. Unlike commercial software developers who can afford to test their systems on many different hardware configurations, Linux developers typically only have access to their personal computers. Luckily, because there are so many Linux developers, most of the standard hardware found in the PC world is supported.

The System's CPU

A basic system requires an IBM compatible PC with an Intel 80386 or later CPU in any of the various CPU types such as the 80386SX, 80486DX/2, and Pentium. Other CPU clones, such as the 80386 clone chips made by Cyrix and Advanced Micro Devices (AMD) are also compatible with Linux. The 80386 and 80486SX processors do not have math coprocessors built in, but Linux does not require a floating point math coprocessor. Linux can emulate the coprocessor using software routines, but at a significant reduction in execution speed. For a fast system you should consider getting a CPU with a math coprocessor built in, such as an 80486DX or Pentium.

The System's Bus

The type of bus used to communicate with the peripherals is also important. Linux only works with the ISA and EISA buses. The MicroChannel Architecture (MCA) bus used on IBM's PS/2 is not supported, although a port is in process. Some newer systems use a faster bus for such items as disk access and video displays, called the *local bus*. Linux does support the VESA Local Bus but may not support a non-VESA Local Bus architecture. Linux also supports the new PCI bus found on many high-end Pentium systems.

Memory Needs

Linux requires surprisingly little RAM to run, especially when compared to comparable operating systems such as OS/2 and Windows NT. Linux requires at least 2M of RAM, although 4M is highly recommended. If you have less than 4M of RAM, you need to use what is called a *swap file*. The basic rule of thumb is: the more memory your system contains, the faster your system runs.

The next memory consideration for Linux is the use of the X Windows clone called XFree86.

Note

This version of X Windows is freely distributable and is included with Linux for that reason. XFree86 is a GUI similar to Microsoft Windows.

▶▶ See "Installing the XFree86 System," p. 141

To productively use XFree86, your Linux system requires at least 16M of virtual memory. Virtual memory is the combination of physical memory and swap space on the hard drive. Again, the more physical memory contained on the system, the more responsive the system, especially when using XFree86.

Disk Drives and Space Requirements

While it is possible to run Linux from a floppy drive-only system, running Linux from your system's floppy drive is not recommended.

Note

You can boot Linux from a floppy drive. Booting a system refers to the process of starting a computer system and loading the operating system into memory to start the system. The term is derived from the phrase *bootstrapping*.

For a home-based system, you need a floppy drive; either a 5 1/4- or a 3 1/2-inch suffices. You need a floppy even if you install and run Linux from your CD-ROM.

For better system performance, you want to install Linux on a hard drive. You must have an IBM AT standard drive controller. This should not be a problem because most modern, non-SCSI controllers are AT compatible. Linux supports all MFM and IDE controllers, as well as most RLL and ESDI controllers. Linux may or may not support the newer, high capacity IDE drives from older 8-bit IDE controllers.

Linux does support a wide range of SCSI hard-drive controllers. If your controller is a true SCSI controller, that is, not a proprietary version of SCSI, Linux can use your controller. Linux currently supports SCSI controllers from Adaptec, Future Domain, Seagate, UltraStor, the SCSI adapter on the ProAudio Spectrum 16 card, and Western Digital. The following list provides card types from several supported vendors:

- Adaptec 152x/1542/1740/274x/284x
- Buslogic
- EATA-DMA (DPT, NEC, AT&T)
- Seagate ST-02
- Future Domain TMC-8xx, 16xx
- Generic NCR5380
- NCR 53c7, 8xx
- Always IN2000
- Pro Audio Spectrum 16
- Qlogic
- Trantor t128/T128F/T228
- Ultrastor
- 7000FASST

▸▸ See "Controllers (SCSI)," p. 721

If you have the proper drive controller, then you must worry about disk space requirements. Linux does support multiple hard drives and can be installed across drives. Unlike other operating systems, Linux does not need to be installed on the same hard drive; pieces can be installed on different drives.

Disk Space. The one item to realize, though, is that Linux cannot reside on the same *partition* as other operating systems such as MS-DOS and OS/2. Partitions are areas of a disk drive specified during initialization of a drive and before formatting a drive. You typically use a program called `fdisk` to partition a drive. There are some commercial products that allow you to repartition a drive and Linux provides a utility called fips to do the same. To use Linux efficiently, you should repartition your hard drive and allocate enough space for the Linux system files and your data files.

Caution

Unless you are installing Linux onto a brand new hard drive, you will need to repartition and reformat the drive. This destroys all information currently stored on that portion of the drive. Thus, it is imperative to back up your files before installing Linux. If space permits, you can split a single hard drive into multiple partitions and copy your files back to one of the partitions.

The amount of disk space required depends on the software you install. Linux requires less disk space than most implementations of UNIX systems. You can run a complete Linux system, without X Windows support, in 20M. For a complete installation, 150 to 200M is recommended.

Swap Space. Finally, as mentioned in the section on memory requirements, if you have limited RAM, you need swap space. While systems such as Microsoft Windows create a swap file that resides on your hard drive as any other file, Linux also allows the swap file to reside on a separate swap partition. Most Linux installations use partitions rather than files. Because you can place multiple partitions on the same physical hard drive, you can place the swap partition on the same drive as Linux. Linux allows up to eight swap partitions that can be no larger than 16M. A rule of thumb is to set the swap file size to twice the amount of physical RAM contained on your system. Thus, if you have 8M of physical RAM, your swap partition should be 16M in size.

Monitor Requirements

For the text-based terminals, Linux supports all standard Hercules, CGA, EGA, VGA, and SuperVGA video cards and monitors. To take advantage of the color-coding directory listings available with Linux, you need a color monitor. So for text-based operation, any video/controller combination should work. The big problems occur when you run the X Windows system distributed with Linux.

To use XFree86, you need a video adapter that uses one of the *chipsets* listed in Table 3.1. Chipsets are a group of integrated circuits, or computer chips, used to take information from the computer and convert the data into a form displayable on a video monitor. To find out the chipset used by your video adapter, check the documentation included with your card to determine if there are any problems using XFree86.

Some other problems encountered by the XFree86 developers are caused by adapter manufacturers who do not provide the necessary information on programming the cards to display information. Without this information, developers are unable to support X Windows on those adapters. Also, some manufacturers provide this information but require either royalty payments or non-disclosure agreements for others to use the information. These types of restrictions make it impossible to support these adapters on a freely distributed system like the XFree86 system for Linux.

Note

The Diamond video cards have not been supported in the past, due to restrictions the company had on giving out proprietary information. The Diamond company has now begun work with the XFree team to support the company's video systems specifically under Linux and XFree86. For further information, look at the file **/sunsite/X11/diamond.faq** on the CD-ROM.

Table 3.1 Video Chipsets Supported by Linux

Manufacturer	Chipset(s)
Tseng	ET3000, ET40000AX, ET4000/W32
Western Digital	WD90C00, WD90C10, WD90C11, WD90C24, WD90C30, WD90C31
Trident	TVGA8800CS, TVGA8900B, TVGA8900C, TVGA8900CL, TVGA9000, TVGA9000i, TVGA9100B, TVGA9200CX, TVGA9320, TVGA9400CX, TVGA9420
ATI	28800-4, 28800-5, 28800-a
NCR	77C22, 77C22E, 77C22E+
Cirrus Logic	CLGD5420, CLGD5422, CLGD5424, CLGD5426, CLGD5428, CLGD6205, CLGD6215, CLGD6225, CLGD6235
OAK	OTI067, OTI077
S3	86C911, 86C924, 86C801, 86C805, 86C805i, 86C928
Compaq	AVGA
Western Digital/Paradise	PVGA1

Note

The release notes for the current version of XFree86 distributed with Linux should contain a more recent list of supported and non-supported chipsets.

▸▸ See "Video Cards," p. 717

CD-ROMs

To install the Linux system included on the accompanying CD-ROM, you must have a CD-ROM drive supported by Linux. While there are other methods used to install Linux, such as floppy and network installation, a CD-ROM is the best medium to support this book. Because most CD-ROMs use a SCSI interface controller, any SCSI controller listed in Table 3.1 should also work with a CD-ROM attached to the controller. Linux also now supports many of the new EIDE and ATAPI CD-ROMS available on the market.

Many of the CD-ROMs included with multimedia packages may or may not work with Linux, depending on whether the controller is a true SCSI adapter or a proprietary adapter. Proprietary adapters for the most part will not work. However, Linux does specifically support the Creative Labs Soundblaster line of CD-ROMs and provides a specific installation configuration for their CD-ROMs. Other CD-ROMs known to work with Linux are the following:

- NEC CDR-74
- Sony CDU-541
- Sony CDU-31a or 33a
- Plextor DM-3024
- Aztech
- Orchid
- Okano
- Wearnes CD with interface card
- Soundblaster, Panasonic Kotobuki, Matsushita, TEAC-55a, or Lasermate
- Most IDE/ATAPI CD-ROMS
- Mitsumi CD-ROMs

▶▶ See "CD-ROM Drives Supported," p. 729

Network Access

There are several ways to connect a Linux system to the world, but the two most popular, and supported, methods are via network controller cards and modems. Network controller cards include token ring, FDDI, TAXI, and Ethernet cards. Most common business networks use an Ethernet controller card.

Network Access via Ethernet. Ethernet is a protocol invented by Xerox, it has gained immense popularity in the networking world. While is it unlikely you will connect Linux to an Ethernet network at home, many business and educational institutions are connected via Ethernet. Several of the Ethernet adapters supported by Linux are listed in Table 3.2.

▶▶ See "Supported—Ethernet," p. 724

Table 3.2 Ethernet Controller Cards Supported by Linux

Manufacturer	Interface Card
3Com	3c503, 3c503/16
Novell	NE1000, NE2000
Western Digital	WD8003, WD8013
Hewlett-Packard	HP27245, HP27247, HP27250

Network Access via Modem. At home, you will more than likely connect to the outside world via a modem and a communication protocol such as SLIP or PPP. Linux supports almost every type of modem on the market, both internal and external. If you can access the modem from MS-DOS, you will have no problem accessing the modem from Linux.

▶▶ See "Requirements for SLIP and PPP," p. 283

Miscellaneous Hardware

The following is a list of miscellaneous hardware supported by Linux. While making Linux easier to use and more robust, such hardware is not required. Such items include mice, tape drives, and printers.

Mice. Using text-based Linux does not require a mouse. However, unlike many UNIX implementations, Linux does allow you to cut text from any area of the screen and paste it to the command line by using a mouse. If you intend to use the X Windows clone, XFree86, you must use a mouse. Linux supports most serial mice, including mice from the following list:

- Logitech
- MM series
- Mouseman
- Microsoft
- Mouse Systems

Linux also supports the Microsoft, Logitech, ATIXL, and PS/2 bus mice. In fact, any pointing devices, such as trackballs and touch screens, which emulate the previously listed mice, should work with Linux.

Tape Drives. As specified earlier in the chapter, tape drives provide a great deal of storage space for backing up your computer system. Linux supports several SCSI-based tape systems, as shown in Table 3.3. Linux also supports the popular Colorado

Memory Systems tape drives, both the 120 and 250 versions, which are plugged into a system's floppy-disk controller. The versions that plug into the printer port are currently not supported. Most drives supporting QIC-02 should also work with Linux.

▶▶ See "Tape Drives—Supported," p. 728

Table 3.3 Tape-Backup Drives Supported by Linux

Manufacturer	Model
Sanko	CP150SE
Tandberg	3600
Wangtek	5525ES, 5150ES, 5099EN

Printers. Linux supports the complete range of parallel printers. Configuring Linux to support serial printers is tedious and error prone. Serial printer support is not well documented or supported by the basic Linux installation programs. If you have a serial printer, you may have problems using it under Linux. If you have a parallel printer, your biggest problem is most likely the *stair-step effect.* The stair-step effect looks like

```
This is line one.
                  This is line two.
                                    This is line three.
```

How UNIX, and hence Linux, treat carriage returns and line feeds produces the stair-step effect. Under most UNIX systems the command to move the paper down one line (line feed) and then position the print head at the beginning of the line (carriage return) are represented by one control character. Under systems such as MS-DOS and Windows, however, each command is represented by a different control character. When you print a UNIX file under a printer configured for MS-DOS systems, you see the stair-step effect because the file only contains the line feed control character and not the carriage return control character.

▶▶ See "Configuring Printers: What You Need," p. 475

Linux Distributions

After you have determined you have the correct hardware to run Linux, you must next choose which distribution of Linux to install. The reason is that Linux is distributed by many different organizations, each with a unique collection of programs, although each provides a core group of files that constitutes a Linux release. A release is identified by a series of numbers in the form of A.BB.CC, where A is either 0 or 1, and BB and ZZ are between 0 and 99. Higher numbers generally indicate newer releases. The current release of Linux on the enclosed CD is kernel version 1.3.18, plus several kernels at release 1.2.13. This distribution may also contain experimental kernels with drivers for unique hardware. You can find the various kernels in the /kernels directory on the CD-ROM.

Luckily for you, the decision is rather easy, because we have included a complete Slackware 3.0 distribution on the accompanying CD-ROM. However, there are other distributions, as follows:

- MCC Interim Linux
- TAMU Linux
- LST
- SLS
- Debian Linux
- Yggdrasil Plug-and-Play Linux CD-ROM and the Linux Bible
- Trans-Ameritech Linux plus BSD CD-ROM
- The Linux Quarterly CD-ROM
- Caldera
- RedHat

Note

This edition of *Special Edition Using Linux* also provides the RedHat distribution on the second CD.

The Distribution HOWTO also provides an exhaustive listing of various Linux distributions. You learn later in this chapter how to access the various HOWTOs that accompany each Linux release.

Welcome to the CD-ROM for Using Linux

The accompanying CD-ROM is published by InfoMagic, Inc. This CD-ROM is an abbreviated version of the InfoMagic Linux Developer's Resource, which is a five CD-ROM set of Linux-related material. For a complete description of InfoMagic's other CD-ROM titles, refer to the file `catalog.txt`.

Note

InfoMagic has provided an upgrade policy for readers of *Special Edition Using Linux,* Second Edition—you'll find a coupon in the book good for a low cost upgrade to InfoMagic's five CD-ROM set of Linux and Linux tools. Thus, you'll be able to upgrade to a future release of Linux.

The distribution of Linux on this disc is Slackware and has been included with the explicit permission of its author, Patrick Volkerding. In addition to the complete binary and source distribution for Linux, this CD-ROM also contains the HOWTO documents and Installation Guide from the Linux Documentation Project, headed by Matt Welsh.

This disc is mastered in the ISO-9660 format with Rock Ridge Extensions to preserve the long, mixed-case file names and deeply nested directory structure. Linux fully supports these extensions, and once you get the system installed and running you can see the long file names on the disc. For use under MS-DOS, every directory includes the file `YMTRANS.TBL` that lists the (ISO-9660) alias and the original long, mixed-case file name. The C language sources in the `YM_UTILS` directory can be used to either copy or create symbolic links on systems that do not support the Rock Ridge extensions, though, as mentioned previously, this is not necessary for Linux.

The HOWTO documents are in a directory directly off the root of the disc. The HOWTO material is also provided in the form of a Microsoft Multimedia Viewer title (along with the Viewer software) for browsing or searching under Microsoft Windows. The Viewer supports both hypertext access to all the HOWTOs and full-text search. You may search for single words or phrases and find all occurrences in any of the documents. The Viewer presents a list of topics that your search phrase was found in as well as highlighting the text in each topic.

A setup program for the Viewer software and HOWTO docs has been provided. From the Program Manager, open the File menu and choose Run. Enter **`x:\viewer\setup.exe`**, where *x* is your CD-ROM drive letter. The viewer may also be run directly from the CD-ROM. To do so, from the Program Manager of Windows, open the File menu and choose Run. Enter **`x:\viewer\mviewer2 HowTo.MVB`**, where *x* is the letter corresponding to your CD-ROM drive. Figure 3.1 illustrates the Linux HowTo Setup program.

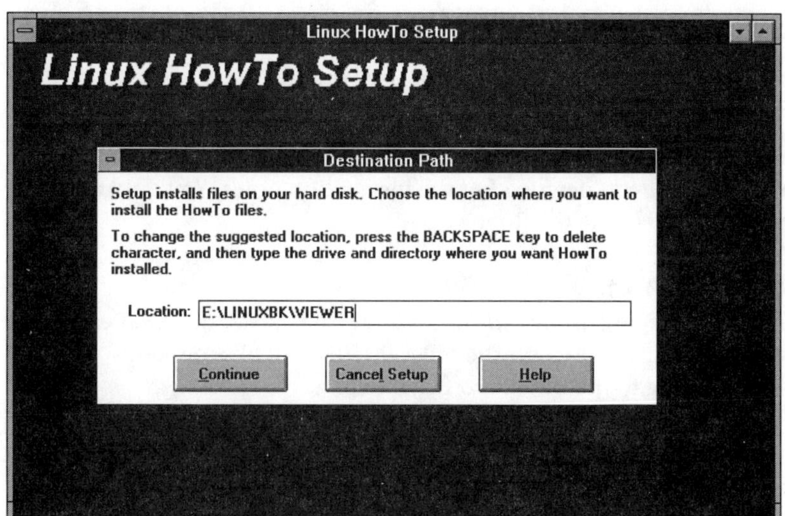

Fig. 3.1

The Linux HowTo Setup program's initial screen.

Slackware 3.0 Notes

Slackware is found below the `distributions` directory. The installation sets are in the directory `slackware` to match the InfoMagic menu option in the CD-ROM installation. The Boot and Root disks are in the directory `slakinst` to make them easier to find under DOS because long file names are not allowed under MS-DOS.

Please refer to the installation notes (`install.txt`) in the `slakinst` directory before proceeding. This is the Installation HOWTO. The Installation HOWTO may also be found in the `howto` directory or viewed using the Microsoft Multimedia Viewer software provided.

In addition to the base system there is a collection of contributed software in the directory `contrib`. The sources for everything in the Slackware distribution are provided in the `slacksrc` directory.

When using the Slackware `setup` utility to install, you are presented with an option to install from CD-ROM. In this CD-ROM installation menu, use the InfoMagic option. If your CD-ROM hardware is not supported by any of the provided Linux kernels, you need to copy the packages to an existing DOS partition (while running DOS) and perform the installation from those copies. The packages appear under DOS as subdirectories of the directory `\distribu`. You should use XCOPY to copy the files in each subdirectory to an identically named subdirectory on your DOS partition. Refer to the file `install.txt` in `slakinst` to decide which packages you want. During the setup process, choose the Install from DOS Partition option.

Notes for Newcomers

In the `howto` subdirectory, there are a series of HOWTO documents that provide detailed instructions on how to configure and install nearly every aspect of Linux. Please refer to these before starting if you have never configured or installed Linux before. The `guide` directory contains an Installation Guide in both text and PostScript format.

The tools used to create the bootable floppies are in the directory `dos_util`. This directory also contains a number of partition manipulation utilities including one called `fips` (in the `dos_util\fips` directory) that can be used to resize DOS partitions without damaging them. Please read the file `fips.doc` before using it.

The boot and root images have been uncompressed on this CD-ROM, you do not need to use the `gzip` program as described in the installation notes. You only need to use the `rawrite` program to create the floppies.

A Roadmap for the CD-ROM

Table 3.4 provides a brief listing of the directories on the CD-ROM and what each contains. You should investigate each in the order listed and look around the CD-ROM before continuing to the installation chapter.

Table 3.4 The Directories on the CD-ROM

Directory	Contents
`bootdsks.12/`	The 1.2 megabyte (5 1/4-inch) bootdisks for installation.
`bootdsks.144/`	The 1.44 megabyte (3 1/2-inch) bootdisks for installation.
`rootdsks/`	The rootdisks for installation.
`contents/`	A list of the files in each installable software package.
`contrib/`	This directory contains extra packages for Slackware, such as the Andrew User Interface System, GNU Fortran 77, GNU Common list, GNU gnat (Ada), GNU Pascal, NCSA httpd, ircll, Lucid `emacs`, SLiRP (a program you can run on a remote UNIX host to emulate a slip/cslip account), and more.
`docs/`	This directory contains the full set of Linux HOWTOs, documents that cover most common Linux maintenance tasks. In addition, you'll find documentation for the MS-DOS VIEW.EXE program, plus our catalog in several languages.
`filename.txt`	A list of all file names on the disc.
`install/`	This directory contains `rawrite`, `gzip`, and `fips`. These are tools that you might find handy if you're running MS-DOS. `gzip` is a UNIX-compatible compession/decompression utility. rawrite enables you to dump a disk image file onto a floppy disk. `fips` lets you shrink the size of an existing MS-DOS partition to make room for a Linux partition.

The Slackware Packages

Slackware is distributed as a series of packages, or sets. Each set contains related files that fit on a series of floppy disks. Each set is designated by a series of letters. The following sections provide a guide to the files contained in each set. You need to be familiar with each package when you install Linux. Not all packages are required to run Linux. Some are required and installed automatically by the setup programs. Some are not required but are highly recommended. Each package requires disk space and if you have space to spare, this should not be a problem; otherwise, you need to pick and choose which packages to install. The following sections help you decide which packages, shown in Table 3.5, to install.

Table 3.5 The Slackware Distribution Packages

Designation	Description
a	Base Linux
ap	Text-based applications
d	Program Development and GCC-C, C++, Objective-C, kernel source, and more
e	emacs
f	FAQs
i	Info pages
iv	InterViews
n	Networking, UUCP, mail, and news
oop	OOP: Smalltalk
q	Extra Kernel images and source
t	TeX
tcl	tcl Script Language/tk Toolkit
x	XFree86 and the X Windows system
xap	X Windows applications
xd	X11 server development
xv	XView (OpenLook Window Manager)
y	Games

Note that each package has a simple name. This name also corresponds to the base name for the directory on the CD-ROM where you can find the package. If you access the files from MS-DOS, the directories are based from `\slackwar\`*`dir-namedisk-number`*. For example, the a package consists of five directories named `a1`, `a2`, `a3`, `a4`, and `a5`.

Also, the files `00_find.unx` and `00_find.dos` contain a complete listing of all files on the disc. The files `ls_lr.unx` and `ls_lr.dos` are exhaustive directory listings in UNIX and DOS format, respectively. The following sections highlight some of the features found in the various packages. For a basic system, however, you need to install the `a`, `ap`, `d`, and `f` packages. You also need to install the `x`, `xd`, and `xap` packages if you want to run the X Windows system.

Slackware unfortunately does not maintain an accounting of the disk space required by each package. Because each disk in the set is usually compressed, and on average compression programs can yield about a 50 percent reduction, you can estimate the space required by multiplying each disk set by 2M (for example, 1.44M x 2=2.8M per disk). Thus, a rough estimate for the minimal system above, without X support, would be about 60M (ignoring such items as swap drive space and user data files).

Note

Please note that while 20M is an estimate, such a system would be slow and prone to crash, overall such a system would not be very usable. 150M of disk space should be more than adequate and with the advent of inexpensive hard drives, should not pose a problem for many users.

The *a* Package: Base Linux

The base Slackware package contains 14 high-density disks, but only three of those disks are represented on the CD-ROM. These packages, `a1`, `a2`, and `a3`, contain the base Linux operating system files. Disk `a1` contains the base operating system in base, all the device drivers in `/devs`, and the necessary UNIX clone files normally found in the `/etc` directory. This disk also contains the kernels for IDE drives and SCSI drives in `idekern` and `scsikern` respectively. `LILO` is Linux Loader and is in this package as well as some initialization and setup files in `sysvinit` and `hdsetup`.

The `a2` package contains the necessary files found in the UNIX `bin` directory. The files needed for terminal operation are found in `getty`. This package also contains the GNU compression utility `gzip`. Various UNIX utilities and shared libraries are also in this package, such as `ps`, `shlibs`, `util`, and `ldso`.

The `a3` package contains more utilities, such as `comms`, `cpio`, `e2fsbn`, `find`, `grep`, `keytbls`, `lpr`, `select`, `shellutl`, `syslogd`, and `tar`. `tar` is another compression/archive utility found in the UNIX world. `select` is a nice terminal utility that lets you cut commands from anywhere on the terminal and paste them to the command line with your mouse. The `find` and `grep` utilities help you find files and information within files.

Table 3.6 specifies which files are automatically added to your system by the setup program (designated with ADD), which files are strongly recommended (designated with REC), which files are optional (designated with OPT), and which files can be skipped (designated with SKP).

Note

The following list of files is typically found in a file called tagfile located in each of the various package subdirectories. The files shipped with the CD for this book might have newer or different files than those listed here. You can edit these tagfiles to suit your needs and thus automate your installation.

Table 3.6 The *a* Package Load Priority

Program	Recommendation	Program	Recomendation
base	ADD	util	ADD
bash	ADD	comms	REC
devs	ADD	cpio	ADD
etc	ADD	e2fsbn	ADD
hdsetup	ADD	find	ADD
idekern	REC	grep	ADD
lilo	ADD	keytbls	OPT
passwd	ADD	lpr	ADD
scsikern	REC	select	REC
sysvinit	ADD	shellutl	ADD
bin	ADD	syslogd	ADD
ldso	ADD	tar	ADD
getty	OPT	tcsh	OPT
gzip	ADD	textutl	ADD
ps	ADD	zoneinfo	ADD
shlibs	ADD	less	ADD

The *ap* Package: Text-Based Applications

The ap package consists of five directories. These files are normally lumped together into a single a package on a typical Slackware distribution, but have been broken up for this version. This package contains important help files, called man pages, an audio-CD player called `workbone`, plus several other useful programs. Table 3.7 indicates the files that are available.

Table 3.7 The *ap* Package

Program	Recommendation	Program	Recomendation
ispell	OPT	gp9600	OPT
jove	OPT	groff	REC
man	REC	quota	OPT
manpgs	REC	diff	REC
termbin	OPT	sc	OPT
termnet	OPT	shlbsvga	REC
termsrc	OPT	workbone	OPT
sudo	OPT	ftape	OPT

Program	Recommendation	Program	Recomendation
ghostscr	OPT	mt_st	OPT
gsfonts1	OPT	vim	OPT
joe	OPT	texinfo	REC
jed	OPT	zsh	OPT
gsfonts2	OPT	ash	OPT
bc	OPT	jpeg	OPT

The *d* Package: Program Development

The d package consists of nine disks, d1-d9, that contain the files needed for program development. These files include the GNU gcc and g++ compilers and support files.

The *e* Package: *emacs*

The e package consists of six disks that contain the executable files and source code to GNU's version 19.27 of emacs. emacs is a full-featured word processor used by many UNIX aficionados, and it is highly recommended that you install this package. This package also includes a version of the lisp programming language that emacs is built with. You may skip loading these portions of the e package, unless you intend to do some emacs hacking.

▶▶ See "Starting emacs," p. 453

The *f* Package: Answers

The f package contains a collection of answers to frequently asked questions on many subjects relating to Linux. This package is added to your Linux system if you select to install the f package. Many of these FAQs are from USENET newsgroups and can help answer many of your questions about Linux.

▶▶ See "What is USENET News?," p. 647

The *n* Package: Networking

The n package contains programs to get you onto the Information Superhighway. If you intend to use Linux to connect to the Internet and use such features as mail, ftp, and USENET news, you need to install this package.

The *oop* Package: Object-Oriented Programming with Smalltalk

The oop package contains GNU's implementation of Smalltalk. Smalltalk is an object-oriented programming environment developed at Xerox Parc.

The *t* Package: *TeX*

The `t` package contains the `TeX` program. `TeX` is a text-formatting package developed by the well-known computer scientist Dr. Donald Knuth.

The *x* Package: XFree86

The `x` package contains the entire implementation of the XFree86 system. This is a free version of X Windows X11R6 clone that provides a graphical user interface to Linux. You do not need to install this package to run Linux, but if you have the necessary hardware, give XFree86 a try.

The *xap* Package: X Applications

The `xap` package contains several X applications. Included are `xgrab`, a screen-capture program used to capture many of the figures for this book, and `xtris`, a version of the popular Tetris game. If you load the `x` package, then it is also recommended that you load the `xap` package to get the most use from X Windows.

The *y* Package: Games

What's a computer without games? The `y` package contains several favorite UNIX games for Linux, including `tetris` and `hunt`.

From Here...

This chapter has introduced the various distributions available for Linux and provided you with a detailed description of the Slackware distribution found on the accompanying CD-ROM. After exploring the CD-ROM you should set your sights on actually installing the Linux system. For more information, see the following chapters:

- Chapter 4, "Installing Linux," provides you with the details to get Linux up and running. Before entering the wonderful world of Linux, you must install the system on your PC, not always an easy task. This chapter will help you plan, install, and configure your system.
- Appendix C, "The Linux Hardware Compatibility HOWTO," for detailed information on what hardware Linux currently supports. If you do not have supported hardware, then getting linux to run correctly is almost impossible. If your hardware is not among those listed in the Appendix, double-check the HowTo on the enclosed CD-ROM to see if your hardware is supported. (The one on the CD-ROM will be newer than the one referenced in Appendix C.)
- Appendix D, "The Linux CD-ROM HOWTO," for detailed information on what CD-ROM drivers Linux currently supports. This HOWTO also provides many troubleshooting tips for getting Linux to communicate with CD-ROMs.
- The "Linux Installation and Getting Started Guide," by Matt Welsh, which is part of the Linux Installation HOWTO provided on the enclosed CD-ROM. This document covers installing Linux from a point of view of the basic system rather than any one distribution. A very good reference for general questions regarding Linux installations.

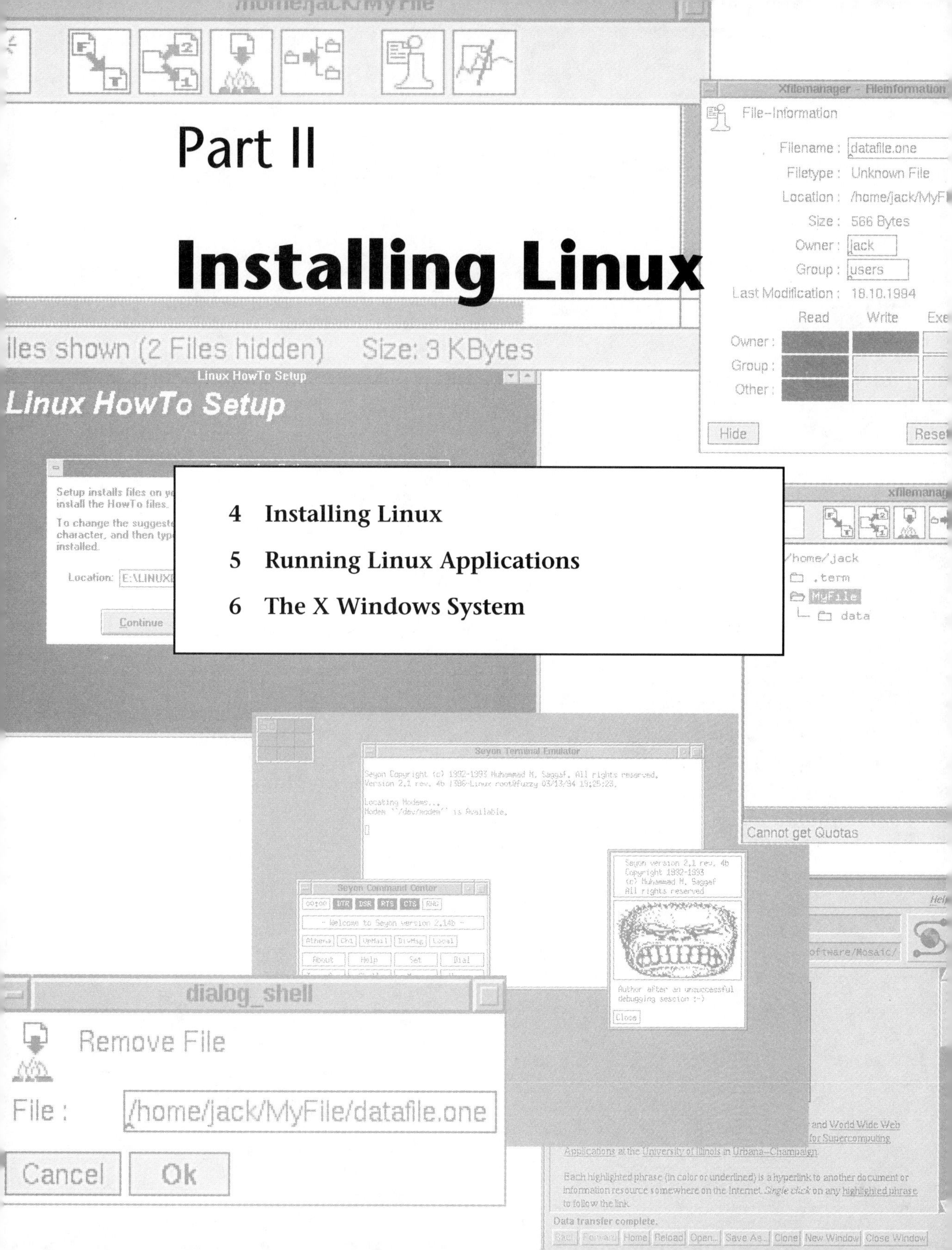

Part II

Installing Linux

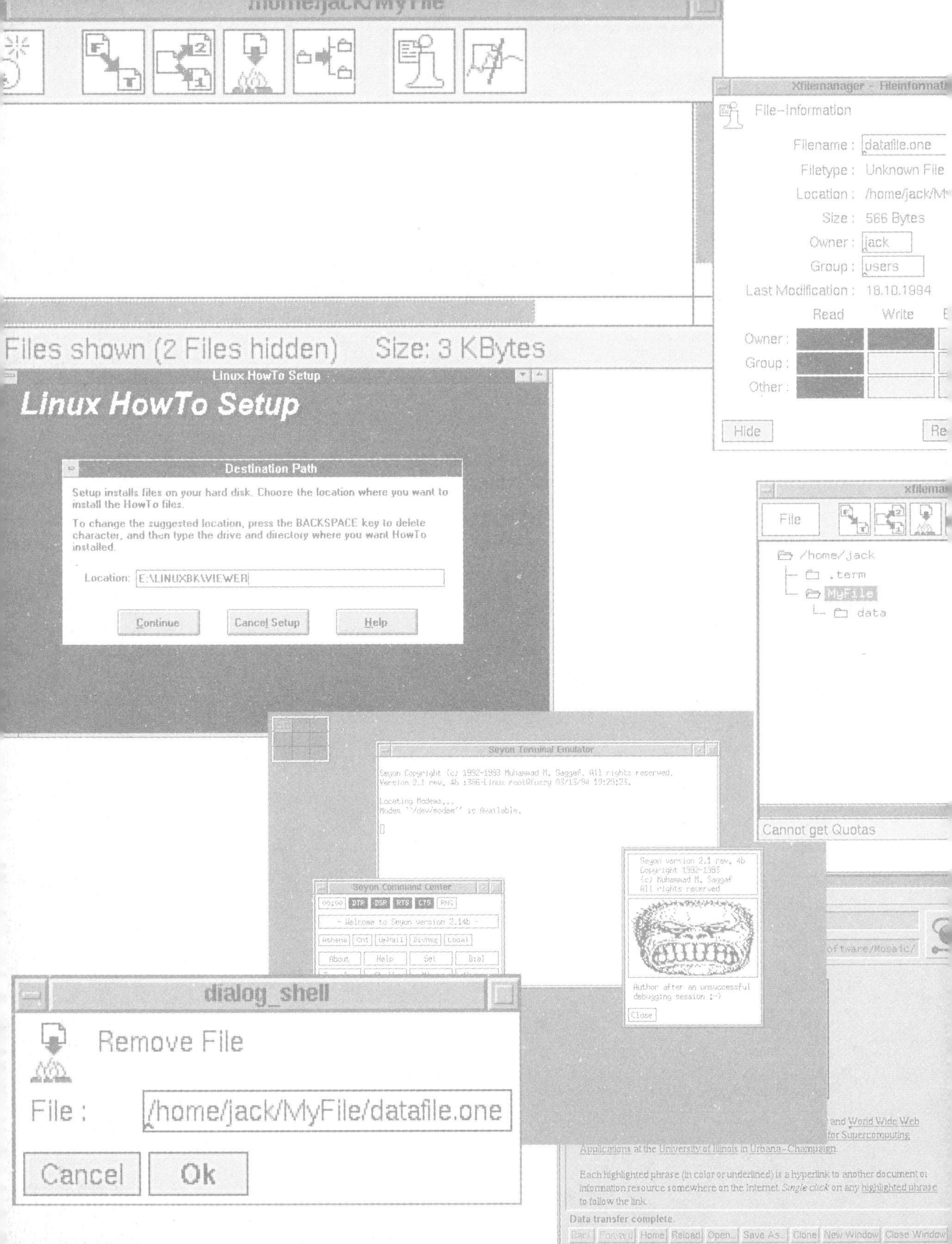

Files shown (2 Files hidden)   Size: 3 KBytes
Xfilemanager - Fileinformati
File-Information
Filename : datafile.one
Filetype : Unknown File
Location : /home/jack/M
Size : 566 Bytes
Owner : jack
Group : users
Last Modification : 18.10.1994
Read Write
Owner :
Group :
Other :
Hide
Linux HowTo Setup
Linux HowTo Setup
Destination Path
Setup installs files on your hard disk. Choose the location where you want to install the HowTo files.
To change the suggested location, press the BACKSPACE key to delete character, and then type the drive and directory where you want HowTo installed.
Location: E:\LINUXBK\VIEWER
Continue
Cancel Setup
Help
File
/home/jack
.term
MyFile
data
Cannot get Quotas
Seyon Terminal Emulator
Seyon Copyright (c) 1992-1993 Muhammad M. Saggaf. All rights reserved.
Version 2.1 rev. 4b i386-Linux root@fuzzy 03/13/94 19:25:23.
Locating Modems...
Modem ``/dev/modem'' is Available.
Seyon Command Center
DTR DSR RTS CTS RNG
- Welcome to Seyon version 2.14b -
Athena Ctrl UxMail DivMsg Local
About Help Set Dial
Seyon version 2.1 rev. 4b
Copyright 1992-1993
(c) Muhammad M. Saggaf
All rights reserved
Author after an unsuccessful debugging session :-)
Close
dialog_shell
Remove File
File : /home/jack/MyFile/datafile.one
Cancel
Ok
oftware/Mosaic/
e and World Wide Web
for Supercomputing
Applications at the University of Illinois in Urbana-Champaign.
Each highlighted phrase (in color or underlined) is a hyperlink to another document or information resource somewhere on the Internet. Single click on any highlighted phrase to follow the link.
Data transfer complete.
Back Forward Home Reload Open... Save As... Clone New Window Close Window

CHAPTER 4

Installing Linux

This chapter gives you the information needed to install Linux. Remember, Linux is not a commercial product and you might find some problems. Though this book leads the way, you may find the need to use the resources provided on the CD-ROM. First, review the hardware requirements from Chapter 3, "Understanding the Linux Distributions," and make sure that you have compatible equipment. If you don't, Linux may work, but more than likely, it won't. But in the hacker world, if a part of Linux doesn't work, you fix it. Hacking kernel code is probably not your forte, but if you have the appropriate hardware, things should go smoothly.

◀◀ See "Choosing the Right Hardware for Linux," p.34

Once you have determined that you have the necessary hardware, you must prepare for the installation. Following the steps provided in this chapter should ensure a smooth installation. In this chapter, you learn:

- How to prepare your system for the installation
- How to partition your hard drives to make room for Linux
- How to install the typical Slackware distribution
- How to use the provided tools to install the Slackware distribution included on the CD-ROM
- What to do if things go wrong

Note

This book assumes that you have a working knowledge of DOS and of such items as formatting your hard drive, partition tables, and sector sizes. If this information sounds like a foreign language, check out *Using MS-DOS 6.2, Special Edition*, or ask a computer guru buddy to help you through this. Again, you are about to make major changes to your system, so be careful.

What You Need To Install Linux

It is a good idea to have paper and pen nearby to take notes just in case something does go wrong; besides, you will need to jot down some numbers along the way. Next, you need a distribution of Linux, which is supplied on the accompanying CD-ROM. To start the installation process, you need two formatted floppy disks, either two 1.44M high-density, 3 1/2-inch disks or two 1.2M, 5 1/4-inch disks. You should also decide how you intend to boot Linux. You have two choices. You can boot Linux from a floppy disk, in which case you need an extra formatted disk—for a total of three disks. The other choice is to use a program called `LILO`, the Linux Loader. `LILO` is a program that allows you to specify which operating system to boot. Such programs as OS/2 and Windows NT provide similar functionality. `LILO` is discussed later in this chapter.

◀◀ See "Linux Distributions," p. 41

Next, you should make sure you have enough disk space to install Linux. You can get a rough estimate using the number of disk images in each package you plan to install and multiplying by 2.5. This provides the number of megabytes of hard drive space you need for the software. You should also factor in swap space and user requirements. While 2.5 is a large multiple, most people can get by with 200M devoted to Linux and less if you plan not to use such applications as `TeX` and X Windows.

◀◀ See "The Slackware Packages," p. 45

For configuring XFree86, you should also write what type of chipset your video card uses. If you have a serial mouse and modem, write the serial port that each is using. You need this information later during the configuration process.

The Preparations

If you have a brand-new system or a system that you don't care what happens to the data already stored on the computer, you can skip most of the following sections and go directly to "Creating the Boot and Root Disks." If, however, you already have a system you are using and simply want to add Linux, you must do some planning. The main reason is that Linux is another operating system, not just a collection of programs. In general, when you install Linux, a new operating system, you must do the following:

Create the Linux boot disk

Repartition the hard drive to make room for Linux

Boot the Linux installation medium

Create the Linux partitions

Create the file systems

Install the Linux system and software applications

The boot disks consist of two floppies that you must create. The reason is you need to *bootstrap* Linux onto the new system. Next, you must repartition your current hard drive to make room for Linux. This may cause problems because repartitioning a hard drive destroys any data contained on the affected partitions. After making room for Linux, you need to boot the Linux system and create its new partitions and file systems. Typically, Linux systems need a primary partition to store the files on and a swap file partition, especially if you have a machine with eight or fewer megabytes of memory. A file system is basically a section of your hard drive specially formatted to hold files. UNIX and Linux use file systems to represent entire sections of the directory tree. This is in contrast to MS-DOS, which places subdirectories in the directory tree on the same logical drive. UNIX systems do this because placing subdirectories on different drives is safer. If one drive malfunctions, only the information on that drive needs to be replaced or fixed. After creating the file systems, you then install the Linux operating system, its support files, and various application packages distributed with the system.

Preparing—Floppies and Backups

First, you must make a system disk for your PC. To install Linux, it is necessary to repartition your hard drive to make room for the new operating system. Unfortunately, you just can't simply copy the files over to an MS-DOS, OS/2, or Windows NT file system.

Create an MS-DOS Boot Disk

When you repartition your hard drive, you should prepare for the worst—the trashing of your hard drive. If your drive crashes, you may not be able to boot up. Thus, you should create a boot floppy with the necessary boot files.

For MS-DOS, place a floppy into the disk drive and type **`format a: /s`**. This creates a boot floppy. Copy your current CONFIG.SYS, AUTOEXEC.BAT, and any driver files needed to start your computer. Also, copy FDISK.EXE and FORMAT.COM to the floppy because you will be repartitioning your hard drive and will then need to reformat the hard disk. Keep this disk in a safe place. If you are backing up your system, also include the necessary file to restore your backup. (You also will probably need your DOS disks to restore DOS to your system.)

You might also want to record the various cmos settings for your system, too. Most Intel-compatible computer systems allow you to access the setup information from the cmos at startup.

> **Note**
>
> If you are using OS/2, you need to reference the OS/2 documentation on how to create an OS/2 boot disk.

Backing Up Your System

Unless you are using a brand-new computer or a computer with a brand-new hard drive containing no software, take the time to make a backup. If you have a tape drive, use the program sold with your tape drive to back up the entire hard drive. If you don't have a tape drive, you can use the MS-DOS backup/restore programs to make a backup of your system. Make sure you have plenty of floppy disks and use the following command syntax:

```
backup from to
```

For example, if you are going to back up all the files *from* C: drive *to* the A: drive, enter **`backup c: a:`**, press <Return>, and start swapping floppies. Of course with the cost of large hard drives dropping, as well as the cost of tape backup units, you should consider doing a tape backup rather than backing up to floppies.

Creating the Boot and Root Disks

Once you have made your DOS boot disk and backed up your system, you must now create the boot disks for Linux. The Slackware distribution of Linux included on this CD-ROM provides a Windows program to automatically create the boot and root disks. There are two floppies needed with Slackware: the boot and root floppies. You create these floppies with a set of MS-DOS programs provided with most Linux distributions, called `gzip` and `rawrite`.

`gzip` is a GNU program very much like PKWare's `pkzip`. `gzip` allows you to compress and uncompress archive files. You need this program because many of the Linux files, especially those needed for installation, are compressed using `gzip`. `rawrite` is a program used to write the contents of a file directly to a floppy without regard to the format. Once you unzip the boot images with `gzip`, you must use `rawrite` to transfer the images to the appropriate floppies.

The Boot Disk. The boot disk is used to start the Linux system for installation. It contains bare-bones device drivers and a basic version of the operating system. This boot disk is specific to the hardware and type of floppy drive your system uses to boot (usually the A: drive under MS-DOS). The various files are shown in Table 4.1. (These files may have been updated prior to the printing of this book. See the README file in the `\boot 12` or `\boot144` directory for details.)

Table 4.1 The Boot Files

Name	Descriptions
`bare.gz`	Contains only IDE hard-drive drivers. (No SCSI, CD-ROM, or networking support.) Use this only if you have an IDE hard-drive controller and are not going to install from a CD-ROM.
`aztech.gz`	Contains IDE, SCSI, and Aztech non-IDE CD-ROM support.
`xt.gz`	Contains IDE and XT hard-drive support.
`cdu31a.gz`	Contains IDE and SCSI drivers, including support for the Sony CDU31/33a CD-ROM.
`cdu535.gz`	Contains IDE and SCSI drivers including drivers for the Sony 535/531 CD-ROMs.
`cd.gz`	Contains IDE hard drive and non-SCSI CD-ROM drivers. Get this if you're going to be installing from a (non-SCSI) CD-ROM.
`idecd.gz`	Supports IDE, SCSI, and IDE/ATAPI CD-ROMs.
`mitsumi.gz`	Contains IDE, SCSI, and Mitsumi CD-ROM drivers.
`cdscsi.gz`	Contains IDE and SCSI hard-drive support, and non-SCSI CD-ROM drivers.
`scsi.gz`	Contains IDE and SCSI hard-drive support.
`net.gz`	Contains IDE hard drive and TCP/IP networking support. Get this if you are going to install over the network using NFS.
`scsinet1.gz`	Contains IDE and SCSI hard-drive support, SCSI CD-ROM drivers, and EtherNet networking support. This kernel supports the Adaptec 152x/1542/1740/274x/248x, the Buslogic, EATA-DMA, Seagate st-02, and Future Domain TCC-8xx-16xx controller cards.
`scsinet1.gz`	Contains IDE and SCSI hard-drive support, SCSI CD-ROM drivers, and EtherNet networking support too. This kernel supports the Generic NCS5380/53C7/8xx, Always, Pro Audio Spectrum 16, Quelogic, Trantor T128/T128F/T1228, Ultrastor, and 7000 FASST controller cards.
`sbpcd.gz`	Contains IDE and CD-ROM support for the Creative Labs Sound Blaster/Panasonic CD-ROM systems.

These files come in two flavors, depending on the size of your boot floppy. Luckily, the uncompressed files are already available for you on the accompanying CD-ROM in the `/slakwar` directory. If your A: drive is a 1.2M 5 1/4-inch drive, look in the `/slakwar/boot12` directory. If you have a 1.44M 3 1/2-inch high-density drive, look in the `/slakwar/boot144` directory. If you use another distribution, you need to copy the compressed files to a directory on your hard drive and use the `gzip` program to unzip them. Table 4.2 illustrates the commands for the `gzip` program, which uses the syntax

```
gzip [-acdfhlLnNtvV19] [-S suffix] [file ...]
```

Table 4.2 Flags for the *gzip* Command

Flag	Name	Description
`-a`	`ascii`	ASCII text; converts end-of-lines using local conventions
`-c`	`stdout`	Writes on standard output, keeps original files unchanged
`-d`	`decompress`	Decompresses
`-f`	`force`	Forces overwrite of output file and compresses links
`-h`	`help`	Gives this help
`-l`	`list`	Lists compressed file contents
`-L`	`license`	Displays software license
`-n`	`no-name`	Does not save or restore the original name and time stamp
`-N`	`name`	Saves or restores the original name and time stamp
`-q`	`quiet`	Suppresses all warnings
`-S` *`suffix`*	`suffix .suf`	Uses `suffix .suf` on compressed files
`-t`	`test`	Tests compressed file integrity
`-v`	`verbose`	Verbose mode
`-V`	`version`	Displays version number
`-1`	`fast`	Compresses faster
`-9`	`best`	Compresses better
`file`		Files to (de)compress. If none given, uses standard input

To create the images for a Sound Blaster installation, you unzip the `sbpcd.gz` file with the following command:

```
gzip -d sbpcd.gz
```

The result is a file called `sbpcd`, without the `gz` extension. As stated earlier, the enclosed CD-ROM already contains the uncompressed files in the appropriate boot directory.

Making the Root Disks. The root disks are needed to create a beginning file system for the first Linux boot. From this file system, you install the full Linux Slackware distribution. You need one of the files listed in Table 4.3 to create your root disk.

Table 4.3 The Root Files

Name	Descriptions
`color144.tgz`	The menu-based color installation disk for 1.44M drives. Most users should use this root disk.

Name	Descriptions
umsds144.tgz	A version of the color144 disk for installing with the UMSDOS file system, which allows you to install Linux onto a directory of an MS-DOS file system. This installation method is not discussed in detail here, but you don't have to repartition your drive. More on this later.
tty144.tgz	The terminal-based installation disk for 1.44M drives. You should use color144.tgz, but a few people have reported problems with it on their system. If color144.tgz doesn't work for you, try tty144.tgz instead. It is a bit dated and the installation procedure isn't identical, but it should work if color144.tgz doesn't.
colrlite.tgz	The menu-based color installation disk for 1.2M drives. Some things have been trimmed off of this disk to make it fit on a 1.2M floppy, but it should work if you only have a 1.2M drive.
umsds12.tgz	A version of the colrlite disk for installing with the UMSDOS file system. See the description of umsds144.tgz.
tty12.tgz	The terminal-based installation disk for 1.2M drives. Use this root disk if you have a 1.2M boot floppy and colrlite.tgz doesn't work for you.

Again, the accompanying CD-ROM already contains the uncompressed images. Depending on the size of your boot floppy, you can find the files in either the root12 or root144 subdirectories underneath the /slakwar/ directory.

Creating the Disks with *rawrite*. Once you have the image file uncompressed, you can transfer the file to floppies. To do this, you need the rawrite program. You can find this program on the accompanying CD-ROM in the /utils subdirectory.

For this step, you need the two floppies you formatted earlier. You must make sure you write the current images to the floppy disks. Thus, you must write the images made for 1.44M disks to 1.44M disks. If you write the images from the 1.2M directories to a 1.44M disks, you won't be able to install Linux.

Label one disk the boot disk and place it in the disk drive. The following sequence assumes a 1.44M, 3 1/2-inch boot disk drive, sbpcd, and color144 installation root/boot disks:

```
E:\LINUX>RAWRITE
RaWrite 1.2 - Write disk file to raw floppy diskette

Enter source file name: COLOR144
Enter destination drive: A:
Please insert a formatted diskette into drive A: and press -ENTER-
: A
Number of sectors per track for this disk is 18
Writing image to drive A:,  Press ^C to abort.
Track: 01  Head:  1 Sector: 10
```

rawrite displays progress information as the program writes the raw image to the disk, and then the program displays done when finished. If you wish to abort the process, simply press <Ctrl-c> to stop. If any errors occur during the operation, the program displays one of the error messages shown in Table 4.4.

Table 4.4 Possible *rawrite* Error Codes

Error	Description
`Operation Successful`	Not an error message, hopefully you will see this message.
`Bad command`	Your hardware I/O system did not understand a command sent by the program. Try a different version of `rawrite` from another distribution package.
`Address mark not found`	Try a different disk.
`Attempt to write on the write-protected disk`	Remove the write protection from disk.
`Sector not found`	Possible bad disk, try a different one.
`Reset failed (hard disk)`	Possible hardware problems, check hardware before continuing.
`Disk changed since last operation`	Do not remove the disk from the `operation` drive until the entire operation is complete.
`Drive parameter activity failed`	Possible hardware problems.
`DMA overrun`	Data was lost on transfer from memory to disk—try operation again. This may be an indication of hardware or low memory problems.
`Attempt to DMA across 64K boundary`	Attempt by DMA chip to write beyond a 64K boundary. May be an indication of hardware or low memory problems.
`Bad sector detected`	Disk is bad—try a new one.
`Bad track detected`	Disk is bad—try a new one
`Unsupported track`	Possible bad disk—try a new one.
`Bad CRC/ECC on disk read`	Bad disk—try a new one.
`CRC/ECC corrected data error`	Possible bad disk or hardware.
`Controller has failed`	Major hardware problems.
`Seek operation failed`	Possible bad disk or hardware problem.
`Attachment failed to respond`	Check drive door—make sure it is closed.
`Drive not ready (hard disk only)`	Possible major hardware problems.
`Undefined error occurred (hard disk only)`	Possible hardware problems.
`Write fault occurred`	Possible bad disk or hardware problems.
`Status error`	Undefined error—could be hardware or disk.
`Sense operation failed`	Possible bad disk or hardware problem.

If rawrite fails, try a new formatted disk. If the problem persists, you should have your hardware checked for possible problems. After writing the boot disk, you need to write the root disk to another disk. Simply use the root image file name as the source file name instead of the boot image file name.

```
RaWrite 1.2 - Write disk file to raw floppy diskette

Enter source file name: scsi
Enter destination drive: A:
Please insert a formatted diskette into drive A: and press -ENTER-
: A
Number of sectors per track for this disk is 18
Writing image to drive A:,  Press ^C to abort.
Track: 01  Head:  1 Sector: 10
```

Partitioning Your Hard Drive

Once you have backed up your system and made the necessary disks, you must prepare your system's hard drive for Linux. This process is the most dangerous because maximum data loss is assured. If you have not backed up your system, do so now. While there is an experimental program, called FIPS, and commercial programs such as Partition Magic, that do nondestructive repartitioning, a full backup is recommended, just in case problems occur.

Why Use Partitions?

In the early days of PCs, hard drives were few and far between. Most computers used floppies to hold the operating system and programs and their data. IBM with the introduction of the IBM PC XT introduced a 10M hard drive. Early operating systems such as DOS could only access a limited amount of space on hard drives. Then hard-drive manufacturers kept expanding the space on their hard drives quicker than the operating system's ability to access the additional space. The operating system got around this problem by letting the user split the hard drive into sections, called partitions. These partitions can hold program files, other operating systems, or data.

Typical MS-DOS systems have one partition, which is referred to as drive C:. If you split the drive into partitions, these partitions are typically referred to in alphabetical order as D:, E:, and so on. MS-DOS also allows you to install multiple hard drives, so that the next drive in this chain might be referred to as F:. UNIX and Linux do not use drive letters to refer to partitions; instead, they use directory names to refer to partitions. Also, as indicated earlier, Linux users can place different directories on different partitions and even on different drives. You can also place different operating systems on different partitions.

Explaining Partitions

Partitions are specified in a section of the hard drive referred to as the boot record in what is called a *partition table*. This table is used by the various operating systems to determine what operating system to boot and where their files can be found physically on the hard drive. The boot record is used to boot, or start up, the machine's operating system. `LILO` and other boot managers use this section of the hard drive, typically found on the first sectors of the drive, to control which operating system to start.

The partition table holds information about the locations and sizes of the various partitions on the hard drive. There are three kinds of partitions: primary, extended, and logical. DOS and some other operating systems must boot from primary partitions. Hard drives can only contain four primary partitions. An extended partition does not contain data itself; instead, it allows the user to define other, logical partitions on the drive. Thus, to get around the four-limit primary partition number, you can define an extended partition and then define other logical partitions within the extended partition. Some operating systems like MS-DOS and versions of OS/2 before version 2.0 require that they be installed in a primary partition, but they can access logical drives in extended partitions. This is important to remember if you are going to have both a DOS system and a Linux system reside on the same drive. DOS must go in a primary partition.

Using FDISK

Partitions are created, destroyed, and managed by a program usually called FDISK. Each operating system has its own version of FDISK, so be sure to use the correct one. If you are currently using DOS or are planning to use DOS, you must first repartition the DOS drive using DOS's FDISK. You later use the Linux version of `fdisk` to create the Linux partitions. If you are using OS/2, you also need to use the OS/2 version of FDISK to prepare the OS/2 partitions.

Partition Requirements. First, you should plan out what partitions you need. DOS requires a primary partition. Linux and OS/2 can reside in other partitions. If you are using the OS/2 boot manager, which also works well with Linux, you must prepare for its use also. You must also be aware if you are shrinking a current DOS partition to make room for Linux that not all of your files can be restored to the new, smaller DOS partition. Please note that you can access DOS partitions from Linux, moving, saving, and editing DOS files under Linux. However, you cannot execute DOS programs under Linux.

> **Note**
>
> There are two experimental components of Linux that allow you to emulate DOS under Linux and also install Linux under DOS. Both systems are still in the implementation stage and are, thus, more suited for Linux hackers. You can also find plenty of information on these topics in the Linux world.

▶▶ See "Running DOS Programs Under Linux," p. 117

Next, you should jot down the number of partitions you need and how much disk space to provide each with.

DOS Requirements. If you want to boot DOS, it must go in a primary partition. A bootable version of DOS does not require much space—just enough for the system files, `COMMAND.COM`, `CONFIG.SYS`, and any driver files needed to start your system. For instance, I provide a 5M DOS partition on my first drive in order to boot DOS. Once DOS is loaded and running, you can access any of the other extended and logical drives on the system. Unfortunately, while Linux can access DOS files in a DOS partition, DOS cannot access Linux files in a Linux partition.

OS/2 Requirements. OS/2 versions 2.0 and later do not need a primary partition. The OS/2 system can install and boot from an extended partition. Thus, you can install DOS on a primary partition and create an extended partition area for OS/2 and Linux. The space required for OS/2 is version- and feature-dependent and you should consult your OS/2 documentation for space requirements. You should also subtract from available space 1M if you intend to use the OS/2 boot manager.

Linux Requirements. As explained earlier, Linux stores files on file systems and these file systems can reside on different partitions, basically as safety precautions. Linux requires one partition for each file system. The next consideration is for a swap partition. Linux, like most operating systems that use disk space for memory (called a virtual memory configuration), needs a swap file or a swap partition to simulate physical memory using disk space. Linux typically uses a swap partition.

The size of the swap partition depends on the amount of physical RAM your system contains. A rule of thumb is to make your swap partition twice the size of your amount of RAM. Thus, if you have 8M of RAM in your system, you should create a swap partition 16M in size. If you have 4M of RAM or less, you must activate a swap partition.

Linux swap partitions can only be 128M in size, so if you need more space, you have to create multiple swap partitions. Thus, if you have a Linux system that needs two partitions for Linux, one for the system files and one for user files, plus a swap partition—you need to define two Linux partitions and one 32M swap partition.

Repartitioning

This section assumes you need to repartition a DOS drive. First, you execute FDISK by typing **`fdisk`** at the DOS prompt, and you see the FDISK Options screen (see fig. 4.1).

The screen shown in Figure 4.1 might appear different depending on which version of MS-DOS you are using. Pick menu option 4, Display Partition Information. The Display Partition Information screen appears (see fig. 4.2).

Write down this information. You need the current partition table information if you decide to abort the Linux installation and put your system back the way it was before you started.

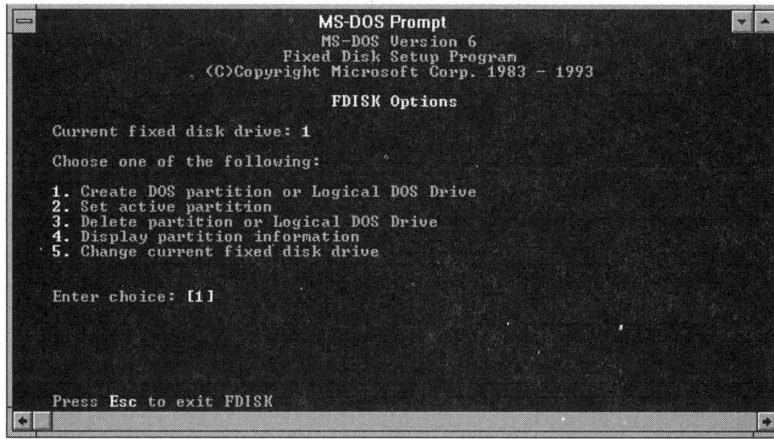

Fig. 4.1

The FDISK Options screen.

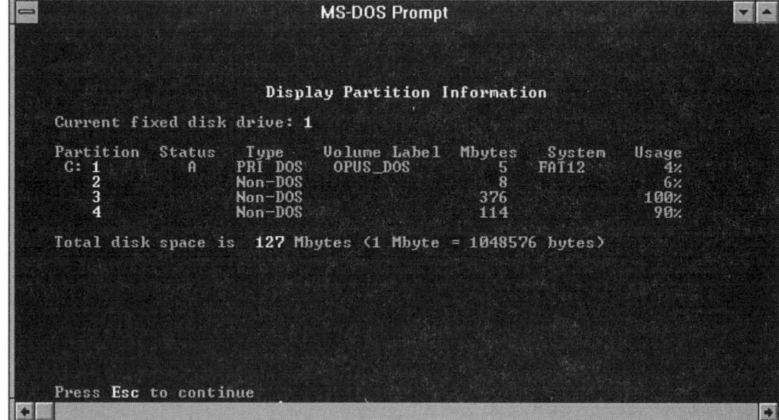

Fig. 4.2

The Display Partition Information screen in MS-DOS 6.0.

Note

You may not need to repartition your hard drive, although it is thought that repartitioning offers the best introduction to Linux. You can either use FIPS to nondestructively repartition your hard drive or install Linux on the same partition as DOS with UMSDOS.

FIPS stands for the First nondestructive Interactive Partition Splitting program. It is a program developed by Arno Schaefer as a result of the Linux project and is used to move around DOS partitions to make room for Linux partitions.

The complete instructions for using FIPS can be found in the document `fips.doc` located on the enclosed CD-ROM in `/utils/fips` directory. This program can help only if you have enough free space left on your drive to install Linux; otherwise, you either need to delete unneeded files or use the process described earlier to repartition your hard drive.

UMSDOS is a project to allow Linux to exist on DOS partitions. UMSDOS allows you to create the Linux root file system under an existing DOS directory. You learn more about using UMSDOS later in this chapter.

Deleting Partitions. Unfortunately, FDISK does not allow you to simply resize a partition; you must first delete the partition and then add it back with the desired size. From the FDISK Options screen, choose menu option 3, Delete Partition or Logical DOS Drive, which deletes the necessary partitions. The Delete DOS Partition or Logical DOS Drive screen appears (see fig. 4.3).

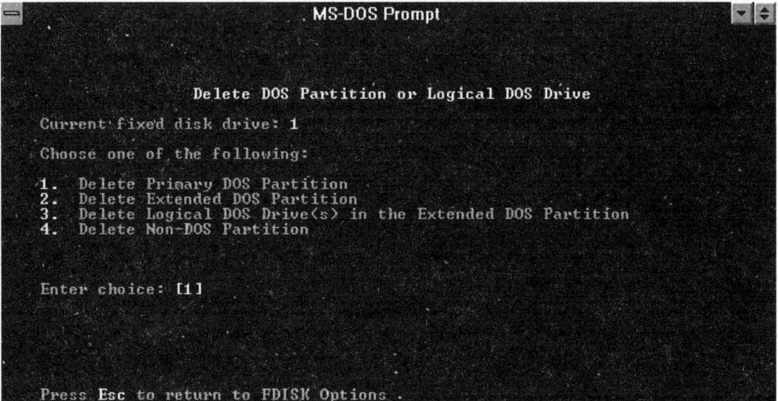

Fig. 4.3

The Delete DOS Partition or Logical DOS Drive screen.

Pick the appropriate menu option for the type of partition you are deleting, such as a primary DOS partition. For example, option 1, Delete Primary DOS Partition, allows you to delete primary DOS partitions. Choosing option 1 displays the Delete Primary DOS Partition screen (see fig. 4.4).

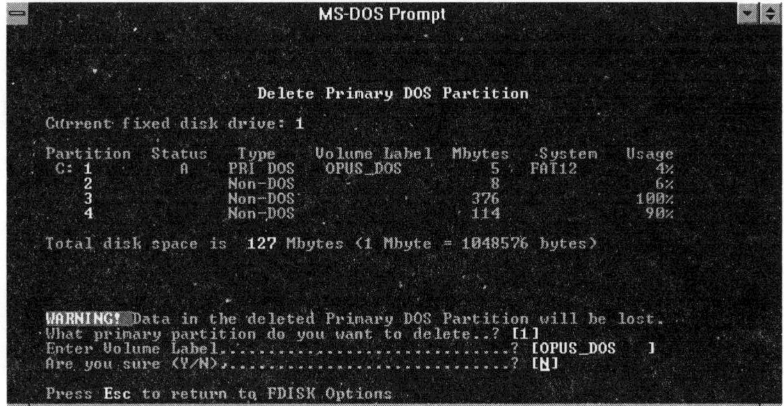

Fig. 4.4

The Delete Primary DOS Partition screen.

The screen asks for a volume name of the partition and then a confirmation to see if you really want to delete the partition. Because all information on the partition will be destroyed, FDISK wants to be absolutely sure that you want to delete the primary DOS partition.

Adding Partitions. Once you have deleted all the necessary partitions, you must then add the appropriate partitions for your DOS system. You cannot add the Linux or OS/2 partitions with the DOS FDISK program. Partitioning the hard drive for Linux is covered later in this chapter. Figure 4.5 shows the Create a DOS Partition or Logical DOS Drive screen.

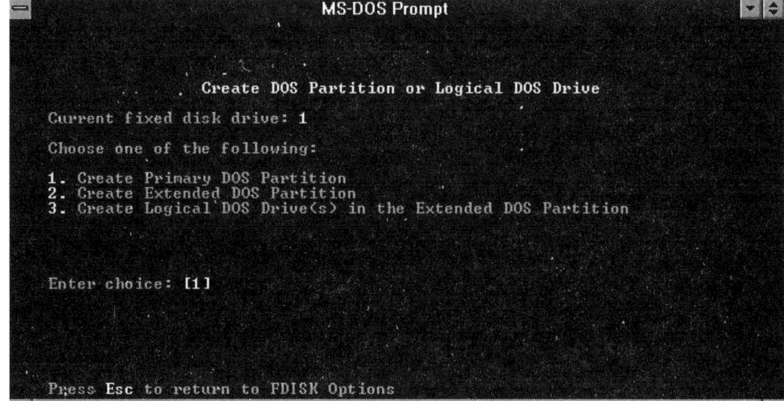

Fig. 4.5

The Create DOS Partition or Logical DOS Drive screen.

Providing all the space available for the partition and making the partition the *active* partition are the FDISK defaults (see fig. 4.6).

Active indicates that the partition is bootable. In order to boot DOS, you must specify the primary partition as active. Say no to this first selection so that you can specify the exact amount of disk space to provide to your DOS partition. Answering no to the question in Figure 4.6 displays the Specify Disk Space for the Partition screen. Specify the desired space for your DOS partition in either megabytes or in percentage of space available and press <Return>.

Next, you must set this partition active. From the FDISK Options screen, choose menu option 2, Set Active Partition, and simply follow the instructions on the set active menu screen.

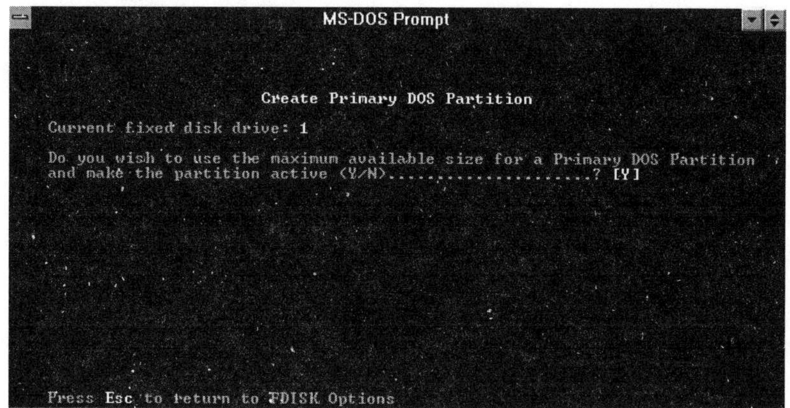

Fig. 4.6

The Create Primary DOS Partition screen.

Formatting the Partition. Once you have repartitioned your hard drive, you need to prepare the new partition for DOS and restore the appropriate files back to the DOS partition. Reboot your computer using the boot disk you made earlier. Then format the appropriate drive and transfer the system files using the following command:

```
format c: /s
```

Once the partition is formatted you can restore your backup to the new drive. Remember, if you shrank the partition, not all the files will fit on the new drive. It might be necessary to place the files that don't fit on the new drive onto other DOS drives or partitions.

Using UMSDOS Instead of Formatting Your Hard Drive

UMSDOS is a full-featured UNIX file system Linux can use that resides on an MS-DOS partition. That means you do not have to repartition your hard drive. The name stands for **U**NIX in **MS-DOS** file system. UMSDOS acts within the constraints of the MS-DOS file system while still providing the long file names, as well as other file system attributes, known to the UNIX world. However, you can not use both your MS-DOS areas on the hard drive and your UMSDOS files at the same time. Of course, by using various Linux utilities and taking advantage of the advance file system, Linux can access your MS-DOS areas. Under MS-DOS, you will be able to see the Linux files, but some may not make much sense, since MS-DOS can only recognize 12-character file names and can not handle multiple periods in a file name, like Linux is able to do.

Caution

When you are using MS-DOS, you will be able to see a file named `--linux-.---`, DO NOT ERASE this file! This file maintains information used by Linux to handle such items as long file names and symbolic links. Deleting this file from under MS-DOS will severely damage your Linux file system!

(continues)

(continued)

Also, Win95 also allows long file names, but at this moment, Win95 and UMDOS have problems working together. If you try to install UMDOS under Win95 beware, you could trash your entire system!

To install the UMSDOS system, first create a Linux root disk containing the UMSDOS kernel. This is the umsdos144.gz file (or the umsdos12 file if you are using 1.2M floppies). Follow the steps detailed in "Making the Root Disks" earlier in the chapter. Next, specify either the MS-DOS partition table or an empty directory on an existing MS-DOS partition on which to install the UMSDOS file system, and later, Linux.

▶▶ See "The Linux File System," p. 300
▶▶ See "Looking at Types of Files," p. 327

Preparing the Hard Drive for Linux

Once you have repartitioned your hard drive and made the Linux boot and root disks, or have prepared a UMSDOS filesystem, now comes the time to install Linux. You must first boot Linux from the disks you have just created. Then you need to use the Linux version of `fdisk` to create the necessary Linux partitions. After preparing the hard drive for installation, you can run the `setup` program to install and configure Linux to your taste.

Booting Linux

To use the disks you made, simply place the boot disk into the drive and reboot your system. The following screen appears:

```
LILO

as "Slackware Linux Installation Disk (v.3.0.0 ELF)

If you have any extra parameters to pass to the kernel, enter them
at the prompt below. For instance, you might need something like
this to detect the hard drives on PS/1 and ValuePoint models from IBM:

      ramdisk hd=cyl,hds,hds,secs
(where "cyl", "hds", and "secs" are the number of
cylinders, sectors, and heads on the drive.)

Also, in a pinch, you can boot your system with a command like:
    mount root=/dev/hda1

If you would rather load the root/install disk from your second
floppy drive:
  drive2
```

```
DON'T SWITCH ANY DISKS YET! This prompt is just for entering
extra parameters. If you don't need to enter any parameters,
hit ENTER to continue.

boot:
```

If you have any parameters, which are discussed later in this chapter, to pass to the kernel before it boots, enter them at the `boot:` prompt. If you don't have any parameters, press <Return> to continue the installation.

Linux then loads itself into a ramdisk and uncompresses before running.

As Linux boots it displays information on-screen to let you know what is happening, including what type of hardware it can detect and use. The system then checks the amount of memory available, which floppy drives are available, and what network protocols are available. The system then checks the floating point processor, and if the system is a 386 it checks for a 387 and how the two processors communicate if available. Linux then displays the identity, date, and time at which the Linux kernel was built. Linux then does a partition check on the available partitions. Finally, since Linux was booted from the boot disk, it displays the following:

```
Please remove the boot kernel disk from your floppy drive, insert the
root/install disk (such as one of the Slackware color144,
colrlite, tty144, or tty12 disks) or some other disk you
wish to load into a ramdisk and boot, and then
press ENTER to continue.
```

Replace the boot disk with the root disk and press <Return>.

The system starts by displaying information messages from the ramdisk, indicating how many bytes of information it is installing and what address it is using. When finished, the system displays the following screen:

```
Welcome to the Slackware Linux Distribution installation disk, (v. 3.0)

###### IMPORTANT! READ THE INFORMATION BELOW CAREFULLY. ######
- You will need one or more partitions of type "Linux Native" prepared.
It is also recommended that you create a swap partition (type
"Linux Swap") prior to installation. Most users can use the Linux
"fdisk" utility to create and tag the types of all these partitions.
OS/2 Boot Manager users, however, should create their Linux partitions
with OS/2 "fdisk", add the bootable (root) partition to the Boot Manager
menu, and then use the Linux "fdisk" to tag the partitions as type
"Linux native".
- If you have 4 megabytes or less of RAM, you MUST activate a swap
partition before running setup. After making the partition with fdisk,
use: mkswap /dev/<partition> <number of blocks> ; swapon /dev/<partition>
- Once you have prepared the disk partitions for Linux, and activated a
swap partition if you need one, type "setup" to begin the installation
process.
- If you want the install program to use monochrome displays, type:
TERM=vt100
   before you start "setup".
```

```
You may now login as "root".

Slackware login:
```

You are now ready to log on to a functioning Linux system. Unlike DOS, UNIX does not boot directly to a system prompt. To gain access to UNIX, you must log on and let the system know you are using it. This is similar to how Microsoft Windows for Workgroups and Windows NT behave, except that you cannot bypass this step.

At the moment, you do not have an account on your own Linux system. Later in this chapter, you learn how to add a simple user account. There is only one account available and this account belongs to the *super user*, also known as root. The root account has the highest privileges in the Linux system. When you log on as root, you can do anything you want. So until you add an account for yourself, type **`root`** and press <Return>.

▶▶ See "Adding a User," p. 179

The system responds with

```
Linux 1.3.18. (Posix)

If you're upgrading an existing Slackware system, you might want to
remove old packages before you run 'setup' to install the new ones.
If you don't your system will still work but there might be some old
files left laying around on your drive.

Just mount your Linux partitions under /mnt and type 'pkgtool'.
If you don't know how to mount your partitions, type 'pkgtool'
and it will tell you how it's done.

To start the main installation, type 'setup'

#
```

The # is the super-user prompt. This is identical to the command prompts found under DOS. Linux is waiting for you to issue a command. The preceding information indicates that you should type **`setup`**, but before you can install the various programs, you must set up your partitions. To do this, you must run the Linux version of `fdisk`.

Partitioning the Drive for Linux

At the # prompt type **`fdisk`** and press <Return>. This starts the `fdisk` program, which displays

```
Using /dev/hda as default device!

Command (m for help)
```

Notice the first information line printed by `fdisk`, `Using /dev/hda as default device!` Remember that DOS refers to most partitions and hard drives via a letter, such as C: or D:. Linux refers to them in a very different manner. Linux refers to drives via a file name, such as /dev/hda.

Linux communicates with hardware via a series of programs called device drivers. In fact, DOS also uses device drivers to communicate with hardware. While DOS device drivers usually have a .SYS extension and can reside anywhere on the system, Linux stores such device drivers in a directory called /dev. The drivers Linux uses in installation were supplied by the boot disk you created. The important point to remember, though, is that because the hard drive, floppy drives, and CD-ROM drives are hardware, Linux uses device drivers in the /dev directory to access the drives. Linux also references these drives with the subdirectory name rather than by a letter. Table 4.5 displays a typical Linux device directory.

Table 4.5 Linux Devices

Device	Name
Floppy drive A:	/dev/fd0
Floppy drive B:	/dev/fd1
First hard drive	/dev/hda
First primary partition on drive A:	/dev/hda1
Second primary partition on drive A:	/dev/hda2
First logical partition on drive A:	/dev/hda3
Second hard drive	/dev/hdb
First primary partition on drive B:	/dev/hdb1
First SCSI hard drive	/dev/sda

Note that the entire drive is referred to as /hd*letter*. The primary partitions are then given the next set of four numbers followed by the logical partitions. Thus, logical partitions always start at /dev/hda4.

Using the Linux *fdisk*

At the fdisk prompt type m for a list of commands. Table 4.6 provides a list of available commands.

Table 4.6 The Linux *fdisk* commands

Command	Description
a	Toggles a bootable flag
c	Toggles the DOS compatibility flag
d	Deletes a partition
l	Lists known partition types

(continues)

Table 4.6 Continued

Command	Description
m	Prints this menu
n	Adds a new partition
p	Prints the partition table
q	Quits without saving changes
t	Changes a partition's system ID
u	Changes display/entry units
v	Verifies the partition table
w	Writes the table to disk and exits
x	Extra functionality (experts only)

To begin the partitioning, select the p command (by pressing the <p> and <Return>) to display the current partition table, which should reflect the drive you partitioned earlier with the DOS FDISK program. The following displays a possible listing from the p command:

```
Disk /dev/hda: 15 heads, 17 sectors, 1024 cylinders
Units = cylinders of 255 * 512 bytes

Device          Boot    Begin     Start     End     Blocks    Id    System
/dev/hda1       *       1         1         41      5219      1     DOS 12-bit FAT
dev/hda2                1024      1024      4040    384667+   51    Novell?
Partition 2 has different physical/logical endings:
     phys=(967, 14, 17) Logical=(4096, 14.17)
```

Note

Your screen may appear different than the preceding one, since the values are different for each type of drive and the partitions already defined on that drive.

The display indicates the various partitions already defined that it can detect, the start and ending locations of the partition, and how big it is in blocks. The display also indicates the partition type. Table 4.7 displays a listing of all the different types of partitions you can define with the Linux `fdisk`. The primary ones you used are 83-Linux Native and 82-Linux Swap. You can get a similar listing with the `l` command.

Notice the note about the different physical and logical endings that Linux prints at the end of the screen. The difference is because on the system used to write this chapter, a prior partition containing the DOS D: drive was left intact, while the C: drive was repartitioned to a smaller C: drive to make room for Linux. Thus, there is space between the C: drive and the D: drive. This is where the necessary partitions required by Linux will be created.

Table 4.7 The Known Linux Partition Types

Reference Number	Type
0	Empty
1	DOS 12-bit FAT
2	XENIX root
3	XENIX usr
4	DOS 16-bit < 32M
5	Extended
6	DOS 16-bit >= 32M
7	OS/2 HPFS
8	AIX
9	AIX bootable
a	OS/2 Boot Manager
40	Venix 80286
51	Novell?
52	Microport
63	GNU HURD
64	Novell
75	PC/IX
80	Old MINIX
81	MINIX/Linux
82	Linux Swap
83	Linux Native
93	Amoeba
94	Amoeba BBT
a5	BSD/386
b7	BSDI fs
b8	BSDI swap
c7	Syrinx
db	CP/M
e1	DOS access
e3	DOS R/O
f2	DOS secondary
ff	BBT

The begin, start, and end numbers from the display are very important and you should write them down. You will need them in a later step in order to specify the necessary sizes of the partitions you will add.

Adding the Necessary Partition

Because you have repartitioned the drive for DOS, you should not have to delete any partitions for Linux. You should only have to add partitions. To add a partition, issue the `n` command, which displays

```
Command Action
  e extended
  p primary(1-4)
```

Press <p> and then <Return>. `fdisk` then asks for the partition number; enter your selection and press <Return>. If you indicate a partition number already in use, `fdisk` reports this fact and asks you to delete the partition before trying to add it to the partition table. For this example, enter **3**, to add a third primary partition that is referred to as `/dev/hda3`.

Next, `fdisk` asks for the location of the first cylinder. This is usually the first available cylinder, and in fact, `fdisk` displays a default range for your selection. For example,

```
First cylinder (42-1024) :
```

If you refer to the prior screen, you see that the first partition ends at cylinder 41 and that the next partition begins at cylinder 1024. Thus, the range supplied by `fdisk` above allows you to start the next partition anywhere in the range of 42–1024. It is a very good idea not to place partitions just anywhere throughout the disk, so choose the next available location, which in this case is cylinder 42. Enter this **42** and press <Return>.

> **Note**
>
> Linux can have trouble booting from partitions defined to start at cylinders above 1024. If you can only create a Linux partition in this range, then you may have to boot Linux from a floppy. You learn how to create a boot floppy (which is different than the boot floppy used for installation) later in this chapter. The only downside is it takes a little longer to boot Linux from floppy than from the hard drive. If you have an IDE drive with more than 1024 cylinders, then read the file /help/big_ide on the slackware 3.0 CD.

Now `fdisk` wants you to specify how much space to allocate for this partition. You can express this size in number of cylinders or by the number of bytes (+*size*), kilobytes (+*size*K), or megabytes (+*size*M). Because you should already know the approximate size you need for the swap file, define this partition first, and then leave the rest of the disk space for the Linux program partitions. Thus, for this example, your machine has 8M of RAM, so you need to specify a 16M partition size by replying as such

```
Last cylinder or +size or +sizeM or +sizeK (42-1023): +16M<Return>
```

You should then use the p command to take a look at the new partition table you have defined. In this example, the new partition table looks like

```
Disk /dev/hda: 15 heads, 17 sectors, 1024 cylinders
Units = cylinders of 255 * 512 bytes

Device       Boot Begin  Start  End   Blocks   Id    System
/dev/hda1    *     1      1      41    5219 1   DOS   12-bit FAT
/dev/hda2          1024   1024   4040  384667+  51    Novell?

Partition 2 has different physical/logical endings:
     phys=(967, 14, 17) Logical=(4039, 14.17)
/dev/hda3          42     42     170   16447+   83     Linux native
```

Note that by default, fdisk made the new partition a Linux Native type. To change this to a swap partition, you need to use the t command. Enter **t** and then enter the partition number you want to change; in this example, enter **3**. fdisk then requests you enter the hexadecimal value of the desired partition type from Table 4.7. If you do not have the table handy you can type **l** and get the list of codes. Because you want a swap partition, enter the **82** at the prompt and press <Return>.

As you can see, fdisk reports the new partition type, but you can also use the p command to double-check that partition 3 is now a Linux Swap partition.

Now you can add your Linux partitions. For this example, add only one partition, but if you wanted to have multiple partitions for various reasons, you could do so at this time. To add a partition, press <n> and specify p for another primary partition, and then the number for this partition, which is 4. To keep from fragmenting different partitions across the drive, start the last partition where the other left off, at cylinder 171. For the last cylinder, because you want to use the rest of the space for the Linux system, you can specify the last cylinder instead of an exact byte count. Thus, enter **1023**, as shown below:

```
Command (m for help):n
Command action
    e    extended
    p    primary partition (1-4)
p
Partition number (1-4): 4<return>
First cylinder (171-1024):171<return>
Last cylinder or +size or +sizeM or +sizeK (171-1023):1023<Return>
```

Now use the p command to verify the new partitions. If you need to make any changes, do so now. Once you are satisfied with the layout of your partitions, you can use the w command to write the partition table information to the hard disk. None of your changes are permanent until you use the w command; thus, if you feel you have made some changes in error, you can use the q command to exit without altering the partition table. If you use the w command, Linux tells you the partition table has been altered and then re-syncs the disks to match the new partition table. If your Linux system hangs at this point, reboot with the install boot and root disks until you are back at the # prompt.

Caution

Do not use the Linux `fdisk` program to create or modify partitions for other operating systems. This could leave the hard drive in a useless state for both operating systems.

Creating the Swap Partition

Some distributions of Slackware, including the one on the accompanying CD-ROM, provide automatic creation and activation of the swap file during installation, so you do not have to worry about creating the swap file. However, if you are using a different distribution, you may need to create and activate the swap file before continuing with the installation.

Note

If you get an "out of memory" type error during the installation procedures that follow, you should increase the size of your swap file. If you already have the maximum of 16M, then you need to create and activate another swap partition following these instructions. Remember, the Slackware Setup program only creates one swap partition.

To create the swap space, use the `mkswap` command and tell it which partition to use and how much size to use for virtual RAM. For example, to create a swap space on the `/dev/hda3` partition that you previously defined, enter the following command at the # prompt:

```
mkswap -c /dev/hda3 16447
```

The `16447` represents 16M and can be found in the blocks column of the `fdisk p` command output screen. The `-c` option is optional and tells `mkswap` to check for bad sections on the partition. Next, you need to activate the swap system with the `swapon` command:

```
# swapon /dev/hda3
```

Again, if you are using the accompanying CD-ROM, you should not have to worry about activating the swap system as long as you create the partition for one. During installation, the install program detects the swap partition and automatically starts the system for installation.

Installing the Linux System

Now that the system is partitioned for Linux, you can install the various packages. The install package allows you to specify what you want to install. It also detects any DOS partitions and can make them visible to Linux if you want. To start the installation, type **`setup`** and press <Return>. Be careful throughout the installation since the Slackware setup program does not recover well from mistyped or extraneous keys.

◀◀ See "The Slackware Packages," p. 45

Next you should see, if you have a color monitor and installed the color root disks, a color display titled Slackware Linux Setup (version FD-2.2.0). The screen provides the following menu selections:

Menu Item	Description
HELP	Read the Slackware Setup Help file
KEYMAP	Remap your keyboard if you're not using a U.S. one
QUICK	Choose quick or verbose install mode [now: VERBOSE]
MAKE TAGS	Experts may customize tagfiles to preselect packages
ADDSWAP	Set up your swap partition(s)
TARGET	Set up your target partitions
SOURCE	Select source media
DISK SETS	Decide which disk sets you wish to install
INSTALL	Install selected disk sets
CONFIGURE	Reconfigure your Linux system
EXIT	Exit Slackware Linux Setup

You can navigate through the menu using the <Up Arrow> and <Down Arrow> keys, the <+> and <-> keys, or the key corresponding to the first letter of the menu item previously listed. Once you have selected an option, the <Spacebar> or the <Return> key activates the selection, that is, performs the tasks associated with that menu item. Your first selection should be to review the help file for the setup program, which is the HELP menu option. Once you have reviewed the help file, the recommended sequence for installing Slackware is ADDSWAP, SOURCE, TARGET, DISK SETS, INSTALL, and CONFIGURE.

Note

By default, the Slackware distribution `setup` program comes up in verbose mode. Unless you are reinstalling at some future date, leave the `isetup` program in verbose mode so that the system provides detailed information along the way as to what it is doing.

The ADDSWAP Selection. Although you can go through the various commands outlined above to set up your swap partition, it is easier to allow the `setup` program to do this work for you. You can set up and configure your swap partition by selecting the ADDSWAP menu item. This command then displays a screen indicating `SWAP SPACE DETECTED` in the title of the screen and provides the following information:

```
Slackware Setup has detected a swap partition:

Device     Boot   Begin   Start   End    Blocks   Id    System
/dev/hda3         42      42      170    16447+   82    Linux Swap

Do you wish to install this as your swap partition?
```

You have two options, yes or no. Choose yes, using the arrow keys, to continue the installation process. Linux `setup` gives the following warning:

```
IMPORTANT NOTE: If you have already made any of your swap partitions
active (using the swapon command), then you should not allow Setup to
use mkswap on your swap partitions, because it may corrupt memory pages
that are currently swapped out. Instead, you will have to make sure
that your swap partitions have been prepared (with mkswap) before they
will work. You might want to do this to any inactive swap partitions
before you reboot.
```

▶▶ See "Using Swap Files and Partitions," p. 321

Choose OK to continue. Then `setup` asks if you want to use `mkswap`. If you have not prepared the swap files, then select yes and continue. `setup` next asks if you want to make the swap partitions active with the `swapon` command. Select yes to continue the installation. Once the program has configured and activated your swap partitions, `setup` indicates to you information that will be added to the `/etc/fstab` file.

Select OK to continue with the installation. Next `setup` asks

```
Now that you've set up your swap space, you may continue on
with the installation. Otherwise, you'll be returned to the
main menu. Would you like to continue the installation and
set up your TARGET drive(s)?
```

Select yes to set up your TARGET partitions on your hard drive.

The TARGET selection. Again, the `setup` program displays a screen with the partition information. If you have used `fdisk` to create multiple partitions, each partition is displayed and `setup` asks you to select one to use for installation. Because this example uses only one partition, the information for the one partition is all that is displayed, as shown here:

```
Device     Boot   Begin   Start   End    Blocks    Id    System
/dev/hda4         171     171     1023   108757+   83    Linux native
```

Next, `setup` asks you to choose a file system. You have two choices, `ext2` and `xiafs`. `setup` displays the following message and asks for a selection:

```
There are two main filesystem types that are used for Linux.
These are the xiafs filesystem, and the second extended
filesystem (ext2). Ext2 seems to be the current standard.
Xiafs hasn't really been changed in quite some time. Ext2 has one
really nice feature that xiafs doesn't have: an ext2 partition is
unmounted, a clean bit is written to it. When the machine is rebooted,
```

```
checking is skipped for any partitions that have the clean bit on them.
Xiafs may be a better choice for machines with low memory, however, so
it's still supported. What filesystem do you plan to use on your root
partition (/dev/hda4 ), ext2fs or ziafs?
```

Installing the ext2 file system is recommended, so select ext2 and choose OK. You are then asked to format the partition:

```
If this partition has not been formatted, you should format it.
NOTE: This will erase all data on it. If you are trying to upgrade
an existing Linux partition, you should use setup from your hard drive,
not from the boot/root disk. (The versions of setup supplied on the
hard drive and the boot/root disk differ.) Would you like to format
this partition?
```

You have three options: Format, to provide a quick format with no checks for bad blocks; Check, which is slower but checks the hard drive for bad blocks; and No, to bypass formatting the partition. Choose Check and then OK to format this partition.

Note

Checking for bad spots probably isn't necessary for newer (that is, IDE) drives because the drives take care of remapping bad spots.

Next, the setup program asks about inode density. Inodes are explained in Chapter 18, "Understanding the File and Directory System," but basically you need one inode for each file on your Linux system. If you are going to have many small files, you need many inodes. The setup program displays the following screen:

▶▶ See "Directories and Physical Disks," p. 328

```
SELECT INODE  DENSITY

Ext2fs default to one inode per 4096 bytes of drive space. If you're
going to have many small files on your drive, then you may need more
inodes (one is used for each file entry). You can change the density
to one inode per 2048 bytes, or even per 1024 bytes. Select '2048' or
'1024', or just hit enter to accept the default of 4096 bytes.
NOTE: If you are going to run from CD using a small (<60MB) partition,
use 1024 to be safe. Each link uses an inode and it's easy to run out
of space.
```

Select the second entry, 2048, and choose OK. The setup program then displays an information screen indicating the formatting choices you have made. (Watch the drive in-use light. Don't press any keys until the program displays the next screen with an option you can select.)

Next, if setup detects any DOS or OS/2 High Performance File System (HPFS) partitions, setup asks if you want to make these partitions visible from Linux. If you have any such partitions on your drive, answering yes is a good idea because you can access the files on these partitions from Linux. Select your choice (yes or no) to continue.

If you selected yes, then the `CHOOSE PARTITION` screen appears, listing the various partitions you can select. In the entry box, type the name of the partition you want to make visible from Linux and press <Return>. If you have more than one partition available, the `setup` program continues to ask for a choice until you enter <q>.

Once you have entered the name, `setup` asks for a place in the directory tree to mount the partition. What this means is that the entire partition is accessed as if it were a subdirectory. You must specify where this subdirectory starts. The following screen appears:

```
SELECT MOUNT POINT

Now this new partition must be mounted somewhere in your directory tree.
Please enter the directory under which you would like to put it. For
instance, you might want to reply /dosc, /dosd, or something like that.
NOTE: This partition won't actually be mounted until you reboot.

Where would you like to mount /dev/hda1?
```

In the entry box, enter the directory where you want to mount the partition. If this is a DOS partition, follow these suggestions: for drive C:, use `/dosc`; for drive D:, use `/dosd`; and so on. If you are mounting an OS/2 partition, you can respond with `/os2c`, `/os2d`, and so on. Also, make sure that you specify the correct slash mark in directory names, `/` and not the DOS backslash `\`.

After entering the mount point, the `setup` program displays an information screen called `CURRENT DOS/HPFS STATUS` to let you know which partitions will be mounted. After dismissing this screen by selecting OK, you are returned to the `CHOOSE PARTITION` screen. If you have other partitions to mount, you can repeat the preceding procedure until all desired partitions are mounted. When all have been processed, press <q> to move on to the next phase of installation, selecting what media to install from.

The SOURCE selection. After formatting and mounting your directories, the `setup` program asks you to continue with installation with the SOURCE selection. This section lets you pick where you will install the Slackware distribution from. If you are using the accompanying CD-ROM, that choice is CD-ROM. If you have the distribution on floppies, you use the floppy drive to install. Select yes to display the `SOURCE MEDIA SELECTION` screen:

```
SOURCE MEDIA SELECTION
Where do you plan to install Slackware Linux from?
1      Install from a hard drive partition
2      Install from floppy disks
3      Install via NFS
4      Install from a pre-mounted directory
5      Install from CD-ROM
```

If you are using the CD-ROM, select choice number 5 and choose OK, which displays the Installing from CD-ROM screen.

```
INSTALLING FROM CD-ROM

In order to install Slackware from a CD-ROM, it must contain the
distribution arranged beneath a source directory in the same way
as if you were to install it from a hard drive or NFS. The source
directory must contain subdirectories for each floppy disk. Your
CD-ROM should be compatible with this format if it contains a mirror
of the Slackware FTP site.

What type of CD-ROM drive do you have?

1      SCSI [/dev/scd0 or /dev/scd1]
2      Sony CDU31A [/dev/sonycd]
3      Sony 535 [/dev/cdu535]
4      Mitsumi [/dev/mcd]
5      Sound Blaster Pro (Panasonic) [dev/sbpcd]
```

Select your CD-ROM drive from those provided, which should match one of the selections you made in the `LININST` program, and choose OK.

Note

If you have problems getting the installation program to detect your CD-ROM, you may have to abort the installation and create a new root disk with another kernel.

▶▶ See "Configuring and Building the Kernel," p. 743

You now need to look up the source directory you saved in the section "Repartitioning" earlier in this chapter. The `setup` program displays the `SELECT SOURCE DIRECTORY` screen.

Note

The following screens may appear different because Linux changes so rapidly it is hard to keep up with improvements. While every effort has been made to assure the book is in step with the CD, this is not always possible. Que wants you to have the most up-to-date software, so that is what is shipped with the book. Alas, things may have changed since the text was written and the CD created.

```
SELECT SOURCE DIRECTORY

Now we need to know which directory on the CD contains the Slackware
sources. This location may vary depending on the cd you have. There
are default selections for the Slackware Professional CD (including
an option to run mostly from the CD), InfoMagic CD, TransAmeritech CD,
and the Linux Quarterly CD-ROM. There may be other directories
containing other versions - enter a custom directory name if you like.
Which option would you like?
```

```
slakware                        Slackware Pro:install to HD
slackpro                        Slackware Pro:run from CD
slackware/slakware              TransAmeritech CD
packages/slackware              Linux Quarterly CD-ROM
distributions/slackware         InfoMagic CD-ROM
Custom                          Enter your own directory name
```

If you are using the accompanying CD-ROM, choose the `distributions/slackware` menu selection and choose OK to continue. The next section asks you to pick the packages to install on your system. You should quickly review the packages that you are interested in installing.

◀◀ See "The Slackware Packages," p. 45

Note

If you enter the wrong directory or do not remember the directory name, the `setup` program alerts you to this and prompts for the correct directory name. If you forgot the name, you need to exit the `setup` program and look on the CD-ROM to find the directory. If you are using the enclosed CD-ROM, you do not need to do this because the `/slackware` directory is the correct directory on the CD-ROM. If you are using another installation media or CD-ROM, then you need to know the directory. You can usually recognize the directory structure because the subdirectories have names similar to the package names, for example, `/a`, `/ap`, `/oop`, and so on.

Selecting the Series to Install. After specifying the installation media and source directory, the `setup` program displays the `SERIES SELECTION` screen. Simply move up and down through the list with the arrow keys and mark the desired packages with the <Spacebar>. When you make a selection with the <Spacebar>, an `X` appears next to the selection. When you have made all your selections, press the <Return> key to continue.

```
SERIES SELECTION

Use the spacebar to select the disk sets you wish to install.
You can use the UP/DOWN arrows to see all the possible choices.
Press the ENTER key when you are finished. If you need to install
a disk set that is not listed here, check the box for custom
additional disk sets.

CUS   Also prompt for CUSTOM disk sets
A     Base Linux system
AP    Various Applications that do not need X
D     Program development (C, C++, Lisp, Perl, etc)
E     GNU Emacs
F     FAQ lists, HOWTO documentation
I     Info files readable with info, JED, or Emacs
IV    Interviews Development + Doc and Idraw Apps for X
N     Networking (TCP/IP, UUCP, Mail, News)
OOP   Object Oriented Programing (GNU Smalltalk 1.1.1)
```

```
Q      Extra Linux kernels with UMSDOS/non-SCSI CD drivers
T      TeX
TCL    Tcl/Tk/TclX, Tcl language, and Tk toolkit for X
X      XFree-86 2.1.1 X Window System
XAP    X Applications
XD     XFree-86 2.1.1 X11 Server Development System
XV     XView 3.2 release 4. (OpenLook window Manager, apps)
Y      Games (that do not require X)
```

Your selections are based on personal preference and the type of hardware you have—that is, if you do not have the hardware to run x, then you should not install the packages that require x (iv, x, xap, xd, xv). You must install package a because this is the base Linux system. Also, if you are interested in programming, you should install the various programming packages such as d, oop, tcl, and xd. If you are not interested in programming, you really don't need these packages. If you want to access the information superhighway, you want to install package n. Strongly recommended packages are f and i because they contain a wealth of information you will need about Linux.

For each package you select, you are led through a series of screens for each package, and each package has programs that it must add, it highly recommends you add, and you can skip. Simply follow the instructions on each screen to install the system. For this example, you install the following packages: a, ap, d, e, f, i, n, t, tcl, x, xap, and y.

Once you have selected the desired packages, choose OK to continue. A simple screen appears telling you that you are about to enter the INSTALL section and that if you have not made all the appropriate selections, you are returned to the main selection menu. Select yes to continue with the setup process.

Install Selections. The setup program next prompts you for the type of prompting you want to have while setup goes through each package installing programs. Each package contains a set of tagfiles that indicate how the file should be treated. For a first-time install, select the HELP mode indicated in the SELECT PROMPTING MODE screen. This helps you decide which mode to use.

◀◀ See "The a Package: Base Linux," p. 47

```
SELECT PROMPTING MODE
Now you must select which type of prompting you would like to use while
installing your software packages. If you're not sure which to use,
read the help file.

Which type of prompting would you like to use?

Normal   Use the default tagfiles
Custom   Use custom tagfiles in the package directories
Path     Use tagfiles in the subdirectories of a custom path
None     Use no tagfiles - install everything
HELP     Read the prompt mode help file
```

After reading the HELP file, select the `Normal` prompting mode and select OK. Then select INSTALL.

Note

The HELP file indicates a `Prompting` mode, but as you can see from the menu selections there is no such item. `Normal` is the closest matching item and that is why you should use that selection for the installation procedure.

At this point the `setup` program is on autopilot and goes through each package you selected earlier and installs the various programs. Those programs marked as `ADD` in the tagfiles are automatically added. `setup` displays a screen indicating what package it is installing and a brief message about what the package is. You cannot stop the `setup` program from installing a program marked as `ADD` in the tagfile.

When the `setup` program comes across a program marked as `OPT`, `REC`, or `SKIP`, it displays a screen telling you what it is about to install, whether it is recommended you install the program, how much space is required to install the program, and then a list of choices. The choices are usually yes, no, or an option to abort the entire program, and the choices are accessible with the arrow keys. Usually, the default selection is `yes, install package` *`XXX`*, where *`XXX`* is the name of the package being installed.

Note

Be careful with your answers. If you select an incorrect choice, you cannot go back and change your mind. If you accidentally install a package you did not want, things are not so bad; you may lose some disk space and gain another program to experiment with. However, if you do not install a package you need, then the best you can do is write down the missed package and then later run the `pkgtool`, to install the desired package. You can also abort the current installation and start over, but that is a rather harsh and time-consuming option.

▶▶ See "Using `pkgtool`," p. 217

Configuring Your System. The `setup` program has now finished loading all the software components you specified. Now it must configure your system. The `setup` program displays

```
CONFIGURE YOUR SYSTEM

Now it's time to configure your Linux system. If this is a new system,
you must configure it now or it will not boot correctly. Otherwise,
you can back out to the main menu if you're sure you want to skip this
step. If you've installed a new kernel image, it's important to
reconfigure you system so that you can install LILO (the Linux Loader)
```

```
or create a bootdisk using the new kernel. Do you want to move on to
the CONFIGURE option?
```

Since this is your first time through, you need to configure your system. Select yes to continue. The next screen asks you to make a boot disk. You should create a boot disk, even if you use the `LILO`. The screen displayed is as follows:

```
MAKE BOOT DISK

It is HIGHLY recommended that you make a standard boot disk for your
Linux system at this time. Such a disk can be very handy if LILO is
ever improperly installed. Since the boot disk will contain a kernel
that is independent of LILO and the kernel on your hard drive, you'll
still be able to use it to boot your system no matter what you do to
LILO or your hard drive kernel. Would you like to make a standard
boot disk?
```

Make sure you have a formatted floppy ready, select yes, and press <Return>. `setup` displays the `BOOT DISK CREATION` screen. Simply put the formatted floppy into the drive and select yes to create the boot disk.

If you skip boot disk creation, `setup` displays the following warning message:

```
SKIPPED BOOT DISK CREATION

Boot disk creation skipped. I hope you already have a boot disk.
If you don't, you have to install LILO if you haven't already,
or you'll have a hard time booting your machine. :^)
```

It is highly recommended that you create a boot disk. If anything goes wrong with the preceding installation or the following configuration, especially when installing the Linux Loader, LILO, you will have an extremely hard time booting your system. In fact, you should also make a boot disk for any other operating systems you may have resident on your system. Typically, with a boot disk you can boot from a floppy if things go bad and correct the problem. Make a boot disk!

Configuring Your Modem. Next, `setup` asks you to configure a modem. You should do this now, even if you do not plan to use a modem at this time. `setup` displays the following screen if you want to configure your modem:

```
MODEM CONFIGURATION

This part of the configuration process will create a link in /dev from
your callout device (cua0, cua1, cua2, cua3) to /dev/modem. You can
change this link later if you put you modem on a different port.
```

Select yes to continue. Next you need to specify the serial port that your modem is hooked to. You do this via the `SELECT CALLOUT DEVICE` screen displayed. The items `cua0-3` represent your serial ports, with `cua0` representing COM1, `cua1` being COM2, and so on. Select the appropriate COM port and select OK.

Configuring the Mouse. You next go through a similar process to configure your mouse. If you have a mouse with your system, you should go ahead and configure it at this time. Select yes from the `MOUSE CONFIGURATION` screen to continue. You are then presented with a screen containing six selections. If you have a mouse that is Microsoft-compatible and not listed in the choices in table 4.8, you can select option 1 and have a good chance of your mouse working.

Table 4.8 Mouse Types Supported by Linux

Option	Description
1	Microsoft compatible serial mouse
2	C&T 82C710 or PS/2 style mouse (auxiliary port)
3	Logitech bus mouse
4	ATI XL bus mouse
5	Microsoft bus mouse
6	Mouse Systems serial mouse

If you select a mouse that requires a serial port, `setup` requires you to specify the port. Like modems, Linux refers to the serial ports with a different name than COM1, COM2, and so on. Linux refers to the ports as `ttyS0` through `ttyS3`. Select the appropriate serial port from the `SELECT SERIAL PORT` screen and select OK to continue with the installation.

***Configuring Linux To Use* ftape.** If you loaded the `ftape` package, `setup` detects this fact and asks if you want to start the program as soon as Linux boots. It does not hurt to start the program at boot time, so if you loaded the `ftape` package, you should have `setup` start the program at boot time. Select yes from the `FTAPE CONFIGURATION` screen to continue.

Configuring Your Modem's Baud Rate. Next, if you installed the `gp9600` package, the `setup` program displays the `SET YOUR MODEM SPEED` to set your modem speed. Simply select the appropriate baud rate and choose OK. If you do not see a rate high enough for your modem needs, then you can later use the `setserial` program to set the baud rate to whatever value you require.

Installing *LILO*

`LILO` stands for the Linux Loader. `LILO` is a program executed at system start-up that allows you to select which operating system is used to boot the computer. You can use `LILO` to boot several different operating systems such as Linux and MS-DOS. With `LILO` you can specify a default operating system to boot and a default time limit before it boots that system. For example, if you had MS-DOS and Linux on your computer, you can configure `LILO` to boot either one. You could then tell `LILO` to boot MS-DOS if no one intervenes after 30 seconds. Before that 30 seconds is up, however, a user could specify another operating system to boot instead of the default. You can press the <Ctrl>, <Alt>, or <Shift> keys to stop the timed process. Press the <Tab> key to get a list of operating systems `LILO` can boot. You specify all this information while configuring LILO. While you can directly edit the lilo.conf file located in the /etc directory, the LILO INSTALLATION screen provides a better interface to editing the file.

Once you have configured your system, setup lets you install LILO. setup displays

```
LILO INSTALLATION

LILO (the Linux Loader) allows you to boot Linux from your hard drive.
To install, you make a new LILO configuration file by creating a new
header and then adding at least one bootable partition to the file.
Once you've done this, you can select the install option, Alternately,
if you already have an /etc/lilo.cfg, you may reinstall using that.
If you make a mistake, you can always start over by choosing 'Begin'.
Which Option would you like?


Begin        Start LILO configuration with a new LILO header
Linux        Add a Linux partition to the LILO config file
OS/2         Add an OS/2 partition to the LILO config file
DOS          Add a DOS partition to the LILO config file
Install      Install LILO
Recycle      Reinstall LILO using the existing lilo.conf
Skip         Skip LILO installation and exit this menu
View         View your current /etc/lilo.cfg
Help         Read the Linux Loader Help file
```

To begin, you should select the Help option first to read the help file. After reading the help file, you should start at the beginning—the Begin option. If you do not want to install LILO at this time but instead want to use a boot floppy, you can select the Skip menu option.

Caution

If you skip installing LILO, you must have a bootable floppy. If you skipped creating a boot floppy earlier, you should install LILO, or once back at the main menu, re-enter the configuration selection and create a boot floppy. If you do leave setup without a way to boot your system, you are forced to configure your system at a later time with the boot and root disks you originally created.

***OPTIONAL append= LINE* screen.** The first item to fill is any additional command-line parameters you need to pass to the kernel when you start the system. This might be needed with certain SCSI hard drives and IBM motherboards. If you need to pass any command-line parameters, enter them in the edit box of the displayed screen. If you have no parameters to pass, press <Return> to continue.

Target Location. Next, you must choose a location to place the LILO program. You can place the program in the Master Boot Record of your first hard drive, in what's called the *super block* of your root Linux partition, or on a floppy disk. If you choose the Floppy Disk option, you need to place a formatted floppy in the drive. You should probably use the Master Boot Record to place LILO.

Delay Option. The next screen allows you to set the amount of time `LILO` waits before booting the default operating system. You have the following choices:

Selection Choice	Description
None	Don't wait at all—boot straight into the first operating system
5	5 seconds
30	30 seconds
Forever	Present a prompt and wait until a choice is made

Select one of the above choices and select OK.

Choosing Your Default Operating System and Add All Partitions

Next, you return to the main `LILO INSTALLATION` screen. You must now choose your default operating system. This is the first operating system located in the `lilo.conf` file. So if you want Linux to be the default operating system, you should select the `Linux` menu option. If you want MS-DOS to be the default, select the `DOS` menu option. Make your selection and the installation program presents a screen consisting of all the possible partitions that you can boot from. Enter the name of the partition just as it appears under the `Device` column heading on the `SELECT` *`XXX`* `PARTITION`, where *`XXX`* indicates the type of partition you are using; for example, if you had selected `DOS`, then the screen reads `SELECT DOS PARTITION` and displays all available, bootable DOS partitions. Once you have entered the correct device name, select OK to continue.

Next, you must select a short name to help identify the operating system when someone presses the <Tab> key at the `LILO` prompt. This is the name a user must enter to select that operating system as the boot operating system from `LILO`. Examples of names are `DOS`, `LINUX`, `OS2`, and so on. The name must be a single word.

After selecting your default operating system, you can continue to add various operating systems to `LILO` using the `Linux`, `OS/2`, and `DOS` menu options. Just remember to add Linux. After you have added all the appropriate operating system partitions, you should use the `View` option to examine your current `/etc/lilo.conf` file. For this example, assume you have specified DOS as the default operating system and added an entry for Linux. You also specified a 30-second delay before booting into DOS. In that case, your `lilo.conf` file looks like

```
# LILO configuration file
# generated by 'liloconfig'
#
# Start LILO global section
boot = /dev/hda
#compact        # faster, but won't work on all systems.
delay = 300
vga = normal    # force sane state
ramdisk = 0     # paranoia setting
```

```
# End LILO global section
# Linux bootable partition config begins
image = /vmlinuz
  root = /dev/hda4
  label = linux
# Linux bootable partition config ends
# DOS bootable partition config begins
other = /dev/hda1
  label = dos
  table = /dev/hda
# DOS bootable partition config ends
```

Once you have added all the needed partitions, select the `Install` option to configure `LILO`.

Un-Installing *LILO*

If you are running `LILO` version 0.14 or newer then you can uninstall `LILO` with the following command:

```
opus:~# lilo -u
```

If you have a previous version, then you must either remove or disable `LILO` from its primary partition. You can use either Linux's or MS-DOS's FDISK program to make another partition active.

If you placed `LILO` within the MBR (master boot record), then you must replace it with another MBR from another operating system. With MS-DOS 5.0 or above, the command

```
c:\>fdisk /mbr
```

restores the MS-DOS MBR.

Once `LILO` is removed from either the active partition or the MBR, you are then free to remove the files from `/etc/lilo`.

▶▶ See "Removing Files or Directories," p. 345

Configuring Your Network. Next, `setup` allows you to configure your network. You may not have all the information available yet since you may have to collect that later, but go ahead and configure as much as possible. The `setup` program tries to configure your system, but in case it cannot, which is very likely the first time, you can configure the network later with the `netconfig` command. You might also want to check out Parts IV, "Networking Administration," and VII, "Using the Internet." Select yes to start the configuration, and select OK on the `NETWORK CONFIGURATION` screen to begin.

The item you need is a name for your machine. This is a personal name and you can be as creative as you want.

Note

It is a good idea to stick with lowercase letters because UNIX and Linux are case-sensitive and most commands and interactions are done with lowercase letters.

At the `ENTER HOSTNAME` prompt enter your selected name and press <Return>.

The next prompt asks for something called a domain name. If you understand this term and have one available, enter the domain name for your system. If you do not have a domain name yet or don't understand what one is, don't worry. Later chapters of this book tell you what an Internet domain name is and how to configure your network with one. If you do not have a domain name, enter the following as a placeholder and press <Return> to continue.

```
tristar.com
```

You must enter a domain name; otherwise, the installation program does not proceed.

▶▶ See "Domains," p. 582

The next question deals with using TCP/IP through loopback. By answering yes to this question, "Only use loopback," you can skip several layers of configuration. But don't worry, later chapters show you how to configure your network to gain access to the Internet. Answering yes to this question and configuring your network later is a good idea. If you select yes, the network configuration is complete and you can continue with the rest of the configuration.

▶▶ See "The `etc/hosts` File," p. 249

***selection*.** If you have a mouse, you can use the `selection` program to cut and paste commands from your terminals. This screen asks if you want to automatically start the program at boot time. If you have a mouse, you should start `selection` at boot time by answering yes at this screen. However, if you have a bus mouse, there are potential problems using `selection` and XFree86. If you have a bus mouse, you shouldn't start `selection` automatically. If you do not choose to start `selection` at boot time, you can execute the program at any time with the following command:

```
selection -f &
```

***sendmail* Configuration.** Next, `setup` asks you to choose a configuration file for `sendmail`. For starters, you might want to preload one of the supplied `sendmail` configuration files. If you know how you are connecting to the Internet, with PPP, via EtherNet and so on, you can choose either the `SMTP-BIND` or the `SMTP` menu selections. If you plan on using a modem and UUCP, select the `UUCP` menu selection. If you do not plan on using a network, select the `SKIP` menu option. If you are unsure, the `SKIP` menu option is a good choice because you can reconfigure the system at a later time.

▶▶ See "Understanding E-Mail," p. 621

Time-Zone Configuration. Next, `setup` requires you to select a time zone that Linux uses to keep track of the date and time. Look through the list of available time zones and choose the most appropriate one. If you are in the United States, there are several selections that begin with `US`. The same applies for Australia, Canada, and those systems that use Greenwich Mean Time or Universal Time. Select your time zone and press <Return>.

Replace *etc/fstab*. The `etc/fstab` is a file-system table that represents each of your partitions. If you modify the table, with `LILO` for example, while using the `setup` program, it may ask you to replace the old one with the new one. This screen only appears if, for some reason, you stop and restart the `setup` program or the configuration process. If you have made no changes to the partition table, answer no to this question; otherwise, answer yes.

Modifying the Kernel with *rdev*

Once configuration is complete, you can rerun setup to add new items, or you can use the `pkgtool` program to view, add, or delete packages.

▶▶ See "Using `pkgtool`," p. 217

However, you might have to change items germane to your kernel, such as the video mode used. One solution is to reinstall Linux, a major undertaking as you've just seen. Or you can recompile and build a new kernel from scratch, but that's not for the novice. Another option is to modify the current kernel, which fortunately, Linux allows you to do with the `rdev` command. `rdev` is a program found in `/sbin` and should only be used when you are logged in as root.

For a complete listing of options, invoke `rdev` with the `\h` or `\?` parameter. This will display a listing of options.

Your kernel file—that is, the actual software—is found in a file named `vmlinux`. The reason for this name is historical, most UNIX systems store the kernel in a file named `vmunix`. A parameter to `rdev` is usually this file name. You can use `rdev` to fix problems such as root and swap partitions and video modes.

Building a New Kernel

Sometimes a problem has only one solution—a new kernel. The Linux kernel is the core operating system for Linux. While not for the faint of heart, sometimes it is necessary to download a new kernel from the Net and build it. If you have some programming experience and know your way around the C programming language, then you should be able to build and install a new kernel. If not, then you can skip this section. You may have to install a new kernel for several reasons: A new patch is provided to run new hardware; or, you wish to remove features from the kernel you don't use, thus lowering the memory requirements for your system. The starting point is to determine what kernel version you are currently running.

You can find out the kernel version with the following command:

```
uname -a
```

The response indicates which version of the kernel is currently running and when it was created. The version numbers are in the form of

```
MajorVersionNumber.MinorVersionNumber.PatchLevel.
```

Linus Torvalds is the official release point for new kernels, even though anyone can modify Linux (due to the GPL). This gives the Linux development and user community a common baseline from which to work and communicate.

Note

Make sure to read the Kernel HOWTO before actually trying to build and configure a new kernel!

To build a new kernel, you need to have the source files in the `/urs/src/linux` directory. You also need to have the C compiler package loaded, which is disk set D. If you did not install that package during installation, use `pkgtool` to do so now.

▶▶ See "Using `pkgtool`," p. 217

First you must get the new kernel sources or patches. The new sources are usually found on the Internet. Check **sunsite.unc.edu** for the latest and greatest kernels. If you are modifying your current kernel, then this step is of course unnecessary. The source files are usually in a `tar` file and will need to be unarchived.

Tip

It is a VERY good idea to make a backup copy of your current kernel with the following commands:

```
cd /usr/src
cp linux linux.sav
```

These commands copy the entire `linux` source directory to another directory called `linux.sav`.

Next, you should use the `patch` command to apply any patch files. After preparing the source files, then you can configure and build your new system. Start by entering the following command from the `/usr/src` directory:

```
make config
```

This command asks you various questions about the drivers you wish to install/configure. Pressing <Enter> accepts the default value for each question; otherwise you must supply the answer. Some of the questions are shown in Table 4.9. You may have to answer other questions depending on the version of the kernel you are installing or the patches you have applied.

Table 4.9 Some Configuration Options

Configuration Option	Description
Kernel Math Emulation	Asks if the kernel should emulate a math coprocessor.
Normal Harddisk Support	Enables drivers for all standard hard drives.
XT Harddisk Support	Applies only if your machine uses an XT class controller class instead of an AT controller.
Networking Support	By answering yes to this question you enable networking support within the kernel.
SCSI Support	Enable support for SCSI controllers.
CD_ROM Drivers	A series of questions dealing with CD-ROMs, especially those not supported within the standard SCSI Support package.
Filesystems	A series of questions dealing with file systems the kernel should support. If your kernel does not have support for the ISO9660 file system then you will not be able to use a CD-ROM.
Parallel Printer Support	Enable printer support via the parallel port.
Mouse Support	Bus mice need their own support from within the kernel.
Sound Card Support	A series of questions about the hardware and software configuration of a sound card.

After you have answered the various questions to configure your new kernel you must compile it.

> **Note**
>
> The build process can take anywhere from 15 minutes to many hours. So relax and order a pizza.

The following commands will build the new kernel:

```
make dep
make clean
make
```

Once the compilation completes you can create a new boot disk as discussed earlier in this chapter. You can either copy this kernel to a new diskette, or use `LILO` to boot the new kernel.

Upgrading from a Previous Version of Slackware

The current version of Slackware, version 3.0, contains the Linux files in a special format, called ELF. Earlier versions of Slackware were in a format called a.out. You can not mix these types of executables on the same system, so if you plan on upgrading from an earlier version, you must reinstall from scratch to be safest. This is especially important when dealing with the A and N packages. The `pkgtool` program can uninstall programs as well as install them, but the safest route is to back up your important configuration files and reinstall Linux from scratch.

If you are upgrading from similar formats—from an ELF based distribution to an ELF base distribution—then you can use `pkgtool` to remove those packages you wish to update, and then use the tool to install the newer versions.

Back to the Beginning

Once you have completed the setup and configuration of your system, the `setup` program returns you to the main menu. From here you can choose the `EXIT` option to leave `setup`. If you want to change options, you can do so here. Choose `EXIT` to leave the setup program.

▶▶ See "Using `pkgtool`," p. 217

Choosing `EXIT` returns you to the system prompt, indicated by the # sign. You are now in Linux and can issue simple commands like `ls` for a directory listing of files. At this time, though, you should reboot the system so that all of your setup and configurations can take effect.

Rebooting Linux is more involved than rebooting DOS. You cannot turn off the power and turn the system back on. If you do in Linux, you can damage the file structures and systems. Linux tries to repair itself on boot-up. Do not turn off the power while running Linux. To exit Linux, use the following command:

```
shutdown [-r] time
```

-r indicates that the system should reboot after shutting down, and *time* indicates the time that the system should shut down. You can use now in place of *time* to indicate immediate shutdown. Linux also recognizes the warm boot keys used by DOS to reboot the machine, <Ctrl-Alt-Delete>, which Linux interprets as the command

```
shutdown -r now
```

Make sure that you have removed the root disk from the drive and reboot your new Linux machine.

Problems

After rebooting your machine, the LILO prompt should appear. Make sure that you can boot to your old operating system if you left it on the hard drive. If that system was DOS, press the <Shift> key and then type in the short word you used to identify the DOS partition when you installed LILO. If you enter an invalid word, press the <Tab> key to get a list of valid operating system types. If you are having problems at this point, place your DOS boot disk in the boot drive and reboot.

You should be able to boot from your boot disk. Once your system is up and running under DOS, try the Linux boot disk you created during installation—not the ones you created to originally install the entire system. If that boot disk does not work, you may have to reinstall Linux. Potential problems to check initially are the kernels and your hardware. Before starting over, make sure you have the appropriate hardware. If you made notes during the installation process, check which kernel you installed against what hardware you have. If you have a SCSI CD-ROM, did you install the idekern instead of the scsikern? But do make sure you have hardware supported by Linux.

From Here...

Once you have your system up and running you can read the following chapters for further information about Linux:

- Chapter 5, "Running Linux Applications," which gets you up to speed on the various programs you just installed.
- Chapter 6, "The X Windows System," is interesting if you have installed the X system.
- Chapter 12, "Upgrading and Installing Software," provides instructions on how to reinstall packages you may have left out during the initial setup of your Linux system.
- Chapter 27, "Understanding the Internet," briefs you on the basics about how to get to the Internet.

CHAPTER 5

Running Linux Applications

Now that you have installed your Linux system, this chapter presents a brief introduction to setting up a user account for you to use and some basic commands to get you moving around in your new system. This is your very own multitasking, multiuser system and experimenting is encouraged. You might never get this type of opportunity on a typical UNIX system. Go ahead and play with your system. However, just playing with an operating system is no fun; it doesn't get your daily job done. After all, you don't use DOS all day, right? You use applications. Linux has access to literally thousands of applications from around the world. You have installed several from the Slackware distribution on the enclosed CD-ROM. There are plenty more where they came from, too. Programs that rival those costing hundreds of dollars for the PC are readily available for Linux. In this chapter, you learn:

- How to maneuver around Linux with basic commands to change directories, list files, add new users, and execute programs
- About the enclosed spreadsheet `sc` which you can install
- How to use the modem communications minicom provided with the CD-ROM
- What types of games are available and how to play them
- About the dosemu and wine emulators that enable you to run MS-DOS and MS Windows programs under Linux

Maneuvering Through Linux

After installing Linux and rebooting, you are faced with a system prompt based on the name you gave your system during installation. The prompt looks similar to

```
Welcome to Linux 1.3.18

opus login:
```

However, the prompt may indicate a different version of Linux since Linux is an evolving system.

You must now supply a user name and a password. A user name identifies you to the operating system because Linux can support many different users, both at different times and concurrently. An account also provides the user with a default directory, called the `home` directory. Many accounts are also set up to restrict the user to only certain directories on the system and prevent them from using certain commands. The primary reason is because Linux is a multiuser system and thus tries to protect the files of one user from the prying eyes of another.

Entering Commands

You enter commands in Linux much as you do in DOS and other command-line-oriented operating systems. Linux, like UNIX, is case-sensitive; if Linux doesn't know a command, make sure you spelled it correctly and that you entered it in the proper case. Most commands are executed after you press the <Return> key.

Command History

Linux also provides a history function to recall previous commands. This history is also kept across sessions, too. You can use the <Up-Arrow> key to recall previous commands and then press the <Return> key to activate that command. To get a complete listing of all the prior commands you have entered, you use the `history` command:

```
opus:~# history<Return>
1 clear
2 adduser
3 history
```

Once you have the preceding history list, you can repeat the command by either using the <Up-Arrow> key and cycling through the commands until the proper one appears on the command line, or you can enter the <!> (called the *bang character*) and the number of the command you want to re-execute. For example, if you wanted to repeat the `adduser` command in the previous list, enter

```
opus:~# !2<Return>
```

The number of entries in the history list is user-defined in the user account's `.profile` configuration file. See Chapter 20, "Understanding Linux Shells," for more information on the `.profile` configuration file.

Selection

If you have a mouse with your system and installed the `selection` program, you can also use your mouse to copy text from other areas of your screen to the command line. To select the text, simply move the mouse cursor, which appears as soon as you click the left mouse button, hold down the left mouse button as you drag the cursor across the desired text, and then press the right mouse button to copy the text to the command line. This is useful if you need to enter a long file name on the command line.

Command Completion

Linux also offers another nice feature when entering commands. You can start to type a file name and then press the <Tab> key. Linux searches the directory for a file beginning with the same letters you have typed and completes the file name it finds. If Linux cannot find a unique file name, it beeps and completes the file name to the last common character. For example, if you wanted to copy a file called `todo_monday` to `todo_today`, you type

```
opus:~# cp to<Tab>
```

Linux beeps and fills out the command line like so

```
opus:~# cp todo_
```

If you typed an **m** and then pressed <Tab>, Linux places the entire file name `todo_monday` on the command line.

Managing Users

On many systems the person responsible for maintaining the user accounts is referred to as the *system administrator*. The system administrator sets up user accounts and performs other activities. For more information on the various aspects of system administration, check out the chapters in Part III, "System Administration." On your Linux system, you are the system administrator, so it is your responsibility to set up accounts for yourself, family, and friends.

To add an account for yourself, you must create that account as the system administrator. The system administrator is also sometimes referred to as the *super user* because they have so much control over the system. While any user can be given super-user status, the only system user who has this power is the root account. So to begin your trek through Linux, you must first log on as the super user via the root account.

Logging On and Off

To log on as root, type **root** at the logon prompt and press the <Return> key. Next Linux asks for a password. By using a password, you prevent unauthorized users from logging onto any account. Linux wants to make sure who the user claims to be is in fact the correct user. You should not share your passwords with just anyone. Linux protects the password you type by not *echoing* (that is, not displaying) the letters to the screen, so make sure you enter the correct password. If you enter an invalid user name or password, Linux gives the following error message and starts the process over:

```
opus login: jack<Return>
Password:password<Return>
Login incorrect

opus login:
```

Because this is your first time logging onto the system since installation, the root account has no password set, so after typing **root** and pressing <Return>, you are presented with a command prompt. You are now able to enter Linux commands. Most commands are entered in the same way as in DOS: type the command with any needed parameters and press the <Return> key.

> **Note**
>
> The default installation of Linux provides a small "fortune" every time someone logs onto the system that displays a short, sometimes amusing, sometimes not, adage about life. You can also get a fortune at any time by using the `fortune` command, providing you have installed the text-based games.

To log off, enter

```
logout<Return>
```

This command returns you to the logon prompt. If this command does not work, try the **exit** command.

Adding Users

Once you have logged on as root, you should add an account for yourself. To add an account enter the following command and follow the prompts.

```
opus:~# adduser<Return>

Adding a new user. The user name should be not exceed 8 characters
in length, or you many run into problems later.

Enter login name for new account (^C to quit):
```

Take a look at this screen for a second. Notice the command prompt after which you entered the command. The prompt begins with the host name of the computer. This is the name you entered while installing the `n` package of disks. The next item is the ~ character. Linux uses this character to refer to the account's *home directory*, which is described later. Here, it represents the directory the user is currently located in. If you issued the `adduser` command from the `/usr/bin` directory, the prompt reads

```
opus:/usr/bin#
```

The next character is the pound sign. This prompt, by convention, belongs to any super-user account. A normal user account usually has `$` as a prompt.

The next item you might notice is the misspellings and grammar in the prompts, for example, `should be not` and `you many run`. These errors do not affect the performance of the system but help highlight the fact that Linux, while fully functional and a great system, is not a commercial venture. Now, enter a user name of up to eight characters and press <Return>. An example session to create an account for Jack Tackett follows:

```
Enter login name for new account (^C to quit): jack<Return>

Editing information for new user [jack]

Full Name: Jack Tackett, Jr.<Return>
GID[100]:<Return>

Checking for an available UID after 500
501...
First unused uid is 502

UID [502]:<Return>

Home Directory [/home/jack]:<Return>

Shell [/bin/bash]:<Return>

Password: opus<Return>

Information for new user [jack]:
Home directory: [/home/jack] Shell: [/bin/bash]
Password: [opus] uid: [502] gid: [100]

Is this correct? [y/N] :y<Return>

Adding login [jack] and making directory [/home/jack]

Adding the files from the /etc/skel directory:
./ .kermc -> /home/jack/ ./ .kermc
./ .less -> /home/jack/ ./ .less
./ .lessrc -> /home/jack/ ./ .lessrc
./ .term -> /home/jack/ ./ .term
./ .term/termrc -> /home/jack/ ./ .termrc
./ .emacs -> /home/jack/ ./ .emacs


opus:~#
```

As you move through the process, you must enter a full name for the user. This helps identify the user account further. Next, you are asked to enter a group ID and a user ID. Do not worry about these items at this time. Linux uses them to determine the directories and files that you have access to by default. You can safely accept the default values, the values within the `[]`, by simply pressing the <Return> key after each request.

Next, you are asked to enter a home directory for the user. This is the area where the user is automatically placed when they first log on. This is the user's account area for storing files and for working storage. Linux provides a default directory based on the user's name. If this default directory is acceptable, press <Return>; otherwise, enter a directory and press <Return>. Accept, for now, the defaults offered by the `adduser` command.

You are now asked to specify a shell for the user. The shell is a command interpreter much like COMMAND.COM is for DOS. The shell accepts the input and runs specified commands. You have been using a shell called the bash shell since installing Linux. For the time being, simply accept the default option bash.

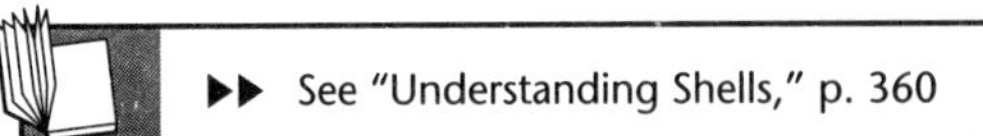
See "Understanding Shells," p. 360

The final parameter is the password for the account. It is highly recommended you provide every account with a password. Linux then displays all the information entered and asks if it is correct. If the information is not correct, enter **n** or press <Return> because No is the default choice and you must go back and correct the errors. If everything is correct, enter **y** and <Return>.

Linux displays a series of files it copies from a skeletal user account located in the ./etc/skel directory to the new user's home directory. These files are configuration files for such items as the user's terminal and how such programs as emacs and less run from their accounts. The users can modify these files at any time to change the default behavior of the programs.

After adding the account, you can verify its existence in one of two ways; the quickest is to use a utility called finger to see if the user has an account. The general form of the command is finger name. For example, you can test for the account created above by entering

```
opus:~# finger jack<Return>

Login: jack   Name Jack Tackett, Jr.
Directory: /home/jack   Shell: /bin/bash
Never logged in.
No Mail.
No Plan.
opus:~#
```

If the user has an account, the appropriate information is displayed; otherwise, a message indicating no such user has an account is displayed.

The next way to verify the account is to actually log on to the account and see if Linux will let you. You can do this in one of several ways. You can log off and then log on as the new user. You can use the command su, which stands for switch user. You can use the login command, and you can use one of the six virtual terminals provided by Linux to log on to a new account. Remember, Linux is *multiuser.* Table 5.1 presents an overview of each method.

Table 5.1 Logging Onto a Newly Created User Account

Command	Description
logout	Logs you off of the root account and brings you back to the logon prompt. You no longer have access to the root account until you log on as root.

Command	Description
su *user-name*	Logs you off of the account, does not ask for the user name to log on as, and then prompts you for the password. If you do not specify user-name, su assumes you are trying to log on as root and expects you to enter the root password.
login *user-name*	Is almost the same as su, except that leaving off user-name merely places you at the normal logon prompt.
<Alt-F*x*>	Using the virtual terminals. You can access a virtual terminal by pressing the <Alt> key and one of the F1 through F6 function keys. This takes you to another logon screen where you can log on as the new user. The best feature of using the virtual terminals is that you are still left in the other account and can swap back and forth using the <Alt-F*x*> keys. You are not logged off of the other account.

Note

If you try to add a user later from the account you now create, you may not be able to use the command `adduser` because certain commands can only be entered by the super user, `adduser` being one of them. If you have trouble adding a user to the system, make sure you are logged on as root.

Changing Passwords

At some future time you may want to change your password or add a password to an account that does not have one, like the current root account. You should always password protect the root account.

▶▶ See "Setting User Passwords," p. 183

To change a password you use the `passwd` command, specifying the old and new password, and then you must verify the new password. If you do not have (or worse do not remember) the old password, you cannot use the `passwd` command to change your password. The typical sequence for `passwd` follows:

```
opus:~$ passwd<Return>
Changing password for jack
Enter old password:password<Return>
Enter new password:new-password<Return>
Re-type new password:new-password<Return>
```

If you make an error, Linux informs you that the password has not been changed. Linux also enforces a minimum number and requires certain types of characters to create a valid password entry for the user.

Caution

Do not forget your passwords. If you forget a user password, you must change the account information. If you forget the root account password, then you must use the boot floppy created during installation to boot the system and change the password. Typically you can set the password to empty and then let the user set a new password with the `passwd` command.

▶▶ See "Setting User Passwords," p. 183

Basic Commands

While Chapter 25, "Command-Line Reference," provides an extensive command-line reference, you need to know some basic commands to get around the system. The following sections provide some of the commands you need to use your Linux system.

cd Change the Current Working Directory

Linux, like DOS and other operating systems, stores files in a tree structure called a directory. You can specify a file via a path from the root directory, specified with the `/` character, to the file itself. Thus, the configuration file for `emacs` for the user `jack` can be exactly specified like so:

```
/home/jack/.emacs
```

If you are familiar with the DOS limits of eight characters for a file name and three characters for an extension, then you will be pleasantly surprised to learn that Linux has no such limit on file names. Linux also uses the concept of a home directory, which is specified when an account is added to the system. A user's home directory is usually specified with the ~ character. You can use this character in place of the directory name, as shown in the following code line, where the user wants to copy a file from the current directory `\usr\home\jack` to their `home` directory:

```
cp .emacs ~.emacs
```

▶▶ See "Understanding File Names," p. 325

To move around the Linux directory structure, you use the change directory command, `cd`. If you enter the `cd` command without any parameters, Linux immediately returns you to your home directory. To move from one directory to another directory, you use the `cd` command much as you do in DOS, that is, `cd new directory`. Linux also uses the single `.` to represent the current directory and the `..` to represent the parent directory. In fact, it is DOS that emulates UNIX, not UNIX/Linux emulating DOS.

> **Note**
>
> Be careful how you specify the directory separator. In DOS, this is the \ character, which Linux uses as the `continue` command on another line character. To separate directory names in Linux you must use the / character.
>
> Also, while DOS does not mind missing spaces when specifying the . and .. parameters, Linux does. Linux does not understand the command `cd..` but does understand the command `cd ..`. Linux needs the space separating the command and the parameter.

Finally, many of the "commands" presented below are actually utility programs that Linux uses to extend its command set. These programs are found in the `/bin` and `/usr/bin` directories.

ls Display Information About Files and Directories

The `ls` stands for list and is used by Linux to display a list of files. This command is the counterpart to the DOS DIR command. Under Linux, the `ls` command displays all the main files in a directory in color. The default colors display the directories in blue and executable programs in green. You can change the default colors by modifying the file `/etc/DIR_COLORS`.

Linux also accepts the command `dir` to list files in a directory. `ls` takes many parameters to specify not only how to display a file but what files to display. The most common parameter is `-la`, which tells `ls` to display information in a long format for every file in a directory.

The command `ls -la` lists all information about every file in the current directory. The command `ls .emacs` lists the file `.emacs`, while `ls -l .emacs` lists all information about the file `.emacs`.

cp Copy Files

The `cp` command is similar to the DOS COPY command. You use this command to copy one or more files from one directory to another directory. The syntax of the `cp` command is

```
cp from-file-name to-file-name
```

You must supply both a *`from-file-name`* and a *`to-file-name`* for the files to be copied. If you want to preserve the file name, use the . as a placeholder for the *`to-file-name`* parameter. This is in contrast to DOS where you could leave off the *`to-file-name`*.

The command `cp fred1 fred1.old` copies the file `fred1` to a backup file named `fred1.old`, while the command `cp ~fred1.old /backup/jack` copies the file `fred1.old` from the home directory to the directory `/backup/jack`.

Installing Linux

II

mv Move Files

The command mv, which is similar to the DOS RENAME command, permits you to move files from one directory to another directory. When you move a file it has the same effect as if you had copied the files to a new directory and then deleted the files in the old directory. mv does not make a copy of the files. The syntax of the mv command is identical to the cp command

```
mv from-file-name to-file-name
```

The command `mv fred1 fred1.old` copies the file `fred1` to a backup file named `fred1.old` and deletes the old `fred1` file, while the command `mv~fred1.old /backup/jack` copies the file `fred1.old` from my home directory to the directory `/backup/jack`.

rm Delete Files

To delete files under Linux, you use the rm command. The rm command is dangerous because once a file is deleted, you can never recover the file, so for safety reasons, you should use the following form of the rm command:

```
rm -i file-name
```

the `-i` parameter tells the command to inquire the user to see if that is the file they really want to remove.

The command `rm fred1` removes the file named `fred1`, while the command `rm -i fred1` deletes the `fred1` file after asking the user if they really want to remove this file.

Caution

Once you delete a file under Linux, that file is gone. You cannot undelete a file or directory under Linux like you can with DOS. If you delete a file, your only hope is a backup copy.

mkdir Create New Directories

Since Linux's file system is based on directories, Linux provides the `mkdir` command to allow users to create new ones. Unlike DOS, which has an alias for the `mkdir` command called MD, Linux requires the full `mkdir` command to be spelled out. You must specify a name for each new directory, as shown in the following example:

```
mkdir /backup
```

Note

Linux does provide a way, via the command shell, to make aliases for command names; thus, if you simply can't live without the `cls` command and hate typing **`clear`**, you can alias `cls` to the `clear` command.

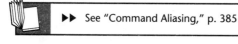

▶▶ See "Command Aliasing," p. 385

rmdir Delete Directories

The `rmdir` command deletes Linux directories. The command takes the name of the directory to delete. This directory must be empty or Linux cannot remove it.

For example, if the `/backup` directory had two directories within it, the command `rmdir /backup` fails. The command `rmdir /backup/jack/*` removes all files in the `jack` directory, while the command `rmdir /backup/jack` removes the now empty directory `/backup/jack`.

Caution

You cannot delete a directory that contains files with the `rmdir` command. Instead, you can use the `-r` parameter to the `rm` command. For example,

```
rm -r *
```

deletes everything from the current directory and every directory below. Be very careful using this command because the moment you delete a directory you cannot recover the directory or the files that were located in the directory. Make backups.

man Display Online Help

To get online help for each of the various Linux commands, you can type **`man`**. Linux then displays, a screen at a time, any information it has on the command. If you are not sure of what command to use, you can try the `-k` parameter and enter a simple keyword that represents the topic of interest. `man` then searches through its help files (called *man pages*) for a topic that contains the keyword. Linux also provides an alias for this command called `apropos`.

If you enter the command **`man ls`**, Linux provides help on the `ls` command, including all its parameters. The command `man -k cls` provides a listing of commands that have the word `cls` in the help file; the command `apropos cls` is the same as `man -k cls`.

more Display File Contents

The `more` command displays a screenful of a text file. You can look through a text file without invoking an editor, printing the file, or trying to pause the terminal as it displays the file. If you try to pass a binary data file to `more`, you could have some unpleasant effects; for example, your terminal can lock up. If your terminal does lock up, try pressing either the <Ctrl-q> or the <Ctrl-s> keys.

A disadvantage with `more` is that you cannot back up to see a screen of information once it passes. For example, to display the contents of your `emacs` configuration file, you can type the following command:

```
more .emacs
```

less A Better *more*

`less` displays information a screen at a time on your terminal. The program's name is a play on words for the program it's meant to replace—`more`. Like `more`, `less` can display a screen of information in a text file, but unlike `more`, `less` allows you to page back and forth within the file. You can use the following command to browse through the `readme` file located in the `info` directory:

```
less .emacs
```

clear Clear Terminal Screen

Sometimes after filling your terminal screen with information, you want a blank screen while you sit and contemplate your next action. Under DOS, you can use the `cls` command, but under Linux, you must use the `clear` command.

Dealing with DOS Files Under Linux

During installation, you were given the chance to make any DOS partitions you had available visible to Linux. These partitions were then placed in a directory you specified during configuration, for example, `/dosc`. If you want to copy these files to a floppy, using the `cp` command may cause problems because UNIX and Linux treat text files a little differently, especially when dealing with carriage returns and linefeeds. To overcome this problem, a group of programs were developed to help deal with MS-DOS files under a UNIX environment. These are the `m-` commands, which include such commands as `mcopy` and `mdir`. `mcopy` works just like the DOS COPY command, and `mdir` provides a directory listing. As you can notice, they resemble their DOS counterparts, except they begin with the letter m, hence the name `m -` commands. The `m-` commands are part of the mtools package, which is a collection of programs, in the public domain, which allows UNIX to interact with DOS files much easier.

These commands also make copying files to floppy disks much easier because you can use the DOS designation, like A:, rather than the Linux designation `/dev/fd0`. For more information on the `m-` commands and other Linux commands, check out Chapter 25, "Command-Line Reference," and Table 5.2 for a brief listing of the various `m-` commands.

Table 5.2 The *m*- Commands

Command	Description
mattrib	Displays the file attributes for the specified file(s)
mcd	Changes directory to the specified path
mcopy	Copies the files specified to the new path
mdel	Deletes the specified files
mdir	Provides a directory listing
mformat	Formats a floppy
mlabel	Labels the DOS filesystem
mmd	Makes a directory
mrd	Removes a directory (must be empty, just as in DOS)
mren	Renames an existing DOS file
mtype	Displays the text contents of a DOS file

Note

While you can see a DOS file with Linux and even do some editing on text files in DOS partitions that Linux can see, you cannot execute DOS or Windows programs under Linux. There are, however, projects underway across the Internet to supply such emulation under Linux. While the prospects look very good for such emulators in the future, at this time DOS and Windows emulation is not fully available. However, you will have a brief introduction to both items later in this chapter.

Shutting Down Linux

When you are finished using a DOS machine, you can typically just turn off the power and walk away. You could also do the same under Windows although there is a great possibility for file damage. Under Linux, there are even more chances for damaging your system, both to hardware and file systems, by simply turning off the power. You must shut down Linux in an orderly fashion, or you might corrupt the operating system to the point where it cannot boot the next time you try.

Linux keeps a lot of information about itself and files in memory, in areas called *buffers*, before writing the information to disk. This process helps to improve system performance and control access to the hardware—something a multitasking operating systems needs to maintain so that one user doesn't try to use a hardware device that another user is using. If you turn off the power, this information is lost and you can damage your file system.

▶▶ See "Shutting Down Linux," p. 176

Since Linux is a multiuser and multitasking operating system, it must make sure that every user stops processing gracefully and save any work in progress before shutting the system down in order to prevent data loss and file damage. This also gives each user logged onto the system time to log off. To shut down Linux in an orderly fashion, you must use the `shutdown` command. The `shutdown` command syntax is

```
opus:~# shutdown [-r] time-to-shutdown [message]
```

The *`time-to-shutdown`* indicates when the system should shut down. The time is specified on a 24-hour clock, so you can tell the machine to shut down at 11 PM by entering

```
shutdown 23:00
```

The `-r` parameter indicates that Linux should immediately reboot after it has shut down. This is useful if you want to quit Linux and boot to another operating system.

The *`message`* parameter is a message sent to each user logged onto the system. This message is displayed on their terminals. This message can be used to let users know why you are shutting down the system. For example, if you needed to do weekly backups, you can use the following message to make sure everyone logs off the system:

```
opus:~# shutdown -r 23:00 Shutting down at 11:00pm for system maintenance
```

Remember, don't simply turn off the computer or press the reset button to exit Linux.

Caution

On some systems, Linux traps the <Ctrl-Alt-Del> reboot keystroke and executes an orderly shutdown as if the user had typed the `shutdown` command. However, on some systems Linux cannot detect this keystroke combination and reboots immediately.

If you do accidentally turn off your system and damage the file structure, there are some things you can do to try and repair the file system.

▶▶ See "Using the *fsck* Command," p. 312

Running Linux Programs

Once you are familiar with moving around Linux and executing basic commands, you can try several applications installed when you set up the systems. These applications cover a broad range of utilities, from a calculator, to full-featured C and C++ compilers. Some of these programs cost hundreds of dollars, but thanks to the GNU philosophy, many are readily available and the only monetary outlay is the cost of getting the program from the Internet. Luckily, many programs for Linux are also available on local bulletin boards, which you can reach via the telecommunications program included with the Slackware distribution of Linux. Also, many CD-ROM vendors supply CD-ROMs with hundreds of UNIX programs in source code. You can retrieve these programs from the CD-ROM and, using the gcc and g++ compilers distributed with Linux, get those programs up and running on your PC—even if you've never compiled a program before.

Finally, these programs are text-based and do not require the X Windows system to operate; thus, they may not have flashy graphics, but they work with most Linux installations.

bc

bc is a command-line calculator for those quick and dirty calculations. bc is actually a sophisticated programming language that allows you to interactively evaluate arithmetic expressions.

When executed, bc responds with a short copyright notice and then leaves you at the command prompt, a blank line. You can then enter simple addition and subtraction functions. You can also perform division and multiplication, but unfortunately, this version of bc truncates the result of division and multiplication operations. This is one of the hazards to be aware of when dealing with GNU software. bc is great for simple calculations as long as you are aware of the possible problems with its division and multiplication operations. Another great feature is the ability to store values from one operation to the next with a simple syntax, *variable-name = expression*. The following example calculates the value of 125 * 5 and stores the result in the var1 variable. To see what the results of the calculation are, you can type the name of the variable and bc prints the value on the next line, as shown in the example. Next the example sets the variable var2 to the contents of var1 divided by 5.

```
var1 = 125 * 5
var1
625
var2 = var1 / 5
var2
```

workbone

If you have a CD-ROM capable of playing audio CDs, then you should give workbone a try. workbone is a text-based CD player written by Thomas McWilliams. He wrote the program for his own enjoyment by hacking an X Windows-based program. Because he did this for his own enjoyment, workbone may not work correctly with every CD-ROM drive. The program uses the numeric keypad to control the CD, so make sure you have the <Num Lock> key engaged. Table 5.3 lists the various controls used.

Table 5.3 *workbone* Commands

Key	Description
0	Exits workbone
DEL	Displays the help screen
1	Goes backward 15 seconds
2	Aborts `workbone`
3	Goes forward 15 seconds
4	Previous selection
5	Restarts current selection
6	Next selection
7	Stops
8	Pauses/resumes
9	Plays

As `workbone` plays, the display updates the time and current selection. If you want to continue working while your CD plays, you have two choices: you can exit `workbone` and leave the music playing (key 0), or if you want to keep the display up and running, you can simply switch to another virtual terminal via the <Alt> key and log onto another account. When you want to check on the display, you can switch back to the proper virtual terminal and check on the status of the CD. You can also stop the CD, and then at a later point, simply re-execute the program to see what tracks are playing, and so on. For more information, check out the man page by typing **`man workbone`**.

sc

Do spiffy computers sell software, or does software sell computers? An age-old question whose answer tends to side with the concept that the proper application can sell thousands of computers. When the program called Visicalc entered the market, PC use in business exploded. Why? Because for years business people had played what-if games with their businesses on pieces of paper called ledgers, or spreadsheets. Visicalc was an electronic version of the paper spreadsheet; it revolutionized how business did its forecasting and planning. Today, the successors of Visicalc, like Microsoft's Excel and Lotus Corp.'s 1-2-3, still carry on the legacy started by Visicalc. And in the world of Linux, `sc` carries on that same legacy.

`sc` is a spreadsheet calculator containing rows and columns of cells. Each cell can contain a numeric value, a label string, or an expression or formula that evaluates to a numeric value or label string. These label strings can also be based on other cells to form complex relationships across a multiple collection of information. If you have worked with other spreadsheet programs, you should have no problem getting up to speed on using sc. If you do need help, you can run a tutorial program to help you learn by entering

```
sc /usr/lib/sc/tutorial.sc
```

This provides an excellent introduction to using sc. If you need a quick reference card, you can print one by entering

```
scqref | your-printer-command
```

your-printer-command for Linux is `lpr`. The solid bar is referred to as a *pipe* since you are piping, or passing on, the results of one command, `scqref`, to another command, `lpr`.

Caution

Check out Chapter 24, "Printing," if you have any problems printing with Linux. The biggest problem you may face, besides the possibility of not being able to print at all, is a bad case of the *jaggies*, which are the stair-step effects caused by how UNIX/Linux treats carriage returns and linefeeds versus how MS-DOS treats them when printing text files containing these characters.

For online help about sc simply type **man sc**.

minicom

Hopefully, once having read the chapters in Part IV, "Network Administration," you will be able to get your Linux system up and running on the Internet, that global information superhighway so much in the news today. Until then, though, you can still connect with the rest of the world if you have a modem and a telecommunications package. Linux supplies the package, called `minicom`, so all you have to do is supply the modem connected to one of your serial ports. `minicom`, like a lot of Linux software, was written by a single person with help from many people on the Internet. The main author of `minicom` is Miquel van Smoorenburg.

`minicom` is a very robust application that rivals many other commercial applications. With it you can connect to a variety of bulletin board services, maintain a list of numbers to dial, and download and upload files once you connect. `minicom` has a very detailed man page, but most of its functionality is available if you learn how to maneuver in `minicom`.

The first item to remember is that `minicom` uses the control-key sequence <Ctrl-A> to access the various functions, such as auto-dial and file down-loading. To get help at anytime while in `minicom`, simply press <Ctrl-a> and then press the <z> key. This displays a brief command summary screen. Table 5.4 lists a few of those commands.

Table 5.4 *minicom* Command Summary

Key	Description
D	Dialing directory
S	Sends files
P	Communication parameters
L	Captures on/off toggle
F	Sends a BREAK to the other terminal
T	Sets terminal emulation between vt100, Minix, or ANSI
W	Linewraps on/off toggle
G	Runs a `minicom` script file
R	Receives a file
A	Adds a linefeed character to the end of lines
H	Hangs up the phone line
M	Initializes the modem
K	Runs kermit
E	Local echo on/off toggle
C	Clears the local screen
O	Configures `minicom`
J	Jumps to a shell
X	Quits and resets the modem
I	Cursor key mode
Z	Displays this screen
B	Scrolls back through the terminal window

While in the help window, you can simply press the above letter to execute the command. From the `minicom` program, however, you must preface the above letters with <Ctrl-a>.

`minicom` has four file transfer protocols: zmodem, ymodem, xmodem, and kermit. If possible, you should try to use the zmodem protocol because of its superior error-recovery capabilities. If zmodem is not available on the other system, you should try each of the protocols in the order given. This is not to say kermit is a bad protocol (it is not), but it is slower than most of the others. The upside to using kermit is that more than likely almost any system you log onto supports kermit.

The next area you should be aware of is that `minicom` takes advantage of some commands that gives it access to the same type of power controlled by the super user (that is `minicom`); thus, anyone running `minicom` has access to certain features of Linux you may not want them to have.

▶▶ See "File Security," p. 204

Playing Games

If you installed the y package, you have access to a myriad of games. Most are text-based so you don't need the X Windows system up and running to enjoy a few minutes of fun. You can get an idea of the variety of games by checking out the `/usr/games` directory. By listing the files, you can see the games that are available. If you do not know what a game is or does, you can try to get help on the game with the `man` command. Of course, if you are adventurous, you can simply start the game and explore. Have fun.

Tetris

Tetris is a game originating from the former Soviet Union. In the game, various shapes drop from the sky and pile up at the bottom. The object of the game is to eradicate those shapes building up and keep the game area from filling. You accomplish the elimination by filling a row across the playing field. When you connect one wall of the playing field with the other so that there are no gaps, that row disappears and all the shapes above it fall down to take up the vacated row. The catch to this is that the shapes fall in a variety of patterns and to fill up a row you must decide how to orient a shape and then where to place it before it touches another block. Once a shape touches another block, it remains at that position. This game has been ported to most platforms, so if you've played the game on other systems, you should have no problem playing Tetris under Linux.

This version of the game is meant to be played only from the terminal, so don't expect fancy graphics. Also the biggest pain is that on other systems you can position and orient the falling shapes with the keyboard arrow keys, not so with this version of Tetris. You must use the keys listed in Table 5.5 for positioning and orienting the various blocks.

Table 5.5 Tetris Command Keys

Direction	Key
Move Left	<,>
Move right	</>
Rotate	<.>
Drop	<Spacebar>
Pause	<s>
Quit	<q>
Refresh	<Ctrl-l>

Dungeon

Dungeon is a text adventure based on the ancient Adventure text games, but instead of caves, you deal with dungeons. You interact with this text-based world in search of treasures and adventure; if you've played other text adventures, then this one is very similar. If you have used only glittery graphics, sit back and use the brain. You interact with the game by issuing commands and requests in the form of verbs and nouns. For instance, at the beginning of the game it tells you that you are in an open field west of a big, white house with a boarded front door. There is a small mailbox here. At the prompt you can issue the following command to read whatever is in the box:

```
There is a small mailbox here.
> open box
Opening the mailbox reveals:
a leaflet.
>read leaflet
```

The game then provides a brief overview of the game and the talented programmers who built it. The last line of the information in the leaflet instructs you to get assistance by entering the command **help** or **info**.

Trek

Trek is a game based on the very popular TV series *Star Trek*. Your goal is to survive the bloody battles with the Klingons and rid your star sector from their scourge. When you start the game, by typing the command **trek**, you are asked a series of questions to set up the game. At any point, either during setup or while playing, you can type a question mark to get help on the possible answers and actions available to you. Some of the possible actions are listed in Table 5.6.

Table 5.6 Trek Commands

Command	Description
abandon	Quits Trek
damages	Lists the damages your starship has sustained
impulse	Goes to impulse power
ram	Ramming speed
srscan	Short-range scan
undock	Leaves starbase
capture	Captures the Klingons
destruct	Self-destructs
lrscan	Long-range scan
dump	Who knows?
visual	Looks at the Klingons

Command	Description
cloak	Cloaks the ship
dock	Enters starbase
move	Plots and follows course
rest	Rests for a while
terminate	Quits
Warp	Engages warp engines
computer	Finds out some information
help	Calls a starbase for help
phasers	Fires phasers
shields	Shields up
torpedo	Fires torpedoes

You are asked for the length of the game you want to play. You can restart a saved game from a log file. You specify a log file on the command line with the name of the game to create a saved game. You are then asked what skill level you want to play. Next, you can enter a password so that others cannot claim your glory; no, really, you need the password so no one but you can blow up the ship.

Because this is a text-based game, there are no glitzy graphics, but you can get a short-range scan with the `srscan`, which displays your sector and all known objects at their respective coordinates. The `srscan` also provides you with valuable information on the condition of your ship. All coordinates refer to a Cartesian matrix you can maintain on paper, or better yet graph paper, so that you do not have to remember from one `srscan` command to the other. The game begins by telling you how many Klingons are in your sector and how many starbases are here and their location. Docking at a starbase can replenish and repair your ship. Unfortunately, the game doesn't tell you where the nasty Klingon warships are located. Make sure you pay attention to energy-use; otherwise, you are in for some bad surprises.

Running DOS Programs Under Linux

After you've had enough of running various Linux applications, you might want to occasionally run some of your DOS or Windows programs. While not yet a complete reality, work is progressing to allow you to do just that, by emulating the various operating systems under Linux. DOSEMU is a program which lets MS-DOS— and their variants, such as PC-DOS—programs run under Linux. DOSEMU stands for DOS EMUlator. There is also a project underway to allow users access to Windows programs under Linux. This project is called WINE and is discussed later in "Running MS Windows Programs under Linux."

Installing DOSEMU

You can find the current version of DOSEMU on the enclosed CD-ROM under the name `/contrib/dosemu_0.000 and contrib/dosemu_0.060`. This file archive and its files need to be placed in the `/usr/src` directory and then unzipped and un-tared using the following commands:

```
opus: gzip -d dosemu_5.tgz
opus: tar -xvf dosemu_5.tar
```

Next you must build the various files using the following commands. You must be logged in as root and have at least 10M of virtual memory available for the build.

Note

You must have installed Package D, the program development package. You need the various compilers and tools within this package to build the DOS emulator.

```
opus: make config
opus: make depend
opus: make most
```

These commands should install the DOSEMU files in the `/var/lib/dosemu` directory.

Configuring DOSEMU

Once the emulator has been built, next you must configure the system. To start, make a bootable DOS disk and copy the following DOS files on the disk: command.com, fdisk.exe, and sys.com.

Next, copy the following DOSEMU files from the dosemu subdirectory onto the floppy: emufs.sys, ems.sys, cdrom.sys, and exitemu.com. You can use the `m-` commands mentioned earlier in "Dealing with DOS Files Under Linux" to copy the files from the Linux partitions to the floppy drive.

Tip

If you have trouble finding these files on Linux, then you can use the `find` command to locate the necessary files, for example,

```
find -name emufs.sys -print
```

This command will display the location of the file on your system, providing it exists.

DOSEMU requires a configuration file, called dosemu.conf, to operate correctly. Next you must customize this file for your system. An example file is located in the examples directory with the name config.dist. The config.dist is shown in Listing 5.1. Remarks are shown with a sharp symbol #, and most options take the form of parameter value. If a parameter has more than one value, then the values are placed within braces {}.

Listing 5.1 A Sample desemu.conf File

```
# Linux dosemu 0.51 configuration file.
# Updated to include QuickStart documentation 5/10/94 by Mark Rejhon
# James MacLean, jmaclean@fox.nstn.ns.ca, 12/31/93
# Robert Sanders, gt8134b@prism.gatech.edu, 5/16/93
#
# NOTICE:
#   - Although QuickStart information is included in this file, you
#     should refer to the documentation in the "doc" subdirectory of the
#     DOSEMU distribution, wherever possible.
#   - This configuration file is designed to be used as a base to make
#     it easier for you to set up DOSEMU for your specific system.
#   - Configuration options between lace brackets { } can be split onto
#     multiple lines.
#   - Comments start with # or ; in column 1. (beginning of a line)
#   - Send Email to the jmaclean address above if you find any errors.


#************************* DEBUG *******************************************
#
# QuickStart:
#  This section is of interest mainly to programmers. This is useful if
#  you are having problems with DOSEMU and you want to enclose debug info
#  when you make bug reports to a member of the DOSEMU development team.
#  Simply set desired flags to "on" or "off", then redirect stderr of
#  DOSEMU to a file using "dos 2>debug" to record the debug information
#  if desired. Skip this section if you're only starting to set up.
#
debug { config off   disk off   warning off   hardware off
    port  off   read  off   general off   IPC   off
    video  off   write  off   xms   off   ems   off
    serial off   keyb  off   dpmi  off
      printer off   mouse  off
   }


#************************ MISCELLANEOUS **********************************
#
#  Want startup DOSEMU banner messages? Of course :-)
dosbanner on
#
#  timint is necessary for many programs to work.
timint on


#************************** KEYBOARD ************************************
#
# QuickStart:
#  With the "layout" keyword, you can specify your country's keyboard
#  layout. The following layouts are implemented:
#    finnish      us      dvorak    sf
#    finnish_latin1  uk      sg      sf_latin1
#    gr       dk      sg_latin1  es
#    gr_latin1     dk_latin1  fr      es_latin1
```

(continues)

Listing 5.1 Continued

```
#    be        no      fr_latin1
#  The us-layout is selected by default if the "layout" keyword is omitted.
#
#  The keyword "keybint" allows more accurate keyboard interrupts,
#  It is a bit unstable, but makes keyboard work better when set to "on".
#
#  The keyword "rawkeyboard" allows for accurate keyboard emulation for
#  DOS programs, and is only activated when DOSEMU starts up at the
#  console. It only becomes a problem when DOSEMU prematurely exits
#  with a "Segmentation Fault" fatal error, because the keyboard would
#  have not been reset properly. In that case, you would have to reboot
#  your Linux system remotely, or using the RESET button. In reality,
#  this should never happen. But if it does, please do report to the
#  dosemu development team, of the problem and detailed circumstances,
#  we're trying our best! If you don't need near complete keyboard
#  emulation (needed by major software package), set it to "off".
#
keyboard { layout us keybint on rawkeyboard on }
# keyboard { layout gr-latin1 keybint on rawkeyboard on }
#
#  If DOSEMU speed is unimportant, and CPU time is very valuable to you,
#  you may want to set HogThreshold to a non-zero value. This means
#  the number of keypress requests in a row before CPU time is given
#  away from DOSEMU. A good value to use could be 10000.
#  A zero disables CPU hogging detection via keyboard requests.
#
HogThreshold 0


#**************************** SERIAL ************************************
#
# QuickStart:
#  You can specify up to 4 simultaneous serial ports here.
#  If more than one ports have the same IRQ, only one of those ports
#  can be used at the same time. Also, you can specify the com port,
#  base address, irq, and device path! The defaults are:
#    COM1 default is base 0x03F8, irq 4, and device /dev/cua0
#    COM2 default is base 0x02F8, irq 3, and device /dev/cua1
#    COM3 default is base 0x03E8, irq 4, and device /dev/cua2
#    COM4 default is base 0x02E8, irq 3, and device /dev/cua3
#  If the "com" keyword is omitted, the next unused COM port is assigned.
#  Also, remember, these are only how you want the ports to be emulated
#  in DOSEMU. That means what is COM3 on IRQ 5 in real DOS, can become
#  COM1 on IRQ 4 in DOSEMU!
#
#  Also, as an example of defaults, these two lines are functionally equal:
#  serial { com 1 mouse }
#  serial { com 1 mouse base 0x03F8 irq 4 device /dev/cua0 }
#
#  If you want to use a serial mouse with DOSEMU, the "mouse" keyword
#  should be specified in only one of the serial lines. (For PS/2
#  mice, it is not necessary, and device path is in mouse line instead.)
#
#  Uncomment/modify any of the following if you want to support a modem
#  (or any other serial device).
```

```
#serial { com 1 device /dev/modem }
#serial { com 2 device /dev/modem }
#serial { com 3 device /dev/modem }
#serial { com 4 device /dev/modem }
#serial { com 3 base 0x03E8 irq 5 device /dev/cua2 }
#
#  If you have a non-PS/2 mouse, uncomment/modify one of the following.
#serial { mouse com 1 device /dev/mouse }
#serial { mouse com 2 device /dev/mouse }
#
#  What type is your mouse? Uncomment one of the following.
#  Use the 'internaldriver' option with ps2 and busmouse options.
#mouse { microsoft }
#mouse { logitech }
#mouse { mmseries }
#mouse { mouseman }
#mouse { hitachi }
#mouse { mousesystems }
#mouse { busmouse }
#mouse { ps2 device /dev/mouse internaldriver }
#  The following line won't run for now, but I hope it will sometime
#mouse { mousesystems device /dev/mouse internaldriver cleardtr }


#************************* NETWORKING SUPPORT *****************************
#
#  Turn the following option 'on' if you require IPX/SPX emulation.
#  Therefore, there is no need to load IPX.COM within the DOS session.
#  The following option does not emulate LSL.COM, IPXODI.COM, etc.
#  NOTE: MUST HAVE IPX PROTOCOL ENABLED IN KERNEL !!
ipxsupport off
#
#  Enable Novell 8137->raw 802.3 translation hack in new packet driver.
#pktdriver novell_hack


#************************* VIDEO ******************************************
#
# !!WARNING!!: A LOT OF THIS VIDEO CODE IS ALPHA! IF YOU ENABLE GRAPHICS
# ON AN INCOMPATIBLE ADAPTOR, YOU COULD GET A BLANK SCREEN OR MESSY SCREEN
# EVEN AFTER EXITING DOSEMU. JUST REBOOT (BLINDLY) AND THEN MODIFY CONFIG.
#
# QuickStart:
#  Start with only text video using the following line, to get started.
#  then when DOSEMU is running, you can set up a better video configura-
#  tion.
#
# video { vga console }     # Use this line, if you are using VGA
# video { cga console }     # Use this line, if you are using CGA
# video { ega console }     # Use this line, if you are using EGA
# video { mda console }     # Use this line, if you are using MDA
#
# Even more basic, like on an xterm or over serial, use one of the
# following :
#
```

(continues)

Listing 5.1 Continued

```
#  For Xterm
# video { vga chunks 25 }
#  For serial at 2400 baud
# video { vga chunks 200 }
#
# QuickStart Notes for Graphics:
#  - If your VGA-Bios resides at E000-EFFF, turn off video BIOS shadow
#    for this address range and add the statement vbios_seg 0xe000
#    to the correct vios-statement, see the example below.
#  - Set "allowvideoportaccess on" earlier in this configuration file
#    if DOSEMU won't boot properly, such as hanging with a blank screen,
#    beeping, or the video card bootup message.
#  - Video BIOS shadowing (in your CMOS setup) at C000-CFFF must be dis-
#    abled.
#
#    *> CAUTION <*: TURN OFF VIDEO BIOS SHADOWING BEFORE ENABLING GRAPHICS!
#
#  It may be necessary to set this to "on" if DOSEMU can't boot up properly
#  on your system when it's set "off" and when graphics are enabled.
#  Note: May interfere with serial ports when using certain video boards.
allowvideoportaccess on
#
#  Any 100% compatible standard VGA card _MAY_ work with this:
#video { vga console graphics }
#
#  If your VGA-BIOS is at segment E000, this may work for you:
#video { vga console graphics vbios_seg 0xe000 }
#
#  Trident SVGA with 1 megabyte on board
#video { vga console graphics chipset trident memsize 1024 }
#
#  Diamond SVGA
#video { vga console graphics chipset diamond }
#
#  ET4000 SVGA card with 1 megabyte on board:
#video { vga console graphics chipset et4000 memsize 1024 }
#
#  S3-based SVGA video card with 1 megabyte on board:
#video { vga console graphics chipset s3 memsize 1024 }


#*************************** MISCELLANEOUS **********************************
#
# QuickStart:
#  For "mathco", set this to "on" to enable the coprocessor during DOSEMU.
#  This really only has an effect on kernels prior to 1.0.3.
#  For "cpu", set this to the CPU you want recognized during DOSEMU.
#  For "bootA"/"bootC", set this to the bootup drive you want to use.
#  It is strongly recommended you start with "bootA" to get DOSEMU
#  going, and during configuration of DOSEMU to recognize hard disks.
#
mathco on       # Math coprocessor valid values: on off
cpu 80386       # CPU emulation valid values: 80286 80386 80486
bootA           # Startup drive valid values: bootA bootC
```

```
#************************ MEMORY ******************************************
#
# QuickStart:
#  These are memory parameters, stated in number of kilobytes.
#  If you get lots of disk swapping while DOSEMU runs, you should
#  reduce these values. Also, DPMI is still somewhat unstable,
#  (as of early April 1994) so be careful with DPMI parameters.
#
xms 1024      # XMS size in K, or "off"
ems 1024      # EMS size in K, or "off"
dpmi off      # DPMI size in K, or "off". Be careful with DPMI!


#*********************** PORT ACCESS **************************************
#
# !!WARNING!!: GIVING ACCESS TO PORTS IS BOTH A SECURITY CONCERN AND
# SOME PORTS ARE DANGEROUS TO USE. PLEASE SKIP THIS SECTION, AND
# DON'T FIDDLE WITH THIS SECTION UNLESS YOU KNOW WHAT YOU'RE DOING.
#
# ports { 0x388 0x389 } # for SimEarth
# ports { 0x21e 0x22e 0x23e 0x24e 0x25e 0x26e 0x27e 0x28e 0x29e } # for
# jill


#******************* SPEAKER **********************************************
#
# These keywoards are allowable on the "speaker" line:
#  native   Enable DOSEMU direct access to the speaker ports.
#  emulated  Enable simple beeps at the terminal.
#  off     Disable speaker emulation.
#
speaker native     # or "off" or "emulated"


#******************* HARD DISKS *******************************************
#
# !!WARNING!!: DAMAGE MIGHT RESULT TO YOUR HARD DISK (LINUX AND/OR DOS)
# IF YOU FIDDLE WITH THIS SECTION WITHOUT KNOWING WHAT YOU'RE DOING!
#
# QuickStart:
#  The best way to get started is to start with a boot floppy, and set
#  "bootA" above in the configuration. Keep using the boot floppy
#  while you are setting this hard disk configuration up for DOSEMU,
#  and testing by using DIR C: or something like that.
#  If you want DOSEMU to be able to access a DOS partition, the
#  safer type of access is "partition" access, because "wholedisk"
#  access gives DOSEMU write access to a whole physical disk,
#  including any vulnerable Linux partitions on that drive!
#
#  !!! IMPORTANT !!!
#  You must not have LILO installed on the partition for dosemu to boot
#  off.
#  As of 04/26/94, doublespace and stacker 3.1 will work with wholedisk
#  or partition only access. Stacker 4.0 has been reported to work with
#  wholedisk access. If you want to use disk compression using partition
```

(continues)

Listing 5.1 Continued

```
#  access, you will need to use the "mkpartition" command included with
#  dosemu to create a partition table datafile for dosemu.
#
#  Please read the documentation in the "doc" subdirectory for info
#  on how to set up access to real hard disk.
#
#  "image" specifies a hard disk image file.
#  "partition" specifies partition access, with device and partition
#   number.
#  "wholedisk" specifies full access to entire hard drive.
#  "readonly" for read only access. A good idea to set up with.
#
#disk { image "/var/lib/dosemu/hdimage" }   # use diskimage file.
#disk { partition "/dev/hda1" 1 readonly }  # 1st partition on 1st IDE.
#disk { partition "/dev/sda2" 1 readonly }  # 1st partition on 2nd SCSI.
#disk { wholedisk "/dev/hda" }              # Entire disk drive unit


#******************* DOSEMU BOOT*********************************************
#
#  Use the following option to boot from the specified file, and then
#  once booted, have bootoff execute in autoexec.bat. Thanks Ted :-).
#  Notice it follows a typical floppy spec. To create this file use
#  dd if=/dev/fd0 of=/var/lib/dosemu/bdisk bs=16k
#
#bootdisk { heads 2 sectors 18 tracks 80 threeinch file /var/lib/dosemu/
#bdisk }
#
#  Specify extensions for the CONFIG and AUTOEXEC files. If the below
#  are uncommented, the extensions become CONFIG.EMU and AUTOEXEC.EMU.
#  NOTE: this feature may affect file naming even after boot time.
#  If you use MSDOS 6+, you may want to use a CONFIG.SYS menu instead.
#
#EmuSys EMU
#EmuBat EMU


#******************* FLOPPY DISKS *****************************************
#
# QuickStart:
#  This part is fairly easy. Make sure that the first (/dev/fd0) and
#  second (/dev/fd1) floppy drives are of the correct size, "threeinch"
#  and/or "fiveinch". A floppy disk image can be used instead, however.
#
#  FOR SAFETY, UNMOUNT ALL FLOPPY DRIVES FROM YOUR FILESYSTEM BEFORE
#  STARTING UP DOSEMU! DAMAGE TO THE FLOPPY MAY RESULT OTHERWISE!
#
floppy { device /dev/fd0 threeinch }
floppy { device /dev/fd1 fiveinch }
#floppy { heads 2 sectors 18 tracks 80
#     threeinch file /var/lib/dosemu/diskimage }
#
#  If floppy disk speed is very important, uncomment the following
#  line. However, this makes the floppy drive a bit unstable. This
```

```
#  is best used if the floppies are write-protected.
#
#FastFloppy on


#****************** PRINTERS *********************************************
#
# QuickStart:
#  Printer is emulated by piping printer data to a file or via a unix
#  command such as "lpr". Don't bother fiddling with this configuration
#  until you've got DOSEMU up and running already.
#
#printer { options "%s" command "lpr" timeout 20 }
#printer { options "-p %s" command "lpr" timeout 10 }  # pr format it
#printer { file "lpt3" }
```

You must then use a text editor to change the settings from the example config file to match your system. Such items as processor type and video cards must match.

> **Note**
>
> You can also boot DOSEMU from a hard drive partition, instead of from a floppy. To access a hard drive, simply configure a drive/partition in the dosemu.conf file.

Running DOSEMU

To run DOSEMU, simply type **dos** at any Linux prompt. To exit, use the `exitemu` command from the prompt. Table 5.7 provides a listing of command-line options you can pass to DOSEMU. You can use `-?` to get a complete, up-to-date listing of command-line parameters too.

Table 5.7 DOSEMU Command-Line Parameters

Parameter	Description
-A	Boot from the A drive
-C	Boot from the hard drive
-c	Optimize video performance from virtual terminals
-D	Set debug options
-e	Specify the amount of EMS memory
-F#	Number (#) of floppies to use from dosemu.conf
-f	Flip the definition of the A and B floppy drives
-H#	Number (#) of hard disks to use from dosemu.conf
-k	Use the raw keyboard console defined in the `rawkeyboard` parameter of dosemu.conf

(continues)

II

Installing Linux

Table 5.7 Continued

Parameter	Description
-P	Copy the debug information to a file
-t	Deliver the time interrupt 9
-V	Activate VGA emulation
-x	Specify the amount of XMS memory
-?	Display summary help for each command
-2	Emulate a 286
-3	Emulate a 386
-4	Emulate a 486

From the DOS prompt supplied by DOSEMU, you can run most DOS programs except those which require DPMI (DOS Protected Mode Support) support. Simply type in the name of the program and, providing dosemu can find the program in your path, dosemu will load and run the program. Table 5.8 shows some of the programs known to operate under Linux, but more are added everyday. Check the file EMUsuccess.txt for an up-to-date listing. Table 5.9 provides a listing of some of the programs which do *not* work with Linux.

Table 5.8 Programs Known to Run with DOSEMU

Name	Function	Success Story Posted by
1st Wordplus	GEM word proc	**jan@janhh.hanse.de**
4desc	4dos desc editor	**piola@di.unito.it**
4DOS 4.2	command interp.	**rideau@clipper.ens.fr**
4dos 5.0c	command interp.	**J1MCPHER@VAXC. STEVENS-TECH.EDU**
ack3d	3-D engine	**martin5@trgcorp.solucorp.qc.ca**
ACU-COBOL	compiler	**fjh@munta.cs.mu.OZ.AU**
Alite 1.10		**ph99jh42@uwrf.edu**
AmTax 93 & 94	tax software	**root@bobspc.canisius.edu**
ansi.sys	screen/kbd drvr (display functions)	**ag173@cleveland.Freenet.Edu**
arj v2.41a	[un]archiver	**tanner@winternet.mpls.mn.us**
As Easy As 5.01	spreadsheet	**ph99jh42@uwrf.edu**
Autoroute Plus	route planner	**hsw1@papa.attmail.com**

Name	Function	Success Story Posted by
Axum	sci. graphics	**miguel@pinon.ccu.uniovi.es**
battle chess	chess game	**jvdbergh@wins.uia.ac.be**
Binkley 2.50eebd	Fidomailer	**stub@linux.rz.tu-clausthal.de**
Blake Stone...	game	**owaddell@cs.indiana.edu**
bnu 1.70	Fossil (Fido)	**stub@linux.rz.tu-clausthal.de**
Borland C++ 2.0	86/286 C/C++ IDE	**rideau@clipper.ens.fr**
Boston Business EDT+		**keegstra@csdr2.fsfc.nasa.gov**
Cardbox Plus	database	**hsw1@papa.attmail.com**
Castle Wolfenstein	3D game	**gt8134b@prism.gatech.EDU**
Checkit diagnostics		
clipper 5.1	dbase compiler	**jvdbergh@wins.uia.ac.be**
COMPRESS	compressed fs	**rideau@clipper.ens.fr**
CCM (Crosstalk)	modem program	
cshow 8.61	picture viewer	**jvdbergh@wins.uia.ac.be**
cview	picture viewer	**lotov@avarice.ugcs.caltech.edu**
d86/a86		
DataPerfect 2.1	database	**fbennett@uk.ac.ulcc.clus1**
Dbase 4		**corey@amiganet.xnet.com**
Derive 1.2	math package	**miguel@pinon.ccu.uniovi.es**
Disk Freedom 4.6	disk utility	
diet 1.45f	file compression	**stub@linux.rz.tu-clausthal.de**
dosnix 2.0	unix utils	**miguel@pinon.ccu.uniovi.es**
Dosshell task	swapper	**jmaclean@fox.nstn.ns.ca**
dtmm	molecular models	**miguel@pinon.ccu.uniovi.es**
Dune 2	game	**COLIN@fs1.in.umist.ac.uk**
dviscr	EMTEX dvi preview	**ub9x@rz.uni-karlsruhe.de**
Easytrax	layout editor	**maehler@wrcd1.urz. uni-wuppertal.de**
Elvis	vi clone	**miguel@pinon.ccu.uniovi.es**
Epic Pinball	game	**krismon@quack.kfu.com**
ETen 3.1	Chinese terminal	**tyuan!root@mp.cs.niu.edu**
Eureka 1.0	math package	**miguel@pinon.ccu.uniovi.es**

(continues)

Table 5.8 Continued

Name	Function	Success Story Posted by
Falcon 3.0	Fighter simulator	**rapatel@rockypc.rutgers.edu**
FastLST 1.03	FidoNdlstcompiler	**stub@linux.rz.tu-clausthal.de**
FormGen II		**root@bobspc.canisius.edu**
freemacs 1.6d	editor	**ph99jh42@uwrf.edu**
Frontier (Elite II)	game	**COLIN@fs1.in.umist.ac.uk**
FW3		**Sebastian.Bunka@ vu-wien.ac.at**
MS Flight Simulator 5	game (runs SLOW!!!)	**newcombe@aa.csc.peachnet.edu**
Foxpro 2.0	database	
Framework 4		**corey@amiganet.xnet.com**
Freelance Graphics 2.1	graph/drawing app	**jwest@jwest.ecen. okstate.edu**
GEM/3	GUI	**jan@janhh.hanse.de**
GEM Draw	GEM drawing app	**jan@janhh.hanse.de**
GEM Paint	GEM painting app	**jan@janhh.hanse.de**
gmouse	mouse driver	**tk@pssparc2.oc.com**
God of Thunder	game	**ensor@cs.utk.edu**
Gravity	simulation pkg	**miguel@pinon.ccu.uniovi.es**
GWS for DOS	graphic file conv	**bchow@bchow.slip**
Gzip 1.1.2	file compression	**miguel@pinon.ccu.uniovi.es**
Harpoon	game	**wielinga@physics.uq.oz.au**
Harvard Graphics 3.0	graph/drawing pkg	**miguel@pinon.ccu.uniovi.es**
Hero's Quest I	game	**lam836@cs.cuhk.hk**
Hijaak 2.0	graphic file conv	**bchow@bchow.slip**
hocus pocus	Apogee Game	**kooper@dutiws.TWI. TUDelft.NL**
Image Alchemy Pro	graphic file conv (-V doesn't work)	**J1MCPHER@VAXC. STEVENS-TECH.EDU**
Incredible Machine	game (slow)	**sdh@po.cwru.edu**
Key Spreadsheet Plus	spreadsheet (on non-doublespaced disks)	**jwest@jwest.ecen.okstate.edu**

Name	Function	Success Story Posted by
Lemmings		**sdh@po.cwru.edu**
less 1.7.7	more than more	**miguel@pinon.ccu.uniovi.es**
LHA	file compression	
Lotus Manuscript	word processor	**miguel@pinon.ccu.uniovi.es**
Managing Your Money	financial	**newcombe@aa.csc.peachnet.edu**
Manifest	(dies during memory timings)	**hsw1@papa.attmail.com**
Mathcad 2.01	math package	**root@bobspc.canisius.edu**
MathCad 2.06	math package	**miguel@pinon.ccu.uniovi.es**
mcafee 9.23 v112	virus scanner	**jvdbergh@wins.uia.ac.be**
Microemacs	editor	**hjstein@MATH.HUJI.AC.IL**
MicroLink Yaht 2.1		**root@bobspc.canisius.edu**
Microsoft C 6.0	compiler	**ronnie@epact.se**
Microsoft Assembler 5.0	assembler	**ronnie@epact.se**
Microsoft Library 2.0		**root@bobspc.canisius.edu**
Microsoft Make	make	**ronnie@epact.se**
MicrosoftMouse Drv 8.2	mouse driver	**hsw1@papa.attmail.com**
MoneyCounts 7.0	accounting pkg	**raeburn@cygnus.com**
mscmouse	mouse driver	**tk@pssparc2.oc.com**
nnansi.com	ANSI driver	**mdrejhon@undergrad.math.uwaterloo.ca**
Netzplan	GEM project mgr	**jan@janhh.hanse.de**
NHL Hockey	game	**krismon@quack.kfu.com**
NJStar 2.1	Chinese word proc	**aab2@cornell.edu**
Norton Utils 4.5	disk utils	**rideau@clipper.ens.fr**
Norton Utils 7.0	disk utils	**rideau@clipper.ens.fr**
PAF	geneology package	**geek+@CMU.EDU**
Paradox	database	**hp@vmars.tuwien.ac.at**

(continues)

II

Installing Linux

Table 5.8 Continued

Name	Function	Success Story Posted by
PC Paintbrush IV	paint program	**bchow@bchow.slip**
PCtools 4.20	disk utils	**rideau@clipper.ens.fr**
pcwdemo		**vinod@cse.iitb.ernet.in**
PC-Write 3.0	word processor	
pcxlab 1.03	PCX viewer	**miguel@pinon.ccu. uniovi.es**
peachtree complete 6.0	accounting	**stjeanp@math.enmu.edu**
Pinball Dreams	game	**ronnie@lysator.liu.se**
PKzip/unzip	file compression	
pklite 1.15	file compression	**stub@linux.rz.tu-clausthal.de**
Pong Kombat	game	**ensor@cs.utk.edu**
PrintShop	greeting card pkg	**geek+@CMU.EDU**
Procomm Plus 2.0	communication	**newcombe@aa.csc. peachnet.edu**
Procomm 2.4.3	communication	**hsw1@papa.attmail.com**
Pspice 5.0	circuit sim.	**root@bobspc. canisius.edu**
Q&A	Word Proc/Databas	**newcombe@aa.csc. peachnet.edu**
Qbasic/edit (from DOS 5.0)	interpreter	
Qedit	editor	
QuickC	compiler	**martin@trcsun3.eas. asu.edu**
Quicken 4.0 for DOS	accounting pkg	**juphoff@nrao.edu**
Quicken 6.0 for DOS	accounting pkg	
Quicken 7.0 for DOS	accounting pkg	**juphoff@astro.phys. vt.edu**
Railroad Tycoon		**juphoff@astro.phys. vt.edu**
Red Baron	game	**wielinga@physics. uq.oz.au**
RM/COBOL	compiler	**fjh@munta.cs.mu.OZ.AU**
Rpro 1.6		**root@bobspc. canisius.edu**

Name	Function	Success Story Posted by
scan109	antivirus	**miguel@pinon.ccu.uniovi.es**
scan112	antivirus	**piola@di.unito.it**
Scorch	tank game	**geek+@CMU.EDU**
Shez94	Arcer-Shell	**stub@linux.rz.tu-clausthal.de**
sled	editor	**piola@di.unito.it**
Space Quest IV	game	**lam836@cs.cuhk.hk**
Spell Casting 301		**mancini@phantom.com**
SPSS/PC+4.0	statistical pkg	**jr@petz.han.de**
Squish 1.01	Fido Scan/Tosser	**stub@linux.rz.tu-clausthal.de**
Stacker 3.1	compressed fs	**mdrejhon@undergrad math.uwaterloo.ca**
Stacker 4.00	compressed fs	**J1MCPHER@VAXC.STEVENS-TECH.EDU**
StatPhys	simulation pkg	**miguel@pinon.ccu.uniovi.es**
STSORBIT	orbit simulation	**troch@gandalf.rutgers.edu**
Stunts	game?	**gt8134b@prism.gatech.EDU**
Superstor	compressed fs	**rideau@clipper.ens.fr**
TAG 2.02	Polish word proc	**rzm@oso.chalmers.se**
TASM 2.51	MACRO assembler	**rideau@clipper.ens.fr**
Telix	modem program	**jou@nematic.ep.nctu.edu.tw**
THelp from BC++2.0	Popup help	**rideau@clipper.ens.fr**
TimED/beta	Fido MSGeditor	**stub@linux.rz.tu-clausthal.de**
TLINK 4.0	LINKER	**rideau@clipper.ens.fr**
Topspeed Modula-2	compiler	**mayersn@hermes.informatik.uni-stuttgart.de**
Turbo Debugger 2.51	realmode debugger	**rideau@clipper.ens.fr**
Turbo Pascal 5.5	compiler	
Turbo Pascal 6.0	compiler	**t2262dj@cd1.lrz-muenchen.de**
Turbo Pascal 7.0	compiler	**mdrejhon@undergrad.math.uwaterloo.ca**

(continues)

Table 5.8 Continued

Name	Function	Success Story Posted by
Turb-opoly 1.43		**root@bobspc. canisius.edu**
Ultima 6	game	**msphil@birds.wm.edu**
Vpic 6.1		**root@bobspc. canisius.edu**
warlords II	game	**buckel@cip. informatik.uni-wuerzburg.de**
Warrior of Destiny	game	**msphil@birds.wm.edu**
WITWI Carmen Sandiego	game	**tillemaj@cae.wisc.edu**
Windows 3.0	windows (real mode)	**cjw1@ukc.ac.uk**
Wolf3d	game	**owaddell@cs.indiana.edu**
WordPerfect 5.1	word processor	**sdh@po.cwru.edu**
WordPerfect 6.0	word processor (needs >1M ram)	**lujian@texmd.minmet. mcgill.ca**
Xtpro 1.1	disk util	**root@bobspc. canisius.edu**
XWing	game (very slow)	**ronnie@lysator.liu.se**
Zarkov 2.6	chess	**a-acero@uchicago.edu**
zoo	file compression	

Table 5.9 Programs Known *Not* to Run with DOSEMU

Name	Function	Posted by
4D-box	boxing game	**jvdbergh@wins.uia.ac.be**
Apple][emulator	emulator	**ph99jh42@uwrf.edu**
Borland C++ 3.1 IDE	compiler	**juphoff@uppieland. async.vt.edu**
brief	editor	**bchow@bchow.slip**
Chuck Yeager Aircombat	flight simulator	**jvdbergh@wins.uia.ac.be**
CIVILIZATION	game	**miguel@pinon.ccu. uniovi.es**
DesqView 2.51 (ALT key doesn't work)		**hsw1@papa.attmail.com**

Name	Function	Posted by
doom	game	**rideau@clipper.ens.fr**
dpms from Stacker 4.0		**J1MCPHER@VAXC.STEVENS-TECH.EDU**
dxma0mod.sys	token-ring driver	**adjihc4@cti.ecp.fr**
dxmc0mod.sys	token-ring driver	**adjihc4@cti.ecp.fr**
ELDB	Economics Database	**hjstein@math.huji.ac.il**
FIPS 0.2.2	disk util(hdimage FAT problem)	
Howitzer	tank game	**geek+@CMU.EDU**
Lahey Fortran	Fortran Compiler	**hjstein@math.huji.ac.il**
Maple V2	math package	**ralf@ark.btbg.sub.de**
MSDOS 5/6 QBASIC/EDIT	editor	**bchow@bchow.slip**
NORTON UTILITIES 7.0	disk utils	**bchow@bchow.slip**
Quattro Pro 4.0	spreadsheet	**jwest@jwest.ecen.okstate.edu**
Raptor	game	**ensor@cs.utk.edu**
Silent Service II	submarine game	**jvdbergh@wins.uia.ac.be**
thunderByte scan	virus scanner	**jvdbergh@wins.uia.ac.be**
Ventura Publisher 3.0	desktop pub	**niemann@swt.ruhr-uni-bochum.de**
wildunix	wildcards	**miguel@pinon.ccu.uniovi.es**
Windows 3.1		**juphoff@uppieland.async.vt.edu**

Running programs under DOSEMU has several problems, mostly due to the fact the computer is emulating DOS and the underlying machine, rather than actually running DOS. This slows down the system. This can become annoying, especially when you are also running other Linux programs in other virtual terminals. Video updates are also rather slow under DOSEMU. Many DOS programs hog the CPU, since they believe they are the only program running. This prevents other Linux programs from receiving access to the CPU. To alieviate this problem, Thomas G. McWilliams wrote a program called Garrot to release access back to Linux from DOS-hogging programs.

Running MS Windows Programs under Linux

DOSEMU cannot run MS Windows programs, so the Linux community has embarked on creating a program that will allow Linux users to run MS Windows programs. This Windows emulator is called Wine. Wine is not a standard acronym and so it can stand as either **WIN**dows **E**mulator or, since Wine can be built as a static library instead of an emulator, **W**ine **I**s **N**ot a Windows **E**mulator. Both these acronyms are from the Windows FAQ, required reading if you wish to experiment with Wine. Why? Because Wine is not as far along in development as DOSEMU. Thus, it is very experimental and error prone. Also, not many Windows programs are supported. In fact, in order to use Wine, you must have MS Windows installed on a partition accessible to Linux. This is because Wine still relies on many parts of MS Windows in order to work. Wine also requires X to be installed and operational. To experiment with Wine you will need the following:

- A Linux kernel, version 99.13 or above
- Source code for Wine since it is only available in source code
- The D package installed for the compiler tools in order to build the source code
- At least 8M of RAM and at least a 12M swap drive
- At least 10M of disk space
- X Windows installed and configured
- A pointing device such as a mouse
- MS Windows installed on a partition accessible to Linux

Since Wine is under heavy development, new versions are released almost weekly. The newest source code is located at **sunsite.unc.edu**, (and other major ftp sites) in the `/pub/Linux/ALPHA/Wine` directory. The file is named after the date of its release, for example, `50606.tar.tgz`.

▶▶ See "Using *ftp* for Remote File Transfer," p. 595

Since Wine is changing so fast and is so unstable, we have not included it on the enclosed CD-ROM. If you wish to experiment with Wine, please feel free to download the newest files and read over the FAQs and HOWTOs. These documents are located on the CD-ROM in the `/docs` directory and provide the information needed to compile, install, configure, and use Wine.

Installing Wine is very similar to installing DOSEMU, with the exception that you can place the source tar file anywhere. Use the `tar` command to unarchive the file in the directory. For example,

```
opus: gzip -d 950606.tar.gz
opus: tar -xvf 950606.tar
```

Building Wine is a little more involved than building DOSEMU; in fact, it is more like building a new kernel. You must answer several questions to configure the build process. The Wine HOWTO explains the full process in detail.

Next you must answer several questions to configure Wine with runtime parameters. These configuration parameters are stored in a file named `/usr/local/etc/wine.conf`. While you can edit this file by hand, it is best to use the supplied configure program to do so.

Once you have configured the compilation files and the runtime parameter file, you can build Wine with the simple command `make`. This process takes several minutes.

To use Wine you invoke the emulator and provide the pathname to a Windows executable file, for example,

```
wine /dosc/windows/winmine.exe
```

The programs currently supported by Wine are calc.exe, clock.exe, notepad.exe, and winmine.exe. This list is continuously expanding so check the FAQ and HOWTO for current programs supported by the Windows emulator.

> **Note**
>
> MS-DOS and MS Windows are not the only operating systems emulated under Linux. There are also emulators for the old Apple II, CPM, and the newer Macintosh operating systems. You can generally find these emulators on ftp sites in the directory `\pub\Linux\system\emulators`.

From Here...

This chapter has just lightly touched on getting started with Linux and the various application programs available. For more information see the following chapters:

- Chapter 6, "The X Windows System," deals with the graphical user interface provided with Linux, Xfree86.
- Chapter 12, "Upgrading and Installing Software," explains how to install new software from CD-ROM or the Internet.
- Chapters 22, "Using the `vi` Editor," and 23, "Using the *emacs* Editor," discuss two of the more popular text editors for Linux.
- Chapter 25, "Command-Line Reference," provides you with a detailed description of many of the available Linux commands.
- Appendix B, "Applications for Linux," gives a wide-ranging list of applications that you can use with Linux.
- The DOSEMU and WINE HOWTOS and FAQs. These documents provide in-depth help on using the various emulators from under Linux. You can find them in the DOCS directory on the enclosed CD-ROM.

CHAPTER 6

The X Windows System

For any operating system to compete for space on today's desktops, it must have an easy-to-use, graphical interface. The most popular systems today are Windows, Macintosh, and OS/2. Although these applications have gained great popularity, they do not have the capability to run graphical applications across a heterogeneous network.

Linux provides the capability to run windowed applications across a heterogeneous network by incorporating the XFree86 implementation of the X11 standard of X Windows created at MIT. This system is much more than a graphical interface used to run applications. It is a very powerful client/server system that enables applications to be run and shared across a network. Although XFree86 is meant to run in a networked environment, it runs fine on a single machine. You do not need a network to run XFree86 or X Windows applications.

In this chapter, you learn:

- What X Windows and XFree86 are
- How to install XFree86
- How to configure the XFree86 system

In order to install, configure, and use XFree86, you need to know some basic Linux commands, such as how to execute programs, move through the directories, and how to copy, view, and delete files. You may even need to modify some of the files with a text editor. If you come across a topic you don't fully understand, this book tries to give you the command you need to perform the operation and then a reference to another chapter to learn, in more detail, how to perform the operation.

Like most parts of Linux, XFree86 also has a HOWTO document. This document is located in the /howto directory on the accompanying CD-ROM and in the /X11 directory when installed under Linux. This HOWTO is maintained by Matt Welsh, **mdw@sunsite.unc.edu**.

> **Caution**
>
> Typically, you do not have to worry about software damaging your hardware. Unfortunately, any software that deals directly with your video system—either the card or the monitor—can cause physical damage, especially if you try to use XFree86 under Linux with an unsupported video card. Make sure you have the necessary hardware before trying to run XFree86. Reading the documentation that comes with the XFree86 system, located in the /usr/X386/lib/X11/etc directory under Linux and the XFree86 HOWTO by Helmut Geyer in /usr/doc/faq/howto/XFree86-HOWTO, is suggested.

What Is X Windows?

The X Windows system is a powerful graphical operating environment that supports many applications across a network. The X Windows system was developed at MIT and can be freely distributed. The version of X Windows discussed in this chapter is X11R6. However, Linux and XFree86 are moving targets, and a newer version of X may be available on the accompanying CD. XFree86, the version used by Linux, is the X11R6 standard ported to Intel-based systems. A wide range of standard PC hardware is supported by XFree86.

The X Windows system grew out of a cooperative effort between two sections at MIT: the section responsible for a networking program called Project Athena, and a section called the Laboratory for Computer Science. Both used large quantities of UNIX workstations and soon realized they were each reinventing the wheel when it came to programming *graphical user interfaces* (GUIs) for UNIX workstations. To cut down on the amount of code both groups were writing, they decided to create one robust, extensible windowing system—X Windows.

In 1987, several vendors—in hopes of creating a single windowing system for UNIX workstations—formed an organization called the X Consortium to promote and standardize X Windows. Thanks to this effort, open computing is a reality. The X Consortium is composed of entities such as IBM, DEC, and MIT. This group of large organizations oversees the construction and release of new versions of X11.

XFree86 is a trademark of the XFree86 Project, Inc. The original programmers who ported X Windows to the 80386 platform decided to found the project in order to gain membership in the X Consortium. By becoming a member of the X Consortium, the XFree86 Project gains access to work in progress and can thus port the new features to XFree86 while the features are being implemented for X Windows, instead of waiting until after the official release to make the port.

X Windows is actually a series of pieces working together to present the user with a GUI. The base window system is a program providing services to the X Windows system. The next piece is a protocol for communicating across the network: the X Network Protocol. On top of the program implementing the X Network Protocol is the low-level interface between the network/base system and higher level programs. This low-level interface is called *Xlib*. Application programs typically use functions in the *Xlib* rather than the lower-level functions. Tying these pieces all together is a window manager. The window manager is an X Windows application whose purpose is to control how windows are presented to users.

The base window system does not provide user interface objects, such as scroll bars, command buttons, or menus. This is different from most other window systems. The user interface items are left to the higher-layer components and the window manager.

X Windows applications include not only window managers, but also games, graphics utilities, programming tools, and many other tidbits. Just about any application that you need has either been written for or ported to X Windows. The setup and use of several of the standard X Windows applications is covered in more detail in Chapter 26, "Using X Windows."

X Windows implements a windows manager to handle the task of creating and controlling the interface that makes up the visual portion of the X Windows system. This is not to be confused with the OS/2 Presentation Manager or the Microsoft Windows Program Manager. Although the windows manager for X Windows does control the behavior and position of the windows, you will not find a system setup icon or control panel for maintaining your Linux system settings.

For the not-so-faint-of-heart, XFree86 also includes programming libraries and includes files for programmers who want to develop their own applications under XFree86. The topic of programming or any of the caveats involved in creating X Windows applications is beyond the scope of this book, but there is ample documentation available on any number of Internet distribution sites, such as **prep.ai.mit.edu**, and on many CD-ROM distributions to gain the foothold necessary to create applications for XFree86.

So just what is X Windows? X Windows is a client/server system controlled by two individual pieces of software with one piece running on the client and the other running on the server. The client and the server pieces of this puzzle can be on different systems or, as is the case with most personal computers, both pieces can reside on the same machine. The following sections discuss what is meant by *client* and *server* in the XFree86 environment.

What Is a Client/Server System?

One of the major buzzwords used in the computer industry today is client/server. This, like most basic concepts in the industry, has been overplayed and overused to the point of confusing the average computer user. In the traditional sense, a server is a machine that just provides resources—disk drive space, printers, modems, and so on—to other computers over a network. A client is the consumer of these services; in other words, a client uses the disk space, printer, or modems provided by a server.

In the world of X Windows, this relationship is the opposite of what you have come to know in the present PC world. The accepted, or more common, notion of a server is that it provides services to a client who uses them. In the most basic form, a client displays the application that is running on the server.

X Windows takes a different view of the client/server relationship. In the world of X Windows, the server displays the application that is running on the client. This may seem a bit confusing at first, but will make sense when you become more intimate with the X Windows system.

So just what is a client? A client is the resource that provides the programs and resources necessary to run an application, what in the traditional sense would be called a server. The resources reside on the client system (remember that the client and server systems can be on the same machine), while the application is displayed and interacted with on the server system.

The capability of an X Windows application, which is the client, to run under a server located on either the same computer or on another computer is called *network transparency*. Thus, an X application does not care whether it runs on a local or remote machine. This capability can be used to run time-consuming tasks on another server, leaving the local client unencumbered to perform other tasks.

Output Capabilities

The base window system provides X Windows with plenty of bitmapped graphical operations. X Windows and X Windows applications use these operations to present information graphically to the users. XFree86 offers overlapping windows, immediate graphics drawings, high-resolution bitmapped graphics and images, and high-quality text. While early X Windows systems were mostly monochrome-based, today X Windows and XFree86 support a wide range of color systems.

X Windows also supports the multiprocessing capabilities of UNIX; thus, XFree86 supports the multiprocessing capabilities of Linux. Each window displayed under X Windows can be a separate task running under Linux.

User Interface Capabilities

The X Consortium left out the standard rules for user interfaces. Today this seems somewhat shortsighted. However, at the time, very little research had been done on user interface technology, so there was no clear interface that was considered the best. In fact, even today unilaterally declaring one interface the best can alienate many people. The look and feel presented by the user interface is a very personal decision. The X Consortium wanted to make X Windows a standard across UNIX workstations, which is one reason X Windows is available freely on the Internet. By making X Windows freely available, it fosters interoperability, which is the cornerstone of open systems. Had the X Consortium dictated a user interface, X Windows may not have gained its current level of popularity.

Input Capabilities

Systems running X Windows typically have some form of pointing device, usually a mouse. XFree86 requires a mouse or other device, such as a trackball, which emulates a mouse. If you do not have such a device, you cannot use the XFree86 system with Linux. X Windows converts signals from the pointing device and from the keyboard, into events. X Windows then responds to these events, performing appropriate actions.

Caution

If your mouse or other hardware pointing device is not among those supported by Linux, you will have problems using XFree86 and using the *selection* program.

◀◀ See "selection," p. 98

Installing the XFree86 System

Hopefully, you installed the XFree86 system while installing the entire Linux Slackware package from the accompanying CD-ROM. The X Windows system is contained in the x and xap distribution packages. If you did not install the X Windows system at that time, you can use the `pkgtool` program to install X Windows.

▶▶ See "Using pkgtool," p. 217

The Software

`pkgtool` is the easiest way to install XFree86, and later in this chapter in the "Installing the X System with `pkgtool`" section are the instructions for installing X using `pkgtool`. But just in case you need to manually install the files (when upgrading to a newer system, for example), then you need to know that the files are located on the CD-ROM in the /slakware/x<#> directories: /slakware/x1 through x16. X consists of several large archived files. The current version of XFree86 for Linux is 3.1.1, which is located on the CD. The main files are shown in Table 6.1. You should log in as the super user (root), and copy the necessary files to /usr/x386. If this directory does not exist, then create it with the mkdir command, as follows:

```
opus#: mkdir /usr/x386
opus#:cd /usr/x386
opus#:cp -r /cdrom/slakware/x1 .
```

II Installing Linux

The above commands also copy all the files from the CD mounted at /cdrom to the current directory.

Note

The CD-ROM included with this book is as up-to-date as possible given the time lag necessary for the production of the book. Nonetheless, there may be a newer version of XFree86 available on the Internet by the time you read this, so check the necessary archive sites—this may save some headaches down the road.

▶▶ See "Using `ftp` for Remote File Transfer," p. 595

Table 6.1 XFree86 Main Distribution Files

Filename	Description
x3270.tgz	IBM 3270 terminal emulation
x_8514.tgz	IBM 8514 server
x_mach32.tgz	Mach32 chip-based server
x_mach8.tgz	Mach8 chip-based server
x_mono.tgz	monochrome monitor server
x_s3.tgz	S3 chip-based server
x_svga.tgz	Server for most SVGA cards, a good basic setup
_vga16.tgz	EGA/VGA 16-color server
xconfig.tgz	Sample Xconfig configuration files, a must have!
xf_bin.tgz	Basic binary files required for X(clients)
xf_cfg.tgz	XDM configuration and FVWM programs
xf_doc.tgz	Documentation for XFree86
xf_kit.tgz	Linker kit for XFree86 (1 of 2)
xf_kit2.tgz	Drivers for Linker kit (2 of 2)
xf_lib.tgz	Dynamic Link Libraries and configuration files
xf_pex.tgz	PEX distribution
xfileman.tgz	File manager program
xfm.tgz	The xfm file manager
xfnt.tgz	X Window fonts
xfnt75	75 point fonts for X
xfract	The xfractint program for displaying fractals
xgames	Games to play under X!

Filename	Description
xgrabsc.tgz	The Xgrabsc and Xgrab programs. Xgrab was used to create most of the images in this book!
xinclude.tgx	Programming header files for X Windows programming
xlock.tgz	The xlock screen password protection program
xman1.tgz	Man pages for X
xman3.tgz	More man pages for X
xpaint.tgz	The Xpaint program, for drawing under X
xpm.tgz	The Xpm libraries, both shared and static
xspread.tgz	The Xspread spreadsheet program
xstatic.tgz	Static libraries for X
xv.tgz	The XV image viewer
xxgdb.tgz	The X Window front end for the GNU debugger

To extract these files, use the following command:

```
opus: gzip -d <filename>.tgz
opus: tar -xvf <filename>.tar
```


Hardware Support for XFree86

Make sure you have the proper hardware to run X Windows, the proper amount of memory, and the necessary disk space. You need about 21M of disk space to install the XFree86 system and the X Windows applications provided.

You need at least 16M of virtual memory to run X Windows. Virtual memory is the combination of the physical RAM on your system and the amount of swap space you have allocated for Linux. You must have at least 4M of physical RAM in order to run XFree86 under Linux, thus requiring a 12M swap file. The more physical RAM you have, the better the performance of your XFree86 system. Next, you need a video card containing a video-driver chipset supported by XFree86.

According to the March 15, 1995, release of Matt Welsh's XFREE86 HOWTO, the video cards with the chipsets listed in Tables 6.2 and 6.3 are supported by XFree86.

Table 6.2 Non-Accelerated Chipsets Supported by XFree86

Manufacturer	Chipsets
ATI	28800-4, 28800-5, 28800-6, 28800-a
Avance Logic	AL2101
Cirrus Logic	CLGD6205, CLGD6215, CLGD6225, CLGD6235
Compaq	AVGA

(continues)

Table 6.2 Continued

Manufacturer	Chipsets
Genoa	GVGA
MX	MX68000, MX680010
NCR	77C22, 77C22E, 77C22E+
OAK	OTI067, OTI077
Trident	TVGA8800CS, TVGA8900B, TVGA8900C, TVGA8900CL, TVGA9000, TVGA9000i, TVGA9100B, TVGA9200CX, TVGA9320, TVGA9400CX, TVGA9420
Tseng	ET3000, ET4000AX, ET4000/W32
Western Digital/Paradise	PVGA1
Western Digital	WD90C00, WD90C10, WD90C11, WD90C24, WD90C30
Video 7	HT216-32

Table 6.3 Accelerated Chipsets Supported by XFree86

Manufacturer	Chipsets
Cirrus	CLGD5420, GLGD5420, CLGD5422, CLGD5424, CLGD5426, CLGD5428
Western Digital	WD90C31
ATI	Mach8, Mach32
S3	86C911, 86C924, 86C801, 86C805, 86C805i, 86C928

Installing the X System with *pkgtool*

To install X Windows, you need to log on as the super user—that is, log on as root. Then you should record the location of the X Windows packages you want to install. These files are located on the accompanying CD-ROM in the /slackware directory. Because Linux mounts the CD-ROM in a directory, the files are relative to that mount point. So a typical Linux installation usually places or mounts the CD-ROM in a directory under the root directory called cdrom. To access the X Windows packages from the enclosed CD-ROM, look in the following directories: /cdrom/slackware/x1, /cdromslackware/x2, and so on. Make sure you remember where these files are located.

▶▶ See "Mounting and Unmounting File Systems," p. 303

Next, from the command prompt, enter **pkgtool**. This command activates the Slackware package tool program that enables you to delete old packages or install new ones. For X Windows, these packages are the x and xap packages contained with the Slackware distribution. A menu with the following options appears:

Menu Item	Description
Current	Installs packages from the current directory
Other	Installs packages from some other directory
Floppy	Installs packages from floppy disks
Remove	Removes packages that are currently installed
View	Views the list of files contained in a package
Exit	Exits package tool

Press <Shift+O> or use the arrow keys to select the Other menu line and press <Return>. `pkgtool` asks for the source directory. Enter the directory you recorded earlier for the first `x` package directory, normally `x1`. Hence, you would enter /cdrom/slackware/x1.

After supplying the initial directory, `pkgtool` first seeks the *xserver* for your graphics card. You can install only one server, so as you move through the screens, choose the No option on the Install screen until you reach the required *xserver*.

Remember that you have to install the appropriate programs from each package. Although not all packages are required, if you are installing XFree86 after installing Linux, you should review the full details on the packages to install. If you have the 21M needed for a full installation, go ahead and install each package, with the exception of the X server; only install one X server for your chipset.

> **Note**
>
> If you have previously installed X Windows, you should first back up important configuration files and then delete the currently installed `x` and `xap` packages.

▶▶ See "Using `pkgtool`," p. 217

Configuring XFree86

After installing XFree86, you must then configure it for your system. XFree86 expects to find a file named XF86Config in one of the following directories:

/etc/XF86Config

/usr/X11R6/lib/X11/XF86Config.<host-name>

/usr/X11R6/lib/X11/XF86Config

You can find the configuration file information in the /etc/X11/etc directory. Before configuring your system, you should check out the files labeled README.Config and README.Linux. If you have the standard, supported equipment listed previously, you should check out the sample Xconfig files from the x3 package. These files are stored in the /usr/X11/lib/X11/Sample-Xconfig-files directory. Check out the Xconfig.Index file to see if your video card is listed. You can do this with the following commands:

```
cd /usr/X11/lib/X11/Sample-Xconfig-files
less Xconfig.Index
```

Caution

You should never use an Xconfig file from someone else, or even one verbatim from this book or any other source, *without* looking the file over for improper values. For example, driving your monitor at unsupported frequencies may damage your equipment.

If your video card is listed, copy the corresponding Xconfig.number file from the sample directory to the /usr/X11/lib/X11 directory. You can use the following command to do this (just substitute the number from the Xconfig.Index file for the number shown below):

```
cp Xconfig.number /usr/X11/lib/X11/Xconfig
```

These are sample configuration files and might work for standard hardware. You can test the configuration file by starting X Windows. To do so, enter **startx**. If the X Windows system starts and runs, congratulations. If for some reason the configuration file is not correct, Linux reports an error. Reboot your system if it just hangs. After a start failure, you need to create a configuration file yourself when you return to the command prompt.

Note

If something does go wrong (and your monitor doesn't explode) then pressing Ctl-Alt-Backspace should terminate the X server and return you to a shell prompt.

Running the SuperProbe Program

If the above installation procedures do not work, you can run a program to configure your system. Slackware provides a program called XF86config to help you configure your XFree86 system, but this program requires you to answer several questions. These questions deal with the type of hardware you have on your system, and incorrect information can cause X to damage that hardware.

There are several document files located in the /usr/X11R6/lib/X11/doc directory that you should read: HOWTO.Config, README.Config, and configxf.doc. You can use the following command to read the files:

```
less file-name
```

You should also gather any manufacturer's manuals for your video card and your monitor.

Next, run the SuperProbe utility.

```
/usr/X11R6/bin/SuperProb
```

This utility scans your system trying to identify the installed video hardware. You should write down the information reported for later use with the XF86Config program. You should also double-check the information generated by SuperProbe with your hardware's documentation. The SuperProbe program will generate information that will be placed in the various sections of the XF86Config file.

The XF86Config Sections

The XF86Config file is a normal ASCII text file read by XFree86 and used to configure the X server to run properly under your hardware system. The file is formatted into the following sections, as shown in Table 6.4:

Table 6.4 XF86Config File Sections

Section	Description
Files	Directories for the font and rgb files.
ServerFlags	Special flags for the X server.
Keyboard	Describes the type of keyboard.
Pointer	Describes your pointing device, typically your mouse.
Monitor	Detailed descriptions about your monitor. This section is very important since incorrect information can severly damage the monitor!
Device	Describes your video card.
Screen	Uses the information from the Monitor and Device sections to describe your physical screen area on the display. This includes such items as number of colors and size of the screen in pixels.

Each section in the file has the following general form:

```
Section "Name"
   data entry values
   data entry values
   more values as needed...
#this is a comment line and is ignored by XFree86
EndSection
```

▶▶ See "Using vi," p. 431

You should build such a file using a text editor like `vi`, following the examples given. After creating the file you run the XF86Config program to generate an XF86Config file for comparison. Finally, you run the X server in a special mode to probe for your system's settings, which you may not be able to determine from the examples, the generated file, or the documentation. These precautions are necessary because of the real threat of damage to your system.

The Files Section. This section lists the various fonts installed on your system in the /usr/X11R6/lib/X11/fonts directory. Each font series will have its own subdirectory here, so you can use the following command to determine which ones are loaded:

```
ls /usr/X11R6/lib/X11/fonts
```

Each directory listed should have a corresponding entry in the Files section.

Luckily, depending on your selections during installation, your font files should go into standard directories and your Files section will appear as in the sample section here:

```
Section "Files"
      RgbPath     "/usr/X11R6/lib/X11/rgb"
      fontPath    "/usr/X11R6/lib/X11/misc/"
      fontPath    "/usr/X11R6/lib/X11/Type1/"
      fontPath    "/usr/X11R6/lib/X11/speedo/"
      fontPath    "/usr/X11R6/lib/X11/75dpi/"
      fontPath    "/usr/X11R6/lib/X11/100dpi/"
EndSection
```

The ServerFlags Section. You will rarely need to edit the default ServerFlags section. This section controls three flags used by the X Server to control its operation. These flags are as shown:

Flag	Description
NoTrapSignals	An advance flag that causes the X Server to "dump core"—create a debugging file, when an operating system software signal is received by the X Server.
DontZap	Disables the use of the <Ctl> - <Alt> - <Backspace> key combination to terminate the X Server.
DontZoom	Disables switching between various graphics modes.

The sample section is shown as follows with each flag commented out and thus disabled.

```
Section "ServerFlags"
      #NoTrapSignals
      #DontZap
      #DontZoom
EndSection
```

The Keyboard Section. The Keyboard section enables you to specify several options for your keyboard such as keymappings. The minimal keyboard section is shown here:

```
Section "Keyboard"
      Protocol     "Standard"
```

```
        AutoRepeat 500 5
        ServerNumLock
EndSection
```

There are many more options available, as shown below, but many are not required for proper operation of your keyboard. For more information on the various options, see the man page for *XF86Config*.

Tip

Type

```
man XF86Config
```

at a shell prompt to see a full description of the various parameters for each section of the XF86Config file.

Option	Parameter/Description
Protocol	Is Standard or Xqueue (standard is the default)
AutoRepeat *delay rate*	Sets the delay before repeating the key at the specified rate
ServerNumLock	Tells the X server to handle the response to the NumLock key internally
VTSysReq	Specifies the X server to handle switching between virtual terminals using the <SysReq> key instead of the <CTL> key

Typcially you use the <ALT>-<Fn> function key method to switch between the various virtual terminals under Linux. But when in X, you must use <CTL>-<ALT>-<Fn> to access the virtual terminal. Of course you might ask why the need for virtual terminals when running a GUI? Well, what happens if your X session locks? If that happens you can then use a virtual terminal to kill your X session.

▶▶ See "Logging On," p. 359

The Pointer Section. The Pointer section deals with your mouse, or other pointing device. XFree86 uses the information here to configure your mouse for use under X. Minimally, you should specify the protocol used by your mouse and the device type. If you have a serial mouse then the device will be the serial port used by the mouse. A sample Pointer section is as follows:

```
Section "Pointer"
      Protocol    "Microsoft"
      Device      "/dev/mouse"
EndSection
```

The various protocols supported by Linux are:

- BusMouse
- Logitech
- MM Series
- Mouseman
- Microsoft
- Mouse Systems
- MMHitTab
- Xqueue
- PS/2

Some of the other options available in the pointer section are shown in the following table, but you should not add them to your XF86Config file unless you are absolutely sure what effect they'll have on your system.

Option	Description
BaudRate rate	Specifies the baud rate for a serial mouse
SampleRate rate	Needed by some Logitech mice
ClearDTR	Required by some mice using MouseSystem protocol
ClearRTS	Same as ClearDTR
ChordMiddle	Needed by some Logitech mice
Emulate3Buttons	Allows a two-button mouse, such as Microsoft mice, to emulate a three-button mouse. The third button is emulated by pressing both buttons at once. Many X applications need a three-button mouse for proper operation.

Note

If you have a Logitech mouse, especially one that does not emulate a Microsoft mouse, then you may have to experiment with some of the options above.

The Monitor Section. This is probably the most important section of the XF86Config file, and probably the most dangerous. Misinformation in this file can cause catastrophic damage to your system, so be careful! The SuperProbe program and your manufacturer's documentation will help greatly in creating this section. You can also use the files /usr/X11R6/lib/X11/doc/modesDB.txt and /usr/X11R6/lib/X11/doc/monitors to search for information on your particular monitor. A typical Monitor section is as follows:

```
Section "Monitor"
      Identifier   "Sanyo 1450 NI"
      VendorName   "Sanyo"
      ModelName    "My 14 inch monitor"
```

```
Bandwidth     60
HorizSync    30-60
VeriRefresh  50-90
#Modes:     Name      dotclock   Horizontal Timing     Vertical Timing
ModeLine    "640x480"    25      640 672 768 800       480 490 492 525
ModeLine    "800x600"    36      800 840 912 1024      600 600 602 625
ModeLine    "1024x768i" 45       1024 1024 1224 1264   768 768 776 816
EndSection
```

Your Monitor section can have more than one monitor defined, so for each monitor you must supply the following information:

Value	Description
Identifier *string*	Monitor identifier.
VendorName *string*	Identifies the manufacturer.
ModelName *string*	Indentifies the make and model.
Bandwidth *value*	The monitor's bandwidth.
HorizSync *range*	The valid horizontal sync frequencies (in kHz). This can be a range if you have a multisync monitor or a series of single values for a fixed-frequency monitor.
VertRefresh *range*	Specifies the vertical refresh frequencies. They can be listed as a range or a series of single values, such as the HorizSync value.
Gamma *value*	The gamma correction value for your monitor.
ModeLine *values*	Specifies a series of values for each resolution to be displayed on the monitor.

For each resolution you will need a ModeLine entry in the Monitor section. The entry has the following format:

```
ModeLine "name" dotclock     Horizontal Freq Vertical Freq
```

The Horizontal and Vertical frequencies are a series of four values expressed in kHz. Most values you can get from running the XF86Config program (discussed in the "Running the XF86Config" section later in this chapter) or from the various documentation files included with the XFree86 package. For your initial test, it's best to enter a standard configuration from the documentation and then let X probe your system for more appropriate values.

The Device Section. The Device section describes the system's video card to XFree86. The Device section for a Standard VGA is as follows:

```
Section "Device"
      Identifier     "SVGA"
      VendorName     "Trident"
      BoardName      "TVG89"
      Chipset        "tvga8900c"
      VideoRam       1024
      Clocks         25.30 28.32 45.00 36.00 57.30 65.10 50.40 39.90
      Option         ...
EndSection
```

The only values that might be hard to come by are the clock values. You can get this value by running X with a special parameter, `-probeonly`. This allows X to scan your system without much chance of physical damage to your system. X then generates a report with most of the values needed for your configuration.

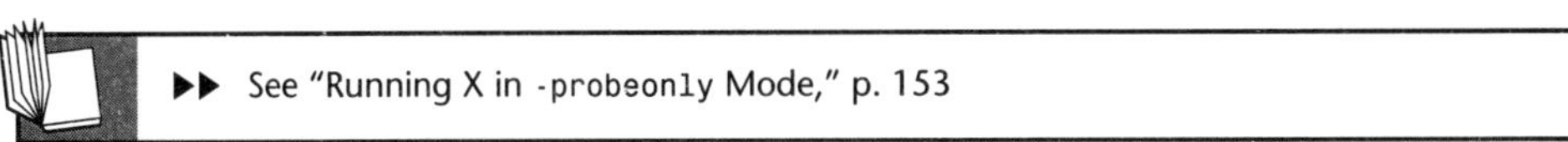
▶▶ See "Running X in `-probeonly` Mode," p. 153

Your server may also require optional parameters. These optional entries in the Device section will be detailed in the appropriate man page for your server.

The Screen Section. Your XF86Config file can contain many monitor and device entries. These entries are tied together in the Screen section to create your X Desktop for your X Server. A sample Screen section is as follows:

```
Section "Screen"
       Driver     "vga2"
       Device     "SVGA"
       Monitor    "Sanyo 1450 NI"
       Subsection "Display"
           Depth      8
           Modes      "1024x768" "800x600" "640x480"
           ViewPort   0 0
           Virtual    1024 768
       EndSubsection
   EndSection
```

The Screen section uses the *identifier* names from each of the Device and the Monitor sections. The Driver value tells what X server you are running and can have one of the following values:

Accel

SVGA

VGA16

VGA2

Mono

Within the Screen section are display subsections, which describe the various modes available for a particular resolution. Each Mode value refers back to each ModeLine value defined in the Monitor section.

X starts up at the position specified by the ViewPort value. A value of 0,0 instructs X to start with position 0,0 in the upper left-hand corner of the display.

The Virtual value enables you to define a virtual screen that is larger than your physical screen. If you specify a larger screen, then X will automatically scroll the screen as needed when you move the pointer to positions outside the range of your physical screen.

Tip

Many programs found on the Internet assume a 3-button mouse and a screen size of 1152 × 900. This screen size is a typical screen size found on a Sun workstation. So, to emulate such a system you would need to specify the *Emulate3Buttons* in the Pointer section and a *Virtual 1152 900* in a Display subsection in the Screen section.

Running the xf86Config Program

After running SuperProbe and building a basic XF86Config file, you then can run the xf86Config program to generate a config file for your system. First, make sure you are not in the /usr/X11R6/lib/X11 directory, because this is where X looks for the XF86Config file first, and you do not want to overwrite the file you just created.

```
/usr/X11R6/bin/xf86Config
```

The xf86Config program asks many questions about your system, which it uses to fill in the various sections of the XF86Config file. After the program finishes you must check to make sure the values are similar to the ones you collected while creating your version of the file. The only items you will need help with are the clock values for your monitor. You can get X itself to help with those values.

Running X in *probe only* Mode

By running X in a special mode, the program generates a file with information about your entire system. You can use the information in this file to complete your XF86Config file. To run X in the special probe only mode, simply enter this command:

```
X -probeonly > /tmp/x.value 2>&1
```

The command redirects the output of X into a file named /tmp/x.value. This is an ASCII file you can edit with any ASCII editor, such as vi. You can cut the clock information from this file and paste the information into your XF86Config file, thus completing your configuration file for X.

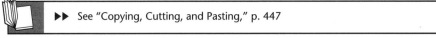

▶▶ See "Copying, Cutting, and Pasting," p. 447

Now copy the file you've created into one of the directories XFree86 looks through, more than likely you can copy the file with this command:

```
cp XF86Config /usr/X11R6/lib/X11/
```

You are now ready to start up your X server with the *startx* command.

The X Windows Resource Files

To operate and use X, you need at least a startup file called .xinitrc. This file provides default settings used by X when running. To override the defaults, you can use a personal file called .Xresources that you place in your home directory. Linux provides a default .xinitrc in/etc/X11/xinit/xinitrc, although you may find the file in /usr/lib/X11/xinit/xinitrc. See the man pages for *startx* and *xrdb* for more information on these files.

From Here...

In this chapter, you learned about the XFree86 implementation of the X Windows XR11R6 standard. You have seen the difference between client and server applications and how they differ from other PC-based client/server applications. The following chapters provide more information:

- Chapter 4, "Installing Linux," explains how to install Linux, which you need to do before installing X Windows. Without a base system, XFree86 is useless.
- Chapter 12, "Upgrading and Installing Software," shows you how to use the `pkgtool` program to install new software systems onto your Linux box. This is useful for installing X if you did not install it with the base Linux system.
- Chapter 22, "Using the `vi` Editor," shows you how to use the vi editor. You need to edit your X configuration file, XF86Config, in order to provide X with the proper information to run on your specific hardware. `vi` is the perfect editor to use for editing the various files needed by X.
- Chapter 23, "Using the `emacs` Editor," shows you how to use the `emacs` editor.

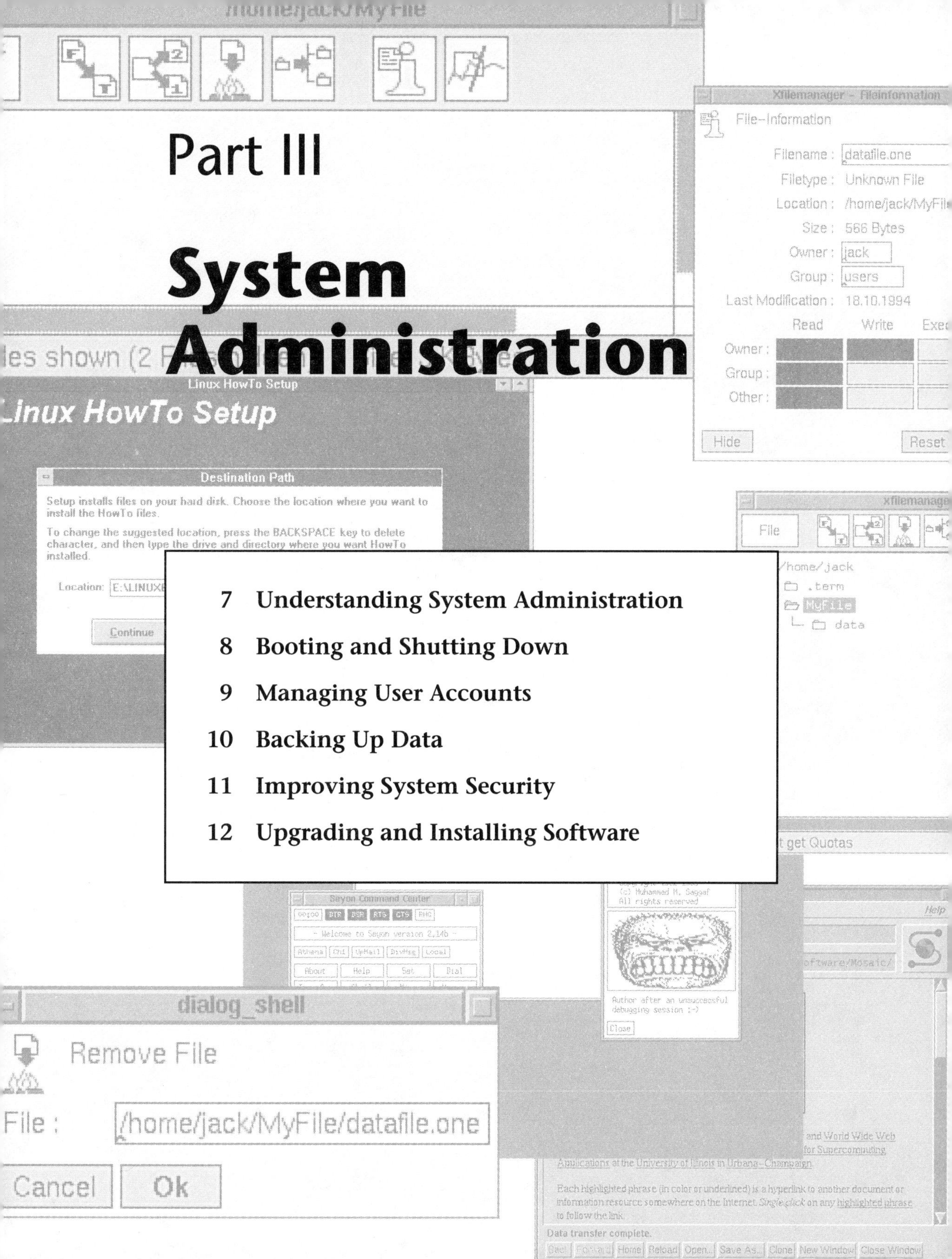

Part III

System Administration

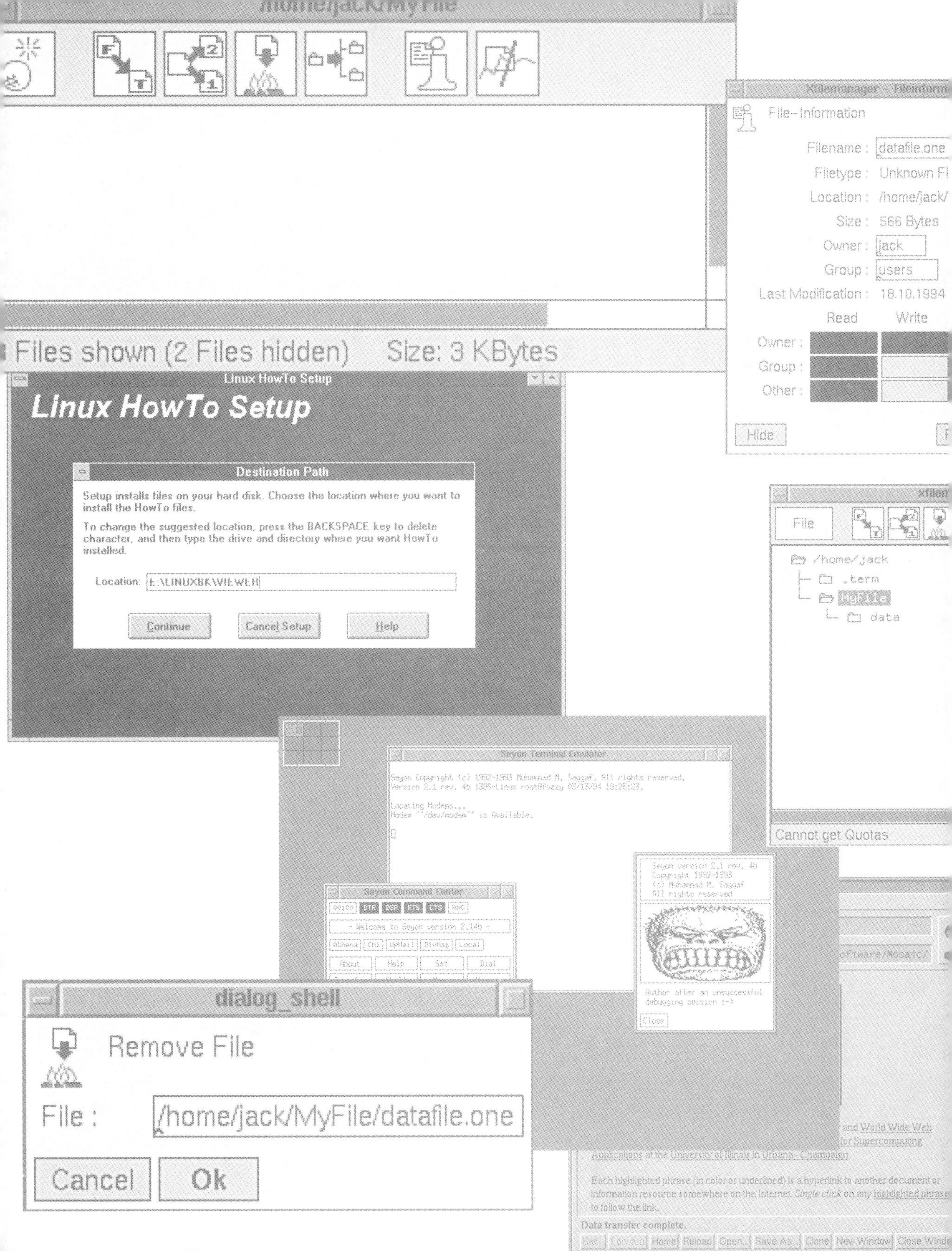

Files shown (2 Files hidden) Size: 3 KBytes
File-Information
Filename : datafile.one
Filetype : Unknown Fi
Location : /home/jack/
Size : 566 Bytes
Owner : jack
Group : users
Last Modification : 18.10.1994
Read
Write
Owner :
Group :
Other :
Hide
Linux HowTo Setup
Linux HowTo Setup
Destination Path
Setup installs files on your hard disk. Choose the location where you want to install the HowTo files.
To change the suggested location, press the BACKSPACE key to delete character, and then type the drive and directory where you want HowTo installed.
Location: E:\LINUXBK\VIEWER
Continue
Cancel Setup
Help
File
/home/jack
.term
MyFile
data
Cannot get Quotas
Seyon Terminal Emulator
Seyon Copyright (c) 1992-1993 Muhammad M. Saggaf. All rights reserved.
Locating Modems...
Seyon Command Center
Welcome to Seyon version 2.14b
About
Help
Set
Dial
Author after an unsuccessful debugging session :-)
Close
dialog_shell
Remove File
File : /home/jack/MyFile/datafile.one
Cancel
Ok
Each highlighted phrase (in color or underlined) is a hyperlink to another document or information resource somewhere on the Internet. Single click on any highlighted phrase to follow the link.
Data transfer complete.
Home
Reload
Open...
Save As...
Clone
New Window

CHAPTER 7

Understanding System Administration

A Linux system should have one or more people designated as the system administrator to manage the system and oversee its performance. The system administrator has the responsibility to see that the system is functioning properly, to know who to call if things can't be fixed locally, and to know how to provide software and hardware facilities to current and new users.

A Linux system requires initial configuration and continuous attention to ensure that the system remains effective, trustworthy, and efficient for all users. The system administrator is the person responsible for attending to the Linux system's needs. As such, this person is responsible for many different tasks.

This chapter discusses some of the major tasks and issues confronting a system administrator in a networked multiuser environment. Assuming that you bought this book to learn about and install Linux, you will probably find yourself in the role of a systems administrator almost immediately. Some of the topics in this chapter are geared to systems administration in a larger organization. However, even if you are a single user who wants to play with Linux at home, you should read about them so that you can be aware of the larger issues involved in systems administration.

In many cases, your Linux system is networked with other computers that are not running Linux. They may be running other types of UNIX, or they may be running a different operating system entirely. Because Linux is a specific flavor of UNIX, much of the information in this chapter is applicable to both Linux and UNIX. In some places in this chapter, UNIX and Linux are used interchangeably.

The following topics are covered in this chapter:

- Why UNIX administration is needed and the most common tasks associated with administration
- Concepts and elements of centralized processing and distributed processing
- The tasks required to set up and maintain a UNIX network
- How to provide users access to your system and support their needs

The Importance of Proper Administration

All UNIX systems are different in one way or another, and each is unique in the way it must be administered. Linux is no exception. Your administrative duties vary, based on, among other things, the number of users you manage, the kinds of peripherals attached to the computer (printers, tape drives, and so on), networking connections, and the level of security you require.

A systems administrator, either alone or with a support staff, must provide a secure, efficient, and reliable environment for system users. The administrator has the power and responsibility to establish and maintain a system that provides effective and dependable service. In a multiuser environment, a number of competing purposes and priorities exist. The administrator exercises the power and responsibility necessary to provide a well-functioning system.

The delegation of administrative responsibilities varies from system to system. On large systems, administration tasks can be divided among several people. Conversely, some small systems do not even require a full-time administrator; such systems simply designate a certain user to act as system administrator. If you work in a networked environment, your system may be administered over the network by a network administrator.

Each Linux system has a single user who can perform virtually any operation on the computer. This user is called the *superuser* and has a special login name called `root`. When logged on to the system, the user named root is logged on to the root directory of the file system.

The system administrator logs on as the superuser to perform privileged work. For normal system work, the system administrator logs on as an ordinary user. The superuser's logon name—root—is used for limited, special purposes only. The number of users who can log on as root should be kept to a minimum (at most two or three). When any person logs on to the system as root, that person is a superuser and has absolute privilege on the system. With this privilege, the superuser can change the attributes of any file, stop the system, start the system, make backups of the system's data, and perform many other tasks.

The administrator must be aware of many of the technical aspects of the computer system. Also, the administrator must be aware of the needs of the users as well as the primary purpose of the system. Any computer system is a finite resource; policies regarding its use must be established and enforced. Thus, the administrator has a technical and policy role to play. That role, combined with the power to perform virtually any possible action, requires a responsible, skillful, and diplomatic person in the role of administrator.

Common Administrative Tasks

The precise job description of the system administrator often depends on the local organization. As system administrator, you may find yourself involved in a wide variety of activities, from setting policy to installing software to moving furniture. However, there are a number of tasks that all system administrators have to either perform or manage, as follows:

- *Manage users.* Adding users, deleting users, and modifying users' capabilities and privileges
- *Configure devices.* Making available and sharing devices such as printers, terminals, modems, tape drives, and so on
- *Make backups.* Scheduling, making, and storing backups for possible restoration if the system's files are lost or damaged
- *Shut down the system.* Shutting down the system in an orderly manner to avoid inconsistencies in the file system
- *Train users.* Providing or obtaining effective training for users so they can use the system effectively and efficiently
- *Secure the system.* Keeping users from interfering with each other through accidental or deliberate actions
- *Log system changes.* Keeping a log book to record any significant activity concerning the system
- *Advise users.* Acting as the "local expert" to aid the system's ordinary users

Understanding Multiuser Concepts

A multiuser system employs two main concepts: multitasking and multiuser services. Linux has the apparent capability to execute multiple tasks concurrently—transparent to the user. For example, you can read your e-mail while compiling a program.

Each task, whether it's a simple command you enter on the command line or a complex application, starts one or more processes. Everything running on a Linux system is associated with a process; hence, because Linux is running many processes simultaneously, Linux is a multitasking operating system.

There are many ways you can connect to a computer running UNIX (referred to as a *server*). You can use either a terminal or a computer; you can be located physically near the server, connected with a cable, or you can be on the other side of the planet connected with high-speed data lines or ordinary phone lines. Whether you're using a terminal or computer and how you are connected to the server determine whether the computer's resources are considered to be distributed or centralized.

A single-user computer operating system, such as DOS, is designed to be used by one person at a time. All the processing is done on one computer that has sole access to resources, such as printers, storage, and processing. Multiuser systems use the centralized- and distributed-processing models to accommodate many users simultaneously.

In a *centralized-processing* environment, many users (large systems can have hundreds of users) access the resources of one computer: storage, printer, memory, and processing.

In the *distributed-processing* environment, processing can occur on the user's own workstation, and the central processor is used to distribute applications and data. Printers and storage can be either connected to the user's workstation or to the main server.

Understanding Centralized-Processing Systems

As technology during the 1950s and 1960s advanced, operating systems began to enable multiple users to share resources from separate terminals. Two users could, in a batch-processing sequence, execute two sets of instructions while sharing a processor, storage, and output.

With the advent of a switched telephone network, computers began to use telephone resources to extend computer resources geographically. With this model, each processor used communications-processing resources to connect with remote terminals. This created a need for computers and terminals to communicate in a better way. The result was the development of *front-end processing* for communications tasks and the centralized-processing model.

Until personal computers became inexpensive, powerful, and ubiquitous, most UNIX systems used the centralized-processing model. With centralized processing, mainframe computers handled all the processing. Users connected to the mainframe share its resources. This model is used less and less today, although it's still appropriate for computing sites where users are separated geographically.

For example, your bank may have one main processing center, yet all of the bank's branches can access the data center regardless of their locations. On each user's desk is a terminal, including a keyboard, a monitor, and a direct connection to the mainframe so that it can access the centralized resources: processing, printing, and storage (see fig. 7.1). The centralized-processing model is usually made up of many elements, such as the server, front-end processors, terminals, modems, and multiport adapters.

As a user requests data, the request is processed by the computer in the bank's main office. Results of the processing are sent back to the terminal in the branch office. All data is processed and stored by the mainframe computer.

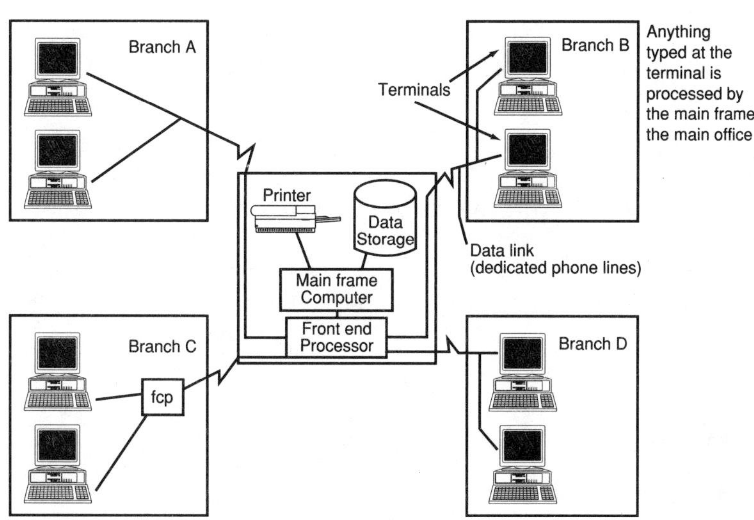

Fig. 7.1

This figure shows the centralized-processing model of a computing environment.

Elements of the Centralized-Processing Model

To make the centralized-processing model work, you need many elements, including the server, front-end processors, terminals, modems, and multiport adapters.

A server can be defined as any computer set up to share its resources (processing power, storage, printers, and so on). For example, you can use an IBM-compatible PC as a server as long as it has enough hard disk space and RAM.

A front-end processor connects the communication channels and the server. It handles the details of communication so that the server is free to process its data.

There are two popular types of terminals used today: *dumb terminals* and *smart terminals*. Traditionally, UNIX is used with dumb terminals, which have keyboards and monitors, but nothing else. The most important thing to realize about dumb terminals is that they have no local processing power. The communications port on the terminal is connected, either directly or through a modem, to the server. When you type on a dumb terminal, each keystroke is transmitted to the server, where it is processed.

Smart terminals can complete minimal processing at the local site. Cash registers and other point-of-sale devices are examples, as are the familiar automated teller machines (ATMs). The local device stores the transaction request and transmits the entire request instead of transmitting each keystroke, as does a dumb terminal.

To connect your terminal to a telephone line, use a modem. Modems translate the digital signals of terminals and computers into analog signals required by telephone lines. Modems are always used in pairs. The first one connects your terminal to the telephone line; the second connects the server to the telephone line. To make the connection, you dial out on the terminal. When the modem on the other end (the one connected to the server) answers, your terminal can communicate with the server.

To expand the number of ports available that users can connect to, install a multiport adapter. For example, a PC typically has only two serial ports: COM1 and COM2. If you want to use a PC as a server for more than two users, you need more ports. The multiport adapter, in this case, consists of a card that you install inside the computer, a small box with eight or more connectors, and a cable that connects the box and the card. Software is supplied with the adapter to permit the added connectors to function as additional serial ports.

Understanding Distributed-Processing Systems

In distributed processing, the terminal is replaced by a workstation—which is itself a computer, usually running either DOS or UNIX. Programs can be located and run from either the server or your workstation. Similarly, files can be located on either system. If you process a file on your workstation, you store it on the server so that others can access it. You can print either on local printers connected to your workstation or on printers connected to the server.

With workstations in common use, your bank probably uses a distributed-processing system instead of the centralized system described in the preceding section. Figure 7.2 shows the same bank with a distributed-processing system.

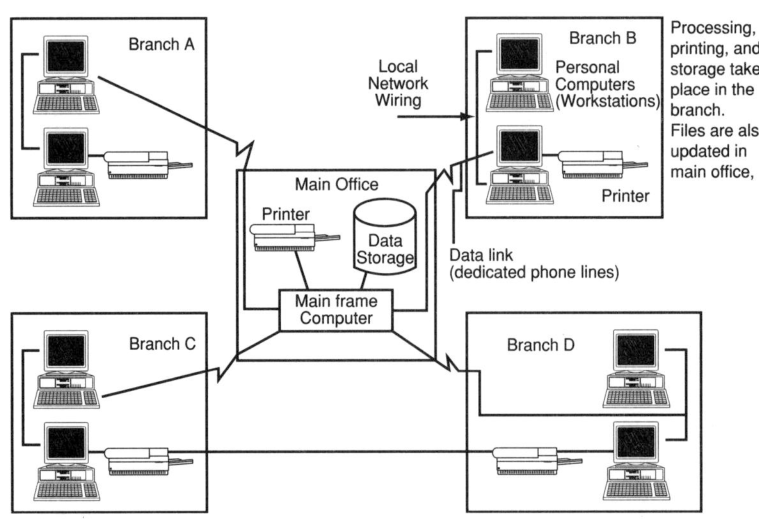

Fig. 7.2

This figure shows the distributed-processing model of a computing environment.

Elements of the Distributed-Processing Model

Distributed processing uses file servers, workstations, network interface cards, hubs, repeaters, bridges, routers, and gateways. The purpose of the file server is to distribute files and segments of programs to workstations, print from a central location, and control flow on the connection between workstations. More than 90 percent of processing occurs at the workstation level, leaving 5 to 10 percent of the load at the file server for administrative tasks. The following sections describe the elements of distributed processing.

Workstations. Besides using it as a file server, you can use a personal computer as a Linux workstation. Linux was designed to run in a very minimal hardware configuration. In fact, you can run Linux with a 386SX microprocessor and 4M of RAM! Since most current systems are more powerful than Linux's minimum requirements, you should have no problem with computing power. The amount of hard drive space required is dependent on how much software you want to install. If you want to run entirely off CD-ROM, you only need about 5M of hard disk space. A minimal hard disk installation takes 10 to 20M of space. A full installation takes over 100M.

Generally, resources should be applied to the workstation level, where most of the processing occurs. The amount of additional resources depends on the types of tasks you plan on doing. For example, word processors take minimal resources (hard drive, RAM, quality of monitor) compared to graphics-intensive tasks, such as multimedia and computer-aided design (CAD) programs. For applications involving CAD, you need very large hard disks (one gigabyte or more), a lot of RAM (16M, 32M, or even 64M), and high-resolution monitors and video cards (1280 × 1024 or higher). You may even want a tape drive for backup and a CD-ROM drive for loading large applications.

Network Interface Cards. A network interface card (NIC) attaches to a slot on the motherboard and is the physical link between the computer and the cabling for the network. Network interface cards are generally available for either coaxial or twisted-pair cabling.

Hubs. The hub serves as a connecting point for coaxial cables and can be either passive or active. A passive hub usually has four connectors. An active hub usually has eight ports and amplifies or relays the signal.

Repeaters. Repeaters amplify or regenerate the signal over the network so that you can extend the normal distance limitations for network cabling.

Bridges. Use a bridge when you need to connect two similar network types together

Routers. Routers are used in large, complex networks where there are many paths for network signals to travel to the same destination. The router determines and sends the signal along the most effective route.

Gateways. Use a gateway when you need to connect dissimilar network types. The gateway performs the necessary protocol conversions so that the two networks can communicate.

Looking at Topologies

Topology refers to how workstations and file servers are connected in a network. The names of various topologies are derived from the pattern the cables make after you connect the various terminals, workstations, and file servers. The most common topologies include *star, bus,* and *ring*. When more than one topology is used in a network, it is referred to as a *hybrid network*.

Star Topology. With the star topology, all workstations are connected to a central file server or hub (see fig. 7.3). You can have either passive or active hubs in this scheme.

A passive hub is simply a connecting point for the workstations. An active hub also offers amplification of the signal. AT&T's Starlan is an example of a network using star topology.

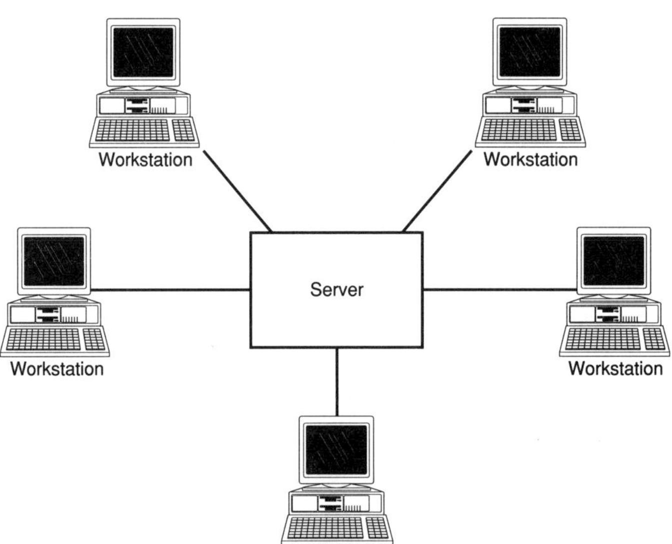

Fig. 7.3

All workstations connect to a central file server in a star topology.

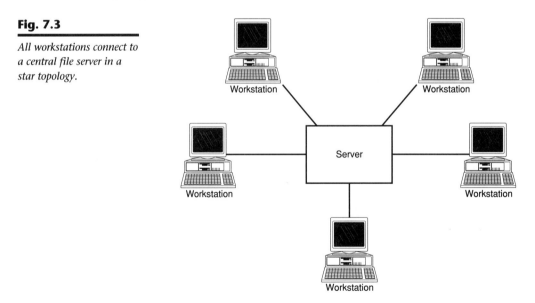

Bus Topology. In a bus topology (see fig. 7.4), all workstations and file servers share a common pathway. They are, in fact, connected directly together. The bus topology is the foundation for Ethernet and token bus.

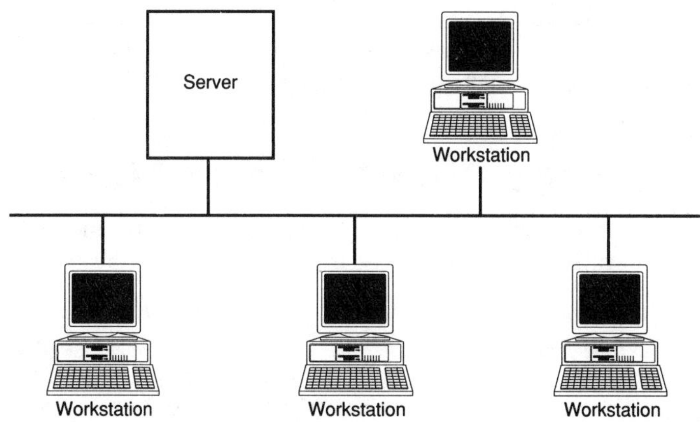

Fig. 7.4

All workstations and file servers share a common pathway in a bus topology.

Ring Topology. A ring topology looks like a wagon wheel without the hub (see fig. 7.5). The server is connected to the workstations in bus fashion; however, the last items along the network are connected together to make a closed loop. Ring topologies use a repeater, which IBM refers to as a Multistation Access Unit (MAU). The IBM Token-Ring Network is an example of a ring topology.

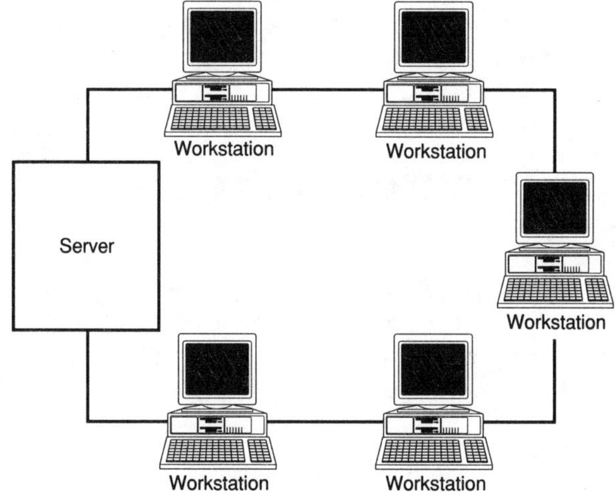

Fig. 7.5

A ring topology has the server connected to the workstations in bus fashion.

Hybrid Topology. In the 1970s and 1980s, firms with decentralized purchasing departments experienced the growth of different topologies on their networks. For example, the accounting department used a bus network; the purchasing department installed token-ring machines; manufacturing used an EtherNet bus; and administration relied on mainframe technology. This combination of networks planted the seeds for enterprise computing and hybrid wide area networks. The integration of these networks linked dissimilar topologies, such as rings, stars, and buses.

Understanding the Client/Server Model

The result of the development of distributed processing is the client/server model. Today, Linux can be used in this model as either the client, the server, or both.

To illustrate a client/server setup, assume that several Linux workstations (the clients) are connected in a bus topology to a server (a high-end PC with lots of disk space, also running Linux). The server has directories for each client where important files can be stored and backed up with the server's nightly backup. The server also has directories from which clients can share files. Connected to the server is a fast laser printer that everyone can access and a tape drive suitable for backing up the large hard disks. In addition, several of the clients have their own slower, less-expensive laser printers connected locally.

> **Note**
>
> The server in this example is a PC running Linux—just like the clients' PCs, although the server is more powerful. There's no reason why the server can't act like a client at times and share resources from the clients. In other words, any Linux system can be both a client and a server.

Administration in a Networked Environment

A UNIX network usually takes the form of many computers, large and small, tied together over directly connected wires or common telephone lines. Administering the network is usually the task of a person or persons located at one of the sites in the network.

Most people can learn Linux and administer a network. In a production environment, it would be nice to find a qualified person right away; however, such people are somewhat rare—and usually well paid. With practice and patience, even people with limited backgrounds in computers can learn how to administer a corporate UNIX/Linux computer.

Defining the Role of the Network Administrator

Any time you have more than a few UNIX/Linux systems connected in a network, you should probably have a dedicated network administrator. Some expertise is needed to decide how systems are connected (LANs or modems), the level of security needed, and how shared peripherals (printers, tape backups, and so on) are distributed. On a day-to-day basis, the administrator maintains lists of system names, network addresses, and user access, and generally makes sure that the network is running properly.

Corporations with networks of 50 to 100 computers can afford to have several administrators with extensive training in selected topics. This can be a necessity if you have complex printing needs, for example. Printers and printing, as an administrative topic, can require extensive knowledge of specific printers and how to interface that equipment to Linux.

Hardware and Software Issues

If, as a system administrator, you are required to choose the networking software and hardware for the computers under your control, there are several things you should consider. As with most things in life, you balance what you need with what you can afford.

If your systems are close together in the same building, a local area network is a low-cost, high-speed means of networking your computers. Put an EtherNet board in each Linux system and use TCP/IP as the networking software. TCP/IP is a standard component of Linux distributions.

To connect over greater distances, you can use modems for lower speed transmissions and the Point-to-Point Protocol (PPP) or the Serial Line Internet Protocol (SLIP) to provide asynchronous TCP/IP connections. UUCP software can also be used for mail, news, and file transfers, although it has limitations. For higher speeds over long distances, you can get leased lines from the telephone company.

Don't buy just any old networking hardware. Although many off-the-shelf networking hardware products come with drivers needed to make them work with DOS, the same isn't true with Linux. As a result, Linux systems have many standard networking drivers built in. Table 7.1 shows the EtherNet cards currently supported by Linux. Check the EtherNet HOWTO for updates to this list.

Table 7.1 Some of the Ethernet cards currently supported under Linux

Manufacturer	Cards
3Com	3c503, 3c503/16, 3c509, 3c579
SMC (Western Digital)	WD8003, WD8013, SMC Elite, SMC Elite Plus, SMC Elite 16 ULTRA

(continues)

Table 7.1 Continued

Manufacturer	Cards
Novell Ethernet	NE1000, NE2000, NE1500, NE2100
D-Link	DE-600, DE-650, DE-100, DE-200, DE-220-T
Hewlett Packard	27245A, 27247B, 27252A, 27247A, J2405A
Digital	DE200, DE210, DE202, DE100, DEPCA (rev. E)
Allied Telesis	AT1500, AT1700
PureData	PDUC8028, PDI8023

Applications that are not integrated with networking products can be used in a network environment. For example, you can install an application on a Linux system and have many users from other computers use the application by running the remote execution commands built into UNIX. Or you can share an application by remotely mounting the file system that contains the application and then running it from the local system.

Common Networking Administrative Tasks

Administration of a network takes on several dimensions. Most networks don't just occur; typically, they evolve. In the ideal situation, the administrators are involved with the purchase of the computers and software so that they know what is expected of them as administrators and what the users are getting.

Setting Up the System. Network software should be installed and ready to connect on-site. If you are using EtherNet for this part of your network, it is a good idea to have the continuity tests completed. If you are using telephone lines, have them tested. Wiring and terminals for users should also be tested and ready. Installation should be Plug-and-Play, but it never is. There are always connection problems.

The advantage of buying a computer for a situation in which the operating system is not yet installed is that you can set up file systems to accommodate your specific needs. You must know what software is going on the computer, the number of users who will be using the system, and the intensity of their usage.

> **Tip**
>
> You have invested time and money in setting up the network to this point. Immediately back up the configuration files you have set up.

When the system is fully functional, the application software should be installed. Software on a Linux computer is often more complex than on a single-user system, so anticipate that installing, tuning, and making the software fully operational will take time. This task can take from a couple of hours to several days—or longer.

You are now ready to start adding users to the system, even though you are still not on-site. Add logon IDs for a few key users and put in a common startup password, such as temp01. This provides some initial security and gives you a chance to get key people onto the system and operational right away when you install the system.

After installation, the computer should be attached to the network. Be sure that you can communicate from any point in the network to any other point. Test communications by moving large and small files from one computer to another. Electronic mail should be directed to and from other nodes in the network. All computers must "know" this new computer in the network. This means that you need to add it to your host name database that is used by any other computers on your network. If you use Domain Name System (DNS) locally, you must add it to the DNS name database. If you are not using DNS, add it to the `/etc/hosts` files on your other systems.

Handling Peripherals. Printers can be a major issue to an administrator. Monitoring and maintaining printers is a significant task and can take a lot of an administrator's time. Understanding the spooling of print jobs, interface tools, and equipment peculiarities requires time and patience.

Modems are the cheapest way to link a network that spans long distances. Modems and PPP or UUCP are tools that can make it practical for a small staff to administer many computers. As with printers, however, there are some problems with modems that require time to get them running right. Choose one or two brand names and really learn their idiosyncrasies.

Monitoring the System. When the installation is complete, you can set up UNIX tools to monitor this new system. The administrators should start getting a feel for how the system is performing.

Monitoring running systems in a network is an ongoing process, but the administrative load should stabilize after a while if you are not constantly adding peripherals or software. Occasionally, something fails or "tweaking" may be necessary. A good administrator learns to determine whether the problem is related to hardware or software.

Coping with Software Upgrades. Some software packages are constantly being updated. While this is a concern with commercial UNIX, it is a special issue under Linux because much of the software is publicly available over the Internet. The good news may be that a bug is fixed. The bad news may be that each system in the network has to be updated. Expect a new challenge with each update.

The best advice is not to immediately put all new versions on your systems, but to test the upgrade or patch on one noncritical system. When you are sure that the new version is okay, upgrade the other systems. A good administrator learns how to install these patches or new versions without going to the other sites in the network. This sounds impossible at first, but you will find that many UNIX tools facilitate this.

Training the Administrator

Training in most organizations is very hit-or-miss. Perhaps the person has some computer background in some computer topic, but there is little done to formally train that person to administer the system. Administration requires attention and a solid knowledge of the following topics:

- *Linux/UNIX design and usage.* The administrator has to have a thorough understanding of such issues as redirection, pipes, background processing, and so on.
- *The `vi` editor.* The vi editor is on virtually every credible UNIX computer put out during the last 10 years, including Linux. Many people criticize it, and many people substitute other editors for their own use, but it is advisable to have an administrator learn and become proficient in the use of `vi` because it is the "common denominator" among UNIX editors.
- *Shell script programming.* Many of the key programs used to administer UNIX are written in shell script language and may require modification for your specific needs. Many of the tools outlined in this chapter require knowledge of how to put together and use a shell program. Almost every user has a favorite shell. Several shells come with the Slackware Linux installation.

  `bash`, the Bourne Again shell, is a Bourne shell clone that is the default shell under Linux. In addition, both the Z and T shells are available in the distribution. You should, however, stay with the common Bourne shell until you master this shell language. Also, virtually all the shell programs written by the Linux creators are written in the Bourne shell. You should also investigate the Perl systems administration language. It provides a very robust set of tools for systems administration in one programming environment.
- *Communications.* Communications training is generally not very good as of this writing. To set up computer networking effectively, knowledge of TCP/IP and the related protocols is essential. Similarly, you will want to understand PPP if you are going to set up an asynchronous Internet connection. Ideally, these protocols should be taught in a laboratory environment with the many options available. Attend classes or at least buy manuals on the subject, but accept that you will be spending much time experimenting.
- *UNIX conventions.* UNIX conventions are not taught or even mentioned in many UNIX classes, and you will probably have to pick them up by observing as you go through training. For example, the bin directories, such as `/usr/bin`, `/bin`, and `/usr/local/bin`, are where binary executable programs are generally located. You can put your own executable programs in `/usr/local/bin`. The lib directories, such as `/usr/lib`, are used for library files. You can put your own

libraries in a directory such as `/usr/local/lib`. Understanding and following standard Linux/UNIX conventions such as these can save time in finding and fixing problems.

Several reputable companies, perhaps including the company that you bought your computer from, offer training on all of these topics. However, this training is probably not specific to Linux. There are a few vendors who sell various distributions of the Linux operating systems and offer classes on selected topics. You should also look for user groups in your area and check the **comp.os.linux** newsgroup hierarchy on UseNet news on the Internet.

Training is best done in small pieces. You should take a course and then come back and use what you learned right away on your network. Linux has an elaborate set of tools that will probably never be completely mastered, but you have to know where to find information in manuals.

From Here...

You can find more information about systems administration topics in the following chapters:

- Chapter 8, "Booting and Shutting Down," discusses proper procedures for starting and stopping the Linux system.
- Chapter 9, "Managing User Accounts," describes how to create and manage user accounts under Linux.
- Chapter 17, "Managing File Systems," shows how to create, update, and manage your file systems.

CHAPTER 8

Booting and Shutting Down

Two of the most common tasks that you encounter when administering a Linux system are booting the system and shutting it down. As you may have guessed, both booting and shutting down Linux are operations that require special consideration.

In this chapter, you learn about:

- Booting Linux
- Booting from the LILO boot manager
- Shutting down a running Linux system

Booting Linux

To use Linux, you must boot the operating system. While this sounds pretty straightforward, there are a few issues to consider. First of all, most people run at least one additional operating system on their PCs other than Linux. This means that you must have some way to specify which operating system you want to boot when you start the system. There are two basic ways to do this: you can boot Linux from a floppy or you can boot from your hard drive using a boot manager.

Booting Linux from a Floppy

Many people use a boot floppy to start Linux. This boot floppy contains a copy of the Linux kernel that points to the root Linux file system on the appropriate hard drive partition on your hard disk. The Slackware Linux installation program gives you the opportunity to create a bootable floppy during the installation process.

Caution

You should make a bootable Linux floppy disk during the installation, even if you intend to install a boot manager on your hard drive. If you should crash your hard disk, this may be the only way to boot your system!

Booting from a Boot Manager

Another way to boot Linux is to use a boot manager program. Linux comes with a boot manager known as LILO, which stands for *Linux Loader*. This program modifies the master boot sector of your boot hard disk and enables you to choose which operating system you want to boot when you turn on your computer.

Boot Managers

There are both advantages and disadvantages to using a boot manager. With a boot manager, you don't need a floppy disk to boot your system. Also, you can choose to boot different operating systems from a menu at boot time or have the system default to a given operating system.

As for the disadvantages, a boot manager adds another level of complexity to the boot process. It must be modified or possibly reinstalled if you add, delete, or upgrade a version of any of the operating systems on your disk. It modifies the master boot record of your hard disk, so if something goes wrong, you may not be able to boot with anything other than a floppy disk until you reformat your hard drive. Also, the boot manager that you choose may not be compatible with some of the more esoteric operating systems.

You should consider your own computing needs carefully before deciding on a floppy or boot manager for booting Linux.

It is also possible to set up LILO so that it can be started from the OS/2 boot manager.

LILO The Linux Loader

LILO is a boot manager that comes bundled as part of the Slackware Linux distribution. It can be installed in the master boot record, on a formatted floppy disk, or on the boot partition's super block for booting OS/2.

◀◀ See "Installing LILO," p. 86

When LILO is installed, the master boot record can be used to select from a set of different operating systems at boot time. Depending on its configuration, LILO counts to a time-out value and then boots a default operating system.

The easiest way to install LILO is to do it via the Slackware Linux installation program, which takes you through a menu-driven system that automates much of the installation process. If you really need to install it from Linux and don't want to use the main Slackware installation program, you can use the shell script `/etc/lilo/QuickInst`, which asks you questions about your setup and generates the appropriate configuration files for you.

Caution

It is highly recommended that you install LILO from the Slackware installation program. Installing a boot manager is an inherently dangerous process—you can easily corrupt data on your hard disk if the installation is not done correctly.

Configuring LILO. LILO reads a configuration file, `/etc/lilo/config`, and uses it to figure out what operating systems are installed on your system and where their boot information is located. The `/etc/lilo/config` file starts with some information that tells LILO how to operate in general. It then contains several sections that list the boot information specific to each operating system that LILO can boot. There is one section for each operating system that LILO is configured to boot on your Linux system.

Two sections from a LILO configuration file follow:

```
# Section for the Linux partition
image=/vmlinuz
label=Linux
root=/dev/hda1

# Section for MS-DOS
other=/dev/hda3
table=/dev/hda
label=msdos
```

The first section gives the boot information for Linux. The `image` line tells LILO where the Linux kernel is located. The `label` lines that appear in both sections give the name of the operating system that appears in the LILO boot menu. The `root` line specifies the location of the Linux root file system.

In the MS-DOS section, the `other` line indicates that the partition for an additional operating system is located on the disk partition `hda3`. The `table` line tells LILO where to find the partition table for `/dev/hda3`.

If you add another operating system to the configuration file, you must then run `/etc/lilo/install` so that LILO can update its information regarding the new operating system.

Using LILO. When you install LILO, you typically want to set a default time-out value and a default operating system to boot. This allows you to have a certain amount of time to select another operating system at boot time. In the event that you do not select an operating system, LILO boots the one that you have set as the default at the end of the time-out count.

When you boot your computer with LILO installed, you get a prompt that reads `LILO:`. At this point, you have several options. You can wait and have Linux boot your default operating system, or you can press <Ctrl>, <Alt>, or <Shift>, and LILO boots the default operating system immediately. You can also type the name of one of the operating systems, and LILO boots the one that you specify. Finally, you can press <Tab>, and LILO displays a list of the different operating systems that are available.

Shutting Down Linux

With a Linux system, you have to be careful when you shut the system down. You can't simply turn the power off. Linux maintains file system I/O information in memory buffers. If you just power down a Linux system, file system corruption can result.

> **Caution**
>
> You should never turn off a Linux system without shutting down properly. The file systems need to synchronize properly when the system is shutting down. You can cause severe damage to the Linux file system if you just power the system off.

The best way to shut down a Linux system is with the shutdown command. The syntax of the command is

```
/sbin/shutdown [flags] time [warning-message]
```

`[warning-message]` is a message sent to all users that are currently logged on, and *`time`* is the time that the shutdown is to occur. The `time` argument can have several different formats. It can be specified as an absolute time in the format hh:mm, where hh is the hour in either one or two digits and mm is the minute of the hour. The mm value must be specified with two digits. The time value can also be given in the format +m, where m is the number of minutes to wait before the shutdown. You can substitute the word `now` for +0. Table 8.1 lists the options that can be used with the shutdown command.

Table 8.1 Command-Line Options for the *shutdown* Command

Flag	Description
-t *sec*	Wait *sec* seconds between sending processes the warning and the kill signal to all processes. This delay gives processes time to finish any shutdown processing that they have to do.
-k	Do not really shut down the system. Just send the warning message to all users.
-r	Reboot after shutdown.
-h	Halt after shutdown.
-n	Do not sync disks before rebooting or halting. Use with caution.
-f	Do a "fast" reboot. This creates the file `/etc/fastboot`. The `rc` boot script should check for this file and not do an `fsck` if it is found.
-c	Cancel an already running `shutdown`. With this option, it is not possible to specify the time argument.

The `shutdown` command prevents any users from logging on, notifies all users on the system that the system will be shut down, waits until the time that you specify, and then sends a `SIGTERM` signal to all processes so that they can exit cleanly. `shutdown` then calls either halt or reboot, depending on your command-line choice in the `shutdown` command. It is possible to halt or reboot the system by entering `halt` or `reboot` directly. However, no warning is given to the users, and the system goes down immediately. These commands should only be used if you are the only user on the system.

From Here...

Obviously, there is more to systems administration than just booting and shutting down the system. You can find more information about system administration in the following chapters:

- Chapter 7, "Understanding System Administration," provides an overview of the various tasks that the average system administrator faces.
- Chapter 9, "Managing User Accounts," shows how to create and maintain user logon accounts on your Linux system.
- Chapter 17, "Managing File Systems," discusses how to properly manage and maintain file systems.

CHAPTER 9

Managing User Accounts

The system administrator is in charge of managing users. This involves adding users so that they can log on to the system, setting user privileges, creating and assigning home directories for users, assigning users to groups, and deleting users when necessary. In this chapter, you explore the various tools and techniques for user account management.

This chapter covers the following topics:

- Adding and deleting users
- Managing user passwords
- Setting and changing user attributes
- Working with groups
- Managing home directories

Working with Users

▸▸ See "Password Security," p. 201

Every user should have a unique logon name. This makes it possible to identify each user and avoids the problem of one person deleting another's files. Furthermore, each user must have a password. About the only exception to this is when there is only one user on a system, and the system has absolutely no connection by modem or network to any other computer. Further, when there is no real reason for a person to have access to your system, you must make sure that individual cannot log on. That person's logon name should be removed, along with any files that your remaining users no longer need.

Adding a User

When you add a user, the result is an entry for the user in the password file, `/etc/passwd`. That entry has the following form:

```
logon_name:encrypted_password:user_ID:group_ID

➥:user_information:logon_directory:logon_shell
```

In this syntax, fields are separated by colons. The fields are listed in Table 9.1.

Table 9.1 Fields in an /etc/passwd File Entry

Field	Description
logon_name	The name used to log on
encrypted_password	The password required to authenticate the user—the primary line of defense against security violations
user_ID	A unique number the operating system uses to identify the user
group_ID	A unique number or name used to identify the primary group for this user. A user can change to other groups if permitted by the administrator
user_information	A description of the user, such as the user's name or title
logon_directory	The user's home directory (where the user ends up after logging on)
logon_shell	The shell used by a user when logging on (for example, /bin/bash if using the bash shell)

Linux provides two commands for adding users: `adduser` and `useradd`. The `adduser` command is an interactive program; you enter the information about a new user in response to a set of prompts. With the `useradd` command, the user information is provided as a set of command-line parameters.

Using the *adduser* Command. When you add a user with the `adduser` command, Linux returns a set of prompts that ask you to enter the necessary information (see Listing 9.1).

Listing 9.1 An Example of an *adduser* Session

```
opus:/# adduser<Return>
Adding a new user. The username should be not exceed
8 characters in length, or you may run into problems later.
Enter login name for new account (^C to quit): jschmoe<Return>
Editing information for new user [jschmoe]
Full Name: Joseph A. Schmoe<Return>
GID [100]:<Return>
Checking for an available UID after 500
501...502...503...
First unused uid is 504
UID [504]:<Return>
Home Directory [/home/jschmoe]:<Return>
Shell [/bin/bash]:<Return>
Password [jschmoe]:<Return>
Information for new user [jschmoe]:<Return>
Home directory: [/home/jschmoe] Shell: [/bin/bash]
```

```
Password: [jschmoe] uid: [504] gid: [100]
Is this correct? [y/N]: y<Return>
Adding login [jschmoe] and making directory [/home/jschmoe]
Adding the files from the /etc/skel directory:
./.kermrc -> /home/jschmoe/./.kermrc
./.less -> /home/jschmoe/./.less
./.lessrc -> /home/jschmoe/./.lessrc
./.term -> /home/jschmoe/./.term
./.term/termrc -> /home/jschmoe/./.term/termrc ./.emacs ->
/home/jschmoe/./.emacs
   opus:/#
```

Throughout the `adduser` session, the program provides default answers in square brackets. To accept the default answer, just press <Return>. Otherwise, enter a different value than the one suggested.

The `adduser` command also copies the files from the directory `/etc/skel` into the user's home directory. The directory, `/etc/skel`, should contain files you want every user to have. These typically include "personal" configuration files, such as `.profile`, `.cshrc`, and `.login` for shell configuration; `.mailrc` for e-mail setup; `.emacs` for your users using Emacs as an editor; and so on.

The `adduser` command is useful for quickly adding user accounts, especially if you only have one or two to add.

Using the *useradd* Command. You can use the `useradd` command to create or add a user to your Linux system. With this command, you can specify all of the information—except the password—that is needed to create the account on the command line. You need to use the `passwd` command to set the password of the new user. Some of these items have default values or values you can set that apply to users you create when you use the command.

Like the `adduser` command, `useradd` also copies the files in the directory `/etc/skel` into the user's home directory.

Table 9.2 lists the options you can use with the `useradd` command.

Table 9.2 Options for Use with the *useradd* Command

Option	Meaning
-u *UID*	Makes *UID* the user ID number of the user. There is no specific default value. If this isn't specified, the next available number above the highest number currently assigned is used.
-g *group*	Makes the *group* the user's primary group instead of the default value. The value for `group` must be either the name or group ID number of an existing group. The default group number is `group 1`.
-c *info*	Puts *info* in the user information field. If `info` contains blanks, enclose it in quotation marks. Colons aren't permitted. There is no default value. If this option isn't specified, the user information field is left blank.
-d *dir*	Makes *dir* the logon or home directory for the user instead of the default. Specify a full path, such as `/users/tuser`, rather than just `tuser`.

Table 9.2 Continued

Option	Meaning
-s *shell*	Makes *shell* the user's logon shell. This must be specified as a full path name, such as /bin/bash.
-G *group*	Makes the *group* the user's supplementary group, so that the user can use the newgrp command with the group(s) listed here. There is no default value. The value for group must be the group ID of an existing group. If you must specify more than one, separate them with commas and leave no intervening spaces—for example, -G 21,31.
-k *dir*	Copies the file from the directory *dir* into the user's logon directory. This option is useful for giving a user an initial .profile file and other files that serve as resources for various commands. The default value is /etc/skel.

You can set default values for useradd by specifying the -D command-line parameter in the following form:

```
useradd -D parameters
```

The parameters you use must be specified with full path names and are the following:

-b *dir*	The logon or home directory
-g *group*	The primary group

With the default home directory, Linux appends the user's logon name to the default directory path. For example, if the default path is /home/admin as set by the command

```
useradd -D -b /home/admin
```

then the default home directory for the user jschmoe created with the command

```
useradd jschmoe
```

is /home/admin/jschmoe.

To add Joe Schmoe's account with home directory, /users/jschmoe, enter

```
useradd -d /users/jschmoe -s /bin/bash -c "Joseph A. Schmoe" jschmoe
```

This creates an entry in the password file that looks like

```
jschmoe:*:123:21:Joseph A. Schmoe:/users/jschmoe:/bin/bash
```

The exact values depend on the defaults for useradd on your system. In any case, with these commands you have the following:

- The user's logon name is jschmoe.
- The * in the password field means that the user cannot log on until a password is set.
- The user ID number is 123.
- The group ID is 21.

- The user's real name is Joseph A. Schmoe.
- The home or logon directory is `/users/jschmoe`.
- The logon shell is `/bin/bash`, which was the value specified on the command line.

When the command is executed, the home directory is created; the files are copied from `/etc/skel` to that directory; the file `/etc/group`, which keeps track of group memberships, is modified to include `jschmoe` in the specified group(s); and `jschmoe` is made the owner of the logon directory and the files it contains.

Setting User Passwords

You set a user's password using the `passwd` command. The system administrator should set a password for each user added to the system. Users can change their passwords when they log on. Use `passwd` as follows:

1. Type the command and logon name (for example, **`passwd jschmoe`**) and press <Return>.
2. You are prompted to enter a password for the user. Type the password and press <Return>; you don't see the password on-screen:

```
Enter new password: newpassword<Return>
```

3. You are prompted to type the password again. Type the password again and press <Return>.

```
Re-type new password: newpassword<Return>
```

The password is encrypted and put into the file `/etc/passwd`. It is important that you take the time to enter passwords that follow the rules for choosing a password, as follows:

- Passwords should be at least six, and preferably eight, characters long.
- Passwords should contain upper- and lowercase letters, punctuation symbols, and numerals.

▶▶ See "Password Security," p. 201

When you're adding a number of users, you'll be tempted to enter short, easy passwords. Don't fall for it. Good passwords are your first line of defense against intruders. Be sure to tell your users why you've assigned that type of password. Further, it's a good idea to change passwords regularly, but remember to educate system users about the choice of good passwords.

After a user is assigned a password, the file entry looks something like

```
jschmoe:Zoie.89&^0gW*:123:21:Joseph A. Schmoe:/users/jschmoe:/bin/bash
```

The second field is the password—not as it was typed, but in encrypted form.

Note

Users occasionally forget passwords. It isn't possible for a system administrator to tell users their own passwords. You can delete a forgotten password by editing the `/etc/passwd` file and deleting the second field in the user's file entry. You can then set the user's password with the `passwd` command. Have a procedure in place to deal with this situation, and let your users know about it.

Removing a User

There are several different degrees of user removal. Removing a user from the system need not be a final, irrevocable act. Here are some possibilities:

- Remove only the capability to log on. This is useful if the user is away for a while and needs to be reinstated some time in the future. The user's directory, files, and group information are kept intact. Edit the password file, `/etc/passwd`, and put an * in the second field of the user's entry, as follows:

  ```
  jschmoe:*:123:21:Joseph A. Schmoe:/users/jschmoe:/bin/bash
  ```

- Remove the user from the password file but keep the user's files on the system. This is useful if the files are used by others. Delete the user's entry from the password file or files. You can do this by using an editor or the `userdel logon_name` command. You then can change the ownership and location of the deleted user's files using the commands `chown` and `mv`.
- Remove the user from the password file and remove all files the user owns. This is the ultimate and complete form of deleting a user. You must delete the user's entry from the password file and delete the user's files from the system. You can do this using the `find` command

  ```
  find users-home-directory -exec rm {} \;<Return>
  ```

  Then remove the directory with `rmdir users-home-directory`, and remove the appropriate entry from the password file or files. Another way to do all this is to use the `-r` option with the command `userdel`, for example, `userdel -r tuser`.

Note

If you use other configuration files at your site, such as e-mail alias files, you have to remove the user from these files manually.

Changing User Attributes

A user's needs, status, and assignments often change. These changes are often reflected in either the password or group file. It may be that a user is assigned to another project and needs access to the files of another group. To modify a user's attributes, use the `usermod` command. The options with this command include some of those available with `useradd` (`-u UID`, `-g group`, `-C info`, `-d dir`, `-s shell`, `-G group`). Two additional options are

-l	Change a user's logon name
-m	Move the user's home or logon directory to the directory specified with the -d option

In the following example, the user name of jschmoe is changed to jas, he is added to the group frstan98, and his home directory has been changed to /research/jas:

```
usermod -l jas -d /research/jas -m -G frstan98 jschmoe
```

The changes take effect the next time the user logs on.

Working with Groups

Each user is a member of a group. You can give different types of groups different capabilities or privileges. For example, it is reasonable to give users of a group that use the system for analysis of a company's sales data access to a different set of files than a group of users whose main function is researching new products.

The password file contains information for a single user. Information about groups is kept in the file, /etc/group. The following is a sample entry:

```
sales::21:tuser, jschmoe, staplr
```

The group name is sales, the group ID number is 21, and the members are tuser, jschmoe, and staplr. Files and directories have permissions associated with them for the owner, group, and others. A user can be a member of more than one group, and you can change group memberships.

Adding a Group

You create a new group by either editing the file, /etc/group, directly or using the groupadd command. To create a new group named sales, enter

```
groupadd sales<Return>
```

The group is added and has a unique group ID number associated with it. The default group ID number is the first available number greater than 99 and greater than that of any other group. If you want to assign the group ID number yourself, including a GID less than 99, use groupadd with the -g option, for example:

```
groupadd -g 21 sales<Return>
```

You still must give a name to the group. You can add users to this group using useradd or usermod.

Deleting a Group

You delete a group by editing the /etc/group file or using the groupdel command. Type the command followed by the name of the group to be removed. To delete the group sales, for example, enter

```
groupdel sales<Return>
```

Modifying Group Attributes

Over time, you may want to change the group ID number associated with a group if that group ID number is to be used for another purpose. To do that, use the following syntax:

```
groupmod -g new-group-id-number group-name
```

To change the name of a group without changing its membership, use the following syntax:

```
groupmod -n new-group-name old-group-name
```

Suppose that you have a group of users working on a project identified as `xf345`, but now they are working together on the project `frstan98`. To change the group, enter

```
groupmod -n frstan98 xf345<Return>
```

Home Directory Management

You should give some thought to grouping your home directories logically if you plan to have a lot of users on your system. In general, you should try to place all the home directories on a given machine under one single top-level directory. That way, they can be grouped according to whatever arrangement makes sense for your needs.

▶▶ See "Mounting and Unmounting File Systems," p. 303

For example, you can specify that `/home` be the top-level directory for user directories. Under `/home`, you can group users by department. The sales users have accounts under `/home/sales`, development is under `/home/develop`, and so on. Your user home directories then fall under these directories or under another set if additional grouping is needed. Because user directories can use a lot of disk space, this enables you to place logical groups of users on different physical file systems. As you need additional space, you can simply create an additional category for home directories and mount it on a file system as a mount point under `/home`.

From Here...

You, as the system administrator, are responsible for managing and supporting the users that log on to your system. Proper user management procedures can help simplify creating and deleting accounts. Linux provides a complete set of tools for managing user account and group information. It is important to understand how user accounts can be grouped logically. By considering how to set up their directory structures so that they reflect this grouping, you can make the most out of limited disk space and make file system maintenance a less taxing job.

You can find more information about systems administration in the following chapters:

- Chapter 7, "Understanding System Administration," gives an introduction to common systems administration tasks.
- Chapter 10, "Backing Up Data," discusses how to plan and implement plans for data backups.
- Chapter 17, "Managing File Systems," describes how to set up and manage file systems on your Linux system.

CHAPTER 10

Backing Up Data

Various kinds of problems can result in loss of data: files get accidentally removed; hardware fails; important information stored in files is no longer available. Users should feel confident that, in such cases, they can access a timely backup of the "lost" files.

Your company's future—and your future with your company—may depend on making those backup files available. At such times, you and others will be thankful that you've taken the time and effort to copy files to some sort of storage media according to a regular, rigorous, and well-documented schedule. Backing up files isn't very glamorous, but no administrator can ignore the process.

The following are several issues to consider in backing up a system:

- *Full or incremental backups.* A *full backup* copies every file. Is it necessary to do that every day? A full backup usually requires a good deal of time and enough media to hold all the files on the system. An *incremental backup* copies the files that have changed since the last full backup.
- *File systems to back up.* Naturally, active file systems must be backed up regularly. Others can be backed up less frequently. Be sure that you have current copies of all the file systems.
- *Types of backup media.* Depending on the devices on your system, you may be able to use 9-track tape, 1/4-inch cartridge tape, 4mm or 8mm DAT tapes, or floppy disks. Each has advantages over the other in terms of sheer bulk, storage capacity, and cost for devices and media. Choose the backup medium to fit your budget, remembering that the least expensive medium may be the most time-consuming.
- *Effect of backups on users.* Performing a backup operation increases the load on a system. Will that be an unreasonable burden on users? Also, files that are changed during the backup process may not be backed up. This can merely be an inconvenience or a very important consideration if you're backing up an active database. Should you perform backups when the system is quiet?

- *Commands to use for backups.* There are some relatively simple, time-honored commands for creating backups such as `tar` and `cpio`. Are they sufficient?
- *Documentation of the backed up files.* You must label all backed up material so that you can use it to recover files when necessary. Some procedures and commands enable you to prepare a table of contents or list of the material that has been backed up.

From an administrator's view, the file system should be backed up according to some automated process with as little operator intervention as possible. It should also be done when the system is relatively quiet so that the backup is as complete as possible. This consideration must be balanced with convenience and costs. Should an operator or administrator have to stay until midnight on Friday to perform a full backup? Is it worth $3,000 for a DAT tape drive so that the entire system can be backed up automatically at 3 AM with no operator intervention?

Consider the alternatives, determine the true costs, and make a decision or recommend a course of action. It's generally a lot cheaper and always easier to restore well-managed backup information than to recreate it or do without it.

In this chapter, you learn about the following topics:

- Planning for backups
- Making a backup schedule
- Using the `tar` command
- Working with `cpio`

Considering Backup Tips

The purpose of performing backups is to be able to restore individual files or complete file systems. Whatever you do about backups should be focused on that central purpose.

Set up a backup plan. Include the files to be backed up, how often they'll be backed up, and document how the files are to be restored. Let all users know the backup schedule and how they can request restoration of files. Be sure to stick with the plan.

Be sure to verify your backups. This could include reading a table of contents from the backup medium after it has been stored or restoring an arbitrarily chosen file from the medium. Remember that it is possible for the backup medium—disk or tape—to have flaws.

Make backups so that files can be restored anywhere on the file system or on another computer system. Use backup or archive utilities that create archives that can be used on other Linux or UNIX computer systems.

Be sure to label all media—tapes, disks, whatever—used in a backup. If you have to use multiple items, be sure that they are numbered sequentially and dated. You must be able to find the file or files you need.

Plan for a disaster. Have copies of the files on your system so that the entire system can be restored in a reasonable amount of time. Store copies of backup tapes or disks off site.

Plan to reevaluate your backup procedures periodically to be sure that they're meeting your needs.

Planning a Backup Schedule

It's important to come up with a backup schedule that meets your needs and that makes it possible to restore recent copies of files. After you decide on a schedule, stick to it.

The ideal situation is to be able to restore any file at any time. Taken to an extreme, that's not possible, but you ought to be able to restore files on a daily basis. To do this, you use a combination of complete and incremental backups. A *complete backup* is one that contains every file on the system. An *incremental backup* is one that contains files that have changed since the last backup. Incremental backups can be at different levels: incremental to the last complete backup or incremental to the last incremental backup. It's convenient to think of backups as occurring at different levels:

Level 0	Complete backup
Level 1	Incremental to the last complete backup
Level 2	Incremental to the last level 1 backup

The following are some sample backup schedules:

- *Full backup one day, incremental other days:*

Day 1	Level 0, complete backup
Day 2	Level 1, incremental backup
Day 3	Level 1, incremental backup
Day 4	Level 1, incremental backup
Day 5	Level 1, incremental backup

  If you create and save an index of each of these backups, you should need only one day's backup to restore an individual file and only two days' backup (day 1 and another day's) to completely restore the system.

- *Full backup once a month, weekly incremental, and daily incremental.* This example is built around Tuesday but can be any specific day of the week.

First Tuesday	Level 0, complete backup
Any other Tuesday	Level 1, incremental backup
Any other day	Level 2, incremental backup

To restore an individual file under this schedule, you may need the complete backup if the file wasn't changed during the month, the level 1 backup if the file was changed the previous week but not this week, or the level 2 backup if the file was changed this week. This schedule is more complex than the previous example, but backups take less time per day.

Performing Backups and Restoring Files

Several different utilities are available for backing up and restoring files in a Linux system. Some are simple and straightforward; others are more complex. The simple methods have their limitations. Choose the one that meets your needs.

Because backing up and restoring files is very important, there are a number of available software systems dedicated to that task. The following sections present two of them:

Command	Description
`tar`	Tape archive utility available on every Linux or UNIX system; this easy-to-use Linux version can use several tapes or disks.
`cpio`	General-purpose utility for copying files; available on every UNIX system; easy to use, more robust than `tar`, and can use several tapes or disks.

Using *tar*

The UNIX `tar` utility was originally designed to create a tape archive (to copy files or directories to tape and then to extract or restore files from the archive). You can use it to copy to any device. It has the following advantages:

- It is simple to use.
- It is reliable and stable.
- Archives can be read on virtually any Linux or UNIX system.

It also has a couple of disadvantages, as follows:

- For some versions of `tar`, the archive must reside on one disk or tape, which means that if a portion of the medium fails—from a bad sector on a disk or bad block on a tape, for example—the entire backup may be lost.
- It cannot back up special files, such as device files.
- On its own, it can only perform complete backups. If you want to do incremental backups, you have to do a little shell programming.

Some of the commonly used options for `tar` are listed in Table 10.1.

Table 10.1 Common Options for the *tar* Command

Option	Description
c	Creates an archive.
x	Extracts or restores files from the archive that is either on the default device or on the device specified by the f option.
f *name*	Creates the archive or reads the archive from *name*, where *name* is either a filename or a device specified in `/dev`, such as `/dev/rmt0`.
Z	Compresses or decompresses the `tar` archive.
z	Compresses or decompresses the `tar` archive with gzip.
M	Creates a multi-volume `tar` backup.
t	Creates an index of all files stored in an archive and lists on stdout.
v	Verbose mode.

There are many additional command parameters that can be used with `tar`. Refer to the man page for a complete list.

Consider some examples of the use of `tar` in backing up and restoring files. The following command copies the directory `/home` to the floppy drive `/dev/fd0`:

```
tar cf /dev/fd0 /home
```

In this case, the `f` option specifies that the archive is created on the floppy drive device `/dev/fd0`. The following command also archives the directory `/home`:

```
tar cvfzM /dev/fd0 /home ¦ tee homeindex
```

The `v` option indicates verbose mode, the `z` option indicates that the archive should be compressed to save space, and the `M` option tells `tar` to create a multi-volume backup. When one floppy disk is full, `tar` prompts you for another. A list of the copied files is directed to `homeindex`. It is a good idea to take a look at that file to see what was copied.

The `find` command is useful for locating files that have been modified within a certain period of time so that they can be scheduled for incremental backups. The following example uses the command `find` to create a list of all files that have been modified in the last day:

```
find /home -mtime -1 -type f -print > bkuplst
➥tar cvfzM /dev/fd0 'cat bkuplst' ¦ tee homeindex
```

To use the list as input to the `tar` command, place the command `cat bkuplst` in back quotes (backward, single quotation marks: `'cat bkuplst'`). This tells the shell to execute the command as a subshell and place the output from the command on the command line in the location of the original back quoted command.

The following command restores the file /home/dave/notes.txt from the device /dev/fd0 (note that you have to give the complete filename to restore it):

```
tar xv /usr2/dave/notes.txt
```

> **Note**
>
> Any of these commands can be automated by putting them in root's cron file. For example, the following entry in the root's cron file performs a backup of /home every day at 1:30 AM:
>
> ```
> 30 01 * * * tar cvfz /def/fd0 /home > homeindex
> ```
>
> If you need to do more complicated backups, you can create shell scripts to control your backups. These shell scripts can also be run via cron.

The tar command can also be used to create archive files in the Linux file system instead of writing to a backup device. This way, you can archive a group of files along with their directory structure in one file. To do this, simply give a filename as the argument to the f option, instead of a device name. The following is an example of archiving a directory and its subdirectories with the tar command:

```
tar cvf /home/backup.tar /home/dave
```

This creates the file /home/backup.tar, which contains a backup of the directory, /home/dave, and all files and subdirectories below it.

> **Note**
>
> The tar command by itself does not perform any file compression. To compress the resulting tar file, either specify the z option with the tar command or use a compression program, such as gzip, on the final tar file.

When you are using tar to make archive files, it is usually a good idea to try to make the top-level entry in the tar file a directory. This way, when you extract the tar file, all the files in it are placed under a central directory in your current working directory. Otherwise, you could end up with hundreds of files in your directory if you extract a tar file in the wrong place.

Suppose that you have a directory below your current directory named data and that data contains several hundred files. There are two basic ways to create a tar file of this directory. You can change directories to data and create the tar file from there.

```
$ pwd<Return>
/home/dave
$ cd data<Return>
$ pwd<Return>
/home/dave/data
$ tar cvf ../data.tar *<Return>
```

This creates a tar file in /home/dave that contains just the contents of data without containing an entry for the directory. When you extract this tar file, you do not create a directory to put the files in—you just get several hundred files in your current directory.

Another way to create the tar file is to start from the parent directory of data and specify the directory name as the thing to archive. For example:

```
$ pwd<Return>
/home/dave
$ tar cvf data.tar data<Return>
```

This still creates an archive of the data directory, but it puts the directory entry as the first thing in the archive. This way, when the tar file is extracted, the first thing that is created is the directory data, and all the files in data are placed in the data subdirectory.

Note

When creating a tar file of all the files in the directory, it is good practice to specify a different location for the tar file other than the current directory. That way, if you try to archive all the files in the current directory, tar won't get confused and try to add its tar file recursively to the tar that it is creating.

Using *cpio*

cpio is a general-purpose command for copying file archives. You can use it to create backups using the -o option or restore files using the -i option. It takes its input from standard input and sends its output to standard output.

Advantages of cpio are as follows:

- It can back up any set of files.
- It can back up special files.
- It stores information in a more efficient manner than tar.
- It skips bad sectors or bad blocks when restoring data.
- Its backups can be restored on almost any Linux or UNIX system.

Some people find cpio's syntax to be a bit more confusing than tar's syntax. Also, to perform incremental backups, you have to do some shell programming.

The following is a list of the commonly used options for cpio:

Option	Description
-o	Copy out. Creates an archive on standard out.
-B	Blocks input or output at 5120 bytes per record. Useful for efficient storage on magnetic tape.

(continues)

III

System Administration

Option	Description
-i	Copy in. Extracts files from standard input (assumed to be the result of a copy out action of `cpio`).
-t	Creates a table of contents of the input.

Consider some examples of `cpio` in backing up and restoring files. The following command copies the files in the directory `/home` to the device `/dev/fd0`:

```
ls /home ¦ cpio -o > /dev/fd0
```

The following example extracts the files on the device `/dev/fd0` and creates an index in the `bkup.indx` file:

```
cpio -it < /dev/fd0 > bkup.indx
```

The following example uses the `find` command to create a list of all files on `/home` that have been modified in the last day:

```
find /home -mtime 1 -type f -print ¦ cpio -oB > /dev/fd0
```

The output of that command is piped to `cpio`, which creates an archive on `/dev/fd0` where the data is stored in 5120 bytes per record.

The following command restores the file `/home/dave/notes.txt` from the device `/dev/fd0`:

```
echo "/home/dave/notes.txt" ¦ cpio -i < /dev/fd0
```

Note

You must give the complete filename to restore it with `cpio`.

Note

Any of these commands can be automated by putting them in `root`'s `cron` file. For example, the following entry in the `root`'s `cron` file performs a backup of `/home` every day at 1:30 AM:

```
30 01 * * * ls /home ¦ cpio -o > /dev/fd0
```

If you need to do more complicated backups, you can create shell scripts to control your backups. These shell scripts can also be run via `cron`.

See the man page for `cpio` for a complete description of the options you can use with this command.

Summary

Performing regular backups of your system is critical to protecting your data. Data can be lost because of hardware failure, software errors, human error, or malicious intrusion into your system. A well-thought-out backup plan can make the job of rebuilding your system much easier.

Both the `tar` and `cpio` commands provide the capability to perform backups on your system. Each command has its own strengths and weaknesses. You should evaluate your own needs and choose accordingly.

There are several tools available that can help automate your backup procedure. Check out the Linux archives on **sunsite.unc.edu** for more information. Also, Linux supports the FTAPE extensions, which are available with the Slackware Distribution. FTAPE enables you to perform backups to QIC-80 magnetic tape units that run off a floppy controller on your system. For detailed information, refer to the FTAPE HOWTO guide.

From Here...

You can find more information about system administration in the following chapters:

- Chapter 7, "Understanding System Administration," gives an overview of the duties of a systems administrator.
- Chapter 9, "Managing User Accounts," shows how to create and manage user access to your Linux system.
- Chapter 17, "Managing File Systems," discusses the ins and outs of file systems and the various issues that you need to consider.

CHAPTER 11

Improving System Security

Unless your system is locked in a closet, you are the only one with a key, and you keep the key on a chain around your neck at all times, you should be concerned about system security. This really is not a joke. If there are multiple users, if the system is connected to the outside world by modems or a network, or if there are times when the system is not attended, then there is the real risk that someone may gain unauthorized access to it.

Sometimes, unauthorized access is benign—but it can still be unnerving. If someone takes the time to gain access to your system, then that person probably has the skill to copy information you want to keep confidential, make unauthorized use of your system's resources, and modify or delete information.

In most organizations, the system administrator has the responsibility for system security. You don't have to be paranoid about it, but you should be aware of the risks and be able to take steps to keep your system secure. Be assertive and professional when addressing security issues.

This chapter discusses ideas and policies for increasing computer security, as well as actual techniques that you can use to make your system more secure. Some of these ideas are of little use to the home computer user and tend to apply to larger installations. Other points in this chapter are very applicable to home users.

In this chapter, you learn about:

- Physical security
- Password security
- Logon security
- File security
- Social engineering threats

> **Note**
>
> Over the past several years, the mass media has changed the meaning of the word *hacker* from "a computer enthusiast" to "someone who breaks into computers." In the computer community, the commonly accepted term for someone who breaks into computers is *cracker*. This is the term used throughout this chapter.

Physical Security

With all the mass media hype about viruses, computer break-ins, and diabolical computer crackers with their modems and network connections, too little attention is paid to the physical security of computer systems.

Computer equipment is fairly sensitive to a variety of environmental conditions. Fire and smoke can obviously mean a quick end for your computing equipment. If you have any sort of business computer installation, you should consider installing smoke detectors, automatic fire extinguishers, and a fire alarm system. In addition to fire and smoke, dust can wreak havoc with computer equipment. Dust is abrasive and can shorten the life of magnetic media and tape and optical drives. Dust can collect in ventilation systems and block the airflow, letting computers overheat. In addition, dust can be electrically conductive and can cause circuit boards to short out and fail.

Electricity poses a special threat to computer equipment. Computers are very sensitive to surges in electrical current. All computer equipment should be connected to surge suppression equipment to reduce the chances of damage. This includes modems connected to telephone lines. Many areas suffer from "dirty power" that fluctuates in both current and voltage.

> **Note**
>
> Although surge suppressors can help protect against spikes in the electrical current, they are virtually worthless against any kind of lightning strike. If lightning hits an incoming line to your house or business, simple surge suppressors are unlikely to save your equipment.

Computers are also common targets for theft. Many computer components are small and expensive. As a result, they are easily stolen and sold. You should evaluate how secure your computers are and try to protect them against theft as you do any valuable possession.

Another aspect of physical computer security is preventing access by unauthorized persons. If someone can walk into your computer room, sit down at a console, and start working unchallenged, you have a problem. By controlling access to your computers, you make it more difficult for someone to steal or damage either data or equipment. Establish access policies for your computing facilities, and educate your users as to these policies.

The following are some steps you can take to improve the physical security at your installation:

- Don't leave a system, tape drives, disk drives, terminals, or workstations unattended for a prolonged period of time. It's a good idea to have some restrictions regarding access to the rooms that house your primary system and associated tape and disk drives. A lock on the door goes a long way in providing security. An unauthorized person can remove backup media—disks or tapes—from an unlocked area.
- Don't leave the system console or other terminal device logged on as root and unattended. If someone knows the system, they can easily give themselves root privileges, modify important software, or remove information from the system.
- Educate system users about physical security risks. Encourage them to report any unauthorized activity they may witness. Feel free to courteously challenge someone you don't recognize who is using the system.
- If possible, don't keep sensitive information on systems that have modem or network connections.
- Keep backups in a secure area, and limit access to that area.

Password Security

The first line of defense against unauthorized access to a system is password protection. This is also often the weakest link in the chain. This section describes some steps you can take to keep passwords secure.

The reality is that users want simple, easy-to-remember passwords. They don't want to change their passwords. They like to write them down so that they can reference them. Unfortunately for you, the system administrator, these are all bad approaches from a computer security standpoint. Password security requires almost constant attention.

The root password is special. Anyone who knows it can access anything on your system and perhaps other systems that your computer is connected to through a network. Change the root password often, choose it wisely, and keep it secure. It's best committed to memory. In most organizations, it's a good idea for two people to know it—but no more than that!

Choosing Passwords

Passwords should be at least six characters long; however, only the first eight characters in any password are recognized. This means that your password is truncated to eight characters if you enter one that is longer than eight characters. It's not too difficult to write a program that can attempt to guess a password. If the password-guessing program is trying to guess a random password, it will take longer to be successful if the password itself is longer.

Computers are very good at doing the same thing over and over, such as encrypting every word in a dictionary and comparing it to your password to try to break into your system. You should never choose a password that is a dictionary word. Also, try not to choose a password that is easily associated with you. Your name, address, spouse's name, child's name, phone number, driver's license number, and so on are all obvious targets for a cracker.

So how do you pick a good password if all the easy ones are also easy to guess? One technique is to pick two random short words and connect them with a punctuation character. This makes an almost random sequence of characters as far as a password guesser is concerned, but is fairly easy for a user to remember. The following are a few examples of passwords that use this technique:

```
joe&day

car!pan

modem!at
```

Another method for picking passwords is to take a phrase that you will remember and use the first letter from each word for the password. This results in a random sequence of characters, but one that you can easily recall. For example, the phrase "Ladies and Gentlemen, Elvis has left the building" translates into the password `L&GEhltb`.

The crucial point is that the password should be remembered. It shouldn't be written down anywhere.

Logon Security

Each account on your Linux system is a door into your computer. All that someone needs is the right key—the password. If you have instituted good password-management practices, you already have a head start toward developing a more secure system. One aspect of computer security that goes hand-in-hand with password security is logon or account security.

Logon or account security involves looking for accounts on your system that may be potential security problems and dealing with them. There are several different kinds of problems that logon security can pose.

Accounts without Passwords

Many computer crackers succeed in breaking into a computer by simply finding an account that does not have a password. You should check your password file regularly for such accounts and disable them. The password is stored in the second field of the password file under Linux. You can check for a blank password field with several tools, such as `grep`, `awk`, or `perl`. You can disable logons to an account by editing the password file and changing the password field to a `*` character. This prevents anyone from logging on with that logon ID.

Unused Accounts

If a logon name won't be used any more, you should delete the account so that it can't be compromised. You can use the command `userdel` to delete the logon name. For example, to remove the logon name `ernie`, use the following command:

```
userdel ernie
```

This deletes the logon name `ernie` and prevents anyone from using it to log on. If you want to remove any files in the `ernie` home directory, use the `-r` option to `userdel`. For example,

```
userdel -r ernie
```

deletes the account and removes the user files associated with it.

◄◄ See "Removing a User," p. 184

Note

If you use other configuration files, such as system mail alias lists, the account that you are deleting has to be removed manually. You can write a shell script that runs `userdel` on the account and then deletes the logon ID from the various custom system files that you use.

Default Accounts

Linux comes with several standard logon IDs that are required for the operating system to work correctly. For example, the root account has no password when Linux is first installed. You should check the password file when you have finished your installations and make sure that all your default accounts either have good passwords or have been disabled by setting the password field to a `*` character.

Some software packages automatically create accounts on your system during their installation processes. Remember to disable them or set their passwords accordingly.

Guest Accounts

It is not uncommon for computer centers to provide some type of guest access accounts for visitors so they can use the local computers temporarily. These accounts usually do not have passwords or have passwords that are the same as the logon ID. For example, the logon `guest` might not have any password or has a password of `guest`. As you might guess, these are security disasters waiting to happen.

Because these accounts and passwords are probably widely known, an intruder could use one to gain initial access to your system. Once a cracker has broken into your system, the intruder can then try to get root access from the inside or use your system as a *waypoint* from which to attack other computers over a network. Tracing an attack back to an open, public account makes it much harder to find the true source of the attack.

Guest or open accounts are really not a good idea on any system. If you really must use one, keep it disabled until it is needed. Randomly generate a password for the account when it needs to be used, and when you can, disable it immediately. Remember not to send the password via e-mail.

Command Accounts

It is common for computers to have several *command accounts:* logon IDs that run a given command and then exit. For example, Finger is an account that has no password. When a user logs on as Finger, the Finger program is run, showing who is on the system, and then the session terminates. Other such accounts may be Sync or Date. These accounts typically do not have passwords. Even though they do not run a shell and run only one command, they can still pose a security risk. If you allow command accounts on your system, you should ensure that none of these commands accepts command-line input. Also, these commands should not have any type of shell escape that could enable a user to get to an interactive shell.

A second reason for not using these types of accounts is that they can give away information about your system that can be useful to an intruder. Using programs such as Finger or Who as command accounts can enable intruders to get the logon IDs of users on your system. Remember that the logon ID/password combination protects your accounts. If an intruder gets the logon ID of a user, they now have half the information that is needed to log on to that account.

Group Accounts

A group account is an account for which more than one person knows the password and logs on under the same ID. You guessed it—a bad idea. If you have an account that is shared by several people and it is broken and is being used as a base to attack other computers, finding the person who gave out the password is difficult. If you have an account that is shared by 5 people, it may in fact be shared by 25. There is no way to know.

Linux gives you the capability to provide file access based on group membership. This way, a group of people who need access to a set of files can share them without needing to share an account. Instead of creating group accounts, make wise use of groups under Linux. Stay with the "One Logon ID—One Person" philosophy.

File Security

The file system under Linux is a tree structure that is built from files and directories. Linux stores several types of information about each file in its file system, including the following:

- The filename
- The file type
- The file size

- The file's physical location on disk
- Various access and modification times
- The owner and group ID of the file
- The access permissions associated with the file

If a user is able to modify some of the file information on certain files, security breaches can occur. As a result, the file system plays a very important role in system security.

Permissions

▶▶ See "chmod," p. 495

Linux file permissions control which users can access which files and commands. These permission bits control access rights for the owner, the associated group members, and other users. By using the `ls -l` command, you can generate a file list that shows the permissions field. The leftmost field shown by `ls -l` specifies the file permissions. For example, this field may look like `-rw-r-r-`. The first `-` in the field shows the file type. For regular files, this field is always `-`.

The next nine characters represent the file access permissions for the owner, group, and world, respectively. Each category takes up three characters in the permissions field, consisting of the characters `r`, `w`, and `x`. Any or all of these characters may be present. These characters represent read permission, write permission, and execute permission, respectively. If one of the permissions has been granted, the corresponding character is present. If permission is not granted, there is a `-` instead.

For example, if a file has a permission field that looks like `-rw-r-r-`, this indicates that the file is a regular file (the first character is `-`), the owner has permissions `rw-` (which means read and write, but no execute), and the other group members and the world at large both have permissions `r-` (which means read permission but no write or execute access). File permissions are changed via the `chmod` command.

Note

You can specify the permissions to the `chmod` command as octal values instead of the `rwx` symbolic values. Simply treat the three characters in a permission field as bits in an octal number—if the character is present, count it as a 1. So, the permissions `-rw-r-r-` are represented numerically as 644.

SUID and SGID Programs

There are two additional permission bits associated with a file—the SUID and SGID bits. SUID stands for Set User ID, and SGID is Set Group ID. Programs with these permissions behave as if they were owned by different UIDs when they are run. When an

SUID program is run, its effective UID is set the same as the user that owns the program on the file system, regardless of who is actually running the program. SGID is similar except that it changes the group ID instead. Although the SUID/SGID feature can be useful, it can present a big security hole. SUID programs are generally used when a program needs special permissions, such as `root` permission, in order to run.

Programmers usually go to great lengths to make sure that their SUID programs are secure. Most security holes in SUID programs occur when the program executes a command line, activates a shell, or runs a file that users can change to contain their own commands. Although some SUID programs are necessary, you should try to keep them to a minimum. You should also regularly scan your file systems to check for new SUID programs by using the `find` command. Refer to the man page for the exact syntax.

Social Engineering Threats

With all the different security features available on a Linux system, the biggest security hole is typically your users. After all, your users already have a valid account.

So what does this have to do with social engineering? What is social engineering, anyway? *Social engineering* is about convincing people to do what you want, either by playing on their assumptions or behavior or by outright misrepresentation and lying. People, in general, want to be helpful. And, if given the opportunity, they usually try to help out as much as possible. Crackers with good social engineering skills play on this characteristic.

Let's look at an example. Assume that you have a computer user, Mr. Jones. He is just your average user—not a guru at all. One day, Mr. Jones gets a call at the office that goes something like this:

Mr Jones: Hello.

Caller: Hello, Mr. Jones. This is Fred Smith in tech support. Due to some disk space constraints, we're going to be moving some user home directories to another disk at 5:30 this evening. Your account will be part of this move and will be temporarily unavailable.

Mr. Jones: Uh, okay. I'll be home by then, anyway.

Caller: Good. Be sure to log off before you go. I just need to check a couple of things. What was your logon ID again, `jones`?

Mr. Jones: Yes. It's `jones`. None of my files will get lost during the move, will they?

Caller: No sir. But I'll check your account just to make sure. What was the password on that account so I can get in to check your files?

Mr. Jones: My password is `tuesday`.

Caller: Okay, Mr. Jones. Thanks for your help. I'll make sure to check your account and verify that all the files are there.

Mr. Jones: Thank you. Bye.

So what just happened here? Someone called one of your users on the phone and managed to get both a valid user name and password in the course of the conversation. And you guessed it; if Mr. Jones calls tech support tomorrow, he will probably find that there is no Fred Smith working there!

How do you prevent things like this from happening? Educate your users. Your users should never give out a password over the phone to a caller. They should never leave one on either e-mail or voice mail. Crackers use social engineering by convincing users to give them what they want; they don't even have to try to break into your system.

Recording Use of the *su* Command

Linux verifies your identity by your logon ID/password combination. As you log on, your process is tagged with an ID that identifies you to the system. It is this UID that is checked for file and directory access. Linux offers the capability to switch to another UID while you are working. When users use the command `su`, they can become root or another user. They must know the password of the user that they are changing to. For example, for a user to change user ID to that of user `ernie`, the command is

```
su ernie
```

The user is then prompted for the password associated with the logon ID `ernie`.

To change to root, the command is

```
su root
```

The user is then prompted for the root password.

Typically, all attempts at using `su` are automatically logged on a system log file, such as `/var/adm/syslog`. Examine this file periodically to check on this sort of activity.

Developing a Secure System

Along with power comes responsibility. If not handled carefully, Linux's power to share information, processing resources, and peripherals can leave your system open to abuse. Your job is to set up system security so that only the right users and systems can connect to yours and that even they can use only the parts of your computer you want to share.

Security Threats

You can monitor your system for security threats. To determine who is using your system and the type of work they are doing, use the `ps` command. Be wary of jobs that seem to be running a very long time or users who seem to be using more resources than normal. These can be an indication that a logon has been compromised and an unauthorized user is running a program to guess passwords.

Controlling the Root

The root logon is reserved for your administrators. The person who logs on as the root has the power to erase any file, restrict use by any person on the network, and to quite literally cause havoc among users. That is the downside of the picture. Linux was designed to give the people having root access the tools to do their jobs better than in other environments.

Many proprietary operating systems have blockages established by the creators to avoid accidental damage to files and other operating factors on the system. The people who created UNIX and Linux took a different attitude toward the administrator. You will find tools that permit you to connect almost any computer device. You will find software that monitors the performance of the computer. You can create an endless array of software and adapt it to just about any business environment.

Additionally, you can force your users to do only specified things on the computer, or you can give them limited rights until they grow in their knowledge. The root user, the administrator, has the power to do these things.

> **Caution**
>
> Because access to the root is so important, some companies restrict use to a select few.

Modems and Crackers. Allowing access from a common modem, similar to those that people have at home, can permit someone to "crack" the system and destroy important data. As a result, many companies insist that the computer have elaborate security mechanisms, which can make these computers almost impossible to work with. Some companies put a dial-back option on the computer so that you must dial the computer and then wait for a return call before you can interact with the system.

Most of the time, a traditional UNIX/Linux approach is recommended. Make sure that all your user logons have passwords. Restrict the systems that can connect to your system. Keep permissions closed on sensitive files. Be careful of set UID bit programs (those that give the user who runs the program the permissions to run as another user). Most break-ins occur because someone left the door open.

Note

Ultimately, security is a problem with people rather than systems. You cannot allow passwords to be etched in the wall near a terminal or have DOS computers with root passwords embedded in communication programs.

Idle Terminals. Users should log off or use some kind of terminal lock program when they leave at the end of the day. Most UNIX systems have such a program that shuts down terminals left on beyond a prescribed length of time.

Enforcing Security. Security in defense firms is clearly understood. Companies that have highly sensitive products in the design cycle understand the need for security. But employees in a small distributor of plumbing parts may have a hard time understanding what everybody is so concerned about. Security in this example is not an issue until you can't figure out who removed a file that included a key proposal.

Employees should have a quick lesson about the sensitivity of data on your computer. A business has a significant investment in the data on the computer. Loss of data can be a distraction or it can mean chaos. Employees who are unwilling to participate in securing a computer should understand that this can be cause for dismissal.

For an administrator, the task becomes apparent. If you are the chief security officer for the network, how can you be sure that files and directories are adequately secured? Fortunately, there are many tools to help you, such as `umask`, `cron`, and UNIX itself.

Permissions seem to be a significant source of worry for most administrators. New administrators typically tighten up permissions and then field calls from people saying they can't gain access to a file they need or they can't execute a program on the system. After a while, these administrators loosen up the permissions so that anybody can do anything. The balancing act of securing the computer while permitting the proper people the tools to do their jobs is sometimes frustrating.

Handling Security Breaches. Security on a computer can require a little detective work. For example, look at the following:

```
# who -u<Return>
root   tty02   Jan 21 08:35   old   15677 Ofc #2
martha ttym1d  Jan 20 13:20   .     591   Payroll #1
ted    ttyp0   Jan 21 08:36   8:25  15763 Warehouse
margo  ttyp2   Jan 21 07:05   9:45  15761 CEO Ofc
root   ttyp4   Jan 21 08:36   .     15767 Modem #1
# date<Return>
Sun Jan 28 19:18:21 CST 1996
```

Suppose that you know that Martha left the office at 5 PM. Has someone found her password or did she leave the terminal on when she left? You can see that she logged on at 13:20 today. It is now 19:18, and somebody is active on the system using her logon. Do you dispatch security?

But what do you do if someone does break into your system? First of all, try to determine if you really do have an intruder. Many times, what you notice may just be the result of human error. If you do have an intruder, you have several options. You need to decide whether any damage was done, and the extent of the damage. Do you prosecute those responsible if you can catch them? If so, you should start trying to gather and protect evidence.

You must decide how to go about securing your system and restoring any damage from your backups. And probably the most important thing of all: document what you do. Start a log immediately. Sign and date any printouts showing evidence of intrusion. These may be useful as evidence. Your log may be invaluable in helping you figure out what you have done when you have to change or restore files.

Two other preventive measures that you should take are to make printouts of your basic system configuration files, such as `/etc/fstab`, and establish a site security policy. You must make sure that your users are aware of your site policy, and that they are reminded frequently.

Another area of concern is when an employee leaves the company. When an employee leaves, for whatever reason, personnel should contact the computer staff to retire the logon.

With all the different security considerations, how much security is enough? Can you have too much? You may be surprised to learn that you can have too much security. In general, if the cost of recovering from a security breach is less than the cost of security, you should reduce the security level for your systems. Note that these cost factors include much more than monetary costs. Among other things, you should take into consideration the content of your files, the amount of time and money that it will take to replace them, any lost productivity time that an attack would produce, and the effect that publicity of a computer security problem will have on your organization.

Backups

◂◂ See "Planning a Backup Schedule," p. 191

Few issues that the typical Linux administrator deals with are as important as the backup or archiving of a system. An administrator can be terminated or a company can literally fail because of the loss of valuable data. The disk or disks on a computer are electromechanical devices, and they will fail at some time.

Most new hard disks are rated at around 150,000 hours mean time between failures—more than five years. But the mean time statistic can be deceptive. Your disk could fail at the 50,000 hour mark or it might last for more than 10 years (highly unlikely). You are gambling if you only occasionally back up your systems, and you take an even greater chance if you aren't checking your backup tapes.

From Here...

You can find more information about security issues in the following chapters:

- Chapter 9, "Managing User Accounts," discusses the issues relating to creating and maintaining user accounts on Linux.
- Chapter 10, "Backing Up Data," describes how to set up and maintain backups of your system.

CHAPTER 12

Upgrading and Installing Software

The base Linux system initially contains only a core set of utilities and data files. The *system administrator* installs additional commands, user application programs, and various data files as required. Applications get updated frequently. System software changes as new features are added and bugs are fixed. The system administrator is responsible for adding, configuring, maintaining, and deleting software from the Linux system.

The word *installing* means copying the associated program files onto the system's hard disk and *configuring* the application (assigning resources) for proper operation on a specific system. The *configuration* of a program instructs it as to where parts of the application are to be installed and how it is to function within the system environment in general.

The Slackware distribution of Linux eases the pain of installing and upgrading software by including the `pkgtool` command. However, you will also find yourself installing software that is not in `pkgtool` format. Many of the software packages that are available on the Internet are in compressed `tar` format.

On large systems, an administrator usually installs applications because most users don't have access to the tape or floppy drives. Administrative permission is also often needed to install components of the applications into system directories. Components may include shared libraries, utilities, and devices that need to go into directories that a normal user can't access.

This chapter covers the following topics:

- Terms you need to know to understand Linux software upgrades and installation
- How to install Linux software packages using the `pkgtool` command
- How to install other software packages
- Concerns and methods for upgrading your Linux system
- Issues involved in upgrading your kernel

Key Terms Used in This Chapter

As you may have surmised if you read the introduction to this chapter, the installation of applications involves an expanded vocabulary. Table 12.1 lists some terms and definitions that you should become familiar with.

Table 12.1 Terms Related to Application Installation

Term	Definition
superuser	The highest privileged user on the system. Also called the *root user.*
system administrator	The person in charge of keeping the UNIX system optimized and properly running. The system administrator has superuser privileges and can install new software onto the system.
installing applications	The initial installation or update of a program for a UNIX system. The process usually requires superuser privileges and access to the computer's tape or floppy disk drive.
configuring	The act of setting up an application to work with your particular system. Configuring can include setting up the application for many users to use, putting it in accessible directories, or sharing it with the network.

The Politics of Upgrading

What software should you upgrade? How often should you upgrade? The answers to these questions are largely determined by the purpose of your system—personal or business—and the demands of your users. Software versions are changing all the time. Various parts of the Linux system are constantly being updated. You wouldn't have time to use your system if you tried to keep up with each and every upgrade that comes out.

Typically, you should not have to completely reinstall the entire Linux system when you upgrade your system software. Usually, only a very small portion of the system software changes with a new release. You may have to upgrade your kernel or upgrade your system libraries, but you probably will not have to do a full reinstall. However, when you upgrade software packages, you quite often have to completely install a new version, especially if you are several versions behind when you upgrade.

Note

It is a good idea to make a current backup of your system before upgrading software. That way, if something goes wrong, you can always get back to your original system.

◀◀ See "Considering Backup Tips," p. 190

In general, you should upgrade your system if a new version of either system or application software becomes available that either fixes a serious problem or adds functionality that you need. It is up to you to determine what constitutes a *serious* problem. If a new release of a software package fixes something that has caused problems on your system or fixes a bug that could damage your system, it is probably worth the time it takes to install it.

Don't try to keep up with every release of every piece of software—upgrading for the sake of upgrading takes too much time and effort. With a little research, you can keep your system working in good condition and update only the parts that need upgrading as you go along.

Installing Software

Installing a major program onto a Linux system is more complicated than installing a similar program on a single-task operating system, such as MS-DOS 6.2 or Apple Macintosh System 7. The multiuser nature of Linux means that every application on the system sometimes receives simultaneous calls for access.

To further complicate installation, most application programs—with the exception of very simple ones—require configuration to your specific system before they can be used. It is up to the system administrator installing the software to identify the items that are specific to the system's configuration when prompted during an application's configuration process.

For example, one user may have only an older character-based terminal while another has a fancy new X Windows terminal. The superuser must make sure that the application responds correctly to the older terminal, sending only characters (that is, letters and numbers), and that the X Windows terminal receives full advantage of the application's colors and graphics. The system administrator manages the system and has the responsibility of keeping it optimized (all programs up to current versions, proper user accounts assigned, and so forth).

As already stated, loading a program onto a Linux system is more complicated than doing so on single-user operating systems. The system administrator who is installing an application may have to create new directories to house the files associated with a particular program. Some software packages call for the configuring or reconfiguring of system devices. Although the end user worries only about learning the new program's features and operating commands, the superuser must make sure that system resources are properly allocated, configured, and maintained for the program (while, of course, not messing up any already installed applications).

Installing software using menus or commands is outwardly a relatively simple task; to the system itself, however, the task is complex. Applications for single-user operating systems, such as DOS programs, usually run only one copy of themselves at a time and have no competing programs. In even a simple Linux installation with only one user logged on, many processes can be running at the same time. Multiply this activity by several users all running programs—including some users who utilize the same application—and the complexity increases dramatically.

The Linux operating system excels at juggling a multitude of processes, programs, users, and peripherals simultaneously. To live in a Linux environment, an application must be properly loaded. An ill-behaved application, or one improperly installed, can cause a system crash (when a process or program goes wild and locks the CPU, causing it to lose control of all the currently running programs). The system shuts down, all users are kicked off, and their programs are interrupted. There is often much wailing and gnashing of teeth from frustrated persons in the midst of some complicated task.

As the one loading a new application, it is the responsibility of the system administrator or superuser to make sure that the application is compatible with the system and to test the application after it is installed.

Understanding the loading of software onto a Linux system first requires a basic knowledge of the responsibilities and privileges of the system administrator.

Understanding the Job of the System Administrator

If you use Linux on a small system, then you are probably your own system administrator. You install and run your applications. It is your responsibility to keep a current backup of files, maintain a proper amount of free space on the hard disk, make sure that the system runs optimally through memory management and other means, and do everything else required in the administration of an efficient and productive system. If you are a user in a larger system environment, there is probably a specific person who handles system administration. The following list briefly summarizes what the system administrator does:

- Starts and stops the system, as needed
- Makes sure that there is enough free disk space and that file systems are free of error
- Tunes the system so that the maximum number of users have access to the system's hardware and software resources, and so that the system operates as fast and as efficiently as possible
- Protects the system from unauthorized entry and destructive actions
- Sets up connections to other computer systems
- Sets up or closes user accounts on the system
- Works with vendors of software and hardware, and those who have training or other support contracts for the system

- Installs, mounts, and troubleshoots terminals, printers, disk drives, and other pieces of both system and peripheral hardware
- Installs and maintains programs, including new application programs, operating system updates, and software-maintenance corrections

Using *pkgtool*

Some Linux software, especially software that is included with a software distribution like Slackware, is bundled into a special package format. Slackware Linux provides the `pkgtool` program that installs software in this special format. If you have installed the Slackware distribution of Linux, you are already familiar with `pkgtool`. It is called by `setup`, the program that you ran to install Linux on your system.

The `pkgtool` program knows how to install the various software packages that make up the full Slackware distribution. These packages are bundled in *disk sets*, with each set represented by some letter code. A complete disk set may contain several different software components, but they are usually related, such as in the disk sets for networking or the disk sets for games. Each disk set also contains a file known as a *tagfile*. The tagfile tells `pkgtool` which software sets to install for a particular package.

If you run `pkgtool` without any arguments, you get an interactive menu system that enables you to select source and destination directories and the various disk sets that you want to install. In addition to running `pkgtool` from the menu system, you can also run `pkgtool` with command-line arguments that specify the various arguments for `pkgtool`. You will probably want to run `pkgtool` from the menu system most of the time. In the event that you should need to run it with command-line arguments, Table 12.2 lists the various arguments to the `pkgtool` command.

Table 12.2 Command-Line Arguments to the *pkgtool* Command

Argument	Description
`-sets` *`setlist`*	Tells `pkgtool` which disk sets to install. The *`setlist`* argument is a list of disk set labels separated by # characters, as in `-sets #A#C`.
`-source_mounted`	Tells `pkgtool` not to unmount and remount the source device with each disk.
`-ignore_tagfiles`	Causes `pkgtool` to ignore the instructions in the tagfiles and install every software component that it finds in a given disk set.
`-source_dir` *`dir`*	If you are installing multiple packages from disk sets, this argument gives the directory where the subdirectories for each disk are found. Not used for installing from floppy.
`-target_dir` *`dir`*	Specifies where the target directory is located.
`-source_device` *`dev`*	Specifies the source device to install from, usually a floppy drive. Not used with the `source_mounted` option.

Installing without *pkgtool*

Most of the different software packages that you will find are not in the form that `pkgtool` can install. Typically, these packages are downloaded via anonymous FTP from some archive site. The process of installing software can range from extremely simple to almost impossible. It all depends on how well the authors of the software wrote their installation scripts and how good their installation documentation is.

Deciphering Software Package Formats. The software packages that you get via anonymous FTP will virtually all be in the form of a compressed `tar` file. These files can be created in a couple of different ways. Typically, a directory tree containing source files, libraries, documentation, executables, and other necessary files is bundled into a `tar` file using the `tar` program. This `tar` file is then usually compressed to save space.

The software package will probably have an extension at the end of the filename that tells you what format it is in. If the file ends in `.gz`, it was compressed with the GNU `gzip` program. This is the most common file compression format for Linux software packages. If the archive name ends with a `.Z`, it was compressed with the `compress` program. Thus, the software package, `foo.tar.gz`, is a `tar` archive that has been compressed with `gzip`.

> **Note**
>
> Sometimes, a `tar` file that has been compressed with `gzip` is written with the `.tgz` extension instead of `.tar.gz`.

Installing the Package. The next thing that you have to do after you figure out the package format is figure out where you want to place the sources so that you can build the software package. Some software packages are fairly large, so it is a good idea to place them on a file system that has a good bit of free space. Some people create a separate file system for sources and mount it under a directory, such as `/usr/local/src` or `/src`. Wherever you decide to build your software packages, make sure that you have enough disk space so the software can be compiled successfully.

At this point, you can go ahead and move the software package to the source tree that you have set up and decompress it and expand the archive. If a file is compressed with `gzip`, you can decompress it with the `gzip -d` command. For example, the command

```
gzip -d foo.tar.gz
```

expands the compressed file `foo.tar.gz` and replaces it with the `tar` archive named `foo.tar`. For files that have been compressed with the `compress` command, use the `uncompress` command to expand them. The command

```
uncompress foo.tar.Z
```

expands the compressed file `foo.tar.Z` and replaces it with the `tar` archive named `foo.tar`.

After you have expanded the compressed file, you need to expand the `tar` file into a directory tree. You want to put the sources for each separate package in its own directory in your source tree. Before untarring the file, you should look at its `tar` listing to see if it was created with a directory as the first entry. Use the command

```
tar -tvf tarfile-name ¦ more
```

and see if the first entry in the `tar` file is a directory. If so, the `tar` file creates the directory when it is expanded. If there is no directory entry at the top level of the `tar` file, all the files at the top level are extracted into the current directory. In this case, you need to make a directory and move the `tar` file into it before you expand it.

Note

Always check for a top-level directory before expanding a `tar` file. It can be quite a mess if the `tar` file expands and places a few hundred files in the current directory instead of in a subdirectory.

Once you have the `tar` file where you want to expand it, you can use the command

```
tar -xvf tarfile
```

to expand the source tree in the tar file. At this point, the next step depends on how the software package that you are installing was written. Typically, you change directory to the top-level directory of the software sources and look for a file named something like `README.1ST`. There should be a few documentation files in the top-level source directory that explain the installation process.

The typical installation process involves editing the file named `makefile` to edit the destination directories where the software places its compiled binaries. You then usually run `make` followed by `make install`.

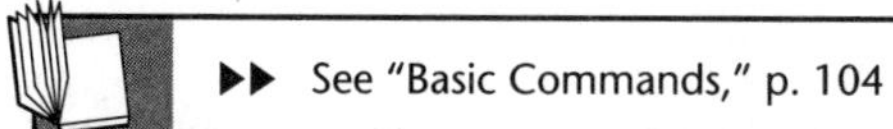

▸▸ See "Basic Commands," p. 104

This process is probably different with each package that you install. For some packages, there may be some sort of configuration shell script that asks you questions and then compiles the software for you. Make sure that you read the documentation files that come with the package.

Reviewing File Permissions

Setting permissions for a software package usually occurs automatically during installation. The installation script that comes with your application usually installs each file with the proper ownership and permissions. Only if something goes wrong and a user who should be able to access the program cannot do so are you required to find the directory the application was copied to and check the permissions.

Typically, the executable file that you run to start the application is installed with permissions that let any user run the file; however, only the superuser can delete or overwrite it. The application is usually installed in a directory that has read and execute permissions, but no write permissions.

Solving Problems

A well-written and well-supported application installs onto your system with minimal requests for information from you. It sets permissions properly so that all you have to do is test the program and inform your users that the application is now available. This is often done through e-mail.

But things can and do go wrong in the installation of programs and their subsequent operation (or nonoperation). If, for whatever reason, the program does not complete the loading process or fails to operate correctly after installation, it is your responsibility to determine why and to fix the problem.

If a program does not install completely, your troubleshooting efforts often require no more than reading the documentation and `README` files supplied with the application and looking for a list of exceptions or problems and their solutions. However, no one expects you to possess expertise and familiarity with the scores of software packages that are available for Linux. Occasionally, you'll require outside help.

If you can't solve the problem by using the information that came with the package, you should try looking on UseNet news to see if there is any discussion of the package in question. A question posted in the appropriate Linux group on UseNet can solve a lot of problems. If you can't find help on the Net, you can try to contact the application developer, usually via e-mail. Remember, Linux is free and so are most of the software packages that exist for Linux. Don't expect shrink-wrapped manuals and 24-hour technical support lines. But if you weren't the adventurous type, you wouldn't be using Linux—right?

Removing Applications

If an application is superseded by another, better package or is no longer used by any user on the system, removing it is a good idea. Disk space is always precious; you certainly don't want old, unused programs to hog space required by new applications.

Removal, like installation, of a program on a Linux system is more complicated than for single-user operating systems. It is sometimes not enough just to erase the application's files and remove its directory. Drivers and other software connections must be disconnected to avoid future problems. By taking notes and capturing the installation messages to a log file, you can usually figure out what was changed when the software was installed. You can then deduce what files to remove and which files to change in order to successfully delete a package.

Upgrading Your Kernel

Along with upgrades for other pieces of software, new versions of the kernel sources are released regularly. These may fix bugs or add new functionality. Alternatively, you may decide to upgrade your kernel because you need to reconfigure it or add new device drivers. In any case, the process is fairly straightforward. You should make sure that you have a backup of your system software and a Linux boot floppy before you start so that you can recover if you should damage your system.

The process for upgrading your kernel is described in detail in the Kernel HOWTO document. This document is regularly posted to the Linux newsgroups on the Internet and is available on the various Linux FTP sites, including **sunsite.unc.edu**. Make sure that you get a copy of this HOWTO and read it thoroughly before you start your kernel upgrade.

The first step in the basic process of upgrading your kernel is getting the new kernel sources. These are available via anonymous FTP from the various Linux archive sites. Once you have the sources, you need to preserve your current kernel sources. To do this, move your `/usr/src/linux` directory to another name, such as `/usr/src/linux.old`. Unpack the kernel sources in the `/usr/src` directory, which creates the `linux` subdirectory in the process. At that point, change to the `linux` directory and look at the documentation and the `README` files. Things may change as new kernels are released, so be sure to read the documentation.

From here, the process may vary a bit. Typically you type **`make config`** and press <Return>, which runs a configuration script and asks you questions about your system. If the configuration phase completes successfully, you then type something similar to **`make dep`** and press <Return>. This checks for all the file dependencies to make sure that the new kernel finds all the files it needs to compile.

After the dependency check is complete, you typically type **`make clean`** and press <Return>. This deletes any old object files that are left lying around in the kernel source directory. If everything has gone okay up to this point, you can type **`make`** and press <Return> to compile the new kernel. Once it compiles, you can install it with the LILO boot manager, and off you go.

Once again, make sure to read the Kernel HOWTO before trying to do this. It goes into deep detail on setting up your kernel and will probably save you hours of frustration. Also, it may keep you from trashing your current Linux system in the process.

From Here...

You can find more information about installing and upgrading software in the following chapters:

- Chapter 4, "Installing Linux," provides a detailed discussion about how to install and set up the Linux operating system.

- Chapter 5, "Running Linux Applications," provides a basic introduction to setting up your Linux system.
- Chapter 10, "Backing Up Data," looks at the process for making system backups.

Part IV

Network Administration

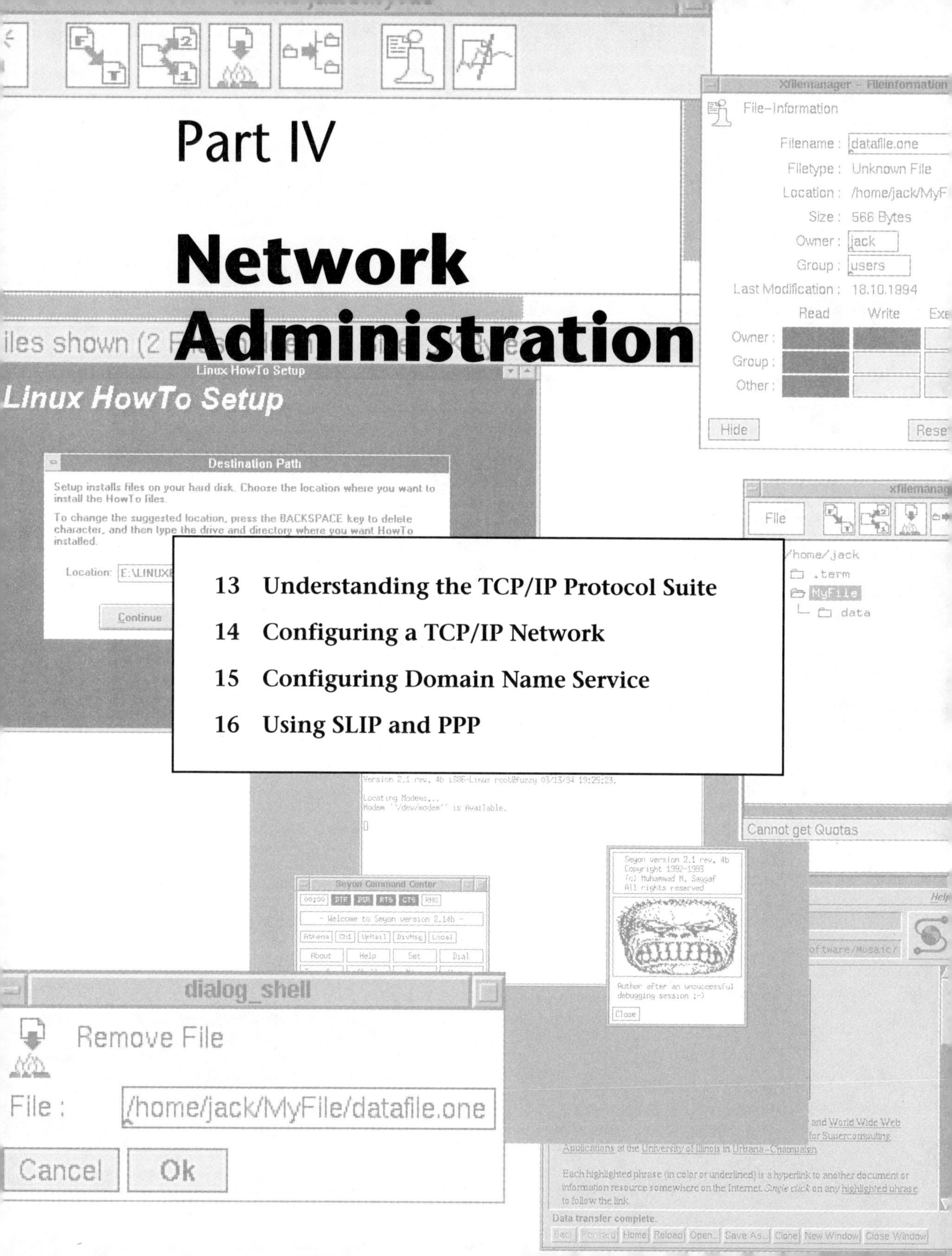

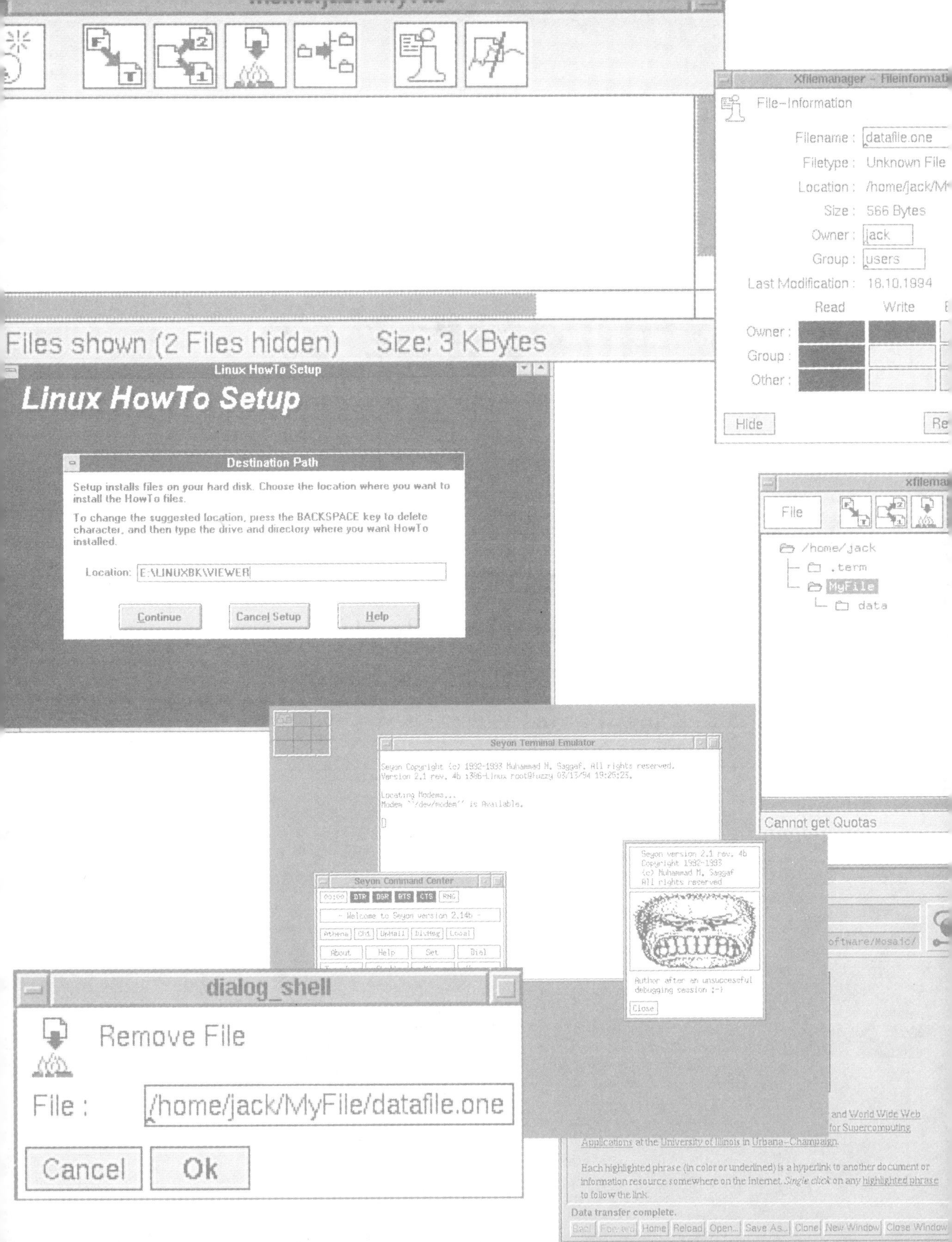

Xfilemanager - Fileinformati
File-Information
Filename : datafile.one
Filetype : Unknown File
Location : /home/jack/M
Size : 566 Bytes
Owner : jack
Group : users
Last Modification : 18.10.1994
Read
Write
Owner :
Group :
Other :
Hide
Files shown (2 Files hidden)
Size: 3 KBytes
Linux HowTo Setup
Linux HowTo Setup
Destination Path
Setup installs files on your hard disk. Choose the location where you want to install the HowTo files.
To change the suggested location, press the BACKSPACE key to delete character, and then type the drive and directory where you want HowTo installed.
Location: E:\LINUXBK\VIEWER
Continue
Cancel Setup
Help
xfilema
File
/home/jack
.term
MyFile
data
Cannot get Quotas
Seyon Terminal Emulator
Seyon Copyright (c) 1992-1993 Muhammad M. Saggaf. All rights reserved.
Locating Modems...
Seyon Command Center
DTR
DSR
RTS
CTS
RNG
About
Help
Set
Dial
Seyon version 2.1 rev. 4b
Copyright 1992-1993
(c) Muhammad M. Saggaf
All rights reserved
Author after an unsuccessful debugging session :-)
Close
dialog_shell
Remove File
File :
/home/jack/MyFile/datafile.one
Cancel
Ok
and World Wide Web
for Supercomputing
Applications at the University of Illinois in Urbana-Champaign.
Each highlighted phrase (in color or underlined) is a hyperlink to another document or information resource somewhere on the Internet. Single click on any highlighted phrase to follow the link.
Data transfer complete.
Home
Reload
Open...
Save As...
Clone
New Window
Close Window

CHAPTER 13

Understanding the TCP/IP Protocol Suite

The suite of widely used protocols known as Transmission Control Protocol/Internet Protocol (TCP/IP) has become increasingly important as national networks, such as the Internet and the proposed information superhighway, depend on it for their communications.

TCP/IP sprouted from initial development as a government-sponsored project to widespread use today, connecting networks of all sizes. Recognized for its ability to enable communication among dissimilar machines, it is found on virtually all workstations, minicomputers, and mainframes. This chapter describes the origins and language of TCP/IP, its addressing and naming conventions, and concepts fundamental to the creation of the Internet.

In this chapter, you learn:

- How TCP/IP has grown from its roots as a U.S. Department of Defense project into the preferred set of protocol suites used to connect to the Internet
- Basic TCP/IP and Internet terms
- The components that make up the TCP/IP protocols and how they compare to the other major computer networking architecture model, Open Systems Interconnection
- How addresses used by TCP/IP to identify systems on the Internet are assigned and used
- How logical networks can be broken down into smaller, physical networks
- How information can be routed from one TCP/IP network to another
- How the parts of a computer network—systems, routers, and other devices—can be put together to form a TCP/IP network that connects to the Internet

History of TCP/IP

In the mid-1970s, the U.S. Department of Defense (DOD) recognized an electronic communication problem developing within their organization. Communicating the ever-increasing volume of electronic information among DOD staff, research labs, universities, and contractors had hit a major obstacle. The various entities had computer systems from different computer manufacturers, running different operating systems, and using different networking topologies and protocols. How could information be shared?

The Advanced Research Projects Agency (ARPA) was assigned to resolve the problem of dealing with different networking equipment and topologies. ARPA formed an alliance with universities and computer manufacturers to develop communication standards. This alliance specified and built a four-node network that is the foundation of today's Internet. During the 1970s, this network migrated to a new, core protocol design that became the basis for TCP/IP.

The mention of TCP/IP requires a brief introduction to the Internet. The Internet connects hundreds of thousands of computers. Nodes include universities, many major corporations, and research labs in the United States and abroad. It is a repository for millions of shareware programs, news on any topic, public forums and information exchanges, and e-mail. Another feature is remote logon to any computer system on the network using the Telnet protocol. Because of the number of systems that are interconnected, massive computer resources can be shared, enabling large programs to be executed on remote systems.

Internet Terminology

The Internet protocol suite is composed of many related protocols based on the foundation formed by TCP and IP. To clarify the relationship of these components, Table 13.1 provides some definitions and notations.

Table 13.1 Networking Terms

Term	Definition
Datagram	Used interchangeably with the words *data packet* or *network message* to identify a unit of information that is exchanged.
DNS	Domain Name Service. A service provided by one or more computers in a network to help in locating a path to a desired node. This saves every system on a network from having to keep a list of every system it wants to talk to. Used by mail gateways.
GOSIP	Government Open System Interconnection Profile. A collection of OSI protocols used in United States government computer networks and projects.
Internet	A computer network based on TCP/IP and related protocols. A public network interconnecting businesses, universities, government facilities, and research centers.

Term	Definition
FTAM	File Transfer, Access, and Management. A file transfer and management protocol as specified by OSI.
FTP	File Transfer Protocol. A protocol that enables file transfer between systems.
IP	Internet Protocol. A protocol responsible for transporting datagrams across the Internet.
NFS	Network File System. A network virtual disk system that enables a client computer to mount remote file systems and directories. Originally developed by Sun Microsystems.
NIC	Network Information Center. Responsible for administering Internet, TCP/IP addresses, and network names.
Node	A computer on a network.
OSI	Open System Interconnection. The ISO standard model for defining data communication.
RFC	Request For Comments. The documentation maintained by the NIC relating to Internet protocols, addressing, routing, configuration, and other related Internet topics.
RIP	Routing Information Protocol. Used to exchange information between routers.
RMON	Remote MONitor. A remote network monitor that enables the collection of information about network traffic.
RPC	Remote Procedure Call. Enables procedures to be executed on a server.
SMTP	Simple Mail Transfer Protocol. Used to transfer electronic mail between systems.
SNMP	Simple Network Management Protocol. A protocol used to manage remote network devices and to collect information from remote devices related to configuration, errors, and alarms.
TCP	Transmission Control Protocol. The protocol between a pair of applications responsible for reliable, connection-oriented data transmission.
Telnet	The protocol used to establish remote terminal connections.
UDP	User DATAGRAM Protocol. A connectionless protocol used to transfer data between agents.
VT	Virtual Terminal. A method for using Telnet to log on to remote systems through the network.

Open Systems Interconnection Model

Many different types of computers are used today. These systems differ in operating systems, CPUs, network interfaces, and many other variables. These differences make the problem of communication between diverse computer systems important. In

1977, the International Organization for Standardization (ISO) created a subcommittee to develop data communication standards to promote multivendor interoperability. The result is the Open Systems Interconnection (OSI) model.

The OSI model does not specify any communication standards or protocols; instead, it provides guidelines that communication tasks follow.

Note

It is important to understand that the OSI model is simply a model—a framework—that specifies the functions that are to be performed. It does not detail *how* these functions are performed. ISO, however, does certify specific protocols that meet OSI standards for parts of the OSI model. For example, the CCITT X.25 protocol is accepted by ISO as an implementation that provides most of the services of the Network layer of the OSI model.

To simplify matters, the ISO subcommittee took the divide-and-conquer approach. By dividing the complex communication process into smaller subtasks, the problem becomes more manageable and each subtask can be optimized individually. The OSI model is divided into seven layers, as follows:

- Physical
- Data Link
- Network
- Transport
- Session
- Presentation
- Application

Tip

One easy way to remember the order of the layers (from the top down) is by making a sentence from the first letters of the layer names: All People Seem To Need Data Processing.

Each layer is assigned a specific set of functions. Each layer uses the services of the layer underneath it and provides services to the layer above it. For example, the Network layer makes use of services from the Data Link layer and provides network-related services to the Transport layer. Table 13.2 explains the services offered at each layer.

Note

The concept of a layer making use of services and providing services to its adjacent layers is simple. Consider how a company operates: the secretary provides secretarial services to the president (the next layer up) to write a memo. The secretary uses the services of a messenger (the next layer down) to deliver the message. By separating these services, the secretary (application) doesn't have to know how the message is actually carried to its recipient. The secretary merely has to ask the messenger (network) to deliver it. Just as many secretaries can send memos in this way by using a standard messenger service, a layered network can send packets by handing them to the network layer for delivery.

Table 13.2 Services Provided at Each OSI Layer

Layer	Description
Physical (Layer 1)	This layer provides the physical connection between a computer system and the network. It specifies connector and pin assignments, voltage levels, and so on.
Data Link (Layer 2)	This layer "packages" and "unpackages" data for transmission. It forms the information into frames. A *frame* represents the exact structure of the data physically transmitted across the wire or other medium.
Network (Layer 3)	This layer provides routing of data through the network.
Transport (Layer 4)	This layer provides sequencing and acknowledgment of transmission.
Session (Layer 5)	This layer establishes and terminates communication links.
Presentation (Layer 6)	This layer does data conversion and ensures that data is exchanged in a universal format.
Application (Layer 7)	This layer provides an interface to the application that a user executes: a "gateway" between user applications and the network communication process.

Caution

Do not confuse the Application layer with application programs you execute on the computer. Remember that the Application layer is part of the OSI model that does not specify *how* the interface between a user and the communication pathway happens; an application program is a specific implementation of this interface. A real application typically does Application, Session, and Presentation layer services, and leaves Transport, Network, Data Link, and Physical layer services to the network.

Each layer communicates with its peer in other computers. For example, Layer 3 in one system communicates with Layer 3 in another computer system.

When information is passed from one layer down to the next, a *header* is added to the data to indicate where the information is coming from and going to. The header-plus-data block of information from one layer becomes the data for the next. For example, when Layer 4 passes data to Layer 3, it adds its own header. When Layer 3 passes the information to Layer 2, it considers the header-plus-data from Layer 4 as data and adds its own header before passing that combination down.

In each layer, the information units are given different names (see Table 13.3). Therefore, by knowing the terms used to reference the data, you know which layer of the model is being discussed.

Table 13.3 Terms Used by OSI Layers to Refer to Information Units

OSI Layer	Information Unit Name
Application	Message
Transport	Segment
Network	Datagram
Data Link	Frame (also called *Packet*)
Physical	Bit

Before the advent of the OSI model, the U.S. Department of Defense defined its own networking model, known as the DOD model (and almost always called the Internet). The DOD model is closely related to the TCP/IP suite of protocols, as explained in the following section.

Looking at the TCP/IP Protocol Stack

The TCP/IP protocol stack represents a network architecture that is similar to the ISO OSI networking model. Figure 13.1 shows the mapping of TCP/IP layers onto the ISO protocol stack.

TCP/IP doesn't make as fine distinctions between the top layers of the protocol stack as does OSI. The top three OSI layers are roughly equivalent to the Internet Process protocols. Some examples of process protocols are Telnet, FTP, SMTP, NFS, SNMP, and DNS.

The Transport layer of the OSI model is responsible for reliable data delivery. In the Internet protocol stack, this corresponds to the host-to-host protocols. Examples of these are TCP and UDP. TCP is used to translate variable-length messages from upper-layer protocols and provides the necessary acknowledgment and connection-oriented flow control between remote systems.

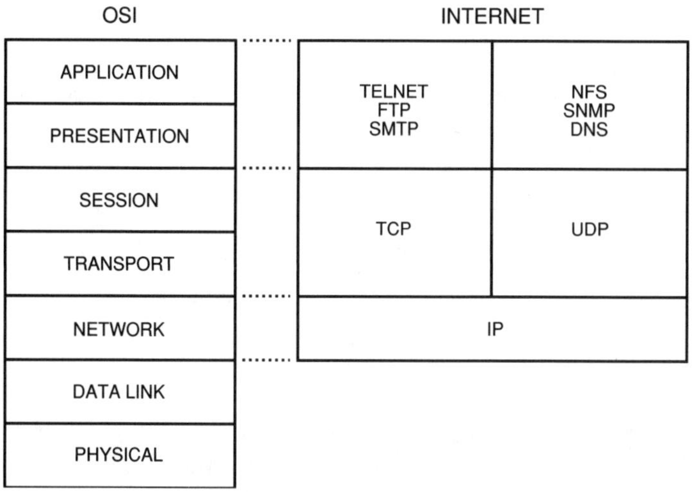

OSI

APPLICATION
PRESENTATION
SESSION
TRANSPORT
NETWORK
DATA LINK
PHYSICAL

INTERNET

TELNET
FTP
SMTP

NFS
SNMP
DNS

TCP

UDP

IP

Fig. 13.1

OSI and TCP/IP compared.

UDP is similar to TCP except that it is not connection-oriented and does not acknowledge data receipt. UDP only receives messages and passes them along to the upper-level protocols. Because UDP does not have any of the overhead related to TCP, it provides a much more efficient interface for such actions as remote disk services.

The Internet Protocol (IP) is responsible for connectionless communications between systems. It maps onto the OSI model as part of the Network layer. The Network layer of the OSI model is responsible for moving information around the network. This is accomplished by examining the Network layer address. This address determines the systems and the path to send the message.

IP provides the same functionality as the Network layer and helps to get the messages between systems—but it does not guarantee the delivery of these messages. IP may also fragment the messages into chunks and then reassemble them at the destination. Each of the fragments may take a different network path between systems. If the fragments arrive out of order, IP reassembles the packets into the correct sequence at the destination.

IP Addresses

The Internet Protocol requires that an address be assigned to every device on the network. This address is known as the *IP address* and is organized as a series of four octets. These octets each define a unique address, with part of the address representing a network (and optionally a subnetwork) and part representing a particular node on the network.

Several addresses have special meanings on the Internet, as follows:

- An address starting with a zero references the local node within its current network. For example, 0.0.0.23 references workstation 23 on the current network. Address 0.0.0.0 references the current workstation.
- The loopback address, 127, is important in troubleshooting and network diagnoses. The network address 127.0.0.0 is the local loopback inside a workstation.
- The ALL address is represented by turning on *all* bits, giving a value of 255. Therefore, 192.18.255.255 sends a message to all nodes on network 192.18; similarly, 255.255.255.255 sends a message to every node on the Internet. These addresses are important to use for multicast messages and service announcements.

Caution

It is important that when assigning node numbers to your workstations, you do not use 0, 127, or 255, as these are reserved numbers and have special meanings.

IP Address Classes

The IP addresses are assigned in ranges referred to as *classes*, depending on the application and the size of an organization. The three most common classes are A, B, and C. These three classes represent the number of locally assignable bits available for the local network. Table 13.4 shows the relationships among the different address classes, the available number of nodes, and the initial address settings.

Table 13.4 IP Address Classes

Class	Available Nodes	Initial Bits	Starting Address
A	2^{24}=167772	0xxx	0–127
B	2^{16}=65536	10xx	128–191
C	2^{8}=256	110x	192–223
D		1110	224–239
E		1111	240–255

Class A addresses are used for very large networks or collections of related networks. All educational facilities are grouped under a class A address. Class B addresses are used for large networks having more than 256 nodes (but less than 65,536 nodes). Class C addresses are used by most organizations. It is a better idea for an organization to get several class C addresses because the number of class B addresses is limited. Class D is reserved for multicast messages on the network, and class E is reserved for experimentation and development.

Obtaining IP Addresses. The administration of Internet addresses is through the Network Information Center (NIC):

Network Solutions
ATTN: InterNIC Registration Services
505 Huntmar Park Drive
Herndon, VA 22070
703-742-4777

It is a good idea to contact the NIC to obtain a unique IP address for your network. This prevents you from having to change all of your node addresses in the future if you decide to connect to the Internet. Having a unique IP address also allows for network management within your organization because you have a pre-allocated set of unique addresses that can be distributed to your computer systems. Getting a unique IP address for your network also prevents the duplication of node addresses and the assignment of addresses outside the range at which your systems can communicate.

The information to be provided to the NIC must be typed and in a certain order. The following is the order and information required:

1. The name of the governmental body sponsoring your connection to the Internet. If your network will not be connected, this information is not required.

   The format is as follows:

   - Sponsoring organization
   - Contact name
   - Contact title
   - Postal mailing address
   - Phone number
   - Net mailbox
   - NIC handle (if one is available)

2. The name, title, mailing address, phone number, and organization of the technical point of contact. This is the information relating to your organization. The information required is as follows:

   - NIC handle if available
   - Your name
   - Your title
   - Postal mailing address
   - Phone number
   - E-mail address if applicable

3. The name of your network. This is usually the company name up to 12 char-acters.
   - Network name
4. The network's geographic location and the responsible organization.
   - Postal address of main network site
   - Name of organization
5. This item is for DOD or military request only. This is for connection to NSFNET.
   - Should MILNET announce your network on NSFNET?
   - Is there an alternate connection to NSFNET?
   - If there is an alternate connection to NSFNET, should MILNET be a backup?
6. Make an estimation of the number of nodes on the network.
   - At time the network is installed
   - Number of connections in one year
   - Number of connections in two years
   - Number of connections in five years
7. This is where you can try to convince the NIC that you need a class B network number. Unless you have compelling reasons to need a class B network number, class C addresses will be assigned.

   What class should you request? Most of us have the notion that we should get what we need for today and the future. Although this is not a bad idea, a limited number of addresses is available. If you have 520 nodes to connect, you don't need a class B address. You should get three class C addresses, for a total of 768 nodes, and then expand in the future as needs dictate by obtaining more class C addresses.
8. Define the type of network, such as educational, research, commercial, defense, or government (non-defense).
9. Purpose of network. This is where you explain what the network will be used for.

After the required information has been submitted to the NIC, it takes about two weeks to obtain your addresses. This information is provided in detail in a document called `internet-number-template.txt` that can be obtained via anonymous FTP from **rs.internic.net** in the `templates` directory. The following section describes how to obtain RFCs.

Obtaining RFCs. In addition to assigning addresses, the NIC can provide other information of value. It is a repository for all technical documentation related to the Internet. It has a collection of documents that describe all the associated protocols, routing methodologies, network-management guidelines, and methods for using different networking technologies.

RFC stands for *Request for Comments*. RFCs can be obtained from the Internet by using the FTP protocol to connect to several different repositories. The RFC series is available on the Internet via anonymous FTP from a variety of sites, such as **ftp.internic.net** in the `/rfc` directory.

Table 13.5 provides a listing of the pertinent RFCs for establishing a network. Some of these documents go into great detail about how the different protocols function and the underlying specifications and theory. Others are more general and provide key information that can be useful to a network manager. At a minimum, an Internet network manager should know where these documents are located and how to obtain them. They provide information that can help in planning and growing an organization's network.

Table 13.5 RFCs of Interest

RFC Name	Description
`RFC791.txt`	Internet Protocol DARPA Internet Program Protocol Specification
`RFC792.txt`	Internet Control Message Protocol
`RFC793.txt`	Transmission Control Protocol DARPA Internet Program Protocol Specification
`RFC950.txt`	Internet Standard Subnetting Procedure
`RFC1058.txt`	Routing Information Protocol
`RFC1178.txt`	Choosing a Name for Your Computer
`RFC1180.txt`	A TCP/IP Tutorial
`RFC1208.txt`	A Glossary of Networking Terms
`RFC1219.txt`	On the Assignment of Subnet Numbers
`RFC1234.txt`	Tunneling IPX Traffic through IP Networks

Network Naming

The naming of network nodes requires some planning. When selecting names, keep network management and user acceptance in mind. Many organizations have network naming standards. If your organization has such standards in place, it is best to follow them to prevent confusion. If not, there is plenty of room for imagination. Computer and network names can be as simple as naming the workstations after the users, such as Diane, Beth, or John.

If you have many similar computers, numbering them (for example, PC1, PC2, ... PC128) may be appropriate. Naming must be done in a way that gives unique names to computer systems. Do not name a computer "thecomputerinthenorthoffice" and expect users not to complain. After all, even the system administrator must type the names of computers from time to time. Avoid names like "oiiomfw932kk." Although such a name may prevent network intruders from connecting to your computer, it may also prevent you from connecting to your workstation.

Names that are distinctive and follow a theme work well, helping the coordination of future expansion and giving the users a sense of connection with their machines. After all, it is a lot easier to have a good relationship with a machine called "sparky" than a machine called "OF1284."

Remember the following points when selecting a naming scheme:

- Keep names simple and short—six to eight characters at most. Although the Internet Protocol allows names up to 255 characters long, you should avoid this. (Each label can be up to 63 characters in length. Each part of a period-separated full domain name for a node is a label.)
- Consider using a theme such as the stars, flowers, or colors, unless other naming standards are required at your site.
- Do not begin the name with numbers.
- Do not use special characters in the name.
- Do not duplicate names.
- Be consistent in your naming policy.

If you follow these guidelines, you can establish a successful naming methodology.

Internet names are representative of the organizations and the functionality of the systems within the network. Following are examples of names that you can use:

```
spanky.engineering.mycompany.com
nic.ddn.mil
```

The following are examples of names that are difficult to use or remember:

```
thisismyworkstation.thelongwindeddepartment.longcompnam.com
34556nx.,m3422.mycompany.com
```

The last listed name could be encoded information about a workstation in room 345 on network 56 with network executive functions, but this type of naming is usually considered poor practice because it can lead to confusion and misdirected messages.

Internet names enable you to reference a user on a particular node, for example,

Eddie@PC28.Programming.mycompany.com

NIC Naming Tree. The NIC maintains a network naming tree. This tree is used to group similar organizations under similar branches of the tree. Figure 13.2 shows the naming tree. Major organizations are grouped under similar branches. This is the source for Internet labels, such as **com**, **edu**, and **gov**, that are seen in Internet names.

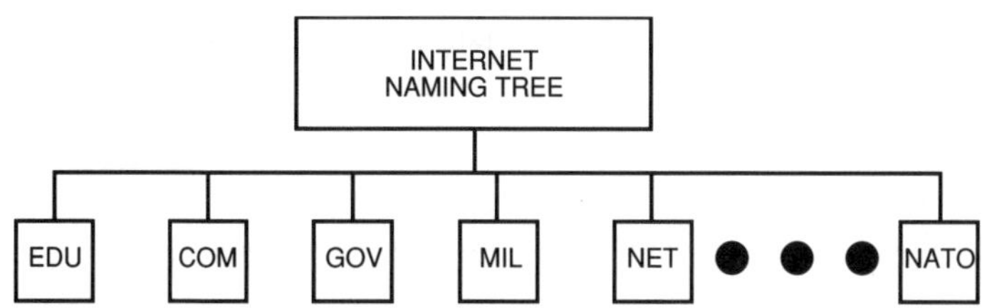

Fig. 13.2

The NIC naming tree.

Table 13.6 shows some of the common leaf names and definitions for the NIC tree. There are many other leaves under the tree, but these are the most common.

Table 13.6 Common NIC Names

Name	Type of Organizations
edu	Educational facilities (such as universities and colleges)
com	Commercial (most corporations)
gov	United States non-military government bodies (White House, Department of Agriculture)
mil	Military (military users and their contractors)
net	Internet network management and administration
org	Other types of organizations (usually non-profit)

Subnetworks

Subnetting is the process of dividing a large logical network into smaller physical networks. Reasons for dividing a network may include electrical limitations of the networking technology, a desire to segment for simplicity by putting a separate network on each floor of a building (or in each department or for each application), or a need for remote locations connected with a high-speed line.

The resulting networks are smaller chunks of the whole and are easier to manage. Smaller subnets communicate among one another through gateways and routers. Also, within an organization there may be several subnetworks that are physically on the same network. This may be done to logically divide the network functions into workgroups.

The individual subnets are a division of the whole. Suppose that a class B network is divided into 64 separate subnets. To accomplish this, the IP address is viewed in two parts: network and host (see fig. 13.3). The network part becomes the assigned IP address and the subnet information bits. These bits are in essence removed from the host's part. The assigned number of bits for a class B network is 16. The subnet part adds 6 bits, for a total of 22 bits to distinguish the subnetwork. This division results in

64 networks with 1,024 nodes in each. The network part can be larger or smaller, depending on the number of networks desired or the number of nodes per network.

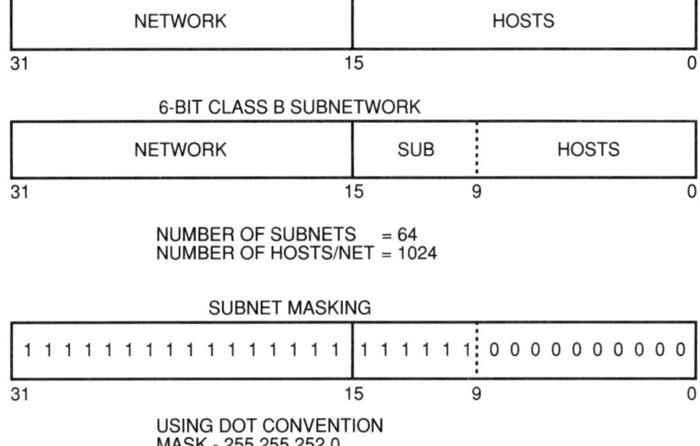

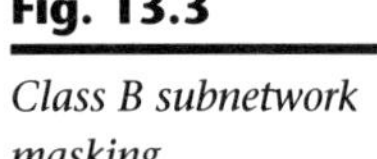

Fig. 13.3

Class B subnetwork masking.

Subnet Masks

Setting a subnet mask is a matter of determining where the network address ends and the host address begins. The subnet mask contains all 1s in the network field and 0s in the host field.

Suppose that a class C network is composed of the following:

```
N = network
H = Host
NNNNNNNN.NNNNNNNN.NNNNNNNN.HHHHHHHH
```

Each position represents a single bit out of the 32-bit address space. If this class C network is to be divided into four class C networks, the pattern resembles the following:

```
NNNNNNNN.NNNNNNNN.NNNNNNNN.NNHHHHHH
```

The subnet mask looks like the following:

```
11111111.11111111.11111111.11000000
```

If this address is written in base-ten dot notation, the subnet mask is 255.255.255.192. This mask is used to communicate among nodes on all subnetworks within this particular network.

If three bits are taken from the host field, eight networks can be formed, and the resulting network mask is as follows:

```
11111111.11111111.11111111.11100000
```

The subnet mask is 255.255.255.224. Each of the eight networks would have 29 nodes because five address bits are available. (It would be 32 except that all 1s, all 0s, and 127 are not legal addresses.)

This concept can be extended to class B and class A networks. The only difference is that the remaining fields are 0 (zero).

Consider a class B network. The address space is divided as follows:

```
NNNNNNNN.NNNNNNNN.HHHHHHHH.HHHHHHHH
```

If two bits are taken from the host field and added to the network part, the following subnet mask is used:

```
11111111.11111111.11000000.00000000
```

The mask is written as 255.255.192.0

The bits needed for the subnet mask can be taken from any of the bit positions within the host field—but this leads to complex subnet masks and address exclusions. You should avoid this if at all possible.

Routing

Routing is a method of transferring information between networks. A router works at the Network layer of network protocols. There are several different means by which data may be routed. The one implemented for an Internet network is the *Routing Information Protocol* (RIP).

Routing Information Protocol (RIP)

Information about routing can be obtained from several RFCs. At this writing, there are 21 different RFCs about routing. The one of most interest to network managers is RFC 1058, Routing Information Protocol (RIP). This RFC is dated June 1988 and discusses the protocol in detail.

The RIP is designed to be used in small to medium-sized networks and is based on Xerox Network Systems (XNS) routing protocols. RIP determines a message route by using a distance-vector routing algorithm. This algorithm assumes that each path is assigned a cost. This cost can be representative of network throughput, type of line, or desirability of the path. The protocol then determines the lowest cost path over which to transmit the message.

How a Routing Protocol Works

To maintain a list of hops to adjacent nodes, an RIP router keeps a routing table in the router or computer memory. This table is updated at 30-second intervals with information from neighboring routers. The information is used to recalculate the lowest cost path between systems. Each router on a network sends out, or advertises, and receives routing information.

The routing protocol is limited in the distance a message can be routed. Each router can route a message only to a cost of 16. If the message sent out on a wire costs more than 16, the host is deemed unreachable. Cost is a method of assigning values to different paths through the network and is a way of ensuring an efficient route to a destination when there is more than one way to get there.

When a network break occurs, the routers must relearn least-cost paths. This takes time and can result in messages being transmitted at higher cost for a period of time. When a node goes down, all routers must readjust their respective routing tables. During this time, messages can be lost in the network. After a period of time, the routers are again synchronized and routing continues.

Router crashes are also a concern. In the event of a crash, adjacent routers update their adjacency to a crashed router in 180 seconds. After that period of time, if no routing information is received from the crashed router, that path is removed from the local router's database.

The RIP does not manage routing distances, just cost. Because of this, the RIP may not use the shortest physical path between two points. Work and modifications have been made to the protocols to help correct this problem. A new routing protocol being developed and tested is *Open Shortest Path First* (OSPF). This protocol has begun to gain acceptance and use. Currently, Novell NetWare implements RIP.

Network Segmentation

Internet networks are divided into segments for a variety of reasons. Some of these reasons are related to the underlying networking technologies. Others are related to geographical locations. Some of the best reasons to isolate network segments are based on network usage. If a lot of traffic in a network is between a few nodes, it is best to isolate those nodes. This isolation drops the usage and provides a more responsive network for the other network users.

Other reasons to segment are to change networking technologies or to communicate between different networking technologies. For example, an office area may be running token ring and the shop floor area may be running Ethernet. Each has a distinct function. The office may require token ring to communicate with an AS/400. The shop floor may have Ethernet to enable shop floor controllers and computers to communicate. The shop floor information then may be uploaded to the office network for order tracking. The connection between the technologies is usually through routers. The routers forward only information that must be exchanged from one network to the other. This information can then be shared between nodes on the respective networks.

Excessive use of routers in a network can become a burden to the network, outweighing their benefits. The use of a router is of little benefit if all the nodes on one network must get to all the nodes on another network and vice versa. In this instance, the advantages of routing would be diminished because of the overhead in the routing protocols. In that kind of situation, a *bridge* is a better alternative.

A bridge enables all information from two networks to be shared. The access is at the Physical layer and not at the Network layer, so address translation and routing overhead are not incurred. A bridge enables all information, including system broadcast messages, to be transmitted. If two networks rarely share information, a router is a better choice; otherwise, a bridge is the proper choice.

Setting Up Internet Networks

The design and configuration of an Internet network is similar to the design of any computer network. It encompasses many types of nodes, including workstations, servers, printers, mainframes, routers, bridges, gateways, print servers, and terminals. The Internet requires that each device have a unique IP address. A device can have more than one address, depending on its function, but at least one address is required for communication with the other devices.

Types of Connections

A TCP/IP network can consist of several systems connected to a local area network or hundreds of systems with connections to thousands of systems on the Internet. Each organization can create the type of network appropriate for its needs.

Figure 13.4 shows a simple network. This network consists of several workstations and a file server. Each station on the network is assigned the network address of 194.62.23. Each device is assigned an individual node address. This network is typical of most departments within a company or even a small office. There is room to connect printers and more workstations to the network. The network has no provisions for connections to other local or wide area networks.

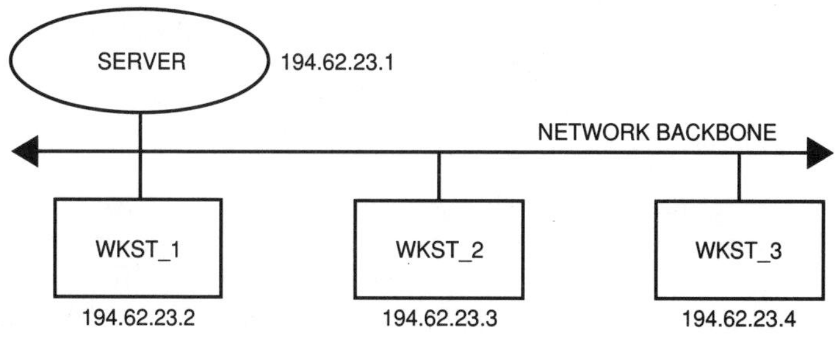

Fig. 13.4

A simple network.

The network in Figure 13.5 is more complex. It includes three separate networks interconnected through a combination of routers and servers. Each of the workstations and computers on each segment may or may not be isolated from using information on one of the other two networks. This is a characteristic of the subnet mask and security enabled on the servers and routers.

Information from one network is routed to one of the other networks on an as-needed basis. This type of configuration is typical of most large corporate networks. It may be chosen based on physical-length limitations of the underlying network technology or individual network loading. One or more of the networks may experience high traffic that must be distributed across several networks.

Fig. 13.5

A more complex network.

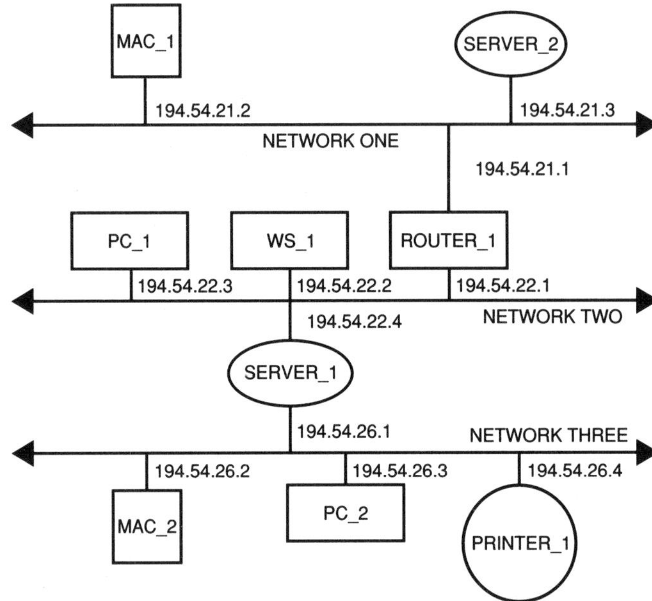

Router 1 between networks 1 and 2 provides for routing information between the two networks. If server 1 connecting networks 2 and 3 has routing enabled, information from network 3 to network 2 is routed. Also, information can be routed from network 3 to network 2 by means of server 1 and from network 2 to network 1 by means of router 1. Server 1, connecting networks 2 and 3, has two IP addresses: one IP address on network 2 and another address on network 3. The same is true for router 1, with addresses on network 2 and network 1.

Consider a situation in which there is a lot of Internet network traffic between network 3 and network 1. In this case, it may be worthwhile to place an additional router between network 1 and network 3. The additional router can eliminate some of the routing overhead on server 1 and enable information to be passed between networks when server 1 is down.

The additional router can add a level of fault tolerance to the network. This fault tolerance is based on the fact that information can still be routed to network 2 from network 3, even when server 1 is down. The path between network 3 and network 2 would be through network 1 and router 1. The addition of router 2 is shown in Figure 13.6.

The fault tolerance of a network improves its integrity and can be of particular importance in certain applications. If time-critical information must be shared between two networks, an alternative path should be provided between the networks. This could be provided through the use of additional routers. Because these paths may be indirect (through a third network), a configuration parameter should be used.

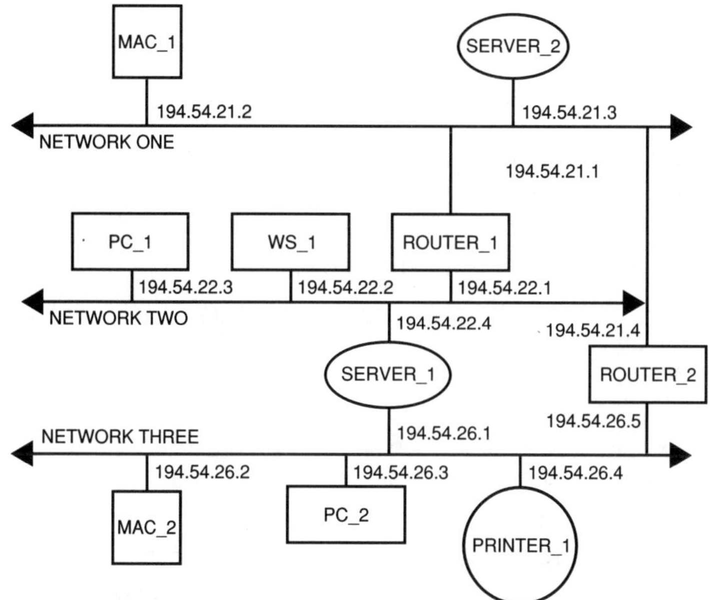

Fig. 13.6

Adding a second router for fault tolerance.

This parameter is usually referred to as *network cost*. The cost of a hop can be increased by increasing the value a packet takes across a network path. The default preferred path is the low-cost path; the alternative path is the high-cost path. This arrangement prevents information from being routed over the high-cost path on a regular basis.

Figure 13.6 shows an additional router added between network 1 and network 3. The desired path for information from network 3 to network 2 is through server 1. Because router 2 connects network 3 and network 1, information can be routed between those two networks. Also, because router 2 is between network 1 and network 2, information is routed through that path. Information from network 3 that is bound for network 2 can go over one of the two paths: either through server 1 or through router 2 and router 1. The latter is not the preferred path, because information can be routed directly over server 1. Therefore, a higher cost is assigned to the path of router 2 and router 1 from network 2. This type of path analysis must be performed in a multiple-segment network.

Choosing a Networking Configuration

The physical media used by an Internet network can be almost any network technology in current use. Internet network traffic is not limited to Ethernet, ARCnet, or token ring. It can travel over asynchronous RS 232, T1 lines, and through frame-relay. Whatever networking topology is selected for the network, the configuration, installation, and operation rules associated with that networking technology must be followed.

Keep in mind the bandwidth that an application requires. Many applications require megabytes of data to be transferred, so bandwidth becomes a prime consideration. Another consideration is the physical location of the network. If all nodes are in the same building, a single LAN can be used. However, if the networks are located across town, a T1 connection may be needed. If the nodes are located in different geographic locations, a frame relay or a packet switched network can be used.

In laying out a network, you must consider the type of information to be carried over the network, the physical location, and network loading. To help determine the capacity of the network, examine the type of workstations, servers, and applications.

If diskless workstations are used in a network, a higher network load is placed on the network for each node. The reason for this is that each remote diskless workstation requires all operating system code to be downloaded through the network. Because all applications and utilities as well as data files are stored remotely, every action on that workstation requires network access.

Also of concern is the amount of NFS traffic that will occur on the network. NFS provides remote virtual disk services, so information retrieved and stored on these remote disks is constantly used on the network.

Other considerations are large graphical images, swapping and page files used for virtual memory, distributed database applications, printer traffic, and terminal traffic. These are all considerations in any network, but the designers and users of PC LANs do not usually have to contend with them. When a network is connected into a general user community, all aspects of the networking environment come into play.

Other items to be examined are the need for dial-up and remote access. If this access is related to terminal and screen traffic, a serial port from an existing system may suffice. If a Serial Line IP (SLIP) connection is made, you must consider how much overhead it will impose on the network when users are loading software utilities, programs, and databases over the phone lines. This is of concern because IP is not limited to a high-speed link like Novell IPX and other networking protocols.

Network Configuration Guidelines

A network must be designed based on guidelines and rules. Some questions to consider when planning a network include the following:

- How will the network be used today?
- How will the network be used next year and the year after?

- What applications are going to be used on the network?
- Will workgroups within the organization require networking resources in the future?
- What types and numbers of workstations will be on the network?
- How many servers, minicomputers, and other hosts will be on the network?
- What other network devices, such as printers and plotters, will be on the network?
- Will shared disk arrays and optical jukeboxes be necessary?
- Will management of the network be centralized?
- Will the network be connected to the Internet or other corporate networks, or will it be the basis for a wide area network?
- What other protocols will utilize the networking technology (IPX, DECNET, LAT, OSI protocols, and TCP/IP)?
- Where will critical data be interchanged (determine several different paths)?
- How will the network grow and change?

After you address all these questions, the network can be defined. The number of nodes indicates how many class C address spaces are needed or whether a class B is needed.

Connection to remote facilities should also be addressed. The load can be distributed across multiple network segments. Try to minimize the traffic that has to go across networks. For example, if you have two systems that exchange a lot of information and hops across three networks are required for them to communicate, consider moving the systems to the same network.

Determine the best networking topology to meet the requirements specified in the network analysis. To allow for growth in the network, the best approach is to determine the maximum load and develop a network in which that load is at a minimum.

Routers and Bridges

Special-purpose devices are used to provide connections between networks and systems. Sometimes the terms *gateway* and *router* are used interchangeably. Strictly speaking, *gateway* describes a system that sends messages between different types of networks; a *router* sends messages between networks of the same type.

In this text, *router* is routinely used to describe any device that takes messages from one network and passes them through to another network. The router contains enough intelligence to know whether the message received must be forwarded to another network or a router.

Routers operate at the Network layer and are usually associated with a protocol, such as IP or IPX. Most routers that route IPX traffic can route IP traffic as well. The router is used to connect multiple local and wide area networks. It provides a method of sharing data between networks. Also, because a router works at the Network layer, it can help reduce broadcast traffic.

If one network uses a lot of different protocols and another network only uses IP, a router that routes only IP messages is needed if those two networks are to communicate. The router prevents messages from being placed on a network that cannot manage them.

Bridges, on the other hand, can be used to interconnect local and wide area networks; they share information regardless of protocol. A bridge allows two interconnected networks to have many different protocols on them at the same time. The messages forwarded by a bridge usually do not contain any further routing information. The messages are usually left undisturbed.

One drawback of bridges is that all network broadcast and multicast messages from all interconnected networks are seen on all legs connected by a bridge. This results in a lot of overhead related to network update messages. Additionally, a bridge forwards messages only to network addresses on the other side of the bridge, but it can forward all network protocols and broadcast messages.

Note

Use bridges only if multiplc protocol packets are to be shared. Otherwise, a router is a better choice because it helps reduce network overhead.

Routers and bridges are used to share information between networks. The appropriateness of each is determined by networking requirements, the protocols involved, network capacity, and user demands. The proper selection of components can help a network operate efficiently, allow for future growth, and help ensure continued reliability.

Summary

Using TCP/IP and related Internet protocols in a network allows for growth and expandability. As the number of computer vendors migrating their systems from proprietary protocols to open communication protocols increases, the need for TCP/IP also increases. Internet Protocols and the suite of related protocols provide the same network services provided by proprietary network schemes in the past. Virtual disk support, network printing, remote booting, routing, and virtual terminal support are offered throughout the Internet Protocol suite.

Applications emerging today and in the future require many different computer systems to share information and programs. Whether these systems are across the hall or across the world, the Internet Protocols can help the information to be shared in a reliable and efficient manner.

The Internet Protocol suite provides for the connection of more than four billion computers. This wide address space has been divided into smaller address segments to help manage addressing and networks. The Internet Protocol suite has been in existence for more than 20 years and continues to expand in functionality.

In the future, there may be a formal convergence of OSI and Internet Protocols. This is being initiated by the U.S. government's adoption of GOSIP (Government OSI Protocol). Networking technology continues to grow and change to meet the needs of the networking community.

From Here...

You can find more information about TCP/IP in the following chapters:

- Chapter 14, "Configuring a TCP/IP Network," shows how to set up and configure your networking system for Linux.
- Chapter 15, "Configuring Domain Name Service (DNS)," explains the Internet name resolution system.
- Chapter 16, "Using SLIP and PPP," shows how to configure asynchronous TCP/IP over serial lines.

CHAPTER 14

Configuring a TCP/IP Network

Configuring a TCP/IP network is one of the more common tasks you will face when administering Linux machines. In the most basic cases, it is not very complex; however, it requires a bit of thought on the design of your network and knowledge of a small number of programs and configuration files. In this chapter, you learn how to do the following:

- Create network configuration files for TCP/IP
- Configure your Ethernet interfaces with the `ifconfig` program
- Specify routes and other networking information using the route program
- Use the `netstat` program to monitor and troubleshoot networking problems
- Use the `netconfig` program to simplify configuring TCP/IP

TCP/IP Configuration Files

TCP/IP networking in Linux is controlled by a set of configuration files in the `/etc` directory. These files tell Linux what its IP address, host name, and domain name are and control the network interfaces. Table 14.1 shows you what each file does. The following sections discuss these files in detail.

Table 14.1 Linux TCP/IP Networking Configuration Files

File	Description
`/etc/hosts`	Maps host names to IP addresses.
`/etc/networks`	Maps domain names to network addresses.
`/etc/rc.d/rc.inet1`	Script that configures and activates your Ethernet interfaces at boot time.

The */etc/hosts* File

Every computer on a TCP/IP network has an IP address, canonical host name, and zero or more host name aliases. The `/etc/hosts` file is the original method for mapping host names to IP addresses. For illustrative purposes, we will examine the network that Tristar, Inc. has built. This network consists of the single Class B network address assigned to Tristar by the NIC; this network has been split into two Class C subnetworks. The format for the hosts file is demonstrated in the following example:

```
# /etc/hosts for unix1.tristar.com
#
# For loopbacking.
127.0.0.1      localhost

# This machine
166.82.1.21      unix1.tristar.com unix1     # the local machine

# Other hosts on our network
166.82.1.20      server.tristar.com server     # the server
166.82.1.22      wk1.tristar.com               # workstation 1
166.82.1.10      netpr1.tristar.com netpr1     # networked printer
166.82.1.1      gateway.tristar.com gateway     # the router
166.82.1.1      gate-if1                # 1st interface on gateway
166.82.2.1      gate-if2                # 2nd interface on gateway
166.82.1.30      unixlt.tristar.com unixlt     # Laptop via PLIP

# end of hosts file
```

Tip

It's a good idea to give a unique name to each network interface on a machine. Doing so makes it easier to see what's going on when you use the `ifconfig` and `route` commands. Note that the preceding gateway has two host names for the IP address `166.82.1.1`.

The format of the hosts file consists of one IP address per line beginning in the first column, the canonical host name associated with that address, and then zero or more aliases. The fields are separated by spaces or tabs. Empty lines and text following a # character are treated as comments and are ignored.

The IP address `127.0.0.1` is known as the local loopback address and is reserved for this purpose. It is normally assigned the name `localhost`. If you are going to use your machine only as a stand-alone system or use SLIP or PPP to connect to the outside world, you need only the `localhost` address in your hosts file.

Note

The function of the `/etc/hosts` file has been mostly taken over by Domain Name Service (DNS) on machines connected to the Internet or large internal networks. However, DNS is not available during boot-up or when you are running in single-user mode, so it's a good idea to place the information for essential machines such as servers and gateways in `/etc/hosts`.

On a network with only a few machines that is not connected to the Internet, it is easier to keep a complete listing of all hosts in `/etc/hosts` instead of configuring and maintaining DNS.

Tip

Naming your networks makes it convenient to do things such as static routing that take either a host name or network name. You don't have to remember the subnets by their IP addresses, just their names.

The */etc/networks* File

Just as hosts have names and IP addresses, networks, and subnets can be named. This naming is handled by the `/etc/networks` file. The following is an example file for `tristar.com`.

```
# /etc/networks for tristar.com

localnet     127.0.0.0      # software loopback network
tristar-c1     166.82.1     # Development Group Network, Class C
tristar-c2     166.82.2     # MIS Network, Class C

# end of networks file
```

First is the `localnet` name and IP address, `127.0.0.0`. If you are not connecting your Linux machine to a TCP/IP network or are only using SLIP or PPP, this is all you need to put in this file. The next lines identify the two Class C subnetworks that Tristar has made from its Class B network.

The IP addresses in the networks file include only the network address portion plus the subnetwork byte.

Initializing Ethernet Interfaces

The `ifconfig` program makes network interfaces such as the software loopback and Ethernet cards known to the Linux kernel. This must be done before Linux can use them. The `ifconfig` program is also used to monitor and change the state of network interfaces. A simple invocation of `ifconfig` is

```
ifconfig interface address
```

This activates the specified network interface and assigns an IP address to it. This is called *bringing up* an interface. The generalized calling syntax for `ifconfig` is

```
ifconfig interface [[-net¦-host] address [options]]
```

The `-net` and `-host` flags force `ifconfig` to treat the address as either a network or host address. Table 14.2 lists the command-line arguments for `ifconfig`.

Table 14.2 Command-Line Arguments for *ifconfig*

Argument	Description
`interface`	The name of the network interface. This is usually the name of the device driver followed by an identification number. This argument is required.
`aftype`	This specifies the address family that should be used for decoding and displaying all protocol addresses. Currently, the inet (TCP/IP) and AX.25 (amateur packet radio) address families are supported. The inet family is the default.
`up`	Using this option activates the specified interface.
`down`	This option deactivates the specified interface.
`[-]arp`	Turns on or off the use of the ARP protocol on the specified interface. The minus sign is used to turn off the flag.
`[-]trailers`	Turns on or off trailers on Ethernet frames. This is not currently implemented in the Linux networking system.
`[-]allmulti`	Turns on or off the promiscuous mode of the interface. Turning this mode on tells the interface to send all traffic on the network to the kernel, not just traffic addressed to your machine.
`metric` *N*	Sets the interface metric to the integer value *N*. The metric value represents the "cost" of sending a packet on this route. Route costing is not currently used by the Linux kernel but is to be implemented at a future date.
`mtu` *N*	Sets the maximum number of bytes the interface can handle in one transfer to the integer value *N*. The current networking code in the kernel does not handle IP fragmentation, so make sure the MTU value is set large enough.
`dstaddr addr`	This sets the IP address of the other end of a point-to-point link. It has been made obsolete by the `pointopoint` keyword.
`netmask addr`	This sets the IP network mask for the specified interface.
`[-]broadcast [`*addr*`]`	This sets the broadcast address for the interface when an address is included. If no address is given, the `IFF_BROADCAST` flag for the specified interface is turned on. A leading minus sign turns off the flag.
`[-]pointopoint [`*addr*`]`	This option turns on point-to-point mode on the specified interface. This tells the kernel that this interface is a direct link to another machine. The address, when included, is assigned to the machine on the other end of the list. If no address is given, the `IFF_POINTOPOINT` flag for the interface is turned on. A leading minus sign turns off the flag.
`hw`	This option sets the hardware address for the specified interface. The name of the hardware class and the ASCII equivalent of the hardware address must follow this keyword. Ethernet (`ether`), AMPR AX.25 (ax25), and PPP (ppp) are currently supported.
`address`	This is the host name or IP address to be assigned to the specified interface. Host names used here are resolved to their IP address equivalents. This parameter is required.

You don't normally need to use all of the options. `ifconfig` can set everything needed from just the interface name, netmask, and IP address assigned. You only need to explicitly set most parameters when `ifconfig` misses or you have a complex network.

Caution

If your Linux machine is on a network, the `ifconfig` program must be kept secure from unauthorized use. Setting a network interface to promiscuous mode allows a person to snoop in your network and get sensitive data such as passwords. This is a serious breach of security.

Using *ifconfig* to Inspect a Network Interface

Running `ifconfig` with just an interface name on the command line prints the status of the interface. Running `ifconfig` with no arguments causes it to output the status of all network interfaces the kernel knows about. The following demonstrates this:

```
$ ifconfig lo
lo        Link encap Local Loopback
          inet addr 127.0.0.1 Bcast 127.255.255.255 Mask 255.0.0.0
          UP LOOPBACK RUNNING MTU 2000 Metric 1
          RX packets 0 errors 0 dropped 0 overruns 0
          TX packets 1658 errors 10 dropped 0 overruns 0
```

This example uses `lo`, the software loopback interface. You can see the assigned IP address (`inet addr`), broadcast address (`Bcast`), and netmask (`Mask`). The interface is `UP` with an `MTU` of `2000` and a `Metric` of `1`. The last two lines give statistics on the number of packets received (`RX`) and transmitted (`TX`), along with packet error, dropped, and overrun counts.

Configuring the Software Loopback Interface

All Linux machines that have the networking layer installed in the kernel have a software loopback interface. This interface is used to test networking applications and to provide a network for local TCP/IP services such as INN when the machine is not connected to a real network.

The network interface name for the loopback system is `lo`. Type the following to run `ifconfig`:

```
ifconfig lo 127.0.0.1<Return>
```

This activates the loopback interface and assigns the address `127.0.0.1` to it. This is the address traditionally used for the loopback because the Class A network, `127.0.0.0`, will never be assigned to anyone by the NIC.

To make the loopback system fully operational, you need to add a route for it with the `route` command, which is discussed later in this chapter.

Configuring a Network Interface

Configuring an Ethernet network interface takes a little bit more work, especially if you are using subnetworks. The basic call to `ifconfig` looks like this for `unix1.tristar.com`:

```
ifconfig eth0 unix1
```

This causes `ifconfig` to activate Ethernet interface 0, look up the IP address for `unix1` in the `/etc/hosts` file, and assign it to this interface. Examining the `eth0` interface at this point reveals the following code:

```
$ ifconfig eth0
eth0      Link encap 10Mbps Ethernet HWaddr 00:00:E1:54:3B:82
          inet addr 166.82.1.21Bcast166.82.1.255 Mask 255.255.255.0
          UP BROADCAST RUNNING MTU 1500 Metric 0
          RX packets 3136 errors 217 dropped 7 overrun 26
          TX packets 1752 errors 25 dropped 0 overrun 0
```

Note that the broadcast address and netmask were set automatically by `ifconfig` based on the IP address it found in `/etc/hosts`. If you are using subnetworks, you need to specify the broadcast address and netmask explicitly. For example, if you have a Class C network and are using the first bit in the host portion of the address to make two subnetworks, then you must specify the broadcast address and netmask when running `ifconfig`.

```
ifconfig eth0 unix1 broadcast 166.82.1.127 netmask 255.255.255.128
```

Configuring Parallel IP Interfaces

The Parallel IP (PLIP), Serial Line IP (SLIP), and Point-to-Point Protocol (PPP) interfaces are managed by `ifconfig` somewhat differently. To bring up a PLIP interface, you add the `pointopoint` option to the `ifconfig` command line. Assume that the Tristar laptop `unixlt` is attached to the first parallel port on `unix1`. You call `ifconfig` like this to activate the PLIP link:

```
ifconfig plip0 unix1 pointopoint unixlt
```

This activates the `plip0` interface with the IP address for `unix1`, sets the `pointopoint` flag, and tells the interface that the IP address for the other end of the link is `unixlt`. `ifconfig` looks up the IP addresses for `unix1` and `unixlt` in `/etc/hosts` and assigns the addresses appropriately. On a laptop, you use the analogous call

```
ifconfig plip0 unixlt pointopoint unix1
```

▶▶ See "Requirements for SLIP and PPP," p. 283

TCP/IP Routing

Routing determines the path a packet takes from its source through the network to its destination. This path is determined by matching the destination IP address against the kernel routing tables and transmitting the packet to the indicated machine, which may or may not be the destination of the packet. The kernel routing table contains information of the form "To get to network X from machine Y, send the packet to machine Z with a cost of 1," along with time-to-live and reliability values for that route.

Routing Policy

The first step in setting up routing on your network is deciding on a routing policy. For small, unconnected networks, using the `route` command to set up static routes on each machine at boot time is sufficient. Large networks with many subnets or networks connected to the Internet need to use dynamic routing. The routed program provides dynamic routing by communicating with routed programs on other machines and installing routes based on what it learns about the topology of the network.

A very common strategy combines static and dynamic routing. Machines on each subnet use static routing to reach their immediate neighbors. The default route, the route used for packets that match no other route in the routing table, is set to a gateway machine that is doing dynamic routing and knows about the rest of the world. Large networks can be constructed this way, minimizing the hassle of configuration files and the amount of bandwidth used by the dynamic routing programs.

Using the */sbin/route* Program

The `/sbin/route` program manipulates the kernel routing table and is used to set static routes to other computers or networks via interfaces that have been configured and activated by `ifconfig`. This is normally done at boot time by the `/etc/rc.d/rc.inet1` script. Table 14.3 describes the command-line arguments for `/sbin/route`.

Table 14.3 Command-Line Arguments for */sbin/route*

Argument	Description
`[none]`	Giving no option to `/sbin/route` causes it to output the current routing table.
`-n`	This causes the same output as giving no option but replaces host names with their numerical IP addresses.
`del`	The `del` argument deletes the route for the specified destination address from the routing table.
`add`	The `add` argument adds to the routing table a route to the specified address or network.

Examining the Kernel Routing Table. Running `/sbin/route` without any command-line arguments or just `-n` outputs the routing table, which looks like this:

```
/sbin/route
Kernel routing table
Destination Gateway Genmask   Flags Metric Ref UseIface
127.0.0.0   *       255.0.0.0 U     0      0   100 lo
```

This is from a machine with just the loopback interface activated. Table 14.4 describes the fields in the routing table report.

Table 14.4 Explanation of the Fields in the Routing Table Report

Field	Description
`Destination`	The destination IP address of the route.
`Gateway`	The host name or IP address of the gateway the route uses. If there is no gateway, a character is output.
`Genmask`	The netmask for the route. The kernel uses this to set the generality of a route by bitwise ANDing the `Genmask` against a packet's IP address before comparing it to the destination IP address of the route.
`Flags`	The flags for the route (U=Up, H=Host, G=Gateway, D=Dynamic route, M=Modified).
`Metric`	The metric cost for the route. This is not currently supported in the kernel networking layer.
`Ref`	The number of other routes that rely on the presence of this route.
`Use`	The number of times the routing table entry has been used.
`Iface`	The network interface to which this route delivers packets.

Returning to the Tristar network, the following is an example from `unixlt`, the laptop, with a SLIP link up and running.

```
/sbin/route
Kernel routing table
Destination     Gateway          Genmask          Flags Metric Ref Use Iface
slip.tristar.c  *                255.255.255.255  UH    0      0   0   sl0
127.0.0.0       *                255.0.0.0        U     0      0   100 lo
default         slip.tristar.c   *                UG    0      0   1   sl0
```

The table entry for the loopback is the same as before, and there are two new entries. The first specifies a route to `slip.tristar.com`. The other new entry specifies a default route using `slip.tristar.com` as a gateway.

Note

Every machine connected to a network must have a default route in its routing table. The default route is used when no other routing table entry matches the destination for a packet.

Adding Static Routes. You add routes to the routing table by running the route program with the `add` argument. The command-line argument syntax for the `route add` command is

```
route add [ -net ¦ -host ] addr [gw gateway] [metric cost]
 [netmask mask] [dev device]
```

Table 14.5 describes the command-line arguments the `route add` command uses.

Table 14.5 Command-Line Arguments Used by the *route add*

Argument	Description
`-net ¦ -host`	Forces the specified address to be treated as either a network or host address.
`addr`	The destination address for the new route. This can be an IP address, host name, or network name.
`gw` *`gateway`*	Specifies that any packets for this address be routed through the specified gateway.
`metric` *`cost`*	This option is not yet implemented.
`netmask` *`mask`*	Specifies the netmask of the route being added. The `route` program will guess what this is, so you don't need to specify it under normal circumstances.
`dev` *`device`*	Forces `route` to associate the new route with the specified network interface device. Again, `route` usually guesses correctly what device to use for the new route, so you won't have to use this often.

Caution

When adding a gateway route to the routing table, you must be sure the specified gateway is reachable. You usually have to add a static route for the gateway before adding the route using the gateway.

Now for some examples, starting with the loopback interface. After configuring the loopback interface with `ifconfig`, you need to add a route to it, as in the following:

```
route add 127.0.0.1
```

Nothing else is needed because `route` compares the address given to it with the addresses for the known interfaces and assigns the loopback interface to the new route. The following example shows how to set the routing for the SLIP link on the Tristar `unixlt` machine after the SLIP link has been established and `ifconfig` has been used to activate the interface:

```
route add slip.tristar.com
route add default gw slip.tristar.com
```

The first command adds a static route for the host **slip.tristar.com**, and the second one tells the kernel to use **slip.tristar.com** as a gateway for all packets with unknown destinations.

Caution

Make sure any host names you use with the `route` command are in the `/etc/hosts` file so that `route` can find the IP addresses for them; otherwise, `route` fails.

If you are subnetting your network by splitting the IP address in the middle of an octet, you will have to specify the required netmask when running `route`. For example, if you have a Class C network and have four subnets using the first two bits of the last octet, you need to run `route` like this:

```
route add hostname netmask 255.255.255.192
```

This ensures that `route` puts the right netmask in the routing table entry.

For Ethernet and other broadcast network interfaces, you need to add routes that tell the kernel what network can be reached via each configured interface. After using `ifconfig` to bring up the `eth0` network interface on **unix1.tristar.com** as you did previously, you need to run `route` to install the route to the network on that interface.

```
route add -net 166.82.1.0
```

That may not look like enough to set the routing table entry correctly; no interface is indicated. `route` handles this by comparing the IP address on the command line to the IP address of each network interface. It assigns the route to the interface that matches it. In this case, `eth0` has been assigned the address `166.82.1.21` with a netmask of `255.255.255.0`. This matches the network address given in the `route` command, so `route` installs a route to the network `166.82.1.0` using interface `eth0`, as shown in the following:

```
$ route
Kernel routing table
Destination     Gateway         Genmask         Flags Metric Ref    UseIface
166.82.1.0      *               255.255.255.0   UN    0      0      0 eth0
127.0.0.0       *               255.0.0.0       U     0      0      100 lo
```

To tell `unix1` how to reach the other subnet, you need two more routing table entries to be safe:

```
route add gateway.tristar.com
route add -net 166.82.2.0 gw gateway.tristar.com
```

This adds a static route to **gateway.tristar.com** and then adds a network route for `166.82.2.0` using **gateway.tristar.com** as the gateway for that network, as shown in the following:

```
$ route
Kernel routing table
Destination     Gateway          Genmask          Flags Metric Ref  UseIface
gateway.tristar *                255.255.255.0    UH    0      0    0 eth0
166.82.1.0      *                255.255.255.0    UN    0      0    0 eth0
166.82.2.0      gateway.tristar  255.255.255.0    UN    0      0    0 eth0
127.0.0.0       *                255.0.0.0        U     0      0    100 lo
```

This shows the static route you added for **gateway.tristar.com** and the gatewayed route to the `166.82.2.0` network.

Deleting Routes with the *route* Command

You delete routes by calling `route` with the `del` option and specifying the destination address of the route you want to delete. For example,

```
route del -net 166.82.2.0
```

deletes the network route for network `166.82.2.0`.

Writing the */etc/rc.d/rc.inet1* Boot Script

Now that you've looked at both the `ifconfig` and `route` commands, you're ready to write the boot-time script that starts up network interfaces, `/etc/rc.d/rc.inet1`. This script is called from `/etc/rc.d/rc.M` when Linux is changing to multiuser mode. You need to put in the `rc.inet1` file the commands that initialize your network interfaces and set any static routes.

If your machine is stand-alone, you need only initialize the loopback interface. The following shows how this can be done:

```
#! /bin/sh
#
# rc.inet1    Initialize the networking system

# Activate the loopback device
/sbin/ifconfig lo 127.0.0.1
/sbin/route add -net 127.0.0.0
```

The next listing is more complex. The following initializes the loopback device, an Ethernet interface, and sets routing for a gateway to the rest of the world:

```
#! /bin/sh
#
# rc.inet1    Initialize the networking system

# Activate the loopback device
/sbin/ifconfig lo 127.0.0.1
/sbin/route add -net 127.0.0.0

# Initialize Ethernet interface 0
/sbin/ifconfig eth0 166.82.1.21 netmask 255.255.255.0
[ccc]broadcast 166.82.1.255
/sbin/route add -net 166.82.1.0 netmask 255.255.255.0

# Now, add route to gateway machine and to rest of world
/sbin/route add -host 166.82.1.1    # Route to gateway machine
/sbin/route add default gw 166.82.1.1    # Route to rest of world
```

This script initializes the loopback device, configures Ethernet interface 0 to use IP address `166.82.1.21`, and adds a route through `eth0` to the network `166.82.1.0`. The last two route commands set a static route to the gateway machine at IP address

166.82.1.1 and then set the default route to the gateway machine. Any packets destined for addresses not in the 166.82.1.0 network will be sent to the gateway, which needs to know how to handle them.

Monitoring a TCP/IP Network *netstat*

The netstat program is an invaluable tool in monitoring your TCP/IP network. It can display the kernel routing table, the status of active network connections, and useful statistics about each network interface. We'll go through each of these functions. Table 14.6 describes the command-line arguments for netstat.

Table 14.6 Command-Line Arguments for the *netstat* Program

Argument	Description
-a	Shows information about all Internet connections, including those that are just listening.
-i	Shows statistics for all network devices.
-c	Shows continually updating network status. This makes netstat output a network status listing once per second until it is interrupted.
-n	Shows remote and local addresses and port information in numeric/raw form instead of resolving host names and service names.
-o	Shows the timer state expiration time and backoff state of each network connection.
-r	Shows the kernel routing table.
-t	Shows TCP socket information only. This includes those that are just listening.
-u	Shows UDP socket information only.
-v	Shows the version information for netstat.
-w	Shows raw socket information.
-x	Shows UNIX domain socket information.

Displaying Active Network Connections

Running netstat with no command-line arguments generates a listing of the active network connections on your machine. The following demonstrates the default output from netstat:

```
$ netstat<Return>
Active Internet connections
Proto Recv-Q Send-Q Local Address          Foreign Address
➥(State)        User
tcp        0      0 unix1.tristar.com:1266 server.tristar.:telnet
➥ESTABLISHED   lance
Active UNIX domain sockets
Proto RefCnt Flags      Type            State       Path
```

```
unix 1        [ ACC ]    SOCK_STREAM    LISTENING    /dev/
printer
unix 2        [ ]        SOCK_STREAM    CONNECTED    /dev/log
unix 2        [ ]        SOCK_STREAM    CONNECTED
unix 1        [ ACC ]    SOCK_STREAM    LISTENING    /dev/log
```

The first section shows an active TCP protocol connection from port 1266 on **unix1.tristar.com** to the `telnet` port on **server.tristar.com** by user `lance`. Table 14.7 describes the fields in the Active Internet Connections listing.

The second section displays active UNIX domain sockets. UNIX domain sockets are an IPC mechanism that uses the UNIX file system as the rendezvous system. Processes create special files in the file system that are then opened by other processes on the machine that wants to communicate. The previous code lines show two sockets listening, one on `/dev/printer` and the other on `/dev/log`. There are also two currently connected sockets, one to `/dev/log` and one which has no specified path associated with it. Table 14.8 describes the fields in the Active UNIX Domain Sockets listing.

Table 14.7 Active Internet Connection Fields

Field	Description
`Proto`	The protocol used by this connection, TCP, or UDP.
`Recv-Q`	The number of bytes received on this socket but not yet copied by the user program.
`Send-Q`	The number of bytes sent to the remote host that have not been acknowledged.
`Local Address`	Local host name and port number assigned to this connection. The socket IP address is resolved to the canonical host name for that address and the port number is translated into the service name unless the `-n` flag is used.
`Foreign Address`	The foreign host name and port number assigned to this connection. The `-n` flag affects this field as it does the `Local Address` field.
	`ESTABLISHED` The connection is fully established.
	`SYN_SENT` The socket is currently trying to make a connection to a remote host.
	`SYN_RECV` The connection is being initialized.
	`FIN_WAIT1` The socket has been closed and is waiting for the connection to shut down.
	`FIN_WAIT2` The connection has been closed. The socket is waiting for a shutdown from the remote host.
	`TIME_WAIT` The socket is closed and is waiting for a remote host shutdown retransmission.
	`CLOSED` The socket is not in use.

(continues)

Table 14.7 Continued

Field	Description	
	CLOSE_WAIT	The remote host has shut down its connection. The local host is waiting for the socket to close.
	LAST_ACK	The remote connection is shut down and the socket is closed. The local host is waiting for an acknowledgment.
	LISTEN	The socket is listening for the incoming connection attempt.
	UNKNOWN	The state of the socket is not known.
User	The logon ID of the user who owns the socket.	

Table 14.8 Fields in the Active UNIX Domain Sockets Listing

Field	Description	
Proto	The protocol in use on this socket. This will usually be unix.	
RefCnt	The number of processes attached to this socket.	
Flags	The flags for this socket. Currently, the only known flag is SO_ACCEPTON (ACC), which indicates that the socket is unconnected and the process that made the socket is waiting for a connection request.	
Type	The mode in which the socket is accessed. This field will contain one of the following keywords:	
	SOCK_DGRAM	Datagram, connectionless mode.
	SOCK_STREAM	Connection-oriented stream mode.
	SOCK_RAW	Raw mode.
	SOCK_RDM	Reliably-delivered message mode.
	SOCK_SEQPACKET	Sequential packet mode.
	UNKNOWN	Mode not known to netstat program.
State	The current state of the socket. The following keywords are used:	
	FREE	The socket is not allocated.
	LISTENING	The socket is waiting for a connection request.
	UNCONNECTED	There is no current connection on the socket.
	CONNECTING	The socket is attempting to make a connection.
	CONNECTED	The socket has a current connection.
	DISCONNECTING	The socket is attempting to shut down a connection.
	UNKNOWN	The state of the socket is unknown. You will not see this under normal operating conditions.
Path	This is the path name used by other processes to connect to the socket.	

Tip

Network interfaces that drop many packets or are getting many overrun errors can be a symptom of an overloaded machine or network. Checking the network interface statistics is a quick way of diagnosing this problem.

Invoking `netstat` with the `-o` option adds the internal state information to the Active Internet Connections listing. The following is an example of this:

```
$ netstat -o<Return>
Active Internet connections
Proto Recv-Q Send-Q Local Address       Foreign Address       (State)
 User
tcp        0      0 localhost:1121      localhost:telnet      ESTABLISHED
 lance  off (0.00/0)
tcp        0      0 localhost:telnet    localhost:1121        ESTABLISHED

 root   on  (673.69/0)
```

The added data is at the end of each line and includes receiver retransmission byte count, transmitter retransmission byte count, timer state (on/off), and (time/backoff) values. The time displayed is the time left before the timer expires. The backoff is the retry count for the current data transmission. This data is useful in diagnosing network problems by making it easy to see which connection is having problems.

Caution

Because the `-o` option outputs the state of internal TCP/IP data, the format of this data may change or this option may be removed in a later release of the networking software.

Examining the Kernel Routing Table

Invoking `netstat` with the `-r` option prints out the kernel routing table. The format is the same as for the `route` command.

Displaying Network Interface Statistics

Invoking `netstat` with the `-i` option prints out usage statistics for each active network interface. This is another excellent tool for debugging network problems. With this command, it is very easy to see when packets are being dropped, overrun, and so on.

The following is an example of using the `-i` option, and Table 14.9 explains each field in the listing:

```
$ netstat -i<Return>
Kernel Interface table
Iface  MTU Met  RX-OK RX-ERR RX-DRP RX-OVR TX-OK TX-ERR TX-DRP TX-OVR Flags
lo     2000  0      0      0      0      0  1558      1      0      0 LRU
```

Table 14.9 Fields in the Kernel Interface Table

Field	Description
`Iface`	The name of the network interface.
`MTU`	The largest number of bytes that can be sent in one transmission by this interface.
`RX-OK`	The number of packets received with no errors.
`RX-ERR`	The number of packets received with errors.
`RX-DRP`	The number of packets dropped.
`RX-OVR`	The number of packet overrun errors.
`TX-OK`	The number of packets transmitted with no errors.
`TX-ERR`	The number of packets transmitted with errors.
`TX-DRP`	The number of packets dropped during transmission.
`TX-OVR`	The number of packets dropped due to overrun errors.
Flags	The following flags can be shown in this field: `A` The interface receives packets for Multicast addresses. `B` The interface receives broadcast packets. `D` The interface debugging feature is currently activated. `L` This is the loopback interface. `M` The interface is in promiscuous mode. `N` The interface does not process trailers on packets. `O` The Address Resolution Protocol is turned off on this interface. `P` This interface is being used as a Point-to-Point connection. `R` The interface is running. `U` The interface has been activated.

Using the *netconfig* Program

Slackware Linux includes a program in `/sbin` called `netconfig` that makes configuring TCP/IP and mail on Linux easy for most situations. It can't handle all possible network configurations, but it does an excellent job on most systems.

Caution

`Netconfig` builds the following configuration files from scratch: `/var/lib/smail/config`, `/var/lib/elm/elm.rc`, `/etc/hosts`, `/etc/networks`, `/etc/rc.d/rc.inet1`, and `/etc/resolve.conf`. If any of these already exist, they are copied to `/tmp/filename.OLD`. This means that if you customize these files and then run `netconfig`, you will have to redo your customizations.

`netconfig` is screen-based. It presents a series of dialog boxes that ask you questions about your TCP/IP configuration. You type the answer to each question using the <Tab> key to move among the fields on-screen. Moving the cursor to the OK field on each screen and pressing <Return> moves you to the next question. Pressing <Return> or the Cancel button aborts `netconfig` and returns you to the prompt.

The following is an opening screen from the `netconfig` program:

```
+--------------------- NETWORK CONFIGURATION -------------------+
|                                                               |
| Now we will attempt to configure your mail and TCP/IP. This   |
| process probably won't work on all possible network           |
| configurations, but should give you a good start. You will be |
| able to reconfigure your system at any time by typing:        |
|                                                               |
| netconfig                                                     |
|                                                               |
+---------------------------------------------------------------+
|                              <OK>                             |
+---------------------------------------------------------------+
```

The next screen asks you for the host name of your machine. You type just the host name without the domain portion. The following shows this dialog box:

```
+------------------------- ENTER HOSTNAME ----------------------+
| First, we'll need the name you'd like to give your host. Only |
| the base hostname is needed right now. (not the domain)       |
|                                                               |
| Enter hostname:                                               |
| +---------------------------------------------------------+   |
| |                                                         |   |
| +---------------------------------------------------------+   |
+---------------------------------------------------------------+
|                         <OK>     <Cancel>                     |
+---------------------------------------------------------------+
```

You can fix any typos by using the <Backspace> key. Be sure you have everything right before clicking OK. You can't go back if you've made a mistake. You will have to cancel `netconfig` and start over.

Figure 14.1 is a flowchart of the questions `netconfig` asks you.

As you can see, if you are using only the loopback interface, or just the loopback and SLIP/PPP, all you need to enter is the host name and domain name of your machine. Otherwise, `netconfig` takes all the TCP/IP configuration information we've talked about and builds the files needed to bring your Linux machine online.

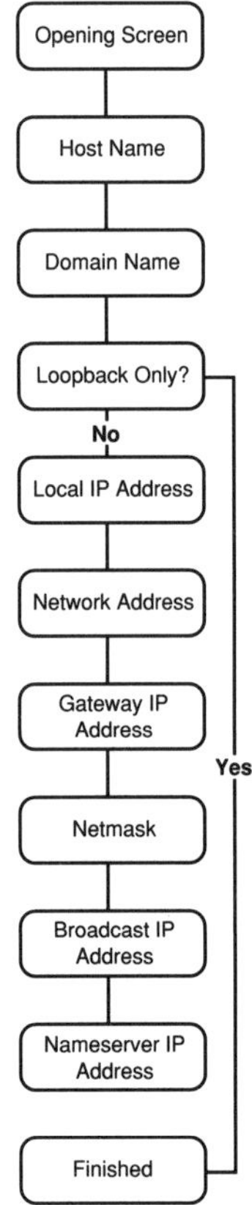

Fig. 14.1

A flowchart of questions `netconfig` asks.

From Here...

This chapter covers the basics of configuring a Linux machine for use on a network. More information can be found in the man pages for the discussed commands. For more information on TCP/IP networking and configuration, see the following chapters:

- Chapter 13, "Understanding the TCP/IP Protocol Suite," explains the details of the TCP/IP Protocols.
- Chapter 15, "Configuring Domain Name Service (DNS)," shows you how to set up Linux as a DNS client and server.
- Chapter 20, "Understanding Linux Shells," gives more details on writing shell scripts.

CHAPTER 15

Configuring Domain Name Service (DNS)

Mapping Internet system names to IP addresses is a task that requires a good degree of consideration. With the explosive growth of the Internet over the past few years, the original system of maintaining host name to IP address mappings in a local flat ASCII file quickly proved impractical. With thousands of computers on the Net, and more being added daily, a new system was needed. That new system was a network-wide distributed database known as BIND, the Berkeley Internet Domain server.

Also referred to variously as the Domain Name Service, the Domain Name System, or DNS, this system provides an effective, relatively transparent host name to the IP address mapping mechanism. DNS is notoriously hard to configure, but once you are successful, it is fairly easy to maintain. This chapter provides a basic overview of how to set up and configure a DNS system. It is, by no means, a complete reference; there are whole books on the subject available. In this chapter, you cover the following:

- Introduction to DNS
- Setting up the resolver
- The various `named` configuration files
- Setting up `named`

Introduction to DNS

DNS provides a mechanism for converting IP addresses into mnemonic names that represent hosts, networks, and mail aliases. It does this by dividing the entire Internet IP and name space into different logical groups. Each of these groups has authority for its own computers and other information.

Since DNS is a complicated topic, it has its own specialized set of terms. Table 15.1 provides the definitions of some commonly used DNS terms.

Table 15.1 Commonly Used DNS Terms

Term	Definition
Domain	The logical entity or organization that represents a part of a network. For example, **unc.edu** is the name of the primary domain for the University of North Carolina at Chapel Hill.
Domain name	The name portion of a host name that represents the domain that contains the host. For example, in the address **sunsite.unc.edu,** the domain name is **unc.edu**. Also used interchangably with `domain`.
Host	A computer on a network.
Node	A computer on a network.
Name server	A computer that provides DNS services to map DNS names to IP addresses.
Resolve	The act of translating a DNS name into its corresponding IP address.
Resolver	A program or library routine that extracts DNS information from a name server.
Reverse resolution	Matching a given IP address to its DNS name.
Spoof	The act of appearing to the network as having a different IP address or domain name.

Originally, when the Internet was first formed, the number of hosts on the Net was very small. It was fairly easy to maintain the name/address mapping. Each host simply had a complete list of all host names and addresses in a local file. As the growth of the Internet accelerated, this system quickly became unwieldy. When a new host was added, it was necessary to update every host file on every computer. In addition, because each new computer resulted in a new line in every host file, the size of the host files began to grow to quite a large size. Clearly a new solution was needed.

DNS can be conceptually divided into the following three parts:

- Domain name space
- Name servers
- Resolvers

The domain name space is a specification for a tree structure that identifies a set of hosts and provides information about them. Conceptually, each node in the tree has a database of information about the hosts under its authority. Queries attempt to extract the appropriate information from this database. In simple terms, this is just the listing of all different types of information, names, IP addresses, mail aliases, and such, that are available for lookup in the DNS system.

Programs that hold and maintain the data located in the domain name space are known as name servers. Each name server has complete information about a subset of the domain name space and has cached information about other portions. A name server has complete information for its area of authority. This authoritative information is divided into areas known as zones, which can be divided among different name servers to provide redundant service for a zone. Each name server knows about other name servers that are responsible for different zones. If a request comes in for information from the zone that a given name server is responsible for, the name server simply returns the information. However, if a request comes in for information from a different zone, the name server contacts the appropriate server with authority for that zone.

Resolvers are simply programs or library routines that extract information from the name servers in response to a query about a host in the domain name space.

The Resolver

The first step in using DNS is to configure the resolver library on your computer. You must configure your local resolver if you intend to use DNS name resolution, even if you are not going to run a local domain name server.

The */etc/host.conf* File

The local resolver libraries are configured via a file named `host.conf` that is located in the `/etc` directory. This file tells the resolver what services to use and in what order. This file is a plain ASCII file that lists resolver options, one per line. Fields in this file may be separated by spaces or tabs. The # character indicates the start of a comment.

Several options may be specified in the `host.conf` file. Table 15.2 lists these options.

Table 15.2 Configuration Options for the */etc/host.conf* File

Option	Description
`order`	Specifies in what order different name resolution mechanisms are tried. The specified resolving services are tried in the order listed. The following name resolution mechanisms are supported: `hosts` Attempt to resolve the name by looking in the local `/etc/host` file `bind` Query a DNS name server to resolve the name. `nis` Use the Network Information Service (NIS) protocol to try to resolve the host name.
`alert`	Takes `off` or `on` as arguments. If turned `on`, any attempt to spoof an IP address is logged via the `syslog` facility.
`nospoof`	If reverse resolution is used to match a host name to a specified address, resolve the host name that is returned to verify that it does match the address that you queried. Prevents "spoofing" of IP addresses. Enabled by specifying `nospoof on`.
`trim`	Takes a domain name as an argument. `trim` removes the domain name before performing an `/etc/hosts` lookup on the name. This allows you to just put the base host name in `/etc/hosts` without specifying the domain name.

(continues)

Table 15.2 Continued

Option	Description
`multi`	Takes `off` or `on` as arguments. Is used to determine if a host is allowed to have more than one IP address specified in `/etc/hosts`. `multi` is used only in conjunction with `host` queries. This option has no effect on either NIS or DNS queries.

The following is an example of an `/etc/host.conf` configuration file that uses these options:

```
# Sample /etc/host.conf file
#
# Lookup names via DNS first then fall back to /etc/hosts
order bind host
# We don't have machines with multiple addresses
multi off
# check for IP address spoofing
nospoof on
# and warn us if someone attempts to spoof
alert on
# Trim the tristar.com domain name for host lookups
trim tristar.com
```

This example shows a general resolver configuration for the domain **tristar.com**. The resolver looks up the host names using DNS first and then tries the local `/etc/hosts` file.

> **Note**
>
> It is a good idea to specify the local `/etc/hosts` file in the resolution search. If for some reason your name servers should be unavailable, you can still resolve the names for hosts that are listed in your local hosts file. You should also keep a list of all your local hosts in your `/etc/hosts` files on each of your local computers.

Multiple IP addresses for a single machine are disabled. This host checks for IP address spoofing by re-resolving the host name that a reverse IP address lookup returns. This is a bit of a performance hit, but it helps make sure that no one is pretending to be a different host than they really are. Also, you've set up the resolver to warn you if an attempt to spoof is detected. Lastly, the resolver trims the domain **tristar.com** from any host names that are looked up in the local `/etc/hosts` file.

The */etc/resolv.conf* File

Now that you have configured the basic behavior of the resolver library, you need to set up some information for the DNS portion of the resolver. You only need to do this if you are using DNS for host name resolution—that is, by specifying `bind` in the `order` statement of the `/etc/host.conf` file. But then you wouldn't be reading this chapter if you were not going to use DNS, would you?

The /etc/resolv.conf controls the way the resolver uses DNS to resolve host names. It specifies the DNS name servers to contact when resolving a host name and in what order to contact them. It also provides the local domain name and some clues as to how to guess at the domain name of hosts that are specified without a domain name.

Table 15.3 lists the valid options for the /etc/resolv.conf file.

Table 15.3 Configuration Options for the */etc/resolv.conf* File

Option	Description
domain	The local domain name of this host. If it is not given, the resolver tries to get the local domain name from the getdomainname() system call.
nameserver	Specifies the IP address of a DNS name server to contact for name resolution. You may list up to three name servers by using the nameserver option multiple times. The name servers are tried in the order listed. You should put your most reliable name server first, so that queries don't time out on a server that is likely to be down.
search	Gives a list of domains to try if no domain name is specified as part of a query host name. If no search option is given, the list of domains is created by using the local domain plus each parent domain of the local domain.

The following is a sample /etc/resolv.conf file for **tristar.com**:

```
# /etc/resolv.conf for tristar.com
#
# Set our local domain name
domain tristar.com
# Specify our primary name server
nameserver 166.82.1.3
```

In this example, you specify the local domain via the domain option and list one name server to use for resolving host names.

Note

You need to specify the IP address of the DNS name server as an argument to the nameserver option—not the host name. If you specify the host name, DNS doesn't know what host to contact to look up the host name of the nameserver.

You did not use the search option to specify the search order. This means that if you try to query the address of a machine, for example skippy, the resolver tries to look up skippy first. If this fails, it looks up **skippy.tristar.com**, and then **skippy.com**.

DNS servers can and do go down unexpectedly. If you rely solely on a DNS server for name resolution, you may find yourself unable to work if it crashes. Make sure that you specify multiple servers and keep a good list of hosts in your local /etc/hosts file just in case.

The *named* Daemon

This is where the real magic starts. You have seen how to set up the basics of resolver configuration and how to tell your resolver which name servers to contact. In this section, you learn the mechanics of setting up a name server.

The DNS name server under Linux is provided by the `named` (pronounced *name-dee'*) daemon. This daemon is typically started at boot time and reads its configuration information from a set of configuration files. `named` typically runs until the machine is shut down. Once `named` has started and is initialized with its configuration information, it writes its process ID to the ASCII file `/etc/named.pid`. It then starts listening for DNS requests on the default network port specified in `/etc/services`.

The *named.boot* File

The first file that `named` reads when it starts is typically `/etc/named.boot`. This is a very small file, but it is the key to all the other configuration files used by `named`. It contains pointers to the various configuration files and to other name servers. In the `named.boot` file, comments start with a semicolon and continue to the end of the line. There are several options that can be listed in the `named.boot` file. Table 15.4 lists these options.

Table 15.4 Configuration Options for the *named.boot* File

Option	Description
`directory`	This is the directory where the DNS zone files are located. You can specify several different directories by using the `directory` option repeatedly. You may give file path names as being relative to these directories.
`primary`	Takes a domain name and file name as arguments. The `primary` option declares `named` to be authoritative for the specified domain and causes `named` to load the zone information from the specified file.
`secondary`	This option tells `named` to act as a secondary server for the specified domain. It takes a domain name, a list of addresses, and a file name as arguments. `named` tries to transfer the zone information from the hosts specified in the address list and then stores the zone information in the file specified on the option line. If `named` is unable to contact any of the hosts, it tries to retrieve the information from the secondary zone file.
`cache`	Sets up caching information for `named`. Takes a domain name and a file name as arguments. The domain name is typically specified as **.**. The file contains a set of records, known as server hints, which list information about the root name servers.
`forwarders`	Takes a list of name servers as arguments. Tells the local name server to try to contact the servers in this list if it is unable to resolve an address from its local information.
`slave`	Turns the local name server into a slave server. If the `slave` option is given, the local server attempts to resolve DNS names via recursive queries. It simply forwards the request to one of the servers listed in the `forwarders` option line.

In addition to these options, there are a few additional options that are not commonly used. Refer to the `named` man page for more information on these options.

Caution

Because **tristar.com** is not attached to the Internet, many of the IP host and network addresses in these examples are fake. When setting up your own name server, make sure that you use the correct addresses assigned to you.

The following is a sample `named.boot` file:

```
; named.boot file
; A sample named.boot for tristar.com
;
directory /var/named
;
cache . named.ca
primary tristar.com named.hosts
primary 197.198.199.in-addr.arpa named.rev
```

This example sets up the primary name server for **tristar.com**. As you can see, comments start with the ; character. The `directory` statement in the file tells `named` that all its working files are located in the `/var/named` directory. Since none of the other files named in the `named.boot` file have directory paths associated with them, they are located in `/var/named`.

The next line sets up the caching information for this name server. This option should be present on almost every machine running as a name server. It tells `named` to enable caching and load the root server information from the file `named.ca`.

Note

The `cache` entry is very important. Without it, no caching is enabled on the local name server. This can cause severe performance problems for name lookups. Also, the local server cannot contact any root name servers and, as a result, is unable to resolve any non-local host names, unless it is set up as a forwarding name server.

The next line in the `named.boot` file tells `named` that this server has primary authority for the domain **tristar.com**. The zone and host information records are in the file `named.hosts`. You learn about these zone authority records in detail in the next section.

There is a second `primary` line in the `named.hosts` file. This line shows that you also have primary zone authority for the zone `197.198.199.in-addr.arpa` with zone information in the `named.rev` file. This strange syntax is `named`'s way of getting information to match IP addresses to DNS names. Because DNS was originally set up to match DNS names to IP addresses, a different `primary` line is needed to do reverse resolution.

> **Note**
>
> The `in-addr.arpa` domain is used to specify reverse, or IP address, to DNS name resolution.

Database Files and Resource Records

All information in the various `named` database files is stored in a format known as a *resource record*. Each resource record has a type associated with it, which tells the record's function. A resource record is the smallest piece of information that is used by `named`.

Most people find the syntax for resource records and master database files in general to be a bit arcane and obscure. It doesn't help matters that some resource records have to appear in certain places in certain files. Most DNS configuration problems can be traced to errors in these master configuration files. All this said, it is time to dive in and take a look at the resource record syntax and the various master files.

> **Note**
>
> Within the master configuration files, you have the option of specifying absolute host names or host names that are relative to this domain. Host names are considered absolute if they end in a **.** character such as **foo,tristar,com.**. Host names that do not end with a period character are considered relative to the local domain, also known as the origin. You can refer to the origin itself by using the **@** character.

Resource records use a general syntax that is consistent across all types of resource records. To add to the confusion, however, several parts of the record are optional depending on the record type, and may assume a default value if not specified. The basic format of a resource record is

```
[owner] [ttl] [class] type data
```

Fields are separated by white space such as spaces or tabs. Table 15.5 discusses what the various fields mean.

Table 15.5 Fields in the Resource Record Data Format

Field	Description
`owner`	The domain or host name that the record applies to. If no name is given, the domain name of the previous resource record is assumed.
`ttl`	The time-to-live field. This field tells how long, in seconds, that the information in this record is valid after it has been retrieved from a DNS server. If no `ttl` value is given, the minimum `ttl` of the last Start of Authority (SOA) record is used.

Field	Description
`class`	Specifies a networking address class. For TCP/IP networks, use the value `IN`. If the class is not given, the class of the previous resource record is used.
`type`	Lists the type of the resource record. This value is required. The various resource record types are listed in the next section.
`data`	Specifies the data associated with this resource record. This value is required. The format of the `data` field depends on the content of the `type` field.

As you can see, the format of a resource record can get quite confusing. There are several optional fields, and the `data` field depends on the type of the resource record. To make matters worse, there are several different types of resource records. Table 15.6 lists the most common resource record types. There are a few additional types, but they are rarely used. If you are interested in the additional types, refer to the appropriate RFCs and the man pages for `named`.

Table 15.6 Commonly Used Resource Record Types

Type	Description
`A`	This is an address record. It associates a host name with an address. The data field holds the address in dotted decimal format. There can be only one `A` record for any given host, as this record is considered authoritative information. Any additional host name or address mappings for this host must be given using the `CNAME` type.
`CNAME`	This field associates an alias for a host with its canonical name, the name specified in the `A` record for this host.
`HINFO`	Provides information about a host. The data field holds the hardware and software information for a particular host.
`MX`	Sets up a mail exchanger record. The data field holds an integer preference value followed by a host name. `MX` records tell a mail transport to send mail to another system that knows how to deliver it to its final destination.
`NS`	This points to a name server for another zone. The data field of the `NS` resource record contains the DNS name of the name server. You need to specify an `A` record as well to match the host name with the address of the name server.
`PTR`	This maps addresses to names, as in the `in-addr.arpa` domain. The host name must be the canonical host name.
`SOA`	The *Start of Authority* or `SOA` record type tells the name server that all the resource records following it are authoritative for this domain. The data field is surrounded by ( ) and is typically a multi-line field. The data field of the SOA record contains the following entries: *`origin`* The canonical name of the primary name server for this domain. It is usually given as an absolute domain name ending with a ., so it is not modified by the `named` daemon.

(continues)

Table 15.6 Continued

Type	Description	
	`contact`	The e-mail contact of the person who is responsible for maintaining this domain. Since the @ character has special meaning in resource records, it is replaced by a . character. If the responsible person for maintaining zone information about **tristar.com** is Dave, the contact address is **dave.tristar.com**.
	`serial`	The version number of the zone information file, which is given as an integer. It is used by secondary name servers to determine when the zone information file has changed. You should increment this number by 1 every time you change the information file.
	`refresh`	The length of time in seconds that a secondary server should wait before trying to check the SOA record of the primary name server. The SOA records do not change very often, so you can usually set this value to be on the order of one day or so.
	`retry`	This is the time in seconds that a secondary server waits to retry a request to a primary server if the primary server was not available. Typically, it should be on the order of a few minutes.
	`expire`	This is the time in seconds that the secondary server should wait before throwing away the zone information if it has been unable to contact the primary server. This number should typically be very large, on the order of 30 days or so.
	`minimum`	This is the default `ttl` value for resource records that do not specify a `ttl`. If your network does not change very much, this number can be set to a fairly large value, such as a couple of weeks. You can always override it by specifying a `ttl` value in your resource records.

As you can see, the format of the resource records gets complicated in a hurry. Hopefully, things get clearer as you look at a few of the master configuration files used by `named`.

The *named.hosts* File

In your `named.boot` file, you listed `named.hosts` as being the file that contains information about your local domain, **tristar.com**. You could have named the file anything you wanted by listing the name on the `primary` line of `named.hosts`. This file contains authoritative information about the hosts in our zone of authority—**tristar.com**. The following is a sample `named.hosts` file that uses several of the resource record types:

```
; named.hosts file for tristar.com
;
@           IN      SOA     ns.tristar.com. dave.tristar.com. (
                                             6 ; serial number
                                             86400 ;refresh 24 hrs
                                             300 ; retry 5 minutes
                                             2592000 ; expire 30 days
                                             86400 ; minimum 24 hrs
                                             )
          IN      NS       ns.tristar.com.
;
; your domain itself tristar.com
;
@           IN      A      199.198.197.1
          IN      MX      100      mailhost.tristar.com
          IN      HINFO      PC-486      Linux
;
; your primary nameserver
;
ns            IN      A      199.198.197.1
nameserver      IN      CNAME      ns.tristar.com.
;
; other hosts
;
mailhost      IN      A      199.198.197.2
opus            IN      A      199.198.197.3
                  IN      MX     100      mailhost.tristar.com
skippy            IN      A      199.198.197.4
          IN      MX      100      mailhost.tristar.com
;
; the localhost
;
localhost        IN      A      127.0.0.1
```

Note

Host names in resource records that end with the `.` character are not translated any further. If the `.` is not the last character in the host name, `named` assumes that the host name that you gave is relative to the origin domain name referred to by **@** and appends the domain name to the host name.

You take a look at this file in detail. The first record that you come to in this file is the `SOA` or *Start of Authority* record for our domain. The first line of this record starts with the @ character which indicates the current origin or domain, **tristar.com**. The definition of the origin comes from the domain listed on the corresponding `primary` line in `named.boot`. After that you see the codes

```
IN SOA
```

This tells `named` that this resource record uses Internet (TCP/IP) addressing and is a Start of Authority record. The next two things on the line are the canonical name of the primary name server for this domain, **ns.tristar.com**, and the e-mail contact with the @ replaced by a ., **dave.tristar.com**. You then list the various fields of the data required by an SOA record, one per line. Refer to table 15.6 for a complete explanation of each of these entries.

After the `SOA` record, the next line is a name-server resource record, which lists **ns.tristar.com** as being a name server for your domain. Because no domain is listed in the domain field, it is assumed to be the last domain specified, which was @, listed in the `SOA` record. And, of course, the @ character really expands to be our local domain, **tristar.com**. What could possibly be easier to understand?

The next three lines set up some information about the **tristar.com** domain itself. Although you have listed the domain name as @ for clarity because it was the last domain name listed in the file, these resource records still apply to it by default if you had left the domain field blank. The line

```
@          IN       A       199.198.197.1
```

allows users to refer to **tristar.com** as though it were a real machine. We have assigned it the IP address of `199.198.197.1`, which, as you will see, is really the IP address of **ns.tristar.com**. The next line sets up a mail exchanger `MX` record for **tristar.com** so that all mail going to it gets forwarded to **mailhost.tristar.com** instead. The last line in this group sets up a host information `HINFO` record for **tristar.com**, which tells the world that it is a PC-486 running Linux.

A few lines earlier in the file, you listed **ns.tristar.com** as being your name server via an `NS` resource record. In order for `named` to work correctly, you must provide an address or `A` record that gives the address of **ns.tristar.com**. The next line in your file does just that. Following the "glue record" that gives the address of the name server, you have a `CNAME` resource record. This record tells you that **nameserver.tristar.com** is an alias for **ns.tristar.com**.

You then proceed to set up address records for three other hosts in your domain: `mailhost`, `opus`, and `skippy`. Notice that after the `A` records for `opus` and `skippy`, there are `MX` records that route any mail received by `opus` or `skippy` to **mailhost.tristar.com**. Because no name was specified in the first field of these `MX` records, they apply to the previous name—`opus` or `skippy`.

> **Note**
>
> Because the owner field of a resource record defaults to the last one specified if it is left blank, it is easy to group records that apply to one host. However, you must be careful if you add new records for new hosts to a file. If you add them to the middle of a file, you may cause the default host to change for some of the existing resource records. Look carefully before you add resource records to an existing file.

Finally, the last host in our `named.hosts` file is the `localhost`, which is mapped to address `127.0.0.1`. As you can see, the syntax for these files gets quite complicated and gives you lots of room for errors.

The *named.rev* File

The `named.rev` file is very similar to the `named.hosts` file, except that it essentially works in reverse. It maps addresses to host names. The following is a sample `named.rev` file for **tristar.com**:

```
; named.rev file for tristar.com
;
@          IN     SOA     ns.tristar.com. dave.tristar.com. (
                                        6 ; serial number
                                        86400 ;refresh 24 hrs
                                        300 ; retry 5 minutes
                                        2592000 ; expire 30 days
                                        86400 ; minimum 24 hrs
                                        )
           IN     NS     ns.tristar.com.
;
; reverse map your IP addresses
;
1          IN     PTR     ns.tristar.com.
2          IN     PTR     mailhost.tristar.com.
3          IN     PTR     opus.tristar.com.
4          IN     PTR     skippy.tristar.com.
```

In this example, you have the same SOA record that you saw in the `named.hosts` file. This just sets up the authority information for our domain. In this case, @, the value of the origin, is set to `197.198.199.in-addr.arpa` from the `primary` line in the `named.boot` file. Recall that the `in-addr.arpa` domain refers to reverse mapping of addresses to names.

> **Note**
>
> The addresses listed as part of your `in-addr.arpa` line is your network address backwards. Your example network for this chapter has the address `199.198.197.0`. When you list it in the reverse mapping data files, you list it as
>
> `197.198.199.in-addr.arpa`

You have the NS record that lists the name server for your domain. Following that are the records that make up the reverse address resolution records. These are PTR records and give the host number (the part of the IP address not listed in the in-addr.arpa value) and the canonical host name that matches it. You must use the canonical host name here instead of a relative host name.

For example, the line

```
2          IN       PTR       mailhost.tristar.com.
```

tells named to map the host address 199.198.197.2 to the host name **mailhost.tristar.com**.

The *named.ca* File

As stated earlier in this chapter, the caching operation of named is very important. Fortunately, the named.ca file that sets up caching is also usually the simplest of the named configuration files. It just lists the root name servers for the various domains along with their IP addresses. It contains a couple of special field indicators that tell named that these are root servers. You can probably just copy the format of the following sample named.ca file. To get a complete current list of the root name servers, use the nslookup utility. The following is a sample named.ca file:

```
; named.ca file
;
.     99999999       IN       NS       NS.NIC.DDN.MIL.
     99999999       IN       NS       NS.NASA.GOV.
     99999999       IN       NS       KAVA.NISC.SRI.COM.
     99999999       IN       NS       TERP.UMD.EDU.
     99999999       IN       NS       C.NYSER.NET.
     99999999       IN       NS       NS.INTERNIC.NET.
;
NS.NIC.DDN.MIL.        99999999       IN      A      192.112.36.4
NS.NASA.GOV.             99999999       IN      A      128.102.16.10
KAVA.NISC.SRI.COM.        99999999       IN      A      192.33.33.24
TERP.UMD.EDU.             99999999       IN      A      128.8.10.90
C.NYSER.NET.             99999999       IN      A      192.33.4.12
NS.INTERNIC.NET.        99999999       IN      A      198.41.0.4
```

As you can see, the named.ca file simply maps NS nameserver records to the appropriate addresses for them.

Troubleshooting

DNS is a very complex system. There are many things that you can do wrong that will cause your system to not behave properly. Many of the problems that occur with a DNS setup will appear to be identical but come from different causes. However, most of the problems result from syntax errors in your configuration files.

Make sure that you specify the host names correctly in your DNS configuration files. If it is an absolute host name, make sure to end it with a period.

Be especially careful with the names used in `SOA` and `CNAME` records. If you make errors here, these resource records can redirect host name queries to computers that don't exist.

Make sure to enter the correct IP address for `A` records, and check to see that it matches your `/etc/hosts` file if you have one. Also, make sure that the DNS name and IP address match the corresponding reverse resolution information in `named.rev`.

Your best tool for figuring out errors is the `nslookup` command. Use `nslookup` to test your DNS server thoroughly. Do both regular and reverse resolution for every address in your DNS database to make sure that all the names and addresses are correct.

From Here...

In this chapter, you have looked at the various components of the DNS system and explored the various configuration files necessary to get a DNS name server running on your Linux system. The syntax for the resource records is fairly arcane and you need to pay close attention to your configuration files as you write them.

You can find more information about networking in the following chapters:

- Chapter 14, "Configuring a TCP/IP Network," shows how to set up and configure TCP/IP networking.
- Chapter 16, "Using SLIP and PPP," shows how to configure SLIP and PPP for dial-up Internet access.
- Chapter 27, "Understanding the Internet," gives an overview of the Internet and DNS.

CHAPTER 16

Using SLIP and PPP

The Linux kernel supports two serial-line protocols for transmitting Internet Protocol (IP) traffic, SLIP (Serial Line Internet Protocol), and PPP (Point-to-Point Protocol). These were developed as a poor man's alternative to expensive leased-line setups for getting Internet connectivity. Anyone with a reasonably high-speed modem and a service provider that supports these protocols can get their Linux machine IP-connected for a very low cost compared to leased-line systems.

SLIP drivers for Linux were available soon after Linux was first released. PPP support has only been recently added but is very stable. In this chapter, you learn the following:

- What is needed to run SLIP or PPP on your Linux machine
- How to initiate and automate SLIP and PPP connections
- How to configure a SLIP and PPP server on your Linux machine
- How to use PPP's security features

Requirements for SLIP and PPP

There are a few things you need to make sure are set up in your Linux kernel or configuration files. TCP/IP networking must be enabled and the loopback interface should be configured. Chapter 14, "Configuring a TCP/IP Network," covers these topics. You will want to have the IP address of your DNS name server included in your `/etc/resolv.conf` file in order to make accessing other machines besides your dial-up host convenient. If your dial-up link is slow or error-prone, you might want to run a name server on your Linux box. This caches any DNS lookups on your Linux box and decreases the amount of DNS IP traffic on your dial-up link.

Using *dip* To Automate SLIP Operations

There are a number of programs available on Linux to manage your SLIP operations. `dip`, the Dial-up IP Protocol Driver is one of the most versatile tools. It provides a scripting language for automating control of the modem and automatically sets up the SLIP network interface and kernel routing tables. `dip` can be used to initiate SLIP connections or provide dial-up SLIP service to other machines. The syntax for `dip` is

```
dip [-tvi] [-m mtu] [scriptfile]
```

Table 16.1 describes `dip`'s command-line arguments.

Table 16.1 *dip* Command-Line Arguments

Arguments	Description
`-t`	Runs `dip` in command mode. Command modes give you full access to everything `dip` can do, allowing you to initiate a SLIP connection manually.
`-v`	Used with `-t` to display the current error level.
`-i`	Instructs `dip` to operate in input mode. This flag is used when `dip` provides SLIP service for others dialing into your machine.
`-m` *`mtu`*	Forces `dip` to use the specified MTU value.
`scriptfile`	Name of the `dip` script to run.

Using *dip* in Command Mode

Invoking `dip` with the `-t` option places it in command mode. This mode lets you control `dip` directly and is an excellent tool for developing and debugging `dip` scripts. The following shows you what `dip`'s command mode looks like:

```
$ /sbin/dip -t<Return>
DIP: Dialup IP Protocol Driver version 3.3.7i-uri (17 Apr 95)
Written by Fred N. van Kempen, MicroWalt Corporation.

DIP>
```

From the `DIP>` prompt, you can run any `dip` command by typing it in and pressing <Return>. The `help` command displays a list of the available commands. Invoking a command with incorrect arguments displays a brief usage statement for that command. Table 16.2 describes the commands available at the command-mode prompt or in `dip` scripts.

Table 16.2 Commands Available in *dip*

Command	Description
`chatkey` *`keyword`* `[`*`code`*`]`	Adds a keyword and error level code to the set of error codes returned by the dial command. This can be used to detect when your modem returns `BUSY`, `VOICE`, or other specific messages.
`config [`*`arguments`*`]`	The `config` command allows you to directly manipulate the SLIP interface `dip` provides. This command is normally disabled because it is a severe security risk. The source code file `command.c` must be modified slightly to enable this command.

Command	Description
`databits` *bits*	Sets the number of bits that can be used as data in each byte. This accommodates 6- and 7-bit dial-up connections.
`default`	Causes `dip` to set a default route in the kernel routing table pointed at the remote host.
`dial` *num*	Dials the specified telephone number.
`echo` *on¦off*	Turns echo on or off. Echo on makes `dip` display what it is sending to and receiving from the modem.
`flush`	Throws away any responses from the modem that have not been read yet.
`get` *$var*	Sets the variable `$var` to either the constant, ask, or remote constant specified, prompts the user for a value, or takes the next word from the serial line and assigns it to `$var`.
`goto` *label*	Jumps to *label* in `dip` script.
`help`	Displays a listing of available commands in command mode.
`if` *$var op number*	Performs a conditional branch in a `goto` label script. `$var` must be one of `$errlvl`, `$locip`, and `$rmtip`. The number must be an integer and the following operators are available and have their traditional C language meanings: ==, !=, <, >, <=, and >=.
`init` *initstring*	Sets the initialization string sent to the modem by the reset command to *initstring*.
`mode SLIP¦CSLIP`	Sets the protocol mode for the connection and makes `dip` go into daemon mode. This command normally causes `dip` to go into daemon mode and not return control to the script or `DIP>` command line.
`modem HAYES`	Sets the modem type. Only the HAYES modem type is currently supported. (HAYES must be capitalized.)
`netmask` *mask*	Sets the netmask for the routes `dip` installs to *mask*.
`parity E¦O¦N`	Sets the parity of the serial line: even, odd, or none.
`password`	Prompts the user for a password and retrieves it in a secure manner. This command does not echo the password as you type it in.
`print`	Echoes text to the console `dip` started on. Variables included in the text are replaced with their values.
`port` *dev*	Sets the device `dip` uses.
`quit`	Exits the `dip` program.
`reset`	Sends the `init` string to the serial line.
`send` *text*	Sends the specified text to the serial line. The traditional C-style backslash sequences are properly handled.
`sleep` *num*	Delays processing for the specified number of seconds.
`speed` *num*	Sets the serial line speed.
`stopbits` *bits*	Sets the number of stopbits used by the serial port.

(continues)

Table 16.2 Continued

Command	Description
`timeout` *num*	Sets the default timeout to the integer value *num*. This is measured in seconds.
`term`	Makes `dip` go into terminal emulation mode. This allows you to interface directly with the serial link. Pressing <Ctrl-]> returns you to the `DIP>` prompt.
`wait` *word num*	Makes `dip` wait for the specified *word* to arrive on the serial line with a timeout of *num* seconds.

`dip` also provides a number of variables for your use. Some, such as the local and remote IP addresses, can be set by you; others are read-only and are used for diagnostic and informational purposes. Each variable begins with a dollar sign and must be written in lowercase letters. Table 16.3 lists these variables and their uses.

Tip

Setting the `$local` or `$remote` variable to a host name causes `dip` to resolve the host name to its IP address and store that in the respective IP address variable. This saves a step in the scripts you write.

Table 16.3 Variables Provided by *dip*

Variable	Description
`$local`	The host name of the local machine
`$locip`	The IP Address assigned to the local machine
`$remote`	The host name of the remote machine
`$rmtip`	The IP Address of the remote machine
`$mtu`	The MTU value for the connection
`$modem`	The modem type being used (read-only)
`$port`	The name of the serial device `dip` is using (read-only)
`$speed`	The speed setting of the serial device (read-only)
`$errlvl`	This variable contains the result code of the last command (read-only) executed; zero indicates success and any other value is an error.

You cannot set the read-only variables directly using the `get` command.

Using *dip* with Static IP Addresses

It is very common to assign individual IP addresses to each machine that uses a SLIP provider. When your machine initiates a SLIP link to the remote host, `dip` configures the SLIP interface with this known address. The following is a `dip` script using static IP addresses for initiating a SLIP link from `unixlt.tristar.com` to `unix1.tristar.com`.

```
# Connect unixlt to unix1 using static IP Addresses
# Configure Communication Parameters
port /dev/cua1 # use modem on /dev/cua1 serial line
speed 38400
modem HAYES
reset                            # Send initialization string to modem
flush                            # Throw away modem response

get $local unixlt                # Set local IP address
get $remote unix1                # Set remote IP address


# Dial number for unix1 modem
dial 555-1234
if $errlvl != 0 goto error       # If the dial command fails, error out
wait CONNECT 75
if $errlvl != 0 goto error       # If we don't get a CONNECT string
                                 # from the modem, error out

send \r\n                        # Wake up login program
wait ogin: 30                    # Wait 30 seconds for login prompt
if $errlvl != 0 goto error       # Error out if we don't get login prompt
send Sunixlt\n                   # Send SLIP login name for unixlt
wait ssword: 5                   # Wait 5 seconds for password prompt
if $errlvl != 0 goto error       # Error out if we don't get password
send be4me\n                     # Send password
wait running 30                  # Wait for indication that SLIP is up
if $errlvl != 0 goto error       # Otherwise error out

# We're in, print out useful information
print Connected to $remote with address $rmtip
default                          # Make this link our default route
mode SLIP                        # Turn on SLIP mode on our end

# Error routine in case things don't work
error:
print SLIP to $remote failed.
```

Tip

Tracking SLIP accounts can be a difficult task. Traditionally, UNIX user accounts are assigned logon names with all lowercase letters. Using the client machine name with a capital S added to the front as the logon name for that machine's SLIP account makes tracking it easier and avoids logon name collisions with normal user accounts.

This script initializes the modem and sets the local and remote IP addresses for the SLIP link. Note that you can use host names here and `dip` resolves them to their IP address equivalents. The script then dials the modem and works its way through the logon sequence. Once logged on and sure that the SLIP link is up on the remote host, the script has dip configure the routing table and then switch the serial line into SLIP mode.

If an error occurs, the error routine at the end of the script prints a warning message and aborts the script. dip is excellent about leaving the serial line in a reasonable state when it is done with it.

Using *dip* with Dynamic IP Addresses

As SLIP became more popular, the task of managing IP addressees for SLIP clients got more and more difficult. This problem got worse when terminal servers supporting SLIP came into use. Now, you might be assigned any one of a range of IP addresses depending on which port the terminal server received your call. This led to changes in dip that captured IP address information from the incoming data on the serial line. The following is a dip script that captures the local and remote IP addresses from the serial line:

```
# Connection script for SLIP to server with dynamic IP address
# assignment. The terminal server prints out:
#
# remote address is XXX.XXX.XXX.XXX the local address is YYY.YYY.YYY.YYY


 # Set the desired serial port and speed.
 port /dev/cua1
 speed 38400

 # Reset the modem and terminal line.
 Reset
 flush

 # Prepare for dialing.
 dial 555-1234
 if $errlvl != 0 goto error
 wait CONNECT 60
 if $errlvl != 0 goto error

 # We are connected. Login to the system.
login:
 wait name: 10                        # Log in to system
 if $errlvl != 0 goto error
 send Sunixlt\n                       # Send user ID
 wait ord: 10
 if $errlvl != 0 goto error
 send be4me\n                         # Send password
 if $errlvl != 0 goto error
 get $remote remote 10                # Get remote IP address
 if $errlvl != 0 goto error
 get $local remote 10                 # Get local IP address
 if $errlvl != 0 goto error
done:
 print CONNECTED to $remote with address $rmtip we are $local
 default                              # Set routing
 mode SLIP                            # Go to SLIP mode
```

```
 goto exit
error:
 print SLIP to $host failed.
exit:
```

This script uses `get $remote remote 10` to watch the serial line and capture the first thing that looks like an IP address in the `$remote` variable. The command times out in ten seconds with an error if it doesn't see an IP address.

Using *diplogin* to Provide SLIP Service

The `dip` program automates starting SLIP links from the client machine. Linux also supports incoming dial-up SLIP links. There are a few packages available for doing this as well. You use the `diplogin` program here, which is really just another name for `dip`.

Providing SLIP service to others requires that you create a specific account for each person on your Linux box and configure that account correctly. You also need to write a `/etc/diphosts` file with appropriate information for each host that you are providing SLIP service for.

Creating SLIP Accounts

You can either manually create the SLIP account or use the `adduser` script with appropriate responses to each question. Here is an example `/etc/passwd` entry for **unixlt.tristar.com** in the `passwd` file on **unix1.tristar.com**.

```
Sunixlt:IdR4gDZ7K7D82:505:100:unixlt SLIP Account:/tmp:/sbin/diplogin
```

It is recommended that `/tmp` be used as the home directory for SLIP accounts to minimize security risks. Make sure you use the correct path to the `diplogin` program.

The */etc/diphosts* File

This file controls access to SLIP on your machine and contains the connection parameters for each account allowed to use SLIP. It contains lines that look similar to the following:

```
Sunixlt::unixlt.tristar.com:unixlt SLIP:SLIP,296
```

The fields in this file are the user ID, secondary password, host name or IP address of the calling machine, an informational field not currently used, and the connection parameters for this account. The connection parameters field contains the protocol (SLIP or CSLIP) and the MTU value for this account.

If the second field is not empty, `diplogin` prompts for an external security password when the specified account logs on to your machine. If the response from the remote host does not match the string in this field, the logon attempt is aborted.

> **Caution**
>
> The `diplogin` program requires superuser privileges to modify the kernel routing table. If you are not running `dip setuid` root then you cannot use a link between `dip` and `diplogin`. You must make a separate copy of `dip` called `diplogin` and have its suid root.

That's all it takes. Setting up SLIP accounts and the `/etc/diphosts` file completely configures your system to support incoming SLIP links.

Using PPP

PPP (Point-to-Point Protocol) is another protocol for sending datagrams across a serial link. Developed after SLIP, PPP contains a number of features SLIP lacks. It can negotiate automatically options such as IP addresses, datagram sizes, and client authorization. It can also transport packets from protocols other than IP.

Automating PPP Links with *pppd* and *chat*

PPP operates in two parts, the PPP driver in the Linux kernel and a program called `pppd` that the user must run. The most basic means of using PPP is to manually log on to the remote host using a communications program and manually start `pppd` on the remote and local hosts. It is much more convenient to use a `chat` script with `pppd` that handles the modem, logging on to the remote host, and starting the remote `pppd`. Before diving into `pppd`, take a short look at `chat`.

Using the *chat* Program. `chat` is a program for automating the interaction between your computer and a modem. It is mainly used to establish the modem connection between the local and remote `pppd` daemon processes. Table 16.4 lists the command-line arguments for the `chat` program. The syntax for `chat` is

```
chat [options] script
```

Table 16.4 *chat* Command-Line Arguments

Argument	Description
`-f` *`file-name`*	Uses the `chat` script in the specified file
`-l` *`lockfile`*	Makes a UUCP style lock file using the specified *`lockfile`*
`-t` *`num`*	Uses the specified number as the timeout in seconds for each expected string
`-v`	Makes `chat` log everything it sends and receives to `syslog`
`script`	The `chat` script to use

You cannot use the `-f` option and specify a `chat` script at the same time. They are mutually exclusive. If you use the `-l` option for `chat`, do not use the `lock` option with pppd because the *lockfile* created by chat causes pppd to fail, thinking that the modem device is already in use.

Tip

When debugging chat scripts, run `tail -f /var/adm/messages` on one virtual console and use the -v option when you run chat in another. You can then watch the conversation chat is having as it comes up on the first virtual console.

Tip

Include only the text necessary in expect strings to positively identify what you are looking for. This minimizes the chance of a mismatch or having your script blow up because of garbled text.

***chat* Scripts.** Chat scripts consist of one or more *expect-reply pairs* of strings separated by spaces. The chat program waits for the expected text and sends the reply text when it receives it. Optional *subexpect-subreply pairs* can be included in the expect portion, separated by hyphens. Here is a typical chat script for logging on to a Linux machine.

```
ogin:-\r\n-ogin: abbet1 word: costello
```

This script says that chat should wait for the string ogin: to appear. If chat times out before receiving it, chat should send a carriage return and linefeed and wait for the string ogin: again. When chat sees the ogin: string it sends abbet1 and then waits for the word: and sends costello in response.

chat normally sends a carriage return after each reply string unless a \c character sequence ends the string. Carriage returns are not looked for in expect strings unless explicitly requested with the \r character sequence in the expect string.

Most modems can report the reason why a call failed when it gets a busy signal or can't detect a carrier. You can use the abort expect string to tell chat to fail if it receives the specified strings. Multiple abort pairs are cumulative. The following script is an example of using the abort expect string.

```
abort 'NO CARRIER' abort 'BUSY' ogin:--ogin: ppp word: be4me
```

This chat script makes chat fail if it receives NO CARRIER or BUSY at any point during the script.

A number of character and escape sequences are recognized by chat. Table 16.5 describes each of these.

Table 16.5 Character and Escape Sequences Recognized by *chat*

Sequence	Description
BREAK	Used as a reply string, this makes chat send a break to the modem. This is a special signal that normally causes the remote host to change its transmission speed.
''	Sends a null string with a single carriage return.
\b	The backspace character.
\c	This suppresses the newline sent after a reply string and must be at the end of the reply string.
\d	Makes chat wait for one second.
\K	Another means of specifying a break signal.
\n	Sends a newline character.
\N	Sends a null character.
\p	Pauses for 1/10th of one second.
\q	This prevents the string it is included in from showing in the syslog file.
\r	Sends or expects a carriage return.
\s	Sends or expects a space character.
\t	Sends or expects a tab character.
\\	Sends or expects a backslash character.
\ddd	Specifies an ASCII character in octal.
^C	Specifies the control character represented by C.

Tip

You can use the abort string to prevent low speed calls on your high speed modem. Configure your modem to return a `CARRIER 14400` string when it makes a connection and add `abort CARRIER 2400` to your `chat` script. This makes `chat` fail if your modem connects at 2400 bps instead of 14400 bps.

Using PPP with *chat*. The `pppd` program has command-line options that control all aspects of the PPP link. Table 16.6 describes the most commonly used options. The syntax for the `pppd` command is

```
pppd [options] [tty_name] [speed]
```

Table 16.6 Frequently Used *pppd* Command-Line Arguments

Argument	Description
device	Uses the specified device. pppd adds /dev/ to the string if needed. When no device is given, pppd uses the controlling terminal.
speed	Sets the modem speed.
asyncmap map	Sets the async character map. This map specifies which control characters can't be sent through the connection and need to be escaped. The map is a 32-bit hex number where each bit represents a character. The 0th bit (00000001) represents character 0 × 00.
auth	Requires the remote host to authenticate itself.
connect *program*	Uses the program or shell command to set up the connection. This is where chat is used.
crtscts	Uses hardware flow control.
xonxoff	Uses software flow control.
defaultroute	Makes pppd set a default route to the remote host in your kernel routing table.
disconnect *program*	Runs the specified program after pppd terminates its link.
escape *c1,c2,...*	Causes the specified characters to be escaped when transmitted. The characters are specified using the ASCII hex equivalent.
file *file-name*	Reads pppd options from the specified file.
lock	Uses UUCP style locking on the serial device.
mru *num*	Sets the maximum receive unit to the specified number.
netmask *mask*	Sets the PPP network interface netmask.
passive	Makes pppd wait for a valid connection instead of failing when it cannot initiate a connection immediately.
silent	Keeps pppd from initiating a connection. pppd waits for a connection attempt from the remote host instead.

There are over 40 other command-line arguments that control all aspects of PPP at all levels. Refer to the man page for information about them.

> **Note**
>
> The pppd program demands that the file /etc/ppp/options exist, even if it is empty. This file is read by pppd and is an excellent place to put options you want pppd to use every time it runs.

There are a number of ways to combine pppd and chat. You can specify all the command-line arguments for both programs on the command line, put the pppd options in a file, or put the chat script in a file. Following is a simple example with everything on the command line:

```
$ pppd connect 'chat "" ATDT5551234 ogin: unixlt word: be4me' \<Return>
/dev/cua1 38400 mru 296 lock debug crtscts modem defaultroute<Return>
```

This runs pppd with a simple chat script that dials a phone number and logs the user unixlt onto the remote host. The device, speed, MRU, and a number of other options are included.

At the other extreme, you can place most of the options for pppd in a file and have chat read a script file. The following is the call to pppd:

```
pppd /dev/cua1 38400 connect 'chat -f unix1.chat'
```

The following lines display the contents of the reference file:

```
# Global PPP Options File
mru 296                                 # Set MRU value
lock                                    # Use UUCP locking
crtscts                                 # Use hardware handshaking
modem                                   # Use modem control lines
defaultroute                            # Make PPP set up default route
```

pppd reads this file and processes the options it finds within. Any text following a # character is treated as a comment and ignored.

```
abort 'NO CARRIER'
abort 'BUSY'
abort 'VOICE'
abort 'CARRIER 2400'
"" ATDT555-1234
CONNECT '\c'
ogin:-BREAK-ogin: ppp
word: ppp-word
```

This chat script sets a number of abort strings, dials the phone number, waits for a logon prompt, and logs the user ppp on to the remote host with password ppp-word.

Providing PPP Service

Configuring your Linux machine to be a PPP server is even easier than setting up a SLIP server. It requires only one new account and a shell script that properly runs the pppd program.

Create an account called ppp with an /etc/passwd entry that looks like

```
$ ppp:*:501:300:PPP Account:/tmp:/etc/ppp/ppplogin
```

and set the passwd appropriately. The uid (501) and gid (300) numbers need not be the same. You can also assign one account to each PPP client you have if you want. The /etc/ppp/ppplogin file should be an executable script such as

```
#!/bin/sh
# PPP Server Login Script
# Turn off messages to this terminal
mesg n
# Turn off echoing
```

```
stty -echo
# Run pppd on top of this sh process
exec pppd -detach silent modem crtscts
```

This script executes pppd with the -detach argument. This keeps pppd from detaching itself from the tty it is on. If pppd detached, the script exits, causing the dial-up connection to close. The silent option makes pppd wait for the remote pppd daemon to initiate the link. The modem options make pppd monitor the modem control lines and crtscts makes pppd use hardware flow control.

That is all there is to it. When users log on to your machine with the proper user ID and password, the PPP link is established automatically on your box.

Security and PPP

Keeping your PPP link secure is very important. Allowing anyone to connect your machine to a PPP server or allowing anyone to connect to your PPP server is as bad as letting anyone put their machine directly on your network. PPP provides a direct IP connection, effectively putting the machines on both ends of the link on the same network.

Two authentication protocols have been developed to make PPP more secure—Password Authentication Protocol (PAP), and the Challenge Handshake Authentication Protocol (CHAP). While a PPP connection is being established, each machine can request the other to authenticate itself. This allows complete control of who can use your PPP service. CHAP is the more secure protocol and is discussed here.

CHAP uses a set of secret keys, which are text strings that are kept secret by the owners of the machines using CHAP, and an encrypted challenge system to authenticate each other. A useful feature of CHAP is that it periodically issues challenge requests as long as the PPP link is up. This, for example, can detect intruders who have replaced the legitimate user by switching phone lines.

The secret keys for CHAP are stored in /etc/ppp/chap-secrets. To use authentication on your PPP link, you add the auth option to the call to pppd and add the appropriate information for the host being authenticated into the chap-secrets file. The following is a sample chap-secrets file for **unixlt.tristar.com**:

```
# unixlt.tristar.com CHAP secrets file
# client/server/secret/IP addr
unixlt.tristar.com unix1.tristar.com "It's Full of Stars"
➥unixlt.tristar.com
unix1.tristar.com unixlt.tristar.com "three stars" unix1.tristar.com
* unixlt.tristar.com "three stars" tristar.com
```

Each line contains up to four fields: the client host name, server host name, secret key, and an optional list of IP addresses that this client can request be assigned to it. The client and server designations in this file are determined by the host that makes the authentication request (the server). The client has to respond to the request.

This file defines three different CHAP secrets. The first line is used when **unix1.tristar.com** requests CHAP authentication from **unixlt.tristar.com** and the second is used for the reverse situation. The last line defines a wild-card situation for the client. This allows any machine that knows the proper secret key to make a PPP link to **unixlt.tristar.com**. The wild-card designator (*) can be used in either the client or server field.

Careful management of the `chap-secrets` file allows you complete control over the machines that can access your PPP server and the machines that you can access with PPP.

Summary

SLIP and PPP are low-cost alternatives to a leased-line IP connectivity solution. You have looked at the requirements for running SLIP and PPP and at how to automate SLIP and PPP links using the `dip` and `chat` commands. You have learned how to configure Linux as a SLIP or PPP server and how to enhance the security of PPP using the CHAP protocol.

From Here...

In this chapter, you explored using SLIP and PPP to connnect your linux machine to a remote network. You can find complete documentation for `dip`, `chat`, and `pppd` in the man pages.

- Chapter 9, "Managing User Accounts," shows you how to add and delete user accounts.
- Chapter 13, "Understanding the TCP/IP Protocol Suite," explains what TCP/IP is and how the protocols work.
- Chapter 14, "Configuring a TCP/IP Network," shows you how to set up a Linux machine for use on a network.
- Chapter 15, "Configuring Domain Name Service (DNS)," shows you how to make Linux use DNS.

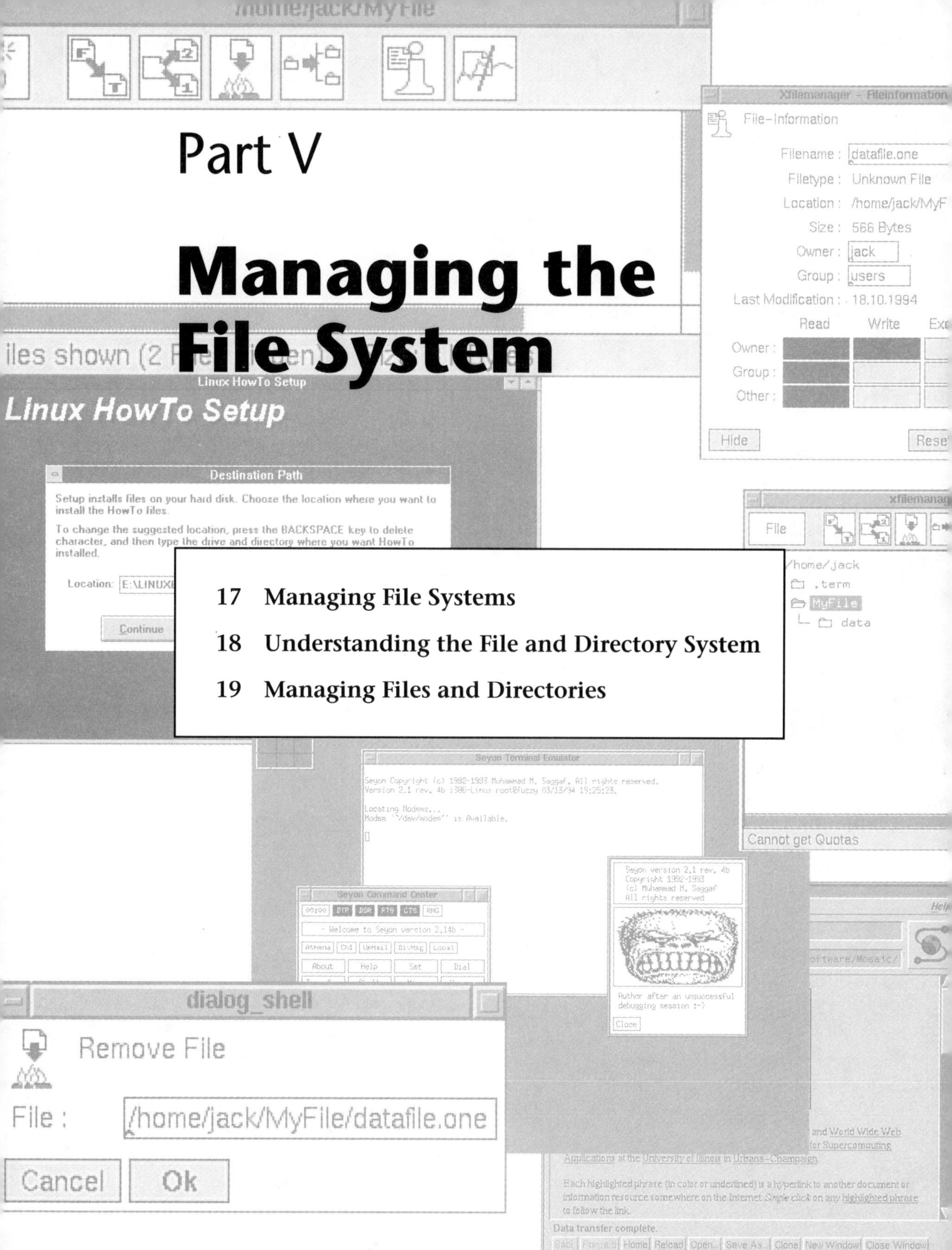

Part V

Managing the File System

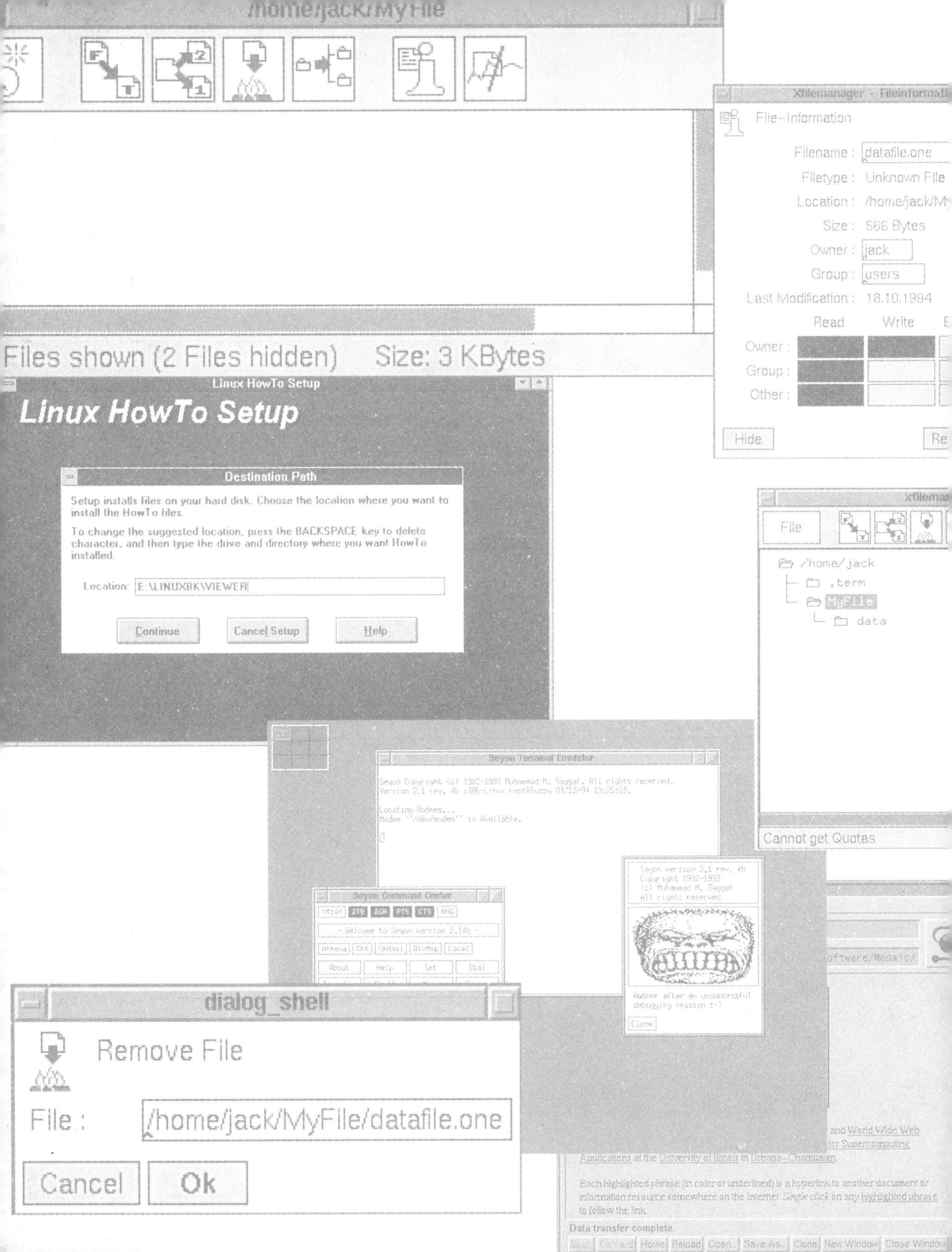

/home/jack/MyFile
Files shown (2 Files hidden)
Size: 3 KBytes
Xfilemanager - Fileinformati
File-Information
Filename : datafile.one
Filetype : Unknown File
Location : /home/jack/M
Size : 566 Bytes
Owner : jack
Group : users
Last Modification : 18.10.1994
Read
Write
Owner :
Group :
Other :
Hide
Linux HowTo Setup
Linux HowTo Setup
Destination Path
Setup installs files on your hard disk. Choose the location where you want to install the HowTo files.
To change the suggested location, press the BACKSPACE key to delete character, and then type the drive and directory where you want HowTo installed.
Location: E:\LINUXBK\VIEWER
Continue
Cancel Setup
Help
xfilema
File
/home/jack
.term
MyFile
data
Cannot get Quotas
Seyon Terminal Emulator
Seyon Command Center
dialog_shell
Remove File
File : /home/jack/MyFile/datafile.one
Cancel
Ok
Close
Data transfer complete.

CHAPTER 17

Managing File Systems

File systems form the basis for all data on a Linux system. Linux programs, libraries, system files, and user files all reside on file systems. Proper management of file systems is critical because all your data and programs exist on top of file systems. Many of the steps outlined in this chapter are performed automatically when you install Linux. However, you should learn to manage your file systems so that you can create or change your Linux system. Understanding file-system management is critical to successful systems administration. Your file system must work properly for your Linux system to work at all. In this chapter, you do the following:

- Learn about file systems
- Tour the Linux file system
- Mount and unmount file systems
- Work with the Network File System (NFS)
- Maintain file systems
- Create and format file systems
- Use swap files and partitions

What Is a File System?

Under Linux, the file space that is visible to users is based on a tree structure, with the root at the top. The various directories and files in this space branch downward from the root. The top directory, /, is known as the root directory. Figure 17.1 gives a graphical example of a tree structure.

Tip

You can visualize the Linux file system as an upside-down tree, with the root at the top and the branches and leaves spreading downward.

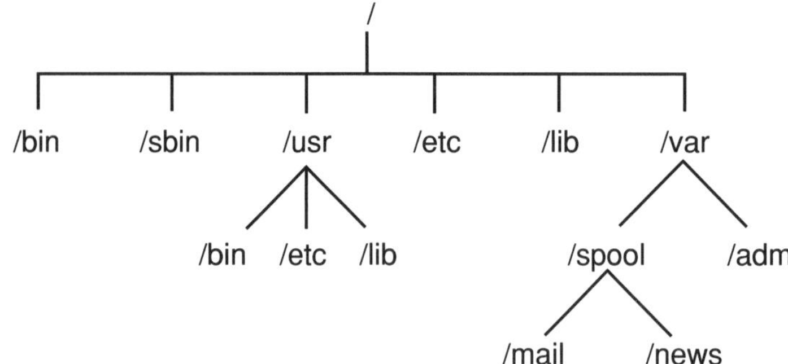

Fig. 17.1

A section of the Linux directory tree.

To the user, this directory tree looks like a seamless entity—the user just sees directories and files. In reality, many of the directories in the file tree are physically located as different partitions on a disk, on different disks, or even on different computers. When one of these disk partitions is attached to the file tree at a directory known as a *mount point*, the mount point and all directories below it are referred to as a file system.

The Linux File System

The Linux operating system is made up of several directories and many different files. Depending on how you selected your installation, these directories may be different file systems. Typically, most all of the operating system resides on two file systems: the root file system, known as `/`, and a file system mounted under `/usr`, pronounced as *user*.

If you change directories to the root directory with the `cd /` command and ask for a directory listing, you see several directories. These make up the contents of the root file system and provide the mount points for other file systems as well.

The `/bin` directory contains executable programs, known as binaries. In fact, the directory named `/bin` is short for binary. These programs are essential system files. Many of the commands, such as `ls`, are actually programs that are found in this directory.

The `/sbin` directory is also used to store system binary files. Most of the files in this directory are used for system administration purposes.

The `/etc` directory is very important, containing many of the Linux system configuration files. Essentially, these are the files that give your Linux system its "personality." The password file, `passwd`, is found here, as is the list of file systems to mount at start up, `fstab`. In addition, this directory contains the startup scripts for Linux, the list of hosts with IP addresses that you want permanently recorded, and many other types of configuration information.

The shared libraries that programs use when they run are stored in the /lib directory. By using shared libraries, many programs can reuse the same code, and these libraries can be stored in a common place, reducing the size of your programs at run time.

The /dev directory contains special files known as device files. These files are used to access all of the different types of hardware on your system. For example, the /dev/mouse file is for reading input from the mouse. By organizing access to hardware devices in this way, Linux effectively makes the interface to a hardware device look like a file. What does this mean, you ask? It means that you, in many cases, can use the same syntax that you use with files to perform operations on computer hardware devices. For example, to create a tape archive of your home directory on a floppy drive, you can use the following command:

```
tar -cdf /dev/fd0 ~tackett
```

▶▶ See "tar," p. 543

Many of the devices in the /dev directory are in logical groups. Table 17.1 lists some of the most commonly used devices in the /dev directory.

Table 17.1 Some of the Most Commonly Used Devices in the */dev* Directory

Device File	Description
/dev/console	Refers to the system console, which is the computer monitor physically connected to your Linux system.
/dev/hd	The device interface to IDE hard drives. The /dev/hda1 device refers to the first partition on hard drive hda. The device /dev/hda refers to the entire hard disk hda.
/dev/sd	This is the device interface for SCSI disks. The same conventions for disks and partitions apply as they do to the /dev/hd devices.
/dev/fd	These devices provide support for floppy drives. /dev/fd0 is the first floppy drive, and /dev/fd1 is the second floppy drive.
/dev/st	This is the device for SCSI tape drives.
/dev/sr	This device provides the interface for SCSI CD-ROM drives.
/dev/tty	These devices provide different consoles for user input. The name comes from when terminals known as teletypes were physically hooked to a UNIX system. Under Linux, they provide support for the virtual consoles that can be accessed by pressing <Alt-F1> through <Alt-F6>. These virtual consoles provide separate simultaneous local logon sessions.
/dev/pty	The pty devices provide support for pseudo-terminals. Psuedo-terminals are used for remote logon sessions such as logon sessions using telnet.
/dev/ttyS	The ttyS devices are the serial interface ports on your computer. /dev/ttyS0 corresponds to COM1 under MS-DOS. If you have a serial mouse, /dev/mouse is a symbolic link to the appropriate ttyS device that your mouse is connected to.

(continues)

Table 17.1 Continued

Device File	Description
/dev/cua	The /dev/cua devices are special call-out devices that are used with modems.
/dev/null	This is a very special device. /dev/null is essentially a black hole. All data written to it is lost forever. This can be very useful if you want to run a command and throw away the standard output or the standard error. Also, if /dev/null is used as an input file, a file of zero length is created.

The /proc directory is actually a virtual file system. It is used to read process information from memory.

The /tmp directory is used to store temporary files that programs create when running. If you have a program that creates a lot of large temporary files, you may want to mount the /tmp directory as a separate file system instead of just having it as a directory on the root file system. If /tmp is left as a directory on the root file system and it has lots of large files written to it, the root file system can fill up.

The /home directory is the base directory for user home directories. It is common to mount this as a separate file system so the users can have plenty of room for their files. In fact, if you have a lot of users on your system, you may need to separate /home into several file systems. To do this, you could create subdirectories such as /home/staff and /home/admin for staff members and administrators, respectively. Mount each of these as different file systems and then create the users' home directories under them.

The /var directory holds files that tend to change in size over time. Typically various system log files are located below this directory.

Note

The directory /var/spool and its subdirectories are used to hold data that is of a transitory nature, such as mail and news that is recently received from or queued for transmission to another site.

Tip

You can create other mount points under the / directory if you want. You might want to create a mount point named /cdrom if you routinely mount CD-ROMs on your system.

The /usr directory and its subdirectories are very important to the operation of your Linux system. It contains several directories with some of the most important programs on your system. Typically, subdirectories of /usr contain the large software packages that you install. Some of the /usr subdirectories are discussed in Table 17.2. The /usr directory is almost always mounted as a separate file system.

Table 17.2 Important Subdirectories in the */usr* File System

Subdirectory	Description
/usr/bin	This directory is used to hold many of the executable programs found on your Linux system.
/usr/etc	This directory contains lots of miscellaneous system configuration files.
/usr/include	Here and in the subdirectories of /usr/include is where you find all of the include files for the C compiler. These are header files that define constants and functions and are critical for C programming.
/usr/g++-include	Contains the include files for the C++ compiler.
/usr/lib	Contains various libraries for programs to use during linking.
/usr/man	This directory contains the various man pages for programs on your Linux system. Below /usr/man are several directories that correspond to the different sections of the man pages.
/usr/src	This directory contains directories that hold the source code for different programs on your system. If you get a package that you want to install, /usr/src/*packagename* is a good place to put the source before you install it.
/usr/local	The /usr/local directory is designed for local customizations to your system. In general, much of your local software is installed in the subdirectories of this directory. The format of this directory is different on almost every UNIX system that you look at. One way to set it up is to have a /usr/local/bin for binaries, a /usr/local/etc for configuration files, a /usr/local/lib for libraries, and a /usr/local/src for source code. The entire /usr/local directory tree may be mounted as a separate file system if you need a lot of room for it.

Mounting and Unmounting File Systems

Tip

If you need to know what file system a directory is located on, you can use the df command. Change directory to the directory in question and type **df .**. The output shows the file system as well as the free space available.

By now, you should have a good feel for what a file system is. So how do you set up a directory as a separate file system?

To mount a file system in the Linux directory tree, you must have a physical disk partition, CD-ROM, or floppy disk that you want to mount. You must also make sure that the directory where you want to attach the file system, known as the *mount point*, actually exists. Mounting a file system does not create the mount point directory. It must exist before you try to mount the file system. For example, suppose that you want to mount the CD-ROM in drive `/dev/sr0` under the mount point `/mnt`. A directory named `/mnt` must exist or the mount fails. After mounting the file system under that directory, all the files and subdirectories on the file system appear under the `/mnt` directory. Otherwise, the `/mnt` directory is empty.

Mounting File Systems Interactively

As you may have guessed by now, Linux uses the `mount` command to mount a file system. The syntax of the `mount` command is

```
mount device mountpoint
```

`device` is the physical device that you want to mount and *`mountpoint`* is the point in the file-system tree where you want it to appear. `mount` accepts several command-line arguments in addition to the two given above. If a needed command is not given, `mount` attempts to figure it out from the `/etc/fstab` file. Table 17.3 lists the command-line arguments for `mount`.

> **Note**
>
> The `mount` command can only be used by the superuser. This is to help ensure system security. There are several software packages available that allow users to mount specific file systems, especially floppy disks.

Table 17.3 Command-Line Arguments for the *mount* Command

Argument	Description
`-f`	Causes everything to be done except for the actual mount system call. This "fakes" mounting the file system.
`-v`	Verbose mode. `mount` provides additional information about what it is trying to do.
`-w`	The file system is to be mounted with read and write permissions.
`-r`	The file system is to be mounted with read-only permission.
`-n`	Mounts without writing in an entry in the `/etc/mtab` file.
`-t` *`type`*	Specifies the type of the file system being mounted. Valid types are `minux`, `ext`, `ext2`, `xiafs`, `msdos`, `hpfs`, `proc`, `nfs`, `umsdos`, `sysv`, and `iso9660`.
`-a`	Causes `mount` to try to mount all file systems in `/etc/fstab`.
`-o` *`list-of-options`*	The `-o` argument followed by a comma-separated list-of-options causes `mount` to apply the options specified to the file system that is being mounted. There are many options available here. For a complete list, refer to the `mount` man page.

Note

There are several forms of the `mount` command that are very common. `mount/dev/hdb3 /mnt` mounts the hard-disk partition `/dev/hdb3` under the directory `/mnt`. `mount -r -t iso9660 /dev/sr0 /mnt` mounts the SCSI CD-ROM drive `/dev/sr0`, which is read-only and of the ISO 9660 file format under the directory `/mnt`. `mount -vat nfs` mounts all the NFS file systems listed in the `/etc/fstab` file.

Note

If a file system doesn't mount correctly, use the command `mount -vf device mountpoint` to see what `mount` is doing. This gives a verbose listing and tells `mount` to do everything except mount the file system. This way you can fake out the `mount` command and get a lot of information about what it is trying to do.

Mounting File Systems at Boot Time

Under most circumstances, the file systems that your Linux system uses won't change frequently. For this reason, you can easily specify a list of file systems that Linux mounts when it boots and that it unmounts when it shuts down. These file systems are listed in a special configuration file named `/etc/fstab` for *file system table*.

The `/etc/fstab` file lists the file systems to be mounted, one file system per line. The fields in each line are separated by spaces or tabs. Table 17.4 lists the different fields in the `/etc/fstab` file.

Table 17.4 Fields in the */etc/fstab* File

Field	Description
File system specifier	Specifies the block special device or the remote file system to be mounted.
Mount point	Specifies the mount point for the file system. For special file systems such as swap files, use the word `none`. This is used to make swap files active but not visible within the file tree.
Type	Gives the file-system type of the specified file system. Currently, the following types of file systems are supported: `minix`, a local file system, supporting file names of 14 or 30 characters; `ext`, a local file system with longer file names and larger inodes (this file system has been replaced by the `ext2` file system, and should no longer be used); `ext2`, a local file system with longer file names, larger inodes, and other features; `xiafs`, a local file system; `msdos`, a local file system for MS-DOS partitions; `hpfs`, a local file system for OS/2 High Performance File System partitions; `iso9660`, a local file system used for CD-ROM drives; `nfs`, a file system for mounting partitions from remote systems; `swap`, a disk partition or special file used for swapping; `umsdos`, a UMSDOS file system; and `sysv`, a System V file

(continues)

Table 17.4 Continued

Field	Description
	system.
Mount Options	A comma-separated list of mount options for the file system. At a minimum, it must contain the type of mount for the file system. See the `mount` man page for more information on this list.
Dump Frequency	Specifies how often the file system should be backed up by the `dump` command. If this field is not present, `dump` assumes that the file system does not need to be backed up.
Pass Number	Specifies in what order the file systems should be checked by the `fsck` command when the system is booted. The root file system should have a value of 1. All other file systems should have a value of 2. If a value is not specified, the file system will not be checked for consistency at boot time.

Tip

It is recommended that you mount your file systems at boot time via the `/etc/fstab` file than by using the `mount` command. Remember, only the superuser can use `mount`.

The following is a sample `fstab` file:

```
# device        directory     type     options
/dev/hda1       /             ext2     defaults
/dev/hda2       /usr          ext2     defaults
/dev/hda3       none          swap     sw
/dev/sda1       /dosc         msdos    defaults
/proc           /proc         proc     none
```

In this sample, you can see several different file systems. First of all, notice that comments in the file are prefixed by a # character. In this `fstab` file, two normal Linux file systems are mounted. These are the disk partitions `/dev/hda1` and `/dev/hda2`. These are listed as being of type `ext2` and are mounted under the root directory, / and `/usr` respectively. The entry defaults listed under the options field indicates that this file system should be mounted using a common set of default options. Specifically, the file system is mounted read/write enabled, it is to be interpreted as a block special device, all file I/O should be done asynchronously, the execution of binaries is permitted, the file system can be mounted with the `mount -a` command, the set UID and set GID bits on files are interpreted on this file system, and ordinary users are not allowed to mount this file system. As you can see, it's a lot easier just to type **`defaults`** for the option instead.

◂◂ See "Creating the Swap Partition," p. 76

The partition /dev/hda3 is a swap partition that is used for kernel virtual-memory swap space. Its mount point is specified as none because you don't want it to appear in the file system tree. It still has to be in the /etc/fstab file so the system knows where it is physically located. Swap partitions are also mounted with the option sw.

The /proc file system is a virtual file system that points to the process information space in memory. As you can see, it does not have a corresponding physical partition to mount.

Tip

For full information on all the options available in the /etc/fstab file, refer to the man page for fstab.

MS-DOS file systems can also be automatically mounted. The partition /dev/sda1 is the first partition on SCSI hard drive sda. It is mounted as an MS-DOS partition by specifying msdos as the type. /dosc is given as its mount point. You can place this mount point anywhere—there is no requirement that it be under the root directory.

Unmounting File Systems

Now that you know all sorts of stuff about mounting file systems, it's time to look at how to unmount. You use the umount command to unmount file systems.

Caution

This command is umount, not "unmount." Make sure that you type it correctly.

There are three forms of the umount command. The basic syntax of the umount command is

```
umount device ¦ mountpoint

umount -a

umount -t fstype
```

device is the name of the physical device to unmount and *mountpoint* is the mount point directory name. You only need to specify one or the other. The umount command has only two additional command-line parameters: -a unmounts all file systems, and -t *fstype* acts only on file systems of the type specified.

Caution

The `umount` command does not unmount a file system that is in use. For example, if you have some file system mounted under `/mnt` and you try

```
cd /mnt<Return>

umount /mnt<Return>
```

You get an error telling you that the file system is busy. You have to change to a different directory in another file system in order to unmount the file system mounted under `/mnt`.

The Network File System

The Network File System (NFS) is a system that allows you to mount file systems from a different computer over a TCP/IP network. Under NFS, a file system on a remote computer is mounted locally and looks just like a local file system to users. This has numerous uses. For example, you can have one machine on your network with a lot of disk space acting as a file server. This computer has all the home directories of all your users on its local disks. By mounting these disks via NFS on all your other computers, your users can access their home directories from any computer.

There are three essential components to NFS. First, the computers that have the file systems that you want to NFS mount must be able to communicate with each other via a TCP/IP network. Second, the computer that has the file system that you are interested in as a local file system must make that file system available to be mounted. This computer is known as the *server*, and the process of making the file system available is known as *exporting* the file system. Third, the computer that wants to mount the exported file system, known as the *client*, must mount the file system as an NFS file system, either via the `/etc/fstab` file at boot time or interactively via the `mount` command. The following sections discuss exporting the file system and mounting it locally.

Exporting an NFS File System

In order for clients to mount an NFS file system, this file system must be made available by the server. Before the file system can be made available, you must ensure that it is mounted on the server. If the file system is always going to an NFS exported file system, you should make sure that you have it listed in the `/etc/fstab` file on the server so that it automatically mounts when the server boots.

Once you have the file system mounted locally, you can make it available via NFS. This is a two-step process. First, you must make sure that the NFS daemons `rpc.mountd` and `rpc.nfsd` are running on your server. These daemons are usually started from the startup `/etc/rc.inet2` script. Usually, all that is needed is to make sure that the following lines are in your `/etc/rc.inet2` script:

```
if [ -x /usr/sbin/rpc.mountd ]; then
     /usr/sbin/rpc.mountd; echo -n " mountd"
```

```
fi
if [ -x /usr/sbin/rpc.nfsd ]; then /usr/sbin/rpc.nfsd; echo -n "nfsd"
fi
```

Note

As RPC-based programs, the `rpc.mountd` and `rpc.nfsd` daemons are not managed by the `inetd` daemon but are started up at boot time, registering themselves with the `portmap` daemon. You must make sure to start them only after `rpc.portmap` is running.

Second, you must enter it in a configuration file named `/etc/exports`. This file contains information about what file systems can be exported, what computers are allowed to access them, and what type and level of access is permitted.

The */etc/exports* File

The `/etc/exports` file is used by the `mountd` and `nfsd` daemons to determine what file systems are to be exported and what restrictions are placed on them. File systems are listed in `/etc/exports`, one per line. The format of each line is the name of the mount point for a local file system followed by a list of computers that are allowed to mount this file system. A comma-separated list of mount options in parentheses may follow each name in the list. Table 17.5 lists the mount options available in the `/etc/exports` file.

Table 17.5 Mount Options Available in the */etc/exports* File

Option	Description
`insecure`	Permits non-authenticated access from this machine.
`unix-rpc`	Requires UNIX-domain RPC authentication from this machine. Default behavior.
`secure-rpc`	Requires secure RPC authentication from this machine. This option is accepted as valid but is not yet implemented under Linux.
`kerberos`	Requires Kerberos authentication on accesses from this machine. This option is accepted as valid but is not yet implemented under Linux.
`root_squash`	Maps any requests from root, `UID 0` on the client, to the `UID NOBODY_UID` on the server.
`no_root_squash`	Don't map any requests from `UID 0`. Default behavior.
`ro`	Mounts the file system read-only. Default behavior.
`rw`	Mounts the file system as read-write.
`link_relative`	Converts absolute symbolic links (where the link contents start with a slash) into relative links by prefixing the link with the necessary number of `../` characters to get from the directory containing the link to the root on the server. Default behavior.
`link_absolute`	Leaves all symbolic links as they are. This is the normal behavior for Sun NFS servers.

(continues)

Table 17.5 Continued

Option	Description
`map_identity`	Assumes the client and server have the same UID/GID information space.
`map_daemon`	Maps local and remote names and numeric IDs using an `lname/uid map` daemon on the client where the NFS request originated. Used to map between the client and server UID spaces.

Here is a sample `/etc/exports` file:

```
# A sample /etc/exports file
/home                bill.tristar.com(rw) fred.tristar.com(rw)
➥george.tristar.com(rw)
/usr/local/bin           *.tristar.com(ro)
/projects            develop.tristar.com(rw) bill.tristar.com(ro)
/pub                 (ro,insecure,root_quash)
```

In this example, the server exports four different file systems. `/home` is mounted with read and write access on three different computers: `bill`, `fred`, and `george`. This directory probably holds user home directories. The `/usr/local/bin` file system is exported as read-only with access allowed for every computer in the `tristar.com` domain. The `/projects` file system is exported with read-write access for the computer `develop.tristar.com` but with read-only access for `bill.tristar.com`. For the `/pub` file system, there is no list of hosts that are allowed access. This means that any host is allowed to mount this file system. It has been exported as read-only, non-authenticated access allowed, and the server remaps any request from root on a remote machine that accesses this file system.

Mounting NFS File Systems

Mounting an NFS file system is very similar to mounting any other type of file system. NFS file systems can be mounted from either the `/etc/fstab` file at boot time or via the `mount` command interactively.

Tip

You must make sure to separate the host-name and file-system-path portions of the remote file-system name with a colon.

Mounting NFS File Systems via */etc/fstab*. When you specify an NFS file system in the `/etc/fstab` file, you identify the file system with the format

```
host-name:/file/system/path
```

`host-name` is the name of the server where the file system is located, and *`x2/file/system/path`* is the file system on the server.

The file-system type is specified as `nfs` in the mount options field of the file system entry. There are several additional options that can be specified as well in addition to `nfs`. The man page for the `mount` command provides an exhaustive list. The most commonly used ones are listed in Table 17.6.

Table 17.6 Commonly Used Options for NFS Mounts

Option	Description
`rsize=`*n*	These specify the datagram size in bytes used by the NFS clients on read requests. The default value is 1024 bytes.
`wsize=`*n*	These specify the datagram size in bytes used by the NFS clients on write requests. The default value is 1024 bytes.
`timeo=`*n*	This sets the time, in tenths of a second, that the NFS client waits for a request to complete. The default value is 0.7 seconds.
`hard`	Mounts this file system using a hard mount. This is the default behavior.
`soft`	Mounts this file system using a soft mount.
`intr`	Allows signals to interrupt an NFS call. This is useful for aborting an operation when an NFS server doesn't respond.

Hard Mounts Versus Soft Mounts

Hard mounts and *soft mounts* determine how an NFS client acts when an NFS server stops responding. NFS file systems are hard mounted by default. If a server stops responding, the client waits until the time-out value specified by the `timeo` option expires and then resends the request. This is known as a *minor time out*. If the requests to the server continue to time out, and the total time out reaches 60 seconds, a *major time out* occurs. Here is where the difference between soft and hard mounts comes into play. If a file system is hard mounted, the client prints a message to the console and starts the mount requests all over again using a time-out value that is twice that of the previous cycle. This has the potential to go on forever. The client keeps trying to remount the NFS file system from the server until it gets it. Period.

Soft mounts, on the other hand, just generate an I/O error to the calling process when a major time out occurs. Linux then continues on its merry way.

Typically, important software packages and utilities that are mounted via NFS should be mounted with hard mounts. This is why hard mounts are the default. You don't want your system to start acting very strange if the Ethernet gets unplugged for a moment—you want it to wait and continue when the network is back up. On the other hand, you might want to mount noncritical data such as remote news spool partitions as soft mounts so that if the remote host goes down, it won't hang your current logon session.

A typical NFS file-system entry in the `/etc/fstab` file might look like

```
mailserver:/var/spool/mail  /var/spool/mail   nfs timeo=20,intr
```

This entry mounts the `/var/spool/mail` file system that is located on the host mailserver at the local mount point `/var/spool/mail`. It specifies that the file system type is `nfs`. In addition, it sets the time-out value to 2 seconds (20 tenths of a second) and makes operations on this file system interruptable.

Mounting NFS File Systems Interactively. NFS file systems can be mounted interactively, just like any other type of file system. However, you should be aware that the NFS `mount` command is not very pretty due to all the options that you can specify on the command line.

Using the previous example, the interactive `mount` command that you use to mount the `/var/spool/mail` file system is

```
# mount -t nfs -o timeo=20,intr mailserver:/var/spool/mail  /var/spool/mail
```

If you need to specify datagram sizes and time outs, interactive `mount` commands can become very complex. It is highly recommended that you place these file systems in your `/etc/fstab` file so that they can be mounted automatically at boot time.

Maintaining File Systems

The system administrator is responsible for maintaining the integrity of the file systems themselves. Typically, this means checking the file systems periodically for damage or corrupted files. Linux automatically checks file systems at boot time if they have a value greater than 0 specified in the pass number field of the `/etc/fstab` file.

> **Note**
>
> The `ext2` file system that is commonly used under Linux has a special flag known as a *clean bit*. If the file system has been synchronized and unmounted cleanly, the clean bit is set on the file system. If the clean bit is set on a file system when Linux boots, it is not checked for integrity.

Using the *fsck* Command

It is a good idea to check your file systems occasionally for damage or corrupt files. Under the Slackware distribution of Linux, you use the `fsck` command to check your file systems. `fsck` is a mnemonic for "file system check." The `fsck` command is really a "front end" for a series of commands that are designed to check specific file systems. The syntax for the `fsck` command is

```
fsck [-A] [-V] [-t fs-type] [-a] [-l] [-r] [-s] filesys
```

However, the most basic form of the command is

```
fsck filesys
```

Table 17.7 describes the command-line options for the `fsck` command.

Table 17.7 Command-Line Arguments for *fsck*

Argument	Description
`-A`	Goes through the `/etc/fstab` file and tries to check all file systems in one pass. This option is typically used during the Linux boot sequence to check all normally mounted file systems. If you use the `-A` option, you cannot use the *`filesys`* argument as well.
`-V`	Verbose mode. Print additional information about what `fsck` is doing.
`-t` *`fs-type`*	Specifies the type of the file system to be checked.
`filesys`	Specifies which file system is to be checked. This argument can be either a block special device name, such as `/dev/hda1`, or a mount point, such as `/usr`.
`-a`	Automatically repair any problems found in the file system without asking any questions. Use this option with caution.
`-l`	Lists all the file names in the file system.
`-r`	Asks for confirmations before repairing the file system.
`-s`	Lists the superblock before checking the file system.

The `fsck` command actually calls a different command to check the file system that you specify. In order to do this, Linux needs to know the file-system type that it is checking. The easiest way to do this is to specify a file-system type with the `-t` option to `fsck`. If you don't do this, Linux tries to figure it out by looking up the file system in the `/etc/fstab` and using the file type specified there. If `fsck` can't find the type information in `/etc/fstab`, it assumes that you are using a Minix file system.

Caution

The `fsck` command assumes that the file system that you are checking is a Minix file system if you don't tell it differently—either with the `-t` argument or by listing the type in `/etc/fstab`. Because your Linux file systems are probably of type `ext2` and not Minix, you should be careful and make sure that `fsck` knows the correct type. This is especially important if you are checking a file system that is not listed in the `/etc/fstab` file.

It is a good idea to unmount a file system before checking it. This ensures that none of the files on the file system are in use when it is being checked.

Note

Remember, you can't unmount a file system if any of the files on it are busy. For example, if a user is currently in a directory on a file system that you try to unmount, you get a message saying that the file system is busy.

Trying to check the root file system presents an additional problem. You cannot directly unmount the root file system, as Linux must be able to access it in order to run. In order to check the root file system, you should boot from a maintenance floppy disk that has a root file system on it and run `fsck` on your real root file system from there by specifying the special device name of your root file system.

If `fsck` makes any changes to your file system, it is very important that you reboot your system immediately. This allows Linux to reread important information about your file system and prevents your file system from further corruption.

Caution

Make sure that you reboot your computer immediately after you run `fsck` if any changes were made to your file system. Use the `shutdown -r` command or the `reboot` command to reboot.

Creating and Formatting File Systems

When you add a new hard disk to your computer or want to change the partition information on an old hard disk, you go through the steps of creating a file system from a raw disk. Assuming that you have added a new hard disk to your system, you must set the disk partition information and then create the actual file systems on the disk before Linux is able to use the disk. In order to change disk partition information, you use the `fdisk` command. For the second step, actually creating the file systems, you use the `mkfs` command.

Using *fdisk* To Create Disk Partitions

The `fdisk` command is used to create disk partitions and set the attributes that tell Linux what type of file system is on a particular partition. If you installed Linux from scratch on an MS-DOS system, you had to run `fdisk` to change the disk partition information before you could install Linux.

Caution

Using `fdisk` on a disk can destroy all data on the disk. Because `fdisk` completely rewrites the file table on the disk, all your former files may be lost. Make sure you have a complete, current backup of your disks.

You should always run the `fdisk` command on an unmounted file system. `fdisk` is an interactive, menu-driven program, not just a single command. To start `fdisk`, type

```
fdisk [drive]<Return>
```

[drive] is the physical disk drive that you want to work on. If you don't specify a disk, the disk `/dev/hda` is assumed. For example, to run `fdisk` on the second IDE hard drive in your system, you type

```
fdisk /dev/hdb<Return>
```

at the superuser command prompt. Since `fdisk` is a menu drive program, there are several different commands that are available when you are using `fdisk`. Table 17.8 summarizes the commands that are available in `fdisk`.

Table 17.8 Commands Available from the *fdisk* Menu

Command	Description
a	Toggles the bootable flag on a partition
c	Toggles the DOS compatibility flag on a partition
d	Deletes a partition
l	Lists partition types known to `fdisk`
m	Displays a menu listing all available commands
n	Adds a new partition
p	Prints the partition table for the current disk
q	Quits without saving any changes
t	Changes the file-system type for a partition
u	Changes display/entry units
v	Verifies the partition table
w	Writes table to disk and exit
x	Additional functions for experts
b	Moves the beginning location of data in a partition (Expert menu only)
c	Changes the number of cylinders (Expert menu only)
d	Prints the raw data in the partition table (Expert menu only)
e	Lists extended partitions on disk (Expert menu only)
h	Changes number of heads on disk (Expert menu only)
r	Returns to main menu (Expert menu only)
s	Changes number of sectors on disk (Expert menu only)

`fdisk` is capable of setting the file-system type of a disk partition to any of several different types. Only use Linux `fdisk` to create partitions that are used under Linux. For MS-DOS or OS/2 partitions, you should use the `fdisk` tool that is native to that operating environment and then use Linux's `fdisk` to tag the partitions as Linux native or Linux swap. Table 17.9 gives a list of the partitions supported by Linux `fdisk`. Each partition has an associated hexadecimal code that identifies it. You must enter the appropriate code in `fdisk` when you want to set a partition type.

Table 17.9 Partition Codes and Types in Linux

Code	Partition Type
0	Empty
1	DOS 12-bit FAT
2	XENIX root
3	XENIX usr
4	DOS 16-bit file system, less than 32M
5	Extended
6	DOS 16-bit file system supporting more than 32M
7	OS/2 High Performance File System (HPFS)
8	AIX
9	AIX bootable
a	OS/2 boot manager
40	Venix 80286
51	Novell?
52	Microport
63	GNU HURD
64	Novell
75	PC/IX
80	Old MINIX
81	Linux/MINIX
82	Linux swap, used for swap files under Linux
83	Linux native, common Linux file system type
93	Amoeba
94	Amoeba BBT
a5	BSD/386
b7	BSDI file system
b8	BSDI swap file system
c7	Syrinx
db	CP/M
e1	DOS access
e3	DOS R/O
f2	DOS secondary
ff	BBT

The following is an example of how to use `fdisk` to set up the partitions on a hard disk for use by Linux. Assume that you want to configure the first IDE drive in your system for Linux. Make sure you have a backup of your data. All data on your hard disk is destroyed in the process. The name of the first IDE hard disk is `/dev/hda`, which is the default device for Linux.

You run `fdisk` with

```
# fdisk
```

`fdisk` responds with

```
Using /dev/hda as default device!
Command (m for help):
```

This tells you that `fdisk` is using disk `/dev/hda` as the device that you are working with. Because this is what you wanted, you are fine. You should always check to make sure that you are really on the disk that you think that you are on. Linux then displays the `fdisk` command prompt.

The first thing you want to do is display the current partition table. This is done with the `p` command.

```
Command (m for help): p<Return>
Disk /dev/hda: 14 heads, 17 sectors, 1024 cylinders
Units = cylinders of 238 * 512 bytes

Device      Boot    Begin     Start     End     Blocks   Id
System

Command (m for help):
```

This listing shows that the current disk, `/dev/hda`, has a geometry of 14 heads, 17 sectors, and 1024 cylinders. The display units are in cylinders of 238 * 512 (121,856) bytes each. Because there are 1024 cylinders and each cylinder is 121,856 bytes, you can deduce that the disk can hold 1024×121,856 = 124,780,544 bytes or about 120M. You can also see that `/dev/hda` has no partitions.

Assume that you want to create a 100M Linux file partition for user home directories and a 20M swap partition. Your next step is to use the `n` command to create a new partition.

```
Command (m for help): n<Return>
Command action
     e   extended
     p   primary partition (1-4)
p<Return>
Partition number (1-4): 1<Return>
First cylinder (1-1023):  1<Return>
Last cylinder or +size or +sizeM or +sizeK (1-1023):  +100M<Return>
```

Using the `n` command to create a new partition displays another menu. You must choose whether you want to create an extended partition or a primary partition. You typically want to create a primary partition unless you have more than four partitions on a disk. `fdisk` then asks you for the partition number that you want to create. Since this is the first partition on the disk, you answer **1**. You are then prompted for the first cylinder for the partition. This determines where on the disk the data area starts. Once again, since this is going to be the first partition on the disk, you can start the partition at cylinder 1.

The next line asks you how large you want the partition to be. You have several options as to how to answer this question. fdisk accepts either a number, which it interprets as the size in cylinders, or the size in bytes, kilobytes, or megabytes. The size in bytes is specified as +bytes, where bytes is the size of the partition. Similarly, +sizeK and +sizeM set the partition size to size kilobytes or size megabytes, respectively. You know that you want a 100M partition, so the easiest answer to the prompt is **+100M**.

Now, you should check the partition table again to see what fdisk has done.

```
Command (m for help): p<Return>
Disk /dev/hda: 14 heads, 17 sectors, 1024 cylinders
Units = cylinders of 238 * 512 bytes

Device     Boot     Begin    Start     End     Blocks      Id
System
/dev/hda1   1          1      861     102400    81     Linux/MINIX
Command (m for help):
```

The partition table shows that you have 1 partition, /dev/hda1, that goes from cylinder 1 to cylinder 861 and uses 102400 blocks. It is listed as being type 81, Linux/MINIX.

Now you need to create the 20M swap partition using the remaining disk space. This is just like creating the first partition.

```
Command (m for help): n<Return>
Command action
    e   extended
    p   primary partition (1-4)
p<Return>
Partition number (1-4): 2<Return>
First cylinder (862-1023):  862<Return>
Last cylinder or +size or +sizeM or +sizeK (862-1023): 1023<Return>
```

Tip

It is usually better to go ahead and enter the size of the last partition in cylinders to make sure that you use all of the disk.

Here you specified partition number 2 for the second partition. When fdisk prompts for the first cylinder, notice that it gives a range of 862 to 1023. This is because the first partition takes up everything before cylinder 862. So enter **862** as the starting cylinder for the second partition. You want to use all of the remaining space on the disk for the swap partition. You should have about 20M left, but if you specify the size in megabytes, the internal fdisk calculations to figure out how many cylinders needed could leave you with a couple of cylinders unused. So you enter **1023** for the last cylinder on the size prompt.

Note

You may see an error similar to

```
Warning: Linux cannot currently use the last xxx sectors of this
partition.
```

where *xxx* is some number. If you see such an error, it can be ignored. It is left over from the days when Linux could not access file systems larger than 64M.

At this point, you have created both of the partitions that you wanted to create. You should take a look at the partition table one more time to check and see that the sizes are correct.

```
Command (m for help): p<Return>
Disk /dev/hda: 14 heads, 17 sectors, 1024 cylinders
Units = cylinders of 238 * 512 bytes

Device      Boot   Begin    Start    End      Blocks     Id
System
/dev/hda1    1      1       861      102400     81      Linux/MINIX
/dev/hda2   862    862      1023      19159     81      Linux/MINIX
Command (m for help):
```

As you can see, /dev/hda1 uses cylinder 1 through cylinder 861 with a size of 102400 blocks, which is approximately 100M. Partition /dev/hda2 goes from cylinder 862 to cylinder 1023 with a size of 19156 blocks or almost 20M.

The next thing that you need to do is change the partition type for each of the partitions. To change the partition type, use the t command at the fdisk command prompt. The most common choice for a standard Linux file system partition is to set it to partition type 83, Linux native. Swap partition should be set to partition type 82, Linux swap.

```
Command (m for help): t<Return>
Partition number (1-4): 1<Return>
Hex code (type L to list codes): 83<Return>
Command (m for help): t<Return>
Partition number (1-4): 2<Return>
Hex code (type L to list codes): 82<Return>
```

When you use the t command, you are prompted for the partition number that you want to change. You are then prompted for the hex code for the file-system ID that you want to set the partition to. Typically, Linux file systems are set to type 83 for normal file systems, and type 82 for swap partitions. You can type **l** at this point to see a list of file systems if you want.

Now that you have created the partitions and labeled them, you should take one last look at the partition table before you exit just to make sure that everything is okay.

```
Command (m for help): p<Return>
Disk /dev/hda: 14 heads, 17 sectors, 1024 cylinders
Units = cylinders of 238 * 512 bytes
```

```
Device      Boot    Begin    Start     End      Blocks      Id
System
/dev/hda1     1       1      861      102400      83      Linux native
/dev/hda2    862     862     1023     19159       82      Linux swap
Command (m for help):
```

As you can see, the partitions are in the right place, they are the right size, and the file-system types are set correctly. The last thing that you need to do is use the `w` command to write the partition table to disk and exit.

```
Command (m for help):  w<Return>

#
```

None of the changes that you make during an `fdisk` session take effect until you write them to disk with the `w` command. You can always quit with the `q` command and not save any changes. This said, you should still always have a backup of any disk that you want to modify with `fdisk`.

After you make changes to a disk with `fdisk`, you should reboot the system just to make sure that Linux has the updated partition information in the kernel.

Using *mkfs* To Build a File System

Once you have created a file-system partition with `fdisk`, you must build a file system on it before you can use it for storing data. This is done with the `mkfs` command. Think of building a parking lot. If you think of `fdisk` as physically building the parking lot, `mkfs` is the part of the process that paints the lines so that the drivers know where to park.

Just like `fsck` is a "front end" program for checking different types of file systems, `mkfs` actually calls different programs to create the file system, depending on what file-system type you want to create. The syntax of the `mkfs` command is

```
mkfs  [-V] [-t fs-type] [fs-options] filesys [blocks]
```

`filesys` is the device special name of the file system that you want to build, such as `/dev/hda1`.

> **Caution**
>
> The `mkfs` command also accepts the name of a mount point, such as `/home`, as the file-system name. You should be extremely careful about doing this. If you run `mkfs` on a mounted "live" file system, you may very well corrupt all the data on that file system.

Table 17.10 lists the various command-line parameters that can be specified with the `mkfs` command.

Table 17.10 Command-Line Parameters for the *mkfs* Command

Option	Description
`-V`	Causes `mkfs` to produce verbose output, including all file-system-specific commands that are executed. Specifying this option more than once inhibits execution of any file-system-specific commands.
`-t` *`fs-type`*	Specifies the type of file system to be built. If the file-system type is not specified, `mkfs` tries to figure it out by searching for *`filesys`* in `/etc/fstab` and using the corresponding entry. If the type cannot be deduced, a MINIX file system is created.
`fs-options`	File-system-specific options that are to be passed to the actual file-system-builder program. Although not guaranteed, the following options are supported by most file system builders.
`-c`	Check the device for bad blocks before building the file system.
`-l` *`file-name`*	Reads a list of the bad blocks on the disk from *`file-name`*.
`-v`	Tells the actual file system builder program to produce verbose output.
`blocks`	The number of blocks to be used for the file system.

Although it is an optional argument, you should get in a habit of specifying the file-system type using the `-t` *`fs-type`* command-line option. Just like `fsck`, `mkfs` tries to figure out the type of the file system from the `/etc/fstab` file. If it can't figure it out, it creates a MINIX file system by default. For a normal Linux file system, you probably want an `ext2` partition instead.

Using Swap Files and Partitions

Swap space on your Linux system is used for virtual memory. A complete discussion of all the issues involved with virtual memory is beyond the scope of this book. Any good general-computer operating systems text book discusses the issue in detail.

Linux supports two types of swap space: swap partition and swap files. A swap partition is a physical disk partition that has its file-system ID set to 82, Linux swap, and is dedicated for use as a swap area. A swap file is a large file on a normal file system that is used for swap space.

You are better off using a swap partition instead of a file. All access to a swap file is performed through the normal Linux file system. The disk blocks that make up the swap file are probably not contiguous and, therefore, performance is not as good as it is with a swap partition. I/O to swap partitions is performed directly to the device, and disk blocks on a swap partition are always contiguous. In addition, by keeping the swap space off a normal file system, you reduce the risk of corrupting your regular file system if something bizarre happens to your swap file.

Creating a Swap Partition

In order to create a swap partition, you must have created a disk partition using `fdisk` and tagged it as having ID 82, Linux swap. Once you have done this, you have two additional steps to do to make the swap partition active. First, you must prepare the partition in a manner similar to creating a file system. Instead of `mkfs`, the command for this operation is `mkswap`. The syntax of the `mkswap` command is

```
mkswap [-c] device size-in-blocks
```

`device` is the name of the swap partition, such as `/dev/hda2`, and *`size-in-blocks`* is the size of the target file system in blocks. You can get the size in blocks by running `fdisk` and looking at the partition table. In the previous example, the size of /dev/hda2 was 19,159 blocks. Linux requires that swap partitions be between 9 and 65,537 blocks in size. The `-c` argument tells `mkswap` to check the file system for bad blocks when creating the swap space, which is a good idea.

Following our previous example, the command for setting up a swap partition on `/dev/hda2` is

```
mkswap -c /dev/hda2 19159
```

After you run `mkswap` to prepare the partition, you must make it active so the Linux kernel can use it. The command to make the swap partition active is `swapon`. The syntax for the `swapon` command is

```
swapon filesys
```

`filesys` is the file system that you want to make available as swap space. Linux makes a call to `swapon -a` during boot, which mounts all available swap partitions that are listed in the `/etc/fstab` file.

> **Note**
>
> Remember to put an entry for any swap partitions or swap files that you create into the `/etc/fstab` file so that Linux can automatically access them at boot time.

Creating a Swap File

Swap files can be useful if you need to expand your swap space and cannot allocate disk space to create a dedicated swap partition. Setting up a swap file is almost identical to creating a swap partition. The main difference is that you have to create the file before you can run `mkswap` and `swapon`.

To create a swap file, you use the `dd` command. For a full description of this command, see the man page for `dd`. The main things that you have to know before creating the file are the name of the swap file you want to create and its size in blocks. A block under Linux is 1024 bytes. For example, to create a 10M swap file named `/swap`, type

```
# dd if=/dev/zero of=/swap bs=1024 count=10240<Return>
```

`of=/swap` specifies that the file to be created is named `/swap`, and `count=10240` sets the size of the output file to be 10240 blocks, or 10M. You then use `mkswap` to prepare the file as a swap space.

```
# mkswap /swap 10240<Return>
```

Remember that you have to tell `mkswap` how big the file is. Before you run `swapon` on the file, you need to make sure that the file is completely written to the disk. Use the `# /etc/sync` command to accomplish this. Now you are ready to make the swap file active. Just as with the swap partition, use the `swapon` command to make the file active, for example

```
# swapon /swap<Return>
```

If you need to get rid of a swap file, you must make sure that it is not active. Use the `swapoff` command to do this, as in

```
# swapoff /swap<Return>
```

You can then safely delete the swap file.

From Here...

In this chapter, you have looked at many different aspects of the Linux file system, from a tour of the basic directory structure, to mounting and unmounting file systems. You have explored accessing remote file systems with NFS and looked in detail at how to create file systems and prepare them for use. Finally, this chapter discussed the creation of swap partitions and swap files.

You can find more information about system administration in the following chapters:

- Chapter 7, "Understanding System Administration," gives an introduction to common systems administration tasks.
- Chapter 9, "Managing User Accounts," describes how to set up and manage user accounts on your Linux system.
- Chapter 10, "Backing Up Data," discusses how to plan and implement plans for data backups.

CHAPTER 18

Understanding the File and Directory System

The words *Linux file system* have two different and often conflicting meanings: the file system of disks and mechanisms that the disks are strung together with, and the logical file system the user sees and manipulates. This chapter is about the logical Linux file system you see and manipulate. Also, if you are familiar with PC operating systems like MS-DOS and OS/2, you will find many of the following topics familiar because the file structures of versions of MS-DOS from version 2.0 onwards were modeled upon those of UNIX, which is the file structure used by Linux.

Every physical and logical entity in Linux is represented as a file in the Linux file system. The physical entities include disks, printers, and terminals; logical entities include directories and, of course, ordinary files—the kind that store documents and programs.

This chapter covers the following topics:

- Linux file names
- Types of Linux files
- File permissions
- Linux directory structure

Understanding File Names

In Linux, just as in other operating systems like MS-DOS, you must distinguish between a file name and a path name. A *file name* consists of a simple series of contiguous letters, numbers, and certain punctuation marks. File names cannot contain spaces or any character that represents a field separator. For example, the file name `johns.letter` is valid; `johns letter` is not.

A file name should not contain any characters that have special meaning to the shell. These special characters are as follows:

```
! @ # $ % ^ & * ( ) [ ] { } ' " \ / ¦ ; < > `
```

Also, the file name cannot contain the / character since this character is used to indicate path names. Path names are discussed later in this section.

Actually, you can use any of these characters by placing double quotes around the file name, for example, `"! johns.letter"`, but you will have a hard time accessing the file with most programs, and the file is not very portable to other UNIX systems.

Most early versions of UNIX, which Linux is based on, limited file names to 14 characters; however, Linux allows 256 characters in a file name. Some recent versions of UNIX, such as the Berkeley version of UNIX (BSD) allow 64-character file names, but only the first 14 are significant. Because one of the goals of Linux is portability, in the interest of writing portable programs and shell scripts, you should limit yourself to 14-character file names.

A *path name* can be any number of characters. In Linux, files don't exist in a vacuum; they exist in a directory. The highest directory is called the *root directory* in Linux and is symbolized by the slash character (/). This directory is simply referred to as root. If a file named `fred` exists in the root directory, its absolute path name is `/fred`. When you add a user to the system with the **`adduser`** command, users are assigned a *home directory*. By convention, this home directory is usually found under root in a directory named, appropriately enough, `home`. If a user named Fred is assigned a directory named `/home/fred`, all files Fred creates are attached to the directory `/home/fred`. An absolute path name for one of Fred's files might be `/home/fred/freds.file`. An *absolute* path name specifies exactly where in the file system you can find a file.

There is another kind of path name: a relative path name. A *relative path name* unambiguously points to a file relative to the current directory. If Fred is in his home directory, the file name `freds.file` is also a relative path name, relative to his current directory. To find out which directory is your current directory, use the command `pwd` (print working directory). You can also check the contents of the `$PWD` environment variable to see which directory is the current working directory with the command `echo $PWD`.

You can define a file anywhere in the Linux file system with relative path names by using the two pseudonyms found in all directories. The single dot (`.`) refers to the current directory; the double dot (`..`) refers to the parent directory. MS-DOS and OS/2 use this same convention.

If Fred is in `/home/fred`, he can point to `/fred` by using `../../fred`. The first double dot points to `/home` (the parent directory of `/home/fred`); the second double dot points to the parent directory of `/home`—namely, the root. The pseudonym for the current directory, the single dot, comes in handy if you want to move files. If Fred wants to move `/fred` to his current directory, he can do so with absolute path names by using this command:

```
mv /fred fred
```

Alternatively, Fred can use the pseudonym for the current directory by using this command:

```
mv /fred .
```

Most Linux commands operate on path names. In most cases, the path name you use is the name of a file in the current directory. The default path name points to your current directory. If Fred is in his home directory, `/home/fred`, all three of the following are equivalent:

```
command freds.letter
command /home/fred/freds.letter
command ./freds.letter
```

Note

Although there is a difference between file names and path names, directories are files, too. When naming directories, remember that they have the same name limitations as ordinary files.

Also note that unlike many PC-based operating systems, Linux does not have the concept of disk-drive letters, only directory paths. The only time Linux deals with disk-drive letters is while dealing with MS-DOS file systems on floppies with the `m-` commands, like `mcopy`. See Chapter 25, "Command-Line Reference," for information on the `m-` commands.

▶▶ See "The Linux File System," p. 300

Looking at Types of Files

There are just four basic types of files: ordinary files, directories, links, and special files. There are several kinds of ordinary files, links, and special files and a large number of standard directories. Each is described in the following sections.

Ordinary Files

Ordinary files are what you spend most of your time manipulating. Ordinary files can contain text, C language source code, shell scripts (programs interpreted by one of the Linux shells), binary executable programs, and data of various types. As far as Linux is concerned, a file is a file. The only difference that Linux knows about is files marked as executable. *Executable files* can be executed directly; provided, of course, that the file contains something to execute and that it is in your search path. Basically the search path is a list of path names you have specified that Linux searches to find an executable file.

▶▶ See "Understanding Shells," p. 360

Executable files are *binary files*; that is, files that execute machine code and shell scripts. The Linux `file` command looks at the data in a file and makes a reasonable guess as to what's inside. If you type **`file *`**, you might see something similar to this:

```
INSTALL:     symbolic link to /var/adm
ghostvw.txt: ascii text
linux:       symbolic link to /usr/src/linux
mbox:        mail text
mterm.txt:   English text
seyon.txt:   English text
xcalc.txt:   English text
xclock.txt:  English text
xeyes.txt:   English text
xgrap.txt:   English text
xlock.txt:   English text
xspread.txt: English text
xtris.txt:   empty
```

All the files named in the first column are ordinary files that contain different kinds of data. All the files are located within a directory.

Directory Files

Directories are files that contain the names of files and subdirectories as well as pointers to those files and subdirectories. Directory files are the only place that Linux stores names of files. When you list the contents of a directory with the `ls` command, all you are doing is listing the contents of the directory file. You never touch the files themselves.

When you rename a file with the `mv` command and that file is in the current directory, all you are doing is changing the entry in the directory file. If you move a file from one directory to another, all you are doing is moving the description of the file from one directory file to another—provided, of course, that the new directory is on the same physical disk or partition.

Directories and Physical Disks

Every file in a Linux system is assigned a unique number called an *inode*. The inode is stored in a table called the *inode table*, which is allocated when the disk is formatted. Every physical disk or partition has its own inode table. An inode contains all the information about a file, including the address of the data on the disk and the file type. File types include such things as ordinary files, directories, and special files.

The Linux file system assigns inode number 1 to the root directory. This gives Linux the address on disk of the root-directory file. The root-directory file contains a list of file and directory names and their respective inode numbers. Linux can find any file in the system by looking up a chain of directories, beginning with the root directory. The contents of the root-directory file might look like this:

```
1    .
1    ..
45   etc
230  dev
```

```
420  home
123  .profile
```

Notice that the files . (dot) and .. (double dot) are represented in the directory. Because this is the root directory, ., and its parent directory, .., are identical. The contents of the /home directory file are different.

```
420  .
1    ..
643  fred
```

Notice that the inode of the current directory, ., matches the inode for /home found in the root-directory file and that the inode for the parent directory, .., is the same as that of the root directory.

Linux navigates its file system by chaining up and down the directory file system. If you want to move a file to a directory on another physical disk, Linux detects this by reading the inode table. In such a case, the file is physically moved to the new disk and assigned a new inode on that disk before being deleted from its original location.

As with the mv command, when you delete a file with the rm command, you never touch the file itself. Instead, Linux marks that inode as free and returns it to the pool of available inodes. The file's entry in the directory is erased.

Links

Ordinary *links* aren't really files at all. They are simply directory entries that point to the same inode. The inode table keeps track of how many links to a file there are and only when the last directory reference is deleted is the inode finally released back to the free pool. Obviously, ordinary links cannot cross device boundaries because all the directory references point to the same inode.

Linux, as well as most modern versions of UNIX, has another kind of link called a *symbolic link*. For such a link, the directory entry contains the inode of a file that is itself a reference to another file somewhere else in the logical Linux file system. A symbolic link can point to another file or directory on the same disk, another disk, or to a file or directory on another computer. One major difference between an ordinary link and a symbolic link is that with ordinary links, every link has equal standing (that is, the system treats every link as though it were the original file) and the actual data is not deleted until the last link to that file is deleted. With symbolic links, when the original file is deleted, all symbolic links to that file are also deleted. Symbolically linked files do not have the same standing as the original.

Other than these subtle differences between links and files, links are treated and accessed exactly as though you were accessing the file directly.

You can tell a file is a link with the ls -l command because the response shows both the local file name and then an indication of the linked file, as shown here:

```
lrwxrwxrwx  1 root   root   4 Oct 17 15:27 Info -> info/
```

The file permission flags also begin with an l to indicate the file is a linked file.

Special Files

Every physical device associated with a Linux system, including disks, terminals, and printers, is represented in the file system. Most, if not all, devices are located in the /dev directory. For example, if you are working on the system console, your associated device is named /dev/console. If you are working on a standard terminal, your device name may be /dev/tty01. Terminals, or serial lines, are called *tty devices* (which stands for *teletype*, the original UNIX terminal). To determine what the name of your tty device is, type the command **tty**. The system responds with the name of the device to which you are connected.

Printers and terminals are called *character-special devices*. They can accept and produce a stream of characters. Disks, on the other hand, store data in blocks addressed by cylinder and sector. You can't access just one character on a disk; you must read and write entire blocks. The same is usually true of magnetic tapes. This kind of device is called a *block-special device*. To make life even more complex, disks and other block-special devices must be able to act like character-oriented devices, so every block-special device has a matching character-special device. Linux makes the translation by reading data being sent to a character device and translating it for the block device. This happens without you doing anything.

There is at least one other type of special device you may run into: a FIFO (first-in-first-out buffer) also known as a *named pipe*. FIFOs look like ordinary files; if you write to them, they grow. But if you read a FIFO, it shrinks in size. FIFOs are used mainly in system processes to allow many programs to send information to a single controlling process. For example, when you print a file with the lp command, the lp command sets up the printing process and signals the lpsched daemon by sending a message to a FIFO. A *daemon*, sometimes called a demon, is a system process that acts without a user requesting an action.

One device-special file is very useful: the *bit bucket*, /dev/null. Anything you send to /dev/null is ignored—useful when you don't want to see the output of a command. For example, if you don't want to see any diagnostic reports printed on the standard error device, you can pour them into the bit bucket with the following command:

```
ls -la> /dev/null
```

File Permissions

File permissions mean more in Linux than just what permissions you have on a file or directory. Although permissions determine who can read, write, or execute a file, they also determine the file type and how the file is executed.

You can display the permission on a file with the long form of the listing command, ls -l. The -l flag tells the ls command to use the long listing. If you type **ls -l**, you might see a directory listing that looks like this:

```
drwx------ 2 sglines  doc    512 Jan 1 13:44  Mail
drwx------ 5 sglines  doc   1024 Jan 17 08:22 News
-rw------- 1 sglines  doc   1268 Dec 7 15:01  biblio
drwx------ 2 sglines  doc    512 Dec 15 21:28 bin
-rw------- 1 sglines  doc  44787 Oct 20 06:59 books
```

```
-rw------   1 sglines  doc  23801 Dec 14 22:50 bots.msg
-rw-r----   1 sglines  doc 105990 Dec 27 21:24 duckie.gif
```

This listing shows virtually everything that can be known about a file from the directory entry and the inode of the file. The first column shows the file permissions, the second column shows the number of links to a file (or extra blocks in a directory), and the third column shows who owns the file. (In Linux, ownership has three possibilities: the owner, the owner's group, and everyone else. Ownership is detailed later in this section.) The fourth column shows the group to which the file belongs. The fifth column shows the number of bytes in the file, the sixth column shows the date and time of creation, and the seventh column shows the name of the file itself.

The permission field (the first column) is broken into four subfields:

```
- rwx rwx rwx
```

The first subfield defines the file type. A normal file has a hyphen (`-`) as a placeholder; directories are marked with a `d`. Table 18.1 shows the permissible values for the file-type subfield.

Table 18.1 Valid Entries for the File-Type Subfield

Character	Meaning
-	Ordinary file
b	Block-special file
c	Character-special file
d	Directory
l	Symbolic link

The next three subfields show the read, write, and execute permissions of the file. For example, an `rwx` in the first of these subfields means that the file has read, write, and execute permission for the *owner*. The next subfield shows the same information for the *group ownership* of the file; the third subfield shows the permissions allowed for *everyone else*.

These permission fields can show more information; in fact, there are several attributes packed into these three fields. Unfortunately, what these attributes mean is determined by the version of Linux you use and whether or not the file is executable.

> **Note**
>
> Normally, a running program is owned by whoever ran it. If the user-ID bit is on, the running program is owned by the owner of the file. This means that the running program has all the permissions of the owner of the file. If you are an ordinary user and the running program is owned by the root user, that running program has automatic permission to read and write any file in the system regardless of your permissions. The same is true of the set-group-ID bit.

The *sticky bit* can also be set in these subfields. The sticky bit tells the system to save a copy of a running program in memory after the program completes. If the program is used often, the sticky bit can save the system a little time because the program does not have to be reloaded into memory from disk each time someone runs it.

You can change permissions on any file you have write permission for by using the `chmod` command. This command has two different syntaxes: absolute and relative. With *absolute permissions*, you define exactly what the permissions on a file will be in octal, or base 8. An octal number can have a value from 0–7. UNIX was originally created on a series of DEC minicomputers that used the octal system, hence the current use of octal numbers. The permissions you want are added together to arrive at a number that defines the permissions. Table 18.2 lists the valid octal permissions.

Table 18.2 Absolute Octal Permissions Used with the Command

Octal Value	Permissions Granted
0001	Execute permission for the owner
0002	Write permission for the owner
0004	Read permission for the owner
0010	Execute permission for the group
0020	Write permission for the group
0040	Read permission for the group
0100	Execute permission for all others
0200	Write permission for all others
0400	Read permission for all others
1000	Sticky bit on
2000	Group-ID bit on if the file is executable; otherwise, mandatory file locking is on
4000	User-ID bit on if the file is executable

Group- and user-IDs refer to who has permission to use, read, or execute a file. These initial file permissions are granted by the system administrator when the user's account is first created. Only users of an indicated group can access files in a group and only if the user has given group members permission to those files.

To give a file read and write permissions for everyone, you must add the required permissions together, as in the following example:

```
0002   Write permission for the owner
0004   Read permission for the owner
0020   Write permission for the group
0040   Read permission for the group
0200   Write permission for all others
0400   Read permission for all others
____
0666   Read and write permission for everyone
```

To give a file these permissions, use the following command:

```
chmod 666 file
```

Relative permissions use a slightly different format. With relative permissions, you must state the following:

- Who you are giving permissions to
- What operation you intend (add, subtract, or set permissions)
- What the permissions are

For example, if you type **`chmod a=rwx file`**, you give read, write, and execute permission to all users. The commands are summarized in Table 18.3.

Table 18.3 Relative Permissions Used with the *chmod* Command

Value	Description
Who	
a	All users (the user, their group, and all others)
g	Owner's group
o	All others
u	Just the user
Operator	
+	Adds the mode
-	Removes the mode
=	Sets the mode absolutely
Permission	
x	Sets execute
r	Sets read
w	Sets write
s	Sets user-ID bit
t	Sets the sticky bit

If a file has been marked as having the user-ID bit on, the permissions displayed by the `ls -l` command look like this:

```
-rws------ 1 sglines   3136 Jan 17 15:42 x
```

If the group-ID bit is added, the permissions look like this:

```
-rws--S--- 1 sglines   3136 Jan 17 15:42 x
```

If you then turn on the sticky bit for the file, the permissions look like this:

```
-rws--S--rws--S--T 1 sglines   3136 Jan 17 15:42 x
```

Note the use of uppercase `S` and `T` to indicate the status of the various bits.

Looking at Linux Standard Directories

You are already familiar with the concept of directories. When you log on, the system places you in your home directory. The `PATH` environment variable is set to point to other directories that contain executable programs. These other directories are part of the standard Linux directory structure.

There is the classic set of directories for UNIX and what can be called the "emerging standard set of directories," which Linux basically follows. Both are described in the following sections.

Classic UNIX Directories

Before UNIX System V Release 4 (for example, UNIX System V Release 3.2 and earlier), most versions of UNIX settled on a regular system of organizing the UNIX directories that looked like this:

```
/
      /etc
      /lib
      /tmp
      /bin
      /usr
            /spool
            /bin
            /include
            /tmp
            /adm
            /lib
```

The `/etc` directory contains most of the system-specific data required to *boot*, or bring the system to life. It contains such files as `passwd` and `inittab`, which are necessary for the proper operation of the system.

The /lib directory contains a library of functions needed by the C compiler. Even if you don't have a C compiler on your system, this directory is important because it contains all the shared libraries that application programs may call. A *shared library* is loaded into memory only when the command calling it is run. This arrangement keeps executable programs small. Otherwise, every running program contains duplicate code, requiring a lot more disk space to store and a lot more memory to run.

The /tmp directory is used for temporary storage. Programs that use /tmp generally clean up after themselves and delete any temporary files. If you use /tmp, be sure to delete any files before logging out. Because the system automatically deletes the contents of this directory periodically, do not keep anything you might need later in this directory.

The /bin directory keeps all the executable programs needed to boot the system and is usually home for the most commonly used Linux commands. Note, however, that an executable program does not have to be binary, which the name *bin* implies. Several smaller programs in /bin are, in fact, shell scripts.

The /usr directory contains everything else. Your PATH variable contains the string /bin:/usr/bin because the /usr/bin directory contains all the Linux commands that are not in the /bin directory. This arrangement has an historical precedence. In the early days of Linux, hard disks weren't very big. Linux needs at least the /etc/tmp/ and /bin directories to bootstrap (that is, start executing) itself. Because the disks of the early Linux era held only those three directories, everything else was on a disk that could be mounted after Linux was up and running. When Linux was still a relatively small operating system, placing additional subdirectories in the /usr directory was not much of a burden. It allowed a moderately sized Linux system to exist with just two disks: a root disk and a /usr disk.

The /usr/adm directory contains all the accounting and diagnostic information needed by the system administrator. If both system accounting and diagnostic programs have been turned off, this directory is effectively empty.

The /include directory contains all the source code used by #include statements in C programs. You will have at least read permission for this directory because it contains all the code fragments and structures that define your system. You should not modify any of the files in this directory because they were crafted (carefully, you can assume) by your system vendor.

The /usr/spool directory contains all the transient data used by the lp print system, the cron daemon, and the UUCP communications system. Files "spooled" to the printer are kept in the /spool directory until they are printed. Any programs waiting to be run by cron, including all the crontab files and pending at and batch jobs, are also stored here.

The /usr/lib directory contains everything else that is part of the standard Linux system. In general, the /usr/lib directory represents the organized chaos hidden beneath the relatively well-disciplined Linux system. This directory contains programs called by other programs found in /bin and /usr/bin as well as configuration files for terminals and printers, the mail system, cron, and the UUCP communications system.

The /usr directory contains all the subdirectories assigned to users. The general convention is this: If your logon ID is mary, your home directory is /usr/mary. This arrangement made a lot of sense when disks were small and expensive but with the advent of very large disks at (relatively) inexpensive prices, there are better ways of organizing Linux, as evidenced by the new directory structure discussed in the next section.

Linux Directories

One of the problems with the classical structure of UNIX is that backing up your data files is difficult with a fragmented /usr directory. There are three different levels of backup generally required in a system: the basic system itself, any changes to the tables that define the basic system for a specific site, and user data.

The basic system can be backed up only once; changes to the controlling tables must be backed up only when there are changes. User data changes all the time and should be backed up frequently. The typical Linux directory structure is shown as follows, but your structure may be a little different, depending on what packages you installed:

```
/
     /etc
          /passwd (the user database)
          /rc     (the system initialization script)
     /sbin
     /bin
     /tmp
     /var
     /lib
     /home
          / <your user name here>(user accounts)
     /install
     /usr
          /bin
     /proc
```

The /bin, /etc, and /tmp, directories have the same function as they do in the classic structure. System definition tables are moved into the /var directory so that whenever the operation of the system changes, you can back up only that directory.

What is new is that all system programs are moved into the /sbin directory. All the standard Linux programs are in /usr/bin, which is linked to /bin. For compatibility, all the classic directories are maintained with symbolic links. The /usr directory, which no longer contains user data, has been reorganized to make sense from the chaos that once was the /usr/lib directory.

From Here...

In this chapter, you examined how Linux uses files and directories and how the file-permission system protects your data. You learned how to change the permissions on files and directories and what the meaning of a special file is. Finally, you looked at the purpose and names of the most common directories found in Linux. For more information, see the following chapters:

- Chapter 7, "Understanding System Administration," explains how to set up new users with file permissions.
- Chapter 17, "Managing File Systems," discusses the concept of file systems and how they are organized.
- Chapter 19, "Managing Files and Directories," discusses how to organize and use your files and directories.

CHAPTER 19

Managing Files and Directories

The vast majority of Linux commands manipulate files and directories. Indeed, Linux shell scripts are particularly adept at manipulating files and directories. File manipulations that are difficult in a conventional language (even in C) are easy from within a shell. This is largely because of the rich selection of file-manipulation commands available in Linux.

File-manipulation commands can be roughly grouped into two categories:

- Commands that manipulate files as objects
- Commands that manipulate the contents of files

This chapter concentrates on commands that manipulate files as objects: commands that move, rename, copy, delete, locate, and change the attributes of files and directories. The chapter also takes a quick look at commands that manipulate the contents of files.

This chapter includes the following topics:

- Listing files
- Organizing files
- Copying files
- Moving and renaming files
- Removing files or directories
- Viewing the contents of a file
- Compressing files
- Manipulating files with the Xfilemanager

Listing Files

The basic command to list files is `ls`. The way `ls` displays files depends on how you are using the command. It also depends on which version of UNIX your copy of `ls` is based upon because many parts of Linux were written by different programmers over time.

If you use the `ls` command in a pipe, every file is displayed on a line by itself. This is also the default for some versions of UNIX like SCO UNIX. Other versions of UNIX list files in several columns. For most uses, the columnar format is more convenient; systems that list files one per row often have an alternative command, usually `lc`, for *list in column* format.

The behavior of the `ls` command is modified with the use of flags that take the form `-abcd`. Again—and unfortunately—what the flags do depends on which version of UNIX your version of `ls` was based on. In general, versions of the `ls` command fall into two categories: versions of `ls` derived from Linux System V and those derived from Berkeley. Because the Berkeley Linux systems are slowly giving way to Linux System V, this chapter concentrates on the flags used by System V. If you are in doubt about which version of `ls` you have, consult the manuals for your system or try the command `man ls`.

Flags used with the `ls` command can be concatenated or listed separately. This means that the following commands are effectively identical:

```
ls -l -F
ls -lF
```

The flags used with `ls` and their uses are listed in Table 19.1 in alphabetical order.

Table 19.1 Flags for the *ls* Command

Flag	Description
`-a`	Lists all entries. In the absence of this or the `-A` option, entries whose names begin with a period (.) are not listed. Linux has a way of "hiding" files: all files that begin with a period are, by default, not listed. Files that begin with a period are generally files used to customize applications. For example, `.profile` is used to customize the Bourne and Korn shells; `.mailrc` is used to customize your e-mail. Because almost every major command you use has a startup file, your home directory looks cluttered if the `ls` command lists them all by default. If you want to see them, use the `-a` flag.
`-A`	Same as `-a`, except that `.` and `..` are not listed. Recall from Chapter 18, "Understanding the File and Directory System," that `.` is a pseudonym for the current directory and `..` is a pseudonym for the parent directory. Because these file names begin with a period, the `-a` flag lists them. If you don't want to see these pseudonyms, use the `-A` flag instead.
`-c`	Uses time of last edit (or last mode change) for sorting or printing. Linux maintains three time and date stamps on every file: the file-creation date, the date of last access, and the date of last modification. Normally, files are listed in ASCII order. (ASCII order is alphabetical order, except that capitals are sorted before lowercase letters.)
`-C`	Forces multicolumn output with entries sorted down the columns. This is the default format of `ls` when output is to a terminal.

Flag	Description
-d	If the argument is a directory, lists only its name (not its contents); often used with the -l flag to get the status of a directory. Normally, the contents of a directory are listed if a directory name is explicitly listed or implied with the use of a wild card. Thus, the simple command ls lists just the directory names themselves but ls * lists files, directories, and the contents of any directories encountered in the current directory.
-F	Marks directories with a trailing slash (/), executable files with a trailing asterisk (*), symbolic links with a trailing at sign (@), FIFOs with a trailing bar (¦), and sockets with a trailing equal sign (=).
-i	Prints each file's inode number (inodes are described in Chapter 18, "Understanding the File and Directory System") in the first column of the report. If you list files that are linked, notice that both files have the same inode number.
-l	Lists in long format, giving mode, number of links, owner, size in bytes, and time of last modification for each file. If the file is a special file, the size field instead contains the major and minor device numbers. If the time of last modification is greater than six months ago, the month, date, and year are shown; otherwise, only the date and time are shown. If the file is a symbolic link, the path name of the linked-to file is printed, preceded by the characters ->. You can combine -l with other options, such as -n, to show user and group ID numbers instead of names.
-n	Lists the user and group ID numbers, instead of names, associated with each file and directory. Usually, only the names are listed. If you are setting up networking products, such as TCP/IP, it is useful to know ID numbers when you are setting up permissions across several systems.
-q	Displays non-graphic characters in file names as the character ?. For ls, this is the default when output is to a terminal. If a file has accidentally been created with non-printable characters, the -q flag displays it.
-r	Reverses the sort order to see files in reverse alphabetical or oldest-file-first order, as appropriate.
-s	Gives the size of each file, including any indirect blocks used to map the file, in kilobytes. If the environment variable POSIX_CORRECT is defined, the block size is 512 bytes.
-t	Sorts by time modified (latest first) instead of by name. If you want to see the oldest file first, use the -rt combination.
-u	Uses time of last access, instead of last modification, for sorting (with the -t option) or printing (with the -l option).
-b	Forces printing of non-graphic characters to be in octal \ddd notation. This is more useful than the -q flag because it allows you to figure out what the characters are.
-x	Forces multicolumn output with entries sorted across rather than down the page.

By default, Linux also provides color descriptions for each file type, provided an appropriate monitor is available. The color definitions are defined in the configuration file DIR_COLORS located in the /etc directory. The default configuration highlights executable files in green, directories in blue, and symbolic links in cyan. To customize the colors, you must copy the DIR_COLORS file to your home directory and change its name to .dir_colors. Table 19.2 provides the color definitions available. See the man pages and the DIR_COLORS file for more information.

Table 19.2 *DIR_COLORS* Values to Create Color Highlighting

Value	Description
0	To restore default color
1	For brighter colors
4	For underlined text
5	For flashing text
30	For black foreground
31	For red foreground
32	For green foreground
33	For yellow (or brown) foreground
34	For blue foreground
35	For purple foreground
36	For cyan foreground
37	For white (or gray) foreground
40	For black background
41	For red background
42	For green background
43	For yellow (or brown) background
44	For blue background
45	For purple background
46	For cyan background
47	For white (or gray) background

There are more options than these shown here, so consult the man pages for ls or check out Chapter 25, "Command-Line Reference."

Organizing Files

There are no fixed rules for organizing files in Linux. Files do not have extensions (such as EXE for executables) as they do in MS-DOS. You can (and perhaps should) make up your own system of naming files, but the classic system of organizing files in Linux is with subdirectories.

More and more, however, Linux applications that have come from the DOS world are bringing their conventions to Linux. Although they may not require it, applications encourage you to name files that you use with their applications with certain extensions.

If you are going to write your own private commands, a useful way to organize your directories is to mimic Linux's use of the `/bin`, `/lib`, and `/etc` directories. Create your own private directories with these names, and follow the Linux tradition of placing executable commands in your `/bin` directory, subsidiary commands in your `/lib` directory, and initialization files in your `/etc` directory. Of course, there is no requirement that you do this, but it is one way of organizing your files.

You create directories with the `mkdir` command. Its syntax is simple:

```
mkdir directory-name
```

In this syntax, *`directory-name`* is replaced by the name you want to assign to the new directory. Of course, you need write permission in the directory before you can create a subdirectory with `mkdir`, but if you are making a subdirectory within your home directory, you should have no problem.

Suppose that you have written three programs called `prog1`, `prog2`, and `prog3`, all of which are found in `$HOME/bin`. Remember that `$HOME` is your home directory; if you want your private programs to run as though they were a standard part of the Linux command set, you must add `$HOME/bin` to your `PATH` environment variable. Do this with the following command in the Bourne or Korn shell:

```
PATH=$PATH:$HOME/bin;export PATH
```

In the C shell, you use this command:

```
setenv PATH "$PATH $HOME/bin"
```

Note

Remember that `$HOME` is the placeholder for the complete path that refers to your home directory. If your home directory is `/home/ams`, `$HOME/bin` is interpreted as `/home/ams/bin`.

If your programs call subsidiary programs, you may want to create subdirectories within your `$HOME/lib` directory. You can create a subdirectory for each program. The private command `pgm1` can then explicitly call, for example, `$HOME/lib/pgm1/pgm1a`.

Similarly, if your command `pgm1` requires a startup table, you can name that table `$HOME/etc/pgm1.rc`; your data can be in your `$HOME/data/pgm1` directory.

Copying Files

The command for copying files is `cp` *`from to`*. You must have read permission for the file you are copying from, and write permission for the directory (and the file if you are overwriting an existing file) you are copying to. Other than that, there are no restrictions on your ability to copy files.

Here are a few things to watch for as you copy files:

- If you copy a file and give it the name of a file that already exists and that you have write permission for, you will overwrite the original file.
- If you give the name of a directory as the destination of the `cp` command, the file is copied into that directory with its original name. For example, if you type the command **`cp file directory`**, the file is copied into *`directory`* as *`directory/file`*.
- You can copy a list of files into a directory with the command `cp` *`file1 file2 file3 . . . directory`*. If the last item in the list is not a directory, an error message appears. Likewise, if any element in the list other than the last item is a directory, an error message appears.
- Be careful when you use wild cards with the `cp` command because you can copy more than you intend to.

Note

Since many Linux users also have MS-DOS files on their systems and usually make the DOS file system accessible from Linux, most of the Linux commands recognize when a file is being copied to or from a DOS partition. Thus, Linux can handle the necessary file translation when copying files. This translation is required since most DOS files embed the carriage return/line feed characters into an ASCII file to indicate a line break. Most Linux and UNIX systems only embed a line-feed character, called `newline`, in the file to indicate a line break.

Moving and Renaming Files

In Linux, moving and renaming files are accomplished with the same command: `mv`. The syntax and rules are the same for `mv` as they are for the copy command, `cp`. That is, you can move as many files as you want to a directory, but the directory name must be last in the list and you must have write permission to that directory.

One thing you can do with `mv` that you can't do with `cp` is move or rename directories. When you move or rename a file, the only thing that happens is the entry in the directory file is changed (unless the new location is on another physical disk or partition, in which case the file and the contents of the directory are physically moved).

If you try to use `rm` (for *remove*) or `cp` without options on a directory, the command fails and displays a message telling you that the item you are dealing with is a directory. To remove or copy directories, you must use the `-r` flag (for *recursive*) with `rm` and `cp`. The `mv` command, however, moves directories quite happily.

Removing Files or Directories

The command to remove a file is `rm`. To delete a file you don't own, you need both read and write permission. If you own the file, you are allowed to delete it, provided that you haven't closed off your own permission to the file. For example, if you turn off write permission to a file by typing **`chmod 000 file`**, you must open permission again with the `chmod` command (by typing **`chmod 644 file`**, for example) before you can delete it.

If you accidentally type **`rm *`**, you delete all the files you have permission to delete in the current directory; you do not delete the subdirectories. To delete subdirectories, you must use the recursive option (`-r`).

Some versions of `rm` stop and ask whether you really want to delete files that you own but don't have at least write permission for. Other versions of `rm` prompt you for any files marked for removal with wild cards. Indeed, you can write a macro or shell script that gives you a second chance before actually deleting a file.

If your version of `rm` balks at removing files you own but don't have write permission for, you can partially protect yourself from accidentally deleting everything in your directory by following these steps:

1. Create a file named `0`. In the ASCII string sequence, the number 0 is listed before any files that begin with letters.
2. Remove all permissions from the file named `0` by typing the command **`chmod 000 0`**. This command removes read, write, and execute permissions for everyone, including yourself.
3. If you type the command **`rm *`**, the file named `0` is the first file that `rm` attempts to remove.

If your version of `rm` balks at removing the `0` file when you type **`rm *`**, you have the chance to think about what you just did. If you didn't intend to delete everything in your directory, press <Del> or <Ctrl-c> to kill the `rm` process. To test this out, try removing just the file named `0`. Don't use `rm *` because, if your version of `rm` doesn't stop at the file `0`, you will erase all the files in your directory.

A better way to protect yourself from accidentally deleting files is to use the `-i` flag with `rm`. The `-i` flag stands for *interactive*. If you give the command **`rm -i file-name`**, you are asked whether you really want to delete the file. You must answer yes before the file is actually deleted. If you type the command **rm -i ***, you must answer yes for every file in your directory. This should give you enough time to think about what you really want to do.

Caution

Think before you delete files. When you delete a file (in most versions of Linux), it's gone and the only way to recover a lost file is from a backup. You did make a backup, didn't you?

If you use the `rm -i` command frequently, there are two ways to implement it: write a shell script or create a shell function. If you write a shell script, remember that the shell searches for commands in the directories listed in your `PATH` variable in the order in which they are listed there. If your `$HOME/bin` directory is listed last, a shell script named `rm` will never be found. You can place your `$HOME/bin` directory first in the `PATH` variable's list or create a new command like `del`. If you create a shell script called `del`, you must mark it as executable with the `chmod` command before the shell can recognize it. When you create your `del` command, you need to give it only one command: `rm -i $*`. If you then type the command **del ***, the shell translates it into `rm -i *`.

▶▶ See "Shell Command Editing and Aliasing," p. 385

Another way to accomplish the same task is with an alias. An *alias* takes precedence over commands that must be looked up; you can think of it as an internal shell command (similar to the *doskey* commands introduced in MS-DOS version 5.0).

To add an alias if you are using the C shell, you must edit the file named `.cshrc`. You can use any text editor, such as the `vi` editor (see Chapter 22, "Using the `vi` Editor"), to edit this file. For the C shell, add the following lines to the top of your `.cshrc` file:

```
rm ()
{
/bin/rm -i $*
}
```

To add an alias to the Korn shell, add the following line to your `$HOME/.kshrc` file:

```
alias rm 'rm -i $*'
```

If you try to delete a directory with the `rm` command, you are told that it is a directory and cannot be deleted. If you want to delete empty directories, use the `rmdir` command (just as with MS-DOS).

Linux offers another way to delete directories and their contents but it is far more dangerous. The `rm -r` command recursively deletes any directories and files it encounters. If you have a directory named `./foo` that contains both files and subdirectories, the command `rm -r foo` deletes the `foo` directory and its contents, including all subdirectories.

If you give the command `rm -i -r`, each directory that the `rm` command encounters triggers a confirmation prompt. You must answer yes before the directory and its contents are deleted. If you left any files in the directory you were attempting to delete, `rm` balks, just as it does if you attempt to remove the non-empty directory with the `rm` command with no options.

Viewing the Contents of a File

Almost every Linux command prints to the standard output. If the command takes its input from a file, after manipulating the file in some way, the command prints the file to your screen. The trick in choosing a Linux command depends on how you want the file displayed. There are three standard commands you can use: `cat`, `more`, and `less`.

Using *cat* to View a File

For displaying short ASCII files, the simplest command is `cat`, which stands for *concatenate*. The `cat` command takes a list of files (or a single file) and prints the contents unaltered on the standard output, one file after another. Its primary purpose is to concatenate files (as in `cat file1 file2>file3`), but it works just as well to send the contents of a short file to your screen.

If you try to display large files using `cat`, the file scrolls past your screen as fast as the screen can handle the character stream. One way to stop the flow of data is to alternatively press <Ctrl-s> and <Ctrl-q> to send start and stop messages to your screen, or you can use one of the page-at-a-time commands: `more` or `less`.

Using *more* to View a File

Both `more` and `less` display one screenful of data at a time. Although they both do roughly the same thing, they do it differently. Both `more` and `less` determine how many lines your terminal can display from the terminal database and from your `TERM` environment variable.

The `more` command is older than `less`, and it is derived from the Berkeley version of UNIX. It proved so useful that, like the `vi` editor, it has become a standard. This section covers just the basics of the command.

The simplest form of the `more` command is `more` *`file-name`*. You see a screenful of the file. If you want to go on to the next screenful, press the <Spacebar>. If you press <Return>, only the next line is displayed. If you are looking through a series of files (with the command `more` *`file1 file2 . . .`*) and want to stop to edit one, you can do so with the `e` or `v` command. The `e` command within `more` uses whatever editor you have defined in your `EDIT` environment variable; the `v` command uses whatever editor has been defined in the `VISUAL` variable. If you have not defined these variables in your environment, `more` defaults to the `ed` editor for the `e` command and to the `vi` editor for the `v` command. The `more` command has only one real drawback: you can't go backward in a file and redisplay a previous screen. However, you can do this with `less`.

Using *less* to View a File

One disadvantage to the `less` command is that you cannot use an editor on a file being displayed. However, `less` makes up for this deficiency by allowing you to move both forward and backward through a file.

The `less` command works almost the same way that `more` does. To page through a file, type the command **`less`** ***`file-name`***. One screenful of data is displayed. To advance to the next screen, press the <Spacebar> as you did with the `more` command. The `less` command has other options, too. To move backward in a file, press the <b> key. To go to a certain position expressed as a percentage of the file, press the <p> key or the <Shift-5> key.

Both the `less` and `more` commands allow you to search for strings in the file being displayed. The `less` command, however, allows you to search backward through the file as well. The search syntax is `/`*`string`*. The `less /`*`string`* command searches backward through the file. With both the `less` and `more` commands, if a string is found, a new page is displayed with the line containing the matching string at the top of the screen. With `less`, pressing the <n> key repeats the previous search.

Both the `more` and `less` commands allow you to escape to the shell with the `!` command. When you escape to the shell with the `!` command, you are actually in a subshell; you must exit the subshell just as you do when you log out from a session. Depending on which shell you are using, you can press <Ctrl-d> or enter the **`exit`** command to return to the same screen in `more` or `less` that you escaped from. If you press <Ctrl-d> and get a message to use `logout` instead of <Ctrl-d>, use the `logout` command.

Viewing Files in Other Forms

Other commands display the contents of files in different forms. For example, if you want to look at the contents of a binary file, display it with the `od` command, which stands for *octal dump*. The `od` command displays a file in octal notation, or base 8. By using various flags, the `od` command can display a file in decimal, ASCII, or hexadecimal (base 16).

Octal, Decimal, and Hexadecimal Notation

Representing binary data is an intriguing problem. If the binary data represents ASCII, you have no problem displaying it (ASCII is, after all, what you expect when you look at most files). If the file is a program, however, the data most likely cannot be represented as ASCII characters. In that case, you have to display it in some numerical form.

The early minicomputers used 12-bit words. Today, of course, the computer world has settled on the 8-bit byte as the standard unit of memory. Although you can represent data in the familiar decimal (base 10) system, the question becomes what to display: a byte, a word, or 32 bits? Displaying a given number of bits compactly requires that base 2 be raised to the required number of bits. With the old 12-bit systems, you could represent all 12 bits with four numbers (represented by 2^3, which was the octal or base 8 format). Because early UNIX systems ran on these kinds of minicomputers, much of the UNIX, and thus, Linux, notation is in octal. Any byte can be represented by a three-digit octal code that looks like this (this example represents the decimal value of 8):

```
\010
```

Because the world has settled on an 8-bit byte, octal is no longer an efficient way to represent data. Hexadecimal (base 16 or 2^4) is a better way. An 8-bit byte can be represented by two hexadecimal digits; a byte whose decimal value is 10 is represented as 0A in hexadecimal.

The `od` command gives you a choice of the way you want binary data to be displayed. It all depends on the flags you use. Table 19.3 summarizes the flags you can use with the `od` command.

Table 19.3 The *od* Command Flags

Flag	Description
`-b`	Displays each byte as a three-digit octal number. This is the default.
`-c`	Displays the ASCII character if the byte can be interpreted as ASCII. Otherwise, it displays bytes according to the codes used in the C language: null (or zero) as `\0`, backspace as `\b`, form feed as `\f`, newline as `\n`, return as `\r`, and tab as `\t`. Any byte that cannot be interpreted by these rules is displayed as a three-digit octal number in the form `\nnn`.
`-d`	Displays each word (two bytes) as an unsigned decimal integer from 0 to 65535.
`-o`	Interprets each word (2 bytes) as octal.
`-s`	Interprets each word (2 bytes) as signed decimal from 32768 to +32767.
`-x`	Displays each byte as a two-character hexadecimal digit.

Searching for Files

If you can't find a file by looking with the `ls` command, you can use the `find` command. The `find` command is an extremely powerful tool. As a result, it is one of the more difficult commands to use. The `find` command has three parts, each of which may consist of multiple subparts. The parts are the following:

- Where to look
- What to look for
- What to do when you find it

If you know the name of a file but don't know where in the Linux file structure it is located, the simplest case of the `find` command works:

```
find / -name file-name -print
```

Be careful when searching from the root directory: on large systems, it can take a long time to search every directory, beginning with the root directory and continuing through every directory and disk (and remotely mounted disk) before finding what you are looking for.

It may be more prudent to limit the search to one or two directories at most. For example, if you know that a file is probably in either the `/usr` or `/usr2` directory, use the following command instead:

```
find /usr /usr2 -name file-name -print
```

There are many different options you can use with `find`; Table 19.4 lists just a few.

Table 19.4 A Sample of the *find* Command Flags

Command	Description
`-name` *`file`*	The *`file`* variable can be either the name of a file or a wild-carded file name. If it is a wild-carded file name, every file that matches the wild cards is selected for processing.
`-links` *n*	Any file that has *n* or more links to it is selected for processing. Replace *n* with the number you want to check.
`-size` *n*`[c]`	Any file that occupies *n* or more 512-byte blocks is selected for processing. A `c` appended to *n* means to select any file that occupies *n* or more characters.
`-atime` *n*	Select any file that has been accessed in the past *n* days. Note that the act of looking for a file with `find` modifies the access date stamp.
`-exec` *cmd*	After you select a list of files, you can run a Linux command that uses the selected files as an argument. You use two simple rules with `-exec`: the name of a selected file is represented by `{ }`, and the command must be terminated by an escaped semicolon. An escaped semicolon is represented by `\;`.
`-print`	This is the most often-used instruction. It simply prints the name and location of any selected files.

The `find` command allows you to perform many logical tests on files as well. For example, if you want to find a selection of file names that cannot be collectively represented with wild cards, you can use the *or* option (`-o`) to obtain a list:

```
find /home ( -name file1 -o -name file2 ) -print
```

You can combine as many selection criteria as you want with the `find` command. Unless you specify the `-o` option, `find` assumes that you mean *and*. For example, the command `find -size 100 -atime 2` means find a file that is at least 100 blocks in size *and* that was last accessed at least two days ago.

Changing File Time and Date Stamps

Each Linux file maintains three time and date stamps: the date of the file's creation, the date of the file's last modification, and the date of the last access. The file creation date cannot be changed artificially except by deliberately copying and renaming a file. Whenever a file is read or opened by a program, the file's access date stamp is modified. As mentioned in the preceding section, using the `find` command also causes the access date to be modified.

If a file is modified in any way (that is, if it is written to—even if the file is actually not modified), both the file modification and file access date stamps are updated. The date stamps on a file are useful if you need to selectively back up only files that have been modified since a given date. The `find` command can be used for this purpose.

If you want to modify the date stamps on a file without actually modifying the file, you can do so with the `touch` command. By default, the `touch` command updates both the access and modification date stamps on a file with the current system date. By default, if you attempt to touch a file that does not exist, the `touch` command creates the file.

You can use the `touch` command to fool a command that checks for dates. For example, if your system runs a backup command that only backs up files modified after a particular date, you can touch a file that hasn't been changed recently to make sure it is picked up.

The `touch` command has the following three flags you can use to modify its default behavior:

`-a`	Updates only the file's access date and time stamp
`-m`	Updates only the file's modification date and time stamp
`-c`	Prevents `touch` from creating a file if it does not already exist

The default syntax for `touch` is `touch -am` *`file-list`*.

Compressing Files

If space is tight on a system, or if you have large ASCII files that are not being used often, you can reduce the size of the files by compressing them. The standard Linux utility for compressing files is `gzip`. The `gzip` command can compress an ASCII file by as much as 80 percent. Compression is also a good thing to do before you mail a file or back it up.

If a file is successfully compressed with the command `gzip` *`file-name`*, the compressed file is named *`file-name`*`.gz` and the original file is deleted. To restore the compressed file to its original components, use the `gunzip` *`file-name`* command. Note that you do not have to append the `.gz` to the file name when you uncompress a file. The `.gz` extension is assumed by the `gzip` command.

If you want to keep the file in its compressed form but want to use the data in a pipeline, use the `zcat` command. The `zcat` command works just like the `cat` command, but expects a compressed file as input, decompresses it, and then prints it on the standard output.

For example, if you have compressed a list of names and addresses stored in a file named `namelist`, the compressed file is named `namelist.gz`. If you want to use the contents of the compressed file as input to a program, use the `zcat` command to begin a pipeline:

```
zcat namelist ¦ program1 ¦ program2 . . .
```

`zcat` suffers from the same limitations as does `cat`—it cannot go backward within a file. Linux does offer a program called `zless` that works just like the command `less`, except `zless` operates on compressed files. The same commands that work with `less` also work with `zless`.

The `compress` command's legal status is in limbo (someone has claimed patent infringement). The compression program of choice for Linux is the freely distributed compression utility `gzip`. The `gzip` command has none of the potential legal problems of `compress`, and almost all the files installed by Linux that are compressed were compressed with `gzip`. `gzip` should work with most compressed files, even those compressed with the older `compress` program.

Manipulating Files with the GUI

If you are using the XFree86 system, chances are you are working with its graphical user interface (GUI). All the file manipulations you do with commands from the shell can be done with mouse actions from the GUI. If you did not install the XFree86 X Windows system, you can skip this section. The program used is called Xfilemanager by Ove Kalkan. See the application's Copyright menu item for information about the program.

To activate the Xfilemanager application, you must press the left mouse button over an open area of the desktop. This action displays the X Windows Utilities menu. Move the cursor to the Applications selection to activate the application's pop-up menu. You then see the Xfilemanager command. Select this command to activate the program.

> **Note**
>
> Using the mouse under X Windows is different than under MS-DOS and Windows. The mouse behaves more like a mouse on the Macintosh. For example, to select a menu item, you must continuously hold down the mouse button, move the cursor to the desired entry, and then release the mouse button. For more information on using X Windows, see Chapter 6, "The X Windows System."

The X Windows application Xfilemanager displays the contents of your directories in *windows* that look like folders. These folders represent your directories.

This chapter, however, is concerned with how you manage the files, directories, and applications that appear in your folder windows. Managing these items includes listing, copying, deleting, and moving.

Figure 19.1 shows an example of a Linux folder window named `MyFile` that exists in your home folder. Note that you can get to this same folder (although you call it a *directory*) from the command line by typing **`cd $HOME/MyFile`**.

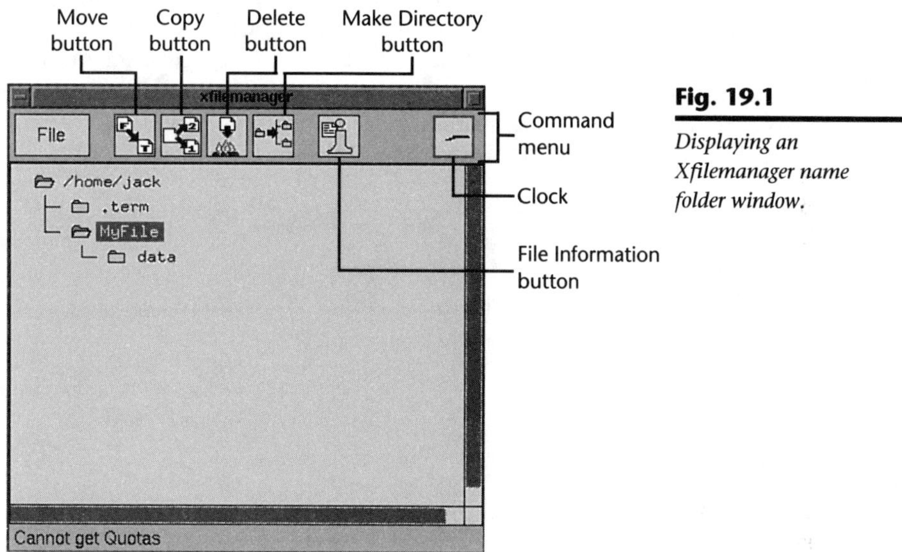

Fig. 19.1

Displaying an Xfilemanager name folder window.

The buttons across the top of the application provide access to a command menu. The first button, named File, allows you to switch directories and exit the application. The Move button allows you to move files, while the Copy button lets you copy files. The Delete button allows you to delete files. The Make Directory button allows you to create a new directory. The File Information button provides information on the selected file, and the final item is a simple clock.

Listing Files with the GUI

You can list the files located in a subdirectory by clicking the folder. This displays a new window (see fig. 19.2). The new window has a similar set of buttons like the first window, and each button performs the same actions. The first button, with the bomb icon, immediately exits the application.

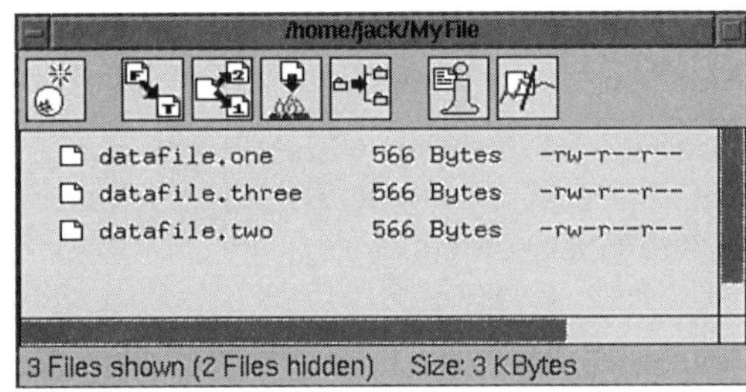

Fig. 19.2

Listing the files located in a subdirectory with the Xfilemanager.

You can display and modify the various file-permission settings by highlighting a file and clicking the File Information button, which displays the File-Information dialog box (see fig. 19.3). To change a file permission, simply move the mouse to the appropriate box and click. A filled box indicates that the permission is set, while an empty box indicates that the permission is not set. When you have changed the permissions, you must click the Apply button for the changes to be made.

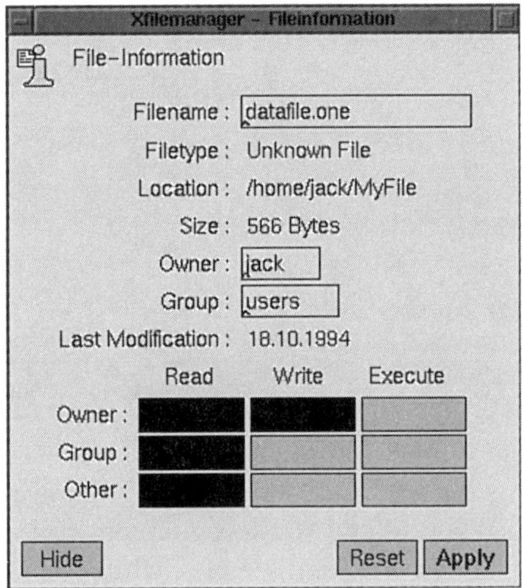

Fig. 19.3

Displaying and modifying file permission settings.

Copying Files in the GUI

To copy files from one folder to another, you click the Copy button, which displays the Copy File dialog box (see fig. 19.4).

The currently selected file name appears in the From text box. You must supply the destination path and file names in the To text box. To cancel the operation, click the Cancel button. To execute the command and actually copy the file, click the Ok button.

Fig. 19.4

The Copy File dialog box.

Moving and Renaming Files in the GUI

To rename a file or move a file from one folder to another, you can select a file and then press the Move button, which displays the Moving & Renaming Files dialog box (see fig. 19.5). Its operation is very similar to the Copy File dialog box. Simply fill in the desired information, and click the Ok button to rename or move the file.

Fig. 19.5

The Moving and Renaming Files dialog box.

Removing Files and Folders

To remove or delete a file or folder from a folder window, the process is the same. Select the desired file or folder, and click the Delete button, which displays the Remove File dialog box (see fig. 19.6). Clicking Ok removes the selected file(s).

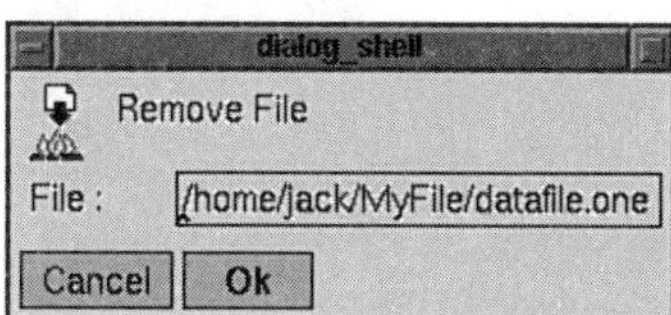

Fig. 19.6

The Remove File dialog box.

Caution

Be careful. Just as with the command-line version of deleting files, if you delete a file by mistake, you cannot recover the file except from a backup. Linux, and any UNIX system for that matter, does not have utilities to "undelete" a file because of the way UNIX systems maintain their file systems. Under MS-DOS, a deleted file only has an entry in the FAT table marked, telling the operating system that the file space is available for use. MS-DOS does not write over this space immediately. However, UNIX, and hence Linux, returns the space (actually the inodes) formerly used by the deleted program back to the free pool. Once the space is moved to the free pool, the file can never be recovered!

From Here...

Managing files and utilities in Linux is a relatively simple chore. Organizing files into directories is easy. Finding, moving, copying, renaming, and deleting files and directories are simple with the commands `find`, `mv`, `cp`, and `rm`. For more information see the following chapters:

- Chapter 25, "Command-Line Reference," explains in detail many of the most common Linux commands.
- Chapter 17, "Managing File Systems," discusses practices for keeping your file system under control.

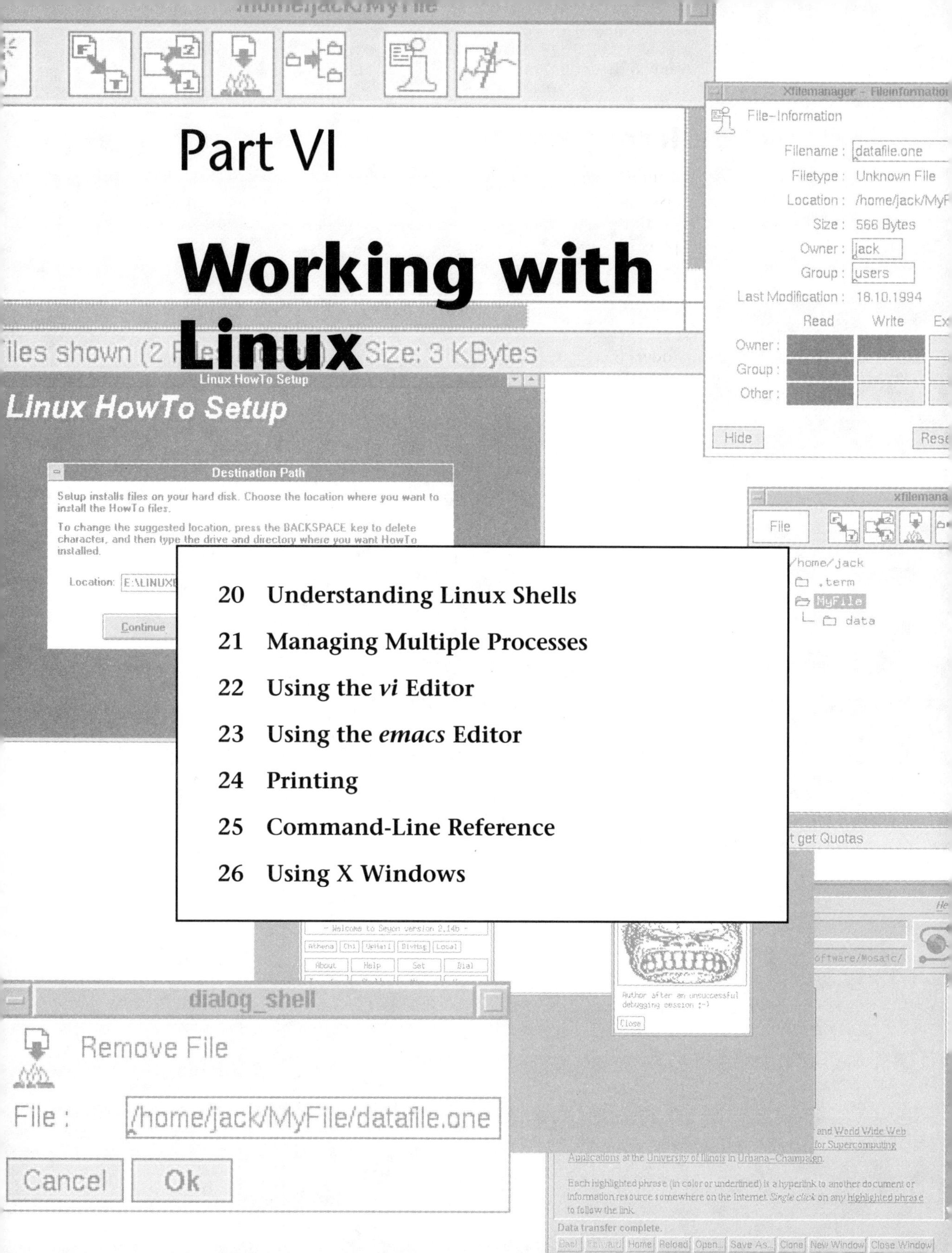

Part VI

Working with Linux

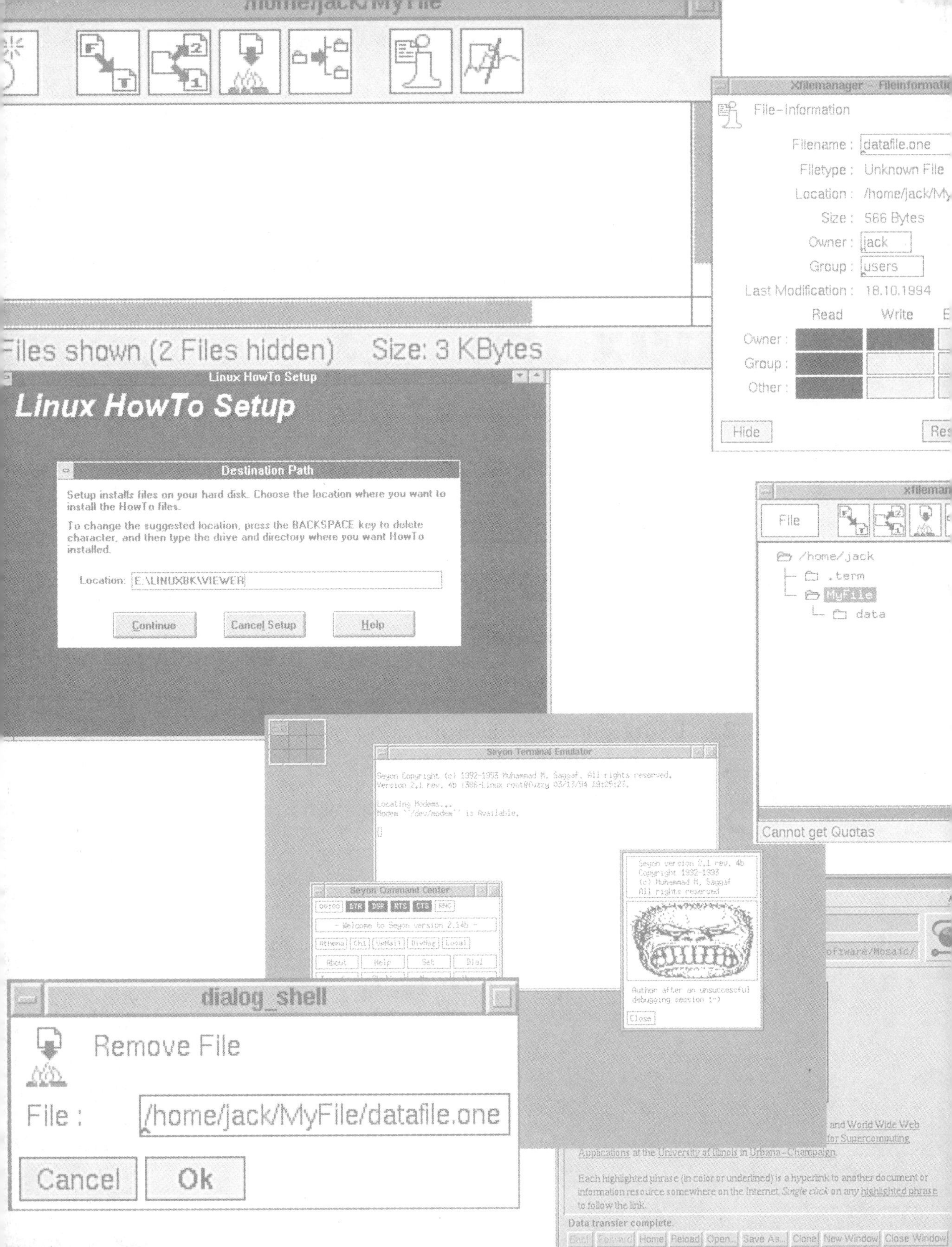

Xfilemanager - Fileinformati
File-Information
Filename : datafile.one
Filetype : Unknown File
Location : /home/jack/My
Size : 566 Bytes
Owner : jack
Group : users
Last Modification : 18.10.1994
Read
Write
Owner :
Group :
Other :
Hide
Files shown (2 Files hidden)
Size: 3 KBytes
Linux HowTo Setup
Linux HowTo Setup
Destination Path
Setup installs files on your hard disk. Choose the location where you want to install the HowTo files.
To change the suggested location, press the BACKSPACE key to delete character, and then type the drive and directory where you want HowTo installed.
Location: E:\LINUXBK\VIEWER
Continue
Cancel Setup
Help
File
/home/jack
.term
MyFile
data
Cannot get Quotas
Seyon Terminal Emulator
Seyon Copyright (c) 1992-1993 Muhammad M. Saggaf. All rights reserved.
Version 2.1 rev. 4b i386-Linux root@fuzzy 03/13/94 18:29:23.
Locating Modems...
Modem ``/dev/modem'' is Available.
Seyon Command Center
00:00
DTR
DSR
RTS
CTS
RNG
- Welcome to Seyon version 2.14b -
About
Help
Set
Dial
Seyon version 2.1 rev. 4b
Copyright 1992-1993
(c) Muhammad M. Saggaf
All rights reserved
Author after an unsuccessful debugging session :-)
Close
dialog_shell
Remove File
File : /home/jack/MyFile/datafile.one
Cancel
Ok
and World Wide Web
for Supercomputing
Applications at the University of Illinois in Urbana-Champaign.
Each highlighted phrase (in color or underlined) is a hyperlink to another document or information resource somewhere on the Internet. Single click on any highlighted phrase to follow the link.
Data transfer complete.
Home
Reload
Open...
Save As...
Clone
New Window
Close Window

CHAPTER 20

Understanding Linux Shells

Though graphical interfaces have been added to the UNIX system in recent years, most of the utilities for using and administering Linux (and other UNIX-like systems) are run by typing commands. In Linux, the command-line interpreter is called the *shell*. This chapter describes how to use features of the shell command environment to work with Linux utilities and file systems.

This chapter covers the following:

- Logging on
- Understanding shells
- Understanding shell command parsing
- Background processing
- Understanding command feedback
- Shell command editing and aliasing
- Understanding shell scripts
- Customizing Linux shells

Logging On

As a new user and novice system administrator on your Linux system you have chosen a logon ID and password. Because Linux is a multiuser operating system, it must be able to distinguish between users and classes of users. Linux uses your logon ID to establish a session in your name and determine the privileges you have. Linux uses your password to verify who you are.

Because any user can log on to any terminal in theory (there *is* an exception), the UNIX operating system begins by displaying a logon prompt on every terminal. Because it is unlikely you will have multiple terminals connected to your initial Linux system (although connecting multiple terminals is certainly possible), you will have the alternate, or virtual, terminals available to you.

To switch to the various *virtual terminals*, simply press the <Alt> key and any of the first six function keys to switch between the various virtual terminals. For example, to log on to virtual terminal one as root, you press <Alt-F1>, which displays the following prompt:

```
Welcome to Linux1.3.18
Opus Login:  root
```

> **Note**
>
> The prompt line in the code line declares this example session to be running under the 1.3.18 version of the Linux kernel. As newer kernels are released, this number is incremented, so you may see a different version on the enclosed CD-ROM. The stable released kernels are given even numbers for the middle number and the odd numbers indicate the latest (and beta) releases.

Enter your user ID (root) and password.

When you log on to any terminal, you own the session on that terminal until you log off. When you log off, Linux displays the logon prompt for the next user. Between logging on and logging off, Linux makes sure that all the programs you run and any files you might create are owned by you. Conversely, Linux does not allow you to read or alter a file owned by another user unless that user or the system administrator has given you permission to do so. Your logon ID and password allow Linux to maintain the security of your files and those of others.

You, as the system administrator for your Linux system, assign every user a user ID, temporary password, group ID, home directory, and shell. This information is kept in a file named `/etc/passwd`, which is owned and controlled by the system administrator, also known as `root`. Once you have successfully logged in, you can change your password, which is then encrypted in a form that no one else can read. If you forget your password, you have to log on as the root user to create a new password. You can change your own password with the `passwd` command (though you have to type in the old password).

> **Note**
>
> For more information on basic system administration duties, such as adding users and fixing forgotten passwords, see Part III, "System Administration," and particularly Chapter 9, "Managing User Accounts."

Understanding Shells

After you log on, Linux places you in your home directory and runs a program called a *shell*. A shell is really nothing more than a program designed to accept commands from you and execute them. Many kinds of programs can be used as shells, but there are several standard shells available with almost all versions of Linux. The following section introduces shells.

Note

Linux shells are equivalent to COMMAND.COM used by MS-DOS. Both accept and execute commands, run batch files, and execute programs.

Looking at Different Shells

One of the shells installed by Linux was the `bash` shell (Bourne Again shell). Linux also provides the T shell (`tsh`) and Z shell (`zsh`). Try each shell and pick one you like.

The shell is a program that starts when you log on and interprets your commands. Because it serves as the primary interface between the operating system and the user, many users identify the shell with Linux. They expect the shell to have the properties mentioned in the first part of this chapter and they expect the shell to be programmable. Remember that the shell is not part of the kernel of the operating system; with enough background in systems programming and knowledge of the Linux operating system, you can write a program that can become a shell.

Although many different shells have been created, there are several prevalent shells: the Bourne, C, T, and Korn shells. They all have the features discussed so far. The Bourne shell is the oldest and the others have some features not in the Bourne shell. In fact, Linux uses a variation of the Bourne shell, the BASH shell, as its default shell. (To the novice user, the Bourne and Korn shells look identical; indeed, the Korn shell grew out of the Bourne shell.)

▶▶ See "Using the `vi` Editor," p. 427

The C shell was developed at the University of California at Berkeley as a shell more suitable for programmers than the Bourne shell. The Korn shell has all the features of the C shell but uses the syntax of the Bourne shell. If all this sounds confusing at the moment, don't worry. You can do a lot without knowing or worrying about the shell you are using.

In their simplest forms, the Bourne and Korn shells use the dollar sign (`$`) as the standard prompt; the C shell uses the percent sign (`%`) as the prompt. Fortunately (or not, depending on your disposition), these prompts can be changed so that you may or may not see either the dollar or the percent sign when you first log on.

The Bourne shell, known as `sh`, is the original UNIX shell. It was written by Steve Bourne with some help and ideas from John Mashey, both of AT&T Bell Laboratories. It is available on all Linux systems. The executable program for this shell is in the file `/bin/sh`. When you use this shell, you usually see a `$` prompt. The fact that the

Bourne shell is available on all Linux systems and that it has all the properties described in the preceding sections—as well as the fact that it has powerful programming capabilities—make this a widely used shell. The examples in the next section are written so that they can be used with the Bourne shell.

The C shell, known as `csh`, was developed by Bill Joy at the University of California at Berkeley. The students and faculty at Berkeley have had a great deal of influence on UNIX and hence Linux. Two results of that influence are the C shell and the `vi` text editor. The Bourne shell has superior shell programming capabilities, but the C shell was developed to reflect the fact that computing was becoming more interactive. The executable program for this shell is in the file `/bin/csh`. When you use this shell, you usually see a `%` prompt. The syntax of the C shell closely resembles the C programming language. This is one reason that shell scripts written for the C shell often cannot run under the Bourne or Korn shell. But the C shell has some desirable features not available in the Bourne shell: command editing, history, and aliasing.

> **Note**
>
> Linux does not provide a copy of the Korn shell by default.

The default Linux shell is the `bash` shell. `bash` is located in `/bin/bash` and provides several enhanced features detailed in the next few paragraphs, such as command editing, command history, and command completion.

Which Shells Are Available?

All Linux systems have the `bash` shell. You may also have installed several other shells during installation, for example, the C shell or the T shell. To determine which shell you are using, enter

```
echo $SHELL
```

The `echo` command prints whatever follows the word `echo` to the terminal screen. `SHELL` is a variable, maintained by the shell, which holds the name of your current shell; `$SHELL` is the value of that variable.

To see whether the C shell is available, enter

```
csh
```

If you see the percent sign (`%`) as the prompt, the C shell is available and running (enter **`exit`** to return to your previous shell). If you get an error message, the C shell isn't available to you.

> **Note**
>
> If you did not install a particular shell during the Linux installation, you can use the `pkgtool` program in `/sbin` to install a program.

◄◄ See "Using pkgtool," p. 217

The shell you use as a logon shell is specified in the password file. Each logon ID is represented by a record or line in the password file; the last field in the record specifies your logon shell. To change your logon shell, you must change that field. The act of changing to another shell is relatively easy. Before you change shells, however, decide whether learning a new syntax and operating method—as well as some incompatibility problems—are worth the change. See the man pages for detailed information on your shell's syntax.

Caution

Never directly edit the password file (`/etc/passwd`) in Linux. Because of the security features added to these releases, the password file should be manipulated only with the appropriate commands. For example, to change to the C shell using `usermod`, enter **`usermod -s /bin/csh`** ***`user`*** where *`user`* is replaced by the user ID of the user for whom you're changing the shell.

A variety of other shells is available; some are proprietary and others are available on the Internet or through other sources. To determine which shell you want to use, simply read the man pages for the various shells and give each a try. Because shells are programs, you can run them just like any other application.

The Logon Environment

Before you see the shell prompt, Linux sets up your default environment. The Linux *environment* contains settings and data that control your session while you are logged on. Of course, as with all things in Linux, you are completely free to change any of these settings to suit your needs.

Your session environment is divided into two components. The first component controls your terminal (more properly, the behavior of the computer's port) that you connect the cable from your terminal to and is called the terminal environment. The second component is called the *shell environment.* It controls various aspects of the shell and any programs you run. You should first know about your terminal environment.

Note

Since Linux runs on a PC, the "terminal" is actually your monitor and keyboard. You may or may not have other terminals connected to your Linux system. Of course, you do have six virtual terminals that you can log on from.

Setting the Terminal Environment. Your logon session actually consists of two separate programs that run side by side to give you the appearance of having the machine to yourself. Although the shell is the program that receives your instructions and executes them, before the shell ever sees your commands, everything you type must first pass through the relatively transparent program called the *device driver.*

The device driver controls your terminal. It receives the characters you type and determines what to do with them—if anything—before passing them on to the shell for interpretation. Likewise, every character generated by the shell must pass through the device driver before being delivered to the terminal. This section is first concerned with how to control the behavior of your device driver.

Linux is unique in that every device connected to the system looks, to a program, just like every other device, and all devices look like files. It is the task of the different device drivers in your system to accomplish this transformation. A hard disk in the system behaves very differently from your terminal, yet it is the job of their respective device drivers to make them look identical to a program.

For example, a disk has blocks, sectors, and cylinders, all of which must be properly addressed when reading and writing data. Your terminal, on the other hand, accepts a continuous stream of characters, but those characters must be delivered to the terminal in an ordered and relatively slow manner. The device driver orders this data and sends it to you at 1200, 2400, 9600, or higher bits per second and inserts stop, start, and parity bits in the data stream.

Because your terminal is always connected to the system, the device driver allows you to define special characters, called *control characters,* that serve as end-of-file and end-of-line markers for your shell. The device driver also allows you to define control characters that send signals to a running process (such as the interrupt signal which can, in most cases, stop a running process and return you to the shell). Figure 20.1 shows one way that the Linux kernel, shell, and device driver behave.

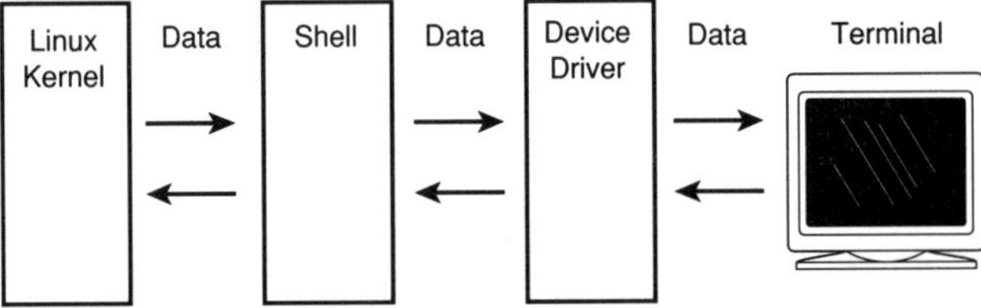

Fig. 20.1

The interaction of the Linux kernel, shell, and device driver.

Dozens of parameters can be set for your terminal but most of them are handled automatically. However, there are a few parameters and modes you should know about.

The device driver has two modes of operation called cooked and raw. In *raw mode,* all the characters you type pass directly to either the shell or a program run by the shell. Programs like editors and spreadsheets require raw mode and set it up automatically. When such programs end, they normally reset your terminal to cooked mode—but not always. When your terminal is in raw mode, it does not respond to control keys like the interrupt key.

When your terminal is in *cooked mode,* every key you type is interpreted by the device driver. Normal keys are stored in a buffer until the end-of-line key is pressed. In most cases, the end-of-line key is the <Enter> or <Return> key (however, this key can be changed). When the device driver receives the end-of-line character, it interprets the entire line before passing the interpreted or *parsed* line on to the shell or application program. Table 20.1 lists the most important control keys.

Table 20.1 Control Keys

Key Name	Description
Interrupt	Uses the interrupt key to interrupt the execution of a running program. When you give Linux a command and press the end-of-line key, a program normally runs until normal completion. If you press the interrupt key, you send a signal to the running program telling it to stop. Some programs ignore this signal; if your terminal is in raw mode, the interrupt key passes directly to the program and may not have the desired effect. The UNIX convention is to use the <Del> key as the interrupt key, but Linux changes this key to <Ctrl-c> for the convenience of people familiar with MS-DOS and other systems that use this key combination.
Erase	The erase control key is defined as the <Backspace> key. When you press the erase key, it deletes the last character in the buffer. The erase key works just like the Backspace key on a typewriter. On some terminals and systems, there is confusion between the <Del> and <Backspace> keys.
Kill	The kill key (normally defined as the @ character) is used to delete everything in the buffer before it passes to the shell or application program. Unlike what happens when you press the interrupt key, you don't see a new shell prompt when you press the kill key. The device driver simply waits for you to type more text.
End-of-line	The end-of-line control key tells the device driver that you have finished entering text and want the text interpreted and passed on to the shell or application program. Linux uses the <Enter> or <Return> key.
End-of-file	Linux treats all devices as though they were files; because your terminal is a source of virtually unlimited characters, Linux provides a way for you to signal you are done with your logon session. When the shell sees an end-of-file character, it exits and you see the logon prompt again. The end-of-file character is the <Ctrl-d> character.

The command used to set and display these parameters is `stty`. The `stty` command stands for *set teletype*. In the "old days," a teletype terminal was the only terminal available; a lot of UNIX terminology is left over from this era. For example, your terminal is defined as a *tty device* with a name like `tty14`. To display all your present settings, type **`stty -a`** from the command line and press <Return>. If you use this command you see something like

```
speed 38400 baud; rows 25; columns 80; line = 0;
intr = ^C; quit = ^\; erase = ^?; kill = ^U; eof = ^D; eol = <undef>;
eol2 = <undef>; start = ^Q; stop = ^S;
➥susp = ^Z; rprnt = ^R; werase = ^W;
lnext = ^V; flush = ^O; min = 1; time = 0;
-parenb -parodd cs8 hupcl -cstopb cread -clocal -crtscts
-ignbrk -brkint -ignpar -parmrk -inpck
➥-istrip -inlcr -igncr icrnl ixon ixoff
-iuclc -ixany -imaxbel
opost -olcuc -ocrnl onlcr -onocr
➥-onlret -ofill -ofdel nl0 cr0 tab0 bs0 vt0 ff0
isig icanon iexten echo echoe echok
➥-echonl -noflsh -xcase -tostop -echoprt
echoctl echoke
```

Tip

If you want a certain setting to take effect every time you log on, place the command in your `.profile` file (located in your home directory) if you're running the `bash` or Bourne shell. For the C shell, place the command in your `.login` file.

Notice that on this system, the interrupt key (`intr`) is defined as <Ctrl-c>, shown as `^C`, and the kill key is <Ctrl-u>. Although you can set all the settings listed here, as a matter of practicality, users usually only reset the interrupt and kill keys. For example, if you want to change the kill key from `^U` to `^C`, enter

```
stty kill '^C'
```

Note

If your terminal is behaving strangely, reset it to a "most reasonable" setting by giving the command **`stty sane`**.

Setting the Shell Environment. Part of the process of *logging on,* that is, of creating a Linux session, is the creation of your environment. All Linux *processes* (as running programs are called) have their own environment separate and distinct from the program itself. It could be said that a program runs from within an environment. The Linux environment, called the *shell environment,* consists of a number of variables and their values. These variables and values allow a running program, like a shell, to determine what the environment looks like.

Environment refers to things like the name of your shell, your home directory, and what type of terminal you are using. Many of these variables are defined during the logon process and either cannot or should not be changed. You can add or change as many variables as you like as long as a variable has not been marked "read only."

Variables are set in the environment in the form *`VARIABLE=value`*. The meaning of *`VARIABLE`* can be set to anything you like. However, many variables have predefined meanings to many standard Linux programs. For example, the `TERM` variable is defined as being the name of your terminal type as specified in one of the standard Linux terminal databases. Digital Equipment Corporation for years made a popular terminal named the VT-100. The characteristics of this terminal have been copied by many other manufacturers and often emulated in software for personal computers. The name of such a terminal type is `vt100`; it is represented in the environment as `TERM=vt100`.

Many other predefined variables exist in your environment. If you use the C shell, you can list these variables with the `printenv` command; with the Bourne or Korn shell, use the `set` command. Table 20.2 lists the most common environment variables and their uses. Note that some of these variables can be changed and some cannot be changed. The first column in the table shows what you type at the command line. The second column describes the variable and how it's used.

Note

If you want an environment variable defined every time you log on, place the definition in your `.profile` file (located in your home directory) if you're running the `bash` or Bourne shell. For the C shell, place the definition in your `.login` file.

Table 20.2 Common Environment Variables

Variable	Description
`HOME=/home/`*`logon`*	Sets your home directory, which is the location that you start out from. Replace *`logon`* with your logon ID. For example, if your logon ID is `jack`, `HOME` is defined as `/home/jack`.
`LOGNAME=`*`logon`*	`LOGNAME` is automatically set the same as your logon ID.
`PATH=`*`path`*	The *`path`* variable represents the list of directories that the shell looks through for commands. For example, you can set the path like this: `PATH=/usr:/bin:/usr/local/bin`.
`PS1=`*`prompt`*	`PS1` is the primary shell prompt. It defines what your prompt looks like. If you don't set it to anything specific, your prompt is the dollar sign ($). If you prefer, you can set it to something more creative. For example, `PS1="Enter Command >"` displays `Enter Command >` as your command-line prompt.
`PWD=`*`directory`*	`PWD` is automatically set for you. It defines where you are in the file system. For example, if you checked PWD (by entering **`echo $PWD`** at the command line) and Linux displays `/usr/bin`, you are in the `/usr/bin` directory. There is also a command, `pwd`, which displays the current directory.
`SHELL=`*`shell`*	`SHELL` identifies the location of the program that serves as your shell. For example, you can set `SHELL` in your `.profile` or `.login` file as `SHELL=/bin/ksh` to make the Korn shell your logon shell.
`TERM=`*`termtype`*	Sets the name of your terminal type, as specified by the terminal database. For example, you can set `TERM` in your `.profile` or `.login` file as `TERM=vt100`.

Perhaps the single most important variable in your environment is the PATH variable. The PATH variable contains a colon-delimited string that points to all the directories that contain the programs you use. The order that these directories are listed in determines which directories are searched first. The list order is important on systems that support several different forms of the same command. Your system may also have locally created commands you may want to access. For example, your PATH variable may contain the following values:

```
/usr/ucb:/bin:/usr/bin:/usr/local/bin
```

This statement instructs your shell to explore the /usr/ucb directory first. If the shell finds the command in the first directory it searches, it stops searching and executes that command. The /bin and /usr/bin directories contain all the standard Linux commands, as detailed in Chapter 25, "Command-Line Reference." The /usr/local/bin directory often contains the local commands added by you and other users of your system. This task of adding local commands is usually the responsibility of the system administrator.

If you intend to create your own commands, you can modify the PATH variable to include directories that contain your own commands. How you do this depends on which shell you use. For example, if you use the Bourne or Korn shell, you can add a directory to your PATH variable by typing

```
PATH=$PATH:newpath
```

When you place a $ in front of the name of a variable, its current value is substituted. In this command, the $PATH variable represents whatever the current path is; the colon and the *newpath* parameters add to the current path.

Several other ways of manipulating variables in your environment are described in the next section. For now, it is sufficient to say that the shell environment contains variables and functions and that these objects can be manipulated by both shells and application programs. Application programs can access and modify the environment, but they generally manipulate variables within the program. Shells, on the other hand, can only manipulate variables in the environment.

Special Shell Variables. The shell keeps track of a number of special variables. You can see what they are with the env command, which lists the variables available to you within your *working environment.* Following is an abbreviated list of what you might see when you enter **env**:

```
HOME=/usr/wrev
SHELL=/bin/sh
MAIL=/usr/mail/wrev
LOGNAME=wrev
PATH=/bin:/usr/bin:.
TZ=PST8PDT
PS1=$
TERM=vt100
```

Any of these special variables can be used in the same way you use any other shell variable. Table 20.3 defines the special variables.

Table 20.3 Environment Variables

Variable Name	Meaning
HOME	Full path name of your home directory
SHELL	Name of your current shell
MAIL	Full path name of your mailbox
LOGNAME	Your logon name
PATH	Directories the shell searches for commands
TZ	Time zone for the `date` command
PS1	System prompt
TERM	The type of terminal you are using

The variable `HOME` always specifies your home directory. When you log on, you are in your home directory. Occasionally, you use the `cd` command to move to other directories. To change to the directory `/usr/local/games`, for example, enter **`cd /usr/local/games`**. To get back to your home directory, all you have to do is enter **`cd`**. You can use the `HOME` variable when you are writing shell scripts that specify files in your home directory. Instead of writing a command such as `grep $number /usr/wrev/sales/data.01`, it is better to write the command as `grep $number $HOME/sales/data.01`. Why is it better to do this?

- The command line is easier to read.
- If your home directory is moved, the command still works.
- `$HOME` always represents the home directory of whoever is using the command. If you write the command using `$HOME`, others can use it as well.

The variable `PATH` lists the directories that the shell searches for commands in. The shell searches those directories in the order they are listed. If `PATH=/bin:/usr/bin/:.`, whenever the shell interprets a command, it first looks in the directory `/bin`. If it can't find the command there, the shell looks in the directory `/usr/bin`. Finally, the shell searches the directory `.` (remember that the period represents your current directory). When you enter **`cal`** to print this month's calendar, the shell first looks in `/bin`. Because the command isn't there, the shell then looks in `/usr/bin` and finds it.

Note that if you had a personalized command named `cal`, the shell never finds it; the shell executes the `cal` command in `/usr/bin` first whenever you give the command. Give your commands names that aren't the same as system commands.

You may want to put all your shell scripts in one directory and change the `PATH` variable to include that directory. This arrangement enables you to execute your shell scripts from whatever directory you happen to be in. To do this, follow these steps:

1. Create a directory to hold the scripts. Use the `mkdir $HOME/bin` command to create the `bin` subdirectory in your home directory.

2. Move each shell script to that subdirectory. For example, to move a shell script named `stamp` to your `bin` subdirectory, use the `mv stamp $HOME/bin` command.
3. Add the script subdirectory to your `PATH` variable with the `PATH=$PATH:$HOME/bin` command. Do this in your `.profile` file so the change takes effect every time you log on to your system.

You need to create that directory and modify the `PATH` variable only once. Under Linux, the directory called `/usr/local/bin` is created to hold "local" commands and scripts that aren't part of the standard Linux package but that you have added locally and are available to all users. In this case, you should expect that `/usr/local/bin` is also part of `PATH`.

The variable `MAIL` contains the name of the file that holds your e-mail. Whenever mail comes into the system for you, it is put into the file specified by the `MAIL` variable. If you have a program that notifies you when new mail has arrived, it checks the file associated with the `MAIL` variable.

The variable `PS1` holds the string of characters you see as your primary prompt. The *prompt* is the string of characters the shell displays whenever it is ready to receive a command. You see how you can change this variable—and any of the others—in the section "Customizing Linux Shells" at the end of this chapter.

The variable `TERM` is used to identify your terminal type. Programs that operate in full-screen mode, such as the `vi` text editor, need this information.

The variable `TZ` holds a string that identifies your time zone. The `date` program and some other programs require this information. The computer system keeps track of time according to Greenwich Mean Time (GMT). If the `TZ` variable is set to `PST8PDT`, the time and date are determined as Pacific Standard Time (PST), eight hours west of GMT, with support for Pacific Daylight Savings Time (PDT). Your computer system automatically changes between daylight savings time and standard time. Remember, during installation you were asked to choose a time zone.

The variable `LOGNAME` holds your logon name, the name or string of characters that the system associates you with. Among the things the `LOGNAME` variable is used for is to identify you as the owner of your files, as the originator of any processes or programs you may be running, and as the author of mail or messages sent by the `write` command.

The following example is an extension of the shell script `safrm` introduced earlier in this chapter. In this new version, the `LOGNAME` variable is used to remove all the files you own from the directory `/tmp`. To do that, the shell script uses the command `find`. The `find` command has a number of options; the shell script uses this `find` command line:

```
find /tmp -user $LOGNAME -exec rm {} \;
```

The first parameter, `/tmp`, is the directory to search. The option `-user` indicates that you want to search for all files that belong to a specified user. Before the command is executed, the shell replaces `$LOGNAME` with the current user's logon name. The option

`-exec` indicates that the following command is to be applied to every file found by the `find` program. In this case, the `rm` program is used to remove the found files. The braces, `{}`, represent the position of each file name passed to the `rm` command. The last two characters, `\;`, are required by the `find` command (an example of using the backslash to pass a character on to a program without being interpreted by the shell). Add this command line to the shell script to obtain a program that removes files safely and also cleans up anything a user has in the `/tmp` directory over 10 days old.

```
# Name:     safrm
# Purpose:  copy files to directory /tmp, remove them
#           from the current directory, clean up /tmp,
#           and finally send mail to user
# first copy all parameters to /tmp
cp $* /tmp
# remove the files
rm $*
# create a file to hold the mail message
#   The file's name is set to msg
#   followed by process ID number of this process
#   For example, msg1208
msgfile=/tmp/msg$$
# construct mail message
date > $msgfile
echo "These files were deleted from /tmp" >>$msgfile
# get list of files to be deleted from tmp
# -mtime +10 gets all files that haven't been
# modified in 10 or more days, -print displays the names.
find /tmp -user $LOGNAME -mtime +10 -print >> $msgfile
# remove the appropriate files from /tmp
find /tmp -user $LOGNAME -mtime +10 -exec rm {} \;
# mail off the message
mail $LOGNAME < $msgfile
# clean up
rm $msgfile
```

Understanding Processes

A running program in Linux is called a *process*. Because Linux is a multitasking system, many processes can run at the same time. To distinguish between processes, Linux assigns each new process a unique ID called a *process ID*.

The process ID is simply a number that uniquely identifies each running process. To see what process IDs are currently associated with your process, use the **ps** command. To get a look at most of the process IDs currently running on your system, issue the command with the following flags, **ps -guax**, and you see something like

```
USER   PID %CPU %MEM SIZE  RSS TTY STAT START   TIME COMMAND
jack    53  3.2  7.0  352  468 p 1 S    02:01   0:01 -bash
jack    65  0.0  3.5   80  240 p 1 R    02:01   0:00 ps -guax
root     1  0.8  3.1   44  208 con S    02:00   0:00 init
root     6  0.0  1.8   24  124 con S    02:00   0:00 bdflush (daemon)
root     7  0.0  1.9   24  128 con S    02:01   0:00 update (bdflush)
root    40  1.0  3.5   65  240 con S    02:01   0:00 /usr/sbin/syslogd
root    42  0.2  2.9   36  200 con S    02:01   0:00 /usr/sbin/klogd
root    44  0.5  3.2   68  216 con S    02:01   0:00 /usr/sbin/inetd
root    46  0.2  3.0   64  204 con S    02:01   0:00 /usr/sbin/lpd
```

```
root    52  0.1  2.0   32  140 con S    02:01   0:00 selection -t ms
root    58  0.2  2.4   37  164 p 6 S    02:01   0:00 /sbin/agetty 38400 tt
```

The process ID is identified by the column titled `PID`. Also note the bold line; this indicates the first process started by the system—`init`. The `init` process is also described later in this chapter.

When Linux is instructed to run a program (that is, to create a process), it does so by making an exact copy of the program making the request. In the simplest case, you request that a program be run by instructing your shell; the shell makes a fork request to the Linux kernel.

Fork and *exec*. A *fork* is the process of cloning an existing process. Linux creates all new processes through the mechanism of forking. When a process is forked, an almost exact duplicate of an existing process (including its environment and any open files) is created; what keeps the duplicate from being exactly the same as its parent application is a flag that tells the forked process which is the parent and which is the child. Because all processes are created in this fashion, all processes have a parent process and a parent-process ID. Every process running on a Linux system can trace its lineage back to `init`, the mother of all processes. `init` itself, process ID `1`, is the only process run directly by the Linux kernel that you as a user have any contact with. Every process you create during a session has your logon shell as an ancestor, and your logon shell has `init` as its parent.

Once a process has successfully forked, the child process calls the `exec` routine to transform itself into the process you requested. The only thing that changes after an `exec` function is the identity of the running process; the environment of the new process is an exact copy of the environment of its parent.

Standard Input and Output. Every new process is created with three open "files." Because Linux treats files and devices exactly the same, an open "file" can be either a real file on a disk or a device such as your terminal. The three open files are defined as *standard input*, *standard output*, and *standard error output*. All Linux commands, as well as application programs, accept input from the standard input and place any output on the standard output. Any diagnostic messages are automatically placed on the standard error output.

When you first log on, the standard input, output, and error files are attached to your terminal; any programs you run (processes you create) inherit your terminal as the three open files.

Understanding Shell Command Parsing

Parsing is the act of splitting the command line, or what you type, into its component parts for processing. In Linux, parsing constitutes a lot more than simply splitting the command line. The command string is first split into its component parts: the file names expanded if you used any wild cards, shell variables expanded, I/O redirection set up, any command groupings or subshells set up, and command substitution performed. Only then can the command line as you typed it be executed.

If these terms such as *wild cards* and *I/O redirection* are new to you, you can find explanations of them, in the order they are performed, later in this chapter. You must first start, however, with the basic command syntax.

Commands, Flags, and Parameters

To execute a Linux command, you merely type the name of the file. The command to list files is `ls`; you can find a file by that name in the `/bin` directory. If `/bin` is listed in your `PATH` variable (and it should be), your shell finds and executes `/bin`. Some Linux commands are not independent files. These commands are built into the shells themselves. For example, the `cd` (change directory) command is built into most shells and executed directly by the shell without looking up a file. Read the man pages for the shell you are using to determine what commands are executed internally or externally. Some shells have a command file that contains commands executed directly by the shell.

Flags. If a command is to execute properly, you must present it to your shell in the proper fashion. The command name itself must be the first item on the line; it is followed by any flags and parameters. *Flags* (sometimes called *options*) are single letters preceded by a hyphen (`-`) that modify the behavior of a command. For example, the list command, `ls`, simply lists the names of the files in the current directory in alphabetical order. By adding various flags, you can list the contents of a directory in many different ways. You can list files and all their attributes with the "long" flag, `-l`. This command takes the following form:

```
ls -l
```

▶▶ See "`ls`: Display Information about Files and Directories," p. 519

The `-l` is the flag. When you want to use more than one flag, simply string the flags together as in `ls -lF` (the `-F` flag displays an asterisk (`*`) if the file is executable, an `@` sign if the file is a symbolic line, and a slash (`/`) if the file is a subdirectory). The man page for every command usually lists all the modifying flags and their meanings before describing any parameters. Flags can also be listed separately; the shell parses them before passing them on to the program. For example, you can write the `ls -lF` command as `ls -l -F`.

> **Note**
>
> Linux provides a feature by default that has become popular in recent years—color highlighting. When you issue the `ls` command, Linux displays files in different colors depending on the file's type. This allows you to quickly identify files that are executable, are actually directories, and are actually linked to other files located in other directories. Also, if you redirect the output from `ls` to a file, this file contains the control codes used to indicate color. This information may cause other programs, such as `less`, problems when used with this file.

One type of flag signals that the next parameter has some special meaning. For example, the `-t` flag in the `sort` command is used to indicate that the next character is a field separator. If you want to sort the `/etc/passwd` file, whose fields are separated by a colon (:), you can enter

```
sort -t: /etc/passwd
```

In the case of the `sort` command, the `-t` flag is needed only if the file uses a field separator other than the default. The default field separator is defined in the `IFS` (Inter Field Separator) environment variable. The shell uses the `IFS` variable to parse the command line so that the shell knows to use the standard field separator unless the `-t` flag indicates otherwise.

Parameters. Flags must be presented to the command before any other parameters. *Parameters* are strings separated by any of the characters defined in the `IFS` environment variable. The default string in `IFS` is a space, a tab, and a newline character. You can place any number of field-separator characters between parameters; when the shell parses the command line, it reduces these characters to one character before proceeding. For example, if a command is followed by three spaces and a tab character and then the first parameter, the shell automatically reduces the three spaces and a tab to one tab character:

```
command<Spacebar><Spacebar><Spacebar><Tab>parameter
```

becomes

```
command<Tab>parameter
```

Parameters are usually either file names or strings that instruct the command to perform some function. If a parameter contains an embedded space, the string must be placed in quotation marks to prevent the shell from expanding it. The following command line contains two parameters; the shell attempts to find the word *New* in a file named `York`:

```
grep New York
```

If the intent is to find the string `New York` in the standard input, the command must be written as

```
grep "New York"
```

In this case, the string `New York` is passed to the `grep` command as one parameter.

File-Name Matching

Most modern operating systems (including all versions of Linux and DOS) support the use of wild cards for file and string searches.

The * Wild Card. The asterisk (*) is the most universal wild card used. It simply means *any and all characters*. For example, the string `a*` means all files beginning with *a*. You can use as many asterisks in a single expression as you need to define a set of files. For example, the expression `*xx*.gif` means any file name with the extension gif that has xx anywhere in the rest of the name. Matches include the file names abxx.gif, xxyyzz.gif, and xx.gif.

Use the asterisk character (*) to represent any sequence of characters. For example, to print all files in your current directory with names that end with .txt, enter

```
lp *.txt
```

Pay attention when using the asterisk wild card. If you enter the following command, you print all files whose names end with txt:

```
lp *txt
```

The file named reportxt is included with the files printed with the second command but not the first. If you enter the following command, the shell passes the name of every file in your directory, as well as the single file named txt, to the command lp (the file named txt in your directory is passed twice to lp):

```
lp * txt
```

In the last example, the lp command first prints the files represented by the *; that is, it prints all files. The lp command then moves to the second item in the list of files it is to print (Linux interprets the space character between the * and txt as a delimiter—in effect, as a comma in an English command). The lp command processes txt as the name of the next file it is to print.

The * symbol can be used anywhere in a string of characters. For example, if you want to use the ls command to list the names of all files in your current directory whose names contain the characters rep, enter

```
ls *rep*
```

Linux lists files with names such as frep.data, report, and janrep. There is one exception: files with names starting with a period aren't listed. To list files with names starting with a period (often called *hidden files*), you must specify the leading period. For example, if you have a file named .reportrc and want to see it listed, enter the following variation of the preceding command:

```
ls .*rep*
```

Caution

Be careful using the asterisk wild card when you are deleting or removing files. The command rm * removes all the files in your directory. An all-too-common mistake is to accidentally delete all files when you mean to delete a collection of files with a common suffix or prefix. If instead of entering rm *txt (which would remove all files with names ending in txt), you enter rm * txt, Linux first deletes all files and then attempts to delete a file named txt. But at that point there aren't any files left. For safety, use the -i option with rm if you use the asterisk for filename completion. The rm -i *txt command prompts you for confirmation before each file is deleted.

The ? Wild Card. Use the question mark (?) wild card to represent a single character. Suppose that you have the files `report1`, `reportb`, `report10`, `reportb3`, `report.dft`, and `report.fin` in your current directory. You know that the `lp rep*` command prints all the files, but to print just the first two (`report1` and `reportb`), enter

```
lp report?
```

To list the names of all files whose names are three characters long and end with the character `x`, enter

```
ls ??x
```

This command lists a file with the name `tax` but not `trax`.

You can also represent a single character by enclosing a range of characters within a pair of square brackets: `[` and `]`. To list the names of all files that begin with an uppercase letter, enter

```
ls [A-Z]*
```

Suppose that you have files named `sales.90`, `sales.91`, `sales.92`, and `sales.93` and you want to copy the first three to a subdirectory named `oldstuff`. Assuming that the subdirectory `oldstuff` exists, enter

```
cp sales.9[0-2] oldstuff
```

Table 20.4 summarizes the file-name completion characters, otherwise known as wild cards.

Table 20.4 Summary of File-Name Completion Characters

Character	Example	Meaning
?	`lp sales.9?`	Represents a single character. The example prints a collection of files with names in the form `sales.`*yy*, where *yy* represents a year in the nineties (`sales.90`, `sales.91`, and so on).
[]	`rm sales.9[0-3]`	Represents a single character in a range. The example removes the collection of files with the names `sales.90`, `sales.91`, `sales.92`, and `sales.93`.
*	`cat sales* > allsales`	Represents any collection of characters except a period when it is the first character in a file name. The example combines into a file named `allsales` all files whose names begin with `sales`.

The question mark represents a single occurrence of any character. Thus, the string `???` represents all files consisting of just three letters. You can generate a list of files with three-letter extensions with the string `*.???`. For example, if you are searching a directory containing graphic images as well as other data, the following command lists all files with extensions like `tif`, `jpg`, and `gif` as well as any other files with three-letter extensions:

```
ls *.???
```

> **Note**
>
> Remember that Linux is not MS-DOS; file names are not limited to eight characters with a three character extension. Remember, file names are case-sensitive under Linux.

The [] Expression. Sometimes you must be more selective than either of the more general-purpose wild cards allow. Suppose that you want to select the files `job1`, `job2`, and `job3` but not `jobx`. You cannot select the right files with the `?` wild card because it represents one occurrence of any character. You can, however, use `job[123]` as the file descriptor. Like the question mark, items inside square brackets (`[]`) represent exactly one character. You can describe a discrete series of permissible values such as `[123]`, which permits only the characters 1, 2, or 3; you can also describe a range of characters such as `[A-Z]`, which represent any character between uppercase A and uppercase Z, inclusive.

You can also specify a set of ranges. For example, if you want to specify only alphabetic characters, you can use `[A-Z,a-z]`. In the ASCII character set, there are special characters between ASCII *Z* and ASCII *a*; if you specified `[A-z]`, you include those special characters in your request.

> **Note**
>
> If you place a file-name wild card or expression inside quotation marks, file-name expansion is suppressed during command-line parsing. For example, if you type **`ls *`**, you get all files in the current directory. On the other hand, if you type **`ls "*"`**, you probably get the error message `file not found` because you are instructing `ls` to search for a file named *.

VI

Working with Linux

Connecting Processes with Pipes

Frequently, you need to use the output of one program or command as the input of another. Instead of entering each command separately and saving results in intermediate files, you can connect a sequence of commands by using a *pipe*. The Linux pipe character is a vertical bar (|).

To sort a file named `allsales` and then print it, enter

```
sort allsales ¦ lp
```

The name *pipe* is appropriate. The output of the program on the left of the pipe (the vertical bar) is sent through the pipe and used as the input of the program on the right. You can connect several processes with pipes.

To print a sorted list of the data in all files with names that begin with `sales`, enter

```
cat sales* | sort | lp
```

Redirecting Input and Output

Many programs expect input from the terminal or keyboard; many programs send their output to the terminal screen. Linux associates keyboard input with a file named `stdin`; it associates terminal output with a file named `stdout`. You can *redirect* input and output so that instead of it coming from or going to the terminal, it comes from a file or is sent to a file.

You use the < (less than) symbol to redirect input into a command or program so that it comes from a file instead of the terminal. Suppose that you want to send a file named `info` by e-mail to someone whose address is `sarah`. Instead of retyping the contents of the file to the `mail` command, give this command to use file `info` as the input (`stdin`) to the `mail` command:

```
mail sarah < info
```

You use the > (greater than) symbol to redirect the output of a program to a file. Instead of the output going to the terminal screen, it is put into a file. The command `date` displays the current time and date on the terminal screen. If you want to store the current time and date in a file named `now`, enter

```
date > now
```

Caution

If the file name on the right side of the > already exists, it is overwritten. Be careful not to destroy useful information this way.

If you want to append information to an existing file, use the two-character >> symbol. To append the current date to a file named `report`, enter

```
date >> report
```

The following is a slightly more lengthy example. Suppose that the file named `sales` consists of sales data; the first field of each line contains a customer ID code. The first command line puts the output of the `date` command into a file named `sales_report`. The second command line uses the `sales` file as input to the `sort` command and appends the output to the `sales_report` file. The last line sends the `sales_report` file to users `sarah` and `brad` by e-mail.

```
date > sales_report
sort < sales >> sales_report
mail sarah brad < sales_report
```

Caution

Be careful not to redirect the same file as both input and output to a command. Most likely, you'll destroy the contents of the file.

Table 20.5 summarizes the redirection symbols used in Linux.

Table 20.5 Summary of Redirection Symbols

Symbol	Meaning	Example
<	Take input from a file	`mail sarah < report`
>	Send output to a file	`date > now`
>>	Append to a file	`date >> report`

Shell Variable Substitution

You learned about shell variable expansion in the first part of this chapter when you set your `PATH` variable to `PATH=$PATH:`*`newpath`*. The shell replaced `$PATH` with the current values of the `PATH` variable. Shells are really interpreted languages, almost like BASIC; the shell variable is the primary object manipulated. Because shell variables are frequently manipulated, each shell provides methods of testing and defining the shell variables.

Shell variables are stored as strings. When two variables are placed together, their respective strings are *concatenated*. For example, if you have two variables, `X=hello` and `Y=world`, the expression `$X$Y` results in the string `helloworld`. If you give the following command, the shell parses the two parameters and the values of `X` and `Y` (the two strings `hello` and `world`) are substituted before being passed to the `echo` command:

```
echo $X $Y
```

The `echo` command then prints `hello world`. Note that if you place a dozen <Tab> characters between `$X` and `$Y`, the output results are still the same.

If the substitution can be ambiguous, the shell picks the most obvious substitution—often with unpredictable results. For example, if you type **`echo $XY`** the shell substitutes `helloY`. If you also had a variable `XY`, its value is substituted instead. To get around these ambiguities, the shell has a simple mechanism to allow you to define exactly what you mean. If you type **`${X}Y`** the shell substitutes the value of `X` before appending the character *Y* to the string.

The Bourne and Korn shells have a rich collection of shell-variable expansion techniques that perform various tests on the variable before making the substitution. See the man pages for `sh` and `ksh` for more details.

Command Substitution

After the shell performs its substitution of variables, it scans the line once more for commands to be run before the command line is finally ready. *Command substitution* means that Linux substitutes the results of a command for a positional parameter. This is specified in the following way:

```
command-1 parameter 'command-2'
```

Be careful in the use of quotation marks ("), apostrophes ('), and accent graves (`). Table 20.6 lists what each mark does.

Table 20.6 Quotation Marks and Apostrophes

Symbol	Meaning
"	The quotation marks disable file-name generation and suppress parameter expansion. However, shell-variable and command substitution still take place.
'	The apostrophe disables all parsing; whatever is enclosed within the apostrophes is passed on as a single parameter.
`	The accent grave, or backquote, implies command substitution. Whatever is enclosed within accent graves is executed as though the command was performed on a line by itself. Any output placed on the standard output then replaces the command. The command line is then parsed again for parameters.

Consider the following command line:

```
echo Today\'s date and time are `date`
```

It produces this output:

```
Today's date and time are Mon May 18 14:35:09 EST 1994
```

To make the `echo` command behave properly, the `'s` (in `Today's`) in the preceding command was preceded by a backslash (\), also called the *escape character* (for example, `Today\'s`). Virtually every non-alphanumeric character on your keyboard has some special meaning to the shell. To use any of the special characters in a string and to prevent the shell from interpreting the character, you must "escape" the character, that is, you must precede it with the escape character `\`. If you wanted to pass the backslash character itself, for example, type `\\`. To pass a dollar sign to a command, type `\$`.

Command Groups, Subshells, and Other Commands

You terminate a simple command with a carriage return. If you want to place more than one command on the command line before pressing <Return>, you can delimit individual commands with a semicolon (;). When the shell parses the command line, it treats the semicolon as an end-of-line character. If you type the following string, the shell executes each command sequentially as though you had typed each on a line by itself:

```
command-1;command-2;command-3
```

For example, you can enter **`clear;ls`** to clear your screen *and* display a directory listing.

Command Groups. If you want to redirect input or output to all the commands as a group, you can do so by making the command line a command group. A *command group* is defined as any number of commands enclosed in braces ({}). For example, the following command string directs the output of both commands to the file `output-file`:

```
{command-1;command-2} > output-file
```

Any form of redirection can also be used. The output of a command group can be placed on a pipe as in the following example:

```
{command-1;command-2} | command-3
```

In this case, the output of *`command-1`* is fed into the pipe; then the output of *`command-2`* is fed into the same pipe; *`command-3`* sees just one stream of data.

> **Note**
>
> Commands executed in a command group run in the current shell. That means that they may modify the environment or change directories.

Subshells. When you run a series of commands as a command group, those commands run in the current shell. If one of the commands modifies the environment or changes directory, the changes are in effect when the command group finishes running. To avoid this problem, run a command group in a subshell. A *subshell* is a clone of the present shell but because child processes cannot modify the environment of their parent process, all commands run in a subshell have no effect on the environment when the command group finishes. To run a command group in a subshell, replace the braces with parentheses. The command-group example used in the preceding section becomes the following:

```
(command-1;command-2) | command-3
```

Only *`command-3`* runs in the current shell but the output of the subshell is piped into the standard input of *`command-3`*.

Background Processing

Because Linux is a multitasking operating system, there are several ways of running commands in the background. The simplest form of background processing allows you to run a command concurrently with a command in the foreground. Other methods place commands deeper and deeper in the background.

Arranging for Processes to Run in the Background

The shell allows you to start one process and, before the first one completes, start another. When you do this, you put the first process *in the background*. You put a process in the background by using the ampersand (&) character as the last character on the line containing the command you want to run in the background. Consider the following command:

```
sort sales > sales.sorted &
```

If you enter this command, you see a number on-screen. This number is the process ID number for the process you put in the background. The PID is the operating system's way of identifying that process.

Normally, when you run a command, the shell suspends operation until the command is complete. If you append the ampersand to the end of a command string, the command string runs concurrently with the shell. By placing the ampersand after a command string, the shell resumes operation as soon as the background command is launched. Unless you use I/O redirection with the background command, both the background command and the present shell expect input from and produce output to your terminal. Unless your background command takes care of I/O itself, the proper syntax for background processing is as follows:

```
command-string [input-file] output-file &
```

For example, to copy a collection of files whose names end with the characters `.txt` to a subdirectory named `oldstuff` and, without waiting for that process to finish, print a sorted list of the data in all files with names that begin with `sales`, enter the following two commands:

```
cp *.txt oldstuff &
cat sales* ¦ sort ¦ lp
```

> **Note**
>
> Put jobs in the background when you don't want to wait for one program to finish before starting another. You can also put jobs in the background when you have a collection of tasks in which at least one can run on its own. Start that one and put it in the background.
>
> You can also use the virtual terminals offered by Linux to execute a command and then log on to another account.

Because the background process is a child of your shell, it is automatically killed when you log off. All child processes are killed when their parent dies.

The *nohup* Command

To place a command deeper in the background than the & operator allows, use the nohup command (which stands for *no hang up*). The nohup command takes as its arguments a command string. However, the nohup command must be used in conjunction with the & operator if you want the command to actually be placed in the background. If a command is run with nohup in the foreground, the command is immune to being killed when you disconnect your terminal or hang up a modem (its original purpose).

The syntax for the nohup command is

```
nohup command-string [input-file] output-file &
```

The *at* and *batch* Commands and the *cron* Daemon

If you run a command with the nohup command, the command executes immediately. If you want to run the command at a later time or on a "time-available" basis, you must invoke the services of the cron daemon.

The cron daemon is a command run in the background by Linux—or, more specifically, by init, the master program. cron provides scheduling services to all Linux processes. You can ask cron to run a program at a specific time, periodically, at a particular time every day, or whenever the load on cron permits.

The *at* Command. The at command expects a time or date as a parameter and takes any number of command strings from its standard input. When the at command detects an end-of-file marker, it creates a Bourne shell script for execution at the time you specified. The at command is flexible about the types of dates and times it accepts. For example, if you enter the command **at now + 1 day**, the next commands, taken from the standard input, are executed tomorrow at this time. One way to use the at command is from within a shell script.

A *shell script* is nothing more than a file containing all the commands necessary to perform a series of commands. The name of the file then becomes your own addition to the Linux command language. One way of using the at command is

```
at now + 1 day <<XX
command-1
command-2
XX
```

When placed in a shell script, these lines let you conveniently run one or more commands the next day. To run different commands, simply change the lines between the first <<XX and last XX lines. You can run any number of commands from this script.

The *batch* Command. The batch command is the logical equivalent of at now. If you attempt to use the at now command, you see an error message that says something like now has passed. The batch command works exactly as at now works if it were logically possible, with one minor exception: the cron daemon maintains a separate queue for commands generated by at, batch, and cron.

The *crontab* Command

One of the best uses of the cron daemon is in automating the maintenance of a system. With cron, you as the system administrator can set up automatic backups of your system every morning at 4 AM, Monday through Saturday. You install, delete, and list commands you want run in this fashion with the crontab command.

To run commands periodically, you must create a file in the crontab format. The crontab file consists of six fields separated by spaces or tabs. The first five fields are integers specifying minute (0–59), hour (0–23), day of the month (1–31), month of the year (1–12), and day of the week (0–6, with 0 referring to Sunday). The sixth field is a command string. Each numeric field can contain an inclusive range of numbers such as 1-5 to indicate Monday through Friday, or discrete sets of numbers such as 0,20,40 to indicate that an instruction should be run every 20 minutes. A field can also contain an asterisk to indicate all legal values. The following example runs the calendar command every 20 minutes starting at midnight Monday and ending at 11:40 PM Friday.

```
0,20,40 * * * 1-5 calendar -
```

> **Note**
>
> The hyphen at the end of this command makes the calendar do its work for *all* users on a system. Although you can invoke the calendar without the hyphen, it's recommended that you use it.

If you name this file cronfile, you can install it in the cron system by issuing the command crontab cronfile.

The cron daemon has a time granularity of one minute, that is, the shortest time duration you can work with is one minute. You, as system administrator, may place limits on the number of commands allowed to be run at any one time. Just because you ask cron to run an at, batch, or crontab file does not mean that it runs at precisely the time you have indicated.

Understanding Command Feedback

Linux provides instant feedback for commands that abort for one reason or another. In most cases, errors are limited to misspellings of the command name or badly formed file names. If you attempt to run a nonexistent command, Linux replies with

```
command: command not found
```

If you try to use a nonexistent file name, Linux responds with

```
command: file: No such file or directory
```

If the error is caused by something other than a command-line error, the command itself usually reports what happened—although not always in an easily decipherable form.

If you attempt to run a command with nohup and you have not redirected the standard error, Linux automatically places any error messages in a file named nohup.out in the directory from which the command was run.

Because commands run by cron have less urgency, any errors—indeed, any output placed on the standard output and not redirected—is sent to you through e-mail.

Shell Command Editing and Aliasing

Different shells include features that provide shortcuts for running commands. Command editing lets you modify commands that have already been typed in. With command history, you can recall commands you have previously entered. Aliasing lets you create commands that represent other commands. Command completion lets you fill in the rest of a file name after you have typed part of it.

Command Editing

Command editing means that after you type a command—and before you press <Return>—you can edit or change parts of the command without having to retype most of it. To edit a command, press <Esc> to get into editing mode and then use any of the line-movement commands from the vi editor to modify the command. You can use <Backspace> to go back to the portion of the command you want to change and other vi commands such as x to delete a character, r to replace a character, and so on.

Command History

The *command history* feature allows you to look back at previously entered commands and recall them. This feature saves you the time and trouble of retyping commands. When you combine this feature with command editing, you can easily correct mistakes in complicated commands and deal effectively with some repetitive tasks. In both shells, the history command displays the list of past commands the shell has saved. The commands are numbered. To execute command 10, for example,type **! 10**. The bash shell also takes advantage of the PC's arrow keys by allowing you to recall previous commands by pressing the <Up-Arrow> key on the keyboard.

Command Aliasing

Command aliasing allows you to define a name for a command. Consider this example: The command man displays Linux documentation or man pages. To make the word help an alias, or alternative, for man, enter

```
alias help=man
```

Now you can enter **help cp** or **man cp** to display Linux man pages about the cp command. Aliases can also be used with commands that have options or arguments. For example, if you want to list the names of all the files in the current directory sorted in descending order by the time they were last modified (so that the most recent files are at the bottom of the list), you can use this command:

```
ls -art
```

The `ls` command is the command to list files; the `-a` option specifies all files, the `-r` option arranges the files in reverse, descending order, and the `-t` option sorts by time last modified. That's a lot to remember. You can assign the alias `timedir` to this complex command with the following command:

```
alias timedir="ls -art"
```

The quotation marks (`" "`) are necessary because the shell expects the alias for `timedir` to be terminated by a space or <Return>. If you enter **`timedir`**, you get the directory listing you want.

> **Note**
>
> Setting an alias from the command line keeps that alias in effect only for the current session. To have the alias active whenever you log on, include the alias definition in the file `.profile` if you use the Bourne shell; keep it in the file `.login` if you use the C shell.

Command Completion

Command completion allows you to type the beginning of a file name and then press the <Tab> key to expand the file name. This can save time and spelling mistakes when entering a command. If two files share a common prefix, Linux expands the command to the last common character, stops expanding the file name, and then beeps. You need to provide the unique file name.

Adding Text with Cut and Paste

Linux also offers a program that can be started at boot time that allows you to use the mouse to select text from anywhere on-screen and then paste the text onto the command line for the shell to interpret. To get a mouse cursor, you simply press one of the mouse buttons. You then select the desired text from anywhere on-screen by first clicking the left mouse button on the beginning of the text and, while holding down the button, dragging the cursor to the desired end point of the text. Once you have selected the text, click the right mouse button to copy the text to the command line.

Understanding Shell Scripts

The shell accepts commands, interprets them, and arranges for the operating system to execute the commands in the manner you specify. In the previous sections, you saw how the shell interprets special characters to complete file names, redirects input and output, connects processes through pipes, and puts jobs or processes in the background.

You can type commands at the terminal or they can come from a file. A *shell script* is a collection of one or more shell commands in a file. To execute the commands, you type the name of the file. The advantages to this approach are the following:

- You don't have to retype a sequence of commands.
- You determine the steps to accomplish a goal once.
- You simplify operations for yourself and others.

By using variables and keywords, you can write programs that the shell can interpret. This is useful because it allows you to create general shell scripts you or others can use in a variety of situations.

Suppose that after you log on, you regularly like to see who is logged on to your system, run a program named `calendar` that displays your appointments for today and tomorrow, and print the current date and time. To do all that, you enter the following commands:

```
who
calendar
date
```

If you put these three commands into a file named `whatsup` and make that file executable, you have a shell script you can execute just like any other command. The file `whatsup` must be a text file. You can use the `vi` or `emacs` text editor to put the commands in the `whatsup` file. To make the file executable, enter

```
chmod +x whatsup
```

The command `chmod` modifies or sets the permissions for a file. The `+x` option makes the file executable, that is, it makes the file work just like a standard Linux command. Putting commands into the file and making the file executable are both one-time operations. From that point on, you can type **`whatsup`** and press <Return> to execute your shell script. You can use the shell script just like any other command. For example, to print the results of the `whatsup` command, enter

```
whatsup | lp
```

To put the results of the `whatsup` command into a file named `info` for future reference, enter

```
whatsup > info
```

To review, follow these steps to create a shell script that you can use whenever you want:

1. Use a text editor, such as `vi` or `emacs`, to put the shell commands into a text or ASCII file. In the preceding example, the commands were put in the file named `whatsup`.
2. Make it so that you have execute permission on the file. Use `chmod +x` *`filename`* (for example, `chmod +x whatsup`).
3. Test the command by typing the name of the command and pressing <Return>.

After using this process a few times, you'll see how easy it is to create useful scripts. Of course, the hardest part is figuring out which shell commands to use and how to use the shell's programming capabilities to express the steps you need to carry out.

You can test a shell script and see all the steps it goes through by entering

```
sh -x script-name
```

In this syntax, `script-name` is the name of the file that holds the script you're considering. The `sh -x` command displays all the steps the script goes through and is useful when you are trying to debug a script.

Writing Programs with the Shell

To write programs using the shells, you must know about variables and control structures. Don't let either of these terms scare you off. A *variable* is an object that, at any one time, has one of possibly many different values assigned to it. *Control structures* specify the way you can control the flow of execution of a script. There are two basic types of control structures: decision structures (such as `if...then...else` structures or `case` structures) and iterative structures or loops (such as a `for` or `while` loop). With a *decision structure*, you choose a course of action from one or more alternatives, usually depending on the value of a variable or the outcome of a command. With an *iterative structure*, you repeat a sequence of commands.

Using *echo*. You can use the `echo` command to display informative messages about what is happening in a shell script. The `echo` command displays its *arguments*, that is, whatever follows the word `echo`, on the terminal screen. Putting a string of characters in quotation marks ensures that all the characters are displayed. You also can redirect the results of `echo` to a file.

```
echo "Please stand by ..."
```

The preceding command displays the following line on the terminal screen:

```
Please stand by ...
```

The following command puts `Please stand by ...` in the file `messg`:

```
echo "Please stand by ..." > messg
```

The `echo` command can make a user feel like something is happening when they enter a command (a particularly good idea if the command doesn't give any output for several seconds or longer). The `echo` command is also useful when you want to trace a shell script. Using the `echo` command at key points tells you what is happening in a script. Here is the file `whatsup` with an `echo` command or two added:

```
echo " Let's see who is on the system."
who
echo " Any appointments? "
calendar
date
echo " All done"
```

When you run the whatsup file, you see the following:

```
$ whatsup<Return>
 Let's see who is on the system.
sarah     tty01     Dec 20 08:51
brad      tty03     Dec 20 08:12
ernie     tty07     Dec 20 08:45
 Any appointments?
12/20     Sales meeting at 1:45
12/21     party after work!
Mon Dec 20 09:02 EST 1993
 All done
$
```

Using Comments. It is always possible that after you write a shell script and don't use it for a while, you'll forget what the shell script does or how it accomplishes its task. Put comments in your shell scripts to explain the purpose of the task and how the task is achieved. A *comment* is a note to yourself or whoever is reading the script. The shell ignores comments; they are important to and for human beings.

The pound sign signals the beginning of a comment to the shell. Every character from the pound sign to the end of the line is part of that comment. Here is how you might comment the shell script whatsup:

```
# Name:      whatsup
# Written:   12/19/93, Patty Stygian
# Purpose:   Display who's logged on, appointments, date
     echo "Let's see who is on the system."
     who          # See who is logged on
     echo " Any appointments? "
     calendar     # Check appointments
     date         # Display date
     echo " All done"
```

Run the shell script again and you see the same results as before. The comments don't change the behavior of the shell script in any way.

Variables in Shell Programs. To use variables, you must know how to give a variable a value and how to access the value stored in a variable.

Using the value of a variable is straightforward, but there are four ways of giving a variable a value:

- Using direct assignment
- Using the read command
- Using command-line parameters
- Substituting the output of a command

Using Direct Assignments. The most direct way to give a variable a value is to write an expression such as

```
myemail=edsgar@crty.com
```

This expression gives the variable `myemail` the value `edsgar@crty.com`. Do not include spaces on either side of the equal sign (=). The direct-assignment method of assigning a value to a variable is of the following form:

```
variable-name=variable-value
```

If *`variable-value`* contains blanks, surround the value with quotation marks. To assign an office address of `Room 21, Suite C` to the variable `myoffice`, for example, use the following command:

```
myoffice="Room 21, Suite C"
```

The shell retrieves the value of the variable whenever it sees a dollar sign ($) followed by the name of a variable. You can see that when the following two statements are executed:

```
echo " My e-mail address is $myemail"
echo " My office is $myoffice"
```

Suppose that you frequently copy files to a directory named `/corporate/info/public/sales`. To copy a file named `current` to that directory, enter

```
cp current /corporate/info/public/sales
```

To make this easier, you can assign the long directory name to the variable `corpsales` with the following expression:

```
corpsales=/corporate/info/public/sales
```

Now to copy the `current` file to that directory, you enter

```
cp current $corpsales
```

The shell replaces `$corpsales` with the value of the variable `corpsales` and then issues the copy command.

Using the read Command. The `read` command takes the next line of input and assigns it to a variable. The following shell script extends the preceding example to ask the user to specify the name of the file to be copied. The `read` command pauses the script and waits for input from the keyboard. When <Return> is pressed, the script continues. If <Ctrl-d> (sometimes represented as ^D) is entered while the `read` command is waiting for input, the script is terminated.

```
# Name: copycorp
# Purpose: copy specified file to
#          /corporate/info/public/sales
     corpsales=/corporate/infor/public/sales
     echo "Enter name of file to copy"     # prompt user
     read filename                         # get file name
     cp $filename $corpsales               # do the copy
```

Using Command-Line Parameters. When the shell interprets a command, it attaches variable names to each item on the command line. The *items* on the command line are the sequences of characters separated by blanks or tab characters. (Use quotation marks to signal that a collection of characters separated by spaces represents one item.) The variables attached to the items in the command line are $0, $1, $2, and so on through $9. These ten variables correspond to the positions of the items on the line. The command name is $0, the first argument or parameter for the command is $1, and so on. To demonstrate this concept, consider the following sample shell script named shovars:

```
# Name:      shovars
# Purpose:   demonstrate command-line variables
     echo $0
     echo $2 $4!
     echo $3
```

Now suppose that you enter

```
shovars -s hello "look at me" bart
```

The output of the shell script is

```
shovars
hello bart!
look at me
```

In this output, the first line is the command's name (variable $0), the second line is the second and fourth arguments (variables $2 and $4). The last line is the third argument (variable $3).

Following is a more serious example. This shell script deletes a file but first copies it to the directory /tmp so that you can retrieve it if necessary.

```
# Name:    safrm
# Purpose: copy file to directory /tmp and then remove it
#          from the current directory
# first copy $1 to /tmp
    cp $1 /tmp
# now remove the file
    rm $1
```

If you type **safrm abc def** and press <Return>, only the file abc is removed from the current directory because the safrm shell script deletes only variable $1. You can, however, represent all the parameters on the command line with $*. Make safrm more general by replacing each occurrence of $1 with $*. If you then enter **safrm abc def xx guio**, all four files (abc, def, xx, and guio) are removed from the current directory.

Substituting the Output of a Command. You can assign to a variable the result of an executed command. To store the name of the current working directory in a variable named cwd, for example, enter

```
cwd= `pwd`
```

Notice that pwd, the print working directory command, is surrounded by accent graves and not apostrophes.

The following shell script changes the name of a file by appending the current month, day, and year to the file name:

```
# Name:      stamp
# Purpose:   rename file: append today's date to its name
# set td to current date in form of mmddyy
     td=`+%m%d%y`
# rename file
     mv $1 $1.$td
```

In this example, the variable `td` is set to the current date. In the final line, this information is appended to variable `$1`. If today is February 24, 1995, and you use this script on a file called `myfile`, the file is renamed (moved) to `myfile.022495`.

Using Special Characters in Shell Programs. You have seen how the shell gives special treatment to certain characters such as >, *, ?, $, and several others. What do you do if you don't want those characters to get special treatment? This section provides a few answers.

You can use the apostrophe to make the shell ignore special characters. Surround the string of characters with a pair of apostrophes, as in this example:

```
grep '^Mary Tuttle' customers
```

The result of this `grep` command is that the lines in the file `customers` that begin with `Mary Tuttle` are displayed. The caret (^) tells `grep` to search from the beginning of the line. If `Mary Tuttle` was not placed within apostrophes, it might be interpreted literally (or as a pipe symbol on some systems). In addition, the space between `Mary` and `Tuttle` isn't interpreted by the shell when it occurs within the apostrophes.

You can also use quotation marks to make the shell ignore most special characters, with the exception of the dollar sign and accent grave. In the following example, the asterisks, spaces, and the greater-than sign are treated as regular characters because the string is surrounded by quotation marks:

```
echo " ** Please enter your response -->"
```

In this next example, however, `$LOGNAME` evaluates correctly, but there is no value for `$5`:

```
echo " >>>Thanks for the $5, $LOGNAME"
```

Use the backslash (\) to make the shell ignore a single character. For example, to make the shell ignore the dollar sign in front of the `5`, issue this command:

```
echo " >>>Thanks for the \$5, $LOGNAME"
```

The result is what you expect:

```
>>>Thanks for the $5, wrev
```

Programming with Control

There are two primary control structures in shell programming: *decision structures* and *iterative structures*. In decision structures, such as `if...then...else` and `case`, you can have the shell script decide which commands to execute based on the value of an expression (such as a variable, the properties associated with a file, the number of parameters in a script, or the result of executing a command). In iterative structures, such as `for` and `while` loops, you can execute a sequence of commands over a collection of files or while some condition holds. The following sections use examples that are not too complicated yet demonstrate the essentials of programming with some control.

Using *case*. The `case` structure is a decision structure that allows you to select one of several courses of action, based on the value of a variable. The following is a short menu program:

```
# Name:     ShrtMenu
# Purpose:  Allow user to print a file, delete a file,
#           or quit the program
# Display menu
     echo "Please choose either P, D, or Q to "
     echo " [P]rint a file"
     echo " [D]elete a file"
     echo " [Q]uit"
# Get response from user
     read response
# Use case to match response to action
     case $response in
        P¦p) echo "Name of file to print?"
             read filename
             lp $filename;;
        D¦d) echo "Name of file to delete?"
             read filename
             rm $filename;;
          *) echo "leaving now";;
     esac
```

The syntax of the `case` statement is

```
case word     in
   pattern) statement(s);;
   pattern) statement(s);;
   ...
   esac
```

The *`word`* parameter is matched against each of the *`pattern`* parameters, starting with the pattern at the top of the list. The statements that execute if *`word`* matches a pattern are terminated by two semicolons (`;;`). The end of the `case` statement is marked by the word `esac` (yes, that's *case* spelled backwards).

In the sample menu, the vertical bar was used to give a choice for a match. For example, `P¦p` means that either an uppercase or lowercase letter *P* is considered a match.

The *`pattern`* `*` is used to represent all other patterns not explicitly stated. If the user presses any key besides <P>, <p>, <D>, or <d>, he exits from the menu.

The following example uses a case statement that makes a selection based on the number of parameters that the shell represents as $#:

```
# Name:     recent
# Purpose:  list the most recent files in a directory
# If user types recent <Return> then the names of
#    the 10 most recently modified files are displayed
# If the user types recent n <Return> then the names of
#    the n most recently modified files are displayed
# Otherwise, user is notified of incorrect usage
#
# Case based on number of parameters
     case $# in
          0) ls -lt ¦ head ;;
               # ls -lt lists names of file in order of
               # most recently modified
               # head displays the first 10 lines of a file
          1) case $1 in
               [0-9]*) ls -lt ¦ head -$1 ;;
               *)echo "Usage: recent number-of-files";;
               esac;;
          *) echo "Usage: recent number-of-files";;
     esac
```

Understanding Exit Status. When a shell command executes, it is either successful or not. If you use the command `grep "American Terms" customers` to see whether the string `American Terms` is in the file `customers`, and the file exits, you have read permission to the file, and `American Terms` is in the file, the shell command has executed *successfully*. If any of those conditions isn't true, the shell command executes *unsuccessfully*. The shell always reports back about the status of the termination of a command, program, or shell script. The value reported back is called the *exit status* of a command and is represented by the variable `#?`. If you enter the following commands, you see the value of `$?`.

```
grep "American Terms" customers
echo $?
```

> **Note**
>
> If `$?` has a value of 0, the previous command was successful; otherwise, the command was unsuccessful.

Following is an example in which the exit status of the command `who¦grep $1` is used in the case statement:

```
# Name:      just.checking
# Purpose:   Determine if person is logged on
# Usage:     just.checking login_name
#
```

```
case 'who ¦ grep $1 > /dev/null` in
     0) echo "$1 is logged on.";;
     *) echo "$1 is not here. Try again later.";;
esac
echo "Have a great day!"
```

If you enter **`just.checking rflame`** and `rflame` is logged on, you see

```
rflame is logged on.
Have a great day!
```

If `rflame` is not logged on, you see

```
rflame is not here. Try again later.
Have a great day!
```

Using the *if* Structure. The `if...then...else...fi` structure is a decision structure that allows you to select one of two courses of action based on the result of a command. The `else` portion of the structure is optional. One or more commands go in place of the ellipsis (...). Provided that the exit status of the last command following the `if` is zero (that is, the command executed successfully), the commands following the `then` and preceding the `else` (if there is one) are executed. Otherwise, the commands following the `else` are executed.

In other words, one or more commands are executed. If the last command was successful, the commands in the `then` portion of the statement are performed and then the commands following the `fi` (the end of the structure) are executed. If the last commands aren't successful, the commands after the `else` are performed.

Here is a familiar example that behaves exactly the same as when it was written using the `case` statement:

```
# Name:     just.checking
# Purpose:  Determine if person is logged on
# Usage:    just.checking login_name
#
if
    who ¦ grep $1 > /dev/null
then
    echo "$1 is logged on."
else
    echo "$1 is not here. Try again later."
fi
echo " Have a great day!"
```

Using the *test* Command. Many of the shell scripts used in this chapter expect the user to behave nicely. The scripts have no check to see whether the user has permission to copy or move files or whether what the user was dealing with was an ordinary file rather than a directory. A command named `test` can deal with these issues as well as some others. For example, `test -f abc` is successful if `abc` exists and is a regular file. You can reverse the meaning of a test by using an exclamation point in front of the option. For example, to test that you do *not* have read permission for file `abc`, use `test ! -r abc`. Table 20.7 lists several options for the `test` command.

Table 20.7 Options for Using the Command with Files

Option	Meaning
-f	Successful if file exists and is a regular file
-d	Successful if file is a directory
-r	Successful if file exists and is readable
-s	Successful if file exists and is not empty
-w	Successful if file exists and can be written to
-x	Successful if file exists and is executable

Here is an example of the use of the `test` command:

```
# Name:    safcopy
# Purpose: Copy file1 to file2
#          Check to see we have read permission on file1
#          If file2 exists then
#               if file2 is a file we can write to
#               then warn user, and get permission to proceed
#               else exit
#          else
#               copy file
#
# Check for proper number of arguments
  case $# in
     2) if test ! -r $1      # cannot read first file;;
        then;;
               exit (1)      # exit with non-zero exit status;;
        fi;;
        if test -f $2        # does second file exist?;;
        then;;
          if test -w $2      # can we write to it?;;
          then;;
               echo " $2 exists, copy over it ? (Y/N)";;
               read     resp              # get permission from user;;
               case $resp in;;
                    Y¦y)     cp $1 $2;;   # go ahead;;
                      *) exit(1);;        # good bye!;;
               esac;;
          else;;
               exit (1)      # Second file exists but can't write;;
          fi
        else     # Second file doesn't exist; go ahead and copy!;
          cp $1 $2;;
        fi;;
     *) echo "Usage: safcopy source destination";;
        exit (1);;
esac
```

You can also use the `test` command to test numbers. To determine whether a value in the variable `hour` is greater than 12, use `test $hour -gt 12`. Table 20.8 lists some options you can use with `test` when you are comparing numbers.

Table 20.8 Options for Using the Command when Comparing Numbers

Option	Meaning
`-eq`	Equal
`-ne`	Not equal
`-ge`	Greater than or equal
`-gt`	Greater than
`-le`	Less than or equal
`-lt`	Less than

The following example shows these options used to display a timely greeting:

```
# Name:     greeting
# Purpose:  Display Good Morning if hour is less than 12
#                   Good Afternoon if hour less than 5PM
#                   Good Evening if hour is greater than 4PM
# Get hour
     hour='date +%H'
# Check for time of day
     if test $hour -lt 12
     then
        echo "Good Morning, $LOGNAME"
     else
        if test $hour -lt 17
        then
           echo "Good Afternoon, $LOGNAME"
        else
           echo "Good Evening, $LOGNAME"
        fi
     fi
```

Using Iterative Structures. Iterative control structures allow you to write shell scripts that contain loops. The two basic types of loops are `for` loops and `while` loops. With `for` loops, you specify a collection of files or values to use with some commands. To copy all the files whose names end with the characters `.txt` to the directory `textdir`, for example, use the following `for` loop:

```
for i in *.txt
do
      cp $i textdir/$i
done
```

The shell interprets the statement `for i in *.txt` and allows the variable `i` to take on the name of any file in the current directory whose name ends with `.txt`. You can then use the variable `$i` with any statements between the `do` and the `done` keywords.

The next example prints a collection of files, each with its own banner page. It also sends mail to the user concerning the status of the print requests. The characters `$*` represent all the parameters given to the shell command.

```
# Name:       Prntel
# Purpose:    Print one or more files
#             each with own title page
#             Notify user which were sent to the printer
#             and which were not.
#             Do this for all parameters to the command
for i in $*
do
     if lp -t $i -dlasers $i > /dev/null
     then
          echo $i >> printed
     else
          echo $i >> notprinted
     fi
done
# end of loop
if test -s printed
then
     echo "These files were sent to the printer " > mes
     cat printed >> mes
     mail $LOGNAME < mes
     rm mes printed
fi
if test -s notprinted
then
     echo "These files were not sent to the printer " >mes
     cat notprinted >> mes
     mail $LOGNAME < mes
     rm mes notprinted
fi
```

A `while` loop looks at the exit status of a command in the same way the `if` statement looks at it. The following script notifies a user when they have received new mail. The script makes the assumption that if the mailbox changes, the user has new mail. The script uses the command `diff` to compare two files and then reports on the differences. If the files are the same, the exit status is zero (the command is successful).

```
# Name:        checkmail
# Purpose:     Notify user if their mail box has changed
# Suggestion:  Run this in the background
# get a size of mail box for comparison
     cp $MAIL omail          # Get set for first time through
# MAIL is a "special" variable indicating the user's mailbox
# while omail and $MAIL are the same, keep looping
     while diff omail $MAIL > /dev/null
     do
          cp $MAIL omail
          sleep 30           # sleep, pause for 30 seconds
     done
# There must be a change in the files
     echo "New mail!!" ¦ write $LOGNAME
```

You can see that some of the commands and concepts used with `if..then..else` statements can be transferred to `while` loops. The difference is, of course, that with `while` loops you are dealing with an iterative, repetitive process.

Customizing Linux Shells

The shell starts when you log on. Other sections in this chapter have shown you that certain special variables are given values by the shell to help define your shell environment. Some of these variables are set by the shell. You can change these settings and give other variables values by editing the file `.profile` if you are using the Bourne or BASH shell. If you are using the C shell, set the variables by editing the file `.login`. You can also use command aliasing to define aliases for commands. Whenever you issue a command, a new shell starts; it inherits many of the characteristics—or much of the environment—of the existing shell. Two things to note about the new shell are the following:

- The new shell runs in your current directory. The `pwd` command returns the same value within a shell as it gives before the shell was started.
- The new shell receives many of its variables from the existing shell. There are ways to make sure that variables set in the existing shell are exported to the new shell.

Exporting Variables to the New Shell

When you create shell variables or give existing variables values, they exist in the running shell. A variable set in the logon shell is available to all command-line arguments. A variable set within a shell has that value only within that shell. The value disappears or is reset when you exit that shell. Consider the following example.

From the command line, enter these two commands, pressing <Return> after each:

```
today=Thursday
echo $today
```

Suppose that the `echo` command displays `Thursday`. Now suppose that you write and execute the following shell script named `whatday`:

```
# Name: whatday
# display the current value of the variable today
     echo "Today is $today."
# set the value of today
     today=Friday
# display the current value of the variable today
     echo "Today is $today."
```

Now enter the following for commands from the command line:

```
chmod +x whatday
today=Thursday
whatday
echo $today
```

The following lines appear on-screen:

```
Today is .
Today is Friday.
Thursday
```

VI

Working with Linux

The value of the variable `today` in the logon shell is `Thursday`. When you execute the shell script `whatday`, you see that initially the variable `today` is not defined (as shown by the display `Today is .`). Then the `today` variable has the value `Friday` in the shell. When the `whatday` script terminates, you return to the logon shell and `today` has its original value `Thursday`.

In order to give the variable `today` the same value it has in the logon shell when the shell script `whatday` starts, use the command `export`. This command "exports," or passes on, the variables from one shell to subsequent shells:

```
export today
```

Now any shell started from the logon shell inherits the value of the variable `today`. Add the `export` command to the preceding sequence of commands:

```
today=Thursday
export today
whatday
echo $today
```

You see the following output:

```
Today is Thursday.
Today is Friday.
Thursday
```

Notice that the value the variable receives in the shell started by the `whatday` script isn't carried back to the logon shell. Exportation or inheritance of variable values goes only in one direction: from a running shell down to the new shell—never back up. That's why when you change your current directory inside one shell, you're back to where you started when that shell terminates.

You can export any variable for one shell down to another shell by using the following syntax:

```
export variable-name
```

In this syntax, *`variable-name`* is the name of the variable you want to export. To change your terminal type from its current setting to a VT-100, for example, enter the following commands to make the new value of `TERM` available to all subsequent shells or programs:

```
TERM=vt100
export TERM
```

When you make changes to or set shell variables in the `.profile` file, be sure to export them. For example, if you want the `PATH` variable to be `PATH=/bin:/usr/bin:/usr/local/bin:.`, set it in the `.profile` file and follow it with this `export` command:

```
export PATH
```

To change the shell prompt, you must set a value for `PS1` in the file `.profile`. To change it from `$` to `Ready $`, for example, use a text editor to put these lines in the file `.profile`:

```
PS1="Ready $"
export PS1
```

Note

Changes you make to `.profile` or `.login` don't take effect until you log off and log on again.

Defining Command Aliases

Command aliases are useful for defining commands you use regularly but for which you don't want to bother remembering the details. Command aliases are also useful for enhancing your working environment with a set of useful tools. This command assigns the alias `recent` to a command that lists the ten most recently modified files in the current directory:

```
alias recent="ls -lat¦head"
```

To avoid typing your command aliases each time you log on, put them in the `.login` file if you are using the C shell or the `.profile` file if you're using the BASH or similar shell. The command aliases are now available to you when you're in your shell.

From Here...

The shell is the primary interface between you and the Linux operating system. Although a shell can be almost any executable program, several standard shells are either supplied with Linux or are freely available in both source code (written in C) or already compiled for your machine. All Linux shells can be viewed as highly sophisticated, special-purpose programming languages containing all the usual constructs found in a programming language. The special purpose of Linux shell languages is to tie together the many small commands and utilities found in the Linux environment. By making use of I/O redirection and background processing, the shell languages allow you to write complex programs with minimal effort. For more information, see:

- Chapter 5, "Running Linux Applications," for basic information on navigating through Linux.
- Chapter 25, "Command-Line Reference," for information on various Linux commands.

CHAPTER 21

Managing Multiple Processes

Linux is a multiuser and multitasking operating system. Multiuser means that several people can use the computer system simultaneously (unlike a single-user operating system such as MS-DOS). Multitasking means that Linux can work on several tasks concurrently; it can begin work on one task and take up another before the first task is finished.

Taking care of several users and multitasking are the jobs of the operating system. Most systems have only one CPU and one collection of chips that make up main memory or RAM. A system may have more than one disk or tape drive for secondary memory and several input/output devices. All of these must be managed and shared between several users. The operating system creates the illusion that each user has the computer system dedicated to them.

In this chapter, you see how to do the following:

- Start multiple processes
- Schedule multiple processes using the commands `at`, `batch`, `cron`, and `crontab`
- Monitor the state of the system using the `who` and `ps` commands
- Use the `nohup` command to allow processes to continue after you log off
- Manage processes by changing their relative priority with the `nice` and `renice` commands
- Terminate processes with the `kill` command

Understanding Multitasking

As mentioned earlier, it's Linux's job to create the illusion that when you make a request, you have the system's undivided attention. In reality, hundreds of requests may be handled between the time you press <Return> and the time the system responds to your command.

Imagine having to keep track of dozens of tasks that you're trying to deal with simultaneously. You have to share the processing power, storage capabilities, and input and output devices among several users or several processes belonging to a single user. Linux monitors a list—also known as a queue—of tasks waiting to be done. These tasks can include user jobs, operating-system tasks, mail, and background jobs. Linux schedules slices of system time for each task. By human standards, each time slice is extremely short—a fraction of a second. In computer time, a time slice is adequate for a program to process hundreds or thousands of instructions. The length of the time slice for each task may depend on the relative priority of each task.

Linux works on one task from the queue for a while, puts the task aside to begin work on another task, and so on. It then returns to the first task and works on it again. Linux continues these cycles until it finishes a task and takes the task out of the queue or until the task is terminated. In this arrangement, sometimes called time-sharing, the resources of the system are shared among all the tasks. Naturally, time-sharing must be done in a reliable and efficient manner.

You've already seen that you can put or run a program in the background. While the program runs in the background, you can continue entering commands and working with other material. This is a feature of multitasking: Linux uses the time-sharing method to balance your immediate commands and the ones running in the background. This chapter shows other ways to schedule jobs or tasks so that they can run without your attention.

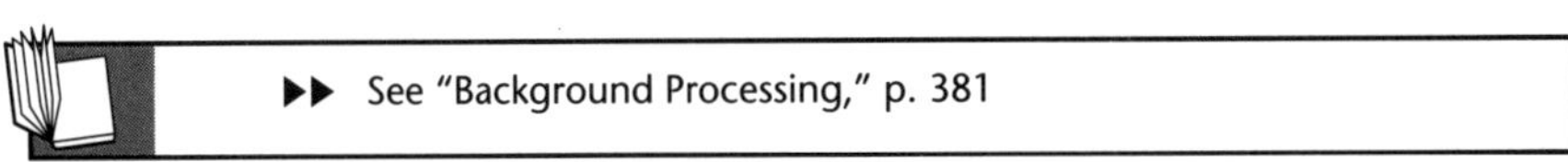
▶▶ See "Background Processing," p. 381

The Linux operating system has the primary responsibility of handling the details of working with several users and several tasks. As a user, you have the power to specify which programs you want to run. Some Linux commands let you specify when you want a job or a process to start. You also have the option of monitoring your processes as well as seeing what other processes are now running. In some cases, you can change the relative priority of jobs. And you can always terminate your processes if the need arises. If you are the system administrator, you have all these capabilities plus the responsibility and power to initiate, monitor, and manage processes that belong to the operating system or any user.

Table 21.1 lists the commands that make it possible to control the multiuser and multitasking capabilities of Linux.

Table 21.1 Multiuser and Multitasking Commands

Command	Action
`at`	Executes commands at a given time
`batch`	Executes commands when system load allows
`cron`	Executes scheduled commands
`kill`	Stops processes
`nice`	Adjusts the priority of a process before it starts
`nohup`	Allows a process to continue after you log off
`ps`	Displays process information
`renice`	Adjusts the priority of a running process
`who`	Displays the system's logged on users

Initiating Multiple Processes

You can start a program running by typing its name and then pressing <Return>. You can also start programs from files that contain shell commands. Running programs can interact with many different parts of the system. A program may read from or write to files, manage its information in RAM, or send information to printers, modems, or other devices. The operating system also attaches information to a process so that the system can keep track of and manage it.

A *process* is a running program. A process is different from a program. In one sense, a process is more than a program because a program is only a set of instructions; a process is dynamic because it uses the resources of a running system. On the other hand, a single Linux program can start several processes.

Linux identifies and keeps track of processes by assigning a *process ID number* (PID) to each process.

Starting Multiple Processes

You've already seen that your logon shell is always running. Whenever you type a command and press <Return>, you start at least one new process while the logon shell continues to run. If you enter the following command, for example, the file named `report.txt` is sent to the `lp` program:

```
lp report.txt
```

▶▶ See "Understanding Shells," p. 360

When the lp program completes its task, the shell prompt reappears. Before the shell prompt reappeared, the logon shell and the lp command were running; you initiated multiple processes in that case. The shell waited until the lp command was finished before putting the shell prompt back on-screen.

Starting a Background Process

You can run a process as a background job by giving the command to start a process and placing an ampersand (&) after the command. For example, if you type the command **lp report.txt &** and press <Return>, the shell responds immediately with a number—the PID for that process. The shell prompt reappears without waiting for the process to complete. The following is a sample of what you would see:

```
$lp report.txt &<Return>
3146
$
```

In this example, 3146 is the PID of the process started by the lp command.

Regardless of whether you run the lp command in the background, the process associated with the lp command is started from the current shell. The lp process is a child process of the current shell. This example points to a common relationship between processes—that of parent and child. Your current shell is the parent process and the running lp process is a child process. Usually, a parent process waits for one or more of its child processes to complete before it continues. If you want the parent to continue without waiting for the child to finish, attach the ampersand (&) to the command that spawns, or initiates, the child process. You can continue with other work or commands while the child runs.

Note

If you're working from a character terminal or a remote logon, your current shell is usually your logon shell. However, if you're using a virtual terminal or a terminal window from a GUI, a separate shell is associated with each session.

Using Pipes to Start Multiple Processes

Another way to start multiple processes is to use one or more pipes on a command line. To print a long listing of the ten most recently modified files in your current directory, enter

```
ls -lt | head | lp
```

This command starts three processes simultaneously—and they're all children of the current shell. A pipe works this way: Commands on either side of the vertical bar (¦) begin at the same time. Neither is the parent of the other; they're both children of the process that was running when they were created. In this sense, you can think of commands on either side of the pipe symbol as sibling processes.

Some programs are written so that they themselves spawn several processes. One example is the `spell` command that lists the words in a document that Linux can't find in a system dictionary. The `spell` command spawns some child processes. Suppose that you enter

```
spell final.rept > final.errs &
```

You see the following results displayed:

```
1286
$
```

Here, `1286` is the PID of the `ispell` process; the `$` prompt indicates that the shell is ready to handle another command from you. Even though `ispell` may spawn some children and wait for them to complete, you don't have to wait. In this example, the current shell is the parent of `spell`, and `ispell`'s children can be thought of as grandchildren of the logon shell. Although a parent can wait for its children, a grandparent doesn't.

All these examples show how it's possible for a user to start multiple processes. You can wait until child processes are finished before continuing or not. If you continue without waiting for the child process to complete, you've made the children background processes. The following section looks at some Linux commands you can use to schedule processes to run at specified times or at a lower relative priority.

Using the Scheduling Commands

The Linux environment provides many ways to handle command execution. Linux lets you create lists of commands and specify when they're to be run. The `at` command, for example, takes a list of commands typed at the keyboard or from a file and runs them at the time specified by the command. The `batch` command is similar to the `at` command, but `batch` runs commands when the system finds time for them rather than allow the user to specify a particular time. The `cron` command allows for commands to be run periodically.

All scheduling commands are useful for running tasks at times when the system isn't too busy. They're also good for executing scripts to external services—such as database queries—at times when it's least expensive to do so.

Running Commands at Specified Times with *at*

To schedule one or more commands for a specified time, use the `at` command. With this command, you can specify a time, a date, or both. The command expects two or more arguments. At a minimum, you specify the time you want the command or commands executed and the command or commands you want to execute.

The following example performs its job at 1:23 AM. If you're working in the wee hours of the morning before 1:23 AM (that is, between midnight and 1:23 AM) the command is done today, at 1:23 AM. Otherwise, it's done at 1:23 AM on the following day. The job prints all files in the directory `/usr/sales/reports` and sends a user named `boss` some mail announcing that the print job was done at 1:23 AM.

```
at 1:23<Return>
lp /usr/sales/reports/*<Return>
echo "Files printed, Boss!" ¦ mailx -s"Job done" boss<Return>
<^D>
```

> **Note**
>
> The `^D` symbol means that <Ctrl-d> was pressed to end the process. Press and hold the <Ctrl> key and then press the <d> key; then release both keys. (Linux may use the `^D` symbol to represent the end of a file. To see exactly which symbol is used, enter the **`stty`** command.)

▶▶ See "Setting the Terminal Environment," p. 363

Commands to be scheduled by `at` are entered as a list of commands on the line following the `at` command; the list of commands are terminated with <Ctrl-d>.

After you terminate the `at` command, you see a display similar to the following:

```
job 756603300.a at Sat Dec 21 01:23:00 1996
```

This response indicates that the job will execute at 1:23 as specified. The job number, `756603300.a`, identifies the job. If you decide you want to cancel the job, do so by using the job number associated with it.

If you have several commands you want to schedule using `at`, it's best to put them in a file. If the name of the file is `getdone`, for example, and you want to schedule the commands for 10:00 AM, enter

```
at 10:00 < getdone
```

Remember that the less-than symbol (<) means to use the contents of the getdone file as input to the at command.

You can also specify a date for an at job. For example, to schedule a job at 5:00 PM on January 24, enter these commands:

```
at 17:00 Jan 24<Return>
lp /usr/sales/reports/*<Return>
echo "Files printed, Boss!" ¦ mailx -s"Job done" boss<Return>
<^D>
```

The jobs you schedule with at are put into a queue that the operating system checks periodically. You don't have to be logged on for the job to be executed. The at command always runs in the background, freeing resources but still accomplishing the job. Any output produced by the commands in your at job is mailed to you.

To see which jobs you scheduled with at, enter **at -l**. Working with the preceding examples, you see the following results:

```
job 756603300.a at Sat Dec 21 01:23:00 1996
job 756604200.a at Fri Jan 24 17:00:00 1997
```

Only your at jobs are listed.

To remove a scheduled at job, enter **at -r** followed by the job number. To remove the second job just listed, for example, enter

```
at -r 756604200.a<Return>
```

Table 21.2 summarizes the different ways to use the at command.

Table 21.2 Summary of *at* Commands

Format	Action
at *hh:mm*	Schedules job at the hour (*hh*) and minute (*mm*) specified using a 24-hour clock.
at *hh:mm month day year*	Schedules job at the hour (*hh*), minute (*mm*), month, day, and year specified.
at -l	Lists scheduled jobs.
at -r *job_id*	Cancels job with job number matching *job_id*.

Running Long Tasks with *batch*

Linux has more than one command for scheduling tasks. The preceding section describes the at command, which gives you the power to decide when a task will run. However, it's always possible that the system can be loaded down with more jobs scheduled at one time than it can comfortably handle.

The `batch` command lets the operating system decide an appropriate time to run a process. When you schedule a job with `batch`, Linux starts and works on the process whenever the system load isn't too great. Jobs run under `batch` execute in the background, just as those run with `at`.

> **Tip**
>
> It's useful to put commands you want to run with `at` or `batch` in a file so that you don't have to retype them. To use `batch` to schedule the commands in the file `getdone`, enter the **`batch < getdone`** command.

The format for `batch` commands is to enter the list of commands on the lines following the `batch` command; you terminate the list of commands with <Ctrl-d>. You can put the list of commands in a file and then redirect the input to `batch` to come from the file. To sort a collection of files, print the results, and notify user `boss` that the job is done, enter the following commands:

```
batch<Return>
sort /usr/sales/reports/* ¦ lp<Return>
echo "Files printed, Boss!" ¦ mailx -s"Job done" boss<Return>
<^D>
```

The system returns the following response:

```
job 7789001234.b at Sat Dec 21 11:43:09 1996
```

The date and time listed are the date and time you pressed <Ctrl-d> to complete the `batch` command. When the job is complete, check your mail: anything that the commands normally display is mailed to you.

Scheduling Commands with *cron* and *crontab*

Both `at` and `batch` schedule commands on a one-time basis. To schedule commands or processes on a regular basis, you indirectly use the program `cron`. You specify the times and dates you want to run a command in `crontab` files. Times can be specified in terms of minutes, hours, days of the month, months of the year, or days of the week.

The `cron` program is started only once, when the system is booted. Individual users shouldn't have permission to run `cron` directly. Also, as the system administrator, you shouldn't start `cron` by typing the name of the command; `cron` should be listed in a shell script as one of the commands to run during a system boot-up sequence.

Once started, `cron` (short for *chronograph*) checks queues for `at` jobs to run and also checks to see whether regular users or the root have scheduled jobs using `crontab` files. If there's nothing to do, `cron` "goes to sleep" and becomes inactive; it "wakes up" every minute to check whether there are commands to run. You can see how important and useful this facility is; also, `cron` uses very few system resources.

Use the `crontab` command to install a list of commands that will be executed on a regular schedule. The commands are scheduled to run at a specified time (such as once a month, once an hour, once a day, and so on). The list of commands to be performed on the specified schedule must be included in the `crontab` file, which is installed with the `crontab` command. Once you install the `crontab` file, `cron` reads and executes the listed commands at the specified times. Also with the `crontab` command, you can view the list of commands included in the file and cancel the list if you want.

Before you install your crontab file with the `crontab` command, create the file containing the list of commands you want to schedule by using a text editor such as `vi` or `emacs`. The `crontab` command handles the placement of the file. Each user has only one `crontab` file, created when the `crontab` command is issued. This file is placed in a directory that's read by the `cron` command.

Each user has one crontab file, stored in the `/usr/spool/cron/crontabs` directory. That file is given the user's name. If your user name is `mcn` and you use a text editor to create a file called `mycron` and install it by typing **`crontab mycron`**, the file `/usr/spool/cron/crontabs/mcn` is created. (In this example, the `mcn` file is created, or overwritten, with the contents of `mycron`, which may contain entries that launch one or more commands.)

Note

For a user to be able to use the `crontab` command, they must be listed in the `/etc/cron.d/cron.allow` file. If you add a user from the command line (by using the `useradd` command), they aren't automatically added to that file. As the root user, you must add the new user to the `cron.allow` file with a text editor.

Once you've created your `crontab` file, modify it using only the `crontab` command. Don't try to replace or modify the file that `cron` examines (that is, the `/usr/spool/cron/crontabs/user` file) by any other means than by using the `crontab` command.

Each line in the `crontab` file contains a time pattern and a command. The command is executed at the specified time pattern. The time pattern is divided into five fields separated by spaces or tabs. Any output that usually appears—that is, information that isn't redirected to `stdout` or `stderr`—is mailed to the user.

Following is the syntax for the commands you enter in a file to be used by `crontab`:

```
minute hour day-of-month month-of-year day-of-week command
```

The first five fields are time-option fields. You must specify all five of these fields. Use an asterisk (*) in a field if you want to ignore that field.

> **Note**
>
> Technically, an asterisk in a `crontab` field means "any valid value" rather than "ignore the value." The `crontab` entry `2 0 1 * * date`, for example, says to run the `date` command at two minutes after midnight (zero hour) on the first day of the month. Because the month and day of the week fields are both asterisks, this entry runs on the first day of every month and any day of the week that the first of the month happens to land on.

Table 21.3 lists the time-field options available with `crontab`.

Table 21.3 Time-Field Options for the *crontab* Command

Field	Range
minute	0 through 59
hour	0 through 23 (midnight is 0)
day-of-month	1 through 31
month-of-year	1 through 12
day-of-week	0 through 6 (Sunday is 0)

You can have as many entries as you want in a `crontab` file and designate them to run at any time you want. This means that you can run as many commands as you want in a single `crontab` file.

To sort a file named `/usr/wwr/sales/weekly` and mail the output to a user named `twool` at 7:30 each Monday, use the following entry in a file:

```
30 07 * * 01 sort /usr/wwr/sales/weekly ¦mailx -s"Weekly Sales"
twool
```

This command specifies the `minute` as 30, the `hour` as 07, any day of the month with the *, any month of the year with another *, and the `day-of-week` as 01 (which represents Monday).

Notice the pipe between the `mailx` and `sort` commands in the preceding example. The command field can contain pipes, semicolons, arrows, or anything else you can enter on a shell command line. At the specified date and time, `cron` runs the entire command field with a standard shell (`bash`).

To specify a sequence of values for one of the first four fields, use commas to separate the values. Suppose that you have a program, `chkquotes`, that accesses a service that provides stock quotes and puts the quotes in a file. To get those quotes at 9 AM, 11 AM, 2 PM, and 4 PM on Monday, Tuesday, and Thursday of every week—and definitely on the 10th of March and September—use the following entry:

```
* 09,11,14,16 10 03,09 01,02,04 chkquotes
```

Put the command lines into a file using `vi` or some other editor that allows you to save files as text files. Assume that you put your commands in a file named `cronjobs`. To use `crontab` to put the file where `cron` can find it, enter

```
crontab cronjobs
```

Each time you use `crontab` this way, it overwrites any `crontab` file you may have already launched.

The `crontab` command has three options: The `-e` option edits the contents of the current `crontab` file. (The `-e` option opens your file using the `ed` editor or whatever is assigned to the `EDITOR` variable in your shell.) The `-r` option removes the current `crontab` file from the `crontabs` directory. The `-l` option lists the contents of the current `crontab` file.

In all these cases, `crontab` works with the `crontab` file that has your logon name. If your logon name is `mcn`, your `crontab` file is `/usr/spool/cron/crontabs/mcn`. The `crontab` command does this automatically; you don't need to know this fact to use the `crontab` command.

The system administrator and users share responsibility for making sure that the system is used appropriately. When you schedule a process, be aware of the impact it may have on the total system. Linux allows you, as the system administrator, to grant access to the `at`, `batch`, and `cron` commands to all users, specific users, or no users (or to deny access to individual users).

Troubleshooting

The commands I put in my crontab file don't work.

The `cron` command runs your `crontab` entries using the Bourne Again shell (`bash`). Your entry fails if you use shell features not supported by `bash`. For example, the Korn shell (`ksh`) allows you to use a tilde (~) to represent a home directory or the `alias` command to designate aliases for certain commands.

When I try to use the `at` *command, I'm told I don't have permission to use it.*

You haven't added your logon ID to the `/etc/cron.d/at.allow` file.

I tried to use the `at now` command to run a command immediately.

No matter how fast you type, `at now` always responds with the message `ERROR: Too late`. The best alternative is to use the `batch` command to run the command for you. You can, however, use `at now +5 min` to run the command in five minutes. After you press <Return>, quickly type to enter your command before the minute expires.

> **Note**
>
> Because Linux doesn't provide the Korn shell and instead uses the bash shell as its default shell, you should have no problems with cron trying to execute unknown commands. However, the bash shell does allow alias, so you should be aware of this troubleshooting tip.

Reporting On and Monitoring the Multitasking Environment

You know that Linux is a multiuser, multitasking operating system. Because so many people can do so many things with the system at the same time, users find it useful to determine who's using the system and what processes are running, as well as to monitor processes.

Knowing that others can keep track of the commands you enter is important. Most users can't access your files without your permission, but they can see the names of commands you enter. Also, you (as the system administrator) or someone else who has the root password can peruse all your files. Although you don't have to be paranoid about privacy on a Linux system, you should know that the system can be monitored by anyone who wants to take the time to do it. The information you can gain about what's going on in the system is more useful than just satisfying curiosity: By seeing what jobs are running, you can appropriately schedule your tasks. You can also see whether a process of yours is still active and whether it's behaving properly.

Finding Out Who's on the System with *who*

The purpose of the who command is to find out who's logged onto the system. The who command lists the logon names, terminal lines, and logon times of users now logged on.

The who command is useful in many situations. If you want to communicate with someone on the computer by using the write command, for example, find out whether that person is on the system by using who. You can also use the command to see when certain users are logged on to the computer to keep track of their time spent on the system.

Using *who* To List Users Logged On to the System. To see everyone who's now logged on to the system, enter who. You see a display similar to the following:

```
$ who<Return>
root       console    Dec 13 08:00
ernie      tty02      Dec 13 10:37
bkraft     tty03      Dec 13 11:02
jdurum     tty05      Dec 13 09:21
ernie      ttys7      Dec 11 18:49
$
```

This listing shows that `root`, `ernie`, `bkraft`, and `jdurum` are now logged on. It shows that `root` logged on at 8 AM, `bkraft` at 11:02, and `jdurum` at 9:21. You can also see that `ernie` is logged on to two terminals and that one logon occurred at 6:49 PM (18:49) two days earlier (which may be some reason for concern or it may just be `ernie`'s usual work habits).

Using Headers in User Listings. Several options are available with `who`, but this chapter describes how to use only two to monitor processes on the system:

- `-u` Lists only users who are now logged on
- `-H` Displays headers above each column

With these options, you can get more information about the users now logged on. The headers displayed with the `-H` option are `NAME`, `LINE`, `TIME`, `IDLE`, `PID`, and `COMMENTS`. Table 21.4 explains the terms appearing in the heading.

Table 21.4 Output Format for the *who* Command

Field	Description
`NAME`	Lists the user's logon name.
`LINE`	Lists the line or terminal being used.
`TIME`	Lists the time the user logged on.
`IDLE`	Lists the hours and minutes since the last activity on that line. A period is displayed if activity occurred within the last minute of system time. If more than 24 hours elapsed since the line was used, the word `old` is displayed.
`PID`	Lists the process ID number of the user's logon shell.
`COMMENT`	Lists the contents of the comment field if comments have been included in `/etc/inittab` or if there are network connections (see the following note).

Note

You probably won't see the `COMMENT` field filled in very often in any recent Linux systems. In the old days, processes that let you log on to UNIX (`getty` or `uugetty`) were started directly from entries in the `/etc/inittab` file and usually listened for logon requests from a particular terminal. The `COMMENT` field might identify the location of that terminal that could tell you who was logged on and at what terminal they were sitting. Today, processes that listen for logon requests are typically handled by the Service Access Facility and are no longer listed in `/etc/inittab`.

The following example uses the -u and -H options and shows the response Linux returns:

```
$ who -uH<Return>
NAME      LINE          TIME        IDLE    PID  COMMENTS
root      console  Dec 13 08:00      .     10340
ernie     tty02    Dec 13 10:37      .     11929  Tech-89.2
bkraft    tty03    Dec 13 11:02    0:04     4761  Sales-23.4
jdurum    tty05    Dec 13 09:21    1:07    10426
ernie     ttys7    Dec 11 18:49     old    10770 oreo.coolt.com
$
```

You can infer from this listing that the last session associated with ernie is from a network site named oreo.coolt.com and that there hasn't been any activity in that session in more than 24 hours (which might signal a problem). The session for root and the first one for ernie have both been accessed within the last minute. The last activity on the session for bkraft was four minutes ago; it has been one hour and seven minutes since any activity was reported on the session for jdurum.

Also note that this listing includes the PID (process ID number) for the logon shell of each user's session. The next section shows how you can use the PID to further monitor the system.

Reporting on the Status of Processes with *ps*

The command ps reports on the status of processes. You can use it to determine which processes are running, see whether a process has completed, see whether a process is hung or having some difficulty, see how long a process has run, see the resources a process is using, determine the relative priority of a process, and find the PID (process ID number) needed before you can kill a process. All this information is useful to a user and very useful to a system administrator. Without any options, ps lists the PID of each process associated with your current shell. It's also possible to see a detailed listing of all the processes running on a system.

Monitoring Processes with *ps*. A common use of the ps command is to monitor background jobs and other processes on the system. Because background processes don't communicate with your screen and keyboard in most cases, you use the ps command to track their progress.

The ps listing displays four default headings as indicators of the information in the fields below each heading: PID, TTY, TIME, and COMMAND. Table 21.5 explains these headings.

Table 21.5 Headings in the Output of *ps*

Field	Explanation
PID	The process identification number
TTY	The terminal that the process originated on
TIME	The cumulative execution time for the process, in minutes and seconds
COMMAND	The name of the command being executed

Suppose that you want to sort a file named `sales.dat`, save a copy of the sorted file in a file named `sales.srt`, and mail the sorted file to the user `sarah`. If you also want to put this job in the background, enter

```
sort sales.dat ¦ tee sales.srt ¦ mailx -s"Sorted Sales Data" sarah &
```

To monitor this process, enter **ps** and see a display such as this one:

```
  PID TTY      TIME COMMAND
16490 tty02    0:15 sort
16489 tty02    0:00 mailx
16492 tty02    0:00 ps
16478 tty02    0:00 bash
16491 tty02    0:06 tee
16480 tty02   96:45 cruncher
```

You see the accumulated time and PID for each process started with the command. You also see information for your logon shell, `bash`, and for `ps` itself. Notice that all the commands in the pipe are running at once—as you would expect (this is the way the piping process works). The last entry is for a command that has been running for more than an hour and a half. If that's a problem, you may want to terminate the process by using the `kill` command (described later in this chapter). If you enter **ps** and see only the following listing, you know the previous job you put into the background is complete:

```
PID     TTY      TIME COMMAND
16492 tty02    0:00 ps
16478 tty02    0:00 bash
16480 tty02   99:45 cruncher
```

> **Note**
>
> Use ps occasionally to check the status of a command. If you use ps every second, however, while waiting to see whether the background job is complete, there isn't much sense putting the job in the background in the first place.

Obtaining More Information About Processes with *ps*. Sometimes, you need to know more about your processes than what the default ps listing provides. To generate additional information, you can invoke some of the options listed in Table 21.6.

Table 21.6 Commonly Used Options for the *ps* Command

Option	Action
-l	Long format
-u	User format—gives user name and start time
-j	Jobs format—pgid sid
-s	Signal format
-v	vm format
-m	Displays memory info (combine with p flag to get number of pages)
-a	Shows processes of other users also
-x	Shows processes without controlling terminal
-S	Adds child CPU time and page faults
-c	Command name from task_struct environment
-w	Wide output—don't truncate command lines to fit on one line
-h	No header
-r	Running processes only
-txx	Processes associated with tty xx only
-n	Numeric output for USER and WCHAN

The ps command gives only an approximate picture of process status because things can and do change while the ps command is running. The ps command gives a snapshot of the process status at the instant the ps command executed. The snapshot includes the ps command itself.

In the following examples, three commands are shown. The first command is the logon shell (bash). The second command is sort (used to sort the file named inventory). The third command is the ps command you're now running.

To find out what processes you're now running, use the following command:

```
$ ps<Return>
PID   TTY      TIME      COMMAND
65    tty01    0:07      -bash
71    tty01    0:14      sort inventory
231   tty01    0:09      ps
```

To obtain a full listing, use the following command:

```
$ ps -uax<Return>
UID      PID    PPID  C    STIME       TTY     TIME    COMD
amanda   65      1    0    11:40:11    tty01   0:06     -bash
amanda   71     65   61    11:42:01    tty01   0:14     sort inventory
amanda 231      65   80    11:46:02    tty01   0:00     ps -f
```

▶▶ See "grep," p. 512

Notice a few things about this full listing. In addition to the PID, the PPID is listed. The PPID is the process ID number of that process's *parent* process. In this example, the first process listed (PID 65) is the parent of the following two. The entry in the fourth column (the column headed C) gives the amount of CPU resources a process has used recently. In selecting the next process to work with, the operating system chooses a process with a low C value over one with a higher value. The entry in the `STIME` column is the time at which the process started.

To monitor every process on the system and get a full listing, enter **`ps -uax`**. (By piping the command through the `grep $LOGNAME` command, the processes belonging to your logon name are displayed while all others are filtered out.) To see a full listing of all your processes, enter

```
ps -uax ¦ grep $LOGNAME
```

To list processes for two terminals (for example, `tty1` and `tty2`), use the following command:

```
$ ps -t "1 2"<Return>
PID  TTY     TIME    COMMAND
32   tty01   0:05      bash
36 ttyty02   0:09      bash
235  tty02   0:16      vi calendar
```

In this example, the `-t` option is used to restrict the listing to the processes associated with terminals `tty1` and `tty2`. Terminal `tty2` is running the shell command (PID 32) and using `vi` to edit the calendar (PID 235). The cumulative time for each process is also listed. If you're using shells from a graphical interface (the `xterm` command), use device names `pts001`, `pts002`, and so on with the `-t` option to see the processes from those sessions.

Sometimes a process is marked as `<defunct>`, which means that the process has terminated and its parent process has been notified, but the parent hasn't acknowledged the fact that the process is "dead." A process like that is called a *zombie process*. It's possible that the parent is busy with something else and the zombie will soon disappear. If you see a number of defunct processes or ones that linger for some time, this is a sign of some difficulty with the operating system.

Controlling Multiple Processes

Linux gives you the power to run several processes concurrently. It also allows a user or an administrator to have control over running processes. This control is advantageous when you need to do the following:

- Initiate a process that continues after its parent quits running (use the `nohup` command)
- Schedule a process with a priority different than other processes (use the `nice` command)
- Terminate or stop a process (use the `kill` command)

Using *nohup* with Background Processes

Normally, the children of a process terminate when the parent dies or terminates. This means that when you start a background process, it terminates when you log off. To have a process continue after you log off, use the `nohup` command. Put `nohup` at the beginning of a command line:

```
nohup sort sales.dat &
```

This sample command tells the `sort` command to ignore the fact that you log off the system; it should run until the process completes. In this way, you can initiate a process that can run for days or even weeks. What's more, you don't have to be logged on as it runs. Naturally, you want to make sure that the job you initiate behaves nicely—that is, it eventually terminates and doesn't create an excessive amount of output.

When you use `nohup`, the command sends all the output and error messages of a command that normally appear on-screen to a file named `nohup.out`. Consider the following example:

```
$ nohup sort sales.dat &<Return>
1252
Sending output to nohup.out
$
```

The sorted file and any error messages are placed in the file `nohup.out`. Now consider this example:

```
$ nohup sort sales.dat > sales.srt &<Return>
1257
Sending output to nohup.out
$
```

Any error messages are placed in the file `nohup.out` but the sorted `sales.dat` file is placed in `sales.srt`.

When you use `nohup` with a pipeline, you must use `nohup` with each command in the pipeline:

```
nohup sort sales.dat ¦ nohup mailx -s"Sorted Sales Data" boss &
```

Scheduling the Priority of Commands with *nice*

Use the `nice` command to run a command at a specific scheduling priority. The `nice` command gives you some control over the priority of one job over another. If you don't use `nice`, processes run at a set priority. You can lower the priority of a process with the `nice` command so that other processes can be scheduled to use the CPU more frequently than the `nice` job. The super user (the person who can log on as the root user) can also raise the priority of a process.

The general form of the `nice` command is as follows:

```
nice -number command
```

The priority level is determined by the *number* argument (a higher number means a lower priority). The default is set to 10. If the *number* argument is present, the priority is incremented by that amount up to a limit of 20. If you enter the following command, the `sort` process starts with a priority of 10:

```
sort sales.dat > sales.srt &
```

If you want to start another process—say, with the `lp` command—but give preference to the `sort` command, you can enter

```
nice -5 lp mail_list &
```

To give the `lp` command the lowest possible priority, enter

```
nice -10 lp mail_list &
```

Only the super user can increase the priority of a process. To do that, they use a negative number as the argument to `nice`. Remember: The lower the `nice` value, the higher the priority (up to a maximum priority of 20). To give a job "top priority," the super user initiates the job as follows:

```
nice --19 job &
```

The ampersand (&) is optional; if *job* is interactive, you as the system administrator wouldn't use the ampersand.

Scheduling the Priority of Running Processes with *renice*

The `renice` command, available on some systems, allows you to modify the priority of a running process. Berkeley UNIX systems have the `renice` command; it's also available in the `/usr/ucb` directory in Linux System V systems for compatibility with Berkeley systems. With `renice`, you can adjust priorities on commands as they execute. The format of `renice` is similar to that of `nice`:

```
renice -number PID
```

To change the priority on a running process, you must know its PID. To find the PID of all your processes, enter

```
ps -e ¦ grep name
```

In this command, *name* is replaced by the name of the running process. The `grep` command filters out all processes that don't contain the name of the process you're looking for. (If several processes of that name are running, you have to determine the one you want by looking at the time it started.)

The entry in the second column of the `ps` listing is the PID of the process. In the following example, three processes are running for the current user (in addition to the shell). The current user's name is `pcoco`.

```
$ ps -ef ¦ grep $LOGNAME<Return>
   pcoco 11805 11804  0  Dec 22   ttysb    0:01 sort sales.dat>sales.srt
   pcoco 19955 19938  4  16:13:02 ttyp0    0:00 grep pcoco
   pcoco 19938     1  0  16:11:04 ttyp0    0:00 bash
   pcoco 19940 19938 142 16:11:04 ttyp0    0:33 find . -name core -exec rm {};
$
```

To lower the priority on the process with PID 19940 (the `find` process), enter

```
renice -5 19940
```

As you would expect, the following are true about `renice`:

- You can use `renice` only with processes you own.
- The super user can use `renice` on any process.
- Only the super user can increase the priority of a process.

Caution

As the system administrator, you change priorities only on jobs you've created. Don't modify priorities on system programs unless you know what you're doing. See Chapter 7, "Understanding System Administration," for more information on the duties system administrators should perform.

Terminating Processes with *kill*

Sometimes, you want or need to terminate a process. The following are some reasons for stopping a process:

- It's using too much CPU time.
- It's running too long without producing expected output.
- It's producing too much output to the screen or to a disk file.
- It appears to have locked a terminal or some other session.
- It's using the wrong files for input or output because of an operator or programming error.
- It's no longer useful.

Most likely, you'll come across a number of other reasons as well. If the process to be stopped is a background process, use the `kill` command to get out of these situations.

To stop a command that isn't in the background, press <Ctrl-c> or <Ctrl-d>, depending on the type of shell you're using. When a command is in the background, however, pressing an interrupt key doesn't stop it. Because a background process isn't under terminal control, keyboard input of any interrupt key is ignored. The only way you can stop background commands is to use the `kill` command.

Normal Termination of Background Processes. The `kill` command sends signals to the program to demand that a process be terminated or killed. To use `kill`, use either of these two forms:

```
kill PID(s)
```

```
kill -signal PID(s)
```

To kill a process whose PID is 123, enter **kill 123**. To kill several processes whose PIDs are 123, 342, and 73, enter **kill 123 342 73**.

By using a *signal* option, you can do more than simply kill a process. Other signals can cause a running process to reread configuration files or stop a process without killing it. Valid signals are listed in the `/usr/include/sys/signal.h` file. An average user, however, will probably use `kill` with no signal or, at most, with the -9 signal (the I-mean-it-so-don't-ignore-me signal, described in the next section).

Caution

Use the correct PID with the `kill` command. Using the wrong PID can stop a process you want to keep running. Remember that killing the wrong process or a system process can have disastrous effects. Also remember that if you're logged on as the system administrator, you can kill *any* process.

If you successfully kill the process, you get no notice from the shell—the shell prompt simply reappears. You see an error message if you try to kill a process you don't have permission to kill or if you try to kill a process that doesn't exist.

Suppose that your logon name is `chris` and that you're now logged on to `tty01`. To see the processes you have running, enter **ps -f** and see the following response:

```
UID      PID   PPID  C    STIME      TTY     TIME    COMMAND
chris    65     1    0    11:40:11   tty01   0:06    -bash
chris    71    65   61    11:42:01   tty01   0:14    total_updt
chris   231    65   80    11:46:02   tty01   0:00    ps -f
chris   187    53   60    15:32:01   tty02 123:45    crunch stats
chris    53     1    0    15:31:34   tty02   1:06    -bash
```

Notice that the program `total_updt` is running at your current terminal. Another program, `crunch`, is running on another terminal, and you think it has used an unusually large amount of CPU time. To kill that process, it may be sufficient to enter **`kill 187`**. To kill the parent of that process, enter **`kill 53`**.

You may want to kill a parent and its child if you logged on as the system administrator and see that someone left their terminal unattended (if you've set up Linux with remote terminals). You can kill a clock process that the user has running (the child process) and the logon shell (the parent process) so that the unattended terminal is no longer logged on.

Stopping the parent of a process sometimes terminates the child process as well. To be sure, stop the parent and its children to halt all activity associated with a parent process. In the preceding example, enter **`kill 187 53`** to terminate both processes.

> **Tip**
>
> If your terminal locks up, log onto another virtual terminal with <Alt-*function key*> (F1-F6), enter **`ps -ef ¦ grep $LOGNAME`**, and kill the logon shell for the locked terminal.

Unconditional Termination of Background Processes. Issuing the `kill` command sends a signal to a process. Linux programs can send or receive more than 20 signals, each of which is represented by a number. For example, when you log off, Linux sends the hang-up signal (signal number 1) to all the background processes started from your logon shell. This signal kills or stops those processes unless they were started with `nohup` (as described earlier in this chapter).

Using `nohup` to start a background process lets the process ignore the signal that tries to stop it. You may be using programs or shell scripts written to ignore some signals. If you don't specify a signal when you use `kill`, signal 15 is sent to the process. The command `kill 1234` sends signal 15 to the process whose PID is 1234. If that process is set to ignore signal 15, however, the process doesn't terminate when you use this command. You can use `kill` in a way that a process "can't refuse," however.

The signal 9 is an unconditional kill signal; it always kills a process. To unconditionally kill a process, use the following format:

```
kill -9 PID
```

Suppose that you enter **`ps -f`** and see the following response listing:

```
UID     PID   PPID  C   STIME      TTY     TIME   COMMAND
chris    65     1   0   11:40:11   tty01   0:06   -bash
chris    71    65  61   11:42:01   tty01   0:14   total_updt inventory
chris   231    65  80   11:46:02   tty01   0:00   ps -f
chris   187    53  60   15:32:01   tty02 123:45   crunch stats
chris    53     1   0   15:31:34   tty02   1:06   -bash
```

To kill process 187, normally you enter **`kill 187`**. If you then enter **`ps -f`** again and see that the process is still there, you know the process is set up to ignore the `kill` command. Kill it unconditionally with **`kill -9 187`**. When you enter **`ps -f`** again, you see that the process is no longer around.

Caution

A disadvantage to using this version of the `kill` command is that `kill -9` doesn't allow a process to finish what it's doing before it terminates. If you use `kill -9` with a program that's updating a file, you loose the updated material. Use the powerful `kill -9` command responsibly. In most cases, you don't need the `-9` option; the `kill` command issued without arguments stops most processes.

Terminating All Background Processes. To kill all background jobs, enter **`kill 0`**.

Commands that run in the background sometimes initiate more than one process; tracking down all the PID numbers associated with the process you want to kill can be tedious. Because the `kill 0` command terminates all processes started by the current shell, it's a faster and less tedious way to terminate processes. Enter the **`jobs`** command to see what commands are running in the background for the current shell.

From Here...

This chapter presented the commands you need to manage multiple processes. You saw that you run multiple processes whenever you put jobs in the background with the ampersand (`&`) or when you use pipes. You can schedule jobs at a specific time with the `at` command, at a time the system feels is appropriate with the `batch` command, and at regularly scheduled times with `cron` and `crontab`. For more information, see:

- Chapter 25, "Command-Line Reference," explains and shows you how to use many of the Linux commands. This chapter also presents you with the various command line parameters each command takes to do its job.

- Part III, "System Administration," discusses how to monitor and maintain your Linux system. System administration is not an easy topic to learn, and in fact requires a hands-on learning approach. This section of the book provides you with a basic understanding of the concepts and the tasks required of a system administrator (often called a sys admin).

CHAPTER 22

Using the *vi* Editor

In earlier chapters, you've seen how convenient and advantageous it is to have sequences of commands or shell programs stored in a file. You probably have to create data, e-mail, lists, memos, notes, reports, and so on; you use some type of text editor to do these tasks. You may have several editors or word processors available on your Linux system to help you with those tasks. To put commands or shell programs in a file, however, you need an editor that can save your work in a *text file*—a file in ASCII format. Linux comes with a standard text editor called `vi`, which you can use for all but the most complex writing and editing projects.

Note

The `vi`, `ex`, and `ed` editors that ship with the Linux distributions are actually other names for an editor called `elvis`. The names `vi`, `ex`, and `ed` are symbolically linked to `elvis`, so when you type **vi**, you actually are running `elvis`.

Your Linux system also has other text editors: a graphical editor for use under the XFree86 system and two standard, non-graphical text editors called `ed` and `ex`. They're both line-oriented editors—that is, you work with only one line at a time. Another editor, called `emacs`, is also supplied with most Linux distributions. `vi` and `emacs` are full-screen editors; when you use them, you see a screen's worth of information, so you can make changes or additions in context. This chapter doesn't discuss `ed` or `ex` very much because you'll find `vi` easier to use.

▶▶ See "Using `emacs`," p. 455

In this chapter, you learn the following:

- What the basic `vi` commands are
- How to create new files and modify existing files
- How to set the `vi` environment

Introducing *vi*

To understand `vi` (pronounced *vee eye*), you need to understand some of `vi`'s history within the UNIX world. And while today's systems, including Linux, have much more user-friendly and robust editors, you should learn how to use `vi` because every UNIX (and thus Linux) system has a copy of `vi` available. Sometimes `vi` is the only editor available at a crucial moment—as a result, you need to know some of its basic operations.

UNIX was developed in an environment in which the user's terminal was a teletype or some other slow, hard-copy terminal; video display monitors generally weren't used. A natural editor for that environment was a *line-oriented editor*—one that the user sees and works on one line of text at a time. Two line-oriented editors are on UNIX systems today: `ed` and `ex`.

In its early days, UNIX was made available to universities essentially free of charge. Students and faculty at several universities made many contributions to the UNIX working environment. Several notable improvements came out of the University of California at Berkeley, including a *full-screen editor*—one that lets you work with a screen of information at once rather than a single line. That full-screen editor is called `vi`, which stands for *visual*. The time was right for the transition to screen-oriented work. Users were working with video terminals rather than hard-copy devices.

Tip

You don't have to become an expert to use `vi`—simply type **man vi** at the command prompt for help.

Note

This chapter doesn't cover all of `vi`'s features—that requires more space than is available. (In fact, entire books are written just on `vi`.) Instead, you learn the commands to do the most necessary editing tasks. If you want to know about the more advanced features of `vi` and advanced text-editing operations, consult the manual pages supplied with Linux.

What Is *vi*?

Because it's part of the standard UNIX environment, `vi` has been learned and used (to one degree or another) by millions of UNIX users. You find that it starts quickly and can be used for simple and complex tasks. As you would expect, you use it to enter, modify, or delete text; search or replace text; and copy, cut, and paste blocks of text. You also see that it can be customized to match your needs. You can move the cursor to any position on-screen and move through the file you're editing. You use the same methods with any text file, regardless of its contents.

The `vi` editor isn't a word processor or desktop publishing system. There aren't any menus and virtually no help facilities. Word-processing systems usually offer screen and hard-copy formatting and printing such as representing text as **bold**, *italic*, or underlined—`vi` doesn't. Other Linux commands can perform some of these functions; for example, `lp` can print and `nroff` can format text. There are some text-processing programs, such as TeX (pronounced tek) and LaTex that can process embedded commands into such items as bold and underlined.

The `vi` editor operates in two modes. In *command mode*, your keystrokes are interpreted as commands to `vi`. Some of the commands you use allow you to save a file, exit `vi`, move the cursor to different positions in a file, and modify, rearrange, delete, substitute, and search for text. In *input* or *text-entry mode*, your keystrokes are accepted as the text of the file you're editing. When `vi` is in input or text-entry mode, the editor acts as a typewriter. In an editing session, you can freely switch between modes. You have to remember the mode you're using and know to change modes. Later in this chapter, you learn about the `showmode` option which tells you `vi`'s current mode. Some people find this uncomfortable at first; there's a learning curve you must deal with. With a little practice, however, you'll find `vi` extremely convenient for editing Linux ASCII files, especially configuration files and shell scripts.

Understanding the Editing Process

You *edit* text by either creating new text or modifying existing text. When you create new text, you place the text in a file with an ordinary Linux file name. When you modify existing text, you use the existing file name to call a copy of the file into the editing session. In either case, as you use the editor, the text is held in the system's memory in a storage area called a *buffer*. Using a buffer prevents you from directly changing the contents of a file until you decide to save the buffer. This is to your benefit if you decide you want to forget the changes you've made and start over.

As you make changes and additions to the text, these edits affect the text in the buffer—not in the file stored on disk. When you're satisfied with your edits, you issue a command to save the text. This command writes the changes to the file on the disk. Only then are the changes made permanent. You can save changes to disk as often as you like. You don't have to exit the editor when you save changes. This chapter shows you that there are several ways to exit the editor; some of those ways write the buffer to the text file on the disk.

The `vi` editor is said to be *interactive* because it interacts with you during the editing session. The editor communicates with you by displaying status messages, error messages, or sometimes nothing on-screen (in typical Linux fashion). The last line on-screen, called the *status line*, holds the messages from Linux. You also see the changes you make in the text on-screen.

You use the editor to modify, rearrange, delete, substitute, and search for text. You conduct these editing operations while using the editor in command mode. In several instances, a command is a single letter that corresponds to the first letter of an action's name. For example, `i` corresponds to the *insert* action and `r` is used when *replacing* a character.

Most commands operate on a single line or range of lines of text. The lines are numbered from 1 (the top line) to the last line in the buffer. When you add or delete lines, the line numbers adjust automatically. A line's number is its *address* in the buffer. An *address range* is simply two addresses or line numbers separated by a comma. If you want to specify the range consisting of the third through the eighth line of the buffer, you use *3,8*.

The position of the *cursor* always indicates your current location in the editing buffer. Some of the commands you issue in command mode affect the character at the cursor position. Unless you move the cursor, changes take place at that position. Naturally, `vi` has several commands for moving the cursor through the edit buffer.

You know now that `vi` is a full-screen editor. You give `vi` commands to move the cursor to different positions in a file and you see the changes you make as you make them. So `vi` has to be able to move to and modify the text on your terminal as well as on a host of other terminal types. It knows what terminal you're using and what its video capabilities are by checking the shell variable `TERM`. Linux uses the `TERM` variable to determine your terminal's capabilities, such as underlining, reverse video, screen-clearing method, function-key assignment, and color capability.

Troubleshooting

My vi *editor doesn't appear to be working correctly with my terminal or screen; I see "strange" characters.*

The `TERM` variable may not be set correctly. Another symptom of an improper terminal setup is that blocks of characters overwrite legible text. The `$TERM` expression gives the value of your current terminal setting. To check the value of `TERM`, enter **`echo $TERM`** and press <Return>. If you work at a terminal that is—or emulates—a `vt100`, this command displays the following result:

```
vt100
```

If that isn't the case, set the value of `TERM` by entering

```
TERM=vt100<Return>
export TERM<Return>
```

Your specific terminal type may be different from `vt100`; set `TERM` accordingly.

I start vi *but don't get the expected responses.*

Check to see whether your terminal is properly set up. Your terminal type isn't the same as the name of your terminal; your terminal type must match one of the terminal types contained in the directory `/usr/lib/terminfo`.

Using *vi*

To start vi, you simply type its name at the shell prompt (command line). If you know the name of the file you want to create or edit, you can issue the vi command with the file name as an argument. For example, to create the file myfile with vi, enter **vi myfile**.

When vi becomes active, the terminal screen clears and a tilde character (~) appears on the left side of every screen line, except for the first. The ~ is the *empty-buffer* line flag. The following is a shortened version of what you should see on your screen (only five lines are listed to save space):

```
_
~
~
~
~
~
```

The cursor is at the leftmost position of the first line (represented here as an underline). You'll probably see 20 to 22 of the tilde characters at the left of the screen. If that's not the case, check the value of TERM (as described in the troubleshooting box at the end of the preceding section) and perhaps talk with your system administrator.

When you see this display, you've successfully started vi; vi is in command mode, waiting for your first command.

> **Note**
>
> Unlike most word processors, vi starts in command mode. Before you start entering text, you must switch to input mode with the <a> or <i> keys, both of which are described in the next section.

Looking at *vi*'s Two Modes

The vi editor operates in two modes: command mode and input mode. In command mode, vi interprets your keystrokes as commands; there are many vi commands. You can use commands to save a file, exit vi, move the cursor to various positions in a file, or modify, rearrange, delete, substitute, or search for text. You can even pass a command to the shell. If you enter a character as a command but the character isn't a command, vi beeps. Don't worry; the beep is an audible indication for you to check what you're doing and correct any errors.

You can enter text in input mode (also called text-entry mode) by *appending* after the cursor or *inserting* before the cursor. At the beginning of the line, this doesn't make much difference. To go from command mode to input mode, press one of the following keys:

<a>	To append text after the cursor
<i>	To insert text in front of the cursor

Use input mode only for entering text. Most word processors start in input mode, but vi doesn't. When you use a word-processing program, you can type away, entering text; to issue a command, you have to use function keys or keys different than those you use when typing normal text. vi doesn't work that way: you must go into input mode by pressing <a> or <i> before you start entering text and then explicitly press <Esc> to return to command mode.

Creating Your First *vi* File

The best way to learn about vi is to use it. This section gives a step-by-step example of how to create a file using vi. In each step, you see an action to perform and then the necessary keystrokes. Don't be concerned with complete accuracy here. The example takes you through the motions and concepts of using vi to create a file, moving between command and input modes, and saving your results. If you run into difficulties, you can quit and start over by pressing <Esc>; then type **:q!** and press <Return>.

1. Start vi. Type **vi** and press <Return>. You see the screen full of flush-left tildes.
2. Go into input mode to place characters on the first line. Press the <a> key. Don't press <Return>. Now you can append characters to the first line. You should not see the character a on-screen.
3. Add lines of text to the buffer. Type

   ```
   Things to do today.<Return>
   a. Practice vi.<Return>
   b. Sort sales data and print the results.
   ```

   You can use the <Backspace> key to correct mistakes on the line you're typing. Don't worry about being precise here: this example is for practice. You learn other ways to make changes in some of the later sections of this chapter.
4. Go from input mode to command mode. Press the <Esc> key. You can press <Esc> more than once without changing modes. You hear a beep from your system if you press <Esc> when you are already in command mode.
5. Save your buffer in a file called vipract.1. Type **:w vipract.1** and press <Return>. The characters :w vipract.1 appear on the bottom line of the screen (the *status line*). The characters should not appear in the text. The :w command writes the buffer to the specified file. This command *saves* or *writes* the buffer to the file vipract.1.
6. See your action confirmed on the status line. You should see the following on the status line:

   ```
   "vipract.1" [New File] 3 lines, 78 characters
   ```

   This statement confirms that the file vipract.1 has been created, is a new file, and contains 3 lines and 78 characters. Your display may be different if you didn't type the information exactly as specified.
7. Exit vi. Type **:q** and press <Return>.

When you type **:q**, you are still in command mode and see these characters on the status line. When you press <Return>, however, `vi` terminates and you return to the logon shell prompt.

The following is a synopsis of the steps to follow:

1. Start `vi`.

   Type **vi** and press <Return>.
2. Go to input mode.

   Press <a>.
3. Enter the text.

   Type the text into the buffer.
4. Go to command mode.

   Press <Esc>.
5. Save buffer to file.

   Type **:w file-name** and press <Return>.
6. Quit `vi`.

   Type **:q** and press <Return>.

You use these steps, or variations of them, for all your editing tasks. Make sure that you can work through them before continuing.

Things to Remember about *vi*

- `vi` starts in command mode.
- To move from command mode to input mode, press <a> (to append text) or <i> (to insert text), respectively.
- You add text when you are in input mode.
- You give commands to `vi` only when you are in command mode.
- You give commands to `vi` to save a file and can quit only when you are in command mode.
- To move from input mode to command mode, press <Esc>.

Starting *vi* Using an Existing File

To edit or look at a file that already exists in your current directory, type **vi** followed by the file name and press <Return>. Try this with the file you created in the preceding section by entering

```
vi vipract.1
```

You see the following display (the number of lines shown here are fewer than you see on-screen):

```
Things to do today.
a. Practice vi.
b. Sort sales data and print the results.
~
~
~
"vipract.1" 3 lines, 78 characters
```

As before, tilde characters appear on the far left of empty lines in the buffer. Look at the status line: it contains the name of the file you're editing and the number of lines and characters.

Troubleshooting

I type a file name that I know exists, but vi *acts as if I'm creating a new file.*

No one is a perfect typist; you may have typed the name of a file that doesn't exist in your current directory. Suppose that you type **vi vipract1.** and press <Return> but there's no file named `vipract1.` in your current directory. You still start `vi`, but `vi` acts as though you were creating a new file.

I try to edit a file, but vi *displays a message about read permission denied and I see the shell prompt again.*

You've tried to edit a file you aren't permitted to read. Also, you can't edit a directory; that is, if you type **vi *directory_name***, where *directory_name* is the name of a directory, `vi` informs you that you opened a directory and doesn't let you edit it. If you try to use `vi` with a file that's an executable program in binary, as opposed to ASCII, you'll see a screen full of strange (control) characters. It won't be something you can read and edit. `vi` expects files to be stored as lines.

I open a file in vi, *but I see a message that the line is too long.*

You're trying to use `vi` on a data file that's just one long string of bytes.

I open a file in vi, *but I'm seeing some very strange characters on-screen.*

You may be using `vi` with a file produced by a word processor.

In all these cases, exit `vi` to return to your logon shell prompt by pressing <Esc> to go to command mode and then typing **:q!** and pressing <Return>. Using `:q!` ensures that you quit `vi` and make no changes to the existing file.

Exiting *vi*

You can exit or quit `vi` in several ways. Remember that you must be in command mode to quit `vi`. To change to command mode, press <Esc>. (If you are already in command mode when you press <Esc>, you hear a harmless beep from the terminal.) Table 22.1 lists the commands you can use to exit `vi`.

Table 22.1 Ways to Quit or Exit *vi*

Command	Action
`:q`	Exits after making no changes to the buffer or exits after the buffer is modified and saved to a file
`:q!`	Exits and abandons all changes to the buffer since it was last saved to a file
`:wq`	Writes buffer to the working file and then exits
`:x`	Same as `:wq`
`ZZ`	Same as `:wq`

As shown in the table, several keystrokes accomplish the same end. To demonstrate, use `vi` to edit the file `vipract.1` created earlier in this chapter. To edit the file, type **`vi vipract.1`** and press <Return>. You see a display similar to

```
Things to do today.
a. Practice vi.
b. Sort sales data and print the results.
~
~
~
"vipract.1" 3 lines, 78 characters
```

The cursor is indicated by an underline character; when you first open the file, it's under the first character of the file, the `T` of `Things`. Because you haven't made any changes to the file since you opened it, you can exit by typing **`:q`** and pressing <Return>. You see the shell prompt. You can also type **`:wq`** to exit the file; if you do so, you see the following message before the shell prompt appears:

```
"vipract.1" 3 lines, 78 characters
```

This message appears because `vi` first writes the buffer to the file `vipract.1` and then exits.

Start `vi` again with the same file (type **`vi vipract.1`** and press <Return>). You see a display similar to

```
Things to do today.
a. Practice vi.
b. Sort sales data and print the results.
~
~
~
"vipract.1" 3 lines, 78 characters
```

Although `vi` starts you off in command mode, just to be sure, press <Esc>. Now press the <Spacebar> enough times so that the cursor moves under the period following `today.` in the first line. To replace that character with an exclamation mark, press <r> (for *replace*) and type `!`. The first line now looks like

```
Things to do today!
```

Because you've changed the buffer, `vi` won't let you exit unless you save the changes or explicitly give a command to quit without saving the changes. If you try to exit `vi` by typing **:q**, `vi` displays the following message to remind you that you haven't written the file to disk since you changed it:

```
No write since last change (:quit! overrides)
```

To abandon the changes you've made to the file, quit by typing **:q!**. To save the changes, quit by typing **:wq** or any other equivalent form (**ZZ** or **:x**).

> **Note**
>
> `vi` doesn't keep backup copies of files. Once you type **:wq** and press <Return>, the original file is modified and can't be restored to its original state. You must make your own backup copies of `vi` files.

◂◂ See "Performing Backups and Restoring Files," p. 192

> **Caution**
>
> Use the `:q!` command sparingly. When you enter **:q!**, all the changes you've made to the file are lost.

Undoing a Command

In `vi`, you can "undo" your most recent action or change to the buffer—as long as you haven't saved that change to the disk file. You do this in command mode. Suppose that you've inadvertently deleted a line of text, changed something you shouldn't have, or added some text incorrectly. Press <Esc> to change to command mode and then press <u>; things are back the way they were before the command that changed the buffer. Just remember that the undo command can undo only the latest action. Also, you can't use the undo command to undo writing something to a file.

The following is an example of the undo command. Start `vi` again with the file `vipract.1`: type **vi vipract.1** and press <Return>. You see a display similar to

```
Things to do today!
a. Practice vi.
b. Sort sales data and print the results.
~
~
~
"vipract.1" 3 lines, 78 characters
```

To add the phrase `for 60 minutes` between `vi` and the period on the second line, move to the second line by pressing <Return>. The cursor now appears under the first character of the second line. Now move the cursor to the period after the `i` in `vi` by pressing the <Spacebar> until the cursor moves to that location. Insert the phrase `for 60 minutes` by pressing <i> to give the input command and then typing the characters of the phrase. Press <Esc> to return to command mode. Your screen looks like

```
Things to do today!
a. Practice vi for 60 minutes.
b. Sort sales data and print the results.
~
~
~
```

Is 60 minutes a good idea? Maybe not. To undo the change to the second line, make sure that you're in command mode (press <Esc>) and then press <u>. The second line of the file now looks like

```
a. Practice vi.
```

Then again, maybe it was a good idea to practice for 60 minutes. Press <u> again (you're already in command mode) and you see the phrase `for 60 minutes` reappear. Will you or won't you practice for that long? You decide. Use the undo command to undo the change (and undo the undo) as many times as you want. Even if you decide to leave the buffer in its original form, `vi` assumes that the buffer has changed and you must exit with **`:q!`** (abandon changes) or `:wq` (save the changes).

If you decide to save the file with the changes, save it to another file. Enter **`:w vipract.2`** and press <Return>.

You can use the <Backspace> key to correct mistakes you make while typing a single line. Unfortunately, as you backspace, you erase all the characters you go back over.

Writing Files and Saving the Buffer

You've seen how to write the buffer to a file and quit `vi`. Sometimes, however, you want to save the buffer to a file without quitting `vi`. You should save the file regularly during an editing session. If the system goes down because of a crash or a power failure, you may lose your work if you haven't saved it recently. To save the buffer, issue the `:w` command from command mode. There are some variations to the steps you follow to save a file. The form of the write command you use depends on the case—of which there are four distinct ones. The following sections describe these cases; Table 22.2 lists the variations of the write command.

Before you issue the write command, first press <Esc> to make sure that you are in command mode, if you aren't already there. If you are already in command mode, you hear a harmless beep.

Table 22.2 Commands to Save or Write a File

Command	Action
`:w`	Writes buffer to the file `vi` is editing
`:w` *file-name*	Writes buffer to the named file
`:w!` *file-name*	Forces `vi` to overwrite the existing file

Saving a New File. If you started `vi` without specifying a file name, you must provide a file name if you want to save the file to disk. The write command you issue in this case has the format

```
:w file-name
```

This command writes the buffer to the file *file-name*. If the command was successful, you see the name of the file and the number of lines and characters in the file. If you specify the name of an existing file, an appropriate message appears on the status line:

```
File exits - use "w! file-name" to overwrite.
```

This condition is described in "Overwriting an Existing File," later in this chapter.

Saving to the Current File. You may want to save the buffer to the file you're now editing. For example, if you started `vi` with an existing file, made some changes to the file, and want to save the changes to the original file, you can simply enter **`:w`**, a form of the write command.

Tip

Save the changes you're making to a file regularly. Use the `:w` command frequently, at least every 15 minutes, during an edit session. You never know when the system might go down.

This command saves the buffer to the file you're now working with (your *working file*). The status line tells you the name of the file and the number of lines and characters written to the file.

Saving as a New File. You may want to save the buffer to a new file—a file different from the one you originally started with. For example, if you started `vi` with the file `vipract.1`, made some changes to the file, and want to save the changes to a new file without losing the original `vipract.1` file, you can save the file as a new file. Type this form of the write command to save the file with a new file name:

```
:w new_file
```

This form of the write command is essentially the same as the original form described in "Saving a New File," earlier in this chapter. The buffer is written to the file named *new_file*. If the command was successful, you see the name of the file and the number of lines and characters in the file. If you specify the name of an existing file, an appropriate message appears on the status line:

```
File exists - use "w! new_file" to overwrite.
```

The following section explains this scenario.

Overwriting an Existing File. If you try to save the buffer to an existing file different from the one you started with, you must explicitly indicate to `vi` that you want to overwrite or replace the existing file. If you specify an existing file name when you try to save the buffer, `vi` displays the following message:

```
File exists - use "w! new_file" to overwrite.
```

If you really want to save the buffer over the existing file, use this form of the write command:

```
:w! existing_file
```

In this syntax, *existing_file* is the name of the file you want to replace. Be careful: once you overwrite a file, you can't automatically bring it back to its original form.

Positioning the Cursor

When you edit text, you need to position the cursor where you want to insert additional text, delete text, correct mistakes, change words, or append text to the end of existing text. The commands you enter in command mode to select the spot you want are called *cursor-positioning commands.*

The Arrow Keys. You can use the arrow keys on many, but not all, systems to position the cursor. It's easy to see whether the arrow keys work: start `vi` with an existing file and see what effects the arrow keys have. You should also be able to use the <Page Up> and <Page Down> keys on the Linux keyboard, providing you have the correct terminal indicated in your `TERMCAP` environment variable.

To create a new file called `vipract.3` that contains a list of the files and directories in the directory `usr`, enter

```
ls /usr > vipract.3
```

You can use this file to experiment with cursor-positioning commands.

Once the file is created, start `vi` with the `vipract.3` file (type **`vi vipract.3`** and press <Return>). Now try using the arrow keys and the <Page Up> and <Page Down> keys to move around the editing buffer.

Tip

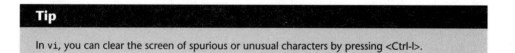

In `vi`, you can clear the screen of spurious or unusual characters by pressing <Ctrl-l>.

It may be the case that, although it appears that the cursor-positioning keys work, they're introducing strange characters into the file. To check whether the keys are entering characters instead of just moving the cursor, press <Esc> to make sure that you are in command mode and then enter **`:q`**. If `vi` allows you to quit and doesn't complain that the file was modified, everything is fine.

Other Cursor-Movement Keys. You can position the cursor in `vi` without using the arrow keys in other ways. You should become familiar with these methods in case you can't or don't want to use the arrow keys. This section also shows you some ways to position the cursor more efficiently than using the arrow keys.

When `vi` was developed, many terminals didn't have arrow keys. Other keys were and still are used to position the cursor. `vi` uses the <h>, <j>, <k>, and <l> keys to position the cursor. Why those keys? They're in a convenient position for touch-typists.

It takes a little practice to get comfortable with these keys, but some experienced `vi` users prefer these keys over the arrow keys.

The following are some other keys that move the cursor:

- Press the <Spacebar> to move the cursor to the right one position.
- Press <Return> or <+> to move to the beginning of the next line. Note that using the <j> key to go down one line preserves your position in the line.
- Press the minus sign (<–>) to move to the beginning of the previous line. Note that using the <k> key to go up one line preserves your position in the line.
- Press <0> (zero) to move to the beginning of a line.
- Press <$> (the dollar sign) to move to the end of a line.

Some `vi` commands allow you to position the cursor relative to words on a line. A *word* is defined as a sequence of characters separated from other characters by spaces or usual punctuation symbols such as

```
. ? , -
```

These commands are the following:

Command	Action
w	Moves forward one word
b	Moves to the beginning of the current word
e	Moves to the end of the current word

The following example demonstrates some of these actions. Start `vi` and open the `vipract.1` file by typing **`vi vipract.1`** and pressing <Return>. Now use any of the cursor-positioning commands just described to move the cursor, indicated by an underline character, to the `t` in the word `data` on the third line of the file. The third line looks like

```
b. Sort sales data and print the results.
```

To move to the beginning of the next word, press <w>; the cursor is positioned under the `a` of the word `and`. To move to the end of that word, press <e>; the cursor is positioned under the `d` in `and`. To move to the beginning of that word, press <b>; the cursor is positioned under the `a` in `and` again.

You can move forward several words to the beginning of another word by typing a whole number before pressing <w>. For example, to move the cursor from its current position (under the `a` of the word `and`) to the beginning of the word three words forward (under the `r` of the word `results`), press <3><w>.

Likewise, you can move backwards four words by pressing <4><b>; you can move forward to the end of the second word by pressing <2><e>.

You can also use this whole-number technique with the keys <h>, <j>, <k>, <l>, <+>, and <–>. For example, press <1><5><j> to position the cursor down 15 lines. If there aren't 15 lines left in the buffer, you hear a beep and the cursor stays where it is.

Big-Movement Keys. You can quickly position the cursor to the top, middle, or bottom of the screen. In each case, the cursor appears at the beginning of the line. The following commands allow you to position the cursor on the screen:

- Press <Shift-h> to move to the first line of the screen. This is sometimes called the home position.
- Press <Shift-m> to move to the line in the middle of the lines now displayed.
- Press <Shift-l> to move to the last line on-screen.

If you want to move through a file one screen at a time, which is more efficient than pressing <Return> or <j> 23 times, use commands that scroll through a file. Pressing <Ctrl-f> moves you forward one screen. Pressing <Ctrl-b> moves you backward one screen.

To move quickly to the last line of the file or buffer, press <Shift-g>. To move to the first line of the file, press <1><Shift-g>. In fact, to move to a specific line in the buffer, type the line number before you press <Shift-g>. To move to line 35 of the file (if there's a line 35), press <3><5><Shift-g>.

> **Note**
>
> Take a little time to practice positioning the cursor using the commands described in these last few sections. Remember that you must be in command mode for the cursor-positioning commands to work. Press <Esc> before you issue a cursor-positioning command.

Adding Text

To add text to the editing buffer, you must go from command mode to input mode. Any usual text characters you type are then added to the buffer. If you press <Return> while you are in input mode, `vi` "opens," or adds, a line to the buffer. Before you start adding text, first position the cursor at the location you want to add text. Press <a> to go to input mode and append text after the cursor position. Press <i> to go to input mode and insert text in front of the cursor position. When you're done adding text, press <Esc> to go back to command mode.

The following are some examples. The position of the cursor is represented by an underline character. For each case, a before and an after view is shown.

1. Example showing the use of <i> (the insert command) to add text.

   Before: `This report is important.`

   Press <i> to insert text in front of the word `important`, type **`very`**, press <Spacebar>, and press <Esc>.

   After: `This report is very_important.`

   Note that the cursor is positioned under the last character you added (in this case, the space).

2. Example showing the use of <a> (the append command) to add text.

   Before: `This report is important.`

   Press <a> to append text after the word `is`, press <Spacebar>, type **`very`**, and press <Esc>.

   After: `This report is very important.`

   Note again that the cursor is positioned under the last character you added (in this case, the `y` in `very`).

When you want to append text at the end of a line, you can position the cursor at the end of a line and press <a>; alternatively, you can position the cursor anywhere in the line and press <Shift-a> to position the cursor at the end of the line, put you in input mode, and allow you to append text—all with one command. Likewise, you can move to the beginning of the current line and insert text at the beginning of a line by pressing <Shift-i>.

To add a line of text below or above the current line, you use the key <o> or <Shift-o>, respectively. Each "opens" a line in the buffer and allows you to add text. In the following two examples, you add a line to some existing text.

1. Example showing the use of <o> to insert lines below the current line.

   Before:
   ```
   All jobs complete
   please call
   if you have any questions.
   ```

   The cursor is on the second line. Press <o> to add a line or lines below that line. Now type the following lines:

   ```
   Jack Tackett, Jr.<Return>
   555-1837
   ```

   Press <Esc>.

   After:
   ```
   All jobs complete
   please call
   Jack Tackett, Jr.
   555-1837
   if you have any questions.
   ```

2. Example showing the use of <Shift-o> to insert lines above the current line.

   Before:
   ```
   All jobs complete
   please call
   if you have any questions.
   ```

   The cursor is on the third line. Press <Shift-o> to add a line or lines above that line. Now type the following lines:

   ```
   Jack Tackett, Jr.<Return>
   555-1837
   ```

   Press <Esc>.

   After:
   ```
   All jobs complete
   please call
   Jack Tackett, Jr.
   555-1837
   if you have any questions.
   ```

In both cases, when you press <Esc>, the cursor was positioned under the last character you typed (the `7` in the phone number). Although you added only two lines, you could have added more lines by pressing <Return> at the end of each line. Naturally, you could have added only one line by not pressing <Return> at all.

Table 22.3 summarizes the commands for adding text. Press <Esc> to make sure that you are in command mode.

Table 22.3 Commands to Add Text

Keystroke	Action
<a>	Appends text after the cursor position
<Shift-a>	Appends text to the end of the current line
<i>	Inserts text in front of the cursor position
<Shift-i>	Inserts text at the beginning of the current line
<o>	Opens a line below the current line to add text
<Shift-o>	Opens a line above the current line to add text

Deleting Text

Making corrections or changes to a file may involve deleting text. You must be in command mode to delete characters. If you are in input mode when you type the delete-character commands, the letters of the commands appear as characters in the buffer file. If that should happen, press <Esc> to go to command mode and press <u> to "undo" the mistake.

With `vi`, you can delete a character, a word, a number of consecutive words, all the text to the end of a line, or an entire line. Because `vi` is a *visual* editor, the characters, words, or lines are removed from the screen as you delete them. Table 22.4 lists the delete commands and describes their actions. They all take effect from the current cursor position. Move the cursor to the character, word, or line you want to change and then issue the desired delete command. Practice using them to see their effect. You'll find they're helpful in making corrections to files.

Table 22.4 Commands to Delete Text

Keystroke	Action
<x>	Deletes character at the cursor position
<d><w>	Deletes from the cursor position in the current word to the beginning of the next word
<d><$>	Deletes from the cursor position to the end of the line
<Shift-d>	Same as <d><$>: deletes the remainder of the current line
<d><d>	Deletes the entire current line, regardless of cursor position in the line

All these commands can be applied to several objects—characters, words, or lines—by typing a whole number before the command. This whole-number technique was introduced earlier in this chapter in the section on positioning the cursor. Some examples are as follows:

- Press <4><x> to delete four characters
- Press <3><d><w> to delete three words
- Press <8><d><d> to delete eight lines

Tip

To have `vi` display line numbers, press <Esc> to make sure that you are in command mode, type **:se number**, and press <Return>. To turn off the line numbers, type **:se nonumber** and press <Return>.

You can also specify a range of lines to delete. You do that by pressing the colon, typing the two line numbers you want to delete (inclusive) separated by a comma, pressing <d>, and pressing <Return>. For example, to delete lines 12 through 36 (inclusive), type **`:12,36d`**; then press <Return>.

When you delete two or more lines, the status line states how many lines were deleted. Remember that you can use <u> to undo the deletion.

Changing and Replacing Text

Another often-faced editing task is changing text or replacing one text string with another (there isn't too much difference between the two operations). The *change* commands in `vi` allow you to change a word or the remainder of a line. In effect, you're replacing one word or the remainder of a line with another. You use the *replace* commands to replace or change a single character or sequence of characters. Table 22.5 summarizes the change and replace commands.

Table 22.5 The Change and Replace Commands

Keystroke	Action
<r>	Replaces a single character
<Shift-r>	Replaces a sequence of characters
<c><w>	Changes the current word, from the cursor position to the end of the word
<c><e>	Changes the current word, from the cursor position to the end of the word (same as <c><w>)
<c><b>	Changes the current word, from the beginning of the word to the character before the cursor position
<c><$>	Changes a line, from the cursor position to the end of the line
<Shift-c>	Changes a line, from the cursor position to the end of the line (same as <c><$>)
<c><c>	Changes the entire line

The changes take place relative to the position of the cursor. You must be in command mode before you can use these commands. Position the cursor at the location in the buffer file you want to correct and press <Esc> before using these commands. Because `vi` is *visual*, the changes are made to the buffer as you execute the commands. Each of these commands puts you into input mode. Except for when you use <r> to replace a single character, you must press <Esc> to finish making changes and return to command mode.

To change several words, use a whole number (representing the number of words to change) before pressing <c><w>.

Here are some examples of how to use the change and replace commands.

1. Example showing the use of <c><e> to change to the end of the word.

   Before: `The report demonstraits thw,strengths of are apporach.`

   The cursor is located at the point in the incorrectly spelled word where corrections are to begin. To change the spelling, press <c><e>, type **tes**, and press <Esc>.

   After: `The report demonstrates thw,strengths of are apporach.`

2. Example showing the use of <Shift-r> to replace a sequence of characters.

   Before: `The report demonstrates thw,strengths of are apporach.`

   The cursor is located at the point in the incorrectly spelled word where you want to start replacing characters. To correct `thw,` to `the` (`the` and a space), press <Shift-r>, type **e**, press <Spacebar>, and press <Esc>.

   After: `The report demonstrates the_strengths of are apporach.`

3. Example showing the use of <c><w> to change text, beginning with the current word and continuing for two words.

   Before: `The report demonstrates thw,strengths of are apporach.`

   The cursor is positioned under the letter of the word where you want to begin changes. To fix the last two words on the line, press <2><c><w>, type **`our approach`**, and press <Esc>.

   After: `The report demonstrates the strengths of our approach.`

Remember to press <Esc> after you make changes to the lines to go back to command mode.

Searching

Finding a word, phrase, or number in a file can be difficult if you have to read through each line yourself. Like most editors and word processors, `vi` has a command that allows you to search for a string of characters. You can search forward or backward from your current position in the buffer. You also can continue searching. `vi` starts searching from the beginning of the buffer file when it reaches the end and vice versa. The commands for searching are summarized in Table 22.6. In each case, `vi` searches for the string you specify, in the direction you specify, and positions the cursor at the beginning of the string.

Table 22.6 The Search Commands

Command	Action
/*string*	Searches forward through the buffer for *string*
?*string*	Searches backward through the buffer for *string*
<n>	Searches again in the current direction
<Shift-n>	Searches again in the opposite direction

When you type the search command, it appears on the status line. To search forward for the string `sales > 100K` in a file, first make sure that you are in command mode and then enter

```
/sales > 100K
```

This command appears on the status line. If the string is in the buffer, `vi` positions the cursor under the first `s` in the word `sales`. If the string isn't in the buffer, `vi` displays the message `Pattern not found` on the status line. To search for another occurrence of the string, press <n>; `vi` either positions the cursor under the next occurrence of the string or, if there's no "next occurrence," the cursor doesn't move.

Troubleshooting

I typed a string I know exists in the file, but vi *doesn't find it.*

The most common cause for this error is that you typed the string incorrectly. `vi` (and computers in general) doesn't do a good job of thinking; `vi` has a terrible time figuring out what you really mean when you type something else. If you're looking for the string vegi-burger but you type **vigi-burger**, `vi` can't find what you want (unless you happened to misspell vegi-burger in the buffer and it matches the search string). Check the search string carefully before you press <Return>.

I searched for a phrase that incorporates a punctuation mark, but vi *returned some odd results.*

Searching in `vi` may not give you the results you want if you're looking for characters that are "special" to `vi`. For example, if you want to find a word you know is located at the end of a sentence (for example, the string `end.`), you must "escape" the period; to `vi`, the period means "any character," not "end of sentence." If you enter **/end.** and press <Return>, `vi` locates `ending`, the word `end` followed by a space, as well as `end` followed by a period. To find only `end` followed by a period, enter **/end\\.**.

Searching in `vi` is also case-sensitive. If you're looking for the word `Tiger` in your buffer, enter **/Tiger** and not **/tiger**.

Copying, Cutting, and Pasting

When you delete or cut characters, words, lines, or a portion of a line, the deleted object is saved in what is called the *general-purpose buffer*. The name isn't too important; what is important is that you can put or *paste* the contents of that buffer anywhere in the text you're editing. You do that with the <p> or <Shift-p> command. The <p> command pastes the object to the right of or after the cursor position; the <Shift-p> command pastes the object to the left of or before the cursor.

Here are some examples of cutting and pasting text:

1. Example showing the use of <p> to paste the contents of the general-purpose buffer after the cursor.

   Before: `Carefully carry these out instructions.`

   Delete the characters `out ` (`out` and a space) by pressing <d><w>. Now move the cursor to the space after the `y` in `carry` and press <p>.

   After: `Carefully carry out_these instructions.`

2. Example showing the use of <Shift-p> to paste the contents of the general-purpose buffer in front of the cursor.

   Before: `Carefully carry these out instructions.`

   Delete the characters `these ` (`these` and a space) by pressing <d><w>. Now move the cursor to the first `i` in `instructions` and press <Shift-p>.

   After: `Carefully carry out these instructions.`

> **Tip**
>
> To change the order of two characters, position the cursor under the first character and press <x><p>. Try it to change the word `tow` to the word `two`.

The preceding examples showed you how to paste after deleting text. But you don't have to delete before you can paste. You can use an operation called *yank*, which is the same as the *copy operation* in some word processors. The forms of the yank command are similar to the forms of the delete command. The idea is that you yank, or copy, a portion of text and then paste it somewhere else using the <p> or <Shift-p> command. The following table lists some of the yank commands (notice that most of the yank commands use the lowercase letter *y*).

Keystroke	Action
<y><w>	Yanks from the cursor position in the current word to the beginning of the next word
<y><$>	Yanks from the cursor position to the end of the line
<Shift-y>	Same as <y><$>: yanks the remainder of current line
<y><y>	Yanks the entire current line

All these commands can be applied to several objects—characters, words, or lines—by typing a whole number before the command.

To copy a sequence of four lines to another portion of the text, follow these steps:

1. Position the cursor at the beginning of the first of the four lines.
2. Press <4><y><y> to yank from the cursor to the end of the line four times. The buffer (what you see on-screen) is unchanged.
3. Position the cursor elsewhere in the text.
4. Press <p> to paste the yanked lines below the line holding the cursor.

Repeating Commands

Not only does `vi` keep the text just deleted or yanked for future use, it also stores the last command you used for future use. You can repeat the last command that changed the buffer by pressing the period.

Suppose that you've completed a report but think it would be a good idea to put two lines containing this text at key points in the report:

```
*************** Please comment ******
*************** On this section ******
```

To do so, follow these steps:

1. Position the cursor in the buffer file where you want to place these lines the first time.
2. Insert the lines: press <o> to open a line and type the two lines of asterisks and text.
3. Press <Esc> to make sure that you are in command mode.
4. As often as necessary, position the cursor to another section of the report and press the period to insert these same two lines again and again.

Setting the *vi* Environment

The `vi` editor has several options you may or may not choose to use. Some of these options can be set on a system-wide basis by the system administrator. You can customize your environment with a number of options that are in effect whenever you start `vi`. Table 22.7 summarizes all the environment options you can set for `vi`. When setting environment options (as described in the next section), you can use either the abbreviation shown in the first column of the table or the full name of the option used in the second column.

Table 22.7 Environment Options for

Abbreviated Option	Function
`ai`	The `autoindent` option indents each line to the same level as the one above. Useful for writing programs. The default is `autoindent off`.
`ap`	The `autoprint` option prints the current line to the screen when the line is changed. The default is `autoprint on`.
`eb`	The `errorbells` option causes the computer to beep when you introduce a command error. The default is `errorbells off`.
`nu`	The `number` option displays line numbers when editing a file. The default is `number off`.
`redraw`	The `redraw` option keeps the screen up-to-date as changes occur. The default is `redraw on`.
`report`	The `report` option sets the size of an editing change that results in a message on the status line. For example, `report=3` triggers a message when you delete three lines but not when less than three lines are deleted. The default is `report=5`.
`sm`	The `showmatch` option shows a matching open parenthesis when the closing parenthesis is entered. This option is mainly useful for programmers writing program code. The default is `showmatch off`.
`smd`	The `showmode` option displays `INPUT`, `REPLACE`, or `CHANGE` on the

(continues)

Table 22.7 Continued

Abbreviated Option	Function
	right side of the status line when the associated command is given. The default is `showmode off`.
`warn`	The `warn` option displays a warning message when an attempt is made to exit `vi` if the buffer has been changed and not saved to the disk file. The default is `warn on`.
`wm=`*n*	The `wrapmargin` option defines the right margin. In the syntax of this command, *n* is a whole number. If *n* is greater than 0, the command forces a carriage return so that no word is *n* or less characters from the right margin. For example, `wm=5` tells `vi` to wrap the line when a character occurs within five characters of the end of the line. Turn this option off by specifying `wm=0`, which is the default.
`ws`	The `word search` (called `wrapscan` on some systems) option wraps from the `<eof>` (end-of-file) character to the `<bof>` (beginning-of-file) character during a search. Default is `word search on`.

Using *set* to See and Set Options

To see the options currently set for your system, type **`:set`** and press <Return> while in command mode in `vi`. The options currently set for this session of `vi` are displayed on the status line. The options displayed with the `set` command vary depending on the options set by default and by your particular implementation of `vi`. Here is an example of what you might see when you issue the `set` command:

```
autoprint errorbells redraw report=1 showmatch showmode term=vt100 wrap
➥margin=5
```

Note

Issuing the `set` command with no arguments results in a display of only the user-set options. You can abbreviate the `set` command as `se`. To set a number of options on the same line, use the `se` command and separate the options with a space, as in the following example:

```
:se ap eb redraw report=1 sm smd warn wm=5 ws
```

Notice that the first character is the colon character, which indicates to `vi` that a command is to be entered.

To see the list of all possible options and their settings, type **`:set all`** and press <Return>. The options and their settings from Table 22.7 are displayed.

Setting the *showmode* Option

One of the most used options is the `showmode` option. To learn about the `showmode` option, start `vi` again with the `vipract.1` file (type **`vi vipract.1`** and press <Return>).

When `vi` executes, you see the text from your first `vi` session on-screen. In your first session, you may have noticed that there was no way to determine whether you were in input mode when you entered the text for this file. You can tell `vi` to inform you when you are in input mode by using the `showmode` option.

The `vi` editor can cause real frustration when you don't know what mode you are in. The `showmode` option identifies the mode you are in. When `showmode` is set on, whenever you are in input mode, the mode displays in the lower corner of the screen.

When you set the `showmode` option, `vi` displays whatever type of input mode it's in: regular `INPUT MODE`, `APPEND MODE`, `REPLACE 1 CHAR` mode, and so on. To set `showmode` in `vi`, press <Esc> to make sure that you are in command mode and then enter **`:set showmode`**. Now go to input mode (press <i>). You should see the message `INPUT MODE` on the status line. Press <Esc> to go back to command mode. You may want to see what happens when you give the commands to replace or change text.

Setting Toggle Options

Any option that doesn't take a number argument is like a toggle switch: it can be turned on or off. For example, as you learned in the preceding section, you set the `showmode` option by entering

```
:se showmode
```

To turn the `showmode` option off you simply add **`no`** in front of the option.

```
:se noshowmode
```

Changing Options for Every *vi* Session

Setting an option during a `vi` session sets that option only for the current session. You can customize your `vi` sessions by putting the `set` commands in a file named `.exrc` in your home directory. To see whether such a file exists, type the following commands:

```
cd<Return>
vi .exrc<Return>
```

The first command takes you to your home directory. The second starts `vi` using the file `.exrc`. If the file exists, it appears on the `vi` screen. If the file doesn't exist, `vi` lets you know it's a new file. The `set` commands in the `.exrc` file start with the word `set` but no colon. For example, the following line sets the options `number` and `showmode`:

```
set number showmode
```

Note

The `.exrc` file is read when you start `vi`. If you create it while you're in `vi`, you must restart `vi` to have the settings take effect.

The options you set and the values you give to some options depend on your preferences and the type of editing you'll be doing. Experiment with some options or talk with more experienced users.

From Here...

Though this chapter could not discuss all the options or features of `vi`, you know where to start and how to use the basic features of `vi`. `Vi` is a very important editor for you to learn because it is available on every Linux/UNIX box. The editor is also quick to load and doesn't require many system resources, so you can use it when other editors may not be able to load. System administrators use vi for many quick and dirty editing task. For more information, see:

- Chapter 10, "Backing Up Data," discusses how to protect your text files from accidental erasure. This chapter will show you how to back up those important files you create with `vi`.
- Chapter 18, "Understanding the File and Directory System," shows you how to deal with files and how those files are treated under Linux. You should have a basic understanding of the file system when using vi or any other editor.
- Chapter 23, "Using the `emacs` Editor," discusses one of the other editors available with Linux. emacs provides many enhancements over vi. Emacs also provides you with an environment from which you can do many tasks you would normally do with other programs, such as read mail and read news.
- Chapter 24, "Printing," shows you how to print your text files once you've created them with `vi`.

CHAPTER 23

Using the *emacs* Editor

The name emacs stands for E ditorMACroS, which began its life as a replacement for an early text editor named teco. emacs is one of the most used, most widely ported editors available in the UNIX/Linux world today. In fact, versions of emacs are available on almost every computing platform known to the industry, from Linux to MS-Windows.

A full version of emacs is very large, taking up several megabytes of disk space. It is a full-featured editor, very powerful, and has been extended for functions beyond text editing. In some installations, you can use it to edit files, keep a calendar, work with e-mail, manage files, read USENET or network news, create outlines, use it as a calculator, and so on. In some ways, emacs is a working environment that contains a text editor. A popular version of emacs is distributed via the GNU license. This is the version Linux installed during installation. In this chapter, you learn the following:

- Basic emacs commands
- How to create new files and modify existing files using emacs
- How to perform basic word processing functions

Starting *emacs*

The emacs editor was created by GNU patriarch Richard Stallman. The source code for emacs is essentially available for free under the GNU licenses. Richard Stallman is the founder and proponent of the Free Software Foundation and the GNU (GNU is Not UNIX) project. The fact that emacs is freely available matches Stallman's philosophy that all software should be free and that computer systems should be open for use by anyone. Users are also encouraged to make modifications but must then share those changes with others.

The emacs editor doesn't have the two basic modes that vi does. That means that anything you type is put into the file buffer. To give the editor commands to save files, search for text, delete text, and so on, you must use other keys. In emacs, you use the control key and various characters (usually <Ctrl-x> and <Ctrl-c>) and the <Esc> key to accomplish the various commands. A variety of common commands are described later in this chapter.

◀◀ See "Looking at vi's Two Modes," p. 431

These emacs commands are actually shortcuts for the full text commands. For example, <Ctrl-x><Ctrl-s>, which saves the current buffer to a file, is actually a shortcut freeing the user from typing the actual emacs command—<Esc>**-x save-buffer**<Return>. As you can see, using the <Ctrl-x><Ctrl-s> key sequence is a lot simpler and easier to remember than the full emacs command. A brief list of the basic commands are presented at the end of this chapter.

emacs also provides the ability to edit multiple buffers, or files, in the same session. That is, you can edit more than one file at a time with emacs. This chapter also covers some of the buffer manipulation commands. emacs also uses buffers to hold deleted text and also to prompt for commands.

Troubleshooting

emacs *is placing the characters I type into the mini buffer and attempting to do strange actions with the characters.*

If you press the <Esc> key twice, emacs enters a lisp programming environment. Lisp is the original language that Stallman used to program emacs, and it is through lisp that programmers can extend and customize emacs. If you press <Esc><Esc>, emacs enters the eval-expression mode and expects the user to enter a lisp command; simply press <Return> to exit this mode.

To start emacs, type **emacs** and press <Return>. A blank screen with a status line at the bottom appears. This chapter doesn't discuss all the keystrokes and commands used in emacs, but you can get help by pressing <Ctrl-h><h>. After that, you can use <Ctrl-x><Ctrl-c> to exit completely or <Ctrl-x><1> to return to your editing session. Thus, unlike vi, emacs has online help facilities and even a tutorial.

Once you have asked for online help, emacs presents another buffer and is ready to provide help. If you press <t>, emacs starts an excellent tutorial. If you press <k>, emacs provides help on the next command/key you enter. Thus, if you pressed <Ctrl-h><k><Ctrl-w>, emacs presents information on deleting a marked region.

To return to your editing session, press <Ctrl-x><1>. This returns emacs to editing only one buffer.

The complete GNU emacs system is large but can be customized to match your local environment. Some smaller versions of emacs that are readily available are Freemacs, by Russell Nelson, and MicroEmacs, originally by Dave Conroy. Remember too that the Linux distribution provides for a few other emacs-like editors, namely JED, and JOVE, which are much smaller in size than the full emacs installation.

Note

This chapter doesn't cover all the features of emacs—that would take more space than is available. In fact, there are entire books written just on emacs. Instead, you learn the commands to do most necessary editing tasks. If you want to know about the more advanced features of emacs and advanced text editing operations, consult the reference manual supplied with your system. You don't have to become an emacs expert to use it. emacs also has a very detailed tutorial as part of the system. More information on running the tutorial is presented later in this chapter.

Using *emacs*

You *edit* text by either creating new text or modifying existing text. When creating new text, you place the text in a file with an ordinary Linux file name. When you modify existing text, you use the existing file name to call a copy of the file into the editing session. In either case, as you use the editor, the text is held in the system's memory in a storage area called a *buffer*.

◀◀ See "Understanding the Editing Process," p. 429

Using a buffer prevents you from directly changing the contents of a file until you decide to save the buffer. This is to your benefit if you decide you want to forget the changes you've made and start over.

emacs allows you to edit multiple buffers at once. This allows you to cut and paste text from one buffer to another, compare text from different files, or merge one file into another file. emacs even uses a special buffer to accept commands and report information to the user. This buffer is referred to as the *mini buffer* and appears at the bottom of the screen.

emacs also allows you to display the contents of various buffers in their own windows; thus, you can see several files at once, even if you are not using a graphical user interface.

Looking Over the *emacs* Screen

Figure 23.1 displays a typical emacs screen as seen by a user. The top portion displays the contents of various buffers, sometimes in multiple windows. Then a mode line is displayed. This line, usually displayed in reverse video, provides the user with information about the buffer, such as the buffer's name, the major and minor mode, and the amount of text displayed in the buffer. Underneath the mode line is the mini buffer. This is a one line buffer where you enter `emacs` commands, and `emacs` reports the outcome of various commands.

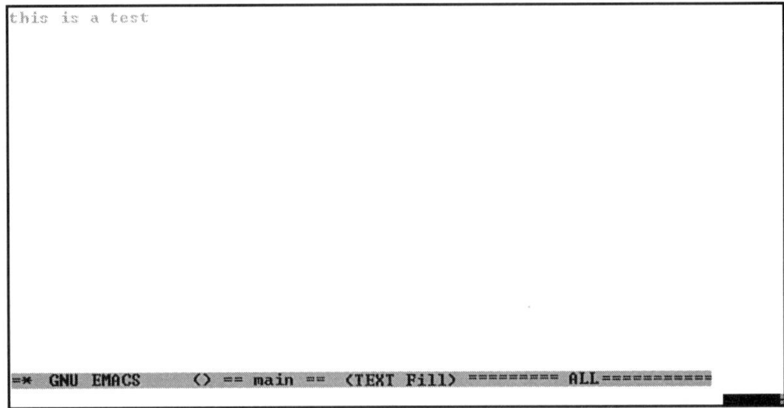

Fig. 23.1

A typical `emacs` *screen.*

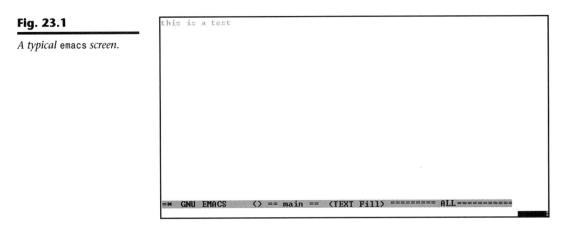

The current position in the buffer is shown by a cursor. `emacs` refers to the cursor as the *point*, especially in the online help system, so it is important to remember this term for the cursor.

Creating Your First *emacs* File

The following instructions allow you to edit your first `emacs` file. If you run into difficulties, you can quit and start over by pressing <Ctrl-x><Ctrl-c>. Notice the mini buffer at the bottom of the screen; your keystrokes are appearing there because you are typing commands to the `emacs` editor.

1. Start `emacs`. Type **`emacs`** and press <Return>. You see the screen shown in Figure 23.1.
2. Add lines of text to the buffer. Type

   ```
   Things to do today.<Return>
   a. Practice emacs.<Return>
   b. Sort sales data and print the results.
   ```

   You can use the <Backspace> key to correct mistakes on the line you are typing. Don't worry about being precise here: this example is for practice. You learn other ways to make changes in some of the later sections of this chapter.
3. Save your buffer in a file called `emacs-pract.1`. Press <Ctrl-x><Ctrl-s>. Notice at the bottom of the screen `emacs-pract.1` appears. Press <Return>. This command *saves* or *writes* the buffer to the file `emacs-pract.1` because it was the specified

file. Note the number of characters in the file name. Unlike MS-DOS and Windows, Linux allows you to enter more than eight characters and a three character extension for a file name.

4. See your action confirmed on the status line. You should see the following on the status line:

```
Wrote /root/emacs-pract.1
```

This statement confirms that the file `emacs-pract.1` has been created, is a new file, contains three lines and 78 characters. Your display may be different if you didn't type the information exactly as specified.

5. Exit `emacs`. Press <Ctrl-x><Ctrl-c> and then <Return>. `emacs` terminates and you return to the logon shell prompt.

The following is a synopsis of the steps you followed:

1. Start `emacs`.

   Type **`emacs`** and press <Return>.

2. Enter the text.

   Type the text into the buffer.

3. Save buffer to file.

   Press <Ctrl-x><Ctrl-s> and answer **y** to the prompt asking to save the file; then press <Return>.

4. Name the file.

   Type the file name and press <Return>.

5. Quit `emacs`.

   Press <Ctrl-x><Ctrl-c>.

You use these steps, or variations of them, for all your editing tasks. Be sure that you can work through them before continuing.

Starting *emacs* Using an Existing File

To edit or look at a file that already exists in your current directory, type **`emacs`** followed by the file name and press <Return>. Try this with the file you created in the preceding section by entering

```
emacs emacs-pract.1<Return>
```

You see the following:

```
Things to do today.
a. Practice emacs.
b. Sort sales data and print the results.
```

Look at the mini buffer: it contains the name of the file you are editing.

Troubleshooting

I typed a file name I know exists, but emacs *acts as if I'm creating a new file.*

You may have typed the name of a file incorrectly or one that doesn't exist in your current directory. Suppose that you type **emacs pract1.** and press <Return>, but there is no file named pract1. in your current directory. You still start emacs, but emacs acts as though you were creating a new file.

I try to edit a file, but emacs *displays a message about read permission denied. Also, the shell prompt appears.*

You have tried to edit a file you are not permitted to read. In addition, you can't edit a directory; that is, if you type **emacs *directory_name***, where *directory_name* is the name of a directory, emacs informs you that you opened a directory and does not let you edit it. If you try to use emacs with a file that is an executable program in binary, as opposed to ASCII, you'll see a screen full of strange (control) characters. It won't be something you can read and edit. emacs expects files to be stored as plain text.

I opened a file in emacs, *but a message about the line being too long appeared.*

You are trying to use emacs on a data file that is just one long string of bytes.

I tried to save a file with the <Ctrl-x><Ctrl-s> keys, but the terminal then hangs, not responding to the keyboard.

Your terminal is probably responding to the flow control characters <Ctrl-s> and <Ctrl-q>. Press <Ctrl-q> to restart your session.

I opened a file in emacs, *but there are some strange characters on-screen.*

You may be using emacs with a file produced by a word processor.

In all these cases, exit emacs to return to your logon shell prompt by pressing <Ctrl-x><Ctrl-c> and then answer **n** to the prompt asking to save the file. Using those keystrokes ensures that you quit emacs and make no changes to the existing file.

Exiting *emacs*

As already stated, to exit emacs press <Ctrl-x><Ctrl-c>. If you have not saved any changes to the file, emacs prompts you to save the buffer. If you type **y**, emacs saves the file and returns you to the Linux shell. If you have not provided a file name, emacs prompts for a file name and then exits. If you respond **n** to the request to save the buffer, emacs prompts again to be sure you want to exit without saving the buffer. This time you must completely type out the response to the prompt, either **yes** or **no**. If you answer yes, emacs returns you to Linux without saving any of the modifications you made to the buffer. Also, if you have multiple buffers open, emacs prompts you for each buffer.

Note

The default installation of `emacs` performs periodic saves while you are editing a buffer. `emacs` does not, per se, make backup copies of files. Once you press <Ctrl-x><Ctrl-s>, the original file is modified and can't be restored to its original state. Thus, you should make your own backup copies of `emacs` files before starting the editing session to make sure the automatic updates do not inadvertently overwrite an important file to the point where you cannot recover a previous version of the file.

Caution

Answer **n** to the exit-without-saving prompt sparingly. When you answer **n**, all the changes you have made to the file since it was last saved are lost.

Perhaps you are not quite finished with your `emacs` session but do need to perform other activities with Linux. In that case, you have several options, you can suspend `emacs` and return to the Linux shell, you can switch to another virtual terminal, or you can issue a shell command from within `emacs`.

Suspending *emacs*. You can suspend `emacs`, in fact almost any Linux application, by pressing <Ctrl-z>. This keystroke combination places the current application into the background and provides you with another shell prompt. To reactivate `emacs` depends on which shell you are executing. You can type the command **`fg`**, which means to bring the background task to the foreground. If the shell you are using does not understand this command, type **`exit`**, which reactivates your `emacs` session with all your files and buffers still intact.

Switching between *emacs* and Other Virtual Terminals. Linux provides the user with six virtual terminals; hence, you have six different sessions. While in `emacs` you can press <Alt-F*x*>, where F*x* is one of the keyboard function keys F1 through F6, to activate another terminal. If you have not already logged on to a session on that terminal, then you must do so, just like when first booting Linux. You then have a completely active Linux session. To switch back to `emacs`, simply repeat the process of pressing <Alt-F*x*>. If you forget which session is running `emacs`, you can simply cycle through each of the virtual terminals. You can also use the `ps` command to display all active processes, as shown below. The output of the `ps -guax` command indicates which terminal each process is currently executing.

◄◄ See "Managing Users," p. 99

```
USER  PID %CPU %MEM SIZE  RSS TTY STAT START   TIME COMMAND
root    1  0.5  3.1   44  208  ?  S    20:48   0:00 init
root    6  0.0  1.8   24  124  ?  S    20:48   0:00 bdflush (daemon)
root    7  0.0  1.9   24  128  ?  S    20:48   0:00 update (bdflush)
root   23  0.0  2.9   56  200  ?  S    20:48   0:00 /usr/sbin/crond -l10
root   36  0.6  3.5   65  240  ?  S    20:48   0:00 /usr/sbin/syslogd
root   38  0.1  2.9   36  200  ?  S    20:48   0:00 /usr/sbin/klogd
root   40  0.3  3.2   68  216  ?  S    20:48   0:00 /usr/sbin/inetd
root   42  0.1  3.0   64  204  ?  S    20:48   0:00 /usr/sbin/lpd
root   47  0.1  6.0  259  404  ?  S    20:48   0:00 sendmail:accepting c
root   51  0.1  2.0   32  140  ?  S    20:48   0:00 selection -t ms
root   52  1.5  7.2  376  484 v01 S    20:48   0:01 -bash
root   53  0.3  3.4   88  232 v02 S    20:48   0:00 /sbin/getty tty2 3840
root   54  0.3  3.4   88  232 v03 S    20:48   0:00 /sbin/getty tty3 3840
root   55  0.2  3.4   88  232 v04 S    20:48   0:00 /sbin/getty tty4 3840
root   56  0.3  3.4   88  232 v05 S    20:48   0:00 /sbin/getty tty5 3840
root   57  0.3  3.4   88  232 v06 S    20:48   0:00 /sbin/getty tty6 3840
root   67  0.0  3.5   80  240 v01 R    20:49   0:00 ps -guax
```

You can then use that value, in the range of v1 to v6, to pick the correct virtual terminal. For example, if the ps command indicates that emacs is currently operating on tty v1 and tty v2, pressing <Alt-F1> or <Alt-F2> brings you back to the appropriate emacs session.

Accessing Linux Commands from within *emacs*. Sometimes all you need to do is a quick check to see if a file exists or some other quick Linux command—you don't need a full shell session to perform the action. In that case, emacs provides a mechanism to execute shell commands from within emacs. To execute a shell within emacs, press <Ctrl-u> <Esc><!>. You are prompted to enter a shell command. Enter the command and press <Return>. emacs passes the command to the Linux shell, which executes the command. If you do not press <Ctrl-u>, emacs places the output into a buffer/window called **Shell Command Output**. You learn more about windows later in this chapter, but basically windows provide you the ability to see multiple buffers at once. emacs provides various commands to move around between windows and to delete windows (without deleting their corresponding buffers). To delete the output window, press <Ctrl-x><1>.

Undoing a Command

In emacs, you can "undo" your most recent action or change to the buffer as long as you haven't saved that change to the disk file. You do this by pressing <Ctrl-x><u>. By repeatedly using this command, you can undo the changes made to the buffer. Unfortunately, you can't use the undo command to undo writing something to a file.

If you want to re-read a file from disk, thus overwriting your current changes, you can use the <Ctrl-x><Ctrl-r> keystroke. This command reads the specified file into the current buffer erasing its previous contents. Thus, if you specify the same file name, emacs replaces the current buffer with the contents of the file on disk. This is a quick way to undo many changes without exiting and restarting emacs. But what if the emacs has auto-saved the file, or you have saved the file, with unwanted changes?

Well, emacs creates a backup file the first time you save a file. The name of this backup file is the same as the file name with a ~ character appended to the end of the name. Thus, if your file was named emacs-prtc.1, the backup file name is emacs-prtc.1~. If you accidentally overwrite your current file with unwanted changes, you may be able to use the backup file to start over.

Writing Files and Saving the Buffer

You have seen how to write the buffer to a file and quit emacs. Sometimes, however, you want to save the buffer to a file without quitting emacs. You should save the file regularly during an editing session. If the system goes down because of a crash or a power failure, you may lose your work if you haven't saved it recently. To save the buffer, press <Ctrl-x><Ctrl-s>.

If you started emacs without specifying a file name, you must provide a file name if you want to save the file to disk. In this case, you press <Ctrl-x><Ctrl-s>.

Saving as a New File. You may want to save the buffer to a new file—a file different from the one you originally started with. For example, if you started emacs with the file emacs-pract.1, made some changes to the file, and want to save the changes to a new file without losing the original emacs-pract.1 file, you can save the file as a new file. To save the file with a new file name, press <Ctrl-x><Ctrl-w>. emacs prompts you for the file name. The buffer is then written to the named file. If the command was successful, you see the name of the file and the number of lines and characters in the file. If you specify the name of an existing file, a message appears in the mini buffer asking if you want to overwrite the file. Simply answer the question appropriately.

Using Files. If you wish to load another file to edit, emacs can either let you load a new file into the current buffer or let you load a file into a new buffer, leaving the current buffer alone. emacs also lets you insert the contents of a file into the current buffer.

To replace the current buffer with the contents of another file, press <Ctrl-x><Ctrl-v>. emacs prompts for a file name in the mini buffer. If you do not remember the entire file name or if the name is rather long, you can use the completion option of emacs. When emacs prompts for a file name you can enter just the first few letters in the name and then press the <Tab> key. emacs then expands the file name to match any files. If more than one file matches, emacs displays a window containing all the files that match the characters you entered and allows you to choose one.

To retrieve a file into a new buffer, press <Ctrl-x><Ctrl-f>. Enter the file name at the mini buffer prompt. emacs normally names the buffer after the file name, but you can change the name of the buffer by pressing <Esc><x>, entering the new name for the buffer, and pressing <Return>. emacs prompts for the new name. Enter the new buffer name and press <Return>. The mode line displays the new name.

Press <Ctrl-x><i> to insert a file into the current buffer. Simply move the cursor to the desired position in the file and press <Ctrl-x><i>.

Positioning the Cursor

When you edit text, you need to position the cursor where you want to insert additional text, delete text, correct mistakes, change words, or append text to the end of existing text. The commands you enter are called *cursor-positioning commands.*

The Arrow Keys. You can use the arrow keys on many, but not all, systems to position the cursor. It's easy to see whether the arrow keys work: start `emacs` with an existing file and see what effects the arrow keys have. You may also be able to use the <Page Up> and <Page Down> keys.

Enter the following command to create a new file called `emacs-pract.3` that contains a list of the files and directories in the directory `/usr`. You can use this file to experiment with cursor-positioning commands.

```
ls /usr > emacs-pract.3
```

If you create the file with the <Ctrl-u><Esc><!> command sequence, you see the message:

```
(Shell command completed with no output)
```

Don't worry about the message because it doesn't mean there is a problem since standard output was redirected to the file and, thus, `emacs` had no output to capture to a buffer. Once the file is created, start `emacs` with the `emacs-pract.3` file (type **`emacs emacs-pract.3`** and press <Return>). Now try using the arrow keys and the <Page Up> and <Page Down> keys (if they are on your keyboard) to move around the editing buffer. If the keys work, you may want to use those keys for cursor positioning.

> **Tip**
>
> In `emacs`, you can clear the screen of spurious or unusual characters by pressing <Ctrl-l>.

It may be the case that, although it appears that the cursor-positioning keys work, they are introducing strange characters into the file. These characters are the codes used by the computer to represent the various keys instead of the characters themselves. If you see such characters, you have to use the various keyboard commands to position the cursor rather than the keyboard keys.

Other Cursor-Movement Keys. There are other ways to position the cursor in `emacs` without using the arrow keys. You should become familiar with these methods in case you can't or don't want to use the arrow keys. This section also shows you some ways to position the cursor more efficiently than using the arrow keys.

When `emacs` was developed in 1975, many terminals did not have arrow keys. Other keys were and still are used to position the cursor. It takes a little practice to get comfortable with these keys, but some experienced `emacs` users prefer these keys over the arrow keys.

Here are some other keys that move the cursor:

- Press <Ctrl-f> to move the cursor to the right one position.
- Press <Ctrl-b> to move the cursor to the left one position.
- Press <Ctrl-n> to move to the beginning of the next line, preserving your position in the line.
- Press <Ctrl-p> to move to the previous line, preserving your position in the line.
- Press <Ctrl-a> to move to the beginning of a line.
- Press <Ctrl-e> to move to the end of a line.

Some `emacs` commands allow you to position the cursor relative to words on a line. A *word* is defined as a sequence of characters separated from other characters by spaces or usual punctuation symbols, such as periods, question marks, commas, and hyphens. These commands are shown in the following table:

Command	Action
<Esc><f>	Moves forward one word
<Esc><b>	Moves backward one word

The following example demonstrates some of these actions. Start `emacs` and open the `emacs-pract.1` file by typing **`emacs emacs-pract.1`** and pressing <Return>. Now use any of the cursor-positioning commands just described to move the cursor, indicated by an underline character, to the `t` in the word `data` on the third line of the file. The third line looks like

```
b. Sort sales data and print the results.
```

To move to the beginning of the next word, press <Esc><f>; the cursor is positioned under the `a` of the word `and` in the previous sentence. Press <Esc><f> to move to the `p` in `print`. To move to the beginning of the word `and`, press <Esc><b>; the cursor is positioned under the `a` in `and` again.

Big-Movement Keys. If you want to move through a file a screen at a time, which is more efficient than pressing <Page Down>, use commands that scroll through a file. The command <Ctrl-x><]> moves you forward one page. The following table illustrates the scrolling keystrokes:

Keystroke	Action
<Ctrl-v>	Moves forward one screen
<Esc><v>	Moves backward one screen

To move quickly to the last line of the file or buffer, press <Esc><Shift-.>. To move to the first line of the file, press <Esc><Shift-,>. In fact, to move to a specific line in the buffer, type the command **goto-line *n***, where *n* is the line number you wish to move to. To move to line 35 of the file (if there is a line 35), press <Esc>, enter **goto-line 35**, and press <Return>.

You can repeat any command you want by pressing <Esc-*n*>, where *n* is the number of times you want to repeat the command, and then entering the command you want to repeat.

> **Note**
>
> Take a little time to practice positioning the cursor using the commands described in these last few sections. Remember that you must be in command mode for the cursor-positioning commands to work.

Adding Text

To add text to the editing buffer, you must position the cursor at the position you wish to start entering text. Any usual text characters you type are then added to the buffer. If you press <Return>, `emacs` "opens," or adds, a line to the buffer. Before you start adding text, first position the cursor at the location you want to add text. You then simply type in the text.

To add a line of text below or above the current line, you use the command <Ctrl-o>. This "opens" a line in the buffer and allows you to add text. In the following two examples, you add a line to some existing text. For each case, a before and an after view is shown.

1. Here's an example showing the use of <Ctrl-o> to insert lines below the current line.

   Before:
   ```
   All jobs complete
   please call
   if you have any questions.
   ```

2. The cursor is on the second line. Press <Ctrl-o> to add a line or lines below that line. Type

   ```
   Lee Nashua<Return>
   555-1837
   ```

   After:
   ```
   All jobs complete
   please call
   Lee Nashua
   555-1837
   if you have any questions.
   ```

Although you added only two lines, you could have added more lines by pressing <Return> at the end of each line. Naturally, you could have added only one line by not pressing <Return> at all.

Deleting Text

Making corrections or modifications to a file may involve deleting text. With `emacs`, you can delete a character, a word, a number of consecutive words, all the text to the end of a line, or an entire line. Because `emacs` is a *visual* editor like `vi`, the characters, words, or lines are removed from the screen as you delete them. Table 23.1 lists the delete commands and describes their actions. They all take effect from the current cursor position. Move the cursor to the character, word, or line you want to change and then issue the desired delete command. Practice using them to see their effect. You will find they are helpful in making corrections to files.

Table 23.1 Commands to Delete Text

Keystroke	Action
<Ctrl-d>	Deletes character at the cursor position
<Esc><d>	Deletes the word the cursor is on
<Ctrl-k>	Deletes from the cursor position to the end of the line
<Esc><k>	Deletes the sentence the cursor is on
<Ctrl-w>	Deletes a marked region

If you use the <Ctrl-k> command, the information just doesn't disappear into the bit bucket. The characters deleted are added to a kill buffer, which you can yank back at any time with the <Ctrl-y> command.

Searching and Replacing Text

Finding a word, a phrase, or a number in a file can be difficult if you have to read through each line yourself. Like most editors and word processors, `emacs` has a command that allows you to search for a string of characters and, if you want, replace those characters with others. You can search forward or backward from your current position in the buffer. You also can continue searching. `emacs` starts searching from the beginning of the buffer file when it reaches the end and vice versa. The commands for searching are summarized in Table 23.2. In each case, `emacs` searches for the string you specify, in the direction you specify, and positions the cursor at the beginning of the string.

Table 23.2 The Search and Replace Commands

Command	Action
<Ctrl-s>	Search forward from current position
<Ctrl-r>	Reverse search from current position
<Ctrl-x><s>	Repeat search forward
<Ctrl-x><r>	Repeat search in reverse

(continues)

Table 23.2 Continued

Command	Action	
<Esc><r>	Replace all instances of first typed in string in mini buffer with second typed in string, ending each string with <Esc>	
<Esc><Ctrl-r *query*>	Before performing the replacement. Answer in the mini-buffer with:	
	<Ctrl-g>	Cancel operation
	<!>	Replace the rest
	<?>	Get a list of options
	<.>	Replace and exit to where command was initiated
	<,>	Replace the rest without asking
	<y>	Replace and continue with replace,operation
	<Spacebar>	Same as <y>
	<n>	Do not replace but continue with operation

Searching. When you type the search command, it appears in the mini buffer. To search forward for the string `sales > 100K` in a file,

```
<Ctrl-s>sales > 100K<Return>
```

This command starts an incremental search through the buffer. Notice as you type in the characters for the search string that `emacs` positions the cursor on the sequence of characters. If `emacs` cannot find the text, the `search failed` message is displayed. If the string is in the buffer, `emacs` positions the cursor under the first `s` in the word `sales`. Once you have found the first occurrence of the string, you must press the <Esc> key to stop the search; otherwise, `emacs` continues looking for a match as you enter other text. `emacs` refers to these types of searches as incremental searches—`emacs` searches as you enter the search string.

`emacs` can also perform non-incremental searches if you preface the search string with the <Esc> key and press the <Return> key at the end, as shown here:

```
<Ctrl-s><Esc>sales > 100K<Return>
```

If you are searching a large file and realize you have entered the wrong search string, `emacs` searches the entire file. To stop the search, you press <Ctrl-g>.

Troubleshooting

I typed a string I know exists in the file, but emacs *can't find it.*

The most common cause for this error is that you typed the string incorrectly. `emacs` (and computers in general) don't do a good job of thinking; `emacs` has a terrible time figuring out what you really mean when you type something else. If you're looking for the string *vegi-burger* but you type **`vigi-burger`**, `emacs` can't find what you want (unless you happened to misspell *vegi-burger* in the buffer and it matches the search string). Check the search string carefully before you press <Return>.

Replacing. While searching for text can help you locate a particular word or section of text, many times you want to replace the found text. An example is if you find a spelling error and want to correct the entire buffer rather than one mistake at a time. For example, to replace every occurrence of the word *misstake* with *mistake*, press <Esc><r>. The mini buffer prompts for the string to search for—type **`misstake`** and press <Return>. `emacs` then prompts for the replacement string, type **`mistake`** and press <Return>. `emacs` proceeds through the file looking for the string `misstake` and replacing it with `mistake`. `emacs` also tries to match capitalization as best as possible. Thus, if `misstake` appeared as `Misstake`, `emacs` replaces it with `Mistake`.

Maybe you do not want to replace every occurrence of a search string with the replacement string, in which case you can instruct `emacs` to query before replacing the string. To have `emacs` replace and query, press <Esc><Ctrl-r>.

For example, if you want to selectively replace the name of your operating system, Linux, with its ancestor UNIX, press <Esc><Ctrl-r>. `emacs` then responds in the mini buffer with `Query replace:`. Now enter the search string **`Linux`** and press <Return>. The `Query replace Linux with:` appears. Enter the replacement string **`UNIX`** and press <Return>. `emacs` begins the search and states, `Query replacing Linux with UNIX`. If you wish to terminate the search and replace operation, press <Ctrl-g>.

Once `emacs` finds an occurrence of `Linux`, it stops and prompts for an action. The possible responses are the following:

Keystroke	Action
<Ctrl-g>	Cancels operation
<!>	Replaces the rest
<?>	Gets a list of options
<.>	Replaces and exits to where the command was initiated
<,>	Replaces the rest without asking
<y>	Replaces and continues with replace operation
<Spacebar>	Same as <y>
<n>	Does not replace but continues with replace operation

Changing Text. Another editing task you often are faced with is changing text or replacing one text string with another (there isn't too much difference between the two operations). You use the replace commands to replace a single character or sequence of characters. You can also use the change commands to fix one of the most common typing mistakes made: transposing two letters. Table 23.3 summarizes the change commands.

Table 23.3 The Change Commands

Keystroke	Action
<Ctrl-t>	Transposes two adjacent letters
<Esc><t>	Transposes two words
<Ctrl-x><Ctrl-t>	Transposes two lines
<Esc><c>	Properly capitalizes the word
<Esc><l>	Lowercases the entire word
<Esc><u>	Uppercases the entire word

The changes take place relative to the position of the cursor. Position the cursor at the location in the buffer file you want to correct before using these commands.

Copying, Cutting, and Pasting

When you delete or cut characters, words, lines, or a portion of a line, the deleted object is saved in what is called the *kill buffer*. The name isn't too important; what is important is that you can put or *paste* the contents of that buffer anywhere in the text you're editing. You do that with <Ctrl-y>. The <Ctrl-y>, or yank command, pastes the object to the right of or after the cursor position.

Here is an example of cutting and pasting text:

1. Example showing the use of <Ctrl-y> to paste the contents of the kill buffer after the cursor.

   Before: `Carefully carry these out instructions.`

2. Delete the characters `out ` (`out` and a space) by pressing <Esc-d>. Now move the cursor to the space after the `y` in `carry` and press <Ctrl-y>.

   After: `Carefully carry out these instructions.`

To copy a sequence of four lines to another portion of the text, you must first mark the four lines of text, delete them to the kill buffer, and then yank them back at the appropriate places. Follow these steps:

1. Position the cursor at the beginning of the first of the four lines.
2. Press <Ctrl-Spacebar> to set the mark.
3. Move the cursor to the end of the fourth line. This creates what `emacs` refers to as a *region*.
4. Delete the text by pressing <Ctrl-w>.
5. Because you want to copy the lines, you must replace the deleted text. Do this with the <Ctrl-y> command.
6. Move the cursor to the point in the buffer you want to copy the text.
7. Press <Ctrl-y> to paste the yanked lines below the line holding the cursor.

Troubleshooting

I deleted the marked region, but the region I marked wasn't deleted.

Unfortunately, GNU `emacs` supplied with Linux does not display any type of marker to indicate the mark, so it is very easy to forget to set the mark or to place it in an inappropriate position. To check the position of the mark use the command <Ctrl-x><Ctrl-x>. This command swaps the position of the cursor and the mark. If the cursor moves to the position you thought the mark was located, you know the mark is properly set. To move the cursor back to the proper position, simply issue the <Ctrl-x><Ctrl-x> to swap them back.

Basic Command Summary

Table 23.4 gives a brief listing of the major functions provided by `emacs`. <Esc><c> means to press and release the meta key, usually the <Esc> key on a PC keyboard, although on some keyboards you can use the <Alt> key and then press the following <c> key. <Ctrl-c> means to press the <Ctrl> key and the <c> key at the same time. Remember, pressing <Ctrl-g> at any time stops the currently executing command.

Table 23.4 Basic Commands

Key Sequence	Descriptions
Saving to Disk	
<Ctrl-x><Ctrl-s>	Saves current buffer to disk
<Ctrl-x><Ctrl-w>	Writes current buffer to disk—ask for new file name
<Ctrl-x><n>	Changes file name of current buffer
<Esc><z>	Writes all changed buffers to disk and exit `emacs`
Reading from Disk	
<Ctrl-x><Ctrl-f>	Finds file, reads into a new buffer created from file name
<Ctrl-x><Ctrl-r>	Reads file into current buffer, erasing previous contents
<Ctrl-x><Ctrl-i>	Inserts file into the current buffer at the cursor's location
Moving the Cursor	
<Ctrl-f>	Moves forward one character
<Ctrl-b>	Moves backward one character
<Ctrl-a>	Moves to front of current line
<Ctrl-e>	Moves to end of current line
<Ctrl-n>	Moves to next line

(continues)

Table 23.4 Continued

Key Sequence	Descriptions
<Ctrl-p>	Moves to previous line
<Esc><f>	Moves forward a word
<Esc><b>	Moves backward a word
<Esc><a>	Goto a line
<Esc><Shift-.>	Moves to beginning of buffer
<Esc><Shift-,>	Moves to end of buffer
Deleting and Inserting	
<Ctrl-d>	Deletes next character
<Ctrl-c>	Inserts a space
<Esc><d>	Deletes next word
<Ctrl-k>	Deletes to end of current line
<Return>	Inserts a new line
<Ctrl-j>	Inserts a new line and indent
<Ctrl-o>	Opens a new line
<Ctrl-w>	Deletes region between mark and cursor
<Esc><w>	Copies region to kill buffer
<Ctrl-x><Ctrl-o>	Deletes lines around cursor
Searching and Replacing	
<Ctrl-s>	Searches forward from current position
<Ctrl-r>	Reverses search from current position
<Ctrl-x><s>	Repeats search forward
<Ctrl-x><r>	Repeats search in reverse
<Esc><r>	Replaces all instances of first typed in string in mini buffer with second typed in string, ending each string with <Esc>
<Esc><Ctrl-r>	Queries before performing the replacement. Answer in the mini buffer with:
Answers to find/replace query	
<Ctrl-g>	Cancels operation
<!>	Replaces the rest
<?>	Gets a list of options
<.>	Exits to where command was initiated
<y>	Replaces and continue with replace operation
<n>	Does not replace but continues with replace operation

Key Sequence	Descriptions
Marked Text	
<Ctrl><Spacebar>	Sets MARK at current cursor position
<Ctrl-x><Ctrl-x>	Exchanges MARK and cursor
<Ctrl-w>	Deletes the marked region
<Esc-w>	Copies marked region to kill buffer
<Ctrl-y>	Inserts the kill buffer at the current cursor position
Buffers	
<Ctrl-x><b>	Switches to another buffer
<Ctrl-x><x>	Switches to next buffer in buffer list
<Esc><Ctrl-n>	Changes name of current buffer
<Ctrl-x><k>	Deletes a non-displayed buffer

Customizing *emacs*

You can customize your version of `emacs` by placing custom functions within a file called `.emacs`. This file must reside in your home directory. This file contains functions written in `emacs` lisp and which personalizes `emacs` to your liking. An example function is as follows:

```
(keyboard-translate ?\C-h ?\C-?)
```

This function is helpful if your terminal translates the backspace key into the <Ctrl-h> characters. These characters are, by default, the sequence used to summon help from within `emacs`. By specifying a new function and binding this function to a key, you can customize how `emacs` responds to these key sequences.

In the above example, `?\C-h` represents the <Ctrl-h> key-press. The `?\C-?` represents the Delete key. On nearly all ASCII keyboards, both of these represent the same ASCII value, namely 8. Once you have entered this function line into your `.emacs` file and saved it, the next time you invoke `emacs` you will be able to delete characters using the backspace key. Of course you will no longer have access to help from the keyboard. To alleviate this problem, you can bind the help function to a new key sequence, just as you did with the delete function. Simply place the following function into your `.emacs` file, specifying your chosen key for *<key>*:

```
(keyboard-translate ?\C-<key> ?\C-h)
```

From Here...

You can find more information on another editor and about Linux's files system in the following chapters:

- Chapter 10, "Backing Up Data," shows you how to properly back up your text files from accidental erasure. This chapter will show you how to back up those important files you create with `vi`.
- Chapter 18, "Understanding the File and Directory System," discusses the basics of files and directories. You should have a basic understanding of the file system when using `vi` or any other editor. While the editor creates and modifies files, it is up to you to name them and place them in the appropriate directories.
- Chapter 22, "Using the `vi` Editor," discusses the basics of using this popular editor. `Vi` is an important editor since it is found on all Linux/UNIX systems. If you know how to use vi then you should be able to edit a file on any system. System administrators also use vi for many sys admin tasks.
- Chapter 24, "Printing," provides information on printing your text files under Linux. Printing files under Linux can be tricky and this chapter helps you prepare your system for printing.

CHAPTER 24

Printing

Although everyone thought the computer revolution would bring the paperless office, it hasn't. More paper is used today than was used 20 years ago. When the UNIX operating system was in its infancy, Bell Labs used it to produce technical documentation. As a result, UNIX, and thus Linux, has a great many utilities designed around printing (or at least formatting data to be printed). This chapter concentrates on the mechanics of actually printing a file.

Because printers are relatively slow, they are called *spooled devices*. When you print a file in Linux, the file doesn't go directly to a printer; instead, it goes to a *queue* to wait its turn to be printed. If your file is the first in the queue, it prints almost immediately.

Because Linux inherits a great deal of UNIX functionality, Linux supports many types of printers, which are shown in Table 24.1.

Table 24.1 Supported Printers under Linux

Linux Device Name	Description
`appledmp`	Apple dot-matrix printer (Imagewriter)
`bj10e`	Canon BubbleJet BJ10e
`bj200`	Canon BubbleJet BJ200
`cdeskjet`	H-P DeskJet 500C with 1-bit/pixel color
`cdjcolor`	H-P DeskJet 500C with 24-bit/pixel color and high-quality color (Floyd-Steinberg) dithering
`cdjmono`	H-P DeskJet 500C printing black only
`cdj500`	H-P DeskJet 500C (same as `cdjcolor`)
`cdj550`	H-P DeskJet 550C
`declj250`	Alternate DEC LJ250 driver
`deskjet`	H-P DeskJet and DeskJet Plus
`dfaxhigh`	DigiBoard, Inc.'s DigiFAX software format

(continues)

Table 24.1 Continued

Linux Device Name	Description
dfaxlow	DigiFAX low (normal) resolution
djet500	H-P DeskJet 500
djet500c	H-P DeskJet 500C
epson	Epson-compatible dot-matrix printers (9- or 24-pin)
eps9high	Epson-compatible 9-pin, interleaved lines
epsonc	Epson LQ-2550 and Fujitsu 3400/2400/1200 color printers
escp2	Epson ESC/P 2 language printers, including Stylus 800
ibmpro	IBM 9-pin Proprinter
jetp3852	IBM Jetprinter ink-jet color printer (Model #3852)
laserjet	H-P LaserJet
la50	DEC LA50 printer
la75	DEC LA75 printer
lbp8	Canon LBP-8II laser printer
ln03	DEC LN03 printer
lj250	DEC LJ250 Companion color printer
ljet2p	H-P LaserJet IId/IIp/III* with TIFF compression
ljet3	H-P LaserJet III* with Delta Row compression
ljet4	H-P LaserJet 4 (defaults to 600 dpi)
ljetplus	H-P LaserJet Plus
m8510	C.Itoh M8510 printer
necp6	NEC P6/P6+/P60 printers at 360 × 360 DPI resolution
nwp533	Sony Microsystems NWP533 laser printer [Sony only]
oki182	Okidata MicroLine 182
paintjet	H-P PaintJet color printer
pj	Alternate PaintJet XL driver
pjxl	H-P PaintJet XL color printer
pjxl300	H-P PaintJet XL300 color printer
r4081	Ricoh 4081 laser printer
sparc	SPARC printer
t4693d2	Tektronix 4693d color printer, 2 bits per R/G/B component
t4693d4	Tektronix 4693d color printer, 4 bits per R/G/B component
t4693d8	Tektronix 4693d color printer, 8 bits per R/G/B component
tek4696	Tektronix 4695/4696 inkjet plotter

> **Note**
>
> Table 24.1 and the following sections in this chapter are adapted from "The Linux Printing-HOWTO: A guide to printing and previewing files under the Linux operating system," copyright 1994 by Grant Taylor and Brian McCauley. See Appendix A, "Sources of Information," on where to find and how to read the various Linux `HOWTO` documents provided on the accompanying CD-ROM.

If your particular printer does not appear in the preceding list, don't fret. If you can access the printer from MS-DOS, you should be able to print ASCII characters to the printer from Linux. The only downside is you may not be able to access certain features of your printer.

The printing systems common to UNIX/Linux are called the *lpr systems*. In this chapter, you learn about the following:

- Configuring your printer
- Sending a file to a printer
- Checking printer status
- Canceling a print job
- Dealing with problems

Configuring Printers: What You Need

This section assumes you know how to edit a text file under Linux and that you have a basic understanding of file ownership and permissions. It also assumes that you have your Linux system set up and running correctly. In particular, if you are going to use remote printing, your networking subsystems must be installed and operating correctly. Check out the man pages on the commands `chmod` and `chown` for more information. Also see chapters 22 and 23 for using the `vi` and `emacs` editors because you need to edit several files when configuring your printers.

How Printing Works under Linux

The simplest way to print under UNIX (and thus under Linux) is to send the print data directly to the printer device. The following command sends a directory listing to the first parallel printer (LPT1 in DOS terms):

```
ls > /dev/lp0
```

This method does not take advantage of the multitasking capabilities of Linux because the time taken for this command to finish is however long it takes the printer to actually physically print the data. On a slow printer or a printer that is deselected or disconnected, this could be a long time.

A better method is to spool the data. That is, to collect the print data into a file and then start up a background process to send the data to the printer.

This is essentially how Linux works. For each printer, a spool area is defined. Data for the printer is collected in the spool area, one file per print job. A background process (called the *printer daemon*) constantly scans the spool areas for new files to print. When one appears, the data is sent to the appropriate printer, or *despooled*. When more than one file is waiting to be printed, they are printed in the order they are completed—first in, first out. Thus, the spool area is effectively a queue, and the waiting jobs are often referred to as being *in the print queue* or *queued*. In the case of remote printing, the data is first spooled locally as for any other print job, but the background process is told to send the data to a particular printer on a particular remote machine.

The necessary information that the printer daemon needs to do its job—the physical device to use, the spool area to look in, the remote machine and printer for remote printing, and so on—is all stored in a file called `/etc/printcap`. The details of this file are discussed below.

In the discussion that follows, the term *printer* is used to mean a printer as specified in `/etc/printcap`. The term *physical printer* is used to mean the thing that actually puts characters on paper. It is possible to have multiple entries in `/etc/printcap` that all describe one physical printer but do so in different ways. If this is not clear to you, read the section on `/etc/printcap`.

The Important Programs for Printing

There are five programs that comprise the UNIX print system. They should be in the locations shown, owned by root, belong to the group daemon, and have the permissions shown in Table 24.2.

Table 24.2 The Important Printing Programs

File Permissions	File Locations
-rwsr-sr-x	/usr/bin/lpr
-rwsr-sr-x	/usr/bin/lpq
-rwsr-sr-x	/usr/bin/lpc
-rwsr-sr-x	/usr/bin/lprm
-rwxr-s---	/usr/sbin/lpd

The first four file permissions in Table 24.2 are used to submit, cancel, and inspect print jobs. `/etc/lpd` is the printer daemon. (The locations, ownerships, and permissions given here are a simplification and may be wrong for your system, so take note of the `lpd` files and permissions.)

There are man pages for all these commands, which you should consult for more information. The important points are that by default `lpr`, `lprm`, `lpc`, and `lpq` operate on a printer called `lp`. If you define an environment variable called `PRINTER`, the name defined is used instead. Both of these may be overridden by specifying the printer name to use on the command line. For example,

```
lpc -PMYPRINTER
```

The *lpd* Daemon

Linux handles all print jobs via the `lpd` deamon. If this process is not running, no printing can place and print files will remain in their spool directories until the `lpd` process is started (there is more information about spool directories later in this chapter). If your system does not load `lpd` at startup, or if for some reason you must kill the `lpd` daemon, the following command starts the printer daemon:

```
lpd [options]
```

The man page on `lpd` gives a list of options, but one important option when configuring your Linux printers is the `-l` option. This option creates a log file that logs each print request to the system. This log file can be useful when debugging your printing system.

The *lpr* Command

The `lpr` command submits a job to the printer, or *queues a print job*. What actually happens is that the file you specify is copied to the spool directory. Each printer specified for your Linux system must have its own spool directory. The size of this spool directory is specified in the `minfree` file located in each directory. The file specifies the number of disk blocks to reserve for spooling files to the printer. This is done to keep the `lpd` daemon from using up the entire hard drive when spooling a print request.

> **Note**
>
> *Spooling* is an acronym for Simultaneous Peripheral Operation Off Line. The term was coined in the early days of the big IBM mainframes when smaller computers were used to print reports offline from the mainframe. This technique allowed expensive mainframes to continue their tasks without wasting time on such trivial matters as printing.

`lpd` finds the file, which then takes care of moving the data to the physical printer. If you don't specify a file, `lpr` uses standard input.

The *lpq* Command

The `lpq` command shows you the contents of the spool directory for a given printer. One important piece of information displayed by `lpq` is the job ID, which identifies a particular job. This number must be specified if you want to cancel a pending job.

lpq also shows a rank for each job in the queue: *active* means the file is actually printing (or at least that lpd is trying to print it). Otherwise, a number shows you where in the queue the job is.

The *lprm* Command

The lprm command removes a job from the queue—that is, it removes unprinted files from the spool directory. You can either specify a job ID (obtained by using the lpq command) or specify - as the job ID; in which case, all jobs belonging to you are canceled. If you do this as root, all jobs for the printer are canceled. If you are root and want to remove all the jobs belonging to a specific user, specify the user's name.

The *lpc* Command

The lpc command lets you check the status of printers and control some aspects of their use. In particular, it lets you start and stop despooling on printers, enable or disable printers, and rearrange the order of jobs in a print queue. The following commands disable printing on myprinter, enable the spool queue on yourprinter, and move job number 37 to the top of the queue.

```
lpc down myprinter
lpc enable yourprinter
lpc topq 37
```

If invoked without any command arguments, lpc is interactive, prompting you for actions to take. Read the man page for complete instructions. Bear in mind that some lpc functions are restricted to root—that is, the super user. Some of the more important commands are shown in Table 24.3. Most lpc commands take the name of the printer, as specified in /etc/printcap, as the parameter.

Table 24.3 Some Common Commands

Command	Parameter	Description
stop	printer	Stops the printer, but print requests are still spooled.
start	printer	Allows the printer to start printing previously spooled files and any new files spooled to this printer.
exit	none	Exits the lpc interactive mode. This command is identical to the quit command.
status	printer	Displays the current status of the printer. The command provides such information as whether the queue is enabled, whether the printer is enabled, and the number, if any, of jobs currently held in the queue waiting to be printed.

lpc is also very unstable in its current implementation under Linux. Some users have reported that lpc can display incorrect status messages and sometimes even hang the system outright.

The Important Directories

There is only one important directory—the spool area where data to be printed is accumulated before `/etc/lpd` prints it. However, typically a system is set up with multiple spool directories, one for each printer. This makes printer management easier. For example, my system is set up to use `/usr/spool/lpd` as the main spool area, with each separate printer having a directory under that with the same name as the printer. Thus, there is a printer called `ps_nff` that has `/usr/spool/lpd/ps_nff` as its spool directory.

The spool directories should belong to the daemon group and be user and group read/writable and world `-readable`. That is, after creating the directory make sure it has the permissions `-rwxrwxr-x` (0775) with the `chmod` command. For the directory `myprinter`, the appropriate command is

```
chmod ug=rwx,o=rx myprinter
chgrp daemon myprinter
```

◀◀ See "File Permissions," p. 330

(The locations, ownerships, and permissions given here are a simplification and may be incorrect for your system, so you should take notes on the `lpd` files and permissions.)

The Important Files

Apart from the programs discussed above, each spool directory contains four files: `.seq`, `errs`, `lock`, and `status`. These files have the permissions `-rw-rw-r-`. The `.seq` file contains the job number counter for `lpr` to assign, and the `status` file contains the message to be reported by `lpc stat`. The `lock` file is used by `lpd` to prevent itself from trying to print two jobs to the same printer at once, and the `errs` file is a log of printer failures.

The file `errs` is not required and can actually be called whatever you like. The name is specified in `/etc/printcap`, but the file must exist for `lpd` to be able to log to the file. So it is usually created manually when setting up the spool area. More on this later in the "Putting It All Together," section.

One very important file is `/etc/printcap`, which is described in detail in the following sections.

More About */etc/printcap*

The file `/etc/printcap` is a text file that may be edited with your favorite editor. `/etc/printcap` should be owned by root and have the permissions `-rw-r-r-`.

The contents of /etc/printcap are typically very cryptic-looking, but once you know how it works, the contents are much easier to understand. The problem is compounded by the fact that in some distributions there is no man page for printcap, and most printcaps are created either by programs or by people with no thought for readability. For your own sanity, make the layout of your printcap file as logical and readable as possible with lots of comments. And get the man page from the lpd sources if you don't already have it.

One printcap entry describes one printer. Essentially, a printcap entry provides a logical name for a physical device and then describes how data to be sent to that device is supposed to be handled. For example, a printcap entry defines what physical device is to be used, what spool directory data for that device should be stored in, what preprocessing should be performed on the data, where errors on the physical device should be logged, and so forth. You can limit the amount of data that may be sent in a single job or limit access to a printer to certain classes of users.

It is perfectly okay to have multiple printcap entries defining several different ways to handle data destined for the same physical printer. For example, a physical printer may support both PostScript and HP Laserjet data formats, depending on some setup sequence being sent to the physical printer before each job. It makes sense to define two printers: one that preprocesses the data by preappending the HP LaserJet sequence, while the other preappends the PostScript sequence. Programs that generate HP data send it to the HP printer, while programs generating PostScript print to the PostScript printer.

Note

If you do not designate a default printer via an environment variable, or do not specify a printer on the lpr command line, then Linux will route the print job to the lp printer. Thus, you should specify one of the printers in the printcap file as the lp printer.

Programs that change the data before it is sent to the physical printer are called *filters*. It is possible for a filter to send no data at all to a physical printer—that is, the filter filters out everything.

```
# Sample printcap entry with two aliases
myprinter¦laserwriter:\
# lp is the device to print to - here the first parallel printer.
              :lp=/dev/lp0: \
# sd means spool directory - where print data is collected
               :sd=/usr/spool/lpd/myprinter:
```

Fields in */etc/printcap*

There are too many fields to describe here in full, so only the most important ones are described. All fields in /etc/printcap (except for the names of the printer) are enclosed between colons and denoted by a two-letter code. The two-letter code is followed by a value that depends on the type of field. There are three types of fields:

string, Boolean, and numeric. Table 24.4 describes the most common and most important fields.

Table 24.4 The Field Descriptions

Field	Type	Description
`lp`	String	Specify the device to print to—for example, `/dev/lp0`
`sd`	String	Specify the name of the spool directory for this printer
`lf`	String	Specify the file that errors on this printer are to be logged to
`if`	String	Specify the input filter name
`rm`	String	Specify the name of a remote printing host
`rp`	String	Specify the name of a remote printer
`sh`	Boolean	Specify this to suppress headers (banner pages)
`sf`	Boolean	Specify this to suppress end-of-job form feeds
`mx`	Numeric	Specify the maximum allowable print job size (in blocks)

More on the *lp* Field. If you specify `/dev/null` as the print device, all other processing is performed correctly, but the final data goes to the bit bucket—that is, to nowhere. This is rarely useful except for test printer configurations or with weird printers. When you are setting up a remote printer (that is, you have specified `rm` and `rp` fields), specify `:lp=:`.

Don't leave the field empty unless you are using a remote printer. The printer daemon complains if you don't specify a print device.

More on the *lf* Field. Whatever file you specify should already exist, or logging does not occur.

More on the *if* Field. Input filters are programs that take print data on their standard input and generate output on their standard output. A typical use of an input filter is to detect plain text and convert it into PostScript. That is, raw text is its input and PostScript is its output.

When you specify an input filter, the printer daemon does not send the spooled print data to the specified device. Instead, it runs the input filter with the spooled data as standard input and the print device as standard output.

More on the *rm* and *rp* Fields. Sending your print data to a printer attached to another machine is as simple as specifying the remote machine `rm` and the remote printer `rp` and making sure that the print device field `lp` is empty. Note that data is still spooled locally before being transferred to the remote machine and any input filters you specify are also run.

More on the *sh* and *sf* Fields. Unless you have a lot of different people using your printer, you are most likely not interested in banner pages.

Suppressing form feeds is most useful if your printer is typically used for output from word-processing packages. Most word-processing packages create complete pages of data, so if the printer daemon is adding a form feed to the end of each job, you get a blank page after each job. If the printer is usually used for program or directory listings, however, having that form feed ensures that the final page is completely ejected, so each listing starts at the top of a new page.

More on the *mx* Field. This field allows you to limit the size of the print data to be spooled. The number you specify is in BUFSIZE blocks (1K under Linux). If you specify zero, the limit is removed, allowing print jobs to be limited only by available disk space. Note that the limit is on the size of the spooled data and not the amount of data sent to the physical printer. If a user tries to exceed this limit the file is truncated. The user sees a message saying

```
(lpr: file-name: copy file is too large)
```

For text physical printers, this is useful if you have users or programs that may deliberately or accidentally create excessively large output but, in most cases, it is not really very applicable.

For PostScript physical printers, the limit is not useful at all because a very small amount of spooled PostScript data can generate a large number of output pages.

Setting the *PRINTER* Environment Variable

You may want to add a line to your logon script—or even to the default user logon script—that sets up a `PRINTER` environment variable. Under the `bash` shell, a suitable line is `export PRINTER=myprinter`. This prevents people having to specify `-Pmyprinter` every time they submit a print job.

To add more printers, just repeat the above process with different printer names. Remember you can have multiple `printcap` entries all using the same physical device. This lets you treat the same device differently, depending on what you call it when you submit a print job to it.

A Test *printcap* Entry

The following shell script is a very simple input filter: it simply concatenates its input onto the end of a file in `/tmp` after an appropriate banner. Specify this filter in the `printcap` entry and specify `/dev/null` as the print device. The print device is never actually used, but you have to set it to something; otherwise, the printer daemon complains.

```
#!/bin/sh
# This file should be placed in the printer's spool directory and
# named input_filter. It should be owned by root, group daemon, and
# be world executable (-rwxr-xr-x).
echo -----------------------------------------------  >> /tmp/
date                                                  >> /tmp/
echo -----------------------------------------------  >> /tmp/
cat                                                   >> /tmp/
```

Here is the printcap entry. Notice the reasonably readable format and the use of the continuation character, \, on all but the last line:

```
myprinter¦myprinter: \
 :lp=/dev/null: \
 :sd=/usr/spool/lpd/myprinter: \
 :lf=/usr/spool/lpd/myprinter/errs: \
 :if=/usr/spool/lpd/myprinter/input_filter: \
 :mx#0: \
 :sh: \
 :sf:
```

Putting It All Together

Putting all the previous bits together, the following is a step-by-step guide to setting up a single printer on /dev/lp0. You can then extend this to other printers. You have to be root to do all this, by the way.

1. Check the permissions and locations of lpr, lprm, lpc, lpq, and lpd.
2. Create the spool directory for your printer, which is called myprinter for now. Make sure that both the directory and printer are owned by root, group daemon, and are user and group writable, read only for others (-rwxrwxr-x). Use the following commands:

   ```
   mkdir /usr/spool/lpd
   mkdir /usr/spool/lpd/myprinter
   chown root.daemon /usr/spool/lpd /usr/spool/lpd/myprinter
   chmod ug=rwx,o=rx /usr/spool/lpd /usr/spool/lpd/myprinter
   ```

3. In the directory /usr/spool/lpd/myprinter, create the necessary files and give them the correct permissions and owner. Use the following commands:

   ```
   cd /usr/spool/lpd/myprinter
   touch .seq errs status lock
   chown root.daemon .seq errs status lock
   chmod ug=rw,o=r .seq errs status lock
   ```

4. Create the shell script input_filter in the directory /usr/spool/lpd/myprinter. Use the input filter given in the "A Test printcap Entry" section for your filter. Make sure that the file is owned by root, group daemon, and is executable by anyone. Use the following commands:

   ```
   cd /usr/spool/lpd/myprinter
   chmod ug=rwx,o=rx input_filter
   ```

5. Create the file /etc/printcap if it doesn't already exist. Remove all entries in it and add the test printcap entry given in the "A Test printcap Entry" section. Make sure the file is owned by root and read only to everyone else (-rw-r-r-).
6. Edit the file rc.local. You can use any ASCII editor such as vi or emacs. Add the line /etc/lpd to the end, which runs the printer daemon each time the system boots. It is not necessary to boot now though—just run it by hand with the following command:

   ```
   lpd
   ```

7. Do a test print by typing

```
ls -l ¦ lpr -Pmyprinter
```

8. Look in /tmp, using the ls command, for a file called testlp.out. It should contain your directory listing, which you can check with the more, less, or cat command. See Chapter 18, "Understanding the File and Directory System," for more information on these commands.
9. Edit /etc/printcap using an ASCII editor such as vi.

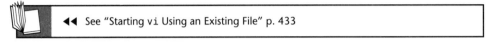

◀◀ See "Starting vi Using an Existing File" p. 433

- In the first printer entry, change both occurrences of myprinter to testlp in the first line only.
- In the second entry, change /dev/null to your real print device—for example, /dev/lp0.
- In the second entry, remove the if line completely.

Now, copy the myprinter entry so that you have two identical entries in the file.

10. Either reboot the system or kill the printer daemon and restart it. You do this because the printer daemon only looks at the /etc/printcap file when it first starts up.
11. Do a test print again. This one should come out on your physical printer. You can use the following command:

```
ls -l ¦ lpr -Pmyprinter
```

Troubleshooting

I get a message saying lpd: connect: No such file or directory.

The printer daemon /etc/lpd is not running. You may have forgotten to add it to your /etc/rc.local file. Alternatively, you did add it but have not booted since. Add it and reboot, or just run /etc/lpd. Remember you have to be root to do this.

I get a message saying Job queued, but cannot start daemon.

This often appears right after the lpd: connect message. Same problem.

I get a message saying lpd: cannot create spooldir/.seq.

You have not created the spool directory specified in the printcap entry, or you have misnamed it. An alternative (though much less likely) answer is that you have too little disk space left.

I get a message saying lpr: Printer queue is disabled.

As root, use lpc enable *printer-name* to enable the printer. Note that as root, you can submit jobs even to a disabled printer.

I submit a print job and there are no error messages, but nothing comes out on the physical printer.

There could be many reasons. Make sure the physical printer is switched on, selected, and physically connected to the device specified in the `/etc/printcap` file. Use the `lpq` command to see whether the entry is in the queue. If it is, the device may be busy, the printer may be down, or there may be an error on the printer. Check the error log specified in the `printcap` entry for clues. You can use the `lpc status` command to check whether the printer is down and `lpc up` *`printer-name`*, or `lpc restart` *`printer-name`*, to bring it back up if it is (you need to be root to do this).

If, after checking, your print jobs still do not come out, make sure that any input filter you have specified is present in the correct directory and has the correct permissions. If you are running `syslogd`, you can look in your logs for messages from `lpd`. If you see log entries saying `cannot` *`execv name of input filter`*, this is almost certainly the problem.

Another possibility is that your printer is a PostScript printer and you are not sending PostScript to it. Most PostScript printers ignore non-PostScript data. You may need to install an appropriate text-to-PostScript input filter.

Lastly (and you'll feel silly if this is the cause), check that your input filter actually generates output and that the output device is not `/dev/null`.

My printer seems to have locked up and none of the above techniques seems to solve the problem.

When all else fails, in the case of a nonprinting printer the next-to-last resort is to kill the `lpd` daemon and restart it. If that does not work then the last resort is to reboot your Linux system with the `shutdown -r now` command. You should make sure no one else is logged on and that you have saved any files before using the `now` option; otherwise, specify a time and also give a message to your other users before shutting down the system.

From Here...

The `lpr` command is the standard Linux interface for printing files. From the command line, you can use `lpr` to print to many different types of printers and to request many different options. Later, you can check the status of your print jobs with the `lpq` command. If you change your mind and want to cancel a print job, you may do so with the `lprm` command. No matter what, you should read the latest edition of the printing HOWTO for more information. For information on related topics, see the following:

- Chapter 4, "Installing Linux," discusses how to install Linux and how to use the Microsoft Windows-based HOWTO viewer.
- Part III, "System Administration," discusses all the details about what a system administrator is and does.
- Appendix A, "Sources of Information," tells you how to locate the printing HOWTO.

CHAPTER 25

Command-Line Reference

This chapter provides a command reference for the Linux environment, a means of covering some of the more common commands you may use. This is not meant to be an exhaustive listing. After the command is listed, the function's purpose is described or reasons are given as to why you would want to use the command. Following this is a syntax line. The syntax line shows what "format" you have to use to type in the command. For example,

```
cp source dest
```

In this example `cp` is the command; *`source`* and *`dest`* are arguments.

When parts of the command are enclosed in square brackets (`[ ]`), this means that these are optional and do not have to be supplied for the command to do something. Words in the syntax in italics are descriptions of arguments you need to supply. After the syntax is a detailed description of what each element of the command means and its effect on the command. A notes section is provided to explain various facets of the command and things to look out for or basic premises needed to be done. A messages section is provided to show you what happens if the command is misused and what those messages are. This is followed by the examples section that demonstrates how to use the command in some real-world situations. Finally, this is followed by a cross-reference of related commands.

at

Schedules jobs to execute at a later time. `batch` runs the command with a lower priority at a point when the system utilization is lower—it may run immediately and it may run later, it depends on the system load.

Syntax

```
at -q queue time

at -l

at -r job-ids

batch
```

Item	Description
`-q queue`	An optional queue designation may be specified. *queue* may be any letter between a to z and A to Z. The c queue is the default for at and the E queue for `batch`. Queues with higher letters run with lower priority for CPU time. If a job is submitted to a queue designated with an uppercase letter, it is treated as if it had been submitted to batch at that time.
time	This is the time when the job starts. The format of *time* is highly flexible, and is divided into three basic parts: *time*, *date*, and *increment*. `at` accepts times in the form of HHMM or HH:MM to run a job at a specific time of day. (If that time is already past, the next day is assumed.) You may also specify `midnight`, `noon`, or `teatime` (4:00 PM), and you can have a time-of-day suffixed with AM or PM for running in the morning or the evening. You can also say what day the job will be run by giving a date in the form *month-name day* with an optional year or giving a date of the form *MMDDYY* or *MM/DD/YY* or DD.MM.YY. You can also give times like `now + count time-units`, where time-units can be minutes, hours, days, or weeks and you can tell `at` to run the job today by suffixing the time with `today` and to run the job tomorrow by suffixing the time with `tomorrow`.
`-l`	Lists your currently scheduled jobs. If you are the super user, all jobs are listed.
`-m`	Sends mail to the user when the job has completed, even if there was no output.
`-r job-ids`	Removes the specified `job-ids` from the queue. Unless you are the super user, you may only remove your own jobs.
`-f file`	Reads the job from `file` rather than standard input.

Notes

Unless the `-f` option is specified, `at` takes all of its commands from standard input. Therefore, the commands are piped to it, redirected to it, or entered interactively.

`at` returns a job ID when it is invoked. This ID may then be used as the *job-ids* parameter described previously.

The super user may use these commands in any case. For other users, permission to use `at` is determined by the files `/etc/at.allow` and `/etc/at.deny`.

If the file `/etc/at.allow` exists, only user names mentioned in it are allowed to use `at`. If `/etc/at.allow` does not exist, `/etc/at.deny` is checked, every user name not mentioned in it is then allowed to use `at`. If neither exists, only the super user is allowed use of `at`. An empty `/etc/at.deny` means that every user is allowed to use these commands. This is the default configuration.

If the `time` specified is less then the current time, the next occurrence of the time is used. For example, if `at noon` is used and it is 1:00 PM, the next day is used.

The standard output and standard error of the commands executed are mailed to the user via UNIX e-mail.

Examples

```
at 4am tomorrow < doit
```

This runs the commands found in the file `doit` tomorrow at 4:00 AM. The file `doit` could also have been specified with the `-f` option as `-f doit`.

```
at noon <doit
```

This runs the commands found in the file `doit` at noon.

```
at -f doit 11am Aug 15
```

This runs the commands found in the file `doit` at on August the 15th at 11:00 AM.

See Also

date, `find`, `mail`

banner

`banner` produces a large banner by "enlarging" the arguments passed to it. As many as ten characters may be specified. These characters are then enlarged using a series of asterisks (*). The output of `banner` is the standard output.

Syntax

```
banner  [-w  [n]] strings
```

Item	Description
`-w` *n*	Changes the width of the banner from the default of 132 columns to *n* columns. If *n* is omitted and `-w` is specified by itself, a width of 80 columns is assumed.
strings	The list of ten character strings to create a banner. Each string, if separated by a space, creates a banner on successive lines. Two strings may be enclosed in quotation marks ("), which causes `banner` to place the strings on the same line.

Examples

```
banner hello
```

Produces the word `hello` in a larger format to the standard output.

```
banner "My Banner" ¦ lpr
```

Prints `My Banner` on the default printer.

bash

sh starts the bash shell, which is a GNU version of the Bourne shell (in fact, bash is an acronym for the Bourne Again shell). The bash shell is one of many command interpreters available under Linux. A shell's job is to take the command line you enter, check its syntax, parse it, and pass it to the kernel in a manner the kernel can understand. sh is also a programming language of sorts; it provides all the control structures found in most high-level languages. It lacks, however, floating point math and robust file reading tools.

Because sh is such a powerful utility, only the basics are discussed here.

Syntax

```
sh [options] file
```

Item	Description	
options	The bash shell is extremely flexible. The *options* field allows you to customize the shell environment. In addition to the options listed here, bash accepts the single character shell options provided by the set built-in command. See the bash man page for a full description.	
	-c *string*	If the -c flag is present, then commands are read from *string*. If there are arguments after the *string*, they are assigned to the positional parameters, starting with $0.
	-i	If the -i flag is used, the shell is interactive.
	-s	If the -s flag is used, or if no arguments remain after option processing, commands are read from the standard input. This option allows the positional parameters to be set when invoking an interactive shell.
	-	A single - signals the end of options and disables further option processing. Any arguments after the - are treated as file names and arguments. An argument of - is equivalent to an argument of -.
	-norc	Do not read and execute the personal initialization file ~/.bashrc if the shell is interactive. This option is on by default if the shell is invoked as sh.
	-noprofile	Do not read either the system-wide startup file /etc/profile or any of the personal initialization files ~/.bash_profile, ~/.bash_login, or ~/.profile. By default, bash normally reads these files when it is invoked as a logon shell.
	-rcfile *file*	Executes commands from file instead of the standard personal initialization file~/.bashrc if the shell is interactive.
	-version	Shows the version number of this instance of bash when starting.

Item	Description	
	-quiet	Do not be verbose when starting up (do not show the shell version or any other information). This is the default.
	-login	Makes the bash shell act as if it had been invoked as a logon shell.
	-nobraceexpansion	Do not perform brace expansion.
	-nolineediting	Do not use the GNU readline library to read command lines if interactive.
	-posix	Changes the behavior of bash where the default operation differs from the POSIX 1003.2 standard to match the standard instead.
file	This is the name of a shell script that contains a sequence of commands for sh to interpret.	

Examples

```
sh
```

Invokes a new shell. You may now work in this shell, changing directories, setting environment variables, and so on. When you return to the original shell by pressing <Ctrl-d> or typing `exit`, you are returned to the directory you started the new shell from and any environment variables you changed are returned to their former values. Applications sometimes let you run a Linux command from the application. Entering `sh` as the command gives you a sub-shell to work in, letting you enter an entire series of commands.

The command

```
sh install.prog
```

runs an installation script.

```
EDITOR=/usr/bin/emacs; export EDITOR
```

This sets the environment variable `EDITOR` to a popular editor called `emacs`. Applications can access variables such as `EDITOR` and alter their behavior based on the variable's values.

See Also

`csh, cd, env, tar`

batch

See `at`.

cal

`cal` displays a calendar on the standard output. The output is small. One year takes less than one 8 1/2 × 11 sheet of paper. This can be useful when you have to quickly compare several years or want to find out on what day of the week a particular date is.

Syntax

```
cal [-j] [-y] [month] [year]
```

Item	Description
`-j`	Displays Julian dates (days are incrementally numbered, starting with one, numbered from January 1).
`-y`	Displays a calendar for the current year.
`month`	May be a number between 1 and 12 or enough letters to represent a unique month. (`J` is not enough to distinguish January, June, and July.) The default is the current month.
`year`	May be any number between 1 and 9999. The default is the current year. All four numbers of the year must be specified. That is, `92` refers to the year 92 not 1992.

Note

A single parameter specifies the year (1–9999) to be displayed. The year must be fully specified: `cal 89` does not display a calendar for 1989 but displays a calendar for the year 89 instead. Two parameters denote the month (1–12) and year. If no parameters are specified, the current month's calendar is displayed.

Examples

```
cal
```

This shows a calendar for the current month.

```
cal 1960
```

Shows the calendar for the year 1960.

```
cal 10 1994
```

Shows the month of October for 1994.

cat

Concatenates files. Also, this is sometimes used to display a file. Some of the options for the `cat` command have both long and short option specifiers. For space reasons, only the short versions of these options have been listed. For more information, refer to the man page.

Syntax

```
cat [options] filelist
```

Item	Description
filelist	This is an optional list of files to concatenate. If no files or a hyphen (-) is specified, the standard input is read.
-b	Numbers all nonblank output lines, starting with 1.
-e	Equivalent to -vE.
-n	Numbers all output lines, starting with 1.
-s	Replaces multiple, adjacent blank lines with a single blank line.
-t	Equivalent to -vT.
-u	Ignored; included for UNIX compatibility.
-v	Displays control characters except for LFD and TAB using ^ notation and precedes characters that have the high bit set with M-.
-A	Equivalent to -vET.
-E	Displays a $ after the end of each line.
-T	Displays TAB characters as ^I.
--help	Prints a usage message and exits with a non-zero status.
--version	Prints version information on standard output then exits.

Note

An output file name must not be the same as any of the input names unless it is a special file.

Examples

```
cat letter-to-dad
```

This concatenates letter-to-dad with nothing and sends the output to the screen.

```
cat letter-to-dad signature >send.let
```

This appends the file `signature` to `letter-to-dad` and creates a new file called `send.let`.

See Also

echo, pr, more, cp

cd

Changes the current working directory.

Syntax

```
cd dirname
```

Item	Description
dirname	Changes to an optional directory name. If no directory is specified, then the user is returned to his home directory.

Note

You must have execute permissions for the directory you want to change to.

See Also

`pwd, bash, chmod, ls`

chgrp

Changes the group ownership of a file. Some of the options for the *chgrp* command have both long and short option specifiers. For space reasons, only the short versions of these options have been listed. For more information, refer to the man page.

Syntax

```
chgrp [options] group filelist
```

Item	Description
`-c`	Verbosely describes only files whose ownership actually changes.
`-f`	Does not print error messages about files whose ownership cannot be changed.
`-v`	Verbosely describes ownership changes.
`-R`	Recursively changes ownership of directories and their contents
`--help`	Prints a usage message on standard output then exits successfully.
`--version`	Prints version information on standard output then exits successfully.
group	The group to change to. This may either be the numerical value of the group ID or the name as found in the file /etc/group.
filelist	A space-seperated list of files to change the group ownership of.

Note

You cannot change the group ownership of a file unless you are the owner of the file or the super user.

Example

```
chgrp sales /usr/salesstuff/*
```

This example changes all the files found in the sales stuff directory to the group ownership of `sales`.

See Also

`chown`, `chmod`

chmod

`chmod` changes the mode of files. The mode of a file controls the access permissions associated with that file. Linux has three levels of security: ownership, group access, and everyone else. Within these three levels are three permissions: read, write, and execute. On standard files, the read permission means you are able to look at the contents of that file, the write permission enables you to modify the file, and the execute permission means you can execute it. Directories behave only slightly differently. The read permission enables you to view the contents of the directory—an `ls` command works. The write permission enables you to create new files in directory and to delete files from the directory. Finally, the execute permission means you can change directory to the directory--the `cd` command works.

Syntax

```
chmod [options] mode filelist

chmod [options] level action permission filelist
```

These are the two formats. The first is less complicated but requires knowledge of the valid numbers to set the various permissions. It is the "absolute" method. It sets the permissions at all levels. The second format is more complicated but lets you use symbols to specify the permissions, and they are specified incrementally. This is the "relative" method because you can add or remove permissions.

Item	Description
`-c`	Verbosely describes only files whose permissions actually change.
`-f`	Does not print error messages about files whose permissions cannot be changed.
`-v`	Verbosely describes changed permissions.
`-R`	Recursively changes permissions of directories and their contents.
`--help`	Prints a usage message on standard output and exits successfully.
`--version`	Prints version information on standard output and then exits successfully.
`filelist`	Lists the files affected by the `chmod` command.

(continues)

Item	Description
mode	The numeric mode, in octal, of the permissions this file has for all levels. Each octal number sets a bit in the mode field stored in the inode table of the file system. Adding the numbers together sets the combination of the permissions. The permissions at the user/owner, group, and other/world levels all follow the same pattern. An additional level controls some special handling. The mode is in the following form: SUGO, where S=special, U=user/owner, G=group, and O=others/world. Each number may be any from the following table (consult the user's reference provided with your system for the Special meaning of the numbers as they differ from the U, G, and O meanings). The available permissions are none, execute, read, and write; the value for these permissions is `0`, `1`, `2`, and `4`, respectively.
level	The level affected by the rest of the command. The different levels are the user/owner of the file, the group, the world, and all levels, which is the default; the codes for these levels are u, g, o, and a, respectively.
action	Specifies what action is to take place on the mode of the file. You can add or remove a permission, or you can set the permission to only what is specified. Use + for adding, - for removing, and = for only what is specified.
permission	The permission to apply to the file. You can grant read, write, or execute permission; the codes for the permissions are `r`, `w`, and `x`, respectively.

Examples

```
chmod 777 letter-to-dad
```

This enables `letter-to-dad` to have all permissions at all levels. Notice how the "special" level isn't specified; this is an implied `0` and no special permissions are granted. The execute permission in this case is nonsense; however, it demonstrates the use of the `7` to mean all possible permissions.

```
chmod 644 letter-to-dad
```

This allows every one to read `letter-to-dad`, but only the owner can change it.

```
chmod a+w letter-to-dad
```

This adds the write permission to the letter for everyone.

```
chmod o-wr,g-wr letter-to-dad
```

This removes both read and write permissions at both the group and world levels.

```
chmod o=r letter-to-dad
```

This sets the other level to allow reading only. All other permissions at this level are taken away.

See Also

`umask`, `ls`

chown

Enables you to change the ownership of the file. In a sense, you are giving the file to someone else.

Syntax

```
chown [options] user filelist
```

Item	Description
-c	Verbosely describes only files whose ownership actually changes.
-f	Does not print error messages about files whose ownership cannot be changed.
-v	Verbosely describes ownership changes.
-R	Recursively changes ownership of directories and their contents.
--help	Prints a usage message on standard output and exits successfully.
--version	Prints version information on standard output then exits successfully.
user	May be a numerical user ID or a valid user name as found in the /etc/passwd file.
filelist	The space-separated list of files to reassign the ownership of.

Note

The ownership of the file can only be changed by the super user.

Example

```
chown pete/usr/acct/pete/*
```

This example changes all the files found in Pete's home directory to the ownership of pete.

See Also

chgrp

clear

Clears the screen, or if you are working at a hard copy terminal, this command form feeds the paper.

Syntax

```
clear
```

Example

```
clear
```

This clears the screen and leaves the prompt in the upper-left corner.

See Also

`echo`

compress

Compresses the specified files or standard input.

Syntax

```
compress [options] [file-name]
```

Item	Description
`-c`	This option causes the results of the compress/uncompress operation to be written to `stdout`; no files are changed.
`-C`	This option prevents subdivision of the file into blocks; this produces an output file that old versions of `compress` can read.
`-d`	Uncompresses files.
`-f`	Overwrites output files if they exist, without prompting for confirmation. Also, changes the name of all files to `.Z` files, even if they did not decrease in size.
`-v`	After each file is compressed, a message is printed giving the percentage of the input file that has been saved by compression.
`file-name`	The file to compress.

Note

Each file is replaced by a file with the extension `.Z`, but only if the file is able to be compressed into a smaller size. If no files are specified, the compression is applied to the standard input and is written to standard output regardless of the results. Compressed files can be restored to their original form by specifying the `-d` option or by running `uncompress` (linked to `compress`), on the `.Z` files or the standard input.

Examples

```
compress bigfile
```

This compresses the file `bigfile` and renames it as `bigfile.Z`.

```
compress -v /home/pete/archive/*
```

This compresses all the files in `/home/pete/archive` and prints information about each file's compression as it is compressed.

```
compress -d bigfile.Z
```

or

```
compress -d bigfile
```

Both of these commands take the compressed input file, `bigfile.Z`, and restore it to its original state.

See Also

gzip

cp

Copies files. You may copy one file to another file or a list of files to a directory.

Syntax

```
cp [options] source-file dest-file

cp [options] source-list dest-directory
```

Item	Description
-a	Preserves as much as possible of the structure and attributes of the original files in the copy.
-b	Makes backups of files that are about to be overwritten or removed.
-d	Copies symbolic links as symbolic links rather than copying the files that they point to, and preserves hard link relationships between source files in the copies.
-f	Removes existing destination files.
-i	Prompts whether to overwrite existing regular destination files.
-l	Makes hard links instead of copies of non-directories.
-P	Forms the name of each destination file by appending to the target directory a slash and the specified name of the source file. The last argument given to cp must be the name of an existing directory.
-p	Preserves the original file's owner, group, permissions, and time-stamps.
-r	Copies directories recursively, copying all non-directories as if they were regular files.
-s	Makes symbolic links instead of copies of non-directories. All source file names must be absolute (starting with '/') unless the destination files are in the current directory. This option produces an error message on systems that do not support symbolic links.
-u	Updates option. Do not copy a non-directory that has an existing destination with the same or newer modification time.
-v	Prints the name of each file before copying it.
-x	Skips subdirectories that are on different file systems from the one that the copy started on.
-R	Copies directories recursively.
--help	Prints a usage message on standard output and exits successfully.
--version	Prints version information on standard output and exits successfully.
-S	The suffix used for making simple backup files can be set with the SIMPLE_BACKUP_SUFFIX environment variable, which can be overridden by this option. If neither of those is given, the default is ~.

(continues)

Item	Description
-V value	The type of backups made can be set with the VERSION_CONTROL environment variable, which can be overridden by this option. If VERSION_CONTROL is not set and this option is not given, the default backup type is existing. The valid values are the following: t or numbered — Always makes numbered backups nil or existing — Makes numbered backups of files that already have them, simple backups of the others never or simple — Always makes simple backups
source-file	The file to copy.
dest-file	The destination name. This may be a directory name as well, in which case, the source file name is used as the name and the file is placed in this directory.
source-list	A space-separated list of files to copy.
dest-directory	The destination directory.

Examples

```
cp letter-to-dad letter.save
```

This copies `letter-to-dad` to a file called `letter.save`.

```
cp letter* /old-letters
```

This copies all the files starting with the word letter to a directory called `old-letters`.

Caution

No verification of a file of the same name already existing in the destination is done. Therefore, if you aren't careful, you can end up overwriting a file in the destination you needed.

See Also

`rm`, `copy`, `ln`, `mv`

crontab

Informs the `cron` daemon of the programs and the schedule that they should run on.

Syntax

```
crontab -l [-u user]

crontab -e [-u user]

crontab -d [-u user]
```

Argument	Description
-l	Lists your crontab file.
-e	Edits crontab file. Uses the vi editor or the editor specified by your VISUAL environment variable.
-d	Deletes a user's crontab file.
-u *user*	Specifies a particular user's crontab file to manipulate. You must be root to use this function.

Note

The crontab file is in the format: M H D m d cmd. Blank lines and lines beginning with # are ignored. A * in a field matches all possible values for the field. Additionally, the crontab file can specify ranges and sub-specifiers as fields. Refer to the crontab man page for full information.

Field	Description
M	The minute of the hour (0–59).
H	The hour of the day (0–23).
D	The day of the month (1–31).
m	The month of the year (1–12).
d	The day of the week (0–6, 0=Sunday).
cmd	The program to run. This command line is passed to sh. The shell is run with only three environment variables: USER, HOME, and SHELL.

csh

See tcsh

cut

Extracts fields from a list of files. Fields may be defined as either character positions or relatively with a field separator.

Syntax

```
cut -cchar-pos filelist

cut -ffields -dfield-sep -s filelist
```

Item	Description
`-c`*char-pos*	The character position to cut out. May be a list separated by commas, a range separated by hyphens, or a combination thereof (for example, `1,4,5`, `1-4`, and `1-4,5-10,25` are all valid).
`-f`*fields*	The fields to cut out. Fields are denoted by a one character separator. If the separator repeats, as in several in a row, they are not treated as one separator. *fields* uses the same syntax as *char-pos*.
`-d`*field-sep*	Specifies the field separator. A tab character is the default. *field-sep* may be any character.
`-s`	Suppresses the line if it doesn't contain *field-sep* characters.
filelist	The list of files to cut from. If no files are specified, `cut` reads from the standard input.

Note

The `-c` and `-f` options are mutually exclusive. See the man page for more options.

Example

```
cut -f1,5 -d: /etc/passwd
```

This command extracts the user ID and names from the password file.

date

Displays the system date and time, or if you are the super user, sets the date and time. You can control how the date is displayed.

Syntax

```
date MMDDhhmm[CC][YY][.ss]

date +format
```

Item	Description
MMDDhhmm[*CC*][*YY*][*.ss*]	This is the format used to set the date and time. The following table explains each variable. Each part must be two digits. *MM* The month (01–12) *DD* The day (01–31) *hh* The hour (00–23) *mm* The minute (00–59) *CC* The first two digits of year (optional) *YY* The year (00–99) (optional) *ss* The second (optional)
+format	Controls how the date is displayed. *+format* is made up of a percent sign followed by any of the following:

Item	Description	
	%	A literal %
	n	A new line
	t	A horizontal tab
	H	The hour in the range (00–23)
	I	The hour in the range (01–12)
	k	The hour in the range (0–23)
	l	The hour in the range (1–12)
	M	The minute in the range (00–59)
	p	AM or PM
	r	The time, 12-hour (*hh:mm:ss* [AP]M)
	s	The number of seconds since 00:00:00, Jan 1, 1970 (a nonstandard Linux extension)
	S	The second (00–61)
	T	The time, 24-hour (*hh:mm:ss*)
	X	The time representation (*%H:%M:%S*)
	Z	The time zone (for example, EDT), or nothing if no time zone is determinable
	a	The abbreviated weekday name (Sun–Sat)
	A	The full weekday name, variable length (Sunday–Saturday)
	b	The abbreviated month name (Jan–Dec)
	B	The full month name, variable length (January–December)
	c	The date and time (Sat Oct 15 10:22:14 EST 1994)
	d	The day of month (01–31)
	D	The date in the format (*mm/dd/yy*)
	h	Same as %b
	j	The day of year (001–366)
	m	The month (01–12)
	U	The week number of the year with Sunday as first day of week (00–53)
	w	The day of the week (0–6) with 0 corresponding to Sunday
	W	The week number of year with Monday as first day of week (00–53)

(continues)

Item	Description	
	x	The date representation (*mm/dd/yy*)
	y	The last two digits of the year (00–99)
	Y	The year (1990...)

Note

Only the super user can set the date.

Examples

```
date 0101130091
```

This sets the date and time to 01/01/91 at 1:00 PM.

The following command

```
date "+Date = %D  Time = %H:%M"
```

results in

```
Date = 01/01/91  Time = 13:00
```

df

Reports the amount of space that is free on the disk.

Syntax

```
df [options] filesystems
```

Item	Description
filesystems	This is an optional list of file systems from which to report the amount of free disk space. If this is left blank, all currently mounted file systems are reported.
-a	Lists file systems that have 0 blocks, which are omitted by default.
-i	Lists inode usage information instead of block usage.
-k	Prints sizes in 1K blocks instead of 512-byte blocks.
-P	Uses the POSIX output format.
-t *fstype*	Limits the listing to file systems of type *fstype*.
-x *fstype*	Limits the listing to file systems not of type *fstype*.
-v	Ignored; included for compatibility with System V versions of df.
--help	Prints a usage message on standard output and exits successfully.
--version	Prints version information on standard output and exits successfully.

Note

`df` reports in blocks rather than bytes.

See Also

`du`

diff

Compares two text files and reports what must be done to the one to make it look like the other. `diff` also can be used to create a script usable by the editor `ed` to re-create the second file from the first. To compare binary files, use `cmp`.

Syntax

```
diff [options] oldfile newfile
```

Item	Description
oldfile	This is the file that you want `diff` to compare and then report what has to be done to it to make it look like *newfile*.
newfile	This is the name of the file you want to use to compare to *oldfile*. In a sense, this is the control file, as `diff` reports what it takes to make *oldfile* look like *newfile*.
-b	Causes leading and trailing blanks and tabs to compare as equal. (For example, `"the   big    tree     "` is the same as `"the big tree"`.)
-e	Generates a script suitable for the `ed` editor.
-f	Similar to the `-e` flag, this produces a script in the opposite order. However, this script is not usable by `ed`.

Notes

The output of `diff` takes any one of the following forms where each form shows a line number range and the text being referenced after:

```
lineno a from-lineno to-lineno
```

The text in the first file at `lineno` has to have the text in the second file `from-lineno` to the `to-lineno` added to it. The text found in the second file is shown preceded by a greater than sign (>). This shows that these lines were only found in the second file.

```
from-lineno to-lineno d lineno
```

The text in the first file found at line number `from-lineno` to the line number `to-lineno` must be deleted. If these lines exist, they fall after the line number in the second file `lineno`. The text to be deleted follows and is preceded by a less than sign (<). This shows that these lines are only found in the first file.

```
from-lineno to-lineno c from-lineno to-lineno
```

In this line, `diff` shows how two sets of lines are different and have to be changed from the first set of line number ranges to match the second set of line number ranges. The text that has to be changed follows and is preceded by <. The text as found in the second file follows this and is preceded by >.

Example

```
diff old-letter letter-to-dad
```

This is a command to change the file `old-letter` so it looks like the file `letter-to-dad`.

See Also

`ed`

du

`du` displays the amount of space being used by the specified directories or files. The information is reported in 1K-byte blocks.

Syntax

```
du [options] names
```

Item	Description
names	The list of directories or files that you want to have the space requirements calculated for. If left blank, the current directory is used.
-s	Causes only a total for each of the specified names. Normally, a number for every subdirectory is displayed.
-a	Causes each file encountered to be displayed with its size.
-b	Prints sizes in bytes.
-x	Only the directories in the currently mounted file system are traversed; other file systems are ignored. May not be supported on some implementations of UNIX.
-L	Shows the disk space used by the file pointed to by a symbolic link instead of the space used by the link itself.

Note

Files with more than one link are only counted once. However, `du` has a maximum number of links it can table, so when this maximum is exceeded, the sizes used by these files are included in the total.

Examples

```
du -s /usr/bin
```

This reports the total space in 512-byte blocks used by the directory `/usr/bin`.

```
du
```

This reports the space usage of the current directory and gives a number for each subdirectory encountered.

See Also

`df`

echo

This command takes the arguments passed to it and writes them to standard output. `echo` is useful in shell scripts to prompt for input or to inform of the status of a process.

Syntax

```
echo [-n] [-e] string
```

Item	Description
`-n`	Normally, `echo` follows all the output with a new line; this option suppresses that.
`-e`	Enables interpretation of the following character sequences in the string: `\a` Alert (bell) `\b` Backspace `\c` Don't print a new line at end `\f` Formfeed `\n` A new line `\r` A carriage return `\t` A tab `\v` A vertical tab `\\` A backslash `\nnn` The character whose octal ASCII code is nnn
`string`	The string of characters you want to output.

Examples

```
echo Hello
```

This prints `Hello` on the standard output.

```
echo -e "enter Y or N \c"
```

This prompts the user for a Y or N response without echoing a new line.

```
echo
```

This simply produces a new line.

```
echo -e 'Can you hear this \07?'
```

This demonstrates the usage of the octal digits. Here, the octal digits are used to sound the terminal bell.

See Also

```
cat
```

ed

A line editor that is useful on systems or terminals that don't support full screen editors such as vi. ed also can be used to edit files in batch by creating ed scripts.

Syntax

```
ed [-] [-s][-x][-p prompt] file-name
```

Item	Description
-	Suppresses the messages produced by the e, r, w, q, and ! commands.
-s	Suppresses diagnostics. This options should be used if ed's input comes from a script.
-x	Prompts for the encryption key to be used in subsequent reads and writes.
-p *prompt*	Enables you to specify your own prompt string.
file-name	The name of the file you want to edit. You may only edit one file at a time.

Note

ed is rather complex and powerful. For more information, see the user's guide and reference book provided with your system, or use a book dedicated to the usage of ed.

Example

```
ed letter-to-dad
```

This starts ed to edit letter-to-dad.

See Also

```
vi, ex
```

See grep.

env

Modifies the environment for the execution of a command without affecting the current environment. It also may be used to display the current environment.

Syntax

```
env [-] [-i][-u name][name=value] [command]
```

Item	Description
-	Restricts the environment to only those values to follow in the *name=value* list.
-u *name*	Removes variable name from the environment if it was in the environment to start with.
-i	Starts with an empty environment, ignoring any environment information inherited by the process.
name=value	Allows you to pass environment variables to the command specifying the value of the variable for this execution of the command. You may pass multiple variables simply by repeating the *name=value* format.
command	The name of command and its arguments to be run with the specified environment.

Example

```
env
```

This prints the current environment in a *name=value* format, one per line.

```
env HOME=/usr/sue sh
```

This runs a new shell with the home directory set up as /usr/sue.

fgrep

See grep.

file

Determines the type of a file. file is able to recognize whether the file is executable, text, data, and so on. Many of the UNIX commands are only shell scripts. file can be used to report the UNIX commands that are and are not scripts. It is also useful to determine if the file is "text" based or not and, therefore, whether it can be viewed or edited.

Syntax

```
file [-c] [-z] [-L] [-f ffile ] [-m mfile] filelist
```

Item	Description
-c	Prints out the parsed form of the magic file. This is usually used in conjunction with -m to debug a new magic file before installing it.
-z	Looks inside a compressed file and tries to figure out its type.
-L	This option causes symbolic links to be followed.
-f *ffile*	Tells file that the list of files to identify is found in *ffile*. This is useful when many files must be identified.

(continues)

Item	Description
`-m` *`mfile`*	Specifies an alternate file of magic numbers to use for determining file types.
`filelist`	A space-separated list of files you want to know the type of.

Example

```
file /home/datafile
```

This examines the file `/home/datafile` and reports what type of file it is.

See Also

The internal `type` command of `bash` as documented in the `bash` man page.

find

`find` is an extremely powerful tool. It traverses the specified directories generating a list of files that match the criteria specified. Files may be matched by name, size, creation time, modification time, and many more criteria. You can even execute a command on the matched files each time a file is found.

Syntax

```
find dirlist match-spec
```

Item	Description	
`dirlist`	A space-separated list of the directories where you want to look for a file or set of files.	
`match-spec`	The matching specification or description of files you want to find.	
	`-name` *`file`*	Tells `find` what file to search for; the file to find is enclosed in quotation marks. Wild cards (`*` and `?`) may be used.
	`-perm` *`mode`*	Matches all files whose mode matches the numeric value of *mode*. All modes must be matched—not just read, write, and execute. If preceded by a negative (`-`), mode takes on the meaning of everything without this mode.
	`-type` *`x`*	Matches all files whose type, *x*, is c (meaning), b (block special), d (directory), p (named pipe), l (symbolic link), s (socket), or f (regular file).
	`-links` *`n`*	Matches all files with *n* number of links.
	`-size` *`n`*	Matches all files of size *n* blocks (512-byte blocks, 1K-byte blocks if `k` follows *n*)
	`-user` *`user-id`*	Matches all files whose user ID is *`user-id`*. May either be the numeric value or the logname of the user.
	`-atime` *`n`*	Matches all files last accessed within the previous *n* days.

Item	Description	
	`-mtime n`	Matches all files modified within the previous *n* days.
	`-exec cmd`	For each file matched, the command *cmd* is executed. The notation `{}` is used to signify where the file name should appear in the command executed. The command must be terminated by an escaped semicolon (`\;`), for example, `-exec ls -d {}\;`. Here, the command `ls` is executed with the `-d` argument and each file is passed to `ls` at the place where the `{}` is found.
	`-newer file`	Matches all files that have been modified more recently than the file *`file`*.

Notes

The options may be grouped together and combined to limit the search criteria. Multiple flags are assumed to be ANDs, meaning that both criteria must be met. To offer more control over selection, the following table describes other options:

`()` Parentheses may be used to group selections. Because the parentheses are special to the shell they must be escaped, `\(`.

`-o` This is the OR operator, overriding the default AND assumption.

`!` This is a NOT operator and negates the expression that follows it.

The `find` command is very complex. There are several different options that are not listed here. Refer to the man page for more information.

Examples

```
find . -name letter-to-dad -print
```

Searches the current directory and its subdirectories for a file called `letter-to-dad`. When and if `find` finds it, the full path name is shown on-screen.

```
find . -name "letter*" -print
```

Looks for all files starting with `letter` (note the use of the `*` wild card). This allows you to do a pattern match of all files starting with the characters `letter`. Such a search results with `letters`, `letter_to_dad`, `letter_to_mom`, and so on.

```
find . -name "letter*" -exec ls -l {} \;
```

This example searches for the files starting with `letter` and executes a long listing on them. Notice the placement of the `{}` and the escaped semicolon, `\;`.

```
find . ! \( -name "letter*" -o -name "*dad" \) -print
```

This example is more complicated. This command looks for a list of files that don't start with `letter` or end with `dad`.

finger

Displays information about users on the system.

Syntax

```
finger [options] users
```

Item	Description
users	This is an optional list of user names. If specified, then additional information about the user is given. Remote users can be specified by giving the user name and the remote host name as in *user@remote.computer*.
-s	Displays the user's logon name, real name, terminal name and write status, idle time, logon time, office location, and office phone number.
-l	Produces a multi-line format displaying all of the information described for the -s option as well as the user's home directory, home phone number, logon shell, mail status, and the contents of the user's .plan and .project files.
-p	Prevents the -l option of finger from displaying the contents of the .plan and .project files.
-m	Restricts matching of the user argument to the logon name.

Notes

If no options are specified, finger defaults to the multi-line output format as specified by the -l argument.

If no arguments are specified, finger prints an entry for each user currently logged onto the system.

See Also

who, w

grep

grep looks for patterns found in files and reports to you when these patterns are found. The name of the command comes from the use of "regular expressions" in the ed family of editors. grep stands for Global Regular Express Printer.

Syntax

```
grep [options] reg-expres filelist

egrep [options] reg-expres filelist

fgrep [options] string filelist
```

Item	Description
filelist	An optional space-separated list of files to search for the given *string* or *reg-expres*. If left blank, the standard input is searched.
reg-expres	The regular expression to search for. Regular expressions are in the form used by `ed`. See the man page for the definition of regular expressions.
string	The string you want to find in the files.
`-v`	Lists the lines that don't match *string* or *reg-expres*.
`-c`	Counts the matching lines.
`-l`	Only the names of the files containing a match are displayed.
`-h`	Suppresses the display of the name of the file the match was found in (`grep` and `egrep` only).
`-n`	Each matching line is displayed along with its relative line number.
`-i`	Causes matching to not be case-sensitive. The default behavior is to be case-sensitive.
`-e` *reg-expres*	Useful when the regular expression or string starts with a hyphen.
`-f` *file*	*file* contains the strings or expressions to search for.

Notes

`fgrep` stands for fast `grep` and can only search for fixed strings. Multiple strings may be searched for by separating each string by a new line or entering them in the `-f file` file.

`egrep` stands for extended `grep` and accepts the following enhancements to regular expressions defined by `ed`:

`+`	If this trails a regular expression, it matches one or more of that occurrence.
`?`	If this trails a regular expression, it matches 0 or 1 occurrences.
`¦`	Used to denote multiple regular expressions.
`()`	May be used to group expressions.

There are several additional command-line options. Refer to the man page for a full description.

Examples

```
grep hello letter-to-dad
```

Searches for the word `hello` in the file `letter-to-dad`.

```
fgrep hello letter-to-dad
```

Does the same thing.

```
grep "[hH]ello" letter-to-dad
```

Searches for the word `hello` or `Hello`.

```
fgrep "hello
Hello" letter-to-dad
```

Does the same thing.

```
egrep "([Ss]ome¦[Aa]ny)one" letter-to-dad
```

This looks for all the words `someone`, `Someone`, `anyone`, or `Anyone` in the file.

```
vi 'fgrep -l hello *'
```

This generates a list of file names in the current directory that have the word `hello` in them and passes this list of names to the editor `vi`.

See Also

`bash`, `ed`

head

`head` prints out the first number of specified lines of a file.

Syntax

```
head -lines filelist
```

Item	Description
-lines	The number of lines to print from the beginning of the file. The default is 10.
filelist	A space-separated list of file names you want displayed. If left blank, the standard input is read.

Example

```
head letter-to-dad
```

This prints the first 10 lines from the file `letter-to-dad`.

See Also

`tail`, `pr`, `cat`, `more`

id

`id` displays your identification to the system. It reports your user name, user ID number, group name, and group ID number.

Syntax

```
id [options]
```

Item	Description
`-g`	Prints only the group ID.
`-G`	Prints only the supplementary groups.
`-n`	Prints the user or group name instead of the ID number. Requires `-u`, `-g`, or `-G`.
`-r`	Prints the real, instead of effective, user or group ID. Requires `-u`, `-g`, or `-G`.
`-u`	Prints only the user ID.
`--help`	Prints a usage message on the standard output and exits successfully.
`--version`	Prints version information on the standard output and then exits successfully.

Example

```
id
```

Shows the `id` information.

join

Extracts the common lines from two sorted files. One line of output is produced for each line in the two files that match, based on the specified keys.

Syntax

```
join [options] file1 file2
```

Item	Description
file1	The first file used in the join, which may be a hyphen (`-`) to tell `join` to read from the standard input; thus, `join` may be a filter in a pipeline.
file2	The second file used in the `join`.
`-a`*n*	The unmatching lines from either *file1* or *file2* also are produced. *n* may be either a 1 or 2.
`-e` *string*	Replaces empty output fields with *string*.
`-j` *n m*	Joins the two files on the *m*th field of file *n*. If *n* is not specified then the *m*th field of each file is used.
`-o` *flist*	Constructs each output line according to the format in *flist*.
`-t` *char*	By default the field separators are tab, new lines, and spaces. This option causes *char* to be used as the field separator. All instances of *char* are significant. Multiple instances of *char* and the default are treated as one.
`-v` *fnumber*	Prints a line for each unpairable line in file *fnumber* (either 1 or 2), instead of the normal output.

Example

```
join to-do-list old-do-list
```

Reports the lines that the two lists have in common.

See Also

`sort`, `uniq`

kill

Allows you to send a signal to a process that is currently executing. Usually, this command is issued to stop the executing process, thus the `kill` name because you use it to "kill" the process.

Syntax

```
kill [-signal] pid
```

```
kill -l
```

Item	Description
-signal	An optional signal that can be sent. The default is `SIGTERM`. Two other popular ones are `SIGHUP`, which is the equivalent of hanging up the phone as if on a modem, and `SIGKILL`, which cannot be ignored by a process.
pid	The process ID of the process you want to send the specified signal. A *pid* is a number used by the system to keep track of the process. The ps command can be used to report the *pid* of a process.
-l	Prints a list of the signal names that can be sent with `kill`.

Tip

Although kill -9 is the sure kill, it is often best to try `SIGTERM` and `SIGHUP` first. These signals can be caught by the applications and after they receive them, properly clean up after themselves. Because kill -9 can't be caught, you may have to do some house cleaning after the process terminates.

Message

```
kill: permission denied
```

You tried to kill a process that you don't own, or you are not the super user.

Examples

```
kill 125
```

This sends the `SIGTERM` signal to the process 125. The default signal is `SIGTERM`.

```
kill -9 125
```

This sends signal `9`, which is the numeric value for `SIGKILL`. This works if no other signals do.

Caution

There are instances when even kill `-9` can't kill the process. This is when the process is using a kernel service and can't receive signals. Periodically processes get locked up in this mode. The only way to resolve this is to shut down the system.

See Also

`sh`, `ps`

less

`less` is a general purpose file pager, similar to `more`. It allows both forward and backward movement through files.

Syntax

`less [options] file-names`

Item	Description
`-?`	This option displays a summary of the commands accepted by less. If this option is given, all other options are ignored, and `less` exits after the help screen is viewed.
`-a`	Causes searches to start after the last line displayed on-screen.
`-c`	Causes full screen repaints to be painted from the top line down.
`-C`	The `-C` option is like `-c`, but the screen is cleared before it is repainted.
`-e`	Causes `less` to automatically exit the second time it reaches end-of-file. By default, the only way to exit `less` is via the `q` command.
`-E`	Causes `less` to automatically exit the first time it reaches the end of the file.
`-i`	Causes searches to be case-insensitive.
`-n`	Suppresses line numbers.
`-o` *`file`*	Causes `less` to copy its input to *`file`* as it is being viewed. This applies only when the input file is a pipe, not an ordinary file.
`-O` *`file`*	The `-O` option is like `-o`, but it overwrites an existing file without asking for confirmation.
`-q`	Causes moderately quiet operation: the terminal bell is not rung if an attempt is made to scroll past the end of the file or before the beginning of the file. The terminal bell is rung on certain other errors, such as typing an invalid character.
`-Q`	Causes totally quiet operation.
`-s`	Causes consecutive blank lines to be squeezed into a single blank line.
`-x` *n*	Sets tab stops every *n* positions. The default for *n* is 8.

Notes

You can specify a set of command options to be used by `less` every time by assigning them to the `LESS` environment variable.

There are many additional command-line and key-command options for the `less` command. Refer to the man page for more information.

Example

```
less letter-to-dad
```

Displays the text of the file `letter-to-dad`.

ln

Creates a link between two files, enabling you to have more than one name to access a file. A directory entry is simply a name to call the file and an inode number. The inode number is an index into the file system's table. Therefore, it is no big deal to have more than one name to inode reference in the same directory or multiple directories.

A benefit of a link over a copy is that only one version of the file exists on the disk; therefore, no additional storage is required. Any file may have multiple links.

`ln` is a link to the `cp` and `mv` commands and behaves in a very similar manner. All the rules for these two commands apply here as well, except that `ln` just makes a link.

`ln` provides two types of links: *hard* links and *symbolic* links. Linux treats hard links just like files. Each hard link is counted as a file entry. This means that the original file will not be deleted until all hard links have been deleted. A symbolic link is treated as a place holder for the file. If a file has symbolic links, and the file is deleted, all symbolic links will be deleted automatically.

Syntax

```
ln [-s]source-file dest-file

ln source-list dest-directory
```

Item	Description
`-s`	Makes a symbolic link instead of a hard link.
`source-file`	The original file.
`dest-file`	The destination name. This is the name you want the file to go by. It is sort of an alias of the original file.
`source-list`	A space-separated list of file to link.
`dest-directory`	The destination directory. This is the directory where you want to have the linked files stored. That is, you want to duplicate the names of the files here just as they were given in the *`source-list`*.

Example

```
ln letter-to-dad my-letter
```

This enables you to edit either the file `letter-to-dad` or the file `my-letter` and modify both of them at the same time.

See Also

`cp, mv`

logname

`logname` reads the `/etc/utmp` file to report what name you used to log onto the system.

Syntax

```
logname
```

Example

```
logname
```

This reports what name you used to log onto the system.

ls

Lists the files found in the file system.

Syntax

```
ls [options] [filelist]
```

Item	Description
`-a`	Shows all files including current directory and the parent directory.
`-C`	Columnar output, sorted down the columns.
`-x`	Columnar output, sorted across the columns.
`-d`	Treats each entry as a directory.
`-l`	Gives a long listing. A long listing shows details about the files, such as the type of the file, the permissions, the link/directory count, the owner, the group, the size in bytes, when the file was last modified, and the file name. The file types are the following: `-` normal file `d` Directory `b` Block-special device (disks) `c` Character special device (terminals) `p` Named pipe `s` Semaphore `m` Shared memory

(continues)

VI

Working with Linux

Item	Description
	The permissions are three clusters of three bytes each. Each cluster represents the permissions for the owner, group, and other. The permissions are as follows: `r` Read access `w` Write access `x` Execute access
`-t`	Sorts by the time last modified. Used with the `-l` flag.
`-u`	Sorts by the time last accessed. Used with the `-t` flag.
`-c`	Sorts by the time the inode information last changed. Used with the `-t` flag.
`-r`	Reverses the sort order.
`-i`	Shows the inode number of the file in the first column.
`-F`	Places a `/` after directory entries, an `*` after executable programs, an `@` after symbolic links, a `¦` after a FIFO, an `=` after sockets, and nothing after regular files.
`filelist`	A list of files to list with `ls`. Wild cards may be used.

Examples

Tip

Use -d when you want to find out the characteristics of a directory. Otherwise, the contents of the directory are shown and not the directory itself.

```
ls
```

Lists the files in the current directory in one long column.

```
ls -C
```

Lists the files in current directory broken up into columns.

```
ls -l
```

Gives a long listing of the files in the current directory.

```
ls -ltr /usr/spool/mail
```

Gives a long listing, sorted by modification time, in descending order of the files found in the directory `/usr/spool/mail`.

See Also

`chmod`

mesg

Enables other users to write to your terminal. This command controls whether you allow a user to use the `write` command to your terminal.

Syntax

```
mesg [n ¦ y]
```

Item	Description
n	Does not allow users to send messages to your terminal.
y	Allows users to send messages to your terminal.

If no option is specified, mesg shows the status of your terminal availability to messages.

Note

mesg -y is the default state of your terminal. This command enables users to write to your terminal.

Messages

```
Is y
```

Your terminal allows others to write to it.

```
Is n
```

Your terminal does not allow others to write to it.

Examples

```
mesg
```

Shows whether users can or cannot write to your terminal.

```
mesg n
```

Disallows the writing of messages to your terminal.

```
mesg y
```

Allows users to write to your terminal.

Caution

It is a good idea to set root's .profile file to include the command mesg n. Many terminals have an escape sequence that puts them into echo command mode—that is, what is supplied by the user writing to root's terminal is in effect, executed by root. This is a grave security hole.

See Also

```
write
```

mcd

`mcd` is used to report and set the current MS-DOS device and directory.

Syntax

```
mcd [msdos-directory]
```

Item	Description
msdos-directory	The new working device and directory relative to an MS-DOS file system.

Example

```
mcd a:/home
```

Sets the working directory to `/home` on MS-DOS drive A:.

Notes

The environment variable `MCWD` may be used to locate the file where the device and current working directory information is stored. The default is `$HOME/.mcwd`. Information in this file is ignored if the file is more than six hours old.

MS-DOS file names are separated by either the `\` or `/` characters. Using the `\` separator or wild-card characters requires that the file name be enclosed in quotes to prevent these characters from being translated by the shell.

See Also

`mcopy`, `mdir`, `mdel`

mcopy

`mcopy` copies files to and from an MS-DOS file system.

Syntax

```
mcopy [options] sourcefile targetfile
```

Item	Description
`-t`	Text file transfer. `mcopy` translates incoming carriage return/line feeds to line feeds.
`-n`	Does not warn the user when overwriting an existing file.
`-v`	Verbose mode.
`-m`	Preserves the file modification time.
sourcefile	The source MS-DOS file to copy.
targetfile	The destination MS-DOS file or directory.

Notes

mcopy uses the drive designation a: to specify the path to the MS-DOS file system. If no drive designation is given, the destination is assumed to be a file under the current working directory.

MS-DOS file names are separated by either the \ or / characters. Using the \ separator or wild-card characters requires that the file name be enclosed in quotes to prevent these characters from being translated by the shell.

The mcd command may be used to establish the device and the current working directory relative to MS-DOS.

Example

```
mcopy -t foo.txt a:foo.txt
```

Copies the Linux file foo.txt to an MS-DOS file in drive A: named foo.txt, translating carriage returns as it copies the file.

See Also

mcd, mdel, mdir

mdel

Deletes an MS-DOS file from a DOS file system.

Syntax

```
mdel [-v] msdos-file
```

Item	Description
-v	Verbose mode. Echo each file name as it is processed.
msdos-file	The file to delete.

Example

```
mdel a:\foo.txt
```

Delete the file foo.txt on drive MS-DOS drive A:.

Notes

mdel uses the drive designation a: to specify the path to the MS-DOS file system. If no drive designation is given, the destination is assumed to be a file under the current working directory.

MS-DOS file names are separated by either the \ or / characters. Using the \ separator or wild-card characters requires that the file name be enclosed in quotes to prevent these characters from being translated by the shell.

The mcd command may be used to establish the device and the current working directory relative to MS-DOS.

See Also

mcopy, mcd, mdir

mdir

Displays the contents of an MS-DOS directory.

Syntax

```
mdir [-w] name
```

Item	Description
-w	Displays the listing in wide format without file size or creation date.
name	The name of the MS-DOS files or directories to list.

Example

```
mdir a:/data
```

Lists the files in the /data directory on the MS-DOS device A:.

Notes

mdir uses the drive designation a: to specify the path to the MS-DOS file system. If no drive designation is given, the destination is assumed to be a file under the current working directory.

MS-DOS file names are separated by either the \ or / characters. Using the \ separator or wild-card characters requires that the file name be enclosed in quotes to prevent these characters from being translated by the shell.

The mcd command may be used to establish the device and the current working directory relative to MS-DOS.

See Also

mdel, mcopy, mcp

mkdir

Creates new directories in the file system.

Syntax

```
mkdir [-m mode] [-p dirnames] dir
```

Item	Description
-m *mode*	Sets the directory permissions to *mode* at the time of creation.
-p *dirnames*	Creates all nonexistent parent directories.
dir	The directory to create.

Examples

```
mkdir letters
```

Creates the directory `letters`.

```
mkdir -p letters/personal letters/work
```

Makes the directories `letters/personal` and `letters/work`. If the directory `letters` do not exist, the `-p` flag causes the directory `letters` to be created; otherwise, an error message results.

See Also

`rm`, `rmdir`, `chmod`

more

`more` is a general-purpose pager. Use `more` to view text that scrolls off the screen. `more` also provides some handy text-search capabilities using regular expressions. `less` can emulate `more` and provides some enhancements.

Syntax

```
more [options] file-names
```

Item	Description
-*n*	*n* is an integer used to set the window size to *n* lines long. The window size is how many lines to show on the screen.
-c	As `more` pages through the text, it draws each line from top to bottom by clearing the line and then drawing the next line. Normally, `more` clears the screen and then draws each line.
-d	Displays the prompt `Press space to continue, 'q' to quit` in place of the default `more` prompt.
-f	Counts logical lines instead of screen lines. Long lines wrap around the screen and are normally counted as a new line by `more`; the `-f` flag turns off the counting of the wrapped portion of long lines.
-l	Does not treat the `^L` (form feed) character specially. Normally `more` treats the `^L` the same as the window filling up by pausing.
-s	Multiple blank lines are suppressed and treated as one.
-p	Does not scroll. Instead, clears the screen and displays the text.
-u	Suppresses underlining.
file-names	A list of files that you want to display with `more`.

Note

For the `-c` option to work the terminal must support the clear-to-end-of-line capa-bility.

Messages

```
file-name: No such file or directory
```

You've tried to view a file that doesn't exist.

```
file-name: Not a text file
```

You've tried to view a file that is not a text file. `more` tries to determine if a file is or is not a text file before allowing you to view it. *`file-name`* is substituted with the name you asked for.

```
dirname: directory
```

You've tried to use `more` to view a directory file. *`dirname`* is substituted with the name you asked for.

Examples

```
more letter-to-dad
```

This displays a text file called `letter-to-dad`.

```
ls -l /dev ¦ more
```

This demonstrates how `more` is used at the end of a pipeline to control the output of the pipeline.

Note

While using the `more` utility, press <h> for a list of other possible actions to use.

Set the environment variable `MORE` to options you want to have set every time you invoke the `more` utility. If, while viewing a file, you realize you want to change something, just press <v>. This boots the `vi` text editor and allows you to make the changes you want. When you exit the editor, you return to the `more` utility at the place you left it.

If you know that you want to look at a section of the text that contains a certain set of characters, enter the / command followed by a regular expression. This searches for the regular expression you entered. See the man page for the `ed` command for a definition of regular expressions.

See Also

`vi`, `ed`, `pr`, `cat`

mv

Renames a file, moves a file to a new directory, or both. `mv` also lets you rename a directory.

Syntax

```
mv [-f] [-i] file1 file2

mv [-f] [-i] dir1 dir2

mv [-f] [-i] filelist dir
```

Item	Description
`-f`	Normally `mv` prompts you if the destination file exists and write permission is turned off. This causes `mv` to do the move without prompting.
`-i`	Interactive mode. Prompt before overwriting a file.
`file1`	The source file name.
`file2`	The destination file name (new name).
`dir1`	The source directory name.
`dir2`	The destination directory name (new name).
`filelist`	A space-separated list of file names. When this option is used the files retain their names but are moved to the new directory *`dir`*.
`dir`	The destination directory.

Note

`mv` cannot physically move a directory; it can only rename it. There are additional options for the `mv` command. Refer to the man page for a full list.

Examples

```
mv letters letter
```

Changes the file name `letters` to `letter`.

```
mv letter $HOME/trashcan
```

Here `trashcan` is a directory in the user's home directory. This is a useful way to remove files because they are easier to recover if you didn't really want to delete them.

Caution

`mv` doesn't prompt for confirmation of the move unless the destination file already exists and the mode of the file prohibits writing or you specify the `-i` flag. Because `mv` first removes the destination file, you may lose a file you didn't mean to lose.

Caution

Because `mv` first removes the destination file, if it exists, before doing the move, any links that had been established with the destination file are lost. If you have to maintain those links, you want to first copy the file to the destination name and then remove the original file.

Note

`ln`, `cp`, and `mv` are linked to each other; they determine their actions based on how they are invoked.

See Also

`rm`, `cp`, `ln`, `copy`, `chmod`

newgrp

Changes your current group ID, allowing you to work with another group's files.

Syntax

```
newgrp group
```

With no options `newgrp` returns you to the group you were in when you logged on.

Item	Description
group	This is the group ID you want to become active under. *group* must be set up in `/etc/group` and the user must be in the list; otherwise, access is denied.

Note

When using the C shell you cannot use the `logout` command, you must use <Ctrl-d> to return to the original group.

Messages

```
No such group.: No such file or directory.
```

This message means you have asked to change to a group ID that does not exist.

```
Passwd:
```

You have asked to change to a group ID that has a password. You must enter the correct group password or access to the group is denied.

```
Sorry
```

Access to the group has been denied. Either your user name is not in the list of valid users for the group or you entered an incorrect group password.

Example

```
newgrp admin
```

This changes your group ID to `admin`.

See Also

```
id
```

passwd

Maintains user passwords. Also, system administrators may use this command to administer user accounts.

Syntax

```
passwd [name]
```

Item	Description
name	Changes the password of the user name. Only the super user can do this.

Notes

You have to be an administrator to change someone else's password.

Passwords should be chosen so that they are easy to remember but hard to guess. This almost seems like a contradiction in terms. However, good password selection is crucial to a secure system.

Tip

A good trick for picking passwords is to pick two unrelated words and join them with a special character, such as `book%car`. You can use the first letter of each word of a phrase. For example, "Four score and seven years ago" translates to `4s&7ya`.

Caution

You should never pick a password that is a real dictionary word in any language. Likewise, you should never use anyone's name. Also, avoid using any identification number associated with yourself.

Example

```
passwd
```

This places you into the password change program. You are first prompted for your old password.

paste

Produces columnar output from one or more files, where each file contributes a column of the output. paste is often used with cut to reorder columns in a file.

Syntax

```
paste -ddelim filelist

paste -s -ddelim filelist
```

Item	Description
-d*delim*	Specifies what character is used to delimit each column (tab is the default).
filelist	A list of files to paste together. May be - to signify standard input.
-s	Causes paste to traverse each file separately. This uses lines in the file for each column. The first line is the first column, the second line the second column, and so on.

Note

The output of paste is always standard output.

Examples

```
ls -l ¦ tee /tmp/tmp.$$ ¦ cut -f5 -d' ' >/tmp/sz.$$

cut -f9 -d' ' /tmp/tmp.$$ ¦ paste - /tmp/sz.$$

rm /tmp/*.$$
```

At first, these code lines might look like a lot to swallow but look at it piece by piece. This command takes the output of l and produces a listing with the name of the file followed by its size in bytes. The result of l is a pipe through tee to allow you to store a copy of the l's output for later use (/tmp/tmp.$$). The pipe flows through tee to the first cut command that extracts the field holding the size and stores that in a file for later use (/tmp/sz.$$). The second cut extracts the name field piping this to paste. paste accepts standard input as its first column and the file /tmp/sz.$$ as the second column. Lastly, clean up by removing the temporary files.

See Also

cut, rm, tee, pr, grep

pr

Allows you to do some formatting to a file while printing it to the standard output. pr also has some of the functionality of paste and nl built into it.

Syntax

```
pr [options] filelist
```

Item	Description
filelist	A space-delimited list of files. If left blank, the standard input is read. - may be used as a file name to tell pr to read from the standard input. You may combine file names and the -. This causes pr to read both from the standard input and from the listed files.
+*page*	Begins printing with page *page*. The default is page 1.
-*col*	Specifies *col* columns of output. This flag assumes the flags -e and -i. The default is 1 column.
-m	Merges the files, printing each file in a column, overriding the -*col* flag.
-d	Double-spaces the output.
-e*ccol*	When reading the input, tabs are replaced with character *c* (of *ccol*) and expanded to positions (*col* + 1), ((2 * *col*)+1), ((3 * *col*)+1), and so on. *c* may be any non-digit character. *col* defaults to every eight positions.
-i*ccol*	Works like -e except on the output of pr, replacing whitespace with the character *c*. Whitespace is spaces, tabs, and so on.
-n*cwidth*	Selects line numbering. *c* is the character to place between the line number and the normal output (the default is a tab). *width* is how many character positions +1 the number occupies (the default is 5).
-w*length*	Sets the length of the line to *length* lines. For columnar output, the default is 72; otherwise, no limit is assumed.
-o*offset*	Offsets each line of output by *offset* character positions (default is 0).
-l*lines*	Sets the length of the page to *lines* lines (the default is 66).
-h *string*	Uses *string* as the header instead of the file name.
-f	Uses a formfeed character between pages. Normally, pr fills the remaining lines with new-line characters to cause a page break.
-t	Doesn't print the header or the footer. Normally, pr prints a five-line header and footer.
-s*char*	Separates multicolumn output with *char*. Tab is the default.

Examples

```
pr -n program.c ¦ lpr
```

This formats the file program.c with line numbers and sends the output to the printer.

```
ls ¦ pr -8 -i\ 6 -w132 -l51 ¦ lpr
```

This command takes the output of the ls command and produces an eight column report separated by a space every six character positions and prints it to a printer that has 11 × 8 1/2-inch paper in it (132 columns by 51 lines).

See Also

cat, grep, fgrep, lpr, paste, more

ps

Reports the status of processes. Because processes rapidly progress in their execution path, this report is only a snapshot view of what was happening when you asked. A subsequent invocation of ps may give different results.

Syntax

```
ps [options]
```

No *options* shows you a picture of the currently executing processes on your terminal. The following *options* are available for the ps command:

Item	Description
-l	Gives you a long listing.
-u	Prints in user format displaying the user name and start time.
-j	Gives output in the jobs format.
-s	Gives output in signal format.
-v	Displays output in virtual memory format.
-m	Displays memory information.
-a	Shows processes of other users as well.
-x	Displays processes without a controlling terminal.
-S	Adds child CPU time and page faults.
-c	Lists the command name from the kernel task_structure.
-e	Shows the environment.
-w	Displays in wide format. Does not truncate command lines to fit on one line.
-h	Does not display a header.
-r	Displays running processes only.
-n	Provides numeric output for USER and WCHAN.
-txx	Displays only processes with the controlling tty xx.

Tip

The -t and -u options are particularly useful for system administrators who have to kill processes for users who have gone astray.

The following columns are reported:

Column	Description
PID	The process ID.
PRI	Process priority.
NI	The Linux process nice value. A positive value means less CPU time.
SIZE	The virtual image size, calculated as the size of text+data+stack.
RSS	The resident set size. The number of kilobytes of the program that is currently resident in memory.
WCHAN	The name of the kernel event that the process is waiting for.
STAT	The process status. Given by one of the following codes: R Runnable S Sleeping D Uninterruptible sleep T Stopped or traced Z Zombie W Process has no resident pages
TT	The name of the controlling `tty` for the process.
PAGEIN	The number of page faults that have caused pages to be read from disk.
TRS	The text resident size.
SWAP	The number of kilobytes on the swap device.

Example

```
ps
```

Shows you the processes running on your terminal.

See Also

`kill`, `more`, `who`

pwd

Reports your present working or current directory.

Syntax

```
pwd
```

Example

```
pwd
```

Shows the current directory you are working in.

See Also

`cd`

rcp

The rcp command is used to copy files between computers.

Syntax

```
rcp [option] file1 file2

rcp [options] files directory
```

There are two forms of the rcp command. One is used to copy a file from one computer to another, and the other form is used to copy one or more files on one computer to a directory on another computer.

Item	Description
-r	Recursively copies subdirectories. For the -r option, the destination must be a directory.
-p	Attempts to preserve modification times and access modes for files.
-k	Requests kerberos tickets.
-x	Turns on DES encryption for all data passed by rcp.
file1, file2	Specification for source and destination files. Local files are simply named with the appropriate path. Remote files are prefaced with the remote host name followed by a colon, as in remotehost:/home/myfile.
files	The source file or files to copy if the destination is a directory. Preface remote files with the remote host name and a colon.
directory	The destination directory. Preface remote files or directory with the remote host name and a colon.

Examples

```
rcp foo.com:/home/dave/myfile localfile.txt
```

Copies the file /home/dave/myfile on the remote computer foo.com to the local file name localfile.txt.

```
rcp /home/data/* foo.com:/home/dave/data
```

Copies all the files from the local directory /home/data to the directory /home/dave/data on the remote computer foo.com.

See Also

cp

rm

Removes files and entire directory structures from the file system.

Syntax

```
rm [options] filelist
```

Item	Description
filelist	A space-delimited list of files you want to delete. It may contain directory names as well.
-r	Deletes the directories specified in *filelist*. Directories won't be deleted unless this flag is used.
-i	Specifies interactive mode. You are prompted for confirmation before the removal takes place. Any response beginning with a Y indicates yes, all others indicate no.
-f	Specifies forced mode. Normally, rm prompts you if you don't have permissions to delete the file. This flag forces the remove without your involvement.
-v	Verbose mode. Echo the name of the file before it is deleted.
--	Indicates the end of all options. Useful if you have to delete a file name that is the same as one of the options. For example, suppose a file named -f got created by accident and you want to delete it. The command, rm -f does not accomplish anything because the -f is interpreted as a flag and not the file name. The command rm -- -f, however, successfully removes the file.

Examples

```
rm letter-to-dad
```

This deletes the file named letter-to-dad.

```
rm -r oldletters
```

In this example, oldletters is a directory. This deletes all the files in this directory substructure.

```
rm -i sue*
```

This prompts you each time it encounters a file starting with the letters sue, to see if the file should be deleted.

```
rm -rf data
```

This deletes the directory data and all files and subdirectories under it. Use with caution.

See Also

rmdir, mv, cp, ln, copy

rmdir

Removes directories.

Syntax

```
rmdir -p dirlist
```

Item	Description
`-p`	Causes `rmdir` to delete any parent directories that also become empty after deleting the directories specified in *`dirlist`*. A status message as to what is, and what is not deleted is displayed.
`dirlist`	A space-delimited list of directory names. Directories must be empty to be deleted.

Messages

```
rmdir: dirname No such file or directory.
```

The directory you tried to remove doesn't exist.

```
rmdir: dirname not a directory
```

You used `rmdir` on a file name that isn't a directory.

```
rmdir: dirname Directory not empty
```

You tried to delete a directory that still contains some files.

Example

```
rmdir letters.1970
```

This deletes a directory that used to hold some old letters.

See Also

`rm`

sh

See `bash`.

shutdown

Linux is an operating system that has to be told that you want to turn it off. You can't just turn off the power on a Linux system—well you can, but you're going to wish you hadn't. `shutdown` lets you control when the shutdown takes place, and it notifies the users on a regular basis. `shutdown` safely brings the system to a point where the power may be turned off.

Syntax

```
shutdown [options] time [warning]
```

Item	Description
time	The time to shut down the system. Refer to the man page for a full description of the available time formats.
warning	A warning message sent out to all users.
-t *n*	Wait *n* seconds between sending processes the warning and the kill signal.
-k	Does not really shut down the system. Just sends the warning messages to everybody.
-r	Reboots after shutdown.
-h	Halts after shutdown.
-n	Doesn't synchronize the disks before rebooting or halting.
-f	Does a fast reboot. Does not check any file systems on reboot.
-c	Cancels an already running shutdown. With this option, it is not possible to give the *time* argument, but you can enter an explanatory message on the command line that is sent to all users.

Note

`shutdown` can only be run by the super user. Messages are sent to the users' terminals at intervals based on the amount of time left till the shutdown.

Examples

```
shutdown -r +15 "System rebooting..."
```

This shuts down the system and reboots it 15 minutes from the time the command was entered. It also sends the message `System rebooting...` to all users.

```
shutdown -h now
```

This shuts down the system and halts it immediately.

See Also

```
wall
```

sleep

Suspends execution for an interval of time.

Syntax

```
sleep n
```

Item	Description
n	Specifies the amount of time to sleep. This must be an integer. The default is measured in seconds. An optional identifier may be used to specify a different time unit. These are as follows: `s` Seconds `m` Minutes `h` Hours `d` Days

Note

`sleep` is not guaranteed to wake up exactly after the amount of time specified.

Example

```
while :
do
    date
    sleep 60
done
```

This shows the date every 60 seconds.

sort

Enables you to sort and merge text files. Sorts may be based on character fields or numeric fields, and multiple sort keys may be specified.

Syntax

```
sort [options] files
```

Item	Description
files	An optional list of files to be sorted or merged. If no files are specified or `-` is used as the file name, the standard input is read.
`-c`	Checks to see if the files are sorted; if they are, no output is generated.
`-m`	Merges the specified files. It is assumed that the files are already sorted.
`-u`	Makes sure only unique lines go to the output. The uniqueness of a line is based on the sort keys.
`-o` *file*	Specifies the output file name. This may be the same as one of the input file names. Normally, the output of sort is the standard output.
`-d`	Sorts in dictionary order. Only letters, digits, and blanks are used for ordering.
`-f`	"Folds," or changes, lowercase letters to uppercase for sort purposes.
`-i`	Ignores non-printable characters in the sort keys.
`-M`	Treats sort key as if it were a month. `JAN` is less than `FEB` which is less than `MAR`, and so on. This implies the `-b` flag.
`-n`	Specifies a key is a numeric key; implies the `-b` flag.

Item	Description
-r	Reverses the sort (descending).
-t *fld-sep*	Specifies that the field separator is the character *fld-sep*, not tabs or blanks.
-b	Ignores leading blanks when determining the value of the sort keys.
+*keybeg*	Specifies that the sort key starts at field number *keybeg*. Fields start counting at zero; the fifth field is a 4. *keybeg* accepts the format *M.NF*, where *M* is the field number, and *N* is the character offset within that field. The absence of *.N* assumes zero. *F* may be any of the following flags: b, d, f, i, n, or r, which have the same meanings as described previously except that they apply only to this key.
-*keyend*	Specifies on what field number the key ends, and follows the same format rules of +*keybeg*. If no ending field number is specified, the end of the line is assumed.

Notes

When multiple keys are used, the keys specified later in the command line are compared when the earlier ones are equal. For example,

```
sort +2 -3  +5 -6
```

The key defined by character positions 5 -6 is compared only when the key defined by positions 2 -3 does not define a uniq record. All comparisons are governed by the locale of the system; this allows support for international usage.

Because sort distinguishes records by looking for the new-line character, the command is not suitable for binary files.

Messages

```
sort: iunrecognized option  option
```

You specified a flag sort doesn't understand.

```
sort: No such file or directory.
```

You specified a file name that doesn't exist.

```
sort: can't create file-name
```

You specified the -o option with a file name in a directory for which you don't have permissions to write in, or the file name exists and you don't have permissions to write to it.

Examples

```
ps -e ¦ sort
```

Because the first column of ps is the PID number, this gives you the processes running on the system in PID order.

```
ps -e ¦ sort +3
```

Because the last column of ps is the name of the command, this gives a list of the processes running by command name.

```
ps -e ¦ sort -u +3
```

This strips out any duplicate process names. In a sense, this answers the question "How many different types of things get used?"

```
ps -e ¦ sort -r +2 -3
```

The third column is the CPU time the process has had. This reverses the sort, placing the processes that have used the most CPU time at the top.

See Also

`uniq`, `join`, `ps`

split

Breaks up a text file into smaller pieces. Periodically, files become too large to load into an editor or some other utility. `split` lets you handle the file in individual, more manageable pieces.

Syntax

`split -numlines file tagname`

Item	Description
-numlines	Specifies the number of lines to include in each piece.
file	The file to split into smaller pieces. If left blank or - is used, standard input is read.
tagname	By default, `split` builds the output pieces by creating the following files: `xaa`, then `xab`, then `xac`, and so on. *tagname*, if specified, replaces the *x* in the previous list, thus building the list: *tagname*`aa`, *tagname*`ab`, *tagname*`ac`, and so on.

Note

There must be enough room for two copies of the file in the current file system.

Message

```
No such file or directory.
```

You supplied `split` with a file name that doesn't exist.

Examples

```
split -1000 letter-to-dad dadletter
```

Apparently, the previous `letter-to-dad` was a large one. This line breaks up that letter into 1,000 line pieces. The output files are `dadletteraa`, `dadletterab`, and so on.

```
cat dadletter* >letter-to-dad
```

This took all the pieces and put them back together again into the file `letter-to-dad`.

See Also

```
cat
```

stty

Sets the terminal device driver line controls. `stty` provides many options to control the `tty` driver. You may set the character size, parity, baud rate, input preprocessing of special characters, and output processing of special characters.

Syntax

```
stty -a -g settings
```

Item	Description
`-a`	Shows all current settings of the currently logged on terminal. Normally, `stty` gives a reduced version of all the settings. `stty` actually reads from the terminal driver. So if you want to see what the terminal settings are for another `tty`, just redirect the input to `stty` (see example that follows).
`-g`	Like `-a` but produces 12 hexadecimal numbers separated by colons. This output is suitable for input to `stty`.
`settings`	The settings may either be the output of a previous `-g` flag, or a series of `stty` commands.

Note

It is important to understand that `stty` changes how the system's `tty` driver behaves in reference to what your terminal is physically set to. There are two ends to having a terminal communicate: the physical settings on the device, and how the system thinks it should talk to the device. If these aren't equal, the communication breaks down. `stty` only affects how the system thinks the device is talking. You use `stty` to enable the system to talk to `tty` devices with varying communication needs.

Message

```
/dev/console: cannot open
```

You tried to manipulate a port you don't have permissions to work with.

Examples

```
stty -a
```

Shows all the settings on this `tty`.

```
stty -a </dev/tty02
```

This shows you all the settings on the second console.

Occasionally, a program crashes and leaves your terminal in a state that doesn't seem to accept your input. In this case, pressing <Ctrl-Shift-j>, typing **`stty sane`**, and pressing <Ctrl-Shift-j> returns your terminal to a usable state.

sync

Writes the current disk image held in the system disk's I/O buffers to the hard disk. You have to make sure that the buffers are written before you shut the machine down; otherwise, the disk does not have a correct image of the information written to it. However, because both `shutdown` and `haltsys` run `sync` on their own, the need to use `sync` is limited.

Syntax

```
sync
```

Example

```
sync
```

This causes the system disk buffers to be written.

See Also

`shutdown`

tail

Enables you to view the end of a text file or track the growth of a text file.

Syntax

```
tail beg-offset -f file
```

Item	Description
beg-offset	The offset, in lines, within the file to begin viewing. If *beg-offset* is preceded with `-`, the offset is relative to the end of the file. If a `+` is used, the offset is relative to the beginning of the file.
`-f`	When this option is used and the input is not standard input, `tail` monitors the growth of the file. This is an endless loop of output and has to be terminated with the interrupt key.
file	The name of the file you want to view the end of or track its growth. If *file* is left blank, the standard input is used.

Message

```
tail: unrecognized option option
```

You tried to invoke `tail` with an option other then `-f`.

Examples

```
tail letter-to-dad
```

Looks at the final ten lines of `letter-to-dad`.

```
tail -20 letter-to-dad
```

Looks at the last twenty lines of `letter-to-dad`.

```
tail +10 letter-to-dad
```

Begins showing `letter-to-dad` after the first ten lines have been read.

```
tail -f growing-file ¦ more
```

Assuming a file called `growing-file` was being built by some other process, this shows you what has been built so far and what is being generated on an ongoing basis. Pipe the output through the pager `more` in case it generates too fast to view on-screen.

See Also

`more`

tar

Used to create tape archives (backups of your file system) or saves and restores files to and from an archive medium.

Syntax

`tar` *`action[options] flag-args filelist`*

Item	Description
`action`	Specifies what action to take on the archive. `action` may be one of the following: `c` Creates a new archive, or overwrites an existing one. `r` Writes the files named in *`filelist`* to the end of the archive, the rear, appending the existing archive. `t` Gives a table of contents of the archive. `u` Updates the archive. Adding the files named in *`filelist`* to the end of the archive if they aren't found in the archive or they have been modified since the last write. (May take quite a bit of time). `x` Extracts the files or directories named in *`filelist`*.
`filelist`	The list of files to manipulate, may contain wild cards (see the Caution later in this section). If *`filelist`* is a directory, that directory is recursively traversed matching all files within that directory's substructure.
`flag-args`	When a flag requires an argument, the arguments are delayed until all the flags have been specified. Then the arguments are listed on the command line in the same order as the flags.
`key`	A number between 0 and 9999. This number is a key to the file `/etc/default/tar` that specifies default options for the device name, blocking factor, device size, and whether the device is a tape.
`b`	Specifies the blocking factor. May be any integer between 1 and 20. The default is 1. Only use this with raw tape/floppy devices. Requires an argument.

(continues)

VI

Working with Linux

Item	Description
f	Specifies the file name to be used as the archive. May be a regular file or a special character device (for example, /dev/rdsk/5h for a high density floppy). If - is used, standard input is read from or written to depending on the action specified. (You cannot pipe a *filelist* to tar as with cpio, or pcpio.) Requires an argument.
m	Tells tar not to restore the modification times. The modification time is the time of extraction.
t	Prints a listing of the contents for the tar file.
v	Places tar into verbose mode. The file names are displayed on the terminal as tar processes them. When used with the t option, tar gives you a listing similar to the long listing of the ls command.
w	Makes tar wait for you to respond with a Y or an N before taking action on the file. Actually, any response starting with the letter Y means yes, and any other response means no. Not valid with the t action.
F	The next argument is a file that holds a list of files to be manipulated.

Note

When listing the file names, you have to be sure you use absolute or relative path names. Files are extracted from the archive in the same way they were created. Furthermore, if you request only a single file to be extracted, you must specify that file name on the command line the same way it was created.

Messages

```
tar: tape write error
```

This usually means one of several things: You don't have a floppy or tape in the drive, you have filled up the floppy or tape, the tape is write-protected, or you need to clean the drive.

```
tar: tape read error
```

This usually means you don't have a floppy/tape in the drive, the door isn't properly shut to the drive, or you have bad media.

```
tar: directory checksum error
```

This usually means one of two things: You have specified the wrong media type for the floppy or tape drive, or the tape has to be rewound. Specifying the wrong media type is a common error. Users have been known to place a 360K floppy disk in the drive and then access it with the /dev/rdsk/5h device.

Example

```
tar cvf /home/joe/backup.tar /home/joe/data.
```

Caution

Special devices are not placed on the archive.

Caution

Wild cards may be used in *`filelist`*. However, the `tar` command doesn't do any wild-card expansion. The shell does the expansion and passes the result to `tar`. This can be a problem for novice users who have deleted files and then want to extract them from the archive. Because the file doesn't exist on the file system, the shell can't expand the wild cards to match the nonexistent files.

See Also

`tar`, `ls`, `wc`, `grep`

tcsh

`tcsh` is a command interpreter similar to `bash`. It is an extension of the popular C shell, with file name completion and command-line editing. Like `bash`, `tcsh` is just about a complete programming language itself. For full information, refer to the online man page.

Syntax

```
tcsh
```

Example

```
tcsh
```

This launches a new shell to work in temporarily. When you exit this shell your environment is returned to what it was before you launched the new shell.

See Also

`bash`

tee

Splits the output in a pipeline to one or more files. This enables you to capture what is going to standard output and place that output into a file while still allowing the output to flow through standard output.

Syntax

`tee [`*`options`*`]` *`filelist`*

Item	Description
filelist	The space-separated list of files that you want to capture the output in.
-i	Causes tee to ignore interrupts.
-a	The files in *filelist* are appended with the output instead of overwritten.

Example

```
ls ¦ tee data.out ¦ more
```

This places a copy of the file listing generated by `ls` in the file `data.out`, while you view the listing through the pager `more`.

See Also

`ls`, `more`

test

Most commonly used in `if` and `while` statements. `if` and `while` are `sh` control constructs used when programming in the Bourne shell. `test` returns a zero exit status if what it tested was true.

Syntax

`test` *expression*

`[`*expression*`]`

Item	Description	
expression	This is the expression that test tests. The following may be used to build a valid expression:	
	-r *file*	True if *file* has read permissions.
	-w *file*	True if *file* has write permissions.
	-x *file*	True if *file* has execute permissions.
	-f *file*	True if *file* is a regular file.
	-d *file*	True if *file* is a directory.
	-b *file*	True if *file* exists and is a block special file.
	-c *file*	True if *file* is a character special file.
	-u *file*	True if *file* has the set-user-ID flag set.
	-g *file*	True if *file* has the set-group-ID set.
	-k *file*	True if *file* has the sticky-bit set.
	-s *file*	True if *file* has a files size greater than zero.
	-t *fd*	True if the file with filedescriptor *fd* is opened and associated with terminal device. The default *fd* is 1.
	-z *str*	True if the length of the string *str* is zero.
	-n *str*	True if the length of the string *str* is nonzero.
	str1 = *str2*	True if string *str1* equals the string *str2*.

Item	Description	
	str1 != *str2*	True if string *str1* doesn't equal the string *str2*.
	str	True if the string *str* is not a null string.
	int1 -eq *int2*	True if the integer *int1* equals the integer *int2*. The following also may be used instead of -eq: -ne Not equal -gt Greater than -ge Greater than or equal -lt Less than -le Less than or equal ! Negates the expression -a A logical AND -o A logical OR () Used for grouping

Note

All the file-oriented tests are false if the file doesn't exist.

Message

```
test: argument expected
```

test was expecting something and you didn't give it. This can be caused by several factors: You gave it an invalid argument, or quite typically, you were testing an environment variable and it wasn't set to anything. It didn't expand in the command line and test expected an argument there.

Examples

Tip

The second form [*expression*] is useful for readability. [is actually a program name found on the file system that is linked to test.

```
if [ -f letter-to-dad ]
then
echo "letter-to-dad exists"
fi
```

This tests to see if the file letter-to-dad exists and is a regular file.

```
if [ -f letter-to-dad -a -f letter-to-mom ]
then
echo "both letters written"
fi
```

This tests to see that letter-to-dad and letter-to-mom have been written.

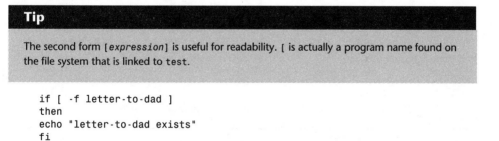

time

Determines how long a program takes to execute.

Syntax

```
time command
```

Item	Description
command	The command you want to time.

Notes

`time` reports three different times:

- `real`—The total elapsed time since you invoked the command. This is sometimes referred to as "wall clock" time because it is the time that has elapsed on the clock on your wall.
- `user`—This is the amount of time actually spent on the CPU outside sys time.
- `sys`—This is the amount of time spent in the kernel, which is the amount of time spent fulfilling system requests.

The total CPU time is `user+sys` time; this is the difference between this and `real` time is the amount of time the CPU spent on other tasks.

Example

```
time compress letter-to-dad
```

This reports the amount of time it took to compress the file `letter-to-dad`.

touch

Changes the access and modification times of a file, or creates a new file with specified times.

Syntax

```
touch [options] MMDDhhmmYY filelist
```

Item	Description
MMDDhhmmYY	This is the time to which to set the file. The format is as follows: *MM* The month *DD* The day *hh* The hour *mm* The minute *YY* The year
filelist	A space-separated list of the files you want to have the specified time.

Item	Description
-a	The specified time changes the access time of the specified files.
-m	Same as -a but for modified time.
-c	If a file in *filelist* doesn't exist, this flag tells touch not to create it.

Note

The flags -am are the default. You cannot modify the creation time of a file. (The term creation time is a bit misleading. The creation time is not really the time the file was created; it is better thought of as when the inode information changed. When the file size changed, the mode changed, the owner changed, and so on.) There are several other options for touch. Refer to the man page for more information.

Message

```
touch: illegal option -- badoption
```

You tried to specify an option, *badoption*, that touch doesn't understand. (*badoption* is substituted with the option you supplied.)

Examples

```
touch letter-to-dad
```

This sets the modification and access times of letter-to-dad to the current date.

```
touch 0101120191 letter-to-dad
```

This sets the modification and access times of letter-to-dad to 01/01/91 at 12:01 PM.

See Also

date

tr

tr translates or maps characters in a file from one form to another. For example, you can use tr to change all tabs to spaces. This command enables you to do some rather robust character handling with a somewhat simple structure.

Syntax

```
tr [options] from-string to-string
```

Item	Description
from-string	This is the string of characters to map from or the characters you want translated. The following special notations may be used and repeated: [c1-*cn*] This specifies a range of characters from c1 to *cn*.

(continues)

VI

Working with Linux

Item	Description
	`[c*n]` This specifies that character `c` repeats *n* times. *n* may be zero or left blank, which assumes a huge number of the character `c`. This is useful for padding the *`to-string`* (see the Notes section for the `tr` command).
`\octal`	Specifies the octal value of a character. This is useful for manipulating the non-printable characters (control characters).
`to-string`	This is the string of characters to map into; the character the *`from-string`* translates to. The special notations noted previously may be used here as well.
`-c`	Normally `tr` substitutes the characters found in *`from-string`* with the characters found in *`to-string`*, with the output showing the original contents of the file with the substitution applied. This option restricts the output to the characters specified in *`from-string`* and effectively appends the characters in *`to-string`*.
`-d`	Deletes the characters specified in *`from-string`*.
`-s`	Strips repeated characters generated in the output by those specified in *`to-string`*, leaving only one of the repeated characters in the output.

Note

The *`to-string`* must be the same number of characters as the *`from-string`*.

Examples

```
tr -d "\015\032" <dosfile >linuxfile
```

Tip

Enclose *`from-string`* and *`to-string`* in quotation marks as shown in the examples to ensure that the special meaning of any characters recognized by the shell are escaped and passed to `tr` instead of being expanded by the shell.

This is one way of translating DOS text files into a format more suitable in Linux. It deletes the carriage returns and the DOS end-of-file marker (^Z).

```
tr -s "\015\032" "[\012*]" <dosfile >unixfile
```

This is a significantly more complicated way of accomplishing the same task as the previous example. However, it demonstrates two features of `tr`. In this example, you replace all the carriage returns and end-of-file markers with the Linux new-line character. The `-s` strips the duplicate new lines producing only one. *`to-string`* uses the "padding" option described previously to ensure that the lengths of the two strings are equal.

Caution

The range notation may be used with the characters representing the digits as well, such as 0–9. However, such notation refers strictly to the digits themselves and not the value they may represent. You cannot use this to replace all tens with nines because ten is two digits and nine is only one digit.

See Also

`ed`

true

Tip

The character `:` in the Bourne shell gives the same results as `true` and doesn't require the execution of a program.

Returns a zero exit status that means true in the shell. This command is useful when programming in the shell to create continuous loops.

Syntax

```
true
```

Example

```
while true
do
     repetitive command
done
```

Rather than typing a command repeatedly, have the computer do the repetitive work for you. This example causes some repetitive command to be executed over and over without you having to type it.

See Also

`bash`

tty

Reports the currently logged on terminal device name, or tests if standard input is a terminal.

Syntax

```
tty -s
```

Item	Description
`-s`	This option causes `tty` to test if the standard input is a terminal device or not. No output is generated. The result code is set to zero if standard input is a terminal, one if it is not.

Message

```
not a tty
```

This is the message displayed when you try to invoke `tty` and haven't used the `-s` flag and the standard input is not a terminal.

Examples

```
tty
```

This simply reports the terminal's device name.

```
if tty -s
then
echo "This is a terminal"
fi
```

This tests if the standard input is a terminal or not.

umask

Specifies what the default permissions of files you create are, or reports what the current defaults are.

Syntax

`umask` *`mask`*

Item	Description
`mask`	This is the mask that is applied when generating the permissions for the files you might create. If left blank, `umask` reports the current setting. *`mask`* is composed of three digits. The digits represent the permissions for the owner of the file (that's you), the group, and the rest of the world. The *`mask`* is called a mask because the value specified is actually masked at the bit level to generate the permissions. However, if you don't think in this way (most people don't), simply think of *`mask`* as the permissions you don't want to give. `0` You don't want to restrict any permissions. `1` You want to restrict execute permissions. `2` You want to restrict write permission. `4` You want to restrict read permissions. Adding any of these numbers together restricts the combination of the permissions. A permission value of 7, which is the sum of 4, 2, and 1, restricts all permissions.

Examples

```
umask
```

This reports the current mask setting.

```
umask 000
```

This gives complete access to everyone on the system to every file you create.

```
umask 022
```

This gives you complete permissions on the files you create. However, everyone else is only able to read and execute those files.

```
umask 007
```

This gives you and the people in your group complete permissions and doesn't allow anyone else to do anything.

See Also

```
chmod
```

uname

Reports the system name and other catalog information.

Syntax

```
uname [options]
```

Item	Description
-s	Reports the system name. This is the default.
-n	Reports the node name of the system. This is used in communications.
-r	Reports the release number of the operating system.
-v	Shows the version number of the operating system.
-m	Reports the machine hardware name.
-a	Reports all the above information, equivalent to -mvrns.

Message

```
uname: illegal option -- badoption
```

You invoked uname with an option it doesn't recognize.

Example

```
uname
```

This reports the system name of the currently logged on machine.

uniq

Strips out lines that are identical, producing only one unique line.

Syntax

```
uniq [options] input output
```

Item	Description
input	The name of the file from which to read; if left blank, the standard input is read.
output	The name of the file to create with the results of the `uniq` command. If left blank, standard output is used. If specified, *output* must not be the same as *input*.
-u	Causes `uniq` to only output those lines that aren't repeated.
-d	Causes `uniq` to only output those lines that were repeated—but only one copy of them.
-c	Produces a report with the left column being the count of the number of times the line repeated and then the line itself.
-*fields*	When doing the comparison for uniqueness, the first *fields* count of fields is skipped. Fields are separated by tabs or spaces.
+*chars*	After skipping any specified fields, also skips *chars* number of characters.

Notes

The default operation is to output all the lines in the input file but with only one copy of any repeated lines.

`uniq` assumes the input file is already sorted.

Examples

```
who ¦ cut -d" " -f1 ¦ uniq
```

This shows a list of users currently logged on the system, but if anyone was logged on more than once, you only see them once.

```
who ¦ cut -d" " -f1 ¦ uniq -d
```

This is a slight twist on the previous command. This is an example showing those who logged on more than once.

```
who ¦ cut -d" " -f1 ¦ uniq -u
```

The following shows only those who are not logged on more than once.

```
who ¦ cut -d" " -f1 ¦ uniq -c
```

With this command you get a list of each user on the system and a count of the number of times they are logged on.

See Also

```
sort
```

uudecode

See uuencode.

uuencode

uuencode is used to format a binary file so that it can be sent over media that do not support any format other than simple ASCII data. Electronic mail or USENET news are examples of such media. The uuencode program encodes the file so that it contains only ASCII characters. The file can then be restored to normal via the uudecode command.

Syntax

```
uuencode [file] name

uudecode [file]
```

Item	Description
file	The name of the file to format with uuencode or uudecode. If no file name is given, uuencode reads from the standard input, and uudecode writes to the standard output.
name	The name to be used for the decoded file when it is converted with uudecode.

Note

When a file is decoded with uudecode, it will be stored with the file name name that was given when it was originally converted with uuencode. The decoded file's original permissions will be restored, except that setuid and execute bits are not retained.

Examples

To convert the compressed file data.Z so that it can be sent via e-mail:

```
uuencode data.Z data.Z > data.uu
```

This tells uuencode that the file to convert is named data.Z and that when the encoded file is uudecoded, it should be stored in a file named data.Z. Since uuencode writes to the standard output, we have redirected the output into a file named data.uu. The file data.uu contains the uuencoded version of data.Z and can now be sent via electronic mail.

To convert the uuencoded file back to its original state:

```
uudecode data.uu
```

This creates a file named data.Z that has the same permissions as the original file.

vi

`vi` stands for visual `ex`. `vi` is the same editor as `ex` except it is full screen and you are able to see the changes you make. `vi` is such a powerful tool that this discussion only provides rudimentary information on `vi`. If you want to work with `vi`, consult the man page and find a good reference book as well.

Syntax

```
vi file-name
```

This invokes the `vi` editor on the specified file.

Item	Description
file-name	This is the name of the file to edit.

The following are a few of the commands available in `vi`:

Command	What It Does
`Esc`	Pressing the <Esc> key puts you back into command mode, allowing you to enter a new command.
`r`	Replaces one character.
`R`	Unlimited replacement in the line.
`i`	Insert mode.
`dd`	Delete the line.
`x`	Delete a character.
`$`	End of the line.
`^`	Beginning of the line.
`:x`	Writes the file and exits `vi`.
`:q!`	Quits `vi` without saving file.
`/`	Allows the entry of a search pattern.

Example

```
vi letter-to-dad
```

This starts `vi` to work on a letter to your dad.

See Also

`ed`

wall

Writes to all users currently logged on the system. The message appears on the terminal of each user. This is a broadcast message.

Syntax

```
wall [file-name]
```

Item	Description
file-name	Reads from this file and send its contents to users.

`wall` reads from a specified file or from standard input until an end-of-file (<Ctrl-d>) is reached. It then broadcasts this message to all users on the system.

Note

You should be the super user to run this. As super user you can override any protection the users have on their terminals to avoid being written to.

Examples

```
wall
Please get off the system in 10 minutes^D
```

This command invokes an interactive version of `wall` and types in a one line message ending with the end-of-file keystroke (<Ctrl-d>). The message doesn't go out until the end-of-file is encountered.

```
wall shutdown-note
```

This causes `wall` to read the file `shutdown-note` and sends the contents of that file to all users.

See Also

```
write
```

wc

Counts the number of characters, words, or lines in a file.

Syntax

```
wc [options] filelist
```

Item	Description
filelist	A space-separated list of file names for counting the contents. If left blank, the standard output is read.
`-c`	Counts only the number of characters.
`-w`	Counts only the number of words. Words are any string of characters separated by a space, tab, or new line.
`-l`	Counts only the number of lines, or more precisely, it counts the number of new-line characters encountered.

Note

Any combination of the flags in the list may be used. The default is all of them. When more than one option is specified, the output is in this order: lines, words, characters.

Message

```
wc: No such file or directory.
```

You invoked `wc` asking it to count in a file that it can't open. Either the file doesn't exist or you don't have permission to read it.

Example

```
wc letter-to-dad
```

This tells you how many lines, words, and characters `letter-to-dad` is.

which

`which` searches through your path for the specified program.

Syntax

```
which program
```

Item	Description
program	A command that you want to find

Note

If you have a long system path, `which` is useful for finding the directory of a command.

Example

```
which chess
```

Looks through your path for an executable program named `chess`.

See Also

```
find
```

who

Reports who is currently on the system and other user and logon information.

Syntax

```
who [options] utmp-like-file

who am i
```

Item	Description
utmp-like-file	This is an alternate file to read to obtain logon information. This is usually /etc/wtmp. /etc/wtmp is a history of what is found in the /etc/utmp file, and as it grows larger, it must be cleaned up periodically.
-u	Reports those users who are currently logged onto the system.
-T	Indicates whether the terminal allows users to send messages to it. A + indicates the terminal may be written to. A - indicates it cannot be written to.
-H	Prints the header line.
-q	Shows a space-separated list of user names and a count. A quick version of the output. All other options are ignored.
-s	Ignored; included for compatibility.

Example

```
who
```

This gives a list of who is on the system.

See Also

```
ps
```

write

Communicates with a user interactively who is otherwise inaccessible.

Syntax

```
write user tty
```

Item	Description
user	The user name of the person to whom you wish to send a message.
tty	When the user is logged onto more than one terminal at a time you may specify the terminal you want the message to go to.

Note

`write` reads from standard input, and each time you press <Return>, it sends that line to the user. When you press the end-of-file key (<Ctrl-d>), `write` exits.

Messages

```
Message from sending-user sending-tty
```

This means someone is writing to you. `write` lets you know who is sending the message and what terminal they are running `write` from.

```
(end of message)
```

The user sending you a message is finished.

```
user is not logged on.
```

You tried to write to a user who is not currently on the system.

```
permission denied
```

The user you want to write to doesn't want to be written to right now. They most likely issued the `mesg n` command.

Note

When you have finished a line of thought and want the person you are communicating with to respond, it is common practice to use the notation `(o)` to signal "over" and when you are done with the conversation `(oo)` to signal "over and out." Multiple new lines are also used. To do this, press the <Return> key at least twice to signal the other user it is their turn.

Note

If the user has a phone it is probably just as easy to simply pick up your phone and call them. `write` is very useful when the phone isn't available but can be quite cumbersome because you can't begin your response until the other user has completed his line of thought.

Novice users tend to get frustrated if they are written to because they are not comfortable enough with the system to respond. This is usually because they believe that the writing is messing up the application they are currently running, and some applications available on Linux don't provide a redraw or shell escape function. This in essence cripples that user, even though no real damage has taken place.

Caution

If a user is logged onto more than one terminal, then `write` assumes the terminal with the most recent logon. This may not actually be the terminal they are currently on. This presents itself as a problem because now you have to track down what the current terminal is, or it may appear as though the user isn't able to respond. This is a problem due to the multiple consoles and screen capabilities of Linux.

See Also

`mesg`

CHAPTER 26

Using X Windows

If you are familiar with other GUIs, such as Microsoft Windows or the Macintosh user interface, you shouldn't find many differences in X Windows. X Windows presents to the user several windows, each showing the output of an X Windows application, called a client. The client can be running on the user's PC, which is more than likely with Linux, or on another workstation on the network.

How you move around in X Windows is very much dependent on window managers, which is discussed later in this chapter. Most windows use an on-screen pointer called a cursor to indicate where you are working. The cursor can take on many shapes depending on what you are doing and what window manager you are running. In this chapter you will learn the following:

- How to use X Windows
- About the different window managers
- About several of the X Window applications available for Linux

Navigating X Windows

X Windows, like most GUIs, allows input from the keyboard and the pointing device, usually a mouse. Typically, in order for a window to accept input, it must be the active window. An active window normally has a different appearance (for example, a highlighted border) than inactive windows. Making a window active is window manager-dependent. Some allow the window to become active by merely moving the cursor into the window. Others require you to move the cursor to the window and click a mouse button, such as you do in Microsoft Windows.

Menus. Many GUIs on PCs today provide drop-down and pop-up menus. Again, such items are window manager-dependent, including the types of menu choices provided. Most X Windows window managers do not have a main menu bar across the top of the system; instead, they use a floating menu. You typically invoke this floating menu by clicking a mouse button over an empty area of the desktop. You hold down the mouse button and drag the cursor through the various menu selections. When you find the desired menu choice, simply release the button, which is very much like how you navigate menus on a Macintosh and very unlike how you navigate menus under Microsoft Windows.

Virtual Terminals and X Windows. Your `xserver` runs on a virtual terminal assigned by Linux. This terminal is assigned to the seventh virtual terminal, which you can reach with the <Alt-F7> key from a character terminal. From X Windows you can reach the other terminals with the <Ctrl-Alt-F*x*> key combination, where *x* represents the number of the virtual terminal you want to access. While this can be a handy feature, accessing the other virtual terminals, X Windows does provide you the ability to start character terminal emulators, called `xterm` sessions. `xterm` is explained later in this chapter.

Window Managers for Linux

As stated earlier in the chapter, X Windows does not specify a window manager. The look and feel of X Windows is left up to the user. In this spirit, Linux does not provide just one window manager for X Windows, although the default installation installs the `fvwm` window manager as the default. Linux provides the various window managers shown in Table 26.1.

Table 26.1 Window Managers Available for Linux

Name	Description
`twm`	Tom's window manager
`fvwm`	Virtual window manager for X11
`mwm`	Motif window manager
`olwm`	`Openlook`'s window manager, based on Sun's Open Look
`olvwm`	`Openlook`'s virtual window manager

twm. `twm` is a window manager for the X Windows System. It provides title bars, shaped windows, several forms of icon management, user-defined macro functions, click-to-type and pointer-driven keyboard focus, and user-specified key and mouse button bindings. This program is usually started by the user's session manager or startup script. When used from `xdm` or `xinit` without a session manager, `twm` is frequently executed in the foreground as the last client. When run this way, exiting `twm` causes the session to be terminated (that is, logged off).

By default, application windows are surrounded by a `'frame'` with a title bar at the top and a special border around the window. The title bar contains the window's name, a rectangle that is lit when the window is receiving keyboard input, and function boxes known as `'titlebuttons'` at the left and right edges of the title bar. Clicking Button1 (usually the leftmost button on the mouse unless it has been changed with `xmodmap`) on a title button invokes the function associated with the button. In the default interface, windows are *iconified* (minimized to an icon) by clicking (pressing and then immediately releasing) the left title button, which looks like a dot. Conversely, windows are *deiconified*, or maximized, by clicking the associated icon or entry in the icon manager.

Windows are resized by pressing the right title button, which resembles a group of nested squares, dragging the pointer over the edge that is to be moved, and releasing the pointer when the outline of the window is the desired size. Similarly, windows are moved by clicking in the title bar, dragging a window outline to the new location, and then releasing when the outline is in the desired position. Just clicking in the title bar raises the window without moving it. When new windows are created, `twm` honors any size and location information requested by the user. Otherwise, an outline of the window's default size, its title bar, and lines dividing the window into a three-by-three grid that track the pointer are displayed. Clicking Button1 positions the window at the current position and gives it the default size. Clicking Button2 (usually the middle mouse button) and dragging the outline gives the window its current position but allows the sides to be resized as described above. Clicking Button3 (usually the right pointer button) gives the window its current position but attempts to make it long enough to touch the bottom of the screen.

fvwm. `fvwm` is a window manager for X11. It is a derivative of `twm`, redesigned to minimize memory consumption, provide a 3-D look to window frames, and provide a simple virtual desktop. Memory consumption is estimated at about one-half to one-third the memory consumption of `twm`, due primarily to a redesign of `twm`'s inefficient method of storing mouse bindings (associating commands to mouse buttons). In addition, many of the configurable options of `twm` have been removed.

XFree86 provides a virtual screen whose operation can be confusing when used in conjunction with the `fvwm` virtual window manager. With XFree86, windows that appear on the virtual screen actually get drawn into video memory, so the virtual screen size is limited by available video memory.

With `fvwm`'s virtual desktop, windows that do not appear on-screen do not actually get drawn into video RAM. The size of the virtual desktop is limited to 32,000 × 32,000 pixels. It is impractical to use a virtual desktop of more than five times the size of the visible screen in each direction. Note that memory usage with the virtual desktop is a function of the number of windows that exist. The size of the desktop makes no difference.

When becoming familiar with `fvwm`, it is recommended that you disable XFree86's virtual screen by setting the virtual screen size to the physical screen size. When familiar with `fvwm`, you may want to reenable XFree86's virtual screen.

`fvwm` provides multiple virtual desktops for users who want to use them. The screen is a viewport onto a desktop that is larger than (or the same size as) the screen. Several distinct desktops can be accessed. The basic concept is one desktop for each project or one desktop for each application when view applications are distinct. Because each desktop can be larger than the physical screen, windows that are larger than the screen or large groups of related windows can be easily viewed.

The size of each virtual desktop must be specified at startup (the default is three times the physical size of the screen). All virtual desktops must be the same size. The total number of distinct desktops need not be specified but is limited to approximately four billion total. All windows on the current desktop can be displayed in a pager, miniature view, or the current desktop. Windows that are not on the current desktop can be listed, along with their geometries, in a window list, accessible as a pop-up menu.

Sticky windows are windows that transcend the virtual desktop by "sticking to the screen's glass." They always stay put on the screen. This is convenient for things like clocks and `xbiffs`, so you only need to run one such utility, and it always stays with you.

Window geometries are specified relative to the current viewport—that is, `xterm`-geometry +0+0 always appears in the upper-left corner of the visible portion of the screen. It is permissible to specify geometries that place windows on the virtual desktop but off the screen. For example, if the visible screen is 1000 × 1000 pixels, the desktop size is three-by-three, and the current viewport is at the upper-left corner of the desktop, invoking `xterm`-geometry +1000+1000 places the window just off the lower-right corner of the screen. It can be found by moving the mouse to the lower-right corner of the screen and waiting for it to scroll into view. There is currently no way to cause a window to map onto a desktop other than the active desk.

A geometry specified as `xterm`-geometry -5-5 generally places the window's lower-right corner five pixels from the lower-right corner of the visible portion of the screen. Not all applications support window geometries with negative offsets.

olwm. `olwm` is a window manager for the X Windows system that implements parts of the `Openlook` graphical user interface. It is the standard window manager for Sun's Open Windows product, but it works properly with any X11 system, including XFree86. The only requirements for running `olwm` are that the server have the OPEN LOOK glyph and cursor fonts available, which should be the case if you installed all the available fonts for X Windows.

X Windows Applications

There are plenty of applications for X Windows on the Internet. The following sections provide a brief overview of several of the X applications furnished either with the Slackware distribution or in the `\contrib` directory on the enclosed CD-ROM.

xterm

`xterm` is a common X Windows application that simulates a common video terminal such as the DEC vt100. When you start an `xterm` session you can run any command-line program or execute any Linux command just as you do on any of the virtual terminals supplied by Linux. Figure 26.1 illustrates an `xterm` session.

The `xterm` program is a terminal emulator for the X Windows system. It provides DEC vt102 and Tektronix 4014 compatible terminals for programs that can't use the window system directly. If the underlying operating system supports terminal resizing capabilities, `xterm` uses the facilities to notify programs running in the window whenever it is resized.

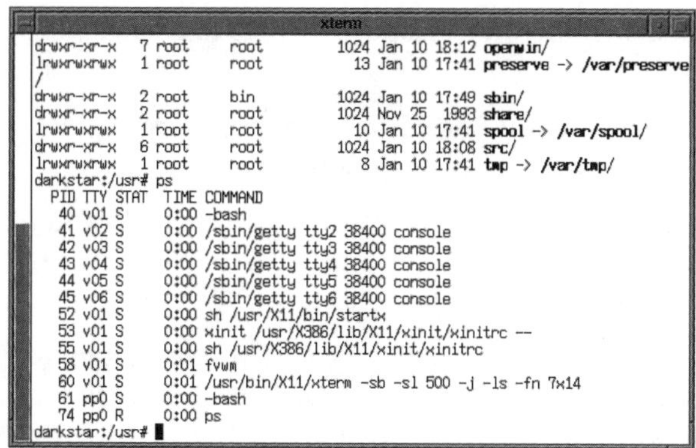

Fig. 26.1

An xterm session under XFree86.

The vt102 and Tektronix 4014 terminals each have their own window so that you can edit text in one and look at graphics in the other at the same time. To maintain the correct *aspect ratio*—the height of the screen in pixels divided by the width of the screen in pixels—Tektronix graphics are restricted to the largest box with a 4014 aspect ratio that fits in the window. This box is located in the upper-left area of the window.

Although both windows may be displayed at the same time, one of them is considered the `'active'` window for receiving keyboard input and terminal output. This is the window that contains the text cursor. The active window can be chosen through escape sequences, the vt Options menu in the vt102 window, and the Tek Options menu in the 4014 window.

Emulations. $TERMCAP entries that work with `xterm` include `xterm`, vt102, vt100, and ansi; `xterm` automatically searches the termcap file in this order for these entries and then sets the TERM and the $TERMCAP environment variables.

Many of the special `xterm` features may be modified under program control through a set of escape sequences different from the standard vt102 escape sequences.

The Tektronix 4014 emulation is also fairly good. Four different font sizes and five different line types are supported. The Tektronix text and graphics commands are recorded internally by `xterm` and may be written to a file by sending the Tektronix COPY escape sequence.

Other Features. `xterm` automatically selects the text cursor when the pointer enters the window and deselects it when the pointer leaves the window. If the window is the focus window, the text cursor is selected no matter where the pointer is.

In vt102 mode, there are escape sequences to activate and deactivate an alternate screen buffer, which is the same size as the display area of the window. When activated, the current screen is saved and replaced with the alternate screen. Saving of lines scrolled off the top of the window is disabled until the normal screen is restored. The termcap entry for `xterm` allows the visual editor `vi` to switch to the alternate screen for editing and to restore the screen on exit.

In either vt102 or Tektronix mode, there are escape sequences to change the name of the windows.

Mouse Usage with *xterm*. Once the vt102 window is created, `xterm` enables you to select text and copy it within the same or other windows.

The selection functions are invoked when the pointer buttons are used with no modifiers, and when they are used with the <Shift> key. The assignment of the functions described below to keys and buttons may be changed through the resource database.

Mouse Button1 (usually the left button) is used to save text into the cut buffer. Move the cursor to the beginning of the text and then hold the button down while moving the cursor to the end of the region and releasing the button. The selected text is highlighted and is saved in the global cut buffer. This selected text is then made the `PRIMARY` selection when the button is released. Double-clicking selects entire words and triple-clicking selects lines. Quadruple-clicking goes back to characters, and so on. A multiple-click is determined by the time from button up to button down.

Mouse Button2 (usually the middle button) pastes the text from the `PRIMARY` selection if any. Otherwise, text is inserted from the cut buffer, inserting it as keyboard input.

By cutting and pasting pieces of text without trailing new lines, you can take text from several places in different windows and form a command to the shell, for example, or take output from a program and insert it into your favorite editor. Because the cut buffer is globally shared among different applications, you should regard it as a file whose contents you know. The terminal emulator and other text programs should be treating it as if it were a text file—that is, the text is delimited by new lines.

The scroll region within the window displaying the `xterm` displays the position and amount of text currently showing in the window relative to the amount of text actually saved. As more text is saved (up to the system-determined maximum), the size of the highlighted area decreases.

Clicking Button1 with the pointer in the scroll region moves the adjacent line to the top of the display window. Clicking Button2 moves the display to a position in the saved text that corresponds to the pointer's position in the scrollbar. Clicking Button3 moves the top line of the display window down to the pointer position.

Unlike the vt102 window, the Tektronix window does not allow the copying of text. It does, however, allow Tektronix GIN mode, and in this mode, the cursor changes from an arrow to a cross. Pressing any key sends that key and the current coordinate of the cross cursor. Clicking Button1, Button2, or Button3 returns the letters `l`, `m`, and `r`, respectively. If the <Shift> key is pressed when a button is pressed, the corresponding uppercase letter is sent. To distinguish a pointer button from a key, the high bit of the character is set.

xcalc

Figure 26.2 displays `xcalc`, a scientific calculator desktop accessory that emulates a TI-30 or HP-10C calculator. Operations may be performed with mouse Button1 or, in some cases, with the keyboard. Many common calculator operations have keyboard accelerators. To quit, click the AC key of the TI calculator with mouse Button3 or click the OFF key of the HP calculator with mouse Button3. In TI mode, the numbered keys; the +/- key; and the +, -, *, /, and = keys all do exactly what you expect them to. It should be noted that the operators obey the standard rules of precedence. Thus, entering **`3+4*5=`** results in `23` and not `35`. The parentheses can be used to override this. For example, entering **`(1+2+3)*(4+5+6)=`** results in `6*15=90`.

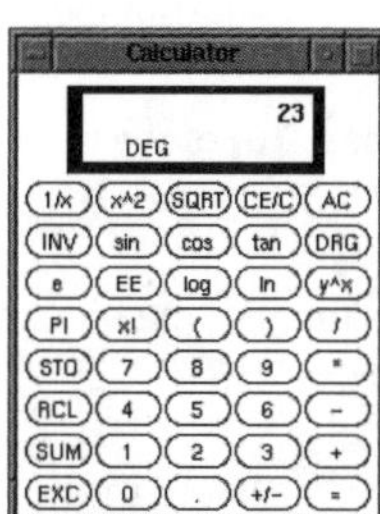

Fig. 26.2

`xcalc` *sessions under XFree86.*

The entire number in the calculator display can be selected for pasting the result of a calculation into text. Table 26.2 lists the various functions for TI emulation.

Table 26.2 TI Emulation

Key/Function	Description
1/x	Replaces the number in the display with its reciprocal.
x^2	Squares the number in the display.
SQR	Takes the square root of the number in the display.
CE/C	When clicked once, clears the number in the display without clearing the state of the machine. Allows you to reenter a number if you make a mistake. Clicking it twice clears the state. Also, AC clears the display, state, and memory. Clicking CE/C with Button3 turns off the calculator, exiting `xcalc`.
INV	Inverts function. See the individual function keys for details.
sin	Computes the sine of the number in the display, as interpreted by the current DRG mode (see DRG). If inverted, it computes the arcsine.
cos	Computes the cosine. When inverted with the INV key, computes the arccosine.
tan	Computes the tangent. When inverted, computes the arctangent.

(continues)

Table 26.2 Continued

Key/Function	Description
DRG	Changes the DRG mode, as indicated by DEG, RAD, or GRAD at the bottom of the calculator display. When in DEG mode, numbers in the display are assumed to be degrees. In RAD mode, numbers are in radians, and in GRAD mode, numbers are in grads. When inverted, the DRG key has a feature of converting degrees to radians to grads and vice versa. For example, put the calculator into DEG mode, and enter `45 INV DRG`. `xcalc` displays `.785398`, which is 45 degrees converted to radians.
e	The constant e, which is 2.7182818.
EE	Used for entering exponential numbers. For example, to get -2.3E-4, you enter **`2 . 3 +/- EE 4 +/-`**.
log	Calculates the log (base 10) of the number in the display. When inverted, it raises 10.0 to the number in the display. For example, entering **`3 INV log`** results in `1000`.
ln	Calculates the log (base e) of the number in the display. When inverted, it raises e to the number in the display. For example, entering **`e ln`** results in `1`.
y^x	Raises the number on the left to the power of the number on the right. For example, entering **`2 y^x 3`** = results in `8`, which is 2^3.
PI	The constant pi, which is 3.1415927.
x!	Computes the factorial of the number in the display. The number in the display must be an integer in the range 0–500; though, depending on your math library, it might overflow long before that.
(	Left parenthesis.
)	Right parenthesis.
/	Division.
*	Multiplication.
-	Subtraction.
+	Addition.
=	Performs calculation.
STO	Copies the number in the display to the memory location.
RCL	Copies the number from the memory location to the display.
SUM	Adds the number in the display to the number in the memory location.
EXC	Swaps the number in the display with the number in the memory location.
+/-	Negate; change sign.
.	Decimal point.

In RPN, or HP, mode, the numbered keys; CHS (change sign); and +, -, *, /, and ENTER keys all do exactly what you expect. Many of the remaining keys are the same as in TI mode. The differences are detailed in Table 26.3.

Table 26.3 HP Emulation

Key/Function	Description
<	This is a backspace key that can be used if you make a mistake while entering a number. It erases digits from the display. If you invert backspace, the x register is cleared.
ON	Clears the display, state, and memory. Pressing it with the Button3 turns off the calculator, exiting `xcalc`.
INV	Inverts the meaning of the function keys. This is the f key on an HP calculator, but `xcalc` does not display multiple legends on each key. See the individual function keys for details.
10^x	Raises 10.0 to the number in the top of the stack. When inverted, it calculates the log (base 10) of the number in the display.
e^x	Raises e to the number in the top of the stack. When inverted, it calculates the log (base e) of the number in the display.
STO	Copies the number in the top of the stack to a memory location. There are ten memory locations. The desired memory is specified by following this key with a digit key.
RCL	Pushes the number from the specified memory location onto the stack.
SUM	Adds the number on top of the stack to the number in the specified memory location.
x:y	Exchanges the numbers in the top two stack positions, the x and y registers.
R v	Rolls the stack downward. When inverted, it rolls the stack upward.
blank	These keys were used for programming functions on the HP-10C. Their functionality has not been duplicated in `xcalc`.

xspread

The program `xspread`, shown in Figure 26.3, is a public domain spreadsheet that runs under X Windows. You must be using an X Windows terminal to be able to run this program. The creators of `xspread` are working on making it use the ASCII screen if it cannot find an X Windows display to use. The `xspread` Reference Manual gives complete documentation for the program. The LaTeX source copy for this manual is in the file `xspread.tex`.

`xspread` supports many standard spreadsheet features. Among these are the following:

- Cell entry and editing
- Worksheet size: 702 columns with unlimited rows
- File reading and writing

- File encryption
- Absolute and relative cell references
- Numeric and label (that is, character string) data in cells
- Left or right justification for labels
- Row and column insertion and deletion
- Hiding and unhiding of rows and columns
- Range names
- Manual or automatic recalculation
- Numeric operators (+, -, *, /, ^, %)
- Relational operators (<, <=, >, >=, =, !=)
- Logical (or Boolean) operators (&, |, ~)
- Function references
- Graphs (XY, Bar, Stack Bar, Pie, and Line graphs)
- Matrix operations (Transpose, Multiply, Add, Subtract, and Inversion)
- Cursor positioning with mouse
- Menu item selection with mouse
- References to external programs, which are called *external functions*

Fig. 26.3

`xspread` *under XFree86.*

The structure and operation of the spreadsheet is similar to but not identical with popular spreadsheets such as Lotus 1-2-3 and its clones. Like other spreadsheets, the workspace is arranged into rows and columns of cells. Each cell can contain a number, a label, or a formula that evaluates to a number or label.

You can start the program with or without specifying a file to be read. This file must be a saved worksheet. If a file is specified on the command line, `xspread` attempts to locate and read the file. If it is successful, `xspread` starts with the file's contents in the workspace. If it is unsuccessful or no file is specified on the command line, `xspread` starts with the workspace empty.

For a tutorial of the spreadsheet program, run one of the demo files: `demo`, `demo_math`, or `demo_matrix` and see the file `Sample_Run` in the `doc` directory.

Seyon

Seyon, as shown in Figure 26.4, is a complete full-featured telecommunications package for the X Windows system. Some of its features are as follows:

- A dialing directory
- Terminal emulation
- A scripting language
- A variety of download protocols, including Z modem
- Various translation modes

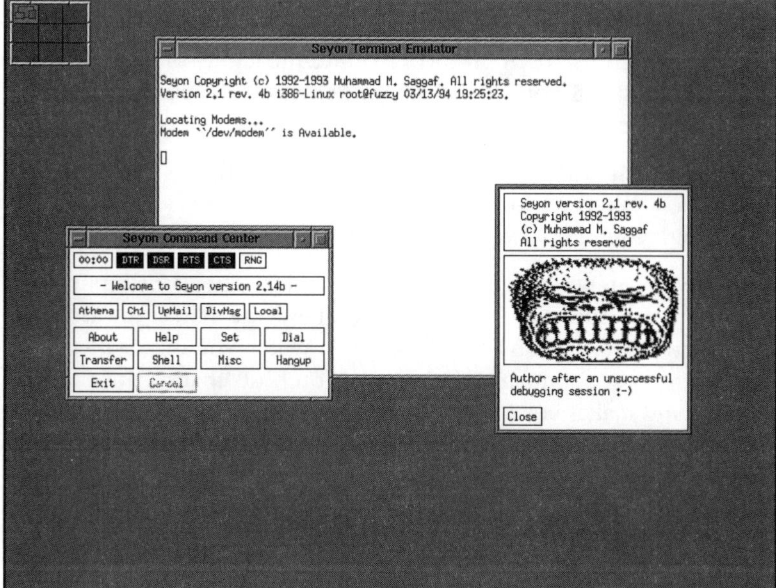

Fig. 26.4

The Seyon program.

Dialing Directory. The dialing directory supports an unlimited number of entries. The directory is fully mouse-driven and features call-progress monitoring, dial time-out, automatic redial, multi-number dialing, and circular redial queue. Each item in the dialing directory can be configured with its own baud rate, bit mask, and script file. The dialing directory uses a plain-text phone book that can be edited from within Seyon. Seyon also supports manual dialing.

Terminal Emulation. Terminal emulation supports DEC vt102, Tektronix 4014, and ANSI. Seyon delegates its terminal emulation to `xterm`, so all the familiar `xterm` functions such as the scroll-back buffer, cut-and-paste utility, and visual bell are available through Seyon's terminal emulation window. Using `xterm` also means that Seyon has a more complete emulation of vt102 than any other UNIX or DOS telecommunications program. Other terminal emulation programs can also be used with Seyon to suit the user's need; for example, color `xterm` can be used to provide emulation for color ANSI (popular on many BBS systems), and `xvt` can be used if memory is a bit tight.

Scripting Language. You can use script language to automate tedious tasks such as logging on to remote hosts. Seyon's script interpreter uses plain-text files and has a syntax similar to that of `sh`, with a few extra additions. It supports many familiar statements such as conditional branching by `if_else` and looping by `goto`. Scripts may be assigned to items in the dialing directory for automatic execution after a connection is made.

File Transfers. Seyon supports an unlimited number of slots for external file transfer protocols. Protocols are activated from a mouse-driven transfer console that uses a plain-text file, editable from within Seyon, for protocol configuration. Seyon prompts the user for file names only if the chosen protocol requires file names or if the transfer operation is an upload for which Seyon also accepts wild cards. Multiple download directories can be specified for the different transfer slots.

Seyon detects incoming Zmodem signatures and automatically activates a user-specified Zmodem protocol to receive incoming files. Zmodem transfers are thus completely automatic and require no user intervention.

Translation Modes. Seyon can perform useful translations with the user's input. For example, Seyon can translate <Backspace> to <Delete>, a new-line marker to carriage-return marker, and meta-key translation—that is, you can switch your <Esc> meta key to the <Alt> key. The latter mode simulates the meta key on hosts that do not support 8-bit-clean connections and makes possible the use of the meta key in programs like `emacs`.

Other Features. Seyon allows you to interactively set program parameters, online help, software (`XONN/XOFF`) and hardware (`RTS/CTS`) flow control; capture a session to a file; and temporarily run a local shell in the terminal emulation window.

Seyon is intended to be both simple and extensively configurable. Almost every aspect of Seyon can be configured via the resources to suit the user's taste.

xgrab

xgrab is an interactive front for xgrabsc, an X Windows image grabber. xgrab was written by Bruce Schuchardt (**bruce@slc.com**) and many other people, who retain a loose copyright on the program. xgrab lets you grab arbitrary rectangular images from an xserver and writes them to files or commands (such as lpr) in a variety of formats.

Read the man page for xgrabsc for a description of the options presented by xgrab. After selecting options from the various categories presented, click the OK button to have xgrab run xgrabsc to let you grab an image from the screen. After you click OK, xgrab's window disappears and xgrabsc gains control until the grabbing process is finished. Afterwards, the xgrab window reappears.

xgrab responds to the standard application options, such as -_display. See the man page for X Windows for a complete list. You can also override the default xgrab settings in your .Xdefaults. See "Examples" later in this chapter for instructions.

Resources. The xgrab resource file, XGrab.ad, contains a complete specification of the resources of all the widgets used in the xgrab window. Widgets are resource specifications for such items as buttons and menus. Global resources, such as default font and color, are at the bottom of the file.

Examples. The ToCommand output option may be used to pipe xgrabsc output to programs. The most common commands are lpr for PostScript output and xwud for X Windows Dump output. Programs that do not accept piped input should not be used in ToCommand.

You can also get fancy and pipe the output through more than one command, such as tee screen.dmp¦ xwud to store the grabbed image and get a preview window.

Default settings for xgrab can be made in your .Xdefaults file. For the Athena toolkit version of xgrab, toggle buttons can be set or unset through their .state attribute, and text-field strings can be set through their *string attribute. For the Motif toolkit version, which has diamond-shaped buttons for radio buttons, toggle buttons can be set or unset through their .set attribute and text-field strings can be set through their *value attribute.

For example, to set the default paper size for PostScript output, put these lines in .Xdefaults (use xrdb to load them into the server):

```
XGrab*.pageWidthText*string: 8.5
XGrab*.pageHeightText*string: 11.0
```

or

```
XGrab*.pageWidthText*value: 8.5
XGrab*.pageHeightText*value: 10.0
```

To set the default output type to XWD, put these lines in .Xdefaults:

```
XGrab*.ps.state: 0
XGrab*.xwd.state: 1
```

xlock

Patrick J. Naughton (**naughton@eng.sun.com**) wrote `xlock` and released it to the world. The `xlock` program locks the local X Windows display until the user enters their password at the keyboard. While `xlock` is running, all new server connections are refused. The screen saver is disabled. The mouse cursor is turned off. The screen is blanked and a changing pattern is put on-screen. If a key or a mouse button is pressed, then the user is prompted for the password of the user who started `xlock`.

If the correct password is entered, the screen is unlocked and the `xserver` is restored. When typing the password, <Ctrl-Shift-u> and <Ctrl-Shift-h> are active as kill and erase commands, respectively. To return to the locked screen, click the small icon version of the changing pattern.

DOOM for Linux

The best is always saved for last. Why run XFree86 under Linux? Because ID Software, Inc. has made a version of their shareware game DOOM available. DOOM is an enthralling shoot-'em-up adventure game that has taken the world by storm. Using realistic 3-D graphics, you are a space marine going into an unholy, terror-filled space colony located on one of the moons of Mars. You must find your way through the labs and various sites, looking for your lost comrades. All you find instead are hideous monsters and other space marines who have turned against you.

The X Windows version supplied on the enclosed CD-ROM in the `contrib` directory is a complete shareware version. While this version does run on 386 computers, it was built to run on high-end 486 systems. If you run DOOM on a 386 with a small amount of physical RAM, be prepared to be disappointed. The game will be too slow to be enjoyable. You need lots of horsepower to play DOOM under Linux.

Installing DOOM. DOOM is stored in a series of archived files under the `///slackware/y2` directory. If you selected to install the games package while installing Linux, then DOOM should already be installed. If not, you can either use `pkgtool` to install it now, or follow these directions. If installing on your own, you first need to copy these files to an area on your hard drive.

First change the directory to the base directory you want to use. The archives extract the files to the `usr/games/doom` directory, so you may as well copy all the files in the `doom` directory on the enclosed CD-ROM to `/usr` with the following commands:

```
cd /usr
cp /cdrom/contrib/linuxdoom/* .
```

Next you need to decompress each of the files in the directory with

```
gzip -d file-name
```

where *`file-name`* is the name of each file in the directory.

This command creates two `tar` files. `tar` files are tape archives but do not necessarily need to be tapes; they can be files. For more information on `tar` see Chapter 10, "Backing Up Data." Now you need to unarchive each of these files with the `tar` command:

```
tar -xfv archive-file
```

This creates the necessary directories and files.

Starting DOOM. X Windows must first be running in order to play DOOM, so enter **`startx`**. Once X Windows is running you can either start an `xterm` session or use the <Ctrl-Alt+-F*x*> key sequence to access one of the virtual character terminals; then enter **`linuxxdoom`**. If this does not work, Linux cannot find the DOOM program—that is, it is not located in your path. If this occurs, simply change the current directory to the directory where you installed DOOM. Then enter the DOOM command again.

If you started DOOM from a virtual terminal, you need to return to the X Windows session using <Alt-F7>. If you started DOOM from an `xterm` session, you should see the DOOM introduction screen in a few seconds. While DOOM is loading, notice a series of messages. One might indicate the inability of DOOM and Linux to start the sound system; thus, you might have to play DOOM without sound. Sound is still not fully supported in this port of DOOM; such is the life of an evolving system such as Linux. For instructions on playing DOOM, see the `README.Linux` file.

From Here...

There are plenty of programs available for Linux out on the Net. You can also use X Windows to multitask different Linux programs easier by using `xterms` rather than the virtual terminals available from the character screens. The following chapters also provide more information:

- Chapter 4, "Installing Linux," explains how to install Linux, which you need to do before installing X Windows.
- Chapter 6, "Installing and Configuring the X Windows System," explains how to install the XFree86 version of X for Linux, which you need to do before installing X Windows.
- To learn how to access the Internet with Linux, check out Chapter 28, "Accessing the Internet with `telnet`, `ftp`, and the `r-` Commands."
- Check out the newsgroups, **comp.windows.x.apps** and **comp.windows.x.intrinsics** for a variety of information about X Windows in general.

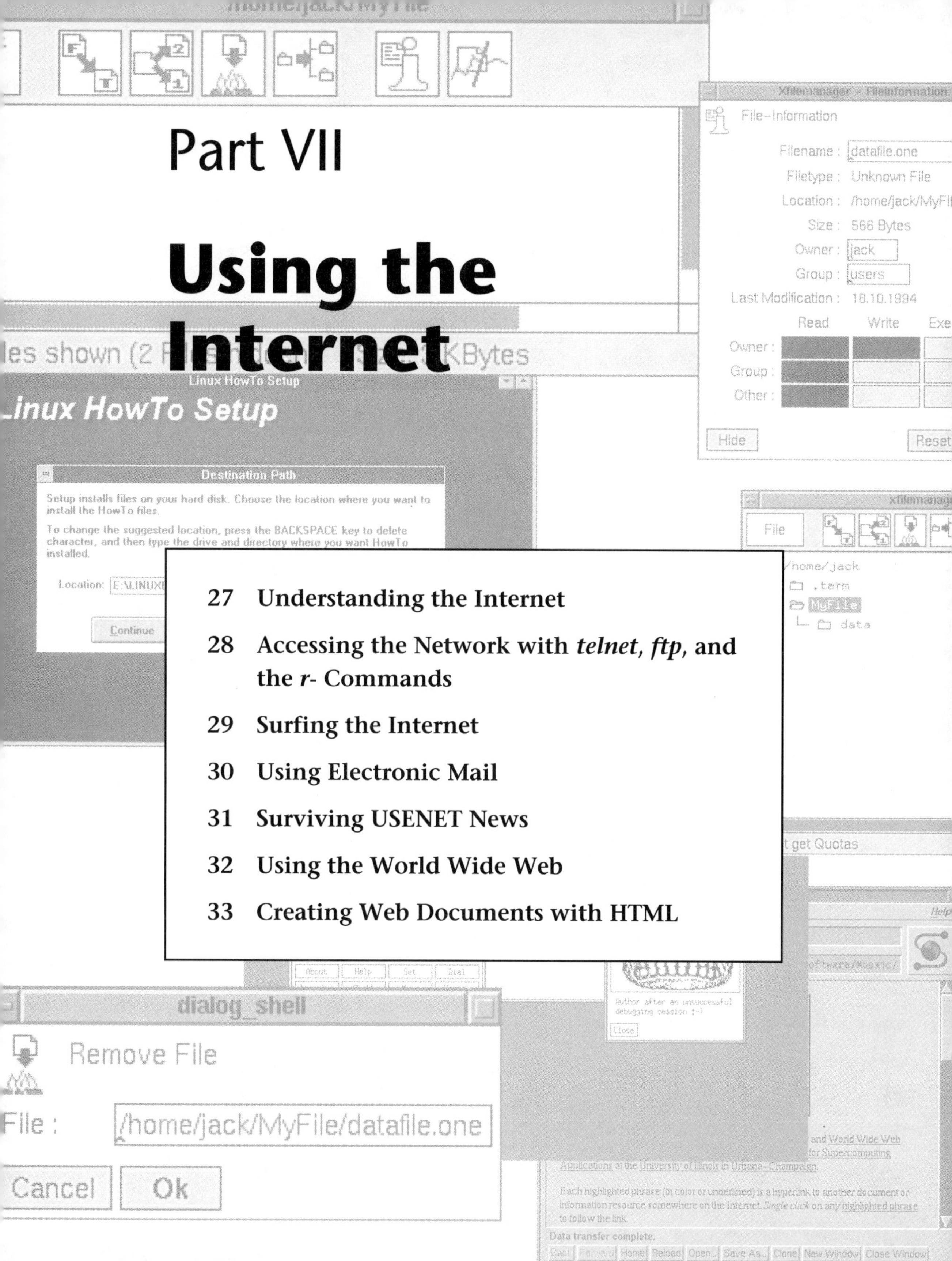

Part VII

Using the Internet

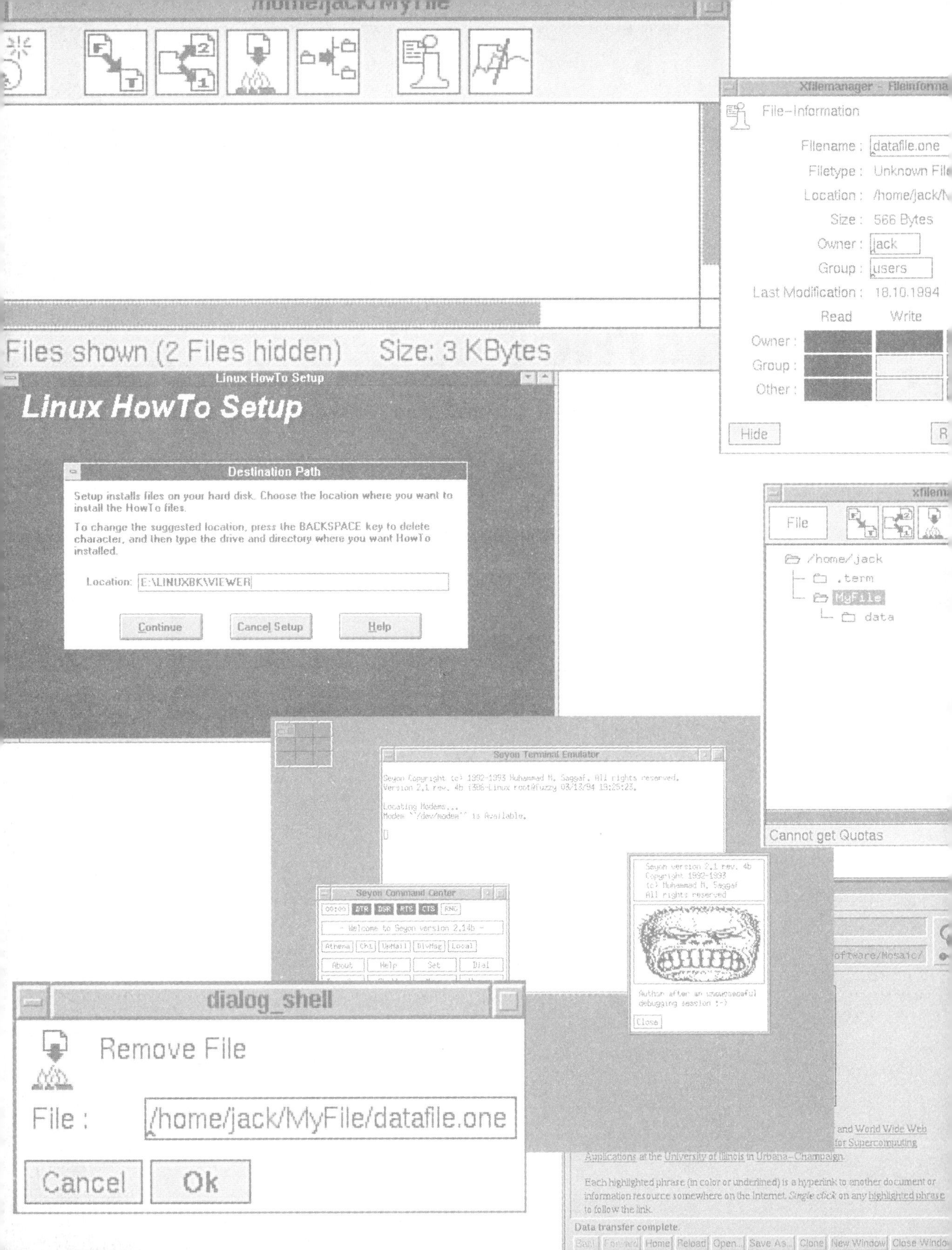

Xfilemanager - Fileinforma
File-Information
Filename : datafile.one
Filetype : Unknown File
Location : /home/jack/M
Size : 566 Bytes
Owner : jack
Group : users
Last Modification : 18.10.1994
Read
Write
Owner :
Group :
Other :
Hide
Files shown (2 Files hidden)
Size: 3 KBytes
Linux HowTo Setup
Linux HowTo Setup
Destination Path
Setup installs files on your hard disk. Choose the location where you want to install the HowTo files.
To change the suggested location, press the BACKSPACE key to delete character, and then type the drive and directory where you want HowTo installed.
Location: E:\LINUXBK\VIEWER
Continue
Cancel Setup
Help
File
/home/jack
.term
MyFile
data
Cannot get Quotas
Seyon Terminal Emulator
Seyon Command Center
dialog_shell
Remove File
File : /home/jack/MyFile/datafile.one
Cancel
Ok
Data transfer complete
Home
Reload
Open...
Save As...
Clone
New Window

CHAPTER 27

Understanding the Internet

Everywhere you turn, you hear about the Internet. Hundreds of books on the market are aimed at getting both novice and more experienced computer users on the Internet. Lots of companies also provide you with a connection—for a small fee, of course. But what is the Internet? How does it work and why is it useful? This chapter addresses these and other questions about this rapidly growing information network, such as the following:

- The structure of the Internet
- The history of the Internet
- The basics of Internet names
- An introduction to the DNS name system
- Using `nslookup` to find hosts on the Internet

Tip

Many computer users refer to the Internet simply as the *Net*.

The Structure of the Internet

The Internet is really a network of computer networks that exchange information with each other. In fact, the word *Internet* comes from the term *internetwork*, which means "to communicate between networks." An easy way to visualize the Internet is to think of a large cloud with computers attached to it (see fig. 27.1). This cloud is constantly changing and growing as new computers and networks are added and existing networks are changed.

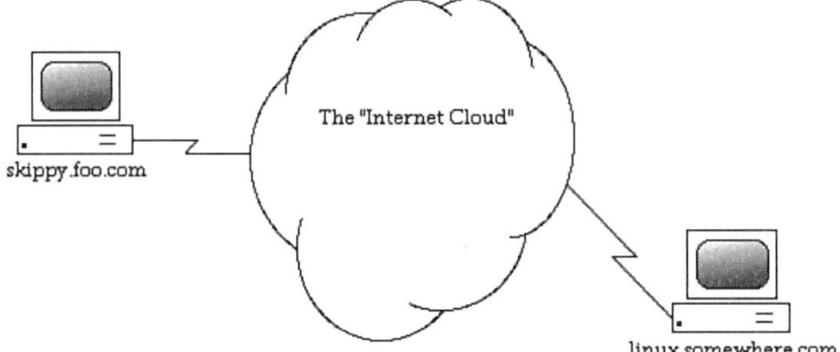

Fig. 27.1

The logical cloud structure of the Internet.

Within this Internet cloud are many computer networks that are connected to each other. These systems use the TCP/IP protocol suite for data communication.

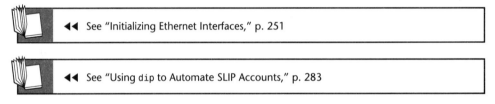

◀◀ See "Initializing Ethernet Interfaces," p. 251

◀◀ See "Using `dip` to Automate SLIP Accounts," p. 283

A Brief History

The Internet grew out of a research program of the U.S. Defense Advanced Research Projects Agency (DARPA), which focused on ways to link various computer networks. The result was the ARPANET, initiated in 1969. By 1971, approximately 40 computers, or hosts, were connected to the ARPANET, and researchers were developing the capability to send e-mail across networks. The ARPANET continued to grow throughout the '70s, and other computer networks began to connect to it as well.

Internetworking research led to the development of the TCP/IP network protocols, which replaced an older protocol suite known as NCP, and became the standard for the ARPANET. As more and more networks connected to the ARPANET and each other, this large complex of networks came to be known as the Internet. The original ARPANET was shut down in 1990, leaving the Internet as its thriving successor.

Size

▶▶ See "Mosaic and the World Wide Web (WWW)," p. 616

The Internet has experienced incredible growth over the last ten years. In 1984, approximately 1,000 hosts were on the Internet. By 1989, this total had grown to more than 100,000. Three years later, in 1992, the total was more than 1 million computers on the Internet. As of July 1994, more than 3.2 million host computers were on the

Net, with an estimated 20 million users. With the development of easy-to-use information-retrieval tools such as Mosaic and the World Wide Web, many non-technical users are discovering that the Internet has vast information resources that they can access.

As to the geographic size of the Internet, it essentially spans the entire world. Almost every industrialized nation has some form of Internet connectivity.

Note

Basically, there are two different levels of Internet connectivity. At the most interactive level, a site has some sort of physical connection to an Internet member network. This site runs the TCP/IP protocol suite as its networking protocols and can make direct network connections in real time to other computers. This is referred to as being *IP connected.* The other type of connection typically uses the UUCP protocol to transfer e-mail and USENET news to and from an IP connected site. Users with this type of connection can't access other computers interactively on the Net.

Internet Names

Tip

Sometimes a domain name might not refer to a specific computer; instead, it might refer to an alias of some sort.

▶▶ See "Internet Documentation," p. 618

With millions of computers on the Internet, how do you specify the one that you want to interact with? You must know the name of the computer, just as you must know the name of someone you want to send a letter to. These names are specified by a convention called the *Domain Name Service* (DNS), which is specified in Internet Request For Comments (RFC) numbers 1032, 1033, 1034, and 1035.

Note

Requests For Comments provide the official documentation, policies, and procedures of the Internet community.

A DNS name has the following format:

```
[subdomain].[subdomain].[...].domain
```

Note

Brackets ([ ]) indicate optional items. Hence, don't type the brackets as part of the name.

Domains

A domain name typically gives a hierarchical structure for a computer or group within an organization. The portion of the name to the far right, the *domain field*, provides the most general category. The United States has eight domain fields, which are listed in Table 27.1.

Table 27.1 Listing of U.S. Domains

Domain	Description
`arpa`	ARPANET members (obsolete)
`com`	Commercial and industrial organizations
`edu`	Universities and educational institutions
`gov`	Non-military government organizations
`mil`	Military
`net`	Network operation organizations
`org`	Other organizations
`us`	United States ISO domain

Tip

Refer to RFC 1480 for more information on the us domain.

Outside the U.S., each nation has a two-letter domain assigned to it based on its country code as defined in the International Standards Organization (ISO) document 3166. For historical reasons, the us domain wasn't widely used initially.

Table 27.2 lists the domains for other nations.

Table 27.2 Listing of International DNS Domains

Country	Domain	Country	Domain
Afghanistan	AF	Andorra	AD
Albania	AL	Angola	AO
Algeria	DZ	Anguilla	AI
American Samoa	AS	Antarctica	AQ

Country	Domain	Country	Domain
Antigua and Barbuda	AG	Chile	CL
Argentina	AR	China	CN
Armenia	AM	Christmas Island	CX
Aruba	AW	Cocos (Keeling) Islands	CC
Australia	AU	Colombia	CO
Austria	AT	Comoros	KM
Azerbaijan	AZ	Congo	CG
Bahamas	BS	Cook Island	CK
Bahrain	BH	Costa Rica	CR
Bangladesh	BD	Cote d'Ivoire (Ivory Coast)	CI
Barbados	BB	Croatia	HR
Belarus	BY	Cuba	CU
Belgium	BE	Cyprus	CY
Belize	BZ	Czech Republic	CZ
Benin	BJ	Denmark	DK
Bermuda	BM	Djibouti	DJ
Bhutan	BT	Dominica	DM
Bolivia	BO	Dominican Republic	DO
Bosnia-Hercegovina	BA	East Timor	TP
Botswana	BW	Ecuador	EC
Bouvet Island	BV	Egypt	EG
Brazil	BR	El Salvador	SV
British Indian Ocean Territory	IO	Equatorial Guinea	GQ
Brunei Darussalam	BN	Estonia	EE
Bulgaria	BG	Ethiopia	ET
Burkina Faso	BF	Falkland Islands	FK
Burundi	BI	Faroe Islands	FO
Cambodia	KH	Fiji	FJ
Cameroon	CM	Finland	FI
Canada	CA	France	FR
Cape Verde	CV	French Guiana	GF
Cayman Islands	KY	French Polynesia	PFF
Central African Republic	CF	French Southern Territories	TF
Chad	TD	Gabon	GA

(continues)

Table 27.2 Continued

Country	Domain	Country	Domain
Gambia	GM	Korea, Democratic People's Republic of (North)	KP
Georgia	GE	Korea, Republic of (South)	KR
Germany	DE	Kuwait	KW
Ghana	GH	Kyrgyzstan	KG
Gibraltar	GI	Lao People's Democratic Republic	LA
Greece	GR	Latvia	LV
Greenland	GL	Lebanon	LB
Grenada	GD	Lesotho	LS
Guadeloupe	GP	Liberia	LR
Guam	GU	Libyan Arab Jamahiriya (Libya)	LY
Guatemala	GT	Liechtenstein	LI
Guinea	GN	Lithuania	LT
Guinea-Bissau	GW	Luxembourg	LU
Guyana	GY	Macau (Macao)	MO
Haiti	HT	Madagascar	MG
Heard and McDonald Islands	HM	Malawi	MW
Honduras	HN	Malaysia	MY
Hong Kong	HK	Maldives	MV
Hungary	HU	Mali	ML
Iceland	IS	Malta	MT
India	IN	Marshall Islands	MH
Indonesia	ID	Martinique	MQ
Iran	IR	Mauritania	MR
Iraq	IQ	Mauritius	MU
Ireland	IE	Mexico	MX
Israel	IL	Micronesia	FM
Italy	IT	Moldovia	MD
Jamaica	JM	Monaco	MC
Japan	JP	Mongolia	MN
Jordan	JO	Montserrat	MS
Kazakhstan	KZ	Morocco	MA
Kenya	KE	Mozambique	MZ
Kiribati	KI		

Country	Domain	Country	Domain
Myanmar	MM	St. Kitts and Nevis	KN
Namibia	NA	St. Lucia	LC
Nauru	NR	St. Pierre and Miquelon	PM
Nepal	NP	St. Vincent and the Grenadines	VC
Netherlands	NL	Samoa	WS
Netherlands Antilles (Dutch West Indies)	AN	San Marino	SM
Neutral Zone	NT	Sao Tome and Principe	ST
New Caledonia	NC	Saudi Arabia	SA
New Zealand	NZ	Senegal	SN
Nicaragua	NI	Seychelles	SC
Niger	NE	Sierra Leone	SL
Nigeria	NG	Singapore	SG
Niue	NU	Slovak Republic	SK
Norfolk Island	NF	Slovenia	SI
Northern Mariana Islands	MP	Solomon Islands	SB
Norway	NO	Somalia	SO
Oman	OM	South Africa	ZA
Pakistan	PK	Spain	ES
Palau	PW	Sri Lanka	LK
Panama	PA	Sudan	SD
Papua New Guinea	PG	Suriname	SR
Paraguay	PY	Svalbard and Jan Mayen Islands	SJ
Peru	PE	Swaziland	SZ
Philippines	PH	Sweden	SE
Pitcairn Island	PN	Switzerland	CH
Poland	PL	Syrian Arab Republic	SY
Portugal	PT	Taiwan	TW
Puerto Rico	PR	Tajkistan	TJ
Qatar	QA	Tanzania	TZ
Reunion Island	RE	Thailand	TH
Romania	RO	Togo	TG
Russian Federation	RU	Tokelau	TK
Rwanda	RW	Tonga	TO
St. Helena	SH	Trinidad and Tobago	TT

(continues)

Table 27.2 Continued

Country	Domain	Country	Domain
Tunisia	TN	Vatican City	VA
Turkey	TR	Venezuela	VE
Turkmenistan	TM	Vietnam	VN
Turks and Caicos Islands	TC	Virgin Islands (British)	VG
Tuvalu	TV	Virgin Islands (U.S.)	VI
Uganda	UG	Wallis and Fortuna Islands	WF
Ukraine	UA	Western Sahara	EH
United Arab Emirates	AE	Yemen	YE
United Kingdom	UK	Yugoslavia (former)	YU
United States	US	Zaire	ZR
Uruguay	UY	Zambia	ZM
Uzbekistan	UZ	Zimbabwe	ZW
Vanuatu	VU		

Subdomains

The subdomain fields of a DNS name serve to identify a specific computer or address within a domain. The subdomains become more specific from right to left in the domain name. The rightmost subdomain field, the one next to the domain field, usually serves to indicate a particular organization within a given domain. The name **ncsu.edu**, for example, refers to the North Carolina State University (**ncsu**) subdomain in the **edu** domain. Secondary subdomain fields specify a department, group, or computer within an organization. These subdomain groupings produce a logical tree structure within the domain.

▶▶ See "Using Electronic Mail," p. 621

To specify a user at a certain location, a special delimiter is used. The @ symbol is used to specify a user, alias, or mailbox in a site's DNS name. For example, Joe Smith has the user account **smith** at the machine **linux1.somewhere.com**. The full address for Joe is

smith@linux1.sales.somewhere.com

The @ symbol is used to separate the destination mailbox from the computer destination.

> **Note**
>
> It's not uncommon for the DNS name portion of an e-mail address to specify a department or organization instead of a machine. In the preceding example, to avoid having to use a specific computer's name in an e-mail address, the system administrator can set up the receiving mailer with an address of **smith@sales.somewhere.com** or even **smith@somewhere.com**.

Basics of Domain Name Service

You've learned how host names are represented by using the DNS convention, but exactly how does Linux know how to communicate with a computer when you send mail to **smith@linux1.somewhere.com**? This simple question really opens up the whole can of worms about networking. However, understanding how DNS translates names is useful for the average user and is absolutely critical for the system administrator.

Names and Numbers

As you recall, this chapter has briefly talked about sites being IP connected to the Internet and using the TCP/IP protocol suite to facilitate communication. TCP/IP identifies each host with a unique number known as an IP address. An IP address is a 32-bit value. Like the DNS name, the address is divided into four 8-bit fields, each separated by a period.

> **Note**
>
> In networking terminology, an 8-bit field is referred to as an *octet* instead of a *byte*. This avoids confusion, as some computers use a byte size of other than 8 bits.

Each computer has exactly one IP address for each physical interface that it has connected to a network.

The IP address of a computer is divided into two parts: a network section, which specifies a particular network, and a host portion, which identifies a particular machine on the network. There now are five categories of IP addresses, based on the type of network address. These are referred to as *Class A* through *Class E*.

In a Class A address, the first octet has a value between 1 and 126, and the network portion consists of the first octet. This obviously limits the number of Class A networks to 126; however, each network can have more than 16 million computers. Class A networks are limited to major corporations and network providers.

Class B networks use the first two octets to specify the network portion and have the first octet in the range of 128 to 191. This leaves the last two octets free for the host

ID. The Class B network space provides for 16,382 network ID numbers, each with 65,534 host IDs. Large companies and organizations such as universities are typically assigned Class B addresses.

Class C addresses use three octets to specify the network portion, with the first octet in the range from 192 to 223. This provides for more than 2 million different Class C networks, but with only 254 hosts per network. Class C networks are usually assigned to small businesses or organizations.

In Class D addresses, the first octet is in the range from 224 to 239 and is used for multicast transmissions.

Class E addresses, with the first octet in the range of 240 to 247, are reserved for future use.

Note

The values 0, 127, and 255 have special meaning in an IP address. A 0 in an octet indicates that the host doesn't know that part of its address. A 127 refers to a loopback or local host address, and a 255 in an octet refers to a broadcast address. When 4.2BSD UNIX was released, the broadcast address was specified by using a 0 in the host portion of the IP address. This was later changed to 255 and is standardized in an RFC. A few old systems may still be around that use the 0 for their broadcast—this is referred to as *Berkeley broadcast*.

When computers communicate using TCP/IP, they use the numeric IP address just described. DNS names are simply a device that helps us poor humans remember which host is which and what network it's connected to. Originally, when the Internet was first formed, the number of hosts on the Net was very small. As a result, each host had a complete list of all host names and addresses in a local file. For obvious reasons, this system quickly became unwieldy. When a new host was added, it was necessary to update every host file on every computer. With the explosive growth of the Internet, the host files also grew quite large. The mapping of DNS names to IP addresses is now accomplished via a distributed database and specific software that performs the lookup.

The distributed database and software that make up the DNS name resolution system is composed of the following three basic parts:

- Domain name space
- Name servers
- Resolvers

Domain Name Space. The *domain name space* is a specification for a tree structure that identifies a set of hosts and provides information about them. Conceptually, each node in the tree has a database of information about the hosts under its authority. Queries try to extract the appropriate information from this database. In simple terms, this is just the listing of all different types of information—names, IP address, mail aliases, and such that's available for lookup in the DNS system.

Name Servers. Programs that hold and maintain the data located in the domain name space are known as *name servers*. Each name server has complete information about a subset of the domain name space and cached information about other portions. Also, a name server has complete information for its area of authority. This authoritative information is divided into areas known as *zones*, which can be divided among different name servers to provide redundant service for a zone. Each name server knows about other name servers that are responsible for different zones. If a request comes in for information from the zone that a given name server is responsible for, the name server simply returns the information. If a request comes in for information from a different zone, however, the name server contacts the appropriate server with authority for that zone.

Resolvers. *Resolvers* are simply programs that extract information from the name servers in response to a query about a host in the domain name space.

Finding Host Information

To find information about a host or domain, you can use two basic sources of information: the `whois` information system and the `nslookup` program.

Using *whois*. `whois` queries the DNS system and returns information on network address numbers, administrative and technical contact information, telephone numbers, and postal and e-mail addresses. The syntax for this command is

```
whois [name]
```

name is a network or domain name or a registered user. The `whois` utility is a local client program that connects to a server and returns the information to your computer. In addition to the `whois` utility, it is possible to connect directly to an information server and get this information. You can telnet to **rs.internic.net** and type **whois** at the first prompt. The `Whois:` prompt appears, where you can make your queries.

Here are a few sample `whois` sessions:

```
Whois: ncsu.edu<Return>
North Carolina State University (NCSU-DOM)
   Computing Center
   Box 7109
   Raleigh, NC 27695-7109

   Domain Name: NCSU.EDU

   Administrative Contact:
      Malstrom, Carl W.  (CWM10)  Carl_Malstrom@ncsu.EDU
      (919) 515-5455
   Technical Contact, Zone Contact:
      Buckland, Randy  (RB424)  randy_buckland@NCSU.EDU
      (919) 515-5491

   Record last updated on 22-Aug-94.
```

```
   Domain servers in listed order:

   FBI.CC.NCSU.EDU              152.1.1.22
   CC00NS.UNITY.NCSU.EDU        152.1.1.161
   EOS01A.EOS.NCSU.EDU          152.1.9.5

Whois: mcnc.org<Return>
Microelectronics Center of North Carolina (MCNC-DOM)
   P.O. Box 12889
   Research Triangle Park, NC 27709

   Domain Name: MCNC.ORG

   Administrative Contact, Technical Contact, Zone Contact:
      Seaver, Tim A.  (TAS8)  tas@NCREN.NET
      919 248 1973


   Record last updated on 15-Sep-92.

   Domain servers in listed order:

   MCNC.MCNC.ORG                128.109.130.3
   PEPE.MCNC.ORG                128.109.130.2
   NCNOC.NCREN.NET              192.101.21.1,128.109.193.1
   SDS.SDSC.EDU                 132.249.20.22

Whois: interpath.net<Return>
   Interpath (INTERPATH-DOM)
   PO Box 12800
   Raleigh, NC  27605

   Domain Name: INTERPATH.NET

   Administrative Contact, Technical Contact, Zone Contact:
      Clegg, Alan B.  (AC178)  abc@INTERPATH.NET
      (919) 890-6310

   Record last updated on 18-Feb-94.

   Domain servers in listed order:

   DNS1.INTERPATH.NET           199.72.1.1
   ICM2.ICP.NET                 192.80.214.224
   NS1.SPRINTLINK.NET           144.228.1.40
   NS2.SPRINTLINK.NET           144.228.8.227
   NS3.SPRINTLINK.NET           199.0.55.3

Whois: ibm.com<Return>
International Business Machines (IBM-DOM)

   Domain Name: IBM.COM

   Administrative Contact, Technical Contact, Zone Contact:
      Trio, Nicholas R.  (NRT1)  nrt@watson.ibm.com
      (914) 945-1850

   Record last updated on 15-Nov-93.
```

```
Domain servers in listed order:

WATSON.IBM.COM              129.34.139.4
NS.AUSTIN.IBM.COM           192.35.232.34
NS.ALMADEN.IBM.COM          198.4.83.134
```

Using *nslookup*. The `nslookup` utility queries the DNS system to return information about specific hosts and networks. Although `nslookup` returns several different types of information, the default behavior is to resolve a DNS name and return its corresponding IP address.

The `nslookup` command has two basic forms: interactive and non-interactive. The non-interactive form has the following syntax:

```
nslookup [hostname]
```

This form of `nslookup` tries to resolve the DNS name ***`hostname`*** and return its IP address.

Interactive mode is selected when either no arguments are given or the first argument starts with a hyphen and the second argument is the name or IP address of a name server. In interactive mode, you can customize the behavior of `nslookup` by specifying the name server to query, changing the type of information to search for, changing the default domain name, enabling debugging, and so forth. Although there are many different options in interactive mode, it's mostly used to search for information other than the IP address. Refer to the `nslookup` man page for all the gory details on the other features.

You can change the search type in `nslookup` interactive mode with the `set type=` command. Table 27.3 lists the types of information that can be specified and the appropriate type code for the `set type=` command.

Table 27.3 Search Information Available in *nslookup*

Information	Type Code
Host's IP address (default)	A
Canonical alias name	CNAME
CPU and operating system info	HINFO
Mail destination	MD
Mail group records	MG
Mail exchanger records	MX
Mail rename domain name	MR
Mailbox or mail list information	MINFO
Name server for zone	NS
Any information found	ANY

There are additional type codes that may be used with `nslookup`. These are specified in the Request For Comments (RFC) number 1035.

From Here...

You can find more information about the Internet in the following chapters:

- Chapter 28, "Accessing the Network with `telnet`, `ftp`, and the `r-` Commands," discusses the different methods for working with the Internet.
- Chapter 29, "Surfing the Internet," describes the different types of information available on the Internet.

CHAPTER 28

Accessing the Network with *telnet*, *ftp*, and the *r-* Commands

The major advantage that you gain from computer networking is the ability to share resources and information and access that information from remote locations. Linux provides a robust set of tools for doing just that.

In this chapter, you learn about the following:

- The `telnet` command
- The `ftp` command
- The `r-` commands

Using *telnet* to Access Remote Computers

The `telnet` command is the basic tool for remote logon under Linux. `telnet` gives you a terminal session on the remote computer that allows you to execute commands as though you were logged on locally.

In order to log on to a computer via `telnet`, you must know a valid user name and password on the remote machine. Although some systems do provide guest logon capabilities, these are fairly rare due to security concerns. When guest logons are allowed, they almost always place the user in a restricted shell or in a menu system. The idea behind both of these guest environments is to provide computer security and protect the system from malicious or careless unknown users. A restricted shell prevents the user from executing specific commands, and a menu system only allows choices from a predefined set of menus, blocking out shell access entirely.

`telnet` also allows users to log on to their own computer from a remote location by entering their user name and password. This allows users to check e-mail, edit files, and run programs on their normal computer as though they were logged on locally. However, you have to make do with a terminal based environment instead of the X Windows system. `telnet` only provides terminal emulation for common terminals such as the DEC VT-100, which does not support graphical environments such as X Windows.

telnet Command Summary

The basic syntax for `telnet` is

```
telnet [host-name]
```

`host-name` is the name of a remote computer. If you do not specify a remote host, `telnet` starts in its *interactive command mode*. If you give a remote host name, `telnet` tries to initiate a session immediately.

`telnet` accepts several command-line arguments in addition to the *`host-name`* argument. Table 28.1 lists the arguments for `telnet`.

Table 28.1 Command-Line Arguments for the *telnet* Command

Argument	Description
`-d`	Turns on debugging.
`-a`	Attempts automatic logon.
`-n` *`tracefile`*	Turns on tracing and saves trace data in *`tracefile`*.
`-e` *`escape char`*	Sets the escape character for the session to be *`escape char`*. If the *`escape char`* character is omitted from the argument, there is no escape character for this `telnet` session.
`-l` *`user`*	Sends the user name *`user`* to the remote system for automatic logon. This argument implies the `-a` argument.
`host-name`	The host name or address of remote system.
`port`	Indicates the port number to connect to on the remote system. Used for specifying different network programs. If not specified, `telnet` connects to the default `telnet` port.

Sample *telnet* Session

It's time to take a walk through a sample `telnet` session. You start the `telnet` session by typing **`telnet`**, followed by the host name of the computer that you want to connect to. `telnet` then returns with the message: `Trying` *`some IP address`*. *`some IP address`* is the address of the computer you specified. If it is successful in connecting to the computer (that is, the computer is up and running and the network isn't down), Linux reports `Connected to` *`computer name`* and then tells you that the escape character is some specific character sequence, almost always <Ctrl-]>. The escape character specifies the character sequence that you type in order to drop from your terminal session into the `telnet` command interpreter. You do this if you want to send commands directly to the `telnet` program and not to your remote computer session.

Once `telnet` has successfully connected to the remote system, the logon information is displayed and the system prompts you for your logon ID and password. Assuming you have a valid user name and password, you successfully log on and can now work interactively on the remote system.

The following is an example of a `telnet` session from a Linux computer that connects to a Linux computer:

```
$ telnet opus.tristar.com<Return>
Trying 127.0.0.1...
Connected to opus.tristar.com.
Escape character is '^]'.

   Linux 1.2.13 (opus.tristar.com) (ttyp1)


   opus login: bubba<Return>
   Password: password<Return>
   Last login: Tue Sep 27 20:50:43 from localhost
   Linux 1.0.9. (Posix).
   opus:~$
   opus:~$ logout<Return>
   Connection closed by foreign host.
$
```

When you are finished with the remote session, be sure to log off. `telnet` then reports that the remote session is closed, and you return to your local shell prompt.

Using *ftp* for Remote File Transfer

File transfer protocol (FTP) is a simple and effective means of transferring files between computers that are connected on a TCP/IP network. FTP allows users to transfer both ASCII and binary files.

During an `ftp` session, you connect to another computer using the `ftp` client program. From this point, you can move up and down through the directory tree, list directory contents, copy files from the remote computer to your computer, and transfer files from your computer to the remote system. Normal file protections apply; you cannot get or put a file on the remote system if you don't have the proper permissions for that file.

◂◂ See "Basics of the Domain Name System," p. 587

In order to use `ftp` to transfer files, you must know a valid user name and password on the remote computer. This user name/password combination is used to validate your `ftp` session and determines what access you have to files for transfer. In addition, you obviously need to know the name of the computer that you want to conduct an `ftp` session with.

You should be aware that `ftp` clients have different command sets depending on the operating system in question. In this chapter, we cover the Linux `ftp` client; however, when you start an `ftp` session with a remote computer, the commands that the remote system expects may be different. It is rare for FTP systems to be completely incompatible with each other. Typically, the commands that you normally use may be slightly different or unavailable.

Anonymous FTP

Due to the explosive growth of the Internet, many organizations have made huge repositories of information available via FTP. These FTP sites have everything from text files to software of every conceivable type available. But how do you access this enormous store house of data if you don't have an account on the remote computer? Do you need to get an account on every FTP site in order to access these files?

In short, the answer is no. There is a common convention on the Internet that allows guest FTP access to file repositories so that users can transfer files. This guest access is referred to as *anonymous FTP*. In order to use anonymous FTP, you start an `ftp` session to the remote system and use the user name of anonymous and your e-mail address as the password.

For example, the user `smith` on `linux.somewhere.com` wants to initiate an `ftp` session with a common FTP site:

```
$ ftp ftp.uu.net<Return>
ftp.uu.net (login:smith): anonymous<Return>
Password: smith@linux.somewhere.com<Return>
```

> **Note**
>
> Many sites do not allow anonymous FTP. Allowing guest users to connect to your computer does involve some risk. In cases where anonymous FTP is not allowed, the `ftp` command fails with a message similar to `Login failed - User "anonymous" unknown`. Sites that do permit anonymous FTP typically place the user in a restricted directory tree that has read-only access. If you are allowed to place files on the remote computer, you usually can only put them in one directory.

ftp Command Summary

The Linux `ftp` command provides a verbose set of command options in interactive mode. As mentioned earlier, some remote hosts may not support all of these commands. Additionally, you probably won't need to use many of them. Table 28.2 lists the commands available while in `ftp`.

Table 28.2 *ftp* Commands Available in Interactive Mode

Command	Description
`!`	Escapes to the shell
`$`	Executes a macro
`account`	Sends the account command to remote server
`append`	Appends to a file
`ascii`	Sets the file-transfer type to ASCII mode
`bell`	Beeps when a command is completed

Command	Description
`binary`	Sets the file-transfer type to binary mode
`bye`	Terminates the `ftp` session and exits
`case`	Toggles `mget` upper- or lowercase file-name mapping
`cd`	Changes working directory on remote computer
`cdup`	Changes remote working directory to parent directory
`chmod`	Changes file permissions of remote file
`close`	Terminates `ftp` session
`cr`	Toggles carriage return stripping when receiving an ASCII file
`delete`	Deletes remote filed
`debug`	Toggles debugging mode
`dir`	Lists the contents of the remote directory (gives size and permissions)
`disconnect`	Terminates `ftp` session (same as close)
`form`	Sets the file-transfer format
`get`	Gets a file from the remote computer
`glob`	Toggles wild-card expansion of local file names
`hash`	Toggles printing the # character for each buffer transferred
`help`	Prints local help information
`idle`	Gets or sets idle timer on the remote computer
`image`	Sets the file transfer type to binary mode (same as binary)
`lcd`	Changes local working directory
`ls`	Lists contents of the remote directory
`macdef`	Defines a macro
`mdelete`	Deletes multiple files on the remote computer
`mdir`	Lists contents of multiple remote directories
`mget`	Gets multiple files from the remote computer
`mkdir`	Makes a directory on the remote machine
`mls`	Lists contents of multiple remote directories
`mode`	Sets the file-transfer mode
`modtime`	Shows last modification time of remote file
`mput`	Sends multiple files to remote computer
`newer`	Gets remote file if the remote file is newer than the corresponding local file
`nmap`	Sets templates for default file-name mapping
`nlist`	Lists contents of the remote directory
`ntrans`	Sets translation table for default file-name mapping

(continues)

Table 28.2 Continued

Command	Description
`open`	Connects to remote `ftp` site
`prompt`	Forces interactive prompting on multiple commands
`proxy`	Issues command on alternate connection
`sendport`	Toggles use of `PORT` command for each data connection
`put`	Sends one file to remote computer
`pwd`	Prints working directory on remote machine
`quit`	Terminates `ftp` session and exits
`quote`	Sends an arbitrary `ftp` command
`recv`	Receives a file
`rget`	Gets file restarting at end of local file
`rstatus`	Shows the status of the remote machine
`rhelp`	Gets help from the remote server
`rename`	Renames a file
`reset`	Clears queued command replies
`restart`	Restarts the file transfer at the specified byte-count
`rmdir`	Removes a directory on the remote machine
`runique`	When retrieving multiple files with the same file name to the same directory, `runique` assigns a unique file name to each file received
`send`	Sends one file to remote computer
`site`	Sends a site specific command to the remote server, one of `umask`, `idle`, `chmod`, `help`, `group`, `gpass`, `newer`, or `minfo`
`size`	Shows the size of the remote file
`status`	Shows the current status
`struct`	Sets the file-transfer structure
`system`	Shows the remote system type
`sunique`	When sending multiple files with the same file name to the same directory, `runique` assigns a unique file name to each file sent
`tenex`	Sets the `tenex` file-transfer type
`trace`	Toggles packet tracing
`type`	Sets the file-transfer type
`user`	Sends new user information
`umask`	Gets or sets the `umask` on the remote computer
`verbose`	Toggles verbose mode
`?`	Prints local help information

As you can see, there are quite a few commands in `ftp`. However, you really only need to take a look at the ones that you use most frequently.

Starting an *ftp* Session. The `open` command is used to open an `ftp` session with a remote host, and its syntax is

```
open host-name
```

You usually only need this command if you are going to connect to more than one site during an `ftp` session. If you only want to connect to one computer during the session, just specify the remote *`host-name`* on the command line as an argument to the `ftp` command.

Ending an *ftp* Session. The `close`, `disconnect`, `quit`, and `bye` commands are used to end an `ftp` session with a remote computer. The `close` and `disconnect` commands close your connection to the remote computer but leave you in the `ftp` program on your local computer. `close` and `disconnect` are identical. `quit` and `bye` close your connection to the remote computer if one is active; then they exit the `ftp` program on your computer.

Changing Directories. The `cd` *`[directory]`* command is used to change directories on the remote computer during your `ftp` session. The `cdup` command takes you to the parent directory of the current directory. The `lcd` command changes your local directory so you can specify where to find or put local files.

Remote Directory Listing. The `ls` command lists the contents of a remote directory, just like `ls` from an interactive shell. The syntax for the `ls` command is

```
ls [directory] [local_file]
```

If a *`directory`* is specified as an argument, the `ls` lists the contents of that directory. If a *`local_file`* name is given, the directory listing is put into the file you specified on your local computer.

The following is an example of an `ls` directory listing:

```
edu
doc
private
systems
packages
multimedia
```

The `dir` command behaves just like the `ls` command except that it provides a long listing giving protections, size, owner, and date. The `ls` command only lists the file names. The syntax of the `dir` command is

```
dir [directory] [local_file]
```

The following is an example of a `dir` directory listing:

```
-rw-r--r--    1 root  archive   2928  May   17   1993   README
-rw-r--r--    1 root  archive   1723  Jun   29   1993   README.NFS
d--x--x--x    2 root  wheel     8192  Jun    6   12:16  bind
rwxr-xr-x     5 root  wheel     8192  Aug    2   06:11  decus
drwxr-xr-x   19 root  archive   8192  Feb    7   1994   doc
drwxr-xr-x    6 root  wheel     8192  Jun   15   15:45  edu
d--x--x--x    7 root  wheel     8192  Sep   28   09:33  etc
```

Getting Files from a Remote System. The `get` and `mget` commands are used to retrieve files from a remote computer. The `get` command retrieves the file that you specify as an argument (*`file-name`*); the `get` command's syntax is

```
get file-name [remote_file-name]
```

You may also give a local file name, which is the name of the file when it is created on your local computer. If you do not give a local file name, the *`remote_file-name`* is used.

The `mget` command retrieves multiple files at once. `mget`'s syntax is

```
mget file-name_list
```

You specify these files by giving a list of file names separated by spaces or a wild-card pattern to `mget`. You are prompted for each file. To turn prompting off, use the `prompt` command before using `mget`. In both cases, the files are transferred as ASCII files unless you have set the transfer mode to something else.

Sending Files to a Remote System. The `put` and `mput` commands are used to send files to a remote computer. The `put` command sends the local file that you specify as an argument. The syntax is

```
put file-name
```

The `mput` command sends a series of local files. The syntax for the `mput` command is

```
mput file-name_list
```

You specify these files by giving a list of file names separated by spaces or a wild-card pattern to `mput`. When using `mput`, you are prompted for each file. To turn prompting off, use the `prompt` command. In both cases, the files are transferred as ASCII files unless you have set the transfer mode to something else.

Changing the File Transfer Mode. FTP transfers files as ASCII files unless you specify something else. This is fine for plain text but renders any binary data useless. The `ascii` and `binary` commands set the transfer mode so that you can prevent damage to your binary files.

Note

Many files that you will want to transfer are in binary format. Files ending with `.tar` are archives created with the `tar` command. Files ending in `.Z` and `.gz` are compressed with either the `compress` command or the GNU `gzip` command, respectively. Files ending in `.zip` are compressed archives created with `PKZIP`. When in doubt, use the binary transfer mode.

Checking Transfer Status. When transferring a large file, you may find it useful to have `ftp` give you feedback on how far along the transfer is. The `hash` command causes `ftp` to print a # character on-screen each time the transmission of a data buffer has been completed. This command works for both sending and receiving files.

Local Commands While in FTP. The `!` character is used to pass a command to the command shell on your local computer while you are in `ftp`. This can be very useful if there is something that you need to do while you are in the midst of an `ftp` session. For example, suppose that you need to create a directory to hold received files. If you type **`!mkdir new_dir`** and press <Return>, Linux makes a directory named `new_dir` in your current local directory.

A Sample *ftp* Session

Here is a short `ftp` session where a user makes an `ftp` connection to another machine and does a directory listing.

```
$ ftp opus<Return>
Connected to opus.
220 opus FTP server (Linux opus 1.0.9 #4
➥Mon Jun 6 16:01:33 CDT 1994 i386) ready.
Name (opus:smith): smith<Return>
Password (opus:smith): password<Return>
331 Password required for smith.
230 User smith logged in.
Remote system type is UNIX.
Using ASCII mode to transfer files.
ftp> ls<Return>
200 PORT command successful.
150 Opening ASCII mode data connection for file list.
bin
usr
dev
etc
pub
README
welcome.msg
226 Transfer complete.
46 bytes received in 0.002 seconds (23 Kbytes/s)
ftp> dir<Return>
200 PORT command successful.
150 Opening ASCII mode data connection for /bin/ls.
total 8
-rw-r--r--  1 root     daemon      1525 Sep 29 15:37 README
dr-xr-xr-x  2 root     wheel        512 Jun 24 11:35 bin
dr--r--r--  2 root     wheel        512 Jun 24 11:18 dev
dr--r--r--  2 root     wheel        512 Jun 24 11:24 etc
dr-xr-xr-x  4 root     wheel        512 Sep 29 15:37 pub
dr-xr-xr-x  3 root     wheel        512 Jun 24 11:15 usr
-r--r--r--  1 root     daemon       461 Jun 24 13:46 welcome.msg
226 Transfer complete.
433 bytes received in 0.027 seconds (16 Kbytes/s)
ftp> get README<Return>
200 PORT command successful.
150 Opening ASCII mode data connection for README (1525 bytes).
```

```
226 Transfer complete.
local: README remote: README
1561 bytes received in 0.0038 seconds (4e+02 Kbytes/s)
ftp> quit<Return>
221 Goodbye.
$
```

In the preceding example, a user opens an `ftp` session to the host opus and logs on as `smith`. The remote `ftp` server prompts for the password, which the user types in. The password does not appear on-screen. `ftp` then logs smith on to the remote system and displays the `ftp>` prompt for interactive mode commands. The user tells `ftp` to list the remote with both the `ls` and `dir` commands and then transfers the file `README` with the `get` command. When finished with the `ftp` session, our intrepid user then logs off with the `quit` command and is returned to the local Linux shell prompt.

A Sample Anonymous FTP Session

In the previous section, you saw a user initiate an `ftp` session with a system and look at some directories. The user had a valid user name and password on the remote system. Take a look at an anonymous FTP session to a major software archive site on the Internet. It is very similar to the one in the previous section, but it has some interesting differences.

```
$ ftp ftp.uu.net<Return>
Connected to ftp.uu.net.
220 ftp.UU.NET FTP server (Version wu-2.4(1)
➥Thu Apr 14 15:45:10 EDT 1994) ready.
Name (ftp.uu.net:bubba): anonymous<Return>
331 Guest login ok, send your complete e-mail address as password.
Password: your e-mail address<Return>
230-
230-                Welcome to the UUNET archive.
230-   A service of UUNET Technologies Inc, Falls Church, Virginia
230-   For information about UUNET, call +1 703 204 8000,
230-  or see the files in /uunet-info
230-
230-   Access is allowed all day.
230-   Local time is Thu Sep 29 15:53:02 1994.
230-
230-   All transfers are logged with your host name and email address.
230-   If you don't like this policy, disconnect now!
230-
230-   If your FTP client crashes or hangs shortly
230-   after login, try using a
230-   dash (-) as the first character of your password.
230-   This will turn off the informational messages which may
230-    be confusing your ftp client.
230-
230-Please read the file /info/README.ftp
230-  it was last modified on Wed Aug 24 17:39:53 1994 - 36 days ago
230-Please read the file /info/README
230-  it was last modified on Wed Aug 24 17:46:00 1994 - 36 days ago
230 Guest login ok, access restrictions apply.
ftp>
```

```
ftp> dir<Return>
200 PORT command successful.
150 Opening ASCII mode data connection for /bin/ls.
total 4149
drwxr-sr-x   2 34   0            512 Jul 26  1992 .forward
-rw-r--r--   1 34   uucp           0 Jul 26  1992 .hushlogin
-rw-r--r--   1 34   archive       59 Jul 31  1992 .kermrc
-rw-r--r--   1 34   archive        0 Jul 26  1992 .notar
drwx--s--x   5 34   archive      512 Jul 23 19:00 admin
lrwxrwxrwx   1 34   archive        1 Jul 26  1992 archive -> .
drwxrws--x   4 0    archive      512 Apr 20 16:29 bin
lrwxrwxrwx   1 34   archive
➥23 Sep 14  1993 by-name.gz -> index/master/by-name.gz
lrwxrwxrwx   1 34   archive
➥23 Sep 14  1993 by-time.gz -> index/master/by-time.gz
-rw-r--r--   1 34   archive   90112 Apr 26  1991 compress.tar
lrwxrwxrwx   1 0   archive        9 Jul 23 18:50 core -> /dev/null
drwxrws--x   2 0   archive      512 Jul 26  1992 dev
drwxrwsr-x  21 34  archive     1024 Sep 29 15:18 doc
drwxrws--x   6 0   archive      512 Apr 14 16:42 etc
lrwxrwxrwx   1 34  archive       31 Dec  8  1993 faces ->
➥/archive/published/usenix/faces
drwxrwsr-x   2 34   archive      512 Jul 26  1992 ftp
drwxrwsr-x   4 34   archive      512 Sep 29 10:34 government
drwxrwsr-x  18 34   archive     1024 Sep 29 10:28 graphics
-rw-rw-r--   1 27   archive   798720 Jul 11 20:54 gzip.tar
lrwxrwxrwx   1 34   archive
➥17 Jul 26  1992 help -> info/archive-help
drwxrwsr-x  20 34   archive     1024 Dec  2  1993 index
drwxrwsr-x  19 34   archive      512 Sep 29 10:30 inet
drwxrwsr-x   4 34   archive      512 Sep 29 15:36 info
drwxrwsr-x  25 34   archive      512 Sep 29 10:29 languages
drwxrwsr-x   4 34   archive      512 Sep 29 10:28 library
drwx--s--x   2 0    0           8192 Jul 26  1992 lost+found
lrwxrwxrwx   1 34   archive
➥20 Aug  2  1992 ls-lR.Z -> index/master/ls-lR.Z
lrwxrwxrwx   1 34   archive
➥21 Sep 14  1993 ls-lR.gz -> index/master/ls-lR.gz
lrwxrwxrwx   1 34   archive
➥21 Aug  2  1992 ls-ltR.Z -> index/master/ls-ltR.Z
lrwxrwxrwx   1 34   archive
➥22 Sep 14  1993 ls-ltR.gz -> index/master/ls-ltR.gz
drwxrwsr-x  24 34   archive     1024 Sep 29 15:10 networking
drwxrwsr-x   2 34   archive      512 Aug 10 09:26 packages
d--xrws--x  17 34   archive      512 Sep 26 12:29 private
drwxrwsr-x  25 34   archive     1536 Sep 29 15:30 pub
drwxrwsr-x  17 34   archive     1024 Sep 29 15:38 published
lrwxrwxrwx   1 34   archive
➥10 Jul 26  1992 sco-archive -> vendor/sco
drwxrwsr-x  20 34   archive      512 Sep 29 04:18 systems
drwxrwxrwx  14 34   archive     1536 Sep 29 15:36 tmp
lrwxrwxrwx   1 34   archive
➥17 Jul 26  1992 unix-today -> vendor/unix-today
lrwxrwxrwx   1 34   archive
➥17 Jul 26  1992 unix-world -> vendor/unix-world
drwxrwsr-x  36 34   archive     1024 Sep 29 15:29 usenet
```

```
drwxrws—x   6 0    archive       512 Oct 22  1992 usr
lrwxrwxrwx   1 34   archive
➥16 Aug  2  1992 uumap -> networking/uumap
-rw-rw-r—    1 34   archive   3279895 Sep 28 21:05 uumap.tar.Z
drwxrwsr-x   3 210  archive      2560 Sep 29 15:36 uunet-info
drwxrwsr-x  64 34   archive      1536 Sep 29 10:29 vendor
226 Transfer complete.
3257 bytes received in 0.76 seconds (4.2 Kbytes/s)
ftp>
ftp> cd systems/unix/linux<Return>
250-Files within this subtree are automatically mirrored from
250-tsx-11.mit.edu:/pub/linux
250-
250 CWD command successful.
ftp>
ftp> binary<Return>
200 Type set to I.
ftp> get sum.Z<Return>
200 PORT command successful.
150 Opening BINARY mode data connection for sum.Z (80959 bytes).
226 Transfer complete.
local: sum.Z remote: sum.Z
80959 bytes received in 5.6 seconds (14 Kbytes/s)
ftp> quit<Return>
221 Goodbye.
$
```

Here an `ftp` session is initiated with `ftp.uu.net`, which is a major FTP archive site on the Internet. The user name given at the logon prompt is anonymous because this is anonymous FTP. For the password, the full e-mail address is used. `ftp.uu.net` then displays a welcome banner that gives some information about the archive. In this example, you can see the user changes directories, sets the file mode to binary, gets a compressed binary file, and exits.

Troubleshooting

I transferred a binary file and it doesn't work properly. I can't unzip *it,* untar *it,* uncompress *it, or anything.*

Make sure that you set the transfer mode to binary. You can do this with the `binary` command at the `ftp>` prompt.

I'm in the process of transferring a large file and I want to check the progress.

Use the `hash` command. `ftp` prints the # character on-screen after every data buffer that is processed.

I was trying to do an anonymous FTP, the site told me that the user anonymous *was unknown and that the logon failed.*

You either misspelled `anonymous`, or the site does not allow anonymous FTP. In the latter case, you must have a valid user name and password on the remote computer.

I want to transfer several files, but I don't want ftp *to prompt me for each one.*

Use the `prompt` command. It toggles prompting on and off.

I tried to use anonymous FTP, and the site told me that I did not enter a valid e-mail address as the password.

In the past, the convention during an anonymous FTP was to enter `guest` as the password. Now, the convention is to enter your e-mail address. Many FTP sites run special FTP server software that checks the password and makes sure that it is in the form **user@host.somewhere.domain**. Try again and make sure that you enter your full e-mail address correctly.

Using the *r-* Commands

In addition to `ftp` and `telnet`, there are several other commands that allow you to access remote computers and exchange files over a network. These commands are known collectively as the `r-` commands.

The `r-` commands deserve special notice because one of their features can cause a severe security loophole if you are not careful. When you issue an `r-` command, the remote system checks a file named `/etc/hosts.equiv` to see if your local host is listed. If it doesn't find your local host, it checks for a file named `.rhosts` in your home directory on the remote machine. The `r-` command then checks to see if your local host name is in the `.rhosts` file. If your local host is listed in either place, the command is executed without checking for a password. While it can be very convenient to not have to type your password every time you need to access a remote computer, it can obviously cause severe security problems. It is recommended that you carefully consider the security implications of the `r-` commands before setting up `/etc/hosts.equiv` and `.rhosts` files on your local system.

rlogin

The `rlogin` command is very similar to the `telnet` command because it allows you to start an interactive command session on a remote system.

The syntax of the `rlogin` command is

```
rlogin [-8EKLdx] [-e char] [-k realm] [-l user-name] host-name
```

Although the most common usage is simply

```
rlogin host-name
```

Table 28.3 explains the various options for `rlogin`.

Table 28.3 Command-Line Options for the *rlogin* Command

Option	Description
`-8`	This option allows an 8-bit input data path at all times. This allows for formatted ANSI characters and other special codes to be sent. If this option is not used, parity bits are stripped except when the remote stop and start characters are other than <Ctrl-s> and <Ctrl-q>.
`-E`	Stops any character from being recognized as an escape character. When used with the `-8` option, this provides a completely transparent connection.
`-K`	Turns off all Kerberos authentication. It is only used when connecting to a host that uses the Kerberos authentication protocol.
`-L`	Allows the `rlogin` session to be run in `litout` mode. Refer to the `tty` manual page for more information.
`-d`	Turns on socket debugging on the TCP sockets used for communication with the remote host. Refer to the `setsockopt` manual page for more information.
`-e`	Used to set the escape character for the `rlogin` session. The escape character is ~ by default. You may specify a literal character or an octal value in the form `\nnn`.
`-k`	This option requests `rlogin` to obtain Kerberos tickets for the remote host in the specified realm instead of the remote host's realm as determined by `krb_realmofhost(3)`.
`-l`	Allows the remote name to be specified. If available, Kerberos authentication is used.
`-x`	Turns on DES encryption for all data passed via the `rlogin` session. This may impact response time and CPU utilization but provides increased security.

rsh

The `rsh` command is an abbreviation for remote shell. This command starts a shell on the specified remote host and executes the command, if any, that you specify on the `rsh` command line. If you do not give a command to execute, you are logged on to the remote machine using `rlogin`.

The syntax of the `rsh` command is

```
rsh [-Kdnx] [-k realm] [-l user-name] host-name [command]
```

Although the most common usage is just

```
rsh host-name [command]
```

Table 28.4 explains the command-line options for `rsh`.

Table 28.4 Command-Line Options for the *rsh* Command

Option	Description
`-K`	Turns off all Kerberos authentication. It is only used when connecting to a host that uses Kerberos.
`-d`	Turns on socket debugging on the TCP sockets used for communication with the remote host. See the `setsockopt` manual page for more information.
`-k`	This option requests `rlogin` to obtain Kerberos tickets for the remote host in the specified realm instead of the remote host's realm as determined by `krb_realmofhost(3)`.
`-l`	Allows the remote name to be specified. If available, Kerberos authentication is used, and authorization is determined as in the `rlogin` command.
`-n`	Redirects input from the special device `/dev/null`.
`-x`	Turns on DES encryption for all data passed. This may impact response time and CPU utilization but provides increased security.

Linux takes the standard input to the `rsh` command and copies it to the standard input of the remotely executed command. It copies the standard output of the remote command to standard output for `rsh`. It also copies the remote standard error to the local standard error file descriptor. Any quit, terminate, and interrupt signals are sent to the remote command. Additionally, any special shell characters that are not surrounded by quotation marks, as in `">>"`, are handled locally. If surrounded by quotation marks, these characters are handled by the remote command.

rcp

The `rcp` command, which stands for *remote copy*, is the last of the `r-` commands that you need to look at. It is used to copy files between computers. `rcp` can be used to copy files from one remote computer to another, without either the source or destination being on the local machine.

There are two forms of the `rcp` command. The first form is used to copy a file to a file. The second form is used when copying files or a directory to a directory. The syntax for the `rcp` command is

```
rcp [-px] [-k realm] file-name1 file-name2
rcp [-px] [-r] [-k realm] file(s)  directory
```

Each file or directory argument is either a remote file name or a local file name. Remote file names have the form `rname@rhost:path`, where `rname` is the remote user name, `rhost` is the remote computer, and `path` is the path to the file. The file name must contain a colon.

Table 28.5 explains the arguments for `rcp`.

Table 28.5 Command-Line Arguments for the *rcp* Command

Option	Description
`-r`	Recursively copies the source directory tree into the destination directory. Note that the destination must be a directory to use this option.
`-p`	Attempts to preserve the modification times and modes of the source files, ignoring the `umask`.
`-k`	This option requests `rcp` to obtain Kerberos tickets for the remote host in the specified realm instead of the remote host's realm as determined by `krb_realmofhost(3)`.
`-x`	The `-x` option turns on DES encryption for all data passed by rcp. This may impact response time and CPU utilization but provides increased security.

If the path specified in the file name is not a full path name, it is interpreted as being relative to the logon directory of the specified user on the remote computer. If no remote user name is given, your current user name is used. If a path on a remote host contains special shell characters, it may be quoted by using `\`, `"`, or `'` as appropriate. This causes all the shell metacharacters to be interpreted remotely.

Note

`rsh` does not prompt for passwords. It performs its copies via the `rsh` command.

From Here...

You can find more information about the Internet in the following chapters:

- Chapter 27, "Understanding the Internet," gives an overview and introduction to the Internet.
- Chapter 29, "Surfing the Internet," describes the various types of information that are available on the Internet and the tools for accessing this information.
- Chapter 30, "Using Electronic Mail," shows how to send and receive e-mail over the Internet.

CHAPTER 29

Surfing the Internet

The Internet is a big place, with lots of information available. What kind of information? Just about everything from software to online shopping. But sorting through all the different services can be very confusing.

In this chapter, you explore some different ways to help you track down the information that you need, such as the following:

- The basics of anonymous FTP
- Using Archie to find files
- Using the Gopher information system
- USENET news
- Interacting via electronic mailing lists
- Searching for information with WAIS
- Using the World Wide Web

There are many different ways to use each of these aspects of the Internet. There are usually several different programs that you can use to access these services, and the features of these different programs vary greatly. For the exact details of your particular software configuration, refer to the online man page for your particular program. Now, grab your virtual surfboard and take a dive into the Internet.

Anonymous FTP

Anonymous FTP provides that basic mechanism for retrieving data from around the Internet. No matter what you are searching for—software, documentation, FAQ lists, programs, or just about anything else—you can probably get a copy via anonymous FTP.

Anonymous FTP is a system that allows you to log on to a file transfer program on many computers, without knowing a user name and password. By using this system, you can access files and data that the system administrators on the remote system have made publicly available.

◄◄ See "Anonymous FTP," p. 596

There are literally thousands of computers on the Internet that provide anonymous FTP access. Almost any kind of information can be found on the Internet, and most of it is available via anonymous FTP. Table 29.1 lists some anonymous FTP sites that you might want to investigate.

Table 29.1 A Brief Listing of Anonymous FTP Sites

Site	Description
sunsite.unc.edu	The major Linux archive site on the Internet
oak.oakland.edu	Large general FTP site
wuarchive.wustl.edu	Large general FTP site
ftp.uu.net	Large general FTP site
rtfm.mit.edu	Has archives of all the USENET FAQs
prep.ai.mit.edu	Distribution point for GNU software

These sites only represent a small sample of the anonymous FTP sites to be found on the Internet.

Archie

One major problem with anonymous FTP is figuring out where the files that you are interested in are located on the Internet. After all, the Internet is a very big place. You could search and search and never find what you are looking for. Clearly, some sort of system is needed to help users find files. It was out of this need that the Archie system was born.

Archie is a database query program that contacts anonymous FTP sites around the world and asks the FTP site for a complete list of all its files. Archie then takes this information and indexes it in its own internal database. You can search this database for the location of files on the Internet. Since updating the Archie database is obviously a time-consuming process, they are usually only updated about once a month. This means that it is possible, though very unlikely, that the location that Archie gives you is not correct.

Archie can be contacted in two different ways. You can run a local client program that connects to an Archie server, or you can connect to a server directly via `telnet`. In general, you should use a client program if you can, because it keeps the system load down on the public access servers.

Archie is a very popular service. The various Archie servers around the world can get very heavily loaded and requests can take a while to complete. Some sites place limits on the number of simultaneous connections, to keep the servers from becoming too slow to use. If you try an Archie server and find that it is fully loaded, you can either try a different server or wait a few minutes and try again. There are several Archie servers around the world that you can connect to for Archie services. Table 29.2 lists these servers.

Table 29.2 Active Archie Servers

Server	IP Address	Location
archie.unl.edu	129.93.1.14	USA (NE)
archie.internic.net	198.49.45.10	USA (NJ)
archie.rutgers.edu	128.6.18.15	USA (NJ)
archie.ans.net	147.225.1.10	USA (NY)
archie.sura.net	128.167.254.179	USA (MD)
archie.au	139.130.4.6	Australia
archie.uni-linz.ac.at	140.78.3.8	Austria
archie.univie.ac.at	131.130.1.23	Austria
archie.cs.mcgill.ca	132.206.51.250	Canada
archie.uqam.ca	132.208.250.10	Canada
archie.funet.fi	128.214.6.102	Finland
archie.univ-rennes1.fr	129.20.128.38	France
archie.th-darmstadt.de	130.83.128.118	Germany
archie.ac.il	132.65.16.18	Israel
archie.unipi.it	131.114.21.10	Italy
archie.wide.ad.jp	133.4.3.6	Japan
archie.hana.nm.kr	128.134.1.1	Korea
archie.sogang.ac.kr	163.239.1.11	Korea
archie.uninett.no	128.39.2.20	Norway
archie.rediris.es	130.206.1.2	Spain
archie.luth.se	130.240.12.30	Sweden
archie.switch.ch	130.59.1.40	Switzerland
archie.twnic.net	192.83.166.10	Taiwan
archie.ncu.edu.tw	192.83.166.12	Taiwan
archie.doc.ic.ac.uk	146.169.11.3	United Kingdom
archie.hensa.ac.uk	129.12.21.25	United Kingdom

To connect to one of these servers, `telnet` to it and log on as `archie`. Each of the servers is slightly different, but most are basically the same. Once you log on to a server, you get a prompt such as

```
archie>
```

where you can enter your search commands. Different servers have different default search values. To determine what the default setup is for the server that you connect to, use the `show search` command. The `show search` command returns one of the following values:

`regex`	Archie interprets your search string as a UNIX regular expression.
`exact`	Your search string must exactly match a file name.
`sub`	Your search string matches if a file name contains it as a substring. This is a case-insensitive search.
`subcase`	Similar to the `sub` search type, except that the case of the letters in the string must match.

You can set the desired search type by using the `set search` command. For example,

```
archie> set search search-type<Return>
```

Once you have your search setup the way you want it, you use the `prog` command to search by file name. For example,

```
archie> set search sub<Return>

archie> prog linux<Return>
```

performs a case-insensitive search of the Archie database for all files that contained the substring `linux`. For each match that Archie finds, it reports the host computer that has the file, along with the full path name of the file on that host.

Once you've found the information that you are looking for, you will need to exit Archie. To do this, you simply type `exit` or `quit` at the `archie>` prompt. For example,

```
archie> exit<Return>
```

If you get confused or just need some assistance when you are using Archie, just type `help` at the `archie>` prompt. This will give you information on how to get help in Archie. From the `help>` prompt, typing a `?` will give you a list of subtopics that you can get help on.

Gopher

Gopher was one of the first Internet services that made a serious attempt at having a user-friendly interface. It is an Internet service that allows you to access information by making selections from a series of menus. When you connect to a site that offers Gopher services, you are given a menu of available choices. You can then just select your choice from the menu without having to know about the name or IP address of the destination site or the directory and file names of the information. Gopher handles this sort of thing transparently.

One disadvantage of Gopher is that there is no standard subject list for the various Gopher servers. The administrators for each individual Gopher server have organized their information in their own way. This means that each Gopher server you access has different subjects. If the server does happen to have some of the same subjects, chances are that they are named different things.

There are not any information resources on the Internet that are actually "Gopher specific." Anything that you can get via Gopher can be made available by other means such as FTP or Telnet. In some cases, sites may have chosen to make resources available only via Gopher for security reasons.

There are two ways to connect to the Gopher system. You can install a local Gopher client program that sends requests to a remote Gopher server, or you can use `telnet` to connect to a remote public access Gopher server. In general, you should use a client program if you can, because it keeps the system load down on the public access servers.

Client software for Gopher is available via anonymous FTP from the site **boombox.micro.umn.edu** in the directory **/pub/gopher**. If you want to try out Gopher before you go to the trouble of installing a client, public access Gopher services are available by using `telnet` to connect to one of the following sites: **consultant.micro.umn,edu**, **ux1.cso.uiuc.edu**, or **gopher.msu.edu**. Log on with the user name `gopher` when you connect to one of these sites.

Look at the following sample Gopher session so that you can get a feel for the interface. By connecting to the Gopher server at **sunsite.unc.edu**, you get the following:

```
Internet Gopher Information Client v2.0.16
Home Gopher server: sunsite.unc.edu

-->  1.  Sun and UNC's Legal Disclaimer
      2.  About the SunSITE Gopher/
      3.  PRESIDENT/
      4.  Search GopherSpace! Archie & Veronica (was Surf the Net!)/
      5.  Internet Dog-Eared Pages (Frequently used resources)/
      6.  Worlds of SunSITE -- by Subject/
      7.  SUN Microsystems News Groups and Archives/
      8.  NEWS! (News, Entertainment, Weather, and Sports)/
      9.  UNC Information Exchange (People and Places)/
      10. The UNC-CH Internet Library/
      11. UNC-Gopherspace/
      12. That Other UNC Gopherspace/
      13. What's New on SunSITE/
      14. Search the UNC Gopherspace with Jughead
<?> Press ? for Help, q to Quit                              Page 1/1
```

The Gopher server at **sunsite.unc.edu** gives you an initial menu with several different selections. An indicator symbol, `-->`, points to the current default menu item. You can select a menu item by moving the indicator with the <Up-Arrow> and <Down-Arrow> keys on your keyboard and then pressing <Return>. You can also just type in the menu choice and press <Return>. At the bottom of the screen, the Gopher server tells you that you can get help by pressing the <?> key, and you can quit Gopher entirely by pressing the <q> key.

Select menu item number 5, `Internet Dog-Eared Pages`, and see where it leads. To do this, move the indicator down to item 5 on the screen and press <Return>. Gopher retrieves the directory for this selection and gives you the following menu:

```
Internet Gopher Client v2.0.16
Internet Dog-Eared Pages (Frequently used resources)

  --> 1.  About Dog-Eared Pages
      2.  Dictionaries and Thesari/
      3.  Search - List of Lists <?>
      4.  1990 Census (not recommended for FTP)/
      5.  ACADEME THIS WEEK/
      6.  Digital Information Infrastructure Guide (DIIG)/
      7.  Economics/
      8.  Electronic Books/
      9.  Guides to the Internet/
      10. InterNIC Directory and Database Services/
      11. Netfind server at the University of Colorado, Boulder <TEL>
      12. Periodic Table of the Elements/
      13. Phone and Fax Index--US Congress <?>
      14. Phone books at other institutions/
      15. Poetry for searching (all of Yeats and Shakespeare plus) <?>
      16. Religious Texts for browsing and searching/
      17. Search  CIA World Fact Book <?>
      18. Search Geographic Name Server by City or ZIP code <?>
Press ? for Help, q to Quit, u to go up a menu              Page 1/2
```

This menu lists pointers to many information resources on the Internet. By repeating the process of simply selecting menu items, you can easily wander all over the Internet and gather information.

As you can see, Gopher provides an easy means to navigate the Internet. Unfortunately, the information that Gopher can retrieve is not well organized, so finding what you want can be a bit of an adventure.

USENET News

In the simplest definition, USENET news, *netnews*, or simply *news*, as it is commonly called, is a forum for online discussion. Many computers around the world exchange chunks of information, called *articles*, on almost every subject imaginable. These computers are not physically connected to the same network; they are logically connected in their ability to exchange data. (See Chapter 31, "Surviving USENET News," for a complete discussion of USENET news.)

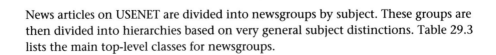

▶▶ See "How USENET Is Structured," p. 650

News articles on USENET are divided into newsgroups by subject. These groups are then divided into hierarchies based on very general subject distinctions. Table 29.3 lists the main top-level classes for newsgroups.

Table 29.3 Top-Level Group Classes in the USENET Hierarchy

Class	Description
alt	A large collection of topics that just don't easily fit into the other classes (short for "alternative").
comp	Many different computer-related topics
misc	Miscellaneous topics that do not easily fit into another category
news	Various topics that relate to the USENET news system itself
rec	Recreational and hobby subjects
soc	Social issues
sci	Various scientific topics
talk	Subjects designed for ongoing conversations

As with everything else on the Internet, there are exceptions to the previous rules. Many other top-level hierarchies exist. Most are devoted to different regions of the world.

USENET news has conversation and discussion on almost any topic that you can think of. It is a great way to find and exchange information.

Mailing Lists

Another avenue for discussion on the Internet comes from e-mail mailing lists. Mailing lists differ from USENET news in that the various messages and discussion articles are sent via e-mail instead of via the USENET news medium.

Why use a mailing list instead of a USENET newsgroup? Usually, mailing lists are targeted at a smaller group of people. It is fairly difficult to set up a new newsgroup on USENET, as there are proposal, discussion, and voting periods required. Any system administrator can set up a mailing list. Also, because each mailing list is maintained on one computer, the system administrator has more control over who can be on the list and can deal with problem users more effectively. Some mailing lists, such as those that discuss computer security issues, are restricted to certain people. If you have a need to be on one of these lists, you have to apply with the list manager to be allowed to subscribe.

As with USENET news, there are mailing lists on a wide variety of subjects. A complete list of publicly available mailing lists is posted regularly to the USENET newsgroup `news.answers`.

Mailing lists are typically set up using a *mail reflector*. A mail reflector is a special e-mail address that is set up to reflect any mail sent to it back out to a group of people. There are usually two e-mail addresses associated with a mailing list: the address of the list maintainer and the address of the list itself. For example, imagine that there is an e-mail address for the users of widgets. The e-mail address for the list might be something like

widgets@somewhere.com

If you send an e-mail message to this list address, it is reflected to all the people that subscribe to the list. By convention, Internet mailing lists use a special e-mail address for administrative requests, such as subscribing to the list. This address is constructed by adding `-request` to the name of the list. So for the imaginary widgets mailing list, the administrative e-mail address would be

widgets-request@somewhere.com

All mail that addresses administrative topics should be sent to the administrative address.

Each mailing list has its own rules and culture. You should become familiar with them before sending mail out onto the list. Usually, you get an introduction message and possibly a list of frequently asked questions (FAQ) when you subscribe to a list. The introduction message contains any special rules that apply to the list. Please make sure that you read the FAQ so that you won't be asking the same questions as hundreds of other people.

Wide Area Information Servers (WAIS)

WAIS stands for Wide Area Information Servers, which is a system for searching a large set of databases for information. The term "wide area" implies being able to use a large network, such as the Internet, to conduct searches using client and server software.

By using WAIS, you can retrieve text or multimedia documents that are stored on databases throughout the Internet. Currently, there are approximately 470 WAIS database servers on the Internet. You can think of WAIS as being similar to Gopher, except that WAIS does the searching for you.

Like Gopher, to use WAIS, you need client software or you have to use `telnet` to connect to a site that provides public access to a WAIS client. There is an interactive UNIX WAIS client known as swais. To use this system, you can telnet to `sunsite.unc.edu` and log on as `swais`. You then get a menu of databases that you can search for topics.

Mosaic and the World Wide Web (WWW)

The World Wide Web, also known as WWW or just the Web, is one of the most exciting developments to happen to the Internet in years. The Web is an interactive *hypermedia* system that connects you to vast amounts of information on the Internet. A hypermedia system is made up of *links* between documents. You can access related information by just selecting one of the links. The information is automatically retrieved for you without you having to know where it is. This section gives a basic introduction to the World Wide Web. For more information, see Chapter 32, "Using the World Wide Web," and Chapter 33, "Creating Web Documents with HTML."

The Web project was started by CERN, the European physics research lab, and has grown at a phenomenal rate. One reason is that information of any type, from text to sound and graphics, can be accessed via the Web.

All About URLs

Resources on the Web are accessed by a descriptive address known as a *Uniform Resource Locator*, or URL. You can think of a URL as a pointer to an object on the Internet that not only tells you where the object is located, but what it is named and how to access it. Everything that you access with the Web has a URL.

The syntax of URLs looks a bit intimidating but it is really pretty straightforward. It consists of a component that specifies which protocol to use, such as **http**, followed by a colon and two slashes, like **://**. It then contains the host name and the path to the file that you want to view. For example, a URL might look like

http://www.boutel.com/faq/www_faq.html

The part to the left of the colon specifies the access method to get to the data. There are several different valid access methods, and they are listed in Table 29.4.

Table 29.4 Valid Access Methods for URLs

Method	Description
`http`	Protocol for accessing most Web pages. Provides interactive hypermedia links to pages written in HTML, the HyperText Markup Language.
`wais`	Used for accessing a WAIS site.
`gopher`	Used for accessing a Gopher server.
`ftp`	Provides an anonymous FTP connection.
`telnet`	Opens a `telnet` connection to a site.
`news`	Used for reading USENET news.

Following the two forward slashes in the URL is the host name and path to the document that you want to view or retrieve. Remember, the document in question can be text, a hypermedia document, sound files, graphics, and so on.

Accessing the Web

In order to access the Web effectively, you need client software known as a *Web browser*. Two common programs are used as browsers, namely Lynx for ANSI terminal access and Mosaic for use with X Windows and other platforms. These Web browsers are found all over the Internet and are available via anonymous FTP. Use Archie to locate a copy at an archive near you.

Using the Web

Once you get a Web browser up and running, retrieve the document:

http://www.boutel.com/faq/www_faq.html

This document provides a list of answers to frequently asked questions concerning the Web. It is also regularly posted to the USENET newsgroup `news.answers`. Here are a few good URLs to check out when you start using the Web.

http://www.ncsa.uiuc.edu/SDG/Software/Mosaic/Docs/whats-new.html

This URL is the unofficial newspaper of the Web that lists new services.

http://www.w3.org/hypertext/DataSources/bySubject/Overview.html

This URL points to the WWW Virtual Library, which provides a good starting point for searching the Web.

Once you find a few Web pages that you like, you can always write your own home page that points to your favorite destinations.

The Web is extremely easy to use—it was designed that way. You can literally be surfing the Net within minutes of setting up your Web browser.

Internet Documentation

As you would expect, the various documents that define how the Internet works are available online. They are available via anonymous FTP from various hosts on the Internet.

The Internet documentation consists of various guides that have been written to make life easier for users and a document series that gives the standards and working notes of the Internet research community. This document series includes the Requests For Comments (RFC) series, the Standards (STD) series, and the For Your Information (FYI) series. These various document series provide information on the procedures, protocols, standards, history, and future of Internet.

The Request For Comments (RFC) Series

The *Requests For Comments*, or RFCs as they are commonly known, are the working documents of the Internet community. These documents cover all aspects of computer communication as related to the Internet. Many RFCs define protocol standards, while others give detailed information on how to implement these standards. Most current standards are published as RFCs. RFCs receive technical review from various Internet task forces and technical experts.

Once a document is assigned an RFC number and published, its number is never reused if the document is updated or reissued. RFC document numbers increase sequentially with each new or revised RFC issued.

The RFC series is available on the Internet via anonymous FTP from a variety of sites, such as **ftp.internic.net** in the **/rfc** directory.

The Standards (STD) Series

The *Standards* series, also known as the STDs, are a series of documents that define the official Internet standards. STD numbers are only assigned to standards documents that have completed the Internet standards approval process. STD numbers are used to help identify the RFCs that are the basis for Internet standards. Sometimes, more than one RFC is included in an STD, and they all have the same STD number. STDs numbers, like RFCs, are never reused. If a standard is revised or updated, it will be issued a new number.

The STD series is available on the Internet via anonymous FTP from a variety of sites, such as **ftp.internic.net** in the **/std** directory.

The For Your Information (FYI) Series

The *For Your Information* series contains a subset of the RFCs that are designed to provide general information about the Internet. These documents tend to be slightly less technical than the RFC series. Each FYI is also assigned an RFC number. Table 29.5 lists some useful FYI documents.

Table 29.5 Useful FYI Documents

Document	Description
FYI 4	Answers to common questions for new Internet users
FYI 6	Information about the X Windows system
FYI 7	Answers to common questions for experienced Internet users
FYI 18	The Internet user's glossary
FYI 24	How to use anonymous FTP

The FYI series is available on the Internet via anonymous FTP from a variety of sites, such as **ftp.internic.net** in the **/fyi** directory.

From Here...

You can find more information about the Internet in the following chapters:

- Chapter 27, "Understanding the Internet," provides an overview of the Internet and a discussion of computer names and addresses.
- Chapter 28, "Accessing the Network with `telnet`, `ftp`, and the `r-` Commands," explains the various tools that you can use to make remote connections on the Internet, including anonymous FTP.
- Chapter 31, "Surviving USENET News," looks at the USENET news system in detail.

CHAPTER 30

Using Electronic Mail

Electronic mail, or e-mail, seems to have taken the world by storm. More than ten million computer users worldwide have access to electronic mail. Most likely, you share your computer system with several users, or it is part of a network maintained by your organization. A number of commercial networks or Internet-access providers can give you or your organization access to electronic mail around the world.

In this chapter, you learn the following:

- How to send e-mail
- How to read e-mail messages
- How to reply to e-mail you have received
- How to print messages, save them to files, and delete messages
- How to route e-mail by forwarding it, creating mailing lists, and sending copies to others

Understanding E-Mail

E-mail is any program that users on a single computer system or a network of systems use to send and receive messages. At a minimum, you provide the program with the address of the recipient and the message you want to send. The address includes the logon name of the person who is to receive the mail. If that user is on another system in a network, the address also includes a means of identifying the target computer system. You either prepare the message while you are using your e-mail program or you prepare it beforehand using a text editor such as `vi`.

There are several advantages to using electronic mail, as follows:

- You can send reports, data, and documents that can reach their destination in a matter of seconds or minutes.
- You don't have to worry about interrupting someone when you send them a message; you aren't necessarily interrupted when you receive messages—that's handled by the computer system.

- You don't need to play phone-tag or make an appointment to communicate with someone.
- You can deal with the messages you receive at a convenient time.
- You can send electronic mail at times convenient for you.

When you send e-mail, it's up to the computer system to make the delivery, which can involve putting your message out on a network to be delivered at some other site. At this point, you say that the mail has been sent. Soon after that, the message arrives at the recipient's machine.

If both the sender and the receiver are on the same computer system, this all takes place on one machine. The e-mail system on the target computer verifies that the addressee exists and the message is added to a file that holds all the e-mail for that user (if no network is involved, the local computer system verifies the addressee). The mail-storage file is called the user's *system mailbox* and has the same name as the user who is receiving the mail. For example, if your logon name is `oliann`, your system mailbox is the file named `oliann` in the directory `/var/spool/mail`. When the message has been "delivered" to the mailbox, you say the mail has been received. Figure 30.1 shows the relationship between sending and receiving e-mail.

Fig. 30.1

Sending and receiving e-mail.

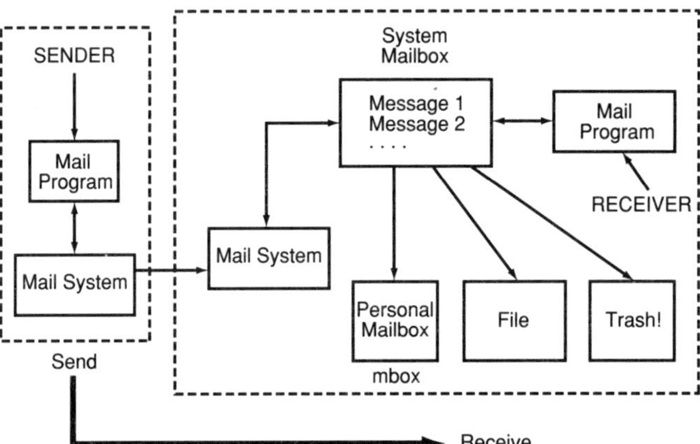

Does the Mail Always Get Through?

When you send e-mail, you may see a message on your screen that says `Mail Sent!`. That means that the mail has been sent—not that it has been received or delivered. Usually, you get e-mail in return if the e-mail system cannot deliver a message.

There can be several reasons that e-mail messages may not go through. If mail is going out to a network, the network address may be correct but the name of the user on that network may not be correct. Or perhaps the complete address is correct, but because of problems with permissions or quotas, the message could not be placed in the user's system mailbox. In both of these cases, the mail was sent but was *undeliverable*. Another scenario is that the e-mail was delivered but the user's mailbox was corrupted or destroyed. A final possibility is that the recipient ignores e-mail or does not log on for several days, weeks, or more.

Your computer system notifies you when you have mail. When you read your mail, you can treat it on a message-by-message basis. Some of the things you can do with your mail are the following:

- Delete individual messages after you read them—or without bothering to read them (using e-mail doesn't mean that you won't get junk mail)
- Keep some messages in the system mailbox
- Keep some messages in a personal mailbox
- Keep other messages in individual files or folders
- Reply directly to the sender of a message
- Do a "group reply" to a group of users who all received the same message
- Forward mail to others
- Print your mail

It's up to you to manage your mail so that it doesn't take up any more disk space than necessary. You really don't have to save every piece of e-mail you get. You'll also see that it is easier to read your incoming mail if you regularly delete or remove messages from your system mailbox.

There are several different e-mail programs available for Linux. The most common e-mail interface, available on virtually every UNIX environment, is `mail`. With the `mail` program, you can do the following:

- Manage and view your e-mail
- Include a `Subject:` header on e-mail you send
- Include a `Cc:` header for sending copies of e-mail to others
- Forward e-mail to others
- Set up mailing lists

This chapter shows examples of `mail`. Later, this chapter introduces another mail program for Linux, the `elm` mailer.

Sending E-Mail with *mail*

You can send e-mail to an individual, a group of individuals, or a mailing list. Just as when you want to send a paper letter, you must specify the address of the recipients with e-mail. Sometimes, you will compose or write a message while you are sending e-mail; at other times, you will send a prepared message; at times you may even send the output of a command or program with e-mail. When using `mail` or `elm`, the message you send has to be a text file, that is, an ASCII file.

> **Note**
>
> The Simple Mail Transport Protocol (SMTP) is used to transfer mail between computers. It currently supports only ASCII files. In order to send a binary file via e-mail, you have to convert the file to ASCII by using the `uuencode` utility.

Regardless of how the message is prepared, you send mail by using a command of the following form:

```
mail address<Return>
```

These commands start the mail system. You can then compose the mail message and send it to the specified *address*. In this syntax, *address* is the e-mail address of the person who is to receive the message. An address can have several different forms. To send e-mail to someone who has a logon ID on the machine you are using, use the logon ID of that person. For example, to send e-mail to someone on your system whose logon name is `anglee`, enter the following command:

```
mail anglee<Return>
```

If `anglee` is on another system you can access through some network or collection of networks, you must include the name by which that system is known on the network. Suppose that `anglee` is the name of a user on a computer system whose network name is `apples.startup.com`. You can send e-mail by entering this command:

```
mail anglee@apples.startup.com<Return>
```

Or you can use this command:

```
mail apples!anglee<Return>
```

The exact form of the address depends on the type of network being used and any local conventions or rules. Ask a local expert or your system administrator about the form of addresses on a network in your company.

To send the same message to several users, include each of their addresses on the line with the `mail` command, as in this example:

```
mail oliver ernie lynn@apples.startup.com kacker tango!charlie!bigjr<Return>
```

Writing a Message while Sending E-Mail

Many users compose or write messages while they are sending e-mail. This is usually the quickest—but not the neatest—way to send mail. It's not neat because you have limited editing capabilities while composing your message. Generally, you can deal with only one line at a time. First, you type the command to send e-mail and specify the address or addresses and press <Return>. Then you type the message, indicating that you're done by typing a period on a line by itself. You can also use <Ctrl-d> to end the message. Here is an example of how to send e-mail to a user named `lynn`. Enter this command to start the mail system and specify the address of user `lynn` on your system:

```
mail lynn<Return>
Subject: Congratulations! Lunch Thursday?<Return>
```

Now type the message, pressing <Return> when you want to end a line. Here is a sample message that you may want to send to `lynn`; notice the use of <Return> to space the paragraphs of the message:

```
Lynn,<Return>
<Return>
Just wanted to tell you that I thought you did a great<Return>
job at the meeting yesterday! It seems as if we're<Return>
finally turning this problem around.<Return>
<Return>
Want to get together for lunch Thursday?<Return>
Give me a call.<Return>
joe<Return>
.<Return>
```

You can also end the message with <Ctrl-d> instead of a period. Remember that the <Ctrl-d> must be on a line by itself, just as the period must be on a line by itself. The computer responds by displaying `EOT`, which means *end of transmission.*

Canceling a Message

You can cancel a message while you're writing it, but you can't cancel it after it's sent. To cancel a message while you are writing it, press whatever key is configured on your system as the interrupt key (usually either <Ctrl-c> or <Del>). When a message is canceled, it is saved in a file named `dead.letter`. You can delete this file or edit it later for another message. When using `mail`, you must press <Ctrl-c> twice to cancel (which is safer in case you press <Ctrl-c> or <Del> by mistake). After canceling your mail message, you see the command-line prompt. The following example shows how the cancel function works:

```
mail lynn<Return>
Subject: Congratulations! Lunch Thursday?<Return>
Lynn,<Return>
<Return>
Just wanted to tell that I thought you did a great<Return>
job<Ctrl-c>
(Interrupt -- one more to kill letter)
```

At this point in the creation of the message, you press <Ctrl-c> or <Del>; the system responds with the message `(Interrupt--one more to kill letter)`. You now must decide whether you want to continue the letter or kill it. If you decide to continue, you just keep typing the text of the letter as follows:

```
at the meeting yesterday! It seems as if we're finally<Return>
turning this problem around.<Return>
<Return>
```

At this point, you decide to cancel the letter again, so you press <Ctrl-c> or <Del>. The system responds with `(Interrupt -- one more to kill letter)`. Because you want to kill the message, press <Ctrl-c> or <Del> a second time; `mail` quits and you see the shell prompt.

Sending a Prepared Message

You may want to use a text editor such as `vi` to compose a message to be sent by electronic mail. If you use a text editor, you have the tools to do things such as format the text and check your spelling. It doesn't matter what program you use to create the text as long as you end up with a text or ASCII file.

Suppose that the file you want to send is named `report.txt` and that the recipient's address is **bigshot@turn.green.com**. There are essentially three ways to send the file, as shown in the following list. In the examples in the following list, the `mail` command uses the option `-s`, and the string that serves as the subject heading is surrounded by quotation marks.

Here are the three methods you can use to send mail using a prepared message file called `report.txt`:

- *Use a pipe.* To send `report.txt` with the `mail` command, enter

  ```
  cat report.txt | mail -s" Sales Report" bigshot@turn.green.com<Return>
  ```

- *Redirect input.* To send `report.txt` with the `mail` command and the `-s` option, enter

  ```
  mail -s" Sales Report" bigshot@turn.green.com < report.txt<Return>
  ```

- *Use `~r` to include a file in a message.* To use `mail` to send the file (using the default `Subject:` prompt), enter these commands:

  ```
  mail bigshot@turn.green.com<Return>
  Subject: Sales Report<Return>
  ~r report.txt<Return>
  ~.<Return>
  EOT
  ```

You see the system prompt after you complete any of these three methods—the result is the same in any case.

> **Note**
>
> In the third example, you use `~r` to *read*, or include, the file `report.txt` in the e-mail message. This is an example of a *tilde command.* To use such commands, you precede a command with the tilde character (~) while you're reading or sending mail. You may find several other tilde commands useful; they are discussed at appropriate points in following sections.

Sending the Result of a Command or Program by E-Mail

◀◀ See "Understanding Shells," p. 360

If you run a command or program that produces results to the screen (known as `stdout`), you can pipe that output to a mail command. Suppose that you have some information in a file called `contrib.lst`, you use the command `sort` to sort it, and then you send the results to yourself (logon name `imgood`) and `bigshot` (whom you've met earlier in this chapter). To do all that, enter

```
sort contrib.lst ¦
➥mail -s "Sorted Contrib Info" imgood bigshot@turn.green.com
```

Reading Your Mail

Most Linux systems notify you when you log on that you have e-mail. It's up to you to read and act on it. You can use either `mail` or another e-mail program to read any mail you have. As you read your mail, the e-mail program marks a message as read. Depending on what commands you use and how you quit the e-mail program, the messages you have read are kept either in your system mailbox, `/var/spool/mail/$LOGNAME`, or in your logon directory in the file named `mbox`.

Using *mail* To Read Mail

To read your mail with `mail`, type **`mail`** and press <Return>. Suppose that your logon name is `imgood`; you'll see a display similar to this (what you type is in bold):

```
mail<Return>
mail     Type ? for help.
"/var/spool/mail/imgood": 5 messages 2 new 1 unread
     1 sarah
     ➥Wed Jan  5 09:17  15/363
     2 croster@turn.green.com
     ➥Thu Jan  6 10:18  26/657   Meeting on Friday
U    3 wjones
➥Fri Jan  7 08:09  32/900   Framistan Order
> N  4 chendric
➥Fri Jan  7 13:22  35/1277  Draft Report
N    5 col.com!kackerma@ps.com
➥Sat Jan  8 13:21  76/3103  Excerpt from GREAT new UNI
?
```

Here are some things to note about the display:

- The first line identifies the program and says to type a question mark for help.
- The second line indicates that `mail` is reading your system mailbox, `/var/spool/mail/imgood`, and that you have five messages. Two have arrived since you last checked your mail, one appeared previously but you have not yet read it, and two messages have already been read.

- The next five lines give information about your mail. Ignore the first few characters for now. Each line holds a message number, the address of the sender, the date the message was sent, the number of lines and characters in the message, and the subject (if one was given). Consider the following line:

  ```
  2 croster@turn.green.com     Thu Jan  6 10:18  26/657   Meeting on Friday
  ```

  This line indicates the message numbered 2 is from **croster@turn.green.com**—an address that indicates the message came to your machine from a network (mail from a local user is marked with just the user's logon ID). The message was sent on Thursday, January 6, at 10:18; it consists of 26 lines and 657 characters. The subject is "Meeting on Friday."
- A message line starting with `N` indicates new mail—mail you didn't know about before.
- A message line starting with `U` indicates unread mail—mail that you know about but haven't read.
- A message line without either `N` or `U` is mail you've read and saved in your system mailbox.
- The greater-than character (>) on a message line marks the current message—the message you'll act on next.
- The question mark (`?`) on the last line is the command prompt from `mail`.

Reading the Current Message. The current message is the message marked by the greater-than character (>). To read that message, just press <Return>. In the preceding example, the current message was number 4. When you open it, you see the following:

```
Message 4:
From chendric Fri, Jan 7 13:22 EST 1994
Received: by your.system.com
Date: Fri, 7 Jan 1994 13:22:01 -0500
From: Carol Hendricks <chendric>
Return-Path: <chendric>
To: aborat, lynn, oackerm, imgood
Subject: Draft Report
Here is a draft of the report I intend to submit next week.
Please take a look at it and let me know your comments.
Thanks.
---------------Report Starts Here---------------
          Opportunities for Expansion
          Prepared by Carol Hendricks
Over the past 6 months, we've seen an indication of an increase in the
demand for our services. Current market trends indicate that the demand
will continue for at least 18 months and possibly longer. The manager of
our service staff states "We're up to our necks in new customers and
:
```

The message is displayed one screen at a time. The colon (`:`) at the bottom of the screen tells you that the message won't fit on one screen. Press <Return> to see the next screenful of the message. Any time you see a colon, you can press <Return> to see the next screen or press <q> to quit viewing the message. When you have seen the last screen, you see `EOF:` (for end of file). Press <q> or <Return> to get back to the `?` prompt. Notice that the greater-than character still points to the message you've just read. The message that was the current message is still the current message.

Some lines were displayed on the screen before the message itself began. This is the header information—and it can be useful. Typically, header information includes the following:

- The message number
- Who sent the message
- When it was sent
- The name of the system that received the message
- The date the message was received
- The "real name" of the sender as well as his or her logon ID
- The `Return-Path`
- Who the message was sent to
- The subject

All this information is passed on with each e-mail message. The sender is always identified, making forgeries difficult. The real name that appears in the `From:` line is taken from a field from the sender's entry in the password file. The `Return-Path` or `Reply-To` information is used by the mail system if you generate a reply (as discussed later in this chapter). The `To:` line contains the address or list of addresses of the recipients of this message. (This sample message was a group message.) The sender provided the `Subject:` line.

Reading the Next Message. There are two ways to read the next message. *Next* refers to the message following the current message in your mailbox. You can press <Return> or <n> to display the next message. It becomes the current message after you read it. You read the next message in the same way you read the current message. After you read the last message in the list, you see the message `At EOF`.

Reading Any Message. All the messages in your mailbox are numbered. You can read messages in any order by typing the message number and pressing <Return> when you see the `?` prompt. For example, to read message number 2, type `2` and press <Return> at the question mark. Message number 2 then becomes the current message.

Reading E-Mail from Other Files

When you start `mail`, you read messages kept in your system mailbox, `/var/spool/mail/$LOGNAME`. Recall from Chapter 20, "Understanding Linux Shells," that `LOGNAME` is the shell variable that holds your logon name. If you log on as `imgood`, your mail is held in `/var/spool/mail/imgood`. You can read mail from other files that hold complete e-mail messages—that is, messages with the headers and text of the messages.

Naturally, you must have read permission for those files.

To read messages from a file, type the command to start the e-mail program, type **-f *file-name*** on the same line, and press <Return>.

For example, to read the e-mail in the file `mbox`, enter

```
mail -f mbox¦<Return>
```

You can read the mail in that file in the same way you read e-mail from your system mailbox.

> **Note**
>
> The `mbox` file is located in your home directory and automatically contains messages you've already read but have not deleted. These messages are saved to `mbox` when you exit `mail`.

Sending Mail while Reading

You can send e-mail while you are using the e-mail program to read your messages. You type **m *address*** and press <Return> when you see the `?` prompt. Then follow these steps:

1. Start the `mail` program: Type ***mail*** and press <Return>.
2. Read some messages or do other things, but at the `?` prompt, type the following to send e-mail to a user whose logon name is `ernie`:

   ```
   m ernie<Return>
   ```

3. At the prompt for a subject, type a subject heading:

   ```
   Subject: Game Time<Return>
   ```

4. Type the message and end it with a period on the last line, as in the following example:

   ```
   Don't forget we're playing V-ball at 6:30<Return>
   .<Return>
   ```

   The computer responds with the following lines:

   ```
   EOT
   ?
   ```

5. Continue using `mail`.

Printing Mail Messages

Using `mail`, you can print the current message to a printer connected to your system. First, make the message you want to print the current message. Then type **¦ lpr** at the `?` prompt and press <Return>. You are, in effect, piping the current message to the `lpr` program.

To print a collection of messages, save them in a file and then print the file. Refer to "Filing and Saving Mail Messages" later in this chapter for information on effective ways to save messages.

Quitting the *mail* Program

As you read e-mail in a mailbox, you can read, skip, or delete messages. (You learn about deleting messages later in this chapter.) These actions don't take place in the mailbox itself, but in a temporary copy of the mailbox. You can quit the e-mail program so that your mailbox is changed by your actions (the modified temporary copy replaces the original mailbox), or you can quit so that your mailbox is unchanged regardless of what you did during your e-mail session.

Quitting and Saving Changes

To quit the `mail` program and save the changes that occur, press <q> and <Return> when you see the `?` prompt. You see the shell prompt again. When you quit `mail` this way, messages you read but didn't delete are saved in a file named `mbox` in your home directory.

Suppose that you use `mail` to read your mail. Assume that your logon name is `imgood` and your home directory is `/home/imgood`. When you type `mail` and press <Return> to start the `mail` program, you see the following screen of information:

```
mail     Type ? for help.
"/var/spool/mail/imgood": 5 messages 2 new 1 unread
      1 sarah
      ➥Wed Jan  5 09:17  15/363
      2 croster@turn.green.com
      ➥Thu Jan  6 10:18  26/657   Meeting on Friday
   U  3 wjones
   ➥Fri Jan  7 08:09  32/900   Framistan Order
> N     4 chendric
➥Fri Jan  7 13:22  35/1277  Draft Report
  N 5 col.com!kackerma@ps.com
   ➥Sat Jan  8 13:21  76/3103  Excerpt from GREAT new UNI
?
```

Now suppose that you read the current message by pressing <Return> and then you read message 1 by typing **1** and pressing <Return> at the `?` prompt. If you then press <q> and <Return> to quit, you see the following information:

```
Saved 2 messages in /home/imgood/mbox
Held 3 messages in /var/spool/mail/imgood
```

The two messages you read are saved in the file `mbox` in your home directory; the other three messages are saved in your system mailbox, `/var/spool/mail/imgood`. The messages that are put in `mbox` are added to that file. If you save messages like this often, `mbox` can become quite large. You may want to print that file occasionally and delete it. You can also read the mail from that file as if it were your system mailbox, as described later in this chapter.

Note

You can read mail and indicate that the current message is to be kept in your system mailbox, `/var/spool/mail/imgood`, and not in the file `mbox`. To do this after you've read a message, type **pre** (for *preserve*) at the `?` prompt and press <Return>.

Quitting and Not Saving Changes

The other way to quit the `mail` program is to press <x> and <Return> at the `?` prompt. When you do that, you exit the program with no changes to your system mailbox or any other file—as if you did not read your mail at all. You then see the shell prompt. You may want to exit the `mail` program in this way when you want to leave the program but save the mail in your system mailbox.

Getting Help

When you type the command to start your e-mail program, you see a `?` prompt. The `mail` program tells you to type `?` for help. To get a list of commands and some information about each command, type `?` and press <Return>. Although you may not use all the commands listed, you can refer to the list when you need some help.

Getting Help with *mail*

To see help messages while you are using `mail`, type `?` and press <Return>. You see a display similar to the following:

```
Mail   Commands
t <message list>     type messages
n               goto and type next message
e <message list>     edit messages
f <message list>     give head lines of messages
d <message list>     delete messages
s <message list>      file append messages to file
u <message list>     undelete messages
R <message list>     reply to message senders
r <message list>     reply to message senders and all recipients
pre <message list>     make messages go back to /usr/spool/mail
p <message list>     print message
m <user list>          mail to specific users
q               quit, saving unresolved messages in mbox
x               quit, do not remove system mailbox
h               print out active message headers
!               shell escape
cd [directory]     chdir to directory or home if none given
A <message list> consists of integers, ranges of same, or user names
separated by spaces. If omitted, Mail uses the last message typed.
A <user list> consists of user names or aliases separated by spaces.
Aliases are defined in .mailrc in your home directory.
&
```

This listing shows you the commands you can use from the `?` prompt. Although some of these commands are explained in later sections of this chapter, here are some things to note right now:

- In each case, you can use the first letter of the command or type the entire command.
- Items in `[ ]` and <> are optional; you don't type the brackets as part of the command.
- You can make the term `message list` refer to all messages by using `*`. For example, to save all messages in a file named `allmail`, type **`s * allmail`** and press <Return>.
- You can make the term `message list` refer to a single message number. For example, to save message number 2 to a file named `meeting`, type **`s 2 meeting`** and press <Return>.
- You can make the term `message list` refer to a range of message numbers by separating the two message numbers with a hyphen. For example, `2-4` refers to messages numbered 2, 3, and 4. To save messages 2, 3, and 4 in a file named `memos`, type **`s 2-4 memos`** and press <Return>.
- The term `print` in the line `print messages` does not mean to print messages on a printer. It means to display the messages on-screen.
- The `edit` command is useful for modifying messages before forwarding them to someone else or saving them in a file.
- If you have so many messages that their headers can't be listed on one screen, use the command `z` to see the next screenful of messages. Use `z-` to see the previous screenful of messages.

Filing and Saving Mail Messages

You will want to save some of the e-mail you receive. It's not practical to keep all your mail in your system mailbox for these reasons:

- You'll have too many messages to wade through whenever you want to read your mail.
- System administrators often put a limit on the size of your system mailbox. If you reach that limit, you may be prevented from receiving any new mail.
- Your mail won't be organized and it can be difficult to find important messages or all messages relating to a specific project or topic.

Earlier in this chapter, you learned that the messages you've read are saved (unless you say otherwise) in the file `mbox`. You also know that you can read these messages by typing **`mail -f mbox`** and pressing <Return>. You can also read messages from other files by using `mail`'s `-f` option.

Saving Files with *mail*

There are two primary ways (with and without a header) to save the current message in a file when you are using `mail`. With both methods, you can specify a file to hold the message and the message is added to that file. If you don't specify a file, the message is added to the file `mbox` (your personal mailbox) in your home directory. If you use `q` to quit the `mail` program, the messages are removed from your system mailbox.

You use the `s` command to save a message with the headers intact (useful if you want to use your e-mail program to read the messages later). You use the `w` command to save a message without the header information (useful when you want to use only the text of the messages in a file that may be processed by some other program).

When you see the `?` prompt, you can use any of the following methods to save a message:

- Type **`s`** to add the current message to `mbox` in your home directory.
- Type **`s`** ***`file-name`*** to add the text of the current message to the file *`file-name`*.
- Type **`w`** ***`file-name`*** to add the text of the current message to the file *`file-name`*.

Tip

To keep messages in your mailbox after you've read them, use the `preserve` command, `pre`. You can use this command with a message list.

You know that messages you have already read are automatically saved to `mbox`, unless you use the `preserve` command.

It's a good idea to get in the habit of specifying a file name when you use the `save` command, `s`. If you don't specify a file name, the current message is added to the file `mbox`. If you include a `msglist` but don't specify a file, `mail` uses `msglist` as the name of the file to which it saves the current message. If you use `q` to quit the e-mail program, the saved messages are removed from your system mailbox.

Deleting Mail Messages

To delete a message from a file of messages you're reading, you use the `d` command. If you quit the e-mail program using `q`, any messages you deleted with the `d` command are removed from the file.

Deleting and Undeleting Messages with *mail*

You use the `d` or `delete` command to mark messages for deletion when you use `mail` to read your e-mail. If you then quit the program with `q`, the marked messages are removed from your mailbox. Unless you have saved them, they're gone for good. For some messages, this is a very good idea.

To delete the current message, type `d` and press <Return>. You can also specify a message list.

Tip

To undelete all the messages you marked for deletion, type **u *** and press <Return> when you see the `?` prompt.

If you mark a message or a group of messages to be deleted, you can change your mind and undelete the message or messages using the `u` command. You must use the `u` command before you enter `q` to quit. Once you enter `q`, the messages are gone for good. Use the `u` or `undelete` command in the same way you use `d` or `delete`.

Replying to Mail

To reply to e-mail, use the address specified in the `Reply-To:` header field. If that field isn't present, use the information in the `Return-Path:` header field. Following are partial headers of two messages; one has both header fields and the other has only the `Return-Path:` header field. The pertinent fields are in bold in each example.

Message 1:

```
From server@malte.abc.com Mon Nov  8 18:31 EST 1993
Received: from MALTE.ABC.COM by s850.mwc.edu with SMTP
Return-Path: <server@matle.ams.com>
Date: Mon, 8 Nov 93 18:17:15 -0500
Comment: From the DuJour List
Originator: dujour@mathe.abc.com
Errors-To: asap@can.org
Reply-To: <dujour@mathe.abc.com>
Sender: dujour@mathe.abc.com
```

Message 2:

```
From chendric Fri, Jan 7 13:22 EST 1994
Received: by your.system.com
Date: Fri, 7 Jan 1994 13:22:01 -0500
From: Carol Hendricks <chendric>
Return-Path: <chendric>
To: aborat, lynn, oackerm, imgood
Subject: Draft Report
```

To reply to the first message, use the `Reply-To` address **dujour@mathe.abc.com**. Note that the `Reply-To` and `Return-Path` fields are different. In the second example, use `chendric` to respond to the sender of the message.

Note

Always use the `Reply-To` address if it is included in the header because it represents the specific address of the sender. When the `Reply-To` address is not available, the `Return-Path` address usually provides an adequate address back to the sender.

Replying to Mail with *mail*

You can let the `mail` program determine the address to use to reply to an electronic mail message. To do this, use either of these commands:

- `R` Addresses a reply to the sender of the message
- `r` Addresses a reply to the sender and all recipients of an e-mail message

With either of these commands, you can use the `msglist` parameter, as explained earlier in this chapter. Otherwise, the `R` or `r` command applies to the current message.

This section shows how to use these two commands by considering the following partial header, excerpted from a message from `chendric`, Carol Hendricks, in which she asks a group to comment on a draft of a report she has prepared:

```
From chendric Fri, Jan 7 13:22 EST 1994
Received: by your.system.com
Date: Fri, 7 Jan 1994 13:22:01 -0500
From: Carol Hendricks <chendric>
Return-Path: <chendric>
To: aborat, lynn, oackerm, imgood
Subject: Draft Report
```

To respond to only `chendric`, type **R** and press <Return> when you see the `?` prompt. You see the following response:

```
To: chendric
Subject: Re: Draft Report
```

These lines tell you the reply is going to one person; the subject header indicates that the message is a reply to the one originally sent.

To make comments for everyone on the distribution list to see, type `r` and press <Return> when you see the `?` prompt. You see the following response lines:

```
To: chendric, aborat, lynn, oackerm, imgood
Subject: Re: Draft Report
```

These lines tell you the reply is going to everyone on the original distribution list as well as the author. The subject header indicates that the message is a reply to the one originally sent.

From then on, you enter your message in the manner described in "Sending E-Mail with `mail`" earlier in this chapter.

Caution

Be careful about using `r` to reply to a message. Whatever you send is sent to *everyone* who got a copy of the original message. Since Linux is case-sensitive, most people aren't used to typing capital letters as commands. It's a very common mistake and is sometimes embarrassing.

Note

Think about what you write and who will read your message before you send a reply. Being sarcastic or scathing doesn't work very well with e-mail. You usually end up sounding like a bully. Using e-mail is not the same as talking with someone: you don't get a chance to see or hear their reactions and they don't get a chance to see or hear you, either. When you use e-mail, it's a lot easier and more effective to be polite and direct. You can see how easy it is to forward mail; once you send something to one person, you can never tell where the message will end up or how many people will see it. Think, and be considerate.

Routing Mail to Others

Electronic mail is distributed by addresses. Tasks such as forwarding a message, sending copies (Cc:) of a message, creating aliases or simpler forms of addresses, and creating mailing lists all involve manipulating addresses. You don't have to do the manipulation directly. The `mail` program has these capabilities built into it.

Forwarding Messages

To forward a message (actually, you're including the message with a message you compose), you must first start `mail` in the same way as when you start it to read your messages. Then you use the `m`, `r`, or `R` command to send a message. As you compose your message, you use a tilde command, `~f`, to forward one or several messages. The general form of the `~f` command is `~f msglist`. Here is a step-by-step example of how to forward a message:

1. Start `mail`: type **`mail`** and press <Return>. The system responds with something similar to the following:

```
mail     Type ? for help.
"/var/spool/mail/imgood": 5 messages 2 new 1 unread
     1 sarah
     ➥Wed Jan  5 09:17  15/363
     2 croster@turn.green.com
     ➥Thu Jan  6 10:18  26/657   Meeting on Friday
U    3 wjones
➥Fri Jan  7 08:09  32/900   Framistan Order
> N   4 chendric
➥Fri Jan  7 13:22  35/1277  Draft Report
    N 5 col.com!kackerma@ps.com
    ➥Sat Jan  8 13:21  76/3103  Excerpt from GREAT new UNI
      ?
```

2. Read message 5 by typing **5** and pressing <Return>. (The text of that message isn't shown here.) But suppose that you want to forward it to your friends with addresses `sarah`, `anglee@hb.com`, and `netcong.com!parsley!lynn`.

3. Use the `m` command to send mail to the addresses listed in Step 2, type a subject, and type a beginning for your message. Here are the commands you enter to achieve this (what you type is in bold):

```
? m sarah anglee@hb.com netcong.com!parsley!lynn
Subject: Forwarding an excerpt from new Que Linux book
Hi!
I'm forwarding an excerpt I came across from a new book by Que.
It's the Special Edition of Using Linux. I'll be getting my
own copy tomorrow,
Do you want me to pick up a copy for you, too?
```

4. Use the command `~f` to forward message number 5. Type **~f 5** and press <Return>. `mail` responds with the following message:

```
Interpolating: 5
(continue)
```

5. The cursor is now under the word `continue`. You can continue with your mail message or end it by typing `~.` and then pressing <Return>. The `?` prompt appears.

Sending a Copy with *mail*

You can send a copy of an e-mail message to one or more addresses by putting those addresses on what is known as the Cc: list. The Cc: list works as you expect it to: the mail is sent to the primary address or addresses (those in the `To:` header) and also to the address or addresses in the `Cc:` header. To include addresses in the Cc: list, use the tilde command `~c` *`address`* while you are sending the message.

This example shows how to send a brief memo to a primary address (`wjones`) and a copy of it to yourself and another address (suppose that your address is `imgood` and the other user's address is `ecarlst`). You send one to yourself so you have a copy of the memo. Follow these steps to add a Cc: list to the list of recipients:

1. Start `mail` to send e-mail to the primary address, `wjones`, and give a subject header. Enter the following commands to achieve this (what you type is in bold):

```
$ mail wjones<Return>
Subject: Memo - Sales Agreement with Framistan<Return>
```

2. Enter the text of the memo you want to send. For example, type the following:

```
TO:         William Jones
Date:     Oct 31, 1994
From:     Henry Charleston
RE:         Sales Agreement With Framistan Motors
On October 29,1994, I held a meeting with the CEO of Framistan Motors.
We concluded and initialed a sales agreement by which Framistan would
purchase 10,000 units of our thermo-embryonic carthurators. The agreement
```

```
has been forwarded to the appropriate parties in our organization and
we intend to formally complete the agreement within two weeks.
```

3. Give the `~c address` command to add addresses to the Cc: list. For example, type the following to send copies to yourself, `imgood`, and to `ecarlst`:

```
~c ecarlst imgood<Return>
```

4. End it and send it: To end the message, type a tilde and period (`~.`) and then press <Return>. The `EOT` message appears, followed by the shell prompt.

Tip

To review and possibly modify the headers on an outgoing message, type **~h** and press <Return> while you are composing the message. You are shown the headers one at a time and you can modify them.

When a message is sent this way, all the recipients can see the headers `To:` and `Cc:`. If someone replies to the message with the `R` or `r` command, they can expect the following results:

- With the `R` command, the reply is sent only to the author of the message.
- With the `r` command, the reply is sent to every address in the `To:` list and the `Cc:` list, as well as to the author.

You can customize `mail` so that it always prompts you for a `Cc:` header in the same way it prompts you for the `Subject:` header. This is discussed in "Customizing Your `mail` Environment" later in this chapter. Of course, you can keep from entering anything in the Cc: list by pressing <Return>.

Using Aliases and Mailing Lists

The `mail` program, like most e-mail programs, allows you to create an alias for an address and a group alias for a list of addresses. You can treat the group alias as a mailing list. Having an alias for an individual address usually makes it easier to use the address because the alias is probably shorter and easier to remember.

You can set an individual or group alias for one `mail` session by using the command `alias` from the `?` prompt while you are reading your e-mail. To make the aliases more useful, put the aliases in a file named `.mailrc` in your home directory (as described in "Customizing Your `mail` Environment" later in this chapter).

Following is an example of setting and using aliases with the `mail` program:

1. Start `mail` by typing **`mail`** and pressing <Return>. After the headers are presented, you see the `?` prompt:

```
mail     Type ? for help.
"/var/spool/mail/imgood": 5 messages 2 new 1 unread
     1 sarah
     ➥Wed Jan  5 09:17  15/363
```

```
    2 croster@turn.green.com
    ➥Thu Jan  6 10:18  26/657   Meeting on Friday
U   3 wjones
➥Fri Jan  7 08:09  32/900   Framistan Order
> N 4 chendric
➥Fri Jan  7 13:22  35/1277  Draft Report
  N 5 col.com!kackerma@ps.com
  ➥Sat Jan  8 13:21  76/3103  Excerpt from GREAT new Linux
   ?
```

2. Set up an individual alias: use the command `alias` followed by the alias for the address. The following example creates the alias `ros` for the address **croster@turn.green.com**:

   ```
   alias ros crsoter@turn.green.com
   ```

3. Use the alias `ros` in an address; `mail` expands it to its complete form. For example, you can enter the `m ros` command to start a message you want to mail to **croster@turn.green.com**.

4. Set up a group alias: use the command `alias` followed by the alias for the addresses. The following example creates the alias `friends` and then forwards some mail to the group (what you type is in bold):

```
alias friends chendric karlack abc.com!homebase!fran eca@xy.srt.edu<Return>
m friends<Return>
Subject: Excerpts from new Linux book - get a copy!<Return>
~f 5<Return>
Interpolating: 5
~.<Return>
EOT
?
```

Customizing Your *mail* Environment

You can customize your `mail` environment by putting commands or `set-environment` variables in the file `.mailrc` in your home directory. The `mail` program checks that file whenever you use the program. Quite a few environment variables and commands can be set in `.mailrc`, and different mail programs will use different commands. Check your manual page for your mail program for a list of all of the `.mailrc` options. Some of the commands `mail` recognizes were given in "Getting Help with `mail`" earlier in this chapter. This section describes a subset of the commands and variables that can be used in the `.mailrc` file. These commands are listed in Table 30.1 and the environment variables are listed in Table 30.2.

You can set a system-wide environment by putting the commands or set variables in the file `/etc/mail.rc`. You can issue any of the commands in Table 30.1 from the `?` prompt any time you use `mail`.

Table 30.1 *mail* Commands

Command	Definition
#	Denotes a comment. No action is taken.
`alias`	Sets an individual or group alias. Used as alias `alias-name address-list`.
`set`	Sets an environment variable. Used as `set variable-name` or `set variable-name=string`.

Table 30.2 *mail* Environment Variables

Variable	Definition
`askcc`	Prompts for the `Cc:` list after the message is entered. Default is `noaskcc`.
`asksub`	Prompts for the `Subject:` list before the message is entered. Enabled by default.
`noheader`	Does not print header information on available messages when you start mail. Disabled by default.
`ignore`	Ignores interrupt characters when you enter messages. This is useful if you have a "noisy" connection over some telephone or other communication lines. Default is `noignore`.
`metoo`	When you have your name in a group alias, a message is normally *not* sent to you. Setting this variable allows you to receive messages sent to a group alias that contains your address. Default is `nometoo`.

The following example sets up the file `.mailrc` so that you use the commands and environment variables listed in tables 30.1 and 30.2. The pound sign (#) is used to document the work. You can create this file using `vi` or any other editor that can produce a text or ASCII file.

```
# .mailrc file for D. Gunter
# make sure interrupts are NOT ignored
set noignore
# set variables so that prompts for Subject and Cc always appear
set asksub
set askcc
# individual aliases
alias billy wbracksto
alias ham jhron@cucumber.abc.com
alias me gunter
# group aliases, mailing list
alias pirates jroger@blackflag.net bbow homebase!lead!bbeard
alias research chendric jreynold eackerma uuport!farplace!consul
alias framistan wjones imgood cornlo@framistan.org imgood
```

Place these statements in the `.mailrc` file. Now when you start `mail`, these command statements are processed. Here is what you might see if you use the group alias `research` to send a message, and use the alias `me` in the Cc: list (what you type is in bold):

```
$ mail<Return>
mail     Type ? for help.
"/var/spool/mail/hwalton": 5 messages 2 new 1 unread
     1 sarah
     ➥Wed Jan  5 09:17  15/363
     2 croster@turn.green.com
     ➥Thu Jan  6 10:18  26/657   Meeting on Friday
U  3 wjones
➥Fri Jan  7 08:09  32/900   Framistan Order
> N  4 chendric
➥Fri Jan  7 13:22  35/1277  Draft Report
  N  5 homebase!lead!bbeard
  ➥Sat Jan  8 10:21  76/3103  What's up?
? m research<Return>
Subject: Meeting Wednesday 1/18/94<Return>
Cc:  me wjones<Return>
We need to get together a week from Wednesday, January 18, 1995<Return>
to discuss plans for the corporate meeting in May. I'll reserve<Return>
Room D-12 for a meeting at 10:00 AM, Wednesday, January 18, 1995<Return>
See you there.<Return>
Dave<Return>
.<Return>
EOT
? x<Return>
$
```

If you read that message, you see something such as this:

```
To: chendric, jreynold, eackerma, uuport!farplace!consul
Cc: gunter, wjones
Subject: Meeting Wednesday 1/18/94
We need to get together a week from Wednesday, January 18, 1995 to
discuss plans for the corporate meeting in May. I'll reserve Room D-12
for a meeting at 10:00 AM, Wednesday, January 18, 1995.
See you there.
Dave
```

The *elm* Mailer

As stated earlier, there are several different mail programs available for Linux. Each has its own advantages and disadvantages. One mail reader that comes with the Slackware Distribution of Linux is the `elm` mailer. This mail program is a screen-oriented mailer rather than a line-oriented one. It provides a set of interactive menu prompts and is extremely easy to use. Virtually everything that you can do with mail can be done under `elm`, and usually much easier! Since `elm` is so easy to use, this section just touches on the highlights of using it. You can find more in-depth information by using `elm`'s online help or by reading the man page.

Starting *elm*

To start a mail session with `elm`, just type **`elm`** at the command prompt. If this is the first time you have used `elm`, it will prompt you for permission to set up a configuration directory in your account and create an mbox mail file if one does not exist. Here is what you see as you start elm for the first time:

```
$ elm<Return>
Notice:
This version of ELM requires the use of a .elm directory in your home
directory to store your elmrc and alias files. Shall I create the
directory .elm for you and set it up (y/n/q)? y<Return>
Great! I'll do it now.

Notice:
ELM requires the use of a folders directory to store your mail folders in.
Shall I create the directory /home/gunter/Mail for you (y/n/q)? y<Return>
Great! I'll do it now.
```

After elm creates its directory and mbox file, it runs the main mail program. This is a full-screen-oriented mailer. Your screen clears and you will see a display similar to the following:

```
Mailbox is '/var/spool/mail/gunter' with 2 messages [ELM 2.4 PL23]
N  1   Nov 11 Jack Tackett    Linux book
N  2   Nov 11 Jack Tackett    more ideas



You can use any of the following commands
by pressing the first character;
d)elete or u)ndelete mail,  m)ail a message,
r)eply or f)orward mail,  q)uit
To read a message, press <return>.  j = move down, k = move up, ? = help

Command:
```

At the top of the screen, elm tells you where your system mail box is located, how many messages are in it, and what version of elm you are running. elm then lists one line for each message in your mailbox. It places the letter N before each new message, just like the mail program. The summary line for each message tells you if the message is new, the message date, the sender, and the subject. As always, your display may vary slightly depending on your version of elm. The current message is highlighted in the list. (In this book, the current message is in boldface in the message list.)

At the bottom of the screen is a command summary that tells you what commands you have available for the current screen. As you can see in this example, you can delete or undelete mail, mail a message, reply to a message, forward mail, or quit. Pressing the j key moves the message selection to the previous message; the k key moves it to the next message. Help is available by pressing the ? key. The Command: prompt at the bottom of the screen tells you to press a command key for elm to do something.

As you can see, elm is very easy to use due to the large number of prompts and on-screen help that is available. Table 30.3 lists all the commands that can be executed from within elm.

Table 30.3 Command Summary for *elm*

Command	Description
`<Return>,<Spacebar>`	Displays current message
`¦`	Pipes current message or tagged messages to a system command
`!`	Shell escape
`$`	Resynchronizes folder
`?`	Displays online help
`+, <Right>`	Displays next index page
`-, <Left>`	Displays previous index page
`=`	Sets current message to first message
`*`	Sets current message to last message
`<Number><Return>`	Sets current message to `<Number>`
`/`	Searches subjects for pattern
`//`	Searches entire message texts for pattern
`>`	Saves current message or tagged messages to a folder
`<`	Scans current message for calendar entries
`a`	Alias, changes to 'alias' mode
`b`	Bounces (remail) current message
`C`	Copies current message or tagged messages to a folder
`c`	Changes to another folder
`d`	Deletes current message
`<Ctrl-d>`	Deletes messages with a specified pattern
`e`	Edits current folder
`f`	Forwards current message
`g`	Groups (all recipients) reply to current message
`h`	Displays header with message
`J`	Increments current message by one
`j, <Down-Arrow>`	Advances to next undeleted message
`K`	Decrements current message by one
`k, <Up-Arrow>`	Advances to previous undeleted message
`l`	Limits messages by specified criteria
`<Ctrl-l>`	Redraws screen
`m`	Mails a message
`n`	Next message, displaying current, then increment
`o`	Changes `elm` options

Command	Description
p	Prints current message or tagged messages
q	Quits, maybe prompting for deleting, storing, and keeping messages
Q	Quick quit—no prompting
r	Replies to current message
s	Saves current message or tagged messages to a folder
t	Tags current message for further operations
T	Tags current message and go to next message
<Ctrl-t>	Tags messages with a specified pattern
u	Undeletes current message
<Ctrl-u>	Undeletes messages with a specified pattern
x, <Ctrl-q>	Exits leaving folder untouched; ask permission if folder changed
X	Exits leaving folder untouched, unconditionally

From Here...

You can find more information about exchanging information over the Internet in the following chapters:

- Chapter 29, "Surfing the Internet," describes the various types of information available on the Internet.
- Chapter 31, "Surviving USENET News," describes the USENET news system that is used to exchange public messages.

CHAPTER 31

Surviving USENET News

With the explosive growth of the Internet, USENET news has attracted lots of attention. Many online services now offer access to USENET. But what is USENET? USENET, which is short for User Network, is a proto-network of machines that exchange information grouped into subject hierarchies. The term proto-network is used because USENET is not a physical network in the normal sense. It is made up of all the computers that exchange USENET news.

The following topics are covered in this chapter:

- What is USENET news?
- The history of USENET
- The newgroup stucture of the USENET news system
- The culture of USENET
- A look at the rn news reader

What Is USENET News?

In the simplest definition, USENET news, netnews, or simply news is a forum for online discussion. Many computers around the world exchange chunks of information, called articles, on almost every subject imaginable. These computers are not physically connected to the same network; they are logically connected in their ability to exchange data. Thus, they form the logical network referred to as USENET. In this chapter, the terms USENET, news, and netnews are used interchangeably.

> **Note**
>
> The software that drives USENET is divided into two parts. There are news readers, the software that users use to read and post news articles, and there is the software that processes articles and transfers them between systems.

Many people initially think of a PC bulletin board system (BBS) when trying to understand USENET. Although USENET news does bear some similarity to a BBS at first glance, there are very substantial and important differences. First of all, the various news articles on different subjects do not reside on one computer as with a BBS. They are sent from computer to computer via a store-and-forward mechanism. Each site that receives news exchanges articles with one or more neighbors in transactions that are known as news feeds. As a result, news articles take time to propagate from place to place. Second, there is no one in charge. Yes, you read that right. USENET has no overall manager, like a BBS sysop. Each site has a good deal of autonomy. USENET news has been described, very accurately, as "organized anarchy."

In general, USENET news is divided into two logical parts: the programs and protocols that make up the mechanism for posting articles and transferring news articles between computers, and the user programs for reading and posting news articles. This chapter deals primarily with the user portion.

A USENET Glossary

USENET news has its own structure and its own culture, which are discussed in another part of this chapter. USENET also has a terminology all its own. These "buzzwords" tend to confuse new users, especially those who use BBS systems. Table 31.1 gives a brief glossary of common terms found on USENET.

Table 31.1 Common Terms Encountered in USENET News

Term	Definition
Article	A single message posted to a newsgroup.
Bandwidth	An engineering term referring to the amount of data a given transmission medium can hold. Commonly used as in "waste of bandwidth" for articles that contain little useful information.
BTW	Acronym for "By the Way."
FAQ	An acronym for the Frequently Asked Questions list. Most newsgroups have an FAQ that they post on a regular basis. It is usually considered impolite to post a question whose answer is in the FAQ for a group.
Flame	An article that is full of rude, angry, insulting statements directed at another person.
FYI	Acronym for "For Your Information."
Hierarchy	USENET's system of grouping newsgroups into a tree structure based on subject.
IMHO	Stands for "In My Humble Opinion."
Newsgroup	A logical group of articles that are about one general subject.
News reader	A user program, such as `rn`, that is used to read and post articles to USENET.
Net.personality	Someone who is famous within the USENET or Internet community.

Net.police	A mythical organization responsible for enforcing the rules on USENET. Typically used as sarcasm.
Netiquette	The etiquette of USENET.
Newbie	Someone who is new to using USENET news.
Quoting	Including parts of a message to which you are responding. Most news readers allow you to quote articles. You should only quote relevant portions of an article to save bandwidth.
ROFL	Acronym for "roll on the Floor Laughing."
RTFM	An acronym for "Read The F***ing Manual." Typically used as in "Here's a short answer to your question. RTFM for more info."
Post	To submit an article to a newsgroup.
Signal-to-noise	Engineering term referring to the ratio of the amount of data to the amount of background noise. On USENET, it refers to how much useful information is in a newsgroup versus the amount of off-topic background chatter. A high signal-to-noise ratio refers to a newsgroup that has lots of useful information and very little off-topic chatter.
Signature	A short file that is included at the end of all your posts. Typically includes your name, e-mail address, and possibly a witty quote of some sort.
Sig file	See *signature*.
Smileys	Common symbols for denoting emotion in a post or e-mail message. For example, :-) and :-(are a happy face and a sad face. (Look at them sideways.)

A Brief History

Note

An excellent reference for the history of USENET news is the news article "Usenet Software: History and Sources," by Dr. Gene Spafford. This article is regularly posted to the newsgroup **news.announce.newusers**.

In late 1979, two graduate students at Duke University began considering how to connect UNIX computers so that they could exchange text messages. Another grad student at the University of North Carolina became involved in this effort and wrote the first news transfer system, which consisted of a collection of shell scripts. This software was installed on the first two USENET sites, **unc** and **duke**. In early 1980, another computer at Duke, **phs**, was added. The news software was eventually rewritten in C for public distribution. This became known as the A News software.

As the news software grew in popularity, it quickly became obvious that the current news transport software could not handle the increasing flow of news. Programmers at the University of California at Berkeley began to rewrite the current A News software to increase its capabilities. This new version, known as B News, was released in 1982.

Throughout this time, news articles were being transferred using the UUCP protocol. As more and more sites joined the news network, the network load grew to unmanageable levels. People soon realized that UUCP no longer worked as the main transport protocol for news, and they began looking toward the Internet and the TCP/IP protocols for help. In 1986 a software package was released that implemented the Network News Transport Protocol, or NNTP. This protocol is defined in RFC 977. NNTP allowed news articles to be exchanged using TCP/IP instead of the slower UUCP protocol. It also allowed users to read and post news from remote machines, so that the main news processing software did not have to be installed on every computer.

◀◀ See "Internet Documentation," p. 618

Now that NNTP was available on the Net, the already rapid growth of the USENET news system exploded. The current news processing software, B News, quickly became too slow to handle the increasing news flow. In 1987, Henry Spencer and Geoff Collyer of the University of Toronto developed a new news processing software, C News.

The USENET news system continues to grow at a rapid pace. Other commercial information service providers are now carrying USENET news as part of their online service. Several BBSs, such as FidoNet, also carry USENET news.

How USENET Is Structured

There are literally thousands of newsgroups. How many, exactly? Well, nobody knows. If you were given a number, it would be obsolete by the time the editors of this book received this chapter. There are thousands of groups on virtually every topic, and that number is growing every day.

Group Hierarchies

With this many different newsgroups, it would be a nightmare trying to find information on the subjects that you were interested in if the newsgroups were not organized in some way. USENET newsgroups are organized in a hierarchy based on subject. The names of the newsgroups are made up of subnames, each separated by a period. These names go from a general category to a specific category as you read the name from left to right. At the top of the hierarchy, there are several standard group categories. These categories are well established. Table 31.2 lists the top-level groups categories in the USENET news system.

Table 31.2 Top-Level Group Classes in the USENET Hierarchy

Class	Description
`comp`	Many different computer-related topics
`misc`	Miscellaneous topics that do not easily fit into another category
`news`	Various topics that relate to the USENET news system itself
`rec`	Recreational and hobby subjects
`soc`	Social issues
`sci`	Various scientific topics
`talk`	Subjects designed for ongoing conversations

As with everything else on the Internet, there are exceptions to the previous table's rules. Many other top-level hierarchies exist. Most are devoted to different regions of the world. For example, the `ba` and `triangle` group hierarchies are concerned with topics of interest to the San Fransisco Bay area and Research Triangle Park North Carolina area, respectively.

One of these additional group hierarchies deserves special discussion. The `alt` hierarchy has very relaxed rules for newsgroup creation. Virtually anyone can create a group under the `alt` hierarchy; however, creating a newsgroup under any other top-level group is extremely difficult. The `alt` hierarchy carries many newsgroups that discuss topics that are out of the mainstream of society. In fact, many people find some of the topics in the `alt` hierarchy to be objectionable. Many Net debates on censorship have started because sites decided to ban part or all of the newsgroups in the `alt` hierarchy.

News Distributions

In addition to grouping articles in hierarchies, USENET also provides a feature for limiting the spread of an article within the news system. New distributions provide a mechanism for limiting articles to a particular geographic area. If a distribution is set to a particular area, only sites within that distribution area receive the article. The system administrator at each site decides what distributions apply to their site.

Why limit the distribution of an article? Suppose that you live in North Carolina and you are posting a meeting announcement for a local user group meeting. It is unlikely that USENET readers in Australia are interested in your meeting. By limiting the distribution of your article to the appropriate geographical area, you can save network bandwidth, reduce the cost of sending your message, and reduce the aggravation of users around the world who have to read your message.

You can limit the distribution of your article by including a `Distribution:` line in the header of your article as you post it. Most news readers ask you for the distribution when you post an article. After the `:` in the `Distribution:` line, enter the appropriate geographical distribution. Table 31.3 lists some commonly used news distributions.

Table 31.3 Commonly Used News Distribution Values

Value	Explanation
`local`	Typically, articles with a `local` distribution are limited to a group of local news servers within your organization. This distribution is often used for local organizational newsgroups.
`nc`	This distribution limits the article to machines within the state of North Carolina. Every state has a statewide distribution that is the same as the postal abbreviation for the state.
`us`	Sends the article to all USENET sites in the United States.
`na`	Sends the article to all USENET sites in North America.
`world`	Sends the article to every reachable USENET site in the world. Typically, this is the default distribution if no other distribution value is specified.

Your site may have some additional distributions that apply. There may be organization-wide or regional distributions that you can use to determine the scope of your article. In general, you should try to pick a distribution that sends your article only to the areas where it will be of interest.

No Central Authority

Many people are mystified by the fact that USENET has no central authority. Your local systems administrator really only has authority over the local system. There is no central group or organization that dictates policy or that you can complain to. In spite of this glaring lack of regulated structure, USENET works remarkably well. In fact, many people argue that it works better than if there were some central authority.

How do things keep working in an orderly manner? USENET is run by cooperation between sites and by customs that have evolved over its life. There are also several people who have gained a great deal of respect and whose opinions are greatly respected.

USENET tends to be very good at policing itself. If a user starts to abuse the network, you can rest assured that both the user and their system administrator will get thousands of e-mail messages and several phone calls about the problem. This usually results in the quick problem resolution.

USENET Culture

USENET has a particular culture all its own. You should take some time to try to become familiar with the facets of this culture before just diving in. Life on USENET will be much easier if you do.

In recent months, several online communication services have added USENET news as a feature of their service. As a result, thousands of people who are new to USENET have started reading and posting USENET news. Many of these users have complained about USENET readers being rude or generally unlike the users of their online service. Well, the culture of USENET is different from almost any other information service that you will find. It is not better or worse—just different. If you try to make allowances for differences in Net culture, you will probably find that your experiences on USENET are a bit easier to handle.

There are well over one million people (probably several million, though no one knows for sure) who read and post USENET news articles daily. These people are from all occupations, all walks of life, and many different countries around the world. Because USENET news is carried on computers all over the world, it truly forms an international community. Many of the people that you encounter on USENET do not speak English as a primary language. You cannot assume that the people reading your articles share your cultural background, ethnic group, religion, or social values. The most that you can assume is that whoever reads your articles is probably very different from you in several ways.

One aspect of USENET culture, the flame, is usually an unpleasant experience for the new user. A *flame* is a rude message, usually degrading and filled with insults that someone posts in response to one of your articles. Unfortunately, as you will see, there is very little that you can do about flames, other than ignore them. USENET is far too large a place for you to try to make everyone happy, and some people really seem to like flaming other people just for the fun of it. Perhaps they find it cheaper than psychotherapy.

Lack of Visual Reference

One problem with electronic communications is that you lack any kind of visual input during the conversation. When people talk to each other in person, you constantly receive information on both a conscious and subconscious level from the other person's body language. Because you cannot see the other people that read and post on USENET, these visual cues are missing. Because you typically use body language and visual cues to represent emotion and feeling, it can be easy to misunderstand someone's post without them.

Fortunately, there are several conventions on USENET that you can use to replace part of the missing visual cues. You can place added emphasis on a particular phrase by surrounding it in asterisks, as in "I *really* mean it!" Also, the use of all capital letters is considered shouting. If you accidentally post an article with your <Caps Lock> key on, several people probably will tell you about it.

You can also express emotions by writing them into your message. For example, if you make a sarcastic statement, you can make sure that it is understood as such by adding `<sarcasm>` at the end of the line. Smileys, also known as emoticons, also work to add emotion to your post. A smiley is an ASCII representation of a face, which you look at sideways in order to see clearly. `:-)` is a happy, smiling face. A sad face is `:-(`. There is a canonical list of smileys out on the Net somewhere. Track it down and look at it if you are really interested; some of them are quite funny and original.

Newsgroup Culture

Just as people are different, each newsgroup on USENET has a different culture. Each newsgroup has a different subject focus and attracts different types of people. In some groups, you may find large numbers of college students, while in others, you may primarily find research scientists.

Some of the more technical hierarchies, such as `comp` and `sci`, tend to be more oriented toward factual discussion, although heated debates do take place. Members of these groups are usually interested in discussing facts and issues related to some technical subject. When you post here, make sure that you take time to carefully compose your article and have references for the various points that you make.

The less technical hierarchies such as `rec` tend to be somewhat more opinion oriented. Remember, you will probably get replies to your articles that reflect other people's opinions that are quite different from your own. Groups in the `talk` hierarchy, along with some of the `misc` groups, get into some very heated discussions. Many of these groups discuss very sensitive topics such as abortion and gun control. Be careful in these groups if you are new to USENET. Make sure you take time to get familiar with the group before posting. Be prepared to receive strongly worded replies and e-mail about your articles. Many of the people here hold very strong beliefs.

When you first start reading a newsgroup, you should take some time to familiarize yourself with the culture of the particular group before posting. Read the group for a few days and try to get a feel for the tone of the articles and the things that appear to be acceptable and unacceptable behavior.

There are a few newsgroups where posting articles is restricted. These are known as moderated newsgroups. Moderated newsgroups are managed by a person known as a moderator. All articles posted to the group must be approved by the moderator prior to posting. The moderator decides if the content of the article is appropriate to the group, and if so, posts the article to the group. Most news software automatically detects if a newsgroup is moderated and e-mails your article to the moderator instead of posting it directly.

Reading and Posting News

Now that you are familiar with USENET, take a look at the basic process for reading and posting news articles. This section discusses reading and posting news in general terms; the exact details depend upon the news reading software that you are using. There are many different software packages available for interacting with news, and each of them is different. These general concepts should apply across all news reading software.

Subscribing to Newsgroups

The first thing that you want to do when you start reading news is to decide which newsgroups you want to read. The process of selecting the newsgroups is known as *subscribing.*

Most news readers will offer you a list of available newsgroups so that you can select the ones in which you are interested. The actual process of subscribing varies between news reading software packages, but it usually involves selecting a series of newsgroups from a list. From then on, only the groups that you have subscribed to are visible when you read news. You can always subscribe to additional groups any time you want or unsubscribe from a group in which you are no longer interested.

Reading News

Once you have subscribed to your newsgroups, you can begin reading news. You select a newsgroup from a list of your subscribed groups. Your news reader displays a list of article subjects for the various articles in the newsgroup. These subjects may be sorted in some order or they may be unsorted, depending on your news reader. Some news readers can sort articles based on subject, showing which articles are replies to other articles. This is known as *threading*.

When you select an article to read, you see several lines of information at the top of the article. These lines make up the article header. The header contains lots of information about the article, including the author, the date it was written, the subject, the newsgroups that the article was posted to, and the path the article took to get to your site. There may be additional information such as the organization that the author is affiliated with, and a set of keywords that identify the content of an article.

Under most news readers, an article is marked as read once you have looked at it. Usually, only new articles are displayed when you select a newsgroup. This means that once you have looked at an article, it probably won't show up in your article list again. If you want to keep the article, you can save it to disk or print it. You can also usually mark the article as unread so that your news reader displays it again the next time that you go into its newsgroup. Many news readers also allow you to list old articles. This gives you a list of old news articles in a newsgroup that are marked as having been read but have not yet been deleted by the news system.

Replying via E-Mail

Once you have read an article, you may decide that you want to add some additional information to it. If your information is not of general interest to everyone in the newsgroup, you may want to reply to the article via e-mail, which most news readers allow you the option of doing.

If you choose to reply through e-mail, the news reader software uses the information in the article header to figure out the e-mail address of the author and then invokes an e-mail editor for you to edit your message. You usually also have the option of including the original article in your reply. If you do include the original article, make sure that you edit the original message to only include the relevant portions. Once you have finished editing your reply, you can send your e-mail message to the article's author.

Posting an Article

The act of creating a news article and sending it out through the USENET system is known as posting an article. When you decide to post an article, you may either post a follow-up article to another article, or you can create a new article on a new subject. Your news reader typically has different commands for the different types of posts that it can perform.

Posting a Follow-Up. A follow-up article is a reply to another article. This article stays in the same subject thread as the original article and is shown as a reply by threaded news readers.

When you post a follow-up, you have the option of including the original post. Including parts of the original post is a good way to provide a frame of reference for your reply. Remember that several days may pass between the time some sites see the original article and your reply. If you do choose to include the original article, try to only include, or quote, the parts of the article that are relevant to your reply. It gets tedious trying to wade through several levels of included files and quotes looking for the new information.

You should check the `Subject` line to make sure that the subject still accurately reflects the content of your post. Also, take a look at the `Newsgroup` line to make sure that your follow-up is going to the appropriate newsgroups.

Posting a New Article. If you decide to start a thread of discussion on a new subject, you want to post a new article instead of a follow-up. The mechanics of posting the article are very similar—you give the appropriate command to your news reader, your news reader asks for some information such as the destination news-groups, subject, and distribution, and you are placed into an editor. The major difference is that you are creating a subject thread instead of replying to one.

> **Tip**
>
> A complete document on USENET writing style is posted regularly to the newsgroup **news.announce.newusers**.

There are several things that you should think about as you write your article. You can think of them as "USENET Style Tips" if you want. These tips cover both the format of your article and its content.

Remember that other users do not have the same equipment as you do. Many people read news with PCs, Macs, terminals, UNIX workstations, and so on. Don't use binary characters in your message. USENET is designed to send ASCII characters only. If you should try to send a binary file, it gets garbled at best, and at worst, it does strange things to other people's displays. If you need to send a binary file through USENET, you should use `uuencode` to format the file into an ASCII format, and then use `split` to break the file into smaller chunks.

You should keep your lines under 80 characters long. Many terminals cannot display lines that are over 80 characters. Similarly, you should try to keep the length of your article under 1000 lines or so. Some sites are still running old versions of the news transport software, and long articles can cause them problems.

You probably want to create a signature file that is automatically included at the end of every post. Most news readers support signature files, although the exact mechanism differs depending on your software. Most people put their name and e-mail address in their signature file, along with their geographical location. Some people add a witty quote or a small ASCII picture. Try to avoid having a large signature file. Some news software limits your signature to four lines or so.

You need to give a subject to your article when you post it. Try to pick a subject line that is short, yet descriptive. Thousands of people scan the subjects in any particular newsgroup, and you want them to be able to pick out your article if it is of interest to them. Also, carefully consider which newsgroups you are going to post your article to. Most news readers allow you to post an article to more than one newsgroup. You should only post to the smallest number of groups that you need. Remember that there are thousands of people reading each newsgroup.

Netiquette Etiquette on USENET

Throughout this chapter, the importance of being aware of how the tone and content of your message are interpreted has been stressed. This general consideration of behavior on USENET has its own term, *netiquette*.

The term netiquette simply refers to "proper and polite" behavior as it applies to USENET news. Most of the time, you should have no real problems on USENET as long as you remember that it is a very big and diverse place. Not everyone on USENET shares your background, beliefs, or values, and you should try to remember this as you post articles.

Make sure that you clearly communicate your ideas in your posts. With the lack of body language and the delay between posts and replies, it is surprisingly easy to interpret someone's meaning incorrectly. Also, remember that many readers do not speak English as a native language and may be unaware of local idioms and sarcasm.

Blatant commercial advertising is frowned upon in USENET news. There are appropriate newsgroups for advertising products and services. Similarly, don't post chain articles, such as the infamous MAKE.MONEY.FAST or the Craig Shergold postcard article. These articles have been circulating around USENET for years, and you (and your systems administrator) will incur the wrath of thousands of people instantly if you post one of them.

Resist the urge to post flames, especially spelling and grammar flames. Even though flames seem to be a permanent part of the USENET "landscape," these personal attacks and raving messages accomplish little. If someone should flame you for one of your posts, take time to calm down and carefully consider how to respond; the best solution might be not to respond at all. If you just zip off another flame in anger, you only escalate the problem. Remember that the person on the other end is really a person, not a computer. If a user is causing a real problem, you can add them to your kill file. A *kill file* is a configuration file for your news reader that contains a list of users or subjects. Anything that appears in your kill file is automatically not displayed when you read news. Most news readers support some version of a kill file. This is a fairly painless way to cut down the noise from really annoying users.

In general, a little common sense and courtesy go a long way to avoiding any problems on USENET. However, remember that USENET is a huge place. There are simply too many people for you to try to make everyone happy. Eventually, someone will get angry over one of your posts and you will probably be flamed.

Using the *rn* News Reader

There are many different types of news reading software available; far too many to describe in this chapter. The `rn` news reader is a very common news reading program that can be found on almost every variant of UNIX. It was developed by Larry Wall and is widely available. While `rn` is not the easiest news reader to use, nor does it have some of the fanciest features, it is still one of the most popular news readers in existence. `rn` allows you to read news via an ASCII interface that is suitable for either local work on a terminal or from a remote network session.

Note

Another news reader, `trn`, is quite popular and is distributed with many distributions of Linux. `trn` is a version of `rn` that supports subject threading. The `trn` news reader is almost identical to `rn` except for the threading support. For compatibility, only the `rn` news reader is discussed in this chapter. For more information on the threading capabilities of `trn`, refer to its Linux man page.

When you start `rn` for the first time, you see a message welcoming you to the program, followed by a list of newsgroups. You have the opportunity to subscribe to different groups at this point. If your site carries a large number of groups, it can be quite time consuming to set up your initial subscription information. `rn` saves your subscription information in your home directory in a file named `.newsrc`.

Once you have completed your subscriptions, `rn` places you in a newsgroup selection mode. The name of each of your subscribed newsgroups are displayed, one at a time. You can enter the newsgroup and start reading articles by pressing <y>, you can skip to the next group by pressing <n>, or you can go to the previous newsgroup by pressing <q>. You can also get a list of subjects in the newsgroup by pressing the <=> key at the newsgroup prompt. Most of the commands in both `rn` and `trn` are one-character commands, and help is available at every command prompt by pressing the <h> key.

Once you have selected a newsgroup to read, you enter the article selection mode. In this mode, there are several commands that can help you navigate the articles in the newsgroup. Table 31.4 lists some of the commands that are available in the article selection mode.

Table 31.4 Some of the Commands That Are Available in Article Selection Mode

Command	Description
<n><Spacebar>	Scans forward for the next unread article. The <Spacebar> only does this at the end of the article at the article selection prompt.
<Spacebar>	Shows the next page of the current article if not at the article selection prompt.
<Shift-n>	Goes to the next article.
<Ctrl-Shift-n>	Goes to the next article with the same subject as the current article.
<p>	Scans backward for the previous unread article. Stays at current article if none is found.
<Shift-p>	Goes to the previous article.
<Ctrl-Shift-r>	Goes to the last previous article with the subject that is the same as the current article.
<h>	Displays help for article selection mode.
<r>	Replies to the article author via e-mail.
<Shift-r>	Replies to the article author via e-mail, including the current article.
<f>	Posts a follow-up article.
<Shift-f>	Posts a follow-up article, including the original article in the new article.
<s>`file-name`	Saves the current article to a file named `file-name`.
<q>	Quits the current group and returns to the newsgroup selection mode.

These are only some of the options that are available within `rn` and `trn`. These are complex programs that allow lots of user customization. Refer to the man pages and the online help for more information.

From Here...

In this chapter, you explored the structure of USENET, the basics of reading and posting articles, the hierarchy of newsgroups, and USENET's general culture. With a little patience, you will find USENET news to be an indispensable source of information. You can find more information about electronic communication and the Internet in the following chapters:

- Chapter 27, "Understanding the Internet," gives an introduction to the Internet and the various services that it provides.
- Chapter 29, "Surfing the Internet," describes the various types of information that can be found on the Internet.
- Chapter 30, "Using Electronic Mail," shows how to communicate with other people using the e-mail system.

CHAPTER 32

Using the World Wide Web

The Internet is a big place, with lots of information available. What kind of information? Everything from new software to online shopping. But sorting through all the services can be confusing.

The *World Wide Web*, also known as *WWW* or simply *the Web*, is one of the most exciting developments to happen to the Internet in years. The Web is an interactive *hypermedia system* that connects you to vast amounts of information on the Internet. A hypermedia system is made up of *links* between documents. You can access related information by selecting any link. The information is automatically retrieved for you without you having to know where it is.

In this chapter, you explore the following topics that will help you use the Web to track down the information you need from the Internet:

- The basics of anonymous FTP
- Using the Gopher information system
- Using the World Wide Web
- Working with Mosaic
- The Netscape Navigator

Introduction to the World Wide Web

The Internet is a completely distributed network, which means that your computer is connected directly not only with the computer down the hallway but with thousands of others all over the world. Your computer connects to another computer, which is connected to a couple of other computers, and so on. To make matters more complex, the Internet is international in scope. Virtually every country in the world has some form of access to the Internet. Something like the World Wide Web was needed as a form of "information navigator," to make it easier for users to access the information on the Internet.

The Web project was started by CERN, a European physics research lab, and has grown at a phenomenal rate. One reason is that information of any type, from text to sound and graphics, can be accessed via the Web. Researchers saw a need for people to be able to share and exchange information and documents in real-time; out of this need, the Web was born.

The Web uses a set of hypertext links that enable users to easily navigate between documents, graphics, files, audio clips, and so on, from sites anywhere on the Internet. When you select one of the hypertext links in a document, whatever item the link points to is automatically retrieved. One link at a time, Internet users quickly find their way to the various bits of information they want.

Of Clients and Servers

The *client/server* relationship is an important concept in networking, and especially in navigation of the Web. A *server* is a computer that offers some services for other computers to use. These services can be just about any kind of programs, routines, or data. A server can provide information from a database, access to file systems that it makes available, access to information archives, and so on.

A *client* is a computer that uses services from a server. The client makes contact with the server, and requests some sort of service. Many times, a client computer uses special software designed to interact with a specially designed server program on the server computer.

Under this client/server model, people with different computers in different locations can access information on the same server. You can even set up different server computers with different types of data. Because people are using a client software program to communicate with the server, you can develop a different client program for each computer platform that they use. That way, people using Windows or a Macintosh can use client software to access information on a UNIX or Linux server just as easily as UNIX or Linux users can.

To access the Web effectively, you need client software known as a *Web browser*. Two common programs are used as browsers: Lynx for ANSI terminal access, and Mosaic for use with the X Windows System and other graphical platforms. These browsers are available from various places; Mosaic can be found at **ftp.ncsa.uiuc.edu** as well as several anonymous FTP locations over the Internet.

Note

One very popular Web browser is *Netscape Navigator*, also known simply as *Netscape*. Netscape is a commercial software package that provides several very useful features. We will talk more about Netscape later in this chapter. The examples in this chapter use Mosaic instead of Netscape, because Mosaic is available for free.

The Web is based on a client/server model. The client software package contacts a server computer, and exchanges messages with that computer through a set of rules that both client and server understand. This set of rules is known as a *protocol*. Web servers and clients communicate through a protocol known as *HyperText Transfer*

Protocol (HTTP). When a Web client program retrieves a document from a Web server, the programs are probably communicating using HTTP.

Web clients such as Mosaic can communicate with other existing protocols in addition to HTTP. It is possible to use these programs to transfer files with the FTP protocol, retrieve documents from Gopher servers, do text searches with WAIS, and read USENET news. All the different protocols and destinations available on the Web can be accessed by using one standard form of address, known as a *uniform resource locator (URL)*.

Using URLs

Resources on the Web are accessed by a descriptive address known as a *uniform resource locator (URL)*. You can think of a URL as a pointer to an object on the Internet telling you not only where the object is located, but also what it is named and how to access it. Everything that you access through the Web has a URL.

The syntax of URLs looks a bit intimidating but is really straightforward. A URL looks like this:

http://www.ncsa.uiuc.edu/SDG/Software/Mosaic/Docs/whats-new.html

Scary? It's really not that bad. The part to the left of the colon specifies the access method to get to the data. This access method essentially defines the protocol used to communicate with the server, and also gives a good clue as to the type of interaction that will take place. There are several different valid access methods; they are listed in Table 32.1

Table 32.1 Valid Access Methods for URLs

Method	Description
http	Protocol for accessing most Web pages. Provides interactive hypermedia links to pages written in HyperText Markup Language (HTML).
wais	Used for accessing a WAIS site
gopher	Used for accessing a Gopher server
ftp	Provides an anonymous FTP connection
telnet	Opens a telnet connection to a site
news	Used for reading USENET news

Following the **://** in the URL is the host name of the server computer you want to contact. After the server name is the directory path to the document you want to view or retrieve. This path depends totally on where the file is located on the remote server. You might not have a path in some cases, if the file is in a default directory. Finally, the filename of the document is given. Remember that the document in question can be text, a hypermedia document, a sound file, a graphic, or the like.

So, take another look at the example. The URL

http://www.ncsa.uiuc.edu/SDG/Software/Mosaic/Docs/whats-new.html

uses the HTTP protocol to contact the server computer **www.ncsa.uiuc.edu**, and says that you are interested in the document named `whats-new.html` located in the directory `/SDG/Software/Mosaic/Docs`. You might be wondering what the `html` extension on the document name means—this extension tells your Web client (for example, Mosaic) that this is a document written in *HyperText Markup Language (HTML)*. HTML is a special syntax used to write hypertext pages for the Web.

You look at HTML in detail in Chapter 33, "Creating Web Documents with HTML."

What's a Home Page?

The term *home page* has a couple of different meanings depending on its context. In general, a home page is the main HTML page that you get when you connect to a Web server. This page contains links to all the available services on the server, and may also have links to other documents of interest throughout the Web. You can think of a home page as a starting point for a particular Web server.

Another definition of home page is the HTML page that's displayed when you start your Web browser client program. You can set this page to be a home page at a Web site that you like, or you can write your own home page that has links to the servers that you prefer.

Your startup home page provides an easy way back to a known location in case you get lost when navigating the Web. Many times you will follow a set of links to a location, and then will not see any obvious way back to another location. By jumping back to your home page, you can navigate again from familiar territory.

Note

Some people write their own *public home page* using HTML, and make it available on the Web. This page acts as their startup home page, and also acts as a Web page that says to other browsers, "Hi. This is who I am." Users usually customize their public home page to describe their interests and hobbies, and some people include photos or sound clips.

Using Gopher

Gopher is an Internet service that allows you to access information by making selections from a series of menus. Gopher was one of the first Internet services that made a serious attempt at having a user-friendly interface.

When you connect to a site that offers Gopher services, you get a menu of available choices. Each menu is either a file or another menu. You can select your choice from the menu without having to know the name or IP address of the destination site, or the directory and file names of the particular information you're asking for. Gopher handles the details.

One disadvantage of Gopher is the lack of a standard subject list for the various Gopher servers. The administrators for each Gopher server have organized their information in their own manner. This means that each Gopher server you access has different subjects. If the server does have some of the same subjects as another server, they might be named different things.

No information resources on the Internet are actually "Gopher specific." Anything you can get through Gopher could be made available by other means, such as an HTML Web page, FTP, or telnet.

Since Gopher existed before the Web came about, you can use Web browsers such as Mosaic to access Gopher services. To access a Gopher server, change the protocol part of the URL so that it says **gopher**. For example, the URL for the Gopher server at **sunsite.unc.edu** is the following:

gopher://sunsite.unc.edu

Gopher provides an easy means to navigate the Internet. Unfortunately, the information that Gopher can retrieve is not well-organized, so finding what you want can be a bit of an adventure. Because the items in *Gopherspace* are presented as a set of menus, you sometimes have to wade through many different menus to get to the file you are searching for. This problem aside, however, there is a lot of good information available through Gopher.

Using FTP

FTP, or *file transfer protocol*, is the method that the Internet uses to exchange files between computers. *Anonymous FTP* is a service that allows you to retrieve data from around the Internet.

No matter what you're searching for—software, documentation, FAQ lists, programs, or just about anything else—you probably can get a copy through anonymous FTP. This service allows you to log on to many computers without knowing a username and password. Using anonymous FTP, you can access any files that the system administrators on the remote system have made publicly available.

Sometimes, a link in a Web document points to an FTP server.

Anonymous FTP

Because of the explosive growth of the Internet, many organizations have made huge repositories of information available through FTP. These FTP sites offer everything from text files to software of every conceivable type.

(continues)

(continued)

How do you access this enormous storehouse of data if you don't have an account on the remote computer? Do you need to set up an account at every FTP site in order to access these files? Absolutely not. There is a common convention on the Internet that allows *guest access* to file repositories so that users can transfer files. This guest access is referred to as *anonymous FTP*. To use anonymous FTP, you start an FTP session to the remote system, using the user name **anonymous** and using your own e-mail address as the password.

Many sites do not allow anonymous FTP, because allowing guest users to connect to your computer does involve some risk. In cases where anonymous FTP is not allowed, the `ftp` command fails with a message like `Login failed - User "anonymous" unknown.`

Sites that do permit anonymous FTP typically place the user in a restricted directory tree that has read-only access. In the rare case that an anonymous FTP user is allowed to place files on the remote computer, the user usually can put files into only one directory.

There are thousands of computers on the Internet that provide anonymous FTP access. Almost any kind of information can be found on the Internet, and most of it is available through anonymous FTP. FTP, like Gopher, predates the Web, so you can use Web browsers such as Mosaic to transfer files via anonymous FTP.

Using FTP for file transfers is a bit confusing and arcane, because files can be transferred in two different transfer modes, and also can be compressed and archived with any of several programs.

FTP supports *ASCII mode transfers* for text files, and *binary mode transfers* for other types of files. Fortunately, most Web clients automatically determine the file type for you, so you don't have to worry about it. You usually can determine the type of archive or compression program that was used on the file by looking at the file extension. Table 32.2 lists the most common file extensions you will encounter.

Table 32.2 Common File Extensions on Files Available through FTP

Extension	Description
`.Z`	File was compressed with the UNIX `compress` program
`.z`	File was probably compressed with either the GNU `gzip` program or the UNIX `compress` program
`.gz`	File was compressed with the GNU `gzip` program
`.tar`	File is an archive of several files created by the UNIX `tar` program
`.zip`	File is an archive of several files created by `pkzip`

Sometimes you will find files that have been created by more than one of these methods. For example, the file `programs.tar.Z` is an archive of several files created by the `tar` utility, and then compressed with the `compress` utility.

To use a Web client such as Mosaic to perform anonymous FTP transfers, replace the protocol portion of the URL with **ftp**. For example, to start an anonymous FTP session to **sunsite.unc.edu**, use the following URL:

ftp://sunsite.unc.edu

This URL causes your Web client to try to make an FTP connection to **sunsite.unc.edu** and log you in as an anonymous FTP session. After your FTP session is established, you can navigate through directories and transfer files by clicking the hyperlinks displayed on your screen.

Note

When you select a text file to transfer from a remote server in an FTP session, most Web clients display the file on your screen. You need to save the file to disk via a menu selection. Some Web browsers allow you to specify loading a file to disk instead of to the screen; for example, to do this in Mosaic, select the `Load to Local Disk` option from the Options menu.

Roadmaps for the Web

How do you find all this neat stuff on the Web? You have to explore and keep track of the locations that interest you. You can create your own home page to store hyperlinks to the various services in which you're interested.

After you get a web browser up and running, retrieve the following document:

http://www.boutell.com/faq/www_faq.html

This document provides answers to frequently asked questions concerning the Web. It is also posted regularly to the USENET newsgroup **news.answers**. Here are a few other good URLs to check out when you start using the Web:

http://www.yahoo.com

This URL points to a service known as *Yahoo*. Yahoo is a huge index of various services available on the Web. The listing is not an exhaustive one—there are too many new services showing up every day—but it is a large, well-organized index. It's a great starting point to search for Web pages on just about any subject.

http://www.ncsa.uiuc.edu/SDG/Software/Mosaic/Docs/whats-new.html

This URL is the unofficial newspaper of the Web that lists new services. The services and announcements at this page are organized by date; the name of each service is displayed along with a short description. A hyperlink connects the description to the service, so you can go there directly.

http://info.cern.ch/hypertext/DataSources/bySubject/Overview.html

This URL points to the WWW Virtual Library, which provides a good starting point for searching the Web.

The Web is extremely easy to use—it was designed that way. You can be surfing the Net within minutes of setting up your Web browser.

Using Mosaic

You're ready to jump on the Web and start surfing the Net. Besides some sort of interactive Internet connection, all you need is a Web client to get you started. This is where Mosaic comes in. Mosaic was developed by the National Center for Supercomputing Applications at the University of Illinois at Urbana-Champaign. The Mosaic project grew out of an effort to develop scientific visualization tools. Even though Mosaic is copyrighted software, it is freely available on the Internet for use for academic, research, and internal business purposes. For complete details, please read the license information that comes with Mosaic.

> **Note**
>
> To use Mosaic, you'll need an interactive Internet connection, such as a SLIP or PPP dialup connection, and the X Windows System installed on your Linux system.

Mosaic was the first easy-to-use multimedia browser for the Internet. It was the first tool that tied all the different parts of the Internet together, and made it easy for users to navigate from place to place. There are other Web browsers available, with many different features, but Mosaic remains one of the most popular.

How To Get Mosaic for Your Linux System

The Mosaic binaries are available via anonymous FTP on the Internet. Although you can find them in many different locations, the official distribution site is **ftp.ncsa.uiuc.edu**. At the time this book was written, the current release of the Mosaic binaries was version 2.6, and was located in the `/Mosaic/Unix/binaries/2.6` directory. The name of the Linux Mosaic file to download is *Mosaic-linux-2.6.Z.*

In addition to the Mosaic binaries, you probably ought to download some additional utility programs that Mosaic uses for various multimedia formats. These programs are used to play sounds, display graphics, and so on. These programs are not supported by NCSA. You can find a list of these viewer utilities via anonymous FTP from **ftp.ncsa.uiuc.edu** in the `/Mosaic/Unix/viewers` directory.

Installing Mosaic

Downloading and installing Mosaic is a straightforward task. You need to install the Mosaic binaries before you can start surfing the Web with Mosaic. As with most software, you need to be `root` on your system to perform some of these steps if you are installing Mosaic as a generally available program. This is only because all users do not have access to places where programs are typically stored (such as `/usr/local/bin` and `/usr/X/bin`).

The first step is to decide where you want to store the Mosaic files you're downloading from the Internet. Depending on your system, you may have a directory tree for source code and software packages, such as `/usr/local/src`, already created. You'll want to create a directory for the Mosaic files in your source tree; for example, `/usr/local/src/Mosaic-2.6`. Change to the directory where you want to store the files, and then download the appropriate binaries from the Internet. Decompress each binary file with the appropriate compression utility.

At this point, you should copy Mosaic to a standard location in your path, such as `/usr/local/bin`. After you've installed the binary in the proper place, set the permissions for Mosaic to **755** so that other users can run the program. That's it.

After you've successfully installed Mosaic, use the following command to start the program from an xterm window during a running X Windows System session (with the `DISPLAY` variable properly set):

```
% Mosaic &
```

Mosaic should display its main window and connect to the default home page on the NCSA Web server.

Configuring Mosaic

The good news is that there are countless ways you can customize Mosaic. The bad news, also, is that there are countless ways you can customize Mosaic. As a new user of Mosaic, you do not need to know every single aspect of Mosaic that you can configure. In fact, most users never make more than very basic changes to their initial Mosaic setup. This section discusses how to configure the window position, default colors, and your default home page.

Setting the Window Position. As with all X-Windows programs, the look and behavior of your window depends on the particular window manager program you are running. The default size for the main Mosaic window is 640 × 700 pixels. Your window manager might place the window automatically in position for you, or you might have to place it yourself.

You can specify the initial size and initial position of the main Mosaic window by using the `-geometry` command-line argument. A example of its use is as follows:

```
% Mosaic -geometry 700x740+50+30 &
```

`700 x 740` specifies the width and height of the window. In this example, the width is 700 pixels and the height is 740 pixels. `+50+30` gives the *offsets* of the starting position of the window; the first number is the *X offset* and the second number is the *Y offset.*

A + character tells Mosaic to measure the offset from either the left or top edge of the screen, depending on whether the parameter is the X or Y offset. Similarly, a - character tells Mosaic to measure the offset from the right or bottom edge of the screen. In the preceding example, the X offset is 50 pixels from the left edge of the screen, and the Y offset is 30 pixels from the top.

Setting the Colors. Mosaic is configured with default color settings for both monochrome and color displays. It tries to determine the type of display you're using and set the colors accordingly. If you ever need to specify monochrome or color operation manually, you can use the `-mono` or `-color` command line parameter when you start Mosaic. These parameters, respectively, force Mosaic to use its default color scheme for a monochrome or color display.

Mosaic automatically sets the foreground color to either black or white, depending on the darkness of the background color. You can manually set the background color by using `-bg` *`color`*, where *color* is a valid color on your system. You can set the foreground to black or white by using `-fg` *`color`*, where *color* is either `Black` or `White`.

Setting the Default Home Page. The *default home page* is the home page that Mosaic brings up when the program starts. If you don't specify a different page, Mosaic defaults to the home page at **www.ncsa.uiuc.edu**.

There are a couple of ways to change your home page. One of the easiest is to use the `-home` *`pagename`* command-line parameter, where *pagename* is the URL for the home page you want as the default.

Another way is to use the `WWW_HOME` environment variable. After you set this variable to the URL of a home page, Mosaic uses it as your home page. The value assigned to the `WWW_HOME` variable is valid until you change it, or until you log out of the session where you set it. You can put it in your shell's startup script to have Mosaic always start with that home page.

Browsing: Navigating with Mosaic

Now that you've installed and configured Mosaic to your liking, you're just about ready to start crawling around the Web. Take a look at the Mosaic interface, and check out a few of its features that help you navigate the Internet.

When you start Mosaic, assuming that you haven't changed the home page, you'll see the default home page at **www.ncsa.uiuc.edu**. Figure 32.1 shows Mosaic with the default Web page loaded.

> **Caution**
>
> The NCSA Web server is very busy. When you try to connect to the default home page, you might get an error message saying that your connection timed out or that Mosaic could not contact the host.

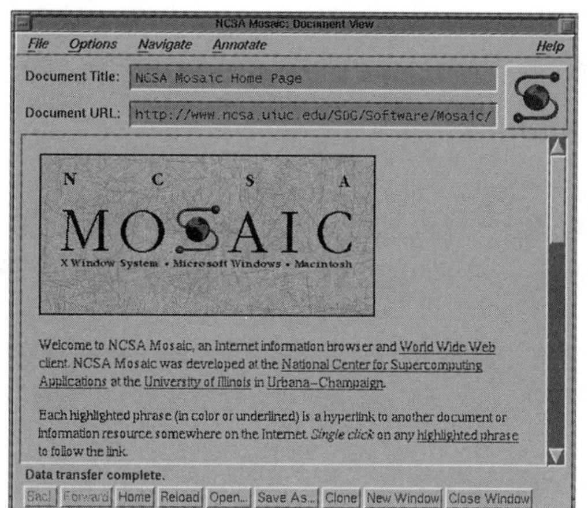

Fig. 32.1

This is the default home page for Mosaic.

The Mosaic Interface. It's important to make a distinction between the Mosaic interface and the document that Mosaic is displaying. The Mosaic interface consists of the menu bar at the top of the window, the Document Title window, the Document URL window, the "spinning globe" activity indicator, the scroll bar on the side of the window, and the status panel and control panel buttons at the bottom. The center section of the window is for displaying documents and error messages.

The Document Title window displays the title of the page currently displayed in the window. The Document URL window displays the URL for this page. The activity indicator to the right of these two windows shows a globe. The globe spins whenever Mosaic is busy retrieving data. If you want to stop an operation such as retrieving a document, click the activity indicator.

The scroll bar at the right allows you to scroll up or down through the document. The status panel at the bottom of the window shows what Mosaic is doing currently. It also displays the URLs associated with hyperlinks in a document as you move the mouse over the hyperlinks.

You use the control panel buttons at the bottom of the window to help you navigate through the Web, as well as to open and save documents. Clicking Back moves you to the last page you were on. After you have moved back, you can move forward to the page you just left by clicking Forward. Clicking Home returns you to your home page.

Tip

If you get lost anywhere on the Web, just click Home and you'll go directly to your home page.

Clicking Reload causes Mosaic to load the current page again. This feature is useful if you ever get an error—or your connection times out—while trying to load a page. The Open and Save As buttons, respectively, allow you to open URLs and save the current document to your local disk. The Clone button opens another Mosaic window with the same document displayed. The New Window button brings up a new window displaying your home page. Finally, the Close Window button closes the current Mosaic window.

Navigating. Moving around in Mosaic is easy. To move to a new page that has a hyperlink, just click the hyperlink; Mosaic opens the URL associated with it. To find out the URL associated with a particular hyperlink, position your mouse over the hyperlink; Mosaic displays the URL in the status panel at the bottom of the window.

If you want to go to a location without using a hyperlink, choose File, Open URL (or click Open on the control panel). Type the URL of the intended destination in the dialog box, and press Enter.

If you are using Mosaic over a SLIP or PPP link, you might want to turn off *image loading* to speed up your session. Normally, Mosaic loads the images that are part of a document when the page is displayed. Figure 32.2 shows a Web page with images displayed.

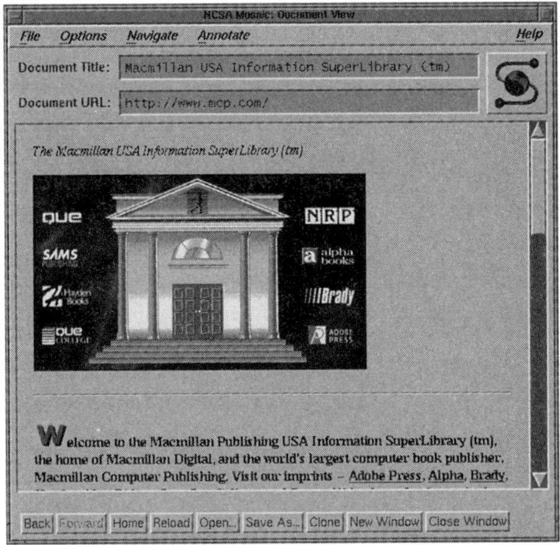

Fig. 32.2

A Web page with images displayed.

Unfortunately, although spiffy graphics look cool, they also take a long time to load over a slow modem link. You can tell Mosaic not to load graphics automatically, by choosing Options, Delay Image Loading. *Delayed image loading* causes Mosaic to display a generic icon in place of each image that normally would be displayed. Figure 32.3 shows a Web page with delayed image loading.

If you decide that you want to see the images for a particular page, choose Options, Load Images In Current.

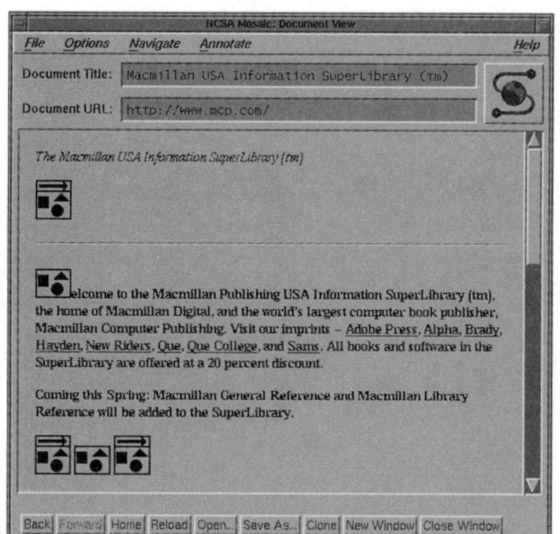

Fig. 32.3

A Web page with delayed image loading.

Like all good Web browsers, Mosaic supports formats such as Gopher and FTP in addition to HTML. The way the information is displayed in Mosaic is somewhat different for Gopher and FTP sites than it is for HTML Web pages. Figure 32.4 shows a Mosaic session connected to a Gopher server.

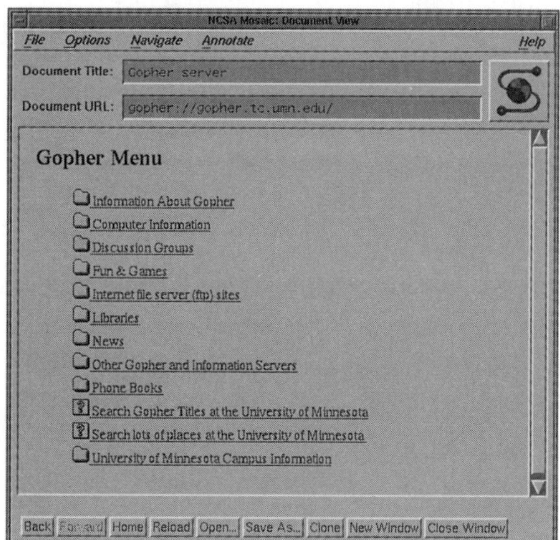

Fig. 32.4

This shows Mosaic connected to a Gopher server.

When you use Mosaic to perform anonymous FTP, you often will want to store files to your local disk instead of displaying them in the Mosaic window. Choose Options, Load To Local Disk to tell Mosaic to save a document to your local disk. Make sure that you deselect this option after you finish storing the file. Figure 32.5 shows an anonymous FTP session conducted by Mosaic.

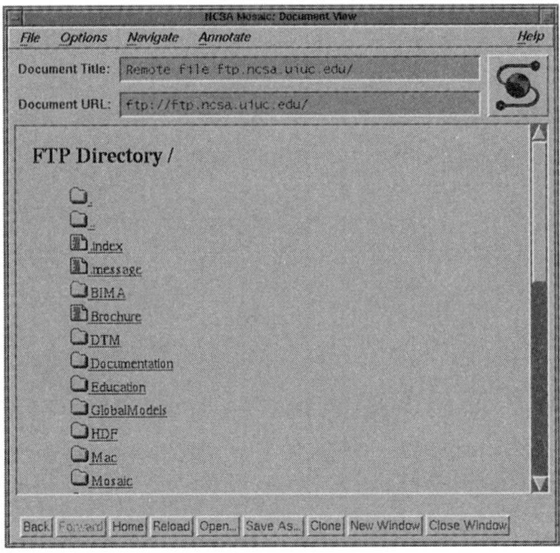

Fig. 32.5

This shows Mosaic performing an anonymous FTP operation.

Hotlists. As you move around the Web, you'll find places that you want to remember so you can visit them again. Instead of writing down the URL of a particularly good Web page, you can take advantage of Mosaic's *hotlist* feature.

A hotlist is a list of URLs you frequently visit. Whenever you find a Web page you like, you can add it to your hotlist. In the future, when you select that page from your hotlist, Mosaic takes you directly there.

Assume that you've navigated to a page on the Internet that you want to come back to often—for example, the Web server for Macmillan Computer Publishing at **http://www.mcp.com**. To add this page to your hotlist, choose Navigate, Add Current To Hotlist.

To use the hotlist to navigate, display it by choosing Navigate, Hotlist. Click to select a page in your hotlist and click Go To. This tells Mosaic to connect to the selected URL.

Several options on the hotlist dialog box allow you to manage your hotlist. You can add the current page to the hotlist, delete an entry, edit a page's title entry in the hotlist, or mail your hotlist to someone else. Using the hotlist to keep track of your favorite places makes it easy for you to navigate the Internet.

Using Netscape Navigator

Mosaic is not the only Web browser available to you. There are several other browser programs, both free and commercial, that you can try if you determine that Mosaic is not exactly what you're looking for. One such Web browser is Netscape Navigator.

What is Netscape Navigator?

Netscape Navigator, often referred to as Netscape, is a commercial Internet browser developed by Netscape Communications Corporation. Netscape provides several enhanced features not found in other Web clients. The program was designed to provide fast access over dialup phone links, and uses on-screen icons and tool bars that store commonly used commands and Web pages. In addition to providing support for other information services, such as Gopher and FTP, Netscape includes a built-in USENET news reader.

One of the interesting features of Netscape is its integrated security features. Netscape has a built-in data security system that protects sensitive information via data encryption. This system works in conjunction with certain Web servers that understand the security protocols built into Netscape.

Where Can You Get Netscape Navigator?

You can get the Netscape software via anonymous FTP from **ftp.mcom.com** in the `/netscape/unix` directory. There is a binary version available for Linux, along with a copy of the current usage license and a `README` file that tells how to install the software.

How To Get the Commercial License

Currently, Netscape Communications Corporation's license for Netscape allows students, faculty, and staff of educational institutions—and employees of non-profit organizations—to use Netscape for free. If you don't fall into one of these categories, you have to purchase the software. You may use it free for an evaluation period, while you are deciding whether to purchase it. For more information about Netscape, including current pricing information, contact Netscape Communications Corporation at 415-528-2555 or via e-mail at **sales@netscape.com**.

From Here...

The World Wide Web is a wonderful way to explore the Internet and tap its vast resources. There are a variety of Web browsers available, as free software or as commercial products. Using a Web browser such as Mosaic or Netscape Navigator makes it easy to surf the Net and find the information you need. You can learn more about the Web and the Internet in the following chapters:

- Chapter 27, "Understanding the Internet," provides an overview of the Internet and its basic services.
- Chapter 29, "Surfing the Internet," shows you how to locate information on the Internet.
- Chapter 33, "Creating Web Documents with HTML," gives an introduction to the HyperText Markup Language that is used to create pages for the Web.

CHAPTER 33

Creating Web Documents with HTML

In Chapter 32, "Using the World Wide Web," you learned how to access the World Wide Web, and were introduced to the various types of information that are available. You can click hypertext links and zip from place to place as fast as you can move your mouse. You can see Web pages with spiffy graphics and sound, lists, forms, and all sorts of neat stuff. But how do you actually create a Web page that other Web users can get to? It's not really as difficult as you might think. All you need is access to a Web server that uses the HTTP protocol, and a set of documents that are written in *HyperText Markup Language (HTML).*

This chapter looks at HTML to see what is involved in writing Web pages using HTML. The following topics are covered in this chapter:

- What is HTML?
- Working with HTML
- Document formatting tags
- Anchors and hypertext links
- Using graphics

What is HTML?

HTML is the language used to develop Web pages and documents. It is a subset of *Standard Generalized Markup Language (SGML)*. HTML, instead of being a conventional programming language, consists of special ASCII tags that are embedded in an ASCII document. These tags are interpreted by Web browser programs, which format and display documents.

HTML thus tells Web browsers how to display Web documents; however, the format information that HTML provides is pretty general. Remember that many different Web browsers are available on the Internet. Many run under graphical interfaces such as the X Windows System or MS Windows. Some, such as Lynx, are ANSI browsers and are limited in terms of which graphical characteristics they can display.

Note

There are several commercial Internet Web browsers that have become very popular. Since we are not in the practice of recommending any specific commercial software, all references to specific Web browsers in this chapter refer to the NCSA Mosaic browser, which can be obtained at no cost.

As you write HTML documents, therefore, remember that they will look different depending on which browser the reader is using. All the available Web browsers try to format HTML documents as properly as possible, but you can't depend on users using a particular browser like Mosaic for the X Windows System or Netscape for Macintosh when they view your page!

Working with HTML

HTML is easy to work with. Because it's an ASCII-based markup language, all you really need is an editor that will let you save files in ASCII format, and a Web browser that you can use to view your Web pages as you develop them. You don't need a network connection to develop Web documents. Any Web browser should let you open a local HTML file and view it just as if you had retrieved it from the Internet.

Before you go any further into the syntax of HTML, take a look at a Web page and its HTML source code. Figure 33.1 shows one of the most frequently visited pages on the Web: the Mosaic home page at NCSA.

Fig. 33.1

This is the Mosaic home page.

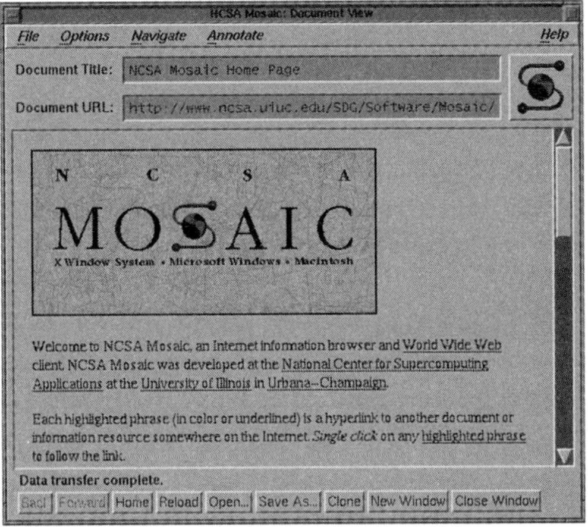

Now, take a look at the HTML for this page. It's easy to see the HTML source code for a Web page. Because a Web browser interprets HTML source code when it gets a page from a Web server, you can tell your Web browser to show you the HTML source code for the page—this is usually done using a menu choice in your browser program. For example, to see a page's HTML source code under Mosaic, choose File, View Source.

Listing 33.1 shows the HTML source code for the Mosaic home page, located at **http://www.ncsa.uiuc.edu/SDG/Software/Mosaic/**.

Listing 33.1 HTML source code for the Mosaic home page

```
<HTML>
<HEAD>
<TITLE>NCSA Mosaic Home Page</TITLE>
</HEAD>

<BODY>
<P ALIGN=CENTER>
<IMG SRC="Images/mosaic.gif" ALT="NCSA Mosaic Image"
WIDTH=383 HEIGHT=179> </P>
<BR>
Welcome to NCSA Mosaic, an Internet information browser and <A
HREF="http://www.w3.org/hypertext/WWW/TheProject.html">World Wide Web</A>
client.  NCSA Mosaic was developed at the <A
HREF="http://www.ncsa.uiuc.edu/General/NCSAHome.html">National Center for
Supercomputing Applications</A> at the <A
HREF="http://www.uiuc.edu/">
University of Illinois</A> in <A
HREF="http://www.prairienet.org/SiliconPrairie/ccnet.html">
Urbana-Champaign</A>.  NCSA Mosaic software is
<A HREF="copyright.html">copyrighted </A>
by The Board of Trustees of the University of Illinois (UI), and
ownership remains with the UI.

<P>

Each highlighted phrase (in color or underlined) is a hyperlink to
another document or information resource somewhere on the Internet.
<i>Single click</i> on any <A HREF="SampleLink.html">highlighted
phrase</A> to follow the link.  <P>

<H2>NCSA Mosaic Flavors</H2>

NCSA Mosaic comes in three flavors.  The most recent version number
follows each hyperlink.
<P>

<UL>
<LI> <A HREF="/SDG/Software/XMosaic/">
NCSA Mosaic for the X Window System</A> (v2.7b2)

<LI> <A HREF="/SDG/Software/MacMosaic/MacMosaicHome.html">
NCSA Mosaic for the Apple Macintosh</A> (v2.0.1)

<LI> <A HREF="/SDG/Software/WinMosaic/HomePage.html">
NCSA Mosaic for Microsoft Windows</A> (v2.0.0)
</UL>

<H2>Starting Points</H2>
```

(continues)

Listing 33.1 Continued

```
The following resources are available to help introduce you to
cyberspace and keep track of its growth:

<UL>
<LI> A <A HREF="Glossary/index.html">glossary</A> of World Wide Web
terms and acronyms

<LI> An
<A HREF="Docs/web-index.html">
INDEX</A> to Mosaic related documents

<LI><A HREF= "http://bucky.aa.uic.edu">NCSA Mosaic Access Page</A> for
persons with disabilities

<LI> Mosaic and WWW related <A HREF="Docs/web-index.html#Tutorials">
Tutorials</A>

<LI><A HREF="MetaIndex.html">Internet Resources Meta-Index</A> at NCSA

<LI>Suggested <A
HREF="http://www.ncsa.uiuc.edu/SDG/Software/Mosaic/StartingPoints/
NetworkStartingPoints.html"
>Starting Points for Internet Exploration</A>

<LI><A HREF="Docs/whats-new.html">What's New</A> with NCSA Mosaic and
     the Internet

</UL>

<H2>Special Notices</H2>

<UL>
<LI>
<A HREF="/WebSGML/WebSGML.html"> SGML on the Web</A> and the first
<A HREF="http://www.oclc.org:5046/oclc/research/panorama/panorama.html">
SGML Web Browser, Panorama</A>

<LI><A HREF="http://jeeves.ncsa.uiuc.edu/Public/IW3C2/">World Wide Web
Conference Information</A>

<LI>NCSA's <A HREF="/General/VRML/VRMLHome.html"> VRML</A> home page

<LI> How to <A HREF="Docs/change-your-home-page.html">change your
home page</A>

<LI> NCSA Mosaic has been winning <a href="Awards/MosaicAwards.html">
awards!
</a>

<LI>NCSA Mosaic Source Code <A HREF="License/LicenseInfo.html">
Licensing Information </A>

</UL>
```

```
<H2>Feedback</H2>

If you have questions or comments concerning NCSA Mosaic, send
e-mail to one of the following addresses: <P>

<UL>
<LI> <b><A HREF="mailto:mosaic@ncsa.uiuc.edu">mosaic@ncsa.uiuc.edu
➥</A></b>
- General information relevant to all Mosaic platforms.
<LI> <b><A HREF="mailto:mosaic-w@ncsa.uiuc.edu">mosaic-w@ncsa.uiuc.edu
➥</A></b>
- Mosaic for Microsoft Windows help
<LI> <b><A HREF="mailto:mosaic-m@ncsa.uiuc.edu">mosaic-m@ncsa.uiuc.edu
➥</A></b>
- Mosaic for Macintosh help
<LI> <b><A HREF="mailto:mosaic-x@ncsa.uiuc.edu">mosaic-x@ncsa.uiuc.edu
➥</A></b>
- Mosaic for the X Windows System
</UL>

<hr>
<ADDRESS>
<A HREF="mailto:mosaic@ncsa.uiuc.edu">mosaic@ncsa.uiuc.edu</A><BR>
<A HREF="http://www.ncsa.uiuc.edu/">
National Center for Supercomputing Applications</A><BR>
<A HREF="http://www.uiuc.edu/">
The University of Illinois at Urbana/Champaign</A>
</ADDRESS>
<P>
Last Modified: July 31, 1995
</BODY>
</HTML>
```

Don't panic! It's not as bad as it looks. HTML is really pretty simple and the syntax won't give you any great headache. You'll notice that in Listing 33.1 there are a lot of items between < and > characters. These items make up most of the HTML-specific entries in the file.

Tip

The <> character combination is often referred to as *angle brackets*.

The basic syntax of HTML is made up of three components: tags, attributes, and URLs. These components, respectively, give the details of how items are to be formatted and displayed, the specifics of certain actions, and the locations of other files and documents.

Tags

Tags are the basic building blocks of HTML. They are the part of HTML that tells Web browsers how to display text and graphics, along with other format information. Tags usually are written between angle brackets. Most tags consist of a *starting tag* and an *ending tag*, which surround the text to be formatted. The first line of the NCSA Mosaic home page shows an example of a starting and ending tag.

```
<TITLE>NCSA Mosaic Home Page</TITLE>
```

This line says to format the text string `NCSA Mosaic Home Page` as a `<TITLE>`. Don't worry about what `<TITLE>` means at the moment—the chapter looks at specific tags in detail a little later.

Notice that there are two tags, `<TITLE>` and `</TITLE>`, in this line. These are starting and ending tags, respectively. The ending tag looks just like the starting tag, except that it has the slash (/) character after the first angle bracket.

Attributes

Sometimes, tags need to specify exact information, such as where a file is located. *Attributes* are used with tags to provide more detail about how the tag is to be implemented. For example, consider the following tag:

```
<IMG SRC="mosaic.gif">
```

This tag, taken from the NCSA Mosaic home page, is an `<IMG>` tag that tells your Web browser to display a graphic image. But which image? That's where the attribute comes in. In this example, the attribute field is `SRC="mosaic.gif"`. This gives detailed information about how the `<IMG>` tag is to be interpreted—the `mosaic.gif` file is to be displayed as the image.

URLs

Resources on the Web are accessed by a descriptive address known as a *uniform resource locator (URL)*. Everything that you access on the Web has a URL. HTML uses URLs to specify the location of needed files or of other Web pages that are connected by hypertext links.

HTML Syntax

As you have seen, HTML breaks down into three basic components: tags, attributes, and URLs. Of these, the basic building block is the tag. Tags are used to give commands to a Web browser, while attributes and URLs are used to provide details about the commands. Tags can be grouped into several categories, depending on their function. Some tags give information about the document as a whole, some are used for formatting text, and some are used for graphics and hypertext links to other documents.

Document Information Tags

The tags that fall into the document information category provide information about a document to Web browsers. This information includes things like where the header or body of the document should start and end, the document title, or even the fact that the Web document is written in HTML. Most Web browsers do not require every one of these tags to be present. In fact, if you review the NCSA Mosaic home page in Listing 33.1, you'll see that most of these tags are not included. You should, however, include them in any Web pages that you write. Standards for HTML are being written, and these tags may very well become a requirement in the future.

The <HTML> and </HTML> tags are used to tell a Web browser that the document it is processing is written in HTML. The <HTML> tag should be the first tag in your document, and the </HTML> tag should be the last.

HTML documents are divided into a header and a body section. The header contains information about the document, and the body contains the document information itself. As you may have guessed, the header section is surrounded by the <HEAD> and </HEAD> tags, while the body is surrounded by the <BODY> and </BODY> tags. There are several tags that can be placed in the header section, but currently only the <TITLE> tag is widely used. The document title—whatever is bracketed by the <TITLE> and </TITLE> tags—appears in the title window of a Web browser.

Note

Because the document title is displayed in a separate window and is not part of the document itself, the title must be plain text and not have any hyperlinks or text formatting. You should make the title descriptive and keep its length below 64 characters.

Text Formatting Tags

HTML provides several different ways to format text for display. Remember that the actual formatting of the text in your Web page is controlled by the Web browser used to view the page.

HTML supports six levels of headings that can be displayed in a document by using the <H1> through <H6> tags. Remember that these headings are displayed differently on different browsers.

Note

It usually is a good idea to use only heading level 1 through heading level 3 in a Web document. If you need more than three levels of headings, consider using additional pages.

At this point, you know enough HTML to start writing a simple HTML document. Listing 33.2 shows a simple HTML sample that uses the tags discussed so far.

Listing 33.2 A simple HTML page

```
<HTML>
<HEAD>
<TITLE>My First Sample HTML Page</TITLE>
</HEAD>
<BODY>
<H1>This is a Level 1 heading</H1>
<H2>This is a Level 2 heading</H2>
<H3>This is a Level 3 heading
</H3>
This is plain text
</BODY>
</HTML>
```

Take a look at the location of the level 2 heading tags and the level 3 heading tags. HTML doesn't care if the tags are at the end of the line, or where they occur. These tags just tell the browser that all the text between them is in the particular heading level that they define. Also, notice that the line `This is plain text` has no tags around it. This line will be displayed as generic text by a browser. Figure 33.2 shows this HTML sample as displayed by Mosaic.

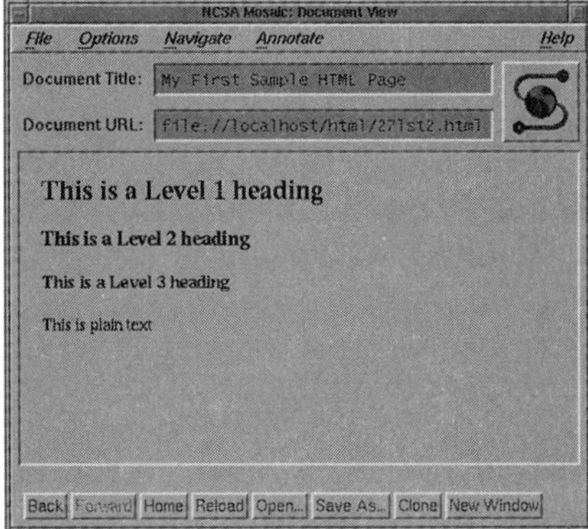

Fig. 33.2

Simple HTML page displayed in Mosaic.

Besides the heading tags, HTML gives you several ways to format normal text in your documents. For one thing, Web browsers completely ignore where the text lines end in your HTML file. Carriage returns also are ignored, so you have to use special tags to indicate where line breaks and paragraphs are to begin.

The `<BR>` tag causes the browser that is displaying your document to insert a line break. Think of this as inserting a carriage return at that point in the line. Subsequent text is moved down to the next line, and placed flush against the left margin.

If you want to create a new paragraph, use the `<P>` tag instead. This has the same effect as the `<BR>` tag, except that most browsers insert a blank line as part of a paragraph break, to visually separate one block of text from another. Because the browsers control the text display, the actual behavior of the <P> tag can vary. With the <P> tag, you do not need a </P> ending tag, as this tag does not bracket any text.

At times you'll want to visually separate different sections of the same page. To do so, HTML provides a way to draw a horizontal line across the document display. The <HR> tag, which stands for *horizontal rule*, is used to draw a horizontal line. It inserts a paragraph break before the line so you don't need the <P> tag. As with the <P> tag, no ending tag is needed for <HR>.

You have looked at several ways to control the format of text in an HTML page. Take a look at another short HTML sample and see the effect of line breaks, paragraph marks, and horizontal rules on the text display. Listing 33.3 shows an HTML sample that uses these formatting tags.

Listing 33.3 An HTML sample showing basic text formatting

```
<HTML>
<HEAD>
<TITLE>A Sample Text Formatting Page</TITLE>
</HEAD>
<BODY>
<H2>Text Sample 1</H2>
Here is some sample text
that is written on separate
lines
without using line breaks. <P>
<H2>Text Sample 2</H2>
This sample text has a <BR>
line break in the middle.<P>
<H2>Text Sample 3</H2>
Text before a paragraph mark.<P>
Text after a paragraph mark.<HR>
Text after a horizontal rule mark.
</BODY>
</HTML>
```

Figure 33.3 shows this sample displayed in Mosaic.

Suppose that you want to display some text, such as a table, and that you want the carriage returns and spacing to be kept exactly as you entered them. You can use the <PRE> and </PRE> tags to define preformatted text. Any text that you surround with these tags gets displayed in a monospace font, and all returns and spaces get used exactly as entered.

You can define to some degree the way text is displayed. HTML provides tags that tell browsers to display text in bold, underline, or italic. These tags are known as *physical styles*. The tags for bold face text are <B> and </B>, the tags for underline are <U> and </U>, and the tags for italic are <I> and </I>. Surround the text that you want to format with the starting and ending tag of the style that you want. You cannot combine styles. Only one style at a time can be applied to text. HTML also provides some *logical styles* for formatting text. The <EM> and </EM> tags are used to mark emphasized text. This style is usually shown in italic. The <STRONG> and </STRONG> tags are used to indicate stronger emphasis. This style is usually shown in bold. In general, you should use the logical styles whenever possible.

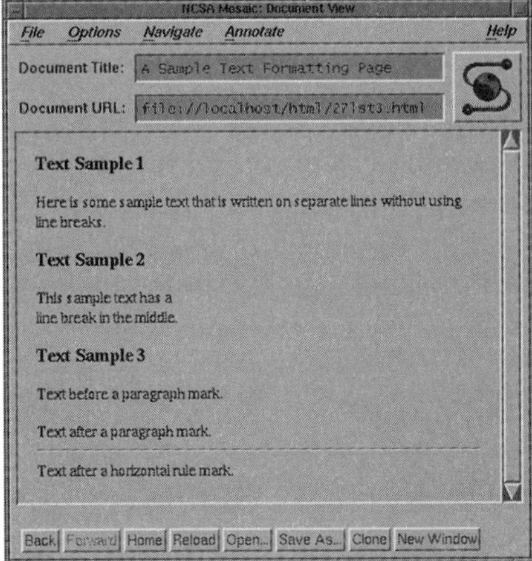

Fig. 33.3

HTML text formatting displayed in Mosaic.

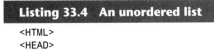

Two formatting tags that don't fit in with other categories of tags are the <ADDRESS> and </ADDRESS> tags. These tags are used to mark addresses, signatures, and so on, within a document. Typically, text with this format is placed at the end of a document, following a horizontal rule mark. The exact formatting of <ADDRESS> text is determined by the individual Web browser.

Organizing Information with Lists

Sometimes you need to deliver information that is logically grouped in some fashion. For example, you might have a list of graphic images to display, or you might want to show a numbered "Top 10" list. HTML provides several different ways to format and display lists of information. Using lists in HTML is a powerful way to deliver information, because the user's Web browser formats all the text in the list in a consistent manner. All you have to do is to decide how the information fits together.

Unordered Lists. An *unordered list* is a list of text displayed separately with a bullet or other formatting character. Each text entry in an unordered list can be several lines long.

Two sets of tags are used to create an unordered list. The <UL> and </UL> tags define the beginning and end of the list, and the <LI> tag is used to mark each list item. Listing 33.4 shows the HTML source for a simple unordered list. Figure 33.4 shows how this list is displayed in Mosaic.

Listing 33.4 An unordered list

```
<HTML>
<HEAD>
```

```
<TITLE>An Unordered List</TITLE>
</HEAD>
<BODY>
<UL>
<LI>This is list item 1.
<LI>This is list item 2.
<LI>This is list item 3.
</UL>
</BODY>
</HTML>
```

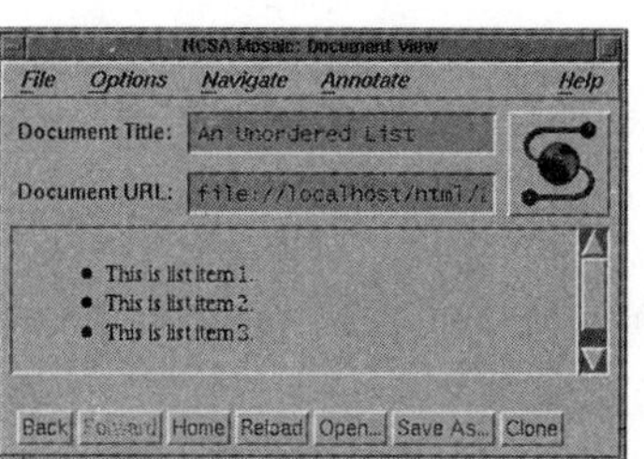

Fig. 33.4

An unordered list viewed in Mosaic.

Ordered Lists. An *ordered list* presents list information in numerical order. Each time a new list item is identified, the number of the list item is incremented. Ordered lists are defined by the <OL> and </OL> tags, and the same <LI> tag used in unordered lists is also used in ordered lists to mark each list item. Listing 33.5 shows the HTML source for a simple ordered list. Figure 33.5 shows how this list is displayed in Mosaic.

Listing 33.5 An ordered list

```
<HTML>
<HEAD>
<TITLE>An Ordered List</TITLE>
</HEAD>
<BODY>
<OL>
<LI>This is list item 1.
<LI>This is list item 2.
<LI>This is list item 3.
</OL>
</BODY>
</HTML>
```

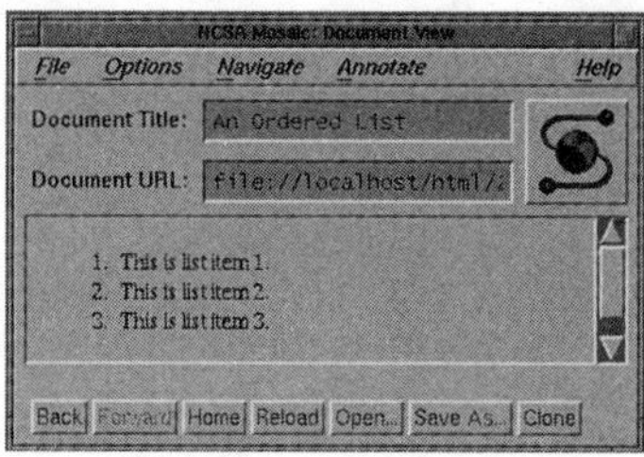

Fig. 33.5

An ordered list viewed in Mosaic.

Glossary Lists. Think of how a glossary in a book looks: You typically have each word or term offset by itself, and then a paragraph giving its definition. HTML *glossary lists* give you a way to do this with your Web pages. A glossary list consists of a *term*—this can be one word or a series of words—followed by a *definition*. The definition is usually a text explanation.

Although glossary lists are particularly useful for glossaries, you can use them to present any kind of information where you need a title and an explanation. One common use is to make the glossary term a hypertext link to another document, and make the definition a description of the linked document. The creation of hypertext links is discussed later in this chapter, so keep this application of a glossary list in mind.

Glossary lists require the `<DL>` and `</DL>` tags to mark the start and end of the list. Instead of a simple list item tag, glossary lists use dual tags: `<DT>` to mark the glossary item, and `<DD>` to mark the definition. Listing 33.6 shows the HTML source for a simple glossary list. Figure 33.6 shows how this list is displayed in Mosaic.

Listing 33.6 A simple glossary list

```
<HTML>
<HEAD>
<TITLE>A Simple Glossary List</TITLE>
</HEAD>
<BODY>
<DL>
<DT>Item 1
<DD>This is the definition field for list item 1.
<DT>Item 2
<DD>This is the definition field for list item 2.
<DT>Item 3
<DD>This is the definition field for list item 3.
</DL>
</BODY>
</HTML>
```

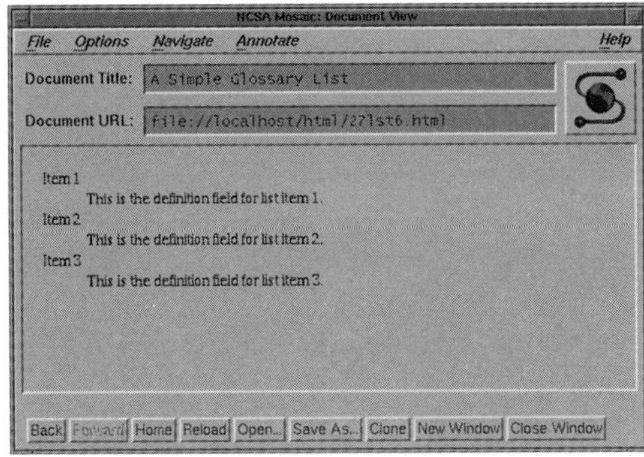

Fig. 33.6

A simple glossary list viewed in Mosaic.

Combining Lists. As you can see, the various lists in HTML give you several ways to present information to a user. In fact, HTML allows you to combine list types to get even more control over how your information is presented. You can nest one list type within another easily.

Suppose that you want to create a section of your home page to tell users your favorite movies and music. You can nest two glossary lists within an unordered list to create a detailed outline. Listing 33.7 shows the HTML source for an example using this type of nesting.

Listing 33.7 Creating a custom list by nesting different list types

```
<HTML>
<HEAD>
<TITLE>A Custom List</TITLE>
</HEAD>
<BODY>
This list shows some of my favorite musicians and movies.
It uses a two glossary lists nested in an unordered list.
It also uses some text formatting tags.<P>
I hope that you enjoy it.<HR>
<UL>
<LI>Here are some of my favorite movies<P>
 <DL>
 <DT>Hopscotch
 <DD>This is a wonderful film about an ex-CIA agent traveling the world
 writing his memoirs
 <DT>Highlander
 <DD>An action adventure about a battle between immortals.
 "There can be only one!"
 </DL>
<P>
<LI>Here are some of my musical groups<P>
 <DL>
 <DT>Tannahill Weavers
 <DD>One of the best Scottish folk bands around.
 <DT>Altan
 <DD>A high energy Irish folk band.
 <DT>Jimmy Buffet
 <DD>Folk hero of parrot-heads everywhere.
 </DL>
</UL>
</BODY>
</HTML>
```

This example is a bit more complicated than the others you have seen, but it still uses only techniques covered so far in this chapter. Notice that the glossary lists are indented in the HTML source code. This is only to make the source code easier to read; recall that Web browsers ignore line breaks and extra spaces when they display the page. Figure 33.7 shows how this page is displayed in Mosaic.

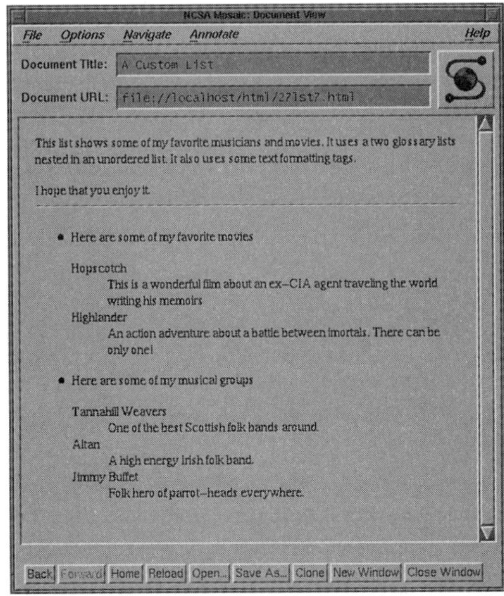

Fig. 33.7

A custom list viewed in Mosaic.

Linking Pages with Anchors

Now comes the neat stuff. This is where you learn how to hook multiple Web pages together and create hypertext links that jump from place to place.

Hypertext links in HTML are known as *anchors*, and the `<A>` and `</A>` tags are used to define an anchor. These tags are placed around the words you want to use for the hypertext link. Web browsers typically underline hypertext links and show them in a different color.

How do you tell the Web browser which document to retrieve when the hypertext link is clicked? It's simple. You use the `HREF` attribute and a URL along with the anchor tag. For example, suppose that you want to create a hypertext link to the NCSA Mosaic home page. If you want to include the sentence `Click` **`here`** `to go to the NCSA Mosaic home page.` where the word **`here`** is the hypertext link, you need the following HTML lines:

```
Click <A HREF="http://www.ncsa.uiuc.edu/SDG/Software/Mosaic/index.html">
here</A> to go to the NCSA Mosaic home page.
```

The anchor tags surround the hypertext link—in this case, the word `here`. The `HREF` attribute is inserted inside the opening anchor tag. That's all there is to it.

> **Note**
>
> Any URL can be placed in the `HREF` attribute. You can link to a Web page, FTP site, Gopher server, or any other location.

In addition to just creating hypertext links, you can also give names to links by using the NAME attribute. *Named links* are very useful for jumping to other locations in a document. You can give a table of contents at the beginning of a long document, and have each entry in the table of contents be a hypertext link to the appropriate place in the document.

Assume that you have a long document, maybe a Frequently Asked Questions (FAQ) list that discusses widgets. You can create a hypertext link from the table of contents to the "How to Use Widgets" section. The first thing you need to do is to create a named anchor in the "How to Use Widgets" section, so that you can jump to it from the table of contents. The HTML to do this looks like the following:

```
<A NAME="howtouse">How to Use Widgets</A>
Widgets are a very powerful tool if used properly.
Unfortunately, no one knows enough about them to use
them properly. Since they have no relevance to HTML, you
don't need to discuss them further in this chapter.
```

Now, all you need to do is to put a hypertext link from the table of contents to this spot. How do you do that? You use the HREF attribute to link to this anchor, and give the anchor's name preceded by a # character. The table of contents entry looks like this:

```
<A HREF="#howtouse">How to Use Widgets</A>
```

When someone clicks the entry **How to Use Widgets** in the table of contents, the browser jumps to the anchor named howtouse later in the document.

Note

You can name an anchor that is a hypertext link to another location. Just use both the NAME and HREF attributes in the same anchor.

Using Graphics

One feature that has made the Web so popular is its ability to incorporate graphics and text in a simple format. HTML makes it easy to insert graphics into your documents. Before you start putting all sorts of graphics images into documents, though, remember that many people access the Web via low-speed telephone lines, and graphics can take a long time to transfer at these rates. Also, a lot of people use text-based browsers, such as Lynx, which cannot display graphics at all. You should make sure that someone can navigate your Web documents easily, even if they have graphics turned off or if their browser does not support graphics. In a moment, you'll learn a technique for checking this.

There are two ways to use graphics in your HTML documents. You can make hypertext links to the graphics files themselves. This method requires the user to have a helper program that can display the graphics file properly. Links for this method are hypertext links that name the graphics image as the destination document.

The other method is to insert the graphics into your HTML document. Graphics inserted in this method are known as *inline images*. Currently, only graphics in the GIF or X Bitmap format can become inline images. HTML uses the `<IMG>` tag to indicate an inline image. This tag is typically combined with the `SRC="filename"` attribute to define which image file gets displayed. HTML also provides the `ALIGN=` attribute to tell Web browsers how they should line up the graphic image with any text that is near it. The valid values for `ALIGN` are `TOP`, `MIDDLE`, and `BOTTOM`.

As mentioned earlier, you need to make your Web pages usable by browsers that don't support graphics. To do this, you should provide some text reference any time you use a graphic image. HTML provides a way for you to define some text to be displayed if a browser cannot display a graphic image. The `ALT="Text"` attribute defines some alternate text that will be displayed when the graphic cannot be displayed.

An example might help pull this all together. Listing 33.8 is a section of HTML that displays an inline GIF image. If a browser can't display the image, then a description of the image is shown instead.

Listing 33.8 Inserting a graphic into your script

```
<HTML>
<HEAD>
<TITLE>Using Graphics</TITLE>
</HEAD>
<BODY>
Here is a picture of a statue by Michaelangelo.
<IMG SRC="statue.gif" ALIGN=BOTTOM ALT="[Photo of statue]">
</BODY>
</HTML>
```

Figure 33.8 shows how this page is displayed in Mosaic.

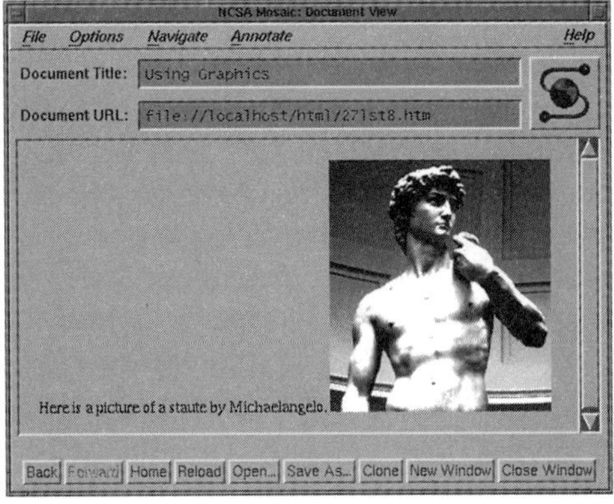

Fig. 33.8

An inline graphic displayed in Mosaic.

You can combine graphic images and anchors to create graphic hypertext links as well. Simply surround the `<IMG>` tag with anchor tags that define which document to load. A picture serves as a hypertext link to another HTML document in the following example:

```
Click the picture to find out more about this statue.
<A HREF="statue.html"><IMG SRC="statue.gif"
ALIGN=BOTTOM ALT="[Photo of statue]">
</A>
```

From Here...

This chapter provided an introduction to basic HTML and how to create a home page. You learned how to use tags, which provide commands to a Web browser, and how to use attributes and URLs, which provide details for the commands. You can find out more about the World Wide Web and the Internet in the following chapters:

- Chapter 27, "Understanding the Internet," provides a basic overview of the Internet.
- Chapter 29, "Surfing the Internet," gives an introduction to various Linux utilities that allow you to navigate the Internet.
- Chapter 32, "Using the World Wide Web," describes ways of navigating the Web under Linux.

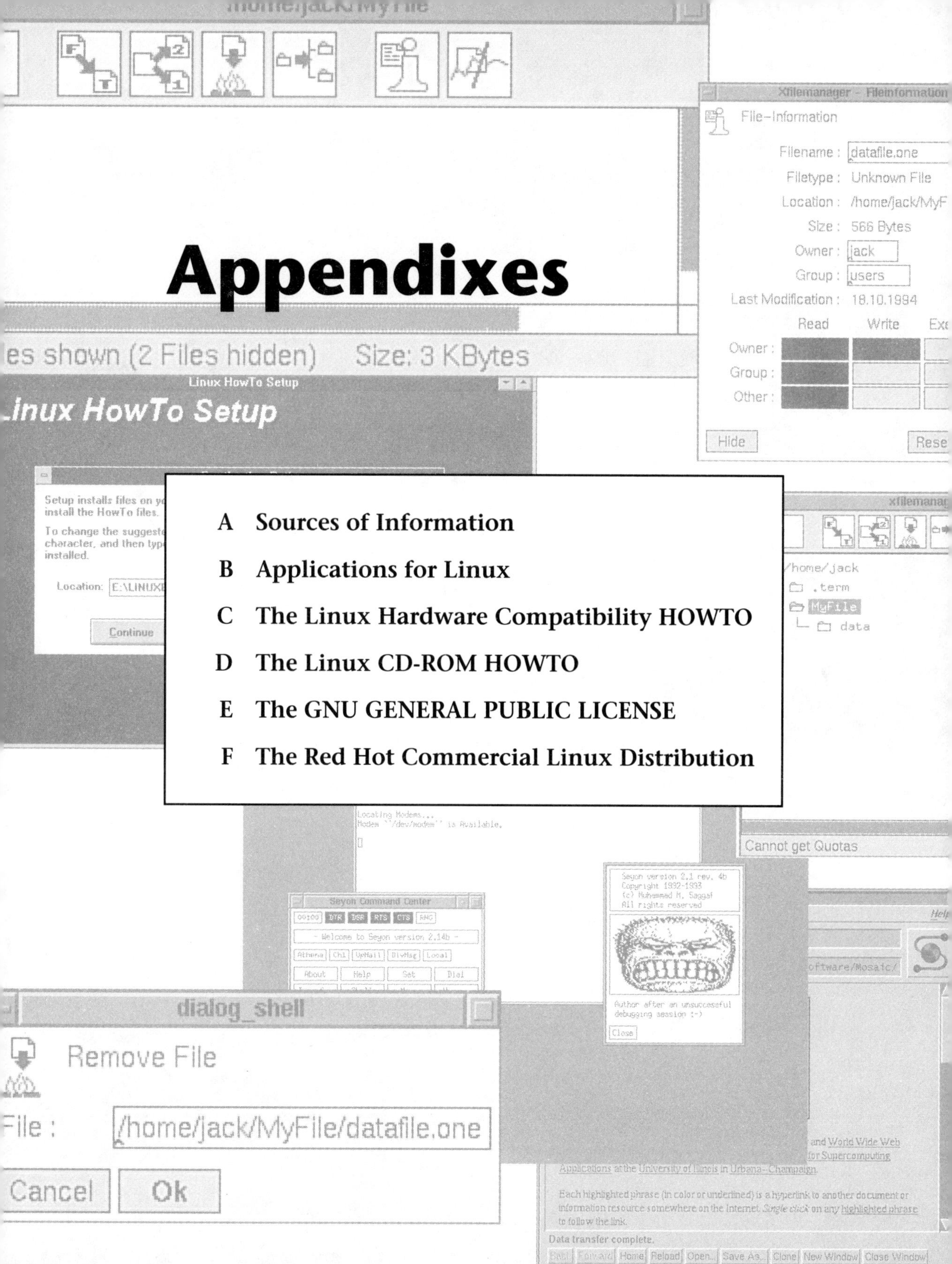

Appendixes

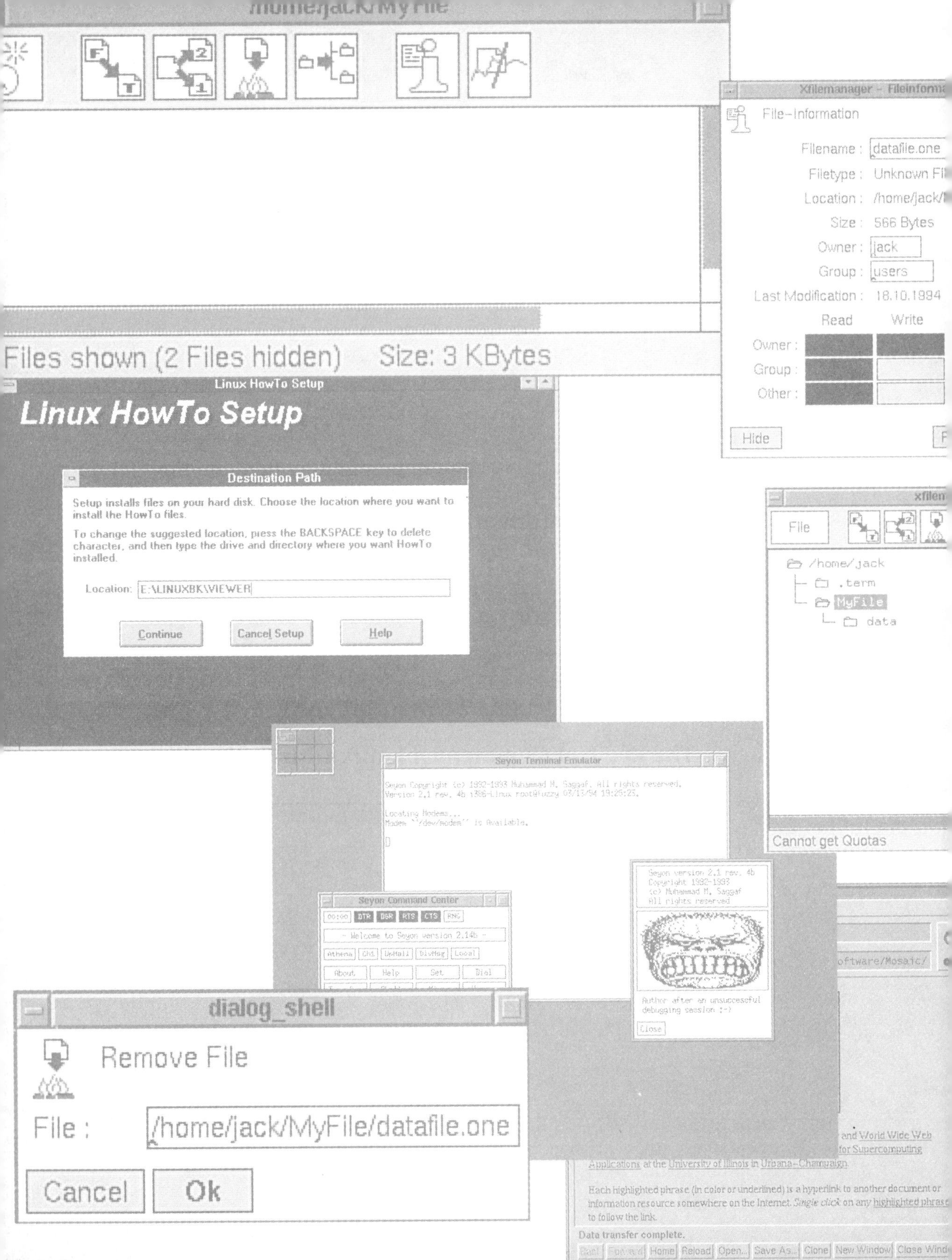
Files shown (2 Files hidden)
Size: 3 KBytes
Xfilemanager - Fileinforma
File-Information
Filename : datafile.one
Filetype : Unknown Fi
Location : /home/jack/
Size : 566 Bytes
Owner : jack
Group : users
Last Modification : 18.10.1994
Read
Write
Owner :
Group :
Other :
Hide
Linux HowTo Setup
Linux HowTo Setup
Destination Path
Setup installs files on your hard disk. Choose the location where you want to install the HowTo files.
To change the suggested location, press the BACKSPACE key to delete character, and then type the drive and directory where you want HowTo installed.
Location: E:\LINUXBK\VIEWER
Continue
Cancel Setup
Help
File
/home/jack
.term
MyFile
data
Cannot get Quotas
Seyon Terminal Emulator
Seyon Command Center
dialog_shell
Remove File
File : /home/jack/MyFile/datafile.one
Cancel
Ok
Data transfer complete.

APPENDIX A

Sources of Information

Because Linux is based on UNIX, almost any UNIX-based book provides some information on Linux. The best source for information, however, is the Linux community itself, which offers everything from updated versions of Linux to extremely active USENET newsgroups. Linux also provides online documents through the *Linux Documentation Project (LDP)*. The LDP is writing a complete set of manuals for Linux. The most recent editions of this project are available via the Internet. The entire project is spearheaded by Matt Welsh, and most of the information is provided in the **\usr\doc\faq** directory.

The following listings provide Internet FTP sites, magazines, and newsgroups from which you can gather more information about Linux.

USENET Newsgroups

If you have access to USENET newsgroups, you'll enjoy the following newsgroups that provide a variety of information about Linux. Only one, **comp.os.linux.announce**, is moderated.

◄◄ See "A USENET Glossary," p. 648

Note

The original Linux-related newsgroup, **comp.os.linux**, no longer exists, since more specific newsgroups have been created.

- **comp.os.linux.announce**—This newsgroup is moderated and used for important announcements like bug fixes.
- **comp.os.linux.answers**—This newsgroup provides answers to any of your Linux questions, especially about setting up Linux. Please read the appropriate Linux documentation and FAQs before posting a question to this group.

- **comp.os.linux.development.system**—This newsgroup is devoted to the many programmers around the world who are developing the Linux system. This group provides a shared communication medium.
- **comp.os.linux.development.apps**—This newsgroup is devoted to the many programmers around the world who are developing applications for Linux.
- **comp.os.linux.hardware**—This newsgroup provides answers to hardware compatibility questions.
- **comp.os.linux.setup**—This newsgroup provides help with Linux setup and installation problems.
- **comp.os.linux.advocacy**—This newsgroup provides a medium to discuss why Linux is the greatest OS.
- **comp.os.linux.networking**—This newsgroup provides answers to networking linux with the rest of the world.
- **comp.os.linux.setup**—This newsgroup provides answers for installing and setting up Linux.
- **comp.os.linux.x**—This newsgroup provides answers to installing and running X under Linux.

Tip

There is a newsgroup named **comp.os.linux.misc** that serves as a catchall for any Linux topic not suited to the other groups. Also, there are over 170 other USENET newsgroups containing the word Linux so you will find many, many more groups. Go exploring!

Online Documents

Matt Welsh spearheads a dedicated group of Linux enthusiasts who are systematically writing a complete set of Linux manuals available on the Internet. The latest versions of the documentation can be found at **sunsite.unc.edu** in the **\pub\Linux\docs** directory. You can also find earlier versions of these documents in your version of Linux's **\docs** directory. Available documents include the following:

- "Linux Installation and Getting Started," by Matt Welsh
- "The Linux System Administrators' Guide," by Lars Wirzenius
- "The Linux Network Administrators' Guide," by Olaf Kirch
- "The Linux Kernel Hackers' Guide," by Michael K. Johnson
- "The Linux Frequently Asked Questions (FAQ) List," maintained by Ian Jackson; it is composed of questions and answers on myriad topics
- "The Linux META-FAQ," maintained by Michael K. Johnson

- "The Linux INFO-SHEET," maintained by Michael K. Johnson
- "The Linux Software Map," maintained by Jeff Kopmanis

Linux HOWTOs

The *Linux HOWTO Index* provides an index to all the available *HOWTO documents*. These HOWTO documents provide a detailed explanation of their topic. Here are some of the titles:

- The Linux Installation HOWTO
- The Linux Distribution HOWTO
- The Linux XFree86 HOWTO
- The Linux Mail, News, and UUCP HOWTOs
- The Linux Hardware HOWTO
- The Linux SCSI HOWTO
- The Linux NET-2 HOWTO
- The Linux Ethernet HOWTO
- The Linux Printing HOWTO

These files are located in the **\usr\doc\faq\howto** directory. Most are archived with `gzip` to save disk space. To read these or other compressed files, enter the **zless** command.

Many FAQs about Linux topics and GNU programs are shipped with Linux and can be found in the **\usr\info** directory.

man Pages

The Linux operating system itself provides plenty of online help via the `man` command. To access online help, enter **`man`** followed by the topic for which you want information.

◂◂ See "man, Display Online Help" p. 107

Magazines

Linux Journal is currently the only periodical devoted explicitly to Linux. Here's where you can request more information about this publication:

Linux Journal
P.O. Box 85867
Seattle, WA 98145
(206) 527-3385

Appendixes

Linux FTP Sites

Linux is a child of the Internet, so naturally the Internet is where you find the greatest amount of up-to-date information regarding Linux. Table A.1 lists the FTP sites that maintain Linux archives. The main archive site is located at the University of North Carolina-Chapel Hill and is named **sunsite.unc.edu**.

◀◀ See "Using `ftp` for Remote File Transfer," p. 595

Table A.1 FTP Sites with Linux Archives

Site Name	Directory
tsx-11.mit.edu	\pub\linux
sunsite.unc.edu	\pub\Linux
nic.funet.fi	\pub\os\Linux
ftp.mcc.ac.uk	\pub\linux
fgb1.fgb.mw.tu-muenchen.de	\pub\linux
ftp.informatik.tu-muenchen.de	\pub\Linux
ftp.dfv.rwth-aachen.de	\pub\linux
ftp.informatik.rwth-aachen.de	\pub\Linux
ftp.ibp.fr	\pub\linux
kirk.bond.edu.au	\pub\os\Linux
ftp.uu.net	\systems\unix
wuarchive.wustl.edu	\systems\linux
ftp.win.tue.nl	\pub\linux
ftp.stack.urc.tue.nl	\pub\linux
ftp.ibr.cs.tu-bs.de	\pub\os\linux
ftp.denet.dk	\pub\os\linux

Linux Web Sites

Since Linux is a child of the Internet, you find not only FTP sites but also Web sites related to Linux. In fact, Linux is a pretty popular subject on the Web. The following URLs access the major Linux information sites on the Web:

URL	Description
http://sunsite.unc.edu/mdw/welcome.html	This is THE site for Linux information!
http://www.cdrom.org	The home for the Slackware Distribution.
http://www.Linux.org.uk	The Web site for European Linux users.

Contacting InfoMagic

InfoMagic produces the CD-ROM enclosed with this book, and they are gracious enough to help support the product. If your disc is damaged, please contact Que Publishing at **http://www.mcp.com**. If you have exhausted the resources above, then contact InfoMagic's support by using their e-mail address:

support@infomagic.com.

For Linux Developers

So you think that Linux is the greatest thing to come along in quite some time, and you want to help develop future releases? Well, you're in luck. There is an active set of mailing lists on the Internet that are devoted to various topics and issues surrounding Linux development. This is a *multichannel mailing list,* meaning that messages on different topics are sent to different groups of people. You must subscribe to each channel that you are interested in. If you think you want to get involved in a Linux development project, you can get more information by sending an e-mail message to:

majordomo@vger.rutgers.edu

with lists in the body to get a list of the lists there; add a line with help to get the standard Majordomo help file which has instructions for subscribing and unsubscribing.

APPENDIX B

Applications for Linux

This appendix provides you with a brief introduction to many of the outstanding application programs available from the GNU project, such as entire C and C++ language compilers, and a graphical debugger. While most GNU software is of interest to programmers, there are also plenty of games and other applications. Most of these items are included with the Slackware distribution you installed from the accompanying CD-ROM. Some are not included due to space but are available either from the distributor (InfoMagic) or can be downloaded from **prep.ai.mit.edu** or **sunsite.unc.edu** via anonymous FTP.

◀◀ See "Anonymous FTP," p. 596

If you did not install every package in your distribution (for lack of disk space, or any other reason), then you can install a needed program at a later time. Chapter 3, "Understanding the Linux Distributions," provides information on exactly what packages are available. Chapter 4, "Installing Linux," shows you how to use the `pkgtool` program to install any applications you did not install with the original installation of Linux. If the CD-ROM does not contain one of the following listed programs, check a local archive site or **prep.ai.mit.edu**, download the program, and then follow the instructions for installing the package. Most of the following programs provide detailed installation instructions, including how to build the program, if necessary.

◀◀ See "`man`, Display Online Help" p. 107

Chapter 25, "Command-Line Reference," provides some instructions for running several of the programs. Otherwise, you can use the man pages to get online help for many of these programs.

Some programs come only in source-code form; that is, only source code is provided and you therefore need to compile and configure the application. In that case, you have to build the program from the source code. Again, most of this process is automated; however, if you do need to compile and link the program, you need one of the

GNU compilers available for your Linux system. If you followed the installation instructions in Chapter 4, "Installing Linux," you should have at least the GNU C compiler (gcc). Many of these programs have been built for versions of UNIX other than Linux, but should work when recompiled under Linux. Following is a list and a brief description of various GNU programs that are available.

Finally, you should constantly check the **sunsite.unc.edu** site because this is the most important Linux site on the Internet. Plenty of GNU- and Linux-specific software is located there. The CD-ROM accompanying this book contains several programs from the **sunsite** archive that are important for Linux users. These programs are described later in this appendix, and are located on the CD-ROM in the **\sunsite** directory.

bash

The bash shell is a POSIX-compatible shell with full Bourne shell (sh) syntax and some C shell commands. The bash shell supports emacs-style command-line editing, job control, functions, and online help. You should not need this program because Linux includes the bash shell as its default shell.

◀◀ See "Understanding Shells," p. 360

bc

bc is an interactive algebraic language with arbitrary precision. GNU bc was implemented from the POSIX 1003.2 draft standard; however, bc has several extensions including multi-character variable names, an else statement, and full boolean expressions. GNU bc does not act as a compiler for the dc calculator. This program should have been installed as part of the Linux installation.

bison

bison is an upwardly compatible replacement for the parser generator yacc but with more features. The file README gives instructions for compiling bison; the files bison.1 (a man page) and bison.texinfo (a GNU texinfo file) have instructions for using it. This program is used to create programming language parsers. bison is used in conjunction with other programs, such as lex or flex, that create lexical analyzers for programming languages.

cpio

cpio is a program for creating, updating, and extracting archives. GNU cpio supports the final POSIX 1003.1 ustar standard. Linux provides cpio in its base installation, but not a man page.

diff

diff compares files, showing line-by-line changes in several flexible formats. GNU diff is much faster than the traditional UNIX versions. Linux installs this program as part of its utilities.

elisp-manual

This is the GNU emacs lisp reference manual with texinfo source and a DVI file that is ready for printing. A copy of makeinfo is usually also provided so that you can make an online version of the manual. The manual documents the extension language used by GNU emacs. If you installed the entire GNU emacs program, then you probably have this file.

elvis

elvis is a clone of vi/ex, the standard UNIX editor. It supports nearly all of the vi/ex commands, in both visual mode and colon mode. elvis runs under BSD UNIX, AT&T SysV UNIX, SCO Xenix, Minix, MS-DOS, Atari TOS, and Linux. The Slackware distribution on the accompanying CD-ROM contains a copy of elvis, from which vi and ex are symbolically linked.

emacs

GNU emacs is an extendible, customizable full-screen editor. Installation of emacs is recommended, despite its size, because almost every UNIX system has emacs installed.

◄◄ See "Using emacs," p. 455

f2c

f2c is a FORTRAN-to-C converter program. Unless you are porting FORTRAN source code to C, there is no need for this program. f2c is included with the Slackware distribution on the accompanying CD-ROM. While f2c can convert FORTRAN to C, the resulting code is not very easy for software engineers to maintain, and the conversion may even fail.

fax

This is a set of software that provides Group 3 fax transmission and reception services for a networked UNIX system. It requires a fax-modem that conforms to the new EIA-592 Asynchronous Facsimile DCE Control Standard, Service Class 2. Linux does not yet support this program, but several Linux-compliant programs are available across the Internet. FlexFax is available from **sgi.com** (**192.48.153.1**). `mgetty+sendfax` is a Linux and SCO-specific `getty` program for fax-modems with a simple `sendfax` program. `mgetty+sendfax` is available from **sunsite.unc.edu** in the file `/pub/Linux/system/serial/mgetty+sendfax-0.16.tar.gz`, and `efax` is available from **sunsite.unc.edu** in the file /pub/Linux/apps/comm/fax/efax07a.tar.gz.

Note

Development within the Linux community moves rapidly, thus the above files may not have the same names as newer versions are released. The files should have similiar names, however, such as efaxXX.tar.gz.

fileutils

These are the GNU file-manipulation utilities. The `fileutils` package contains the following programs: `chgrp`, `chmod`, `chown`, `cp`, `dd`, `df`, `dir`, `du`, `ginstall`, `ln`, `ls`, `mkdir`, `mkfifo`, `mknod`, `mv`, `rm`, `rmdir`, `touch`, and `vdir`. All Linux distributions include this GNU package because Linux uses these utilities. See the respective man pages for information on using these utilities. Also see Chapter 25, "Command-Line Reference."

find

This is a POSIX-compliant implementation (with many extensions) of `find`, a program used for searching file systems for files that match certain criteria, and for performing operations (like showing the path) when they are found. Also included in this distribution are `xargs` and `locate`. Linux includes `find` in its base distribution.

◀◀ See "Searching for Files," p. 349

finger

GNU `finger` is a utility program designed to allow users of UNIX hosts on the Internet to get information about each other. It is a direct replacement for the Berkeley 4.3 `finger` program. Linux installs this utility as part of its basic installation.

flex

`flex` is a faster (but not completely compatible) replacement for `lex`, a lexical-analyzer compiler. `flex` and `bison` are the principal components used for constructing compilers.

gas

`gas` is the GNU assembler, and includes several features designed to optimize the output of a C compiler. In particular, it automatically chooses the correct size for branch instructions (when it knows where it is branching to) and automatically modifies jump-table entries that are out-of-bounds. `gas` works on the following family of processors: VAX, 68020, 80386, and 320xx. This program is part of the GNU compiler suite, but is not required unless you intend to do programming with your Linux system. Linux does not provide this program in its base installation.

gawk

This version of GNU `awk` is upwardly compatible with the SVR4 version. Instructions for using `gawk` are in the file `gawk.texinfo` in your `\doc` directory. You can also get help with the man pages.

gcc

This is version 2 of `gcc`, the GNU C Compiler. In addition to supporting ANSI C, `gcc 2` includes support for the C++ and Objective-C languages, provided you install the required programs. `gcc` extends the C language to support nested functions and non-local go-tos, taking the address of program labels and unnamed structures as function arguments (among other things). There are also many new warnings for frequent programming mistakes. `gcc 2` can generate output files in a.out, COFF, ECOFF, ELF, XCOFF, VAX-VMS, and OSF-Rose formats when used with a suitable assembler. It can produce debugging information in several formats: BSD stabs, COFF, ECOFF, ECOFF with stabs symbols, VAX-VMS, and DWARF. (Support for XCOFF for the RS/6000 is in the future.) `gcc` easily can be configured as a cross-compiler, running on one platform while generating code for another. `gcc 2` supports compatible calling conventions for function calling and return values on Sparc (unlike `gcc 1`) as well as the other machine types. Early testing of `gcc 2` indicates that it produces faster code for Sparc computers than Sun's latest released compilers (both bundled and unbundled). It is also the fastest known compiler for the Motorola 88k. `gcc` can produce position-independent code for several families of CPUs: 68000, 88000, 80386, Sparc, and RS/6000. Supporting PIC on additional suitable CPU types is not too difficult a task. The `gcc` program is one of the GNU's crowning achievements and is available on your Linux system. If you are interested in learning how to program in C, C++, or Objective-C, `gcc` is one program that can do it all...and for a price that's hard to beat (free).

gdb

`gdb` is the GNU source-level debugger. Programmers use a debugger to help them find errors in their programs. Linux includes this debugger in the base distribution but does not require its installation. Linux also provides a graphical front end (that is, a windowing user interface) to the `gdb` debugger when running under X Windows.

ghostscript

The `ghostscript` program is an interpreter for a language that is intended to be—and very nearly is—compatible with the PostScript language. `ghostscript` runs under X Windows on UNIX, Linux, and VMS systems, as well as on MS-DOS machines. It drives displays or low-to-medium-resolution printers. Linux includes `ghostscript` in its base distribution but does not require you to install the program. If you intend to use high-quality printing or graphics with your Linux system, its installation is highly recommended. Fonts for `ghostscript` are included in the base distribution.

ghostview

`ghostview` allows you to view PostScript files on XFree86 displays. `ghostview` handles the user interface details and calls the `ghostscript` interpreter to render the image.

gnuchess

`gnuchess` is a chess-playing program with X Windows, Suntools, curses, ASCII, and IBM PC character set displays available.

gnuplot

`gnuplot` is an interactive program for plotting mathematical expressions and data. Oddly enough, this program was neither created for nor named for the GNU Project—the name is a coincidence.

grep

This is the GNU high-speed `grep` program, which is similar to its UNIX counterpart but usually is faster. Linux installs this program as part of its basic installation. See the man pages for more information on using the program.

groff

This is the GNU `roff` document formatting system. Included in this release are implementations of `troff`, `pic`, `eqn`, and `tbl`; the `-man` and `-ms` macros; and drivers for PostScript, TeX DVI format, and typewriter-like devices. Also included is a modified version of the Berkeley `-me` macros, and an enhanced version of the X11R4 `xditview`.

gzip

This is a new compression program free of known patents that the GNU Project is using instead of the traditional `compress` program, which has patent problems. `gzip` can uncompress LZW-compressed files but uses a different algorithm for compression that generally yields more highly compressed files. This is the standard compression program in the GNU system. Linux makes extensive use of `gzip`, both in building the boot disks required for installation, and in archiving large text files such as the FAQs and HOWTOs.

◄◄ See "Compressing Files," p. 351

indent

This is the GNU modified version of the freely distributable `indent` program from BSD. The `indent.texinfo` file contains instructions on using `indent`.

ispell

`ispell` is an interactive spelling corrector based on the ITS SPELL program. Linux provides both `ispell` and another English version of the program during installation. The programs are not required to operate Linux, but their installation is recommended.

less

`less` is a paginator similar to `more` and `pg`, but with various features (such as the ability to scroll backwards) that some other paginators lack. Linux includes `less` in the basic distribution.

◄◄ See "Using `less` to View a File," p. 348

m4

`m4` is a macro processor, in the sense that it copies its input to the output, expanding macros as it goes. Macros are either built-in or user-defined and can take any number of arguments. Besides just doing macro expansion, `m4` has built-in functions for including named files, running UNIX commands, doing integer arithmetic, manipulating text in various ways, recursion, and so on.

make

GNU `make` supports many more options and features than the UNIX `make`. Programmers use this program to help automate the construction of their programs. All the programs listed here usually have GNU-supplied *makefiles* that automate the compilation of the program. Makefiles are text files that form the input to the `make` program. Linux includes `make` in its base installation.

mtools

`mtools` is a public domain collection of programs to allow UNIX systems to read, write, and manipulate files on an MS-DOS file system (typically a floppy disk). Linux supports many of the `m` commands when dealing with floppy disks. You do not have to use `m` commands when dealing with an MS-DOS partition you have instructed Linux to mount. Linux handles any needed file conversions internally.

nethack

This is the famous game of `nethack`. Instructions for compiling and using `nethack` may be found in the `README` file that accompanies the source code to the program. Linux does not provide this program.

patch

`patch` takes a patch file containing any of the four forms of difference listing that can be produced by the `diff` program, and applies those differences to an original file, producing a patched version. Programmers use `patch` to help update their programs around the world. Instead of sending out an entire new program, programmers can simply send out the changes made since the last distribution. `patch` is available in Linux distributions.

perl

This is a version of Larry Wall's `perl` programming language. `perl` is intended as a faster replacement for `sed`, `awk`, and similar languages. Linux provides `perl` but does not require you to install the package.

rcs

`rcs` is *revision control system,* a program to manage multiple versions of a software project. This program keeps the changes from one version to another rather than multiple copies of the entire file; this saves disk space.

sed

`sed` is a text editor much like `ed`, except `sed` is stream-oriented. It is used copiously in shell scripts. Although GNU `sed` has fewer static limitations in terms of buffer size, command length, and so on, it is a little slower than most implementations. Linux includes `sed` as part of its basic installation.

smalltalk

`smalltalk` is the GNU implementation of Smalltalk, an object-oriented programming language developed by Xerox. Linux includes the `smalltalk` package but does not require you to install it.

tar

`tar` is a program used for archiving many files into a single file, making them easier to transport. GNU `tar` includes multivolume support, the ability to archive sparse files, automatic archive compression/decompression, remote archives, and special features to allow `tar` to be used for incremental and full backups. Unfortunately, GNU `tar` implements an early draft of the POSIX 1003.1 `ustar` standard, which is different from the final standard. Adding support for the new changes in a backward-compatible fashion is not trivial.

Linux includes `tar` in its basic installation. Also, while the destination of a `tar` archive does not have to be a tape drive, if you have a supported tape drive and load the `ftape` program at startup, Linux's `tar` program can create `tar` archives on your tape drive.

texinfo

The `texinfo` package contains a set of utilities related to `texinfo`, which is used to generate printed manuals and online hypertext-style manuals (called *info*). Programs and interfaces for writing, reading, and formatting `texinfo` files are available as both standalone programs and GNU `emacs` interfaces. Linux makes use of such `texinfo` files in its documentation efforts.

time

`time` is used to measure the amount of time a command takes to execute. The program reports statistics about, among other things, the number of users on the system and approximate real time used by a process. Instructions for making `time` (no pun intended) are in the file `README` that accompanies the source code for `time`. Linux provides `time` as part of the basic installation.

uucp

This version of UUCP was written by Ian Lance Taylor and is the standard UUCP system for GNU. It currently supports the `f`, `g` (in all window and packet sizes), `G`, `t`, and `e` protocols, as well as a `Zmodem` protocol and two new bidirectional protocols. If you have a Berkeley sockets library, you can make TCP connections. If you have TLI libraries, you can make TLI connections. Linux provides `uucp` as part of its base installation.

xboard

`xboard` is an X11R4-based user interface for `gnuchess`. It uses R4 Athena widgets and XT Intrinsics to provide an interactive referee for managing a `chess` game between a user and a computer opponent, or between two computers. You can also use `xboard` without a `chess` program to play through games in files, or to play through games manually (force mode)—in this case, moves aren't validated by `xboard`. `xboard` manages a digital chess clock for each player, and resets the clocks if the proper number of moves are played within the time-control period. A game can be started with the initial chess position, a series of moves from a game file, or a position from a position file. The `match` shell script runs a series of games between two machines, alternating sides. The man page `xboard.man` describes the features of `xboard`. Linux makes `xboard` available as part of its X Windows-based applications and games. You must have installed `gnuchess` to take advantage of `xboard`. If you have not installed `gnuchess` or `xboard`, see Chapter 4, "Installing Linux," for information on installing packages after the initial Linux installation.

Surfing the Internet

Chapter 29, "Surfing the Internet," provides information on several popular Internet access tools, such as Archie, Gopher, and Mosaic. Unfortunately, many Linux distributions do not include these tools in their packages—this includes the Slackware distribution on the accompanying CD-ROM. So you will find several files in the `\sunsite` directory on the CD-ROM that do provide these tools. The files are listed in Table B.1. Most have been compressed with the program `gzip`, so you need to unzip the various programs before you can install and use them. Once unzipped, most provide detailed instructions for their installation and use.

Table B.1 Programs for Surfing the Internet

Filename	Description
archie-1.4.1p-bin.tar.gz	Binaries for the Archie FTP site search program
gopher-2.1a.bin.gz	Binaries for the Gopher program
httpd_1.3.tar.gz	NCSA httpd (World Wide Web server) for Linux
lynx-2.3.bin2.tar.gz	Non-X11 World Wide Web client (Xmosaic for terminals) with term support
Mosaic-2.4+term.bin.tar.gz	Mosaic binaries with term support
Mosaic-2.4-R6.tar.gz	Mosaic compiled with X11R6 libraries
Mosaic-2.4.bin2.tar.gz	Mosaic with both term and TCP/IP support

Backing Up Your System

The file Linux-Bkp-Util-v1.10.tgz is a gzip file containing the executable for the Linux-Bkp-Util program. This program provides a full menu-driven interface to the tar command. The Linux-Bkp-Util-v1.10.Readme file contains instructions for the Linux-Bkp-Util program.

The CD-ROM accompanying this book contains gzipped files named backscri.tgz and backup-1.03.tar.gz. These files contain shell script files for automating the tedious job of backing up your system.

◀◀ See "Performing Backups and Restoring Files," p. 192

APPENDIX C

The Linux Hardware Compatibility HOWTO

This document lists most of the hardware supported by Linux and helps you locate any necessary drivers.

Welcome to the Linux Hardware Compatibility HOWTO. This document lists most of the hardware supported by Linux; if only people would read this first before posting their questions on USENET!

Subsections titled "Others" list hardware with alpha or beta drivers in varying degrees of usability, or list drivers that aren't included in standard kernels. Also note that some drivers only exist in alpha kernels, so if you see something listed as supported that isn't in your version of the Linux kernel, you should upgrade.

The latest version of this document can be found on the Net at the usual sites where the Linux HOWTOs are kept.

If you know of any Linux hardware (in)compatibilities not listed here, please let me know—send e-mail or find me on IRC. Thanks.

System Architectures

This document only deals with Linux for Intel platforms; for other platforms, check the following:

Platform	Site
Linux/ARM	http://whirligig.ecs.soton.ac.uk/~rmk92/armlinux.html
Linux/68k	http://www-users.informatik.rwth-aachen.de/~hn/linux68k.html
Linux/MIPS	http://www.waldorf-gmbh.de/linux-mips-faq.html
Linux/PowerPC	http://liber.stanford.edu/linuxppc/
Linux/8086	http://www.linux.org.uk/Linux8086.html
Linux/Alpha	http://www.azstarnet.com/~axplinux/
Linux for Acorn	http://www.ph.kcl.ac.uk/~amb/linux.html
MacLinux	http://www.ibg.uu.se/maclinux/

Computers/Motherboards/BIOS

ISA, VLB, EISA, and PCI buses all are supported.

PS/2 and Microchannel (MCA) are not supported in the standard kernel. Alpha test PS/2 MCA kernels are available but not yet recommended for beginners or serious users.

Specific Systems

- Compaq Deskpro XL **http://www-c724.uibk.ac.at/XL/**
- IBM PS/2 MCA systems **ftp://invaders.dcrl.nd.edu/pub/misc/**

Laptops

Some laptops have unusual video adapters or power management—it is not uncommon to be unable to use the power management features. PCMCIA drivers currently support all common PCMCIA controllers, including Databook TCIC/2, Intel i82365SL, Cirrus PD67xx, and Vadem VG-468 chipsets. The Motorola 6AHC05GA controller used in some Hyundai laptops is not supported. (Read the PCMCIA HOWTO.)

Controller	Site
APM	ftp://tsx-11.mit.edu/pub/linux/packages/laptops/apm/
PCMCIA	ftp://cb-iris.stanford.edu/pub/pcmcia/
Non-blinking cursor	ftp://sunsite.unc.edu/pub/Linux/kernel/patches/console/ noblink-1.5.tar.gz
Power savings (WD7600 chipset)	ftp://sunsite.unc.edu/pub/Linux/system/Misc/ low- level/pwrm-1.0.tar.Z
Other general info	ftp://tsx-11.mit.edu/pub/linux/packages/laptops/

Specific Laptops

Laptop Make and Model	Site
Compaq Contura Aero	http://domen.uninett.no/~hta/linux/aero-faq.html
IBM ThinkPad	http://peipa.essex.ac.uk/tp-linux/tp-linux.html
NEC Versa M and P	http://www.santafe.edu:80/~nelson/versa-linux/
Tadpole P1000	http://peipa.essex.ac.uk/tadpole-linux/tadpole-linux.html

CPU/FPU

Intel/AMD/Cyrix 386SX/DX/SL/DXL/SLC, 486SX/DX/SL/SX2/DX2/DX4, Pentium—Basically all 386 or better processors will work. Linux has built-in FPU emulation if you don't have a math coprocessor.

Experimental SMP (multiple CPU) support is included in kernel 1.3.31 and newer. Check the Linux/SMP Project page for details and updates.

Controller	Site
Linux/SMP Project	http://www.linux.org.uk/SMP/title.html

A few very early AMD 486DXs might hang in some special situations. All current chips should be okay, and getting a chip swap for old CPUs should not be a problem.

ULSI Math*Co series has a bug in the FSAVE and FRSTOR instructions that causes problems with all protected mode operating systems. Some older IIT and Cyrix chips might also have this problem.

There are problems with TLB flushing in UMC U5S chips in very old kernels (1.1.x).

Processor	Site
Enable cache on Cyrix processors	ftp://sunsite.unc.edu/pub/Linux/kernel/patches/CxPatch030.tar.z
Cyrix software cache control	ftp://sunsite.unc.edu/pub/Linux/kernel/patches/linux.cxpatch

Video Cards

Linux works with all video cards in text mode. VGA cards not listed below probably will still work with mono VGA and/or standard VGA drivers.

If you're looking into buying a cheap video card to run X, keep in mind that accelerated cards (such as ATI Mach, ET4000/W32p, and S3) are *much* faster than unaccelerated or partially accelerated cards (for example, Cirrus and WD). S3 801 (ISA), S3 805 (VLB), ET4000/W32p, and ATI Graphics Wonder (Mach32) are good low-end accelerated cards.

"32 bpp" is actually 24-bit color aligned on 32-bit boundaries. It does NOT mean the cards are capable of 32-bit color—it's still 24-bit color (16,777,216 colors). 24-bit packed-pixel modes are not supported in XFree86, so cards that can do 24-bit color modes in other OSs may not be able to do this in X using Xfree86. These cards include Mach32, Cirrus 542x, S3 801/805/868/968, ET4000, and others.

Diamond Video Cards

Most currently available Diamond cards *are* supported by the current release of XFree86. Early Diamond cards may not be officially supported by XFree86, but there are ways of getting them to work. Diamond is now actively supporting the XFree86 Project. The supported cards are shown in the following table:

Video Card	Site
Diamond support for Xfree86	http://www.diamondmm.com/linux.html
Diamond FAQ (for older cards)	ftp://sunsite.unc.edu/pub/Linux/X11/Diamond.FAQ
Diamond Disgruntled Users Page (for older cards)	http://gladstone.uoregon.edu/~trenton/diamond/

SVGALIB (Graphics for Console)

- VGA
- EGA
- ARK Logic ARK1000PV/2000PV
- ATI VGA Wonder
- ATI Mach32
- Cirrus 542x, 543x
- OAK OTI-037/67/77/87
- S3 (limited support)
- Trident TVGA8900/9000
- Tseng ET3000/ET4000/W32

XFree86 3.1.2, Accelerated

- ATI Mach8
- ATI Mach32 (16 bpp—does not work with all Mach32 cards)
- ATI Mach64 (16/32 bpp)
- Cirrus Logic 5420, 542x/5430 (16 bpp), 5434 (16/32 bpp), 62x5
- IBM 8514/A
- IBM XGA, XGA-II
- IIT AGX-010/014/015/016
- Oak OTI-087
- S3 911, 924, 801, 805, 928, 864, 964, Trio32, Trio64, 868, 968
- See Appendix A of this Howto for a list of supported S3 cards
- Tseng ET4000/W32/W32i/W32p
- Weitek P9000 (16/32 bpp)
- Diamond Viper VLB/PCI
- Orchid P9000
- Western Digital WD90C31/33

XFree86 3.1.1, Unaccelerated

- ARK Logic ARK1000PV/VL, ARK2000PV
- ATI VGA Wonder series
- Avance Logic AL2101/2228/2301/2302/2308/2401
- Chips & Technologies 65520/65530/65540/65545
- Cirrus Logic 6420/6440
- Compaq AVGA
- Genoa GVGA
- MCGA (320 × 200)
- MX MX68000/MX68010
- NCR 77C22, 77C22E, 77C22E+
- Oak OTI-067, OTI-077
- RealTek RTG3106
- Trident TVGA8800, TVGA8900, TVGA9xxx (no support for TGUI chipsets)
- Tseng ET3000, ET4000AX
- VGA (standard VGA, 4-bit, slow)
- Video 7/Headland Technologies HT216-32
- Western Digital/Paradise PVGA1, WD90C00/10/11/24/30/31/33

Monochrome

- Hercules mono
- Hyundai HGC-1280
- Sigma LaserView PLUS
- VGA mono

Others

- EGA (ancient, from c. 1992)
  ftp://ftp.funet.fi/pub/OS/Linux/BETA/Xega/
- ET4000/W32 and ICS5341 GenDAC
  ftp://sunsite.unc.edu/pub/Linux/X11/X-servers/
- Trident TGUI9440
  ftp://sunsite.unc.edu/pub/Linux/X11/X-servers/

Works in Progress

- Compaq QVision
- Number Nine Imagine 128

I don't know when support for these cards will be finished, so please don't ask me. If you want support for these cards now, get Accelerated-X.

Commercial X Servers

Commercial X servers provide support for cards not supported by XFree86, and might give better performances for cards that are supported by XFree86. In general, they support many more cards than XFree86, so here I'll only list cards that aren't supported by Xfree86. Contact the vendors directly or check the Commercial HOWTO for more info.

Accelerated-X 1.2

- Chips & Technologies 82C45x, 82C48x, F655xx
- Compaq QVision 2000
- Matrox MGA-I, MGA-II
- Number Nine I-128
- Weitek P9100

$199, X Inside, Inc. **info@xinside.com**

Accel-X supports most cards in 16- and 32- bpp modes and it also supports 24-bit packed pixel modes for cards that have these modes, including ATI Mach32, Mach64 (1280 × 1024@24bpp), ET4000/W32p, S3-866/868/968, and more. Accel-X also supports other input hardware like graphics tablets and touchscreens.

Accel-X also supports XVideo (Xv) extensions (on Matrox Comet, Marvel-II, and SPEA ShowTime Plus), PEX, and XIE.

Metro-X 2.3.2

$199, Metro Link **sales@metrolink.com.**
Metro-X supports more boards than XFree but less than Accel-X; however, I don't have much more information as I can't seem to view the PostScript files they sent me. Mail them directly for more info.

Controllers (Hard Drive)

Linux will work with standard IDE, MFM, and RLL controllers. When using MFM/RLL controllers it is important to use ext2fs and the bad block checking options when formatting the disk. Enhanced IDE (EIDE) interfaces are supported. With up to two IDE interfaces and up to four hard drives and/or CD-ROM drives. Linux will detect these EIDE interfaces:

- CMD-640
- DTC 2278D
- FGI/Holtek HT-6560B
- RZ1000
- Triton (82371FB) IDE (with busmaster DMA)

ESDI controllers that emulate the ST-506 (MFM/RLL/IDE) interface will also work. The bad block checking comment also applies to these controllers. Generic 8-bit XT controllers also work.

Controllers (SCSI)

It is important to pick a SCSI controller carefully. Many cheap ISA SCSI controllers are designed to drive CD-ROMs rather than anything else. Such low-end SCSI controllers are no better than IDE. See the SCSI HOWTO and look at performance figures before buying an SCSI card.

Supported

- AMI Fast Disk VLB/EISA (BusLogic compatible)
- Adaptec AVA-1505/1515 (ISA) (Adaptec 152x compatible)
- Adaptec AHA-1510/152x (ISA) (AIC-6260/6360)
- Adaptec AHA-154x (ISA) (all models)
- Adaptec AHA-174x (EISA) (in enhanced mode)
- Adaptec AHA-274x (EISA)/284x (VLB) (AIC-7770)
- Adaptec AHA-2940/3940 (PCI) (AIC-7870) (since 1.3.6)
- Always IN2000
- BusLogic (ISA/EISA/VLB/PCI) (all models)
- DPT PM2001, PM2012A (EATA-PIO)
- DPT Smartcache (EATA-DMA) (ISA/EISA/PCI) (all models)
- DTC 329x (EISA) (Adaptec 154x compatible)
- Future Domain TMC-16x0, TMC-3260 (PCI)
- Future Domain TMC-8xx, TMC-950
- Media Vision Pro Audio Spectrum 16 SCSI (ISA)
- NCR 5380 generic cards
- NCR 53c400 (Trantor T130B) (use generic NCR 5380 SCSI support)
- NCR 53c406a (Acculogic ISApport / Media Vision Premium 3D SCSI)
- NCR 53c7x0, 53c8x0 (PCI)
- Qlogic/Control Concepts SCSI/IDE (FAS408) (ISA/VLB/PCMCIA) does not work with PCI (different chipset). PCMCIA cards must boot DOS to init card
- Seagate ST-01/ST-02 (ISA)
- SoundBlaster 16 SCSI-2 (Adaptec 152x compatible) (ISA)
- Trantor T128/T128F/T228 (ISA)
- UltraStor 14F (ISA), 24F (EISA), 34F (VLB)
- Western Digital WD7000 SCSI

Others

Processor	Site
AMD AM53C974, AM79C974 (PCI) (Compaq, Zeos onboard SCSI)	ftp://sunsite.unc.edu/pub/Linux/kernel/patches/scsi/AM53C974-0.3.tgz
Adaptec ACB-40xx SCSI-MFM/RLL bridgeboard	ftp://sunsite.unc.edu/pub/Linux/kernel/patches/scsi/adaptec-40XX.tar.gz
Adaptec AHA-2940 (PCI) (AIC-7870)	ftp://remus.nrl.navy.mil/pub/Linux/
Adaptec APA-1460 SlimSCSI (PCMCIA)	ftp://cb-iris.stanford.edu/pub/pcmcia/
Acculogic ISApport/MV Premium 3D SCSI (NCR 53c406a)	ftp://sunsite.unc.edu/pub/Linux/kernel/patches/scsi/ncr53c406-0.10.patch.gz
Always AL-500	ftp://sunsite.unc.edu/pub/Linux/kernel/patches/scsi/al500_0.1.tar.gz
Iomega PC2/2B	ftp://sunsite.unc.edu/pub/Linux/kernel/patches/scsi/iomega_pc2-1.1.x.tar.gz
New Media Bus Toaster PCMCIA	ftp://lamont.ldeo.columbia.edu/pub/linux/bus_toaster-1.5.tgz
Ricoh GSI-8	ftp://tsx-11.mit.edu/pub/linux/ALPHA/scsi/gsi8.tar.gz
Trantor T130B (NCR 53c400)	ftp://sunsite.unc.edu/pub/Linux/kernel/patches/scsi/53c400.tar.gz

Unsupported

- Parallel port SCSI adapters
- Non-Adaptec-compatible DTC boards (327x, 328x)

Controllers (I/O)

Any standard serial/parallel/joystick/IDE combo cards. Linux supports 8250, 16450, 16550, and 16550A UARTs. Cards that support non-standard IRQs (IRQ > 9) can be used.

See National Semiconductor's *Application Note AN-493* by Martin S. Michael. Section 5.0 describes in detail the differences between the NS16550 and NS16550A. Briefly, the NS16550 had bugs in the FIFO circuits, but the NS16550A (and later) chips fixed those. However, there were very few NS16550s produced by National, long ago, so these should be very rare. Many of the "16550" parts in modern boards are from the many manufacturers of compatible parts, which may not use the National "A" suffix. Also, some multiport boards use 16552, 16554, or various other multiport or multi-function chips from National or other suppliers (generally, in a dense package soldered to the board, not a 40-pin DIP). Don't worry about it unless you encounter a very old 40-pin DIP National NS16550 (no A) chip loose or in an old board, in which case treat it as a 16450 (no FIFO) rather than a 16550A.—Zhahai Stewart at **zstewart@hisys.com**.

Controllers (Multiport) Supported—Unintelligent

- AST FourPort and clones
- Accent Async-4
- Arnet Multiport-8 (8 port)
- Bell Technologies HUB6
- Boca BB-1004, 1008 (4, 8 port)—no DTR, DSR, and CD
- Boca BB-2016 (16 port)
- Boca IO/AT66 (6 port)
- Boca IO 2 × 4 (4S/2P)—works with modems, but uses 5 IRQs
- Computone ValuePort (4, 6, 8 port) (AST FourPort compatible)
- DigiBoard PC/X (4, 8, 16 port)
- Comtrol Hostess 550 (4, 8 port)
- SIIG I/O Expander 4S (4 port, uses 4 IRQs)
- PC-COMM 4-port
- STB 4-COM
- Twincom ACI/550
- Usenet Serial Board II

Non-intelligent cards usually come in two varieties, one using standard com port addresses and use 4 IRQs, and another that's AST FourPort compatible and uses a selectable block of addresses and a single IRQ. (Addresses and IRQs are set by using setserial.) If you're getting one of these cards, be sure to check which standard it conforms to; prices are no indication.

Controllers (Multiport) Supported—Intelligent

- Cyclades Cyclom-8Y/16Y (8, 16 port) (ISA/PCI)
- Stallion EasyIO (ISA) / EasyConnection 8/32 (ISA/MCA)
- Stallion EasyConnection 8/64 / ONboard (ISA/EISA/MCA) / Brumby / Stallion (ISA)

Others

Controller	Site
Comtrol RocketPort (8/16/32 port)	ftp://tsx-11.mit.edu/pub/linux/packages/comtrol/
DigiBoard COM/Xi—Contact Simon Park	si@wimpol.demon.co.uk (e-mail address)
DigiBoard PC/Xe (ISA) and PC/Xi (EISA)	ftp://ftp.digibd.com/drivers/linux/
Hayes ESP8	contact Dennis Boylan at dennis@lan.com
Moxa C218 (8 port) / C320 (8/16/24/32 expandable)	<ftp://ftp.moxa.com.tw/drivers/c-218-320/linux/>

(continues)

(continued)

Controller	Site
Specialix SIO/XIO (modular, 4 to 32 ports)	ftp://sunsite.unc.edu/pub/Linux/kernel/patches/serial/sidrv0_5.taz
Stallion Technologies EasyIO/EasyConnection 8/32	ftp://sunsite.unc.edu/pub/Linux/kernel/patches/serial/stallion-0.1.9.tar.gz

Network Adapters

Ethernet adapters vary greatly in performance. In general, the newer the design, the better the adapter performs. Some very old cards like the 3C501 are useful only because they can be found in junk heaps for $5 a pop. Be careful with clones—not all are good clones, and bad clones often cause erratic lockups under Linux. Read the Ethernet HOWTO for detailed descriptions of various cards.

Supported—Ethernet

- 3Com 3C501—Avoid like the plague
- 3Com 3C503, 3C505, 3C507, 3C509/3C509B (ISA)/3C579 (EISA)
- AMD LANCE (79C960)/PCnet-ISA/PCI (AT1500, HP J2405A, NE1500/NE2100)
- AT&T GIS WaveLAN
- Allied Telesis AT1700
- Ansel Communications AC3200 EISA
- Apricot Xen-II
- Cabletron E21xx
- DEC DE425 (EISA)/DE434/DE435 (PCI)
- DEC DEPCA and EtherWORKS
- HP PCLAN (27245 and 27xxx series)
- HP PCLAN PLUS (27247B and 27252A)
- HP 10/100VG PCLAN (ISA/EISA/PCI)
- Intel EtherExpress
- Intel EtherExpress Pro
- NE2000/NE1000 (be careful with clones)
- New Media Ethernet
- Racal-Interlan NI5210 (i82586 Ethernet chip)
- Racal-Interlan NI6510 (am7990 lance chip)—Doesn't work with more than 16MB of RAM
- PureData PDUC8028, PDI8023
- SEEQ 8005

- SMC Ultra
- Schneider & Koch G16
- Western Digital WD80x3
- Zenith Z-Note/IBM ThinkPad 300 built-in adapter

Pocket and Portable Adapters

- AT-Lan-Tec/RealTek parallel port adapter
- D-Link DE600/DE620 parallel port adapter

Slotless

- SLIP/CSLIP/PPP (serial port)
- EQL (serial IP load balancing)
- PLIP (parallel port)—Using LapLink or bi-directional cable

ARCnet

- Works with all ARCnet cards

Token Ring

- IBM Tropic chipset cards

Amateur Radio (AX.25)

- Ottawa PI/PI2
- Most generic 8530-based HDLC boards

Others

Adapter	Site
Ethernet 3Com Vortex Ethercards (3C590, 3C595 (100 mbps)) (PCI)	http://cesdis.gsfc.nasa.gov/pub/linux/drivers/vortex.html
DEC 21040/21140 "Tulip"/SMC PCI EtherPower 10/100	http://cesdis.gsfc.nasa.gov/linux/drivers/tulip.html

ISDN

Check out the Linux ISDN WWW page at: **http://www.ix.de/ix/linux/linux-isdn.html**

ISDN Card	Site
3Com Sonix Arpeggio	ftp://sunsite.unc.edu/pub/Linux/kernel/patches/network/sonix.tgz
Combinet EVERYWARE 1000 ISDN	ftp://sunsite.unc.edu/pub/Linux/patches/network/combinet1000isdn-1.02.tar.gz

(continues)

Appendixes

(continued)

ISDN Card	Site
Diehl SCOM card	ftp://sunsite.unc.edu/pub/Linux/kernel/patches/network/isdndrv-0.1.1.tar.gz
ICN ISDN card	ftp://ftp.franken.de/pub/isdn4linux/
Teles ISDN card	ftp://ftp.franken.de/pub/isdn4linux/

ISDN cards that emulate standard modems or common Ethernet adapters don't need any special drivers to work.

PCMCIA Cards

See Appendix B for a complete list.

ATM

- Efficient Networks ENI155P-MF 155 mbps ATM adapter **http://lrcwww.epfl.ch/linux-atm/**

Frame Relay

- Sangoma S502 56K Frame Relay card **ftp://ftp.sovereign.org/pub/wan/fr/**

Load Balancing

- `eql` (load balancing driver) **ftp://sunsite.unc.edu/pub/Linux/system/Network/serial/eql-1.2.tar.gz**

Unsupported

- Xircom adapters (PCMCIA and parallel port) are not supported.

Sound Cards—Supported

- 6850 UART MIDI
- Adlib (OPL2)
- Audio Excell DSP16
- ATI Stereo F/X (Sound Blaster compatible)
- Aztech Sound Galaxy NX Pro
- Crystal CS4232 (PnP) based cards
- ECHO-PSS (Orchid SW32, Cardinal DSP16, and so on)
- Ensoniq SoundScape (boot DOS to initialize card)
- Gravis Ultrasound

- Gravis Ultrasound 16-bit sampling daughterboard
- Gravis Ultrasound MAX
- Logitech SoundMan Games (SBPro, 44kHz stereo support)
- Logitech SoundMan Wave (SBPro/MPU-401) (OPL4)
- Logitech SoundMan 16 (PAS-16 compatible)
- Microsoft Sound System (AD1848)
- MPU-401 MIDI
- MediaTrix AudioTriX Pro
- Media Vision Premium 3D (Jazz16) (SBPro compatible)
- Media Vision Pro Sonic 16 (Jazz)
- Media Vision Pro Audio Spectrum 16
- OAK OTI-601D cards (Mozart)
- OPTi 82C928/82C929 cards (MAD16/MAD16 Pro)
- SoundBlaster
- SoundBlaster Pro
- SoundBlaster 16 family
- Sound Galaxy NX Pro
- Turtle Beach Wavefront cards (Maui, Tropez)
- WaveBlaster (and other SB16 daughterboards)

Others

Card	Site
MPU-401 MIDI (intelligent mode)	ftp://sunsite.unc.edu/pub/Linux/kernel/sound/mpu401.0.11a.tar.gz
PC speaker/Parallel port DAC	ftp://ftp.informatik.hu-berlin.de/pub/os/linux/hu-sound/
Turtle Beach MultiSound/Tahiti/Monterey	ftp://ftp.cs.colorado.edu/users/mccreary/archive/tbeach/multisound/

Unsupported

The ASP chip on SoundBlaster 16 series and AWE32 is not supported. AWE32's onboard E-mu MIDI synthesizer is not supported. Nathan Laredo (**laredo@gnu.ai.mit.edu**) is willing to write AWE32 drivers if you send him a complimentary card. He is also willing to write drivers for almost any hardware if you send him free samples of your hardware.

SoundBlaster 16 cards with DSP 4.11 have a hardware bug that causes hung/stuck notes when you use a WaveBlaster or other MIDI device attached to it. There is no known fix.

Hard Drives

All hard drives should work if the controller is supported (from the SCSI HOWTO). All direct-access SCSI devices with a block size of 256, 512, or 1,024 bytes should work. Other block sizes will not work (but often this can be fixed by changing the block and/or sector size using the MODE SELECT SCSI command).

Large IDE (EIDE) drives work fine with newer kernels. The boot partition must lie in the first 1024 cylinders due to PC BIOS limitations.

Some Conner CFP1060S drives may have problems with Linux and `ext2fs`. The symptoms are inode errors during `e2fsck`, and corrupt file systems. Conner has released a fix for this problem; contact Conner at 1-800-4CONNER (USA) or +44-1294-315333 (Europe). Have the microcode version (found on the drive label, 9WA1.6x) handy when you call.

Certain Micropolis drives have problems with Adaptec and BusLogic cards; contact the manufacturers for firmware upgrades if you suspect problems.

- Multiple device driver (RAID-0)
  ftp://sweet-smoke.ufr-info-p7.ibp.fr/public/Linux/

Tape Drives—Supported

- SCSI tape drives (from the SCSI HOWTO)—Drives using both fixed- and variable-length blocks smaller than the driver buffer length (set to 32KB in the distribution sources) are supported. Virtually all drives should work. (Please send e-mail if you know of any incompatible drives.)
- QIC-02
- QIC-117, QIC-40/80 drives (Ftape)
  ftp://sunsite.unc.edu/pub/Linux/kernel/tapes—Most tape drives using the floppy controller should work. Check the Ftape HOWTO for details. Various dedicated QIC-80 controllers
  (such as Colorado FC-10 and Iomega Tape Controller II) are also supported.

Unsupported

- Emerald and Tecmar QIC-02 tape controller cards—Chris Ulrich (**insom@math.ucr.edu**)
- Drives that connect to the parallel port (for example, Colorado Trakker)
- Some high-speed tape controllers (such as Colorado TC-15/FC-20)
- Irwin AX250L/Accutrak 250 (not QIC-80)
- IBM Internal Tape Backup Unit (not QIC-80)
- COREtape Light

CD-ROM Drives Supported

- SCSI CD-ROM drives (from the CD-ROM HOWTO)—Any SCSI CD-ROM drive with a block size of 512 or 2048 bytes should work under Linux; this includes the vast majority of CD-ROM drives on the market.
- EIDE (ATAPI) CD-ROM drives
- Aztech CDA268, Orchid CDS-3110, Okano/Wearnes CDD-110
- Goldstar R420
- LMS Philips CM 206
- Matsushita/Panasonic, Creative Labs, Longshine, Kotobuki (SBPCD)
- Mitsumi
- Optics Storage Dolphin 8000AT
- Sanyo H94A
- Sony CDU31A/CDU33A
- Sony CDU-535/CDU-531
- Teac CD-55A SuperQuad

Others

CD-ROM Drive	Site
GoldStar R420	ftp://ftp.gwdg.de/pub/linux/cdrom/drivers/goldstar/
LMS/Philips CM 205/225/202	ftp://sunsite.unc.edu/pub/Linux/kernel/patches/cdrom/lmscd0.3d.tar.gz
LMS Philips CM 206	ftp://sunsite.unc.edu/pub/Linux/kernel/patches/cdrom/cm206.0.22b.tar.gz
Mitsumi (alternate drivers)	ftp://ftp.gwdg.de/pub/linux/cdrom/drivers/mitsumi/
Mitsumi (module)	ftp://ftp.gwdg.de/pub/linux/cdrom/drivers/mitsumi-1.2.x/
NEC CDR-35D (old)	ftp://sunsite.unc.edu/pub/Linux/kernel/patches/cdrom/linux-neccdr35d.patch
Sony SCSI multisession CD-XA	ftp://tsx-11.mit.edu/pub/linux/patches/sony-multi-0.00.tar.gz
Teac CD-55A SuperQuad	ftp://ftp.gwdg.de/pub/linux/cdrom/develop/teac/

Notes

PhotoCD (XA) is supported.

All CD-ROM drives should work similarly for reading data. There are various compatibility problems with audio CD-playing utilities (especially with some NEC drives). Some alpha drivers do not have audio support yet.

Early (single-speed) NEC CD-ROM drives may have trouble with currently available SCSI controllers.

Removable Drives

All SCSI drives should work if the controller is supported, including optical drives, WORM, CD-R, floptical, and others. Iomega Bernoulli and Zip drives work fine, and so do SyQuest drives.

Linux supports both 512 and 1024 bytes/sector disks. There's a problem with MS-DOS filesystems on 1024 bytes/sector disks on some recent kernels (fixed in 1.1.75).

- Parallel port Zip drives **ftp://gear.torque.net/pub/**

Removable drives work like floppies: just fdisk/mkfs and mount the disks. Linux provides drive locking if your drives support it. mtools can also be used if the disks are in MS-DOS format.

CD-R drives require special software to work. Read the CD-R Mini-HOWTO.

Mice

- Microsoft serial mouse
- Mouse Systems serial mouse
- Logitech Mouseman serial mouse
- Logitech serial mouse
- ATI XL Inport busmouse
- C&T 82C710 (QuickPort) (Toshiba, TI Travelmate)
- Microsoft busmouse
- Logitech busmouse
- PS/2 (auxiliary device) mouse

Others

Mouse	Site
Sejin J-mouse	ftp://sunsite.unc.edu/pub/Linux/kernel/patches/console/jmouse.1.1.70-jmouse.tar.gz
MultiMouse—Use multiple mouse devices as a single mouse	ftp://sunsite.unc.edu/pub/Linux/system/Misc/MultiMouse-1.0.tgz

Notes

Touchpad devices like Alps Glidepoint also work, as long as they're compatible with another mouse protocol.

Newer Logitech mice (except the Mouseman) use the Microsoft protocol, and all three buttons work. Even though Microsoft's mice have only two buttons, the protocol allows three buttons. The mouse port on the ATI Graphics Ultra and Ultra Pro use the Logitech busmouse protocol. (See the Busmouse HOWTO for details.)

Modems

All internal modems or external modems are connected to the serial port. A small number of modems come with DOS software that downloads the control program at runtime. These normally can be used by loading the program under DOS and doing a warm boot. Such modems are probably best avoided, since you won't be able to use them with non-PC hardware in the future. PCMCIA modems should work with the PCMCIA drivers. Fax/modems need appropriate fax software to operate.

- Digicom Connection 96+/14.4+—DSP code downloading program **ftp://sunsite.unc.edu/pub/Linux/system/Serial/smdl- linux.1.02.tar.gz**
- ZyXEL U-1496 series—ZyXEL 1.4, modem/fax/voice control program **ftp://sunsite.unc.edu/pub/Linux/system/Serial/ZyXEL-1.4.tar.gz**

Printers and Plotters

Any printer or plotter connected to the parallel or serial port should work.

- HP LaserJet 4 series—free-lj4, printing modes control program **ftp://sunsite.unc.edu/pub/Linux/system/Printing/free-lj4-1.1p1.tar.gz**
- BiTronics parallel port interface **ftp://sunsite.unc.edu/pub/Linux/kernel/misc/bt-ALPHA-0.0.1.tar.gz**

Ghostscript

Many Linux programs output PostScript files. Non-PostScript printers can emulate PostScript Level 2 using Ghostscript.

- Ghostscript **ftp://ftp.cs.wisc.edu/pub/ghost/aladdin/**

Ghostscript-supported printers:

- Apple Imagewriter
- C Itoh M8510
- Canon BubbleJet BJ10e, BJ200
- Canon LBP-8II, LIPS III
- DEC LA50/70/75/75plus
- DEC LN03, LJ250

- Epson 9-pin, 24-pin, LQ series, Stylus, AP3250
- HP 2563B
- HP DesignJet 650C
- HP DeskJet/Plus/500
- HP DeskJet 500C/520C/550C/1200C color
- HP LaserJet/Plus/II/III/4
- HP PaintJet/XL/XL300 color
- IBM Jetprinter color
- IBM Proprinter
- Imagen ImPress
- Mitsubishi CP50 color
- NEC P6/P6+/P60
- Okidata MicroLine 182
- Ricoh 4081
- SPARCprinter
- StarJet 48 inkjet printer
- Tektronix 4693d color 2/4/8-bit
- Tektronix 4695/4696 inkjet plotter
- Xerox XES printers (2700, 3700, 4045, and so on)

Others:

- Canon BJC600 and Epson ESC/P color printers **ftp://petole.imag.fr/pub/postscript/**

Scanners

Scanner	Site
A4 Tech AC 4096	ftp://ftp.informatik.hu-berlin.de/pub/local/linux/ac4096.tgz
Fujitsu SCSI-2 scanners—Contact Dr. G.W. Wettstein	greg%wind.UUCP@plains.nodak.edu
Genius GS-B105G	ftp://tsx-11.mit.edu/pub/linux/ALPHA/scanner/gs105-0.0.1.tar.gz
Genius GeniScan GS4500 handheld scanner	ftp://tsx-11.mit.edu/pub/linux/ALPHA/scanner/gs4500-1.3.tar.gz
HP ScanJet, ScanJet Plus	ftp://ftp.ctrl-c.liu.se/unix/linux/wingel/
HP ScanJet II series SCSI	ftp://sunsite.unc.edu/pub/Linux/apps/graphics/scanners/hpscanpbm-0.3a.tar.gz

Scanner	Site
Logitech Scanman 32/256	ftp://tsx-11.mit.edu/pub/linux/ALPHA/scanner/logiscan-0.0.2.tar.gz
Mustek M105 handheld scanner with GI1904 interface	ftp://tsx-11.mit.edu/pub/linux/ALPHA/scanner/scan- driver-0.1.8.tar.gz
UMAX SCSI scanners—Contact Craig Johnston	mkshenk@u.washington.edu

Other Hardware

- VESA Power Savings Protocol (DPMS) monitors

Support for power savings is included in the Linux kernel. Just use `setterm` to enable support.

Joysticks

- Joystick driver **ftp://sunsite.unc.edu/pub/Linux/kernel/patches/console/joystick-0.7.2.tgz**
- Joystick driver (module) **ftp://sunsite.unc.edu/pub/Linux/kernel/patches/console/joyfixed.tgz**

Video Capture Boards

Video Board	Site
FAST Screen Machine II	ftp://sunsite.unc.edu/pub/Linux/apps/video/ScreenMachineII_1.1.tgz
ProMovie Studio	ftp://sunsite.unc.edu/pub/Linux/apps/video/PMS-grabber.tgz
VideoBlaster, Rombo Media Pro+	ftp://sunsite.unc.edu/pub/Linux/apps/video/vid_src.gz
WinVision video capture card	ftp://sunsite.unc.edu/pub/Linux/apps/video/fgrabber-1.0.tgz
VT1500 TV	ftp://sunsite.unc.edu/pub/Linux/apps/video/vt1500-1.0.5.tgz

Uninterruptible Power Supplies (UPSs)

- APC SmartUPS **ftp://sunsite.unc.edu/pub/Linux/system/UPS/apcd-0.1.tar.gz**
- UPSs with RS-232 monitoring port (unipower package) **ftp://sunsite.unc.edu/pub/Linux/system/UPS/unipower-1.0.0.tgz**
- Various other UPSs are supported—read the UPS HOWTO

Appendixes

Data Acquisition

The Linux Lab Project site collects drivers for hardware dealing with data acquisition; and they also maintain some mailing lists dealing with the subject. I have no experience with data acquisition so please check the site for more details.

- Linux Lab Project **ftp://koala.chemie.fu-berlin.de/pub/linux/LINUX-LAB/**
- CED 1401
- DBCC CAMAC
- IEEE-488 (GPIB, HPIB) boards
- Keithley DAS-1200
- National Instruments AT-MIO-16F / Lab-PC+
- Analog Devices RTI-800/815 ADC/DAC board contact Paul Gortmaker (**gpg109@anu.edu.au**)

Miscellaneous

Device	Site
HP IEEE-488 (HP-IB) interface	ftp://beaver.chemie.fu-berlin.de/pub/linux/IEEE488/
Maralu chip-card reader/writer	ftp://ftp.thp.uni-koeln.de/pub/linux/chip/
Mattel Powerglove	ftp://sunsite.unc.edu/pub/Linux/apps/linux-powerglove.tgz
Reveal FM Radio card	ftp://magoo.uwsuper.edu/pub/fm-radio/
Videotext cards	ftp://sunsite.unc.edu/pub/Linux/apps/video/videoteXt-0.4.tar.gz

Related Sources of Information

Information	Site
Cameron Spitzer's hardware FAQ archive	ftp://rahul.net/pub/cameron/PC-info/
Computer hardware and software vendor phone numbers	http://mtmis1.mis.semi.harris.com/comp_ph1.html
Guide to computer vendors	http://www.ronin.com/SBA/
System optimization information	http://www.dfw.net/~sdw/

Acknowledgments

Thanks to all the authors and contributors of other HOWTOs—many things here are shamelessly stolen from their works! To Zane Healy and Ed Carp, the original authors of this list; and to everyone else who sent in updates and feedbacks. Special thanks to Eric Boerner and lilo (the person, not the program) for the sanity checks. Thanks also to Dan Quinlan for the original SGML conversion.

S3 Cards Supported by XFree86 3.1.2

- CHIPSET RAMDACCLOCKCHIP BPP CARD
- 801/805 AT&T 20C49016Actix GE 32
- Orchid Fahrenheit 1280+
- 801/805 AT&T 20C490 ICD2061A 16STB PowerGraph X.24
- 805 S3 GENDAC16Miro 10SD VLB/PCI SPEA Mirage VLB
- 805 SS2410ICD2061A 8 Diamond Stealth 24 VLB
- 928 AT&T 20C49016Actix Ultra
- 928 Sierra SC15025ICD2061A 32ELSA Winner 1000 ISA/VLB/EISA
- 928 Bt485 ICD2061A 32STB Pegasus VL
- 928 Bt485 SC1141216SPEA Mercury VLB
- 928 Bt485 ICD2061A 32#9 GXE Level 10/11/12
- 928 Ti3020ICD2061A 32#9 GXE Level 14/16
- 864 AT&T 20C498 ICS249432Miro 20SD (BIOS 1.x)
- 864 AT&T 20C498/ICD2061A/32ELSA Winner 1000 PRO VLB/PCI
- STG1700 ICS9161MIRO 20SD (BIOS 2.x)
- 864 STG1700 ICD2061A 32Actix GE 64 VLB
- 864 AT&T 20C498/ICS259516SPEA Mirage P64 DRAM (BIOS 3.x)
- AT&T 21C498
- 864 S3 86C716 SDAC 32ELSA Winner 1000 PRO Miro 20SD (BIOS 3.x) SPEA Mirage P64 DRAM (BIOS 4.x)
- Diamond Stealth 64 DRAM
- 864 ICS5342 ICS534232Diamond Stealth 64 DRAM (some)
- 864 AT&T 20C490 ICD2061A 32#9 GXE64
- 864 AT&T 20C498-13ICD2061A 32#9 GXE64 PCI
- 964 AT&T 20C505 ICD2061A 32Miro Crystal 20SV PCI
- 964 Bt485 ICD2061A 32Diamond Stealth 64
- 964 Bt9485ICS9161A 32SPEA Mercury 64

- 964 Ti3020ICD2061A 8 ELSA Winner 2000 PRO PCI
- 964 Ti3025Ti3025 32#9 GXE64 Pro VLB/PCI Miro Crystal 40SV
- 764 (Trio64) 32SPEA Mirage P64 (BIOS 5.x)
- Diamond Stealth 64 DRAM #9 GXE64 Trio64 STB PowerGraph 64

Supported PCMCIA Cards

These cards are supported by David Hinds' PCMCIA package and this list is taken from his Web page.

Ethernet Cards

- 3Com 3c589, 3c589
- Accton EN2212
- EtherCardCNet CN30BC
- EthernetD-Link DE-650EFA
- InfoExpress SPT
- EFA 205 10baseTEP-210
- Ethernet Farallon
- EtherwaveGVC NIC-2000P
- Ethernet ComboHYPERTEC
- HyperEnetIBM CreditCard
- Ethernet AdapterIC-Card
- EthernetKatron PE-520
- EthernetKingston KNE-PCM/MLANEED
- EthernetLinksys
- EtherCardMaxtech PCN2000
- EthernetNetwork General "Sniffer"
- New Media
- EthernetNovell/National NE4100
- InfoMoverProteon
- EthernetPreMax PE-200
- EthernetRPTI EP400
- EthernetSocket Communications Socket EA LAN AdapterThomas-Conrad
- EthernetVolktek Ethernet

Modem Cards

All modem cards should work.

Memory Cards

- New Media SRAMEpson 2MB SRAMIntel Series 2 and Series 2+ Flash

SCSI Adapters

- Qlogic FastSCSI PCMCIANew Media Bus Toaster SCSIAdaptec APA-1460 SlimSCSI

Unsupported

- Xircom ethernet and ethernet/modem cards
- Canon/Compaq PCMCIA floppy drive

APPENDIX D

The Linux CD-ROM HOWTO

This document describes how to install, configure, and use CD-ROM drives under Linux. It lists the supported hardware, and answers a number of frequently asked questions. The intent is to bring new users quickly up-to-speed and reduce the amount of traffic in the USENET newsgroups.

Introduction

This is the Linux CD-ROM HOWTO document. It is intended as a quick reference covering everything you need to know to install and configure CD-ROM hardware under Linux. Frequently asked questions related to CD-ROM technology are answered, and references are given to other sources of information related to CD-ROM applications and technology.

Acknowledgments

Much of this information came from the file `README.sbpcd` provided with the Linux kernel source code, written by Eberhard Moenkeberg (**eberhard_moenkeberg@rollo.central.de**), the Internet **alt.cd-rom** FAQ, and input from Linux users.

Thanks to the Linuxdoc-SGML package, this HOWTO is available in several formats, all generated from a common source file.

Revision History

Here's a brief revision history of this document:

Version 1.0. First version made publicly available

Version 1.1. CDU33A is explicitly supported as of 1.1.20 kernel; notes on Reveal FX; information on reading audio tracks; information on some alpha drivers; added troubleshooting section; a few other minor additions

Version 1.2. ISO9660 file systems must be mounted read-only starting with 1.1.33 kernel; clarified that SB16 SCSI is supported and newer Aztech drives are not supported; references to `photocd` and `xpcd` programs; note on new `sbpcd` auto-eject feature

Version 1.3. Minor change to the way `sbpcd` auto-eject feature is disabled starting with the 1.1.49 kernel; added information on XA discs and how to identify them

Version 1.4. HOWTO now available in other languages; IBM and Longshine drives now supported by `sbpcd`; alpha driver for Aztech drives; CDU-33 driver no longer auto-probes, supports PhotoCD and audio; more than two SCSI drives are supported; new driver for IDE; reminder to check drive jumpers; can now set `sbpcd` auto-eject with IOCTL; list of drivers with multisession support; question on flashing light on CDU-33

New Versions of This Document

New versions of this document periodically will be posted to **comp.os.linux.announce**. They also will be uploaded to various anonymous ftp sites that archive such information, including **sunsite.unc.edu:/pub/Linux/docs/HOWTO**.

Hypertext versions of this and other Linux HOWTOs are available on many World Wide Web sites. You can also buy printed copies from several vendors.

A French translation of this HOWTO, by Bruno Cornec (**cornec@stna7.stna.dgac.fr**), is available at **ftp.ibp.fr:/pub2/linux/french/docs/HOWTO**. A Japanese translation is in progress.

Feedback

I rely on you, the users, to make this HOWTO useful. If you have any suggestions, corrections, or comments, please send them to me and I will try to incorporate them in the next revision.

CD-ROM Technology

> *CD-ROM is read-only memory, and audio compact disc system is available as package-media of digital data for those purpose. For playing audio CD, please insert Head-phone jack.*
>
> - From a CD-ROM instruction manual

Don't panic! The world of CD-ROM technology is not as confusing as your instruction manual.

CD-ROM stands for *compact disc read-only memory*, a mass storage medium utilizing an optical laser to read microscopic pits on the aluminized layer of a polycarbonate disc.

The same format is used for audio compact discs. Because of its high storage capacity, reliability, and low cost, CD-ROM has become an increasingly popular storage medium.

The storage capacity of a CD-ROM disc is approximately 650 megabytes, equivalent to over 500 high-density 3.5" floppy disks, or roughly 250,000 typed pages.

First-generation CD-ROM drives (known as *single-speed drives*), provide a transfer rate of approximately 150 kilobytes per second (kbps), but are mostly obsolete now. *Double-speed drives* and *quad-speed drives* are commonly available, and 8X drives have recently been introduced.

Most CD-ROM drives use either the *Small Computer Systems Interface (SCSI)* or a *vendor-proprietary interface*. They also typically support playing audio CDs via an external headphone jack or line-level output. CD-ROMs usually are formatted with an ISO-9660 (formerly called *High Sierra*) file system. This format restricts filenames to the MS-DOS style (8+3 characters). The Rock Ridge Extensions use undefined fields in the ISO-9660 standard to support longer filenames and additional Unix style information (such as file ownership, symbolic links, and so on).

PhotoCD is a standard developed by Kodak for storing photographic images as digital data on a CD-ROM. With appropriate software, you can view the images on a computer, manipulate them, or send them to a printer.

CD recorders (CD-R) have recently become available. They use a different medium and specialized equipment for recording, but the resulting disc can be read by any CD-ROM drive.

Supported Hardware

This section lists the CD-ROM drivers and interfaces that currently are supported under Linux. The information here is based on the latest Linux kernel, which at the time of this writing was version 1.1.69.

SCSI CD-ROM Drives

Small Computer Systems Interface (SCSI) is a popular format for CD-ROM drives. Its chief advantages are a reasonably fast transfer rate, multiple-device capability, and support on a variety of computer platforms.

Any SCSI CD-ROM drive with a block size of 512 or 2048 bytes should work under Linux; this includes the vast majority of CD-ROM drives on the market.

You also will need a supported SCSI controller card; see the SCSI HOWTO for more information on interface hardware.

Note that some CD-ROM drives include a controller with a modified interface that is not fully SCSI-compatible (for example, it may not support adding other SCSI devices on the bus).

Proprietary CD-ROM Drives

Several CD-ROM drives using proprietary interfaces are available; often, the interface is provided on a sound card. Simple interface cards equivalent to the interface provided on the sound card are also available. These drives tend to be lower in cost and smaller than SCSI drives.

The following proprietary CD-ROM drives are supported by the Linux kernel (drives listed together are compatible):

- Matsushita/Kotobuki/Panasonic/Creative Labs models CR-521, CR-522, CR-523, CR-562, CR-563, Longshine LCS-7260, IBM
- Mitsumi/Radio Shack
- Sony CDU31A and CDU33A
- Sony CDU535 and CDU531 (driver is available as a kernel patch)
- LMS/Philips CD205/225/202 (driver is available as a kernel patch)
- NEC CDR-260 (driver is available as a kernel patch)
- Aztech CD268A (driver is available as a kernel patch)

The following sound card interfaces are supported:

- SoundBlaster/Pro
- SoundBlaster/16 (both the proprietary interface and SCSI versions)
- Galaxy
- SoundFX
- Spea Media FX sound card (Sequoia S-1000)

The following interface cards are also supported:

- Panasonic CI-101P
- LaserMate
- Aztech (see below)
- WDH-7001C

IBM sells an external CD-ROM drive and interface card that are compatible with the Panasonic CR-562 driver.

Only the older Aztech drives are compatible with the Matsushita/Panasonic driver. There is an ALPHA driver available separately for the CD268A drive. You can find it at **ftp.gwdg.de** in the directory **pub/linux/cdrom/drivers/aztech**.

Drivers for some additional devices are in development and might soon be available as kernel patches. They most likely can be found at **sunsite.unc.edu** in the directory **/pub/Linux/kernel/patches/cdrom**. Check the Linux Software Map for availability.

IDE CD-ROM Drives

CD-ROM drives based on a modified version of the IDE hard disk (ATAPI) standard have recently been introduced—one such drive is the NEC CDR-260. An alpha release of a Linux kernel driver for IDE hard disks and CD-ROM drives is available at **sunsite.unc.edu**. It works with the NEC CDR-260 and possibly others.

> **Note**
>
> The proprietary interfaces are sometimes erroneously referred to as *IDE interfaces* because, like IDE, they use a simple interface based on the PC/AT bus.

Installation

Installation of CD-ROM under Linux consists of the following steps:

1. Installing the hardware
2. Configuring and building the Linux kernel
3. Creating the necessary device files
4. Mounting the media

Installing the Hardware

Follow the manufacturer's instructions for installing the hardware, or have your dealer perform the installation. The details vary depending upon whether the drive is internal or external, and what type of interface is used. There are no special installation requirements for Linux. You might need to set jumpers on the drive and/or interface card for correct operation.

Configuring and Building the Kernel

In order to use a CD-ROM drive, you need the appropriate device drivers. To mount most CD-ROM drives you also need the ISO-9660 file system support in the kernel. Follow your usual procedure for building the kernel: do a **`make config`** and select the appropriate drivers when prompted.

For SCSI CD-ROMs you need to answer Yes to `SCSI support?`, and then enable `SCSI CDROM support` and the driver for the appropriate SCSI interface (for example, `Adaptec AHA1542 support`).

For the proprietary interface drives, select `Sony CDU31A/CDU33A CDROM driver support`, `Mitsumi CDROM driver support`, or `Matsushita/Panasonic CDROM driver support`, according to your drive type. The Matsushita driver supports up to four controllers. For other drive types, you must obtain the driver separately and apply it as a kernel patch.

If you are using the Matsushita/Panasonic drive, you have the choice of letting the kernel auto-probe for the drive, passing it on the kernel command line, or explicitly setting it in the file /usr/src/linux/include/linux/sbpcd.h. It is recommended that you initially set it to auto-probe. Later you can set the type to save some time during bootup.

As of the 1.1.64 kernel, auto-probing for the CDU31A drives has been removed. You now need to do either of the following: add your drive to the configuration table in the driver, or use a lilo boot-line configuration. The format of the lilo command line is:

```
cdu31a=<I/O address>,<interrupt>[,PAS]
```

Setting the interrupt to 0 disables the interrupts and uses polled I/O. The PAS option is for ProAudioSpectum16 sound card users that are not using the sound driver. A typical card would have a configuration like one of the following:

```
cdu31a=0x340,0
cdu31a=0x340,5
```

The easiest way to set this up is to add a line such as the following to your lilo configuration file:

```
append="cdu31a=0x1f88,0,PAS"
```

Again, remember to compile in the ISO-9660 file system support. The Rock Ridge extensions are fully supported by the kernel driver.

If you have a sound card that is supported under Linux, you also should enable and configure the kernel sound driver at this time.

After selecting the device drivers, compile the kernel and install it following your usual procedure.

Creating the Device Files

If you are running a standard Linux distribution, you may have created the necessary device files during installation. Under Slackware Linux, for example, there is a menu-based setup tool that includes CD-ROM setup, and most systems have a /dev/MAKEDEV script. It is recommended that you at least verify the device files against the information in this section.

Create the device file by running the shell commands indicated for your drive type. This should be done as user root. Some Linux distributions may use slightly different CD-ROM device names from those listed here.

It is recommended that you also create a symbolic link to the CD-ROM device to make it easier to remember. For example, for a Panasonic CD-ROM drive, the link could be created using the following:

```
% ln -s /dev/sbpcd /dev/cdrom
```

If you want to play audio CDs, you need to set the protection on the device files to allow users to read and write, by doing something like the following:

```
% chmod 666 /dev/sbpcd
```

Matsushita/Kotobuki/Panasonic/Creative Labs/IBM. With this driver, up to four drives per controller are supported. Only the first device is needed if you have only one drive. If you have more than one controller, create devices with major numbers 26, 27, and 28, up to a maximum of 4 controllers (this is 16 CD-ROM drives in total—hopefully enough for most users).

```
% mknod /dev/sbpcdb 25 0
% mknod /dev/sbpcd0 b 25 0
% mknod /dev/sbpcd1 b 25 1
% mknod /dev/sbpcd2 b 25 2
% mknod /dev/sbpcd3 b 25 3
```

Sony CDU31A/CDU33A. Only one drive is supported by this kernel driver. See the comments in the file `/usr/src/linux/drivers/block/cdu31a.c` for information on configuring the interface card. As of the 1.1.60 kernel, the driver supports playing audio CDs and PhotoCD (but not multisession).

```
% mknod /dev/cdu31a b 15 0
```

See the kernel source file `cdu31a.c` for information on configuring the drive interface card. Also see the notes earlier in this HOWTO about specifying the configuration on the `lilo` command line.

Sony CDU535/CDU531. This driver currently is available only as a kernel patch.

```
% mknod /dev/cdu535 b 24 0
```

Some Linux distributions use `/dev/sonycd` for this device. Older versions of the driver used major device number 21; make sure that your device file is correct.

Mitsumi. The kernel supports one Mitsumi drive. Recent kernels (1.1.25) have incorporated some changes to improve performance.

```
% mknod /dev/mcd b 23 0
```

LMS/Philips. This driver currently is available only as a kernel patch. See the `README` file included with the patches for more information.

```
% mknod /dev/lmscd b 24 0
```

SCSI. Multiple drives are supported (up to the limit of the number of devices on the SCSI bus). Create device files with major number 11 and minor numbers starting at 0.

```
% mknod /dev/scd0 b 11 0
% mknod /dev/scd1 b 11 1
```

IDE Drives. Information on creating the device files are included with the kernel patch for these drives.

Mounting/Unmounting/Ejecting Devices

You can reboot with the new kernel. Watch for a message such as the following indicating that the CD-ROM has been found by the device driver (the message varies depending on the drive type):

```
SBPCD version 2.5 Eberhard Moenkeberg <emoenke@gwdg.de>
SBPCD: Looking for a SoundBlaster/Matsushita CD-ROM drive
SBPCD:
SBPCD: = = = = = = = = = = W A R N I N G = = = = = = = = = =
SBPCD: Auto-Probing can cause a hang (f.e. touching an ethernet card).
SBPCD: If that happens, you have to reboot and use the
SBPCD: LILO (kernel) command line feature like:
SBPCD:
SBPCD:LILO boot: linux sbpcd=0x230,SoundBlaster
SBPCD: or like:
SBPCD:LILO boot: linux sbpcd=0x300,LaserMate
SBPCD: or like:
SBPCD:LILO boot: linux sbpcd=0x330,SPEA
SBPCD:
SBPCD: with your REAL address.
SBPCD: = = = = = = = = = = END of WARNING = = = = = = = = =
SBPCD:
SBPCD: Trying to detect a SoundBlaster CD-ROM drive at 0x230.
SBPCD: - Drive 0: CR-562-x (0.76)
SBPCD: 1 SoundBlaster CD-ROM drive(s) at 0x0230.
SBPCD: init done.
```

Tip

If the bootup messages scroll by too quickly to read, you should be able to retrieve them with the `dmesg` command.

To mount a CD-ROM, insert a disc in the drive, and run the mount command as `root` (this assumes you have created a symbolic link to your device file as recommended earlier in this HOWTO):

```
% mount -t iso9660 -r /dev/cdrom /mnt
```

The CD-ROM now can be accessed under the directory `/mnt`. Note that `/mnt` is commonly used as a temporary mount point; a more suitable name for a permanent installation might be something like `/cdrom`. There are other options to the `mount` command that you may want to use; see the `mount(8)` man page for details.

You can add an entry to `/etc/fstab` to automatically mount a CD-ROM when Linux boots, or to specify parameters for Linux to use when a CD-ROM is mounted; see the `fstab(5)` man page for details.

Caution

To play audio CDs, you should not try to mount them.

To unmount a CD-ROM, use the umount command as root:

```
% umount /mnt
```

The disc can only be unmounted if no processes are currently accessing the drive (including having their default directory set to the mounted drive). You then can eject the disc. Most drives have an eject button; there also is a stand-alone eject program that allows ejecting CD-ROMs under software control.

You should not eject a disc while it is mounted (this may not be possible depending on the type of drive). The sbpcd driver automatically ejects a CD-ROM when it is unmounted, and inserts the CD tray when a disc is mounted (you can turn this feature off when compiling the kernel, or by using a software command).

Troubleshooting

If you still encounter problems, here are some things to check:

If you recompiled the kernel yourself, verify that you are running the new kernel by looking at the time stamp:

```
% uname -a
Linux fizzbin 1.1.31 #1 Wed Jul 20 16:53:35 EDT 1994 i386
```

With recent 1.1.x kernels, you can see what drivers have been compiled by looking at /proc/devices:

```
% cat /proc/devices
Character devices:
1 mem
4 tty
5 cua
6 lp
14 sound
15 Joystick
Block devices:
2 fd
3 hd
25 sbpcd
```

If your drive has hardware jumpers for addressing, check that they are set correctly (for example, set to drive 0 if you have only one drive).

Try reading from the CD-ROM drive. Typing the following command should cause the drive activity light to come on, and no errors should be reported. Use whatever device file is appropriate for your drive, and make sure that a CD-ROM is inserted. Press Ctrl-c to exit.

```
dd if=/dev/cdrom of=/dev/null bs=2048
^C
124+0 records in
124+0 records out
```

If you can read from the drive but cannot mount it, verify that you have compiled in the ISO9660 file system support. With the 1.1.x kernels, this can be done as follows:

```
% cat /proc/filesystems
ext2
msdos
nodev proc
iso9660
```

Make sure that you are mounting the drive with the `-t iso9660` and `-r` options, and that a CD (not an audio CD) known to be good is inserted in the drive.

Make sure that the CD-ROM device files are correct, according to the information in the previous section.

If you are running the syslog daemon, there might be error messages from the kernel that you are not seeing. Try using the `dmesg` command as follows:

```
% dmesg
SBPCD: sbpcd_open: no disk in drive
```

There also might be errors logged to files in `/var/adm`, depending on how your system is configured.

Applications

This section briefly lists some of the key applications available under Linux that are related to CD-ROM drives. Check the Linux Software Map for the latest versions and archive sites.

Audio CD Players

Several programs are available for playing audio CDs through either a headphone jack or an attached sound card.

Program	Specifications
Workman	A graphical player running under X11 and supporting a CD database and many other features
WorkBone	An interactive text-mode player
xcdplayer	A simple X11-based player
cdplayer	A very simple command line-based player

Program	Specifications
Xmcd	An X11/Motif-based player
xmitsumi	Another X11-based player for Mitsumi drives
xplaycd	Another X11-based player, bundled with sound mixer and VU meter programs
cdtool	A set of command line tools for playing audio CDs

Some of these programs are coded to use a specific device file for the CD-ROM (such as `/dev/cdrom`). You may be able to pass the correct device name as a parameter, or you can create a symbolic link in the `/dev` directory. If you are sending the CD output to a sound card, you may want to use a mixer program to set volume settings or select the CD-ROM input for recording.

Inheriting File System

The *Inheriting File System (IFS)* is a kernel driver that allows mounting multiple file systems at the same point. It is similar to the *Translucent File System* provided under SunOS. By mounting a hard disk directory over a CD-ROM file system, you can effectively obtain a writable CD-ROM file system.

The current version is experimental and was written for the 0.99pl11 and pl12 kernels; it might not work with more recent revisions. The author is Werner Almesberger (**almesber@bernina.ethz.ch**).

PhotoCD

PhotoCDs use an ISO-9660 file system containing image files in a proprietary format.

> **Note**
>
> You should be careful about choosing a CD-ROM to use because not all CD-ROM drives support reading PhotoCDs. You should check your manufacturer's documentation before buying a drive.

The `hpcdtoppm` program by Hadmut Danisch converts PhotoCD files to the portable `pixmap` format. It can be obtained from **ftp.gwdg.de:/pub/linux/hpcdtoppm** or as part of the *portable bitmap (PBM) utilities* available on many archive sites (look for `pbm` or `netpbm`).

The `photocd` program by Gerd Knorr (**kraxel@cs.tu-berlin.de**) can convert PhotoCD images into `targa` or Windows and OS/2 bitmap files.

The same author has written the program `xpcd`, an X11-based program for handling PhotoCD images. You can select an image with the mouse, preview the image in a small window, and load the image with any of five possible resolutions. You can also mark a part of the image, then load only the selected part. Look for these packages at **ftp.cs.tu-berlin.de:/pub/linux/Local/misc**.

Mkisofs

Eric Youngdale's `mkisofs` package allows creating an ISO-9660 file system on a hard disk partition. This can then be used to assist in creating and testing CD-ROM file systems before mastering discs.

The tools for actually writing data to writable CD-ROM drives tend to be vendor-specific. They also require writing the data with no interruptions, so a multitasking operating system like Linux is not particularly well-suited.

9660_u

These are some utilities for verifying the format of ISO-9660 formatted discs; you may find them useful for testing suspect CDs. The package can be found on `ftp.cdrom.com` in the `/pub/ptf` directory. They were written by Bill Siegmund and Rich Morin.

Answers to Frequently Asked Questions

The following sections provide answers to some common questions and problems encounter with CD-ROM drives under Linux.

How Can a Non-Root User Mount and Unmount CDs?

Some `mount` commands support the `user` option. For example, consider the following entry in `/etc/fstab`:

```
/dev/sbpcd/cdrom iso9660 user,noauto,ro
```

An ordinary user is then allowed to mount and unmount the drive using these commands:

```
% mount /cdrom
% umount /cdrom
```

The disc will be mounted with some options that ensure security (for example, programs cannot be executed, and device files are ignored)—in some cases this might be too restrictive.

Another method is to get the `usermount` package, which allows non-root users to mount and unmount removable devices such as floppies and CD-ROM drives, but restricts access to other devices (such as hard disk partitions). It is available on major archive sites.

The archive site **ftp.cdrom.com** has the source file `mount.c`, which allows mounting and unmounting of CD-ROM drives (only) by normal users. It runs as a `setuid` executable.

Why Do I Get *device is busy* when Unmounting a CD-ROM?

The disc cannot be unmounted if any processes are accessing the drive, including having their default directory set to the mounted file system. If you cannot identify the processes using the disc, you can use the `fuser` command, as shown in the following example:

```
% umount /cdrom
umount: /dev/sbpcd: device is busy
% fuser -v /cdrom
/cdrom: USER PID ACCESS COMMAND
tranter 50 ..c..bash
```

How Do I Export a CD-ROM to Other Hosts over NFS?

You need to add an entry to the `/etc/exports` file; see the `exports(5)` man page for details.

Can I Boot Linux from CD-ROM?

The easiest way to boot from CD-ROM is to use a boot floppy. Several of the Linux CD-ROM distributions (for example, `Yggdrasil`) include one, or you can use the boot disk(s) from one of the Linux distributions (such as Slackware) that includes the necessary CD-ROM drivers for your system. In the future, it may be possible to boot from IDE CD-ROM drives that have the appropriate ROM BIOS functions.

Why Doesn't the Kernel Recognize My CD-ROM Drive?

If you have a proprietary interface at a non-standard address, you might need to set the I/O port location in the appropriate kernel header file. Similarly, auto-probing by the kernel driver might conflict with another device (such as a network card) and cause your system to hang.

For the Matsushita/Kotubuki/Panasonic/Creative Labs drives, you need to edit the file `sbpcd.h`. For Mitsumi drives it is `mcd.h` and for Sony drives it is `cdu31a.h`. All these files are normally installed in `/usr/include/linux`. Alternatively, you can set the drive parameters on the `lilo` command line.

How Can I Read Digital Data from Audio CDs?

Only a few CD-ROM drives support this. Heiko Eissfeldt **(heiko@colossus.escape.de)** and Olaf Kindel have written a utility that reads audio data and saves it as WAV format sound files. It only works with Toshiba XM3401 and XM4101 SCSI drives. The package is named cdda2wav.tar.gz and can be found at **sunsite.unc.edu.**

The Panasonic `sbpcd` driver also has support for reading sound data, beginning with the 2.0 driver included in the 1.1.22 kernel. A modified version of the `cdda2wav` program that works with this can be found at **ftp.gwdg.de in /pub/linux/misc/cdda2wav-sbpcd.2.tar.gz.**

Even though the standard `cdda2wav` program claims to support the Panasonic drives, it does not yet work properly, because of the need to handle "overlap" of the data.

The CDU-33 driver now supports reading audio data, and is said to work with the `cdda2wav` program.

For more information on this subject, see the **alt.cd-rom** FAQ listed in the "References" section at the end of this document.

How Do I Turn Off the Auto-Probing Messages on Boot?

The `sbpcd` driver displays a lot of information during bootup. If you want to suppress this, set the `sbpcd_debug` variable in the file `sbpcd.c`. The comments in the file explain the various values that can be set for this variable.

Why Doesn't the *find* Command Work Properly?

On ISO-9660 formatted discs without the Rock Ridge Extensions, you need to add the `-noleaf` option to the `find` command.

The reason is that the number of links for each directory file is not easily obtainable, so it is set to 2. The default behavior for the `find` program is to look for `i_links-2` subdirectories in each directory, and then to assume that the rest are regular files. The `-noleaf` option disables this optimization.

Is the Reveal Multimedia Effects Kit CD-ROM Supported?

The answer is provided by **Horne@leader.pfc.mit.edu**:

Reveal Multimedia kits are available fairly cheaply ($300 or so) from department stores. After some thrashing I discovered how to make the following CD-ROM drive work under Linux:

This is a Reveal Multimedia FX kit, which includes a SoundFX SC400 sound card, which has interfaces for Sony CDU33A, Panasonic CR-563, and Mitsumi LU005s. My kit includes Sony.

The tricks to making the Sony CD-ROM work are as follows:

Decide which kernel to patch. I pulled the 1.0 kernel off the Trans-Ameritech CD-ROM via DOS (my system started out as SLS a long time ago).

Add addresses `0x634` and `0x654` to the table at the top of the `cdu31a` driver:

```
static unsigned short cdu31a_addresses[] =
{
0x340, /* Standard configuration Sony Interface */
0x1f88,/* Fusion CD-16 */
0x230, /* SoundBlaster 16 card */
0x360, /* Secondary standard Sony Interface */
0x320, /* Secondary standard Sony Interface */
0x330, /* Secondary standard Sony Interface */
0x634,
0x654,
0
 };
```

Recompile your kernel, specifying Sony CDU31A and ISO9960 support. Create the device file (use major number 15, not 21 as specified in the Trans-Ameritech docs):

```
% mknod /dev/cd b 15 0
```

Mount the drive:

```
% mount -t iso9660 -r /dev/cd /cdrom
```

I'm still working on the actual sound support (I don't really need it yet) but that should be much easier.

Thanks to Reveal technical support for the information that the CD interface is at `0x414` off of the soundcard base address, to Roman at Trans-Ameritech (**roman@btr.btr.com**) who suggested patching the `cdu31a` driver, and to Dale Elrod (**dale@post.dungeon.com**) who provided an existence proof (Dale, your `zImage` didn't recognize the drive—I expect you actually have slightly different hardware.)

The original driver is due to **minyard@wf-rch.cirr.com**, and Linus made it all possible.

Does Linux Support Any Recordable CD-ROM Drives?

The answer is provided by Adam J. Richter (**adam@yggdrasil.com**):

The `Yggdrasil` distribution can drive a Philips CD writer with an Adaptec 154x SCSI controller. I am not sure which other SCSI controllers, if any, will work. You can use `mkisofs` to make an ISO-9660 file system and use `cd write` to write it to the CD. If you want us to help you set this up, you can call us at our technical support number: 900-446-6075, ext. 835 (this costs $2.95/minute, U.S. only).

The Eject Function (for example, from Workman) Does Not Work!

The `sbpcd` driver used to have a problem where the drive could be locked and the eject `ioctl()` would fail. This appears to have been corrected starting with the version 1.1.29 kernel.

You Say I Need to Configure and Build a Kernel—How Do I Do That?

This is not the kernel HOWTO (any volunteers?). Until one is written, try reading the file `/usr/src/linux/README`; it is reasonably complete. If you really don't want to compile a kernel, you may be able to find a precompiled kernel that has the drivers you need as part of a Linux distribution (for example, the Slackware "q" series of disks).

▶▶ See "Building a New Kernel," p. 91

Why Do I Get *Mount: Read-only file system* When Mounting a CD-ROM?

With older kernels you could mount a CD-ROM for read/write; attempts to write data to the CD would not generate any errors. As of kernel version 1.1.33, this was corrected so that CD-ROMs must be mounted read only (using the `-r` option to mount).

Why Does the Disc Tray Open When I Shut Down the System?

As of the 1.1.38 kernel, the `sbpcd` driver ejects the CD when it is unmounted or closed. If you shut down the system, a mounted CD is unmounted. This feature is for convenience when changing discs. If the tray is open when you mount or read a CD, it also is automatically closed.

I found that this caused problems with a few programs (such as `cdplay` and `workbone`). As of the 1.1.60 kernel you can control this feature with software. A sample program is included in the `README.sbpcd` file (or you can use the eject program).

How Do I Mount a "Special" CD?

The "special" CD is likely an XA disc (like all Photo CDs or *one-offs* created using CD-R drives). Most of the Linux kernel CD-ROM drivers do not support XA discs, although you might be able to find a patch on one of the archive sites to add support for XA discs.

The `sbpcd` driver does support XA. If you are using this driver, you can determine if the disc is XA by using the following procedure: go into the file `sbpcd.c` and enable the display of the "Table of Contents" (`DBG_TOC`). Build and install the new kernel, and then boot from it. During each mount the TOC info will be written (either to the console or to a log file). If the first displayed value in the TOC header line is `20`, then it is an XA disc. That byte is `00` with normal disks. If the TOC display shows different tracks, this is also a sign that you have an XA disc.

(Thanks to Eberhard Moenkeberg for this information.)

Which Kernel Drivers Support Multisession?

The `sbpcd` driver supports multisession. The SCSI CD-ROM driver supports multisession with NEC and TOSHIBA drives. The `cdu31a` driver has some multisession support written, but it does not yet work.

Some drivers available as kernel patches may support multisession for other drives.

Why Does the Drive Light Flash on My CDU33 Drive?

This is normal and was added in a recent revision of the driver. It flashes the drive light when a CD is mounted (it's not a bug, it's a feature...).

References

Information on the Panasonic CD-ROM driver can be found in the `/usr/src/linux/drivers/block/README.sbpcd` file.

The following USENET FAQs are posted periodically to `news.answers` and archived at Internet FTP sites such as **rtfm.mit.edu**:

- **alt.cd-rom** FAQ
- **comp.periphs.scsi** FAQ

Several other Linux HOWTOs have useful information relevant to CD-ROM applications and technology:

- SCSI HOWTO
- Hardware Compatibility HOWTO
- Sound HOWTO
- Distribution HOWTO

At least ten companies sell Linux distributions on CD-ROM; most of them are listed in the Distribution HOWTO.

The following USENET newsgroups cover CD-ROM related topics:

comp.publish.cdrom.hardware

comp.publish.cdrom.multimedia

comp.publish.cdrom.software

comp.sys.ibm.pc.hardware.cd-rom

alt.cd-rom

alt.cd-rom.reviews

The Internet site **ftp.cdrom.com** has a large archive of CD-ROM information and software; look in the directory **/pub/cdrom**.

The Linux Documentation Project has produced several books on Linux, including *Linux Installation* and *Getting Started*. These are available at no charge by anonymous FTP from major Linux archive sites, and also can be purchased in hardcopy format.

The Linux Software Map (LSM) is an invaluable reference for locating Linux software. The LSM can be found on various anonymous FTP sites, including **sunsite.unc.edu:/pub/Linux/docs/LSM.gz**.

APPENDIX E

The GNU GENERAL PUBLIC LICENSE

Version 2, June 1991

Preamble

The licenses for most software are designed to take away your freedom to share and change it. By contrast, the GNU General Public License is intended to guarantee your freedom to share and change free software—to make sure the software is free for all its users. This General Public License applies to most of the Free Software Foundation's software and to any other program whose authors commit to using it. (Some other Free Software Foundation software is covered by the GNU Library General Public License instead.) You can apply it to your programs, too.

When we speak of free software, we are referring to freedom, not price. Our General Public Licenses are designed to make sure that you have the freedom to distribute copies of free software (and charge for this service if you wish), that you receive source code or can get it if you want it, that you can change the software or use pieces of it in new free programs; and that you know you can do these things.

To protect your rights, we need to make restrictions that forbid anyone to deny you these rights or to ask you to surrender the rights. These restrictions translate to certain responsibilities for you if you distribute copies of the software, or if you modify it.

For example, if you distribute copies of such a program, whether gratis or for a fee, you must give the recipients all the rights that you have. You must make sure that they, too, receive or can get the source code. And you must show them these terms so they know their rights.

We protect your rights with two steps: (1) copyright the software, and (2) offer you this license which gives you legal permission to copy, distribute and/or modify the software.

Also, for each author's protection and ours, we want to make certain that everyone understands that there is no warranty for this free software. If the software is modified by someone else and passed on, we want its recipients to know that what they have is not the original, so that any problems introduced by others will not reflect on the original authors' reputations.

Finally, any free program is threatened constantly by software patents. We wish to avoid the danger that redistributors of a free program will individually obtain patent licenses, in effect making the program proprietary. To prevent this, we have made it clear that any patent must be licensed for everyone's free use or not licensed at all.

The precise terms and conditions for copying, distribution and modification follow.

GNU GENERAL PUBLIC LICENSE TERMS AND CONDITIONS FOR COPYING, DISTRIBUTION, AND MODIFICATION

0. This License applies to any program or other work which contains a notice placed by the copyright holder saying it may be distributed under the terms of this General Public License. The "Program," below, refers to any such program or work, and a "work based on the Program" means either the Program or any derivative work under copyright law: that is to say, a work containing the Program or a portion of it, either verbatim or with modifications and/or translated into another language. (Hereinafter, translation is included without limitation in the term "modification.") Each licensee is addressed as "you."

Activities other than copying, distribution and modification are not covered by this License; they are outside its scope. The act of running the Program is not restricted, and the output from the Program is covered only if its contents constitute a work based on the Program (independent of having been made by running the Program). Whether that is true depends on what the Program does.

1. You may copy and distribute verbatim copies of the Program's source code as you receive it, in any medium, provided that you conspicuously and appropriately publish on each copy an appropriate copyright notice and disclaimer of warranty; keep intact all the notices that refer to this License and to the absence of any warranty; and give any other recipients of the Program a copy of this License along with the Program.

You may charge a fee for the physical act of transferring a copy, and you may at your option offer warranty protection in exchange for a fee.

2. You may modify your copy or copies of the Program or any portion of it, thus forming a work based on the Program, and copy and distribute such modifications or work under the terms of Section 1 above, provided that you also meet all of these conditions:

> a) You must cause the modified files to carry prominent notices stating that you changed the files and the date of any change.

b) You must cause any work that you distribute or publish, that in whole or in part contains or is derived from the Program or any part thereof, to be licensed as a whole at no charge to all third parties under the terms of this License.

c) If the modified program normally reads commands interactively when run, you must cause it, when started running for such interactive use in the most ordinary way, to print or display an announcement including an appropriate copyright notice and a notice that there is no warranty (or else, saying that you provide a warranty) and that users may redistribute the program under these conditions, and telling the user how to view a copy of this License. (Exception: if the Program itself is interactive but does not normally print such an announcement, your work based on the Program is not required to print an announcement.)

These requirements apply to the modified work as a whole. If identifiable sections of that work are not derived from the Program, and can be reasonably considered independent and separate works in themselves, then this License, and its terms, do not apply to those sections when you distribute them as separate works. But when you distribute the same sections as part of a whole which is a work based on the Program, the distribution of the whole must be on the terms of this License, whose permissions for other licensees extend to the entire whole, and thus to each and every part regardless of who wrote it.

Thus, it is not the intent of this section to claim rights or contest your rights to work written entirely by you; rather, the intent is to exercise the right to control the distribution of derivative or collective works based on the Program.

In addition, mere aggregation of another work not based on the Program with the Program (or with a work based on the Program) on a volume of a storage or distribution medium does not bring the other work under the scope of this License.

3. You may copy and distribute the Program (or a work based on it, under Section 2) in object code or executable form under the terms of Sections 1 and 2 above, provided that you also do one of the following:

a) Accompany it with the complete corresponding machine-readable source code, which must be distributed under the terms of Sections 1 and 2 above on a medium customarily used for software interchange; or,

b) Accompany it with a written offer, valid for at least three years, to give any third party, for a charge no more than your cost of physically performing source distribution, a complete machine-readable copy of the corresponding source code, to be distributed under the terms of Sections 1 and 2 above on a medium customarily used for software interchange; or,

c) Accompany it with the information you received as to the offer to distribute corresponding source code. (This alternative is allowed only for noncommercial distribution and only if you received the program in object code or executable form with such an offer, in accord with Subsection b above.)

The source code for a work means the preferred form of the work for making modifications to it. For an executable work, complete source code means all the source code for all modules it contains, plus any associated interface definition files, plus the scripts used to control compilation and installation of the executable. However, as a special exception, the source code distributed need not include anything that is normally distributed (in either source or binary form) with the major components (compiler, kernel, and so on) of the operating system on which the executable runs, unless that component itself accompanies the executable.

If distribution of executable or object code is made by offering access to copy from a designated place, then offering equivalent access to copy the source code from the same place counts as distribution of the source code, even though third parties are not compelled to copy the source along with the object code.

4. You may not copy, modify, sublicense, or distribute the Program except as expressly provided under this License. Any attempt otherwise to copy, modify, sublicense or distribute the Program is void, and will automatically terminate your rights under this License. However, parties who have received copies, or rights, from you under this License will not have their licenses terminated so long as such parties remain in full compliance.

5. You are not required to accept this License, since you have not signed it. However, nothing else grants you permission to modify or distribute the Program or its derivative works. These actions are prohibited by law if you do not accept this License. Therefore, by modifying or distributing the Program (or any work based on the Program), you indicate your acceptance of this License to do so, and all its terms and conditions for copying, distributing or modifying the Program or works based on it.

6. Each time you redistribute the Program (or any work based on the Program), the recipient automatically receives a license from the original licensor to copy, distribute or modify the Program subject to these terms and conditions. You may not impose any further restrictions on the recipients' exercise of the rights granted herein. You are not responsible for enforcing compliance by third parties to this License.

7. If, as a consequence of a court judgment or allegation of patent infringement or for any other reason (not limited to patent issues), conditions are imposed on you (whether by court order, agreement or otherwise) that contradict the conditions of this License, they do not excuse you from the conditions of this License. If you cannot distribute so as to satisfy simultaneously your obligations under this License and any other pertinent obligations, then as a consequence you may not distribute the Program at all. For example, if a patent license would not permit royalty-free redistribution of the Program by all those who receive copies directly or indirectly through you, then the only way you could satisfy both it and this License would be to refrain entirely from distribution of the Program.

If any portion of this section is held invalid or unenforceable under any particular circumstance, the balance of the section is intended to apply and the section as a whole is intended to apply in other circumstances.

It is not the purpose of this section to induce you to infringe any patents or other property right claims or to contest validity of any such claims; this section has the sole purpose of protecting the integrity of the free software distribution system, which is implemented by public license practices. Many people have made generous contributions to the wide range of software distributed through that system in reliance on consistent application of that system; it is up to the author/donor to decide if he or she is willing to distribute software through any other system, and a licensee cannot impose that choice.

This section is intended to make thoroughly clear what is believed to be a consequence of the rest of this License.

8. If the distribution and/or use of the Program is restricted in certain countries either by patents or by copyrighted interfaces, the original copyright holder who places the Program under this License may add an explicit geographical distribution limitation excluding those countries, so that distribution is permitted only in or among countries not thus excluded. In such case, this License incorporates the limitation as if written in the body of this License.

9. The Free Software Foundation may publish revised and/or new versions of the General Public License from time to time. Such new versions will be similar in spirit to the present version, but may differ in detail to address new problems or concerns.

Each version is given a distinguishing version number. If the Program specifies a version number of this License which applies to it and "any later version," you have the option of following the terms and conditions either of that version or of any later version published by the Free Software Foundation. If the Program does not specify a version number of this License, you may choose any version ever published by the Free Software Foundation.

10. If you wish to incorporate parts of the Program into other free programs whose distribution conditions are different, write to the author to ask for permission. For software which is copyrighted by the Free Software Foundation, write to the Free Software Foundation; we sometimes make exceptions for this. Our decision will be guided by the two goals of preserving the free status of all derivatives of our free software and of promoting the sharing and reuse of software generally.

NO WARRANTY

11. BECAUSE THE PROGRAM IS LICENSED FREE OF CHARGE, THERE IS NO WARRANTY FOR THE PROGRAM, TO THE EXTENT PERMITTED BY APPLICABLE LAW. EXCEPT WHEN OTHERWISE STATED IN WRITING THE COPYRIGHT HOLDERS AND/OR OTHER PARTIES PROVIDE THE PROGRAM "AS IS" WITHOUT WARRANTY OF ANY KIND, EITHER EXPRESSED OR IMPLIED, INCLUDING, BUT NOT LIMITED TO, THE IMPLIED WARRANTIES OF MERCHANTABILITY AND FITNESS FOR A PARTICULAR PURPOSE. THE ENTIRE RISK AS TO THE QUALITY AND PERFORMANCE OF THE PROGRAM IS WITH YOU. SHOULD THE PROGRAM PROVE DEFECTIVE, YOU ASSUME THE COST OF ALL NECESSARY SERVICING, REPAIR OR CORRECTION.

12. IN NO EVENT UNLESS REQUIRED BY APPLICABLE LAW OR AGREED TO IN WRITING WILL ANY COPYRIGHT HOLDER, OR ANY OTHER PARTY WHO MAY MODIFY AND/OR REDISTRIBUTE THE PROGRAM AS PERMITTED ABOVE, BE LIABLE TO YOU FOR DAMAGES, INCLUDING ANY GENERAL, SPECIAL, INCIDENTAL OR CONSEQUENTIAL DAMAGES ARISING OUT OF THE USE OR INABILITY TO USE THE PROGRAM (INCLUDING BUT NOT LIMITED TO LOSS OF DATA OR DATA BEING RENDERED INACCURATE OR LOSSES SUSTAINED BY YOU OR THIRD PARTIES OR A FAILURE OF THE PROGRAM TO OPERATE WITH ANY OTHER PROGRAMS), EVEN IF SUCH HOLDER OR OTHER PARTY HAS BEEN ADVISED OF THE POSSIBILITY OF SUCH DAMAGES.

END OF TERMS AND CONDITIONS

How to Apply These Terms to Your New Programs

If you develop a new program, and you want it to be of the greatest possible use to the public, the best way to achieve this is to make it free software which everyone can redistribute and change under these terms.

To do so, attach the following notices to the program. It is safest to attach them to the start of each source file to most effectively convey the exclusion of warranty; and each file should have at least the "copyright" line and a pointer to where the full notice is found.

```
<one line to give the program's name and a brief idea of what it does.>
     Copyright (C) 19yy  <name of author>
```

This program is free software; you can redistribute it and/or modify it under the terms of the GNU General Public License as published by the Free Software Foundation; either version 2 of the License, or (at your option) any later version.

This program is distributed in the hope that it will be useful, but WITHOUT ANY WARRANTY; without even the implied warranty of MERCHANTABILITY or FITNESS FOR A PARTICULAR PURPOSE. See the GNU General Public License for more details.

You should have received a copy of the GNU General Public License along with this program; if not, write to the Free Software Foundation, Inc., 675 Mass Ave, Cambridge MA 02139 USA.

Also add information on how to contact you by electronic and paper mail.

If the program is interactive, make it output a short notice like this when it starts in an interactive mode:

```
Gnomovision version 69, Copyright (C) 19yy name of author
Gnomovision comes with ABSOLUTELY NO WARRANTY; for details type 'show w'.
This is free software, and you are welcome to redistribute it
under certain conditions; type 'show c' for details.
```

The hypothetical commands 'show w' and 'show c' should show the appropriate parts of the General Public License. Of course, the commands you use may be called something other than 'show w' and 'show c;' they could even be mouse-clicks or menu items—whatever suits your program.

You should also get your employer (if you work as a programmer) or your school, if any, to sign a "copyright disclaimer" for the program, if necessary. Here is a sample; alter the names:

```
Yoyodyne, Inc., hereby disclaims all copyright interest in the program
'Gnomovision' (which makes passes at compilers) written by James Hacker.

<signature of Ty Coon>, 1 April 1989
Ty Coon, President of Vice
```

This General Public License does not permit incorporating your program into proprietary programs. If your program is a subroutine library, you may consider it more useful to permit linking proprietary applications with the library. If this is what you want to do, use the GNU Library General Public License instead of this License.

APPENDIX F

The Red Hat Commercial Linux Distribution

The second CD-ROM accompanying this book contains the entire Red Hat 2.1 distribution of Linux. This is another distribution, much as the Slackware distribution on which this book is based. We've included this second distribution in case you have problems installing Slackware.

The directory structure for the CD is shown below:

```
/mnt/redhat
  ¦----> RedHat
           ¦----> RPMS          -- binary packages
           ¦----> SRPMS         -- source packages
           ¦----> base          -- small filesystem setup archives
           ¦----> instimage     -- image used for graphical installs
           ¦----> sets          -- symlinks to rpms, divided by series
  ¦----> trees                  -- filesystems used for boot and ramdisks
  ¦----> images                 -- boot and ramdisk images
           ¦----> floppies      -- floppy disk images for floppy install
  ¦----> dosutils               -- installation utilities for DOS
  ¦----> doc                    -- various FAQs and HOWTOs
```

Quick Installation

The following is from the readme file in the root directory of the RedHat CD-ROM:

First select a boot image from images/1213/image.txt and write it to a floppy using 'dd' (or 'dosutils\rawrite.exe' on DOS). You also need to make two ramdisk floppies from images/ramdisk1.img and images/ramdisk2.img. Note that PCMCIA support is included and will work with any of the boot disks you use. [Also Note: If you use a PCMCIA SCSI card you need to use boot image with "Adaptec" support.]

The images in images/1213/image.txt are listed with supported devices:

SCSI Support

Ethernet Support

CD-ROM Support

Find the image that best matches your system.

If you are already running Linux, use the mkfloppies.pl script in the *images* directory to do this automatically. It will also save important system information for later use.

After creating the three floppies, insert the boot floppy and reboot your computer. Follow the online instructions to install your Red Hat system.

Red Hat Documentation

The Red Hat distribution provides documentation in several forms, such as ASCII text, HTML, and postscript. You can find the various manuals in the `/doc` directory. Many of the documents are accessible from any web browser by simply loading the document into the browser with the *file* `url` type.

◀◀ See "Using URLs," p. 663

If you did not receive documentation with this product, you can order the manual from the Red Hat Software. Red Hat Software can be reached at:

phone: (203) 454-5500
(800) 454-5502
fax: (203) 454-2582
email: info@redhat.com
FTP: ftp://ftp.redhat.com
WWW: http://www.redhat.com

Red Hat Software
Suite 113
3201 Yorktown Road
Durham, NC 27713

The Red Hat Commercial Linux Installation HOWTO provides an in-depth coverage of how to install Red Hat. You can find this file at /doc/redhat-h.

Using *Special Edition Using Linux*, Second Edition with RedHat

You must rely on the RedHat documentation to install this distribution since most of the installation chapters in this book are based on the Slackware Distribution. However, once you have RedHat installed, the rest of the book will be very useful to you in learning how to use Linux. The following table illustrates which chapters are useful for **S**lackware, **R**edHat, **L**inux, and **U**NIX.

Chapter	Title	Useful with:
1	Understanding Linux	S,L
2	Overview of Features	S,L
3	Understanding the Linux Distributions	S,L
4	Installing Linux	S,L
5	Running Linux Applications	S,R,L
6	The X Windows System	S,R,L
7	Understanding System Administration	S,R,L,U
8	Booting and Shutting Down	S,R,L
9	Managing User Accounts,	S,R,L,U
10	Backing Up Data	S,R,L,U
11	Improving System Security	S,R,L,U
12	Upgrading and Installing Software	S,L
13	Understanding the TCP/IP Protocol Suite	S,R,L,U
14	Configuring a TCP/IP Network	S,R,L,U
15	Configuring Domain Name Service	S,R,L,U
16	Using SLIP and PPP	S,R,L
17	Managing File Systems	S,R,L,U
18	Understanding the File and Directory System	S,R,L,U
19	Managing Files and Directories	S,R,L,U
20	Understanding Linux Shells	S,R,L,U
21	Managing Multiple Processes	S,R,L,U
22	Using the `vi` Editor	S,R,L,U
23	Using the `emacs` Editor	S,R,L,U
24	Printing	S,R,L
25	Command-Line Reference	S,R,L,U
26	Using X Windows	S,R,L
27	Understanding the Internet	S,R,L,U
28	Accessing the Network with `telnet`, `ftp`, and the `r-` Commands	S,R,L,U
29	Surfing the Internet	S,R,L,U
30	Using Electronic Mail	S,R,L,U
31	Surviving USENET News	S,R,L,U
32	Using the World Wide Web	S,R,L,U
33	Creating Web Documents with HTML	S,R,L,U

Index

Symbols

A

B

E

F

G

J

K

L

N

O

P

Q

R

S

T

U

V

W

X

Y

Z

GET CONNECTED
to the ultimate source of computer information!

The MCP Forum on CompuServe

Go online with the world's leading computer book publisher! Macmillan Computer Publishing offers everything you need for computer success!

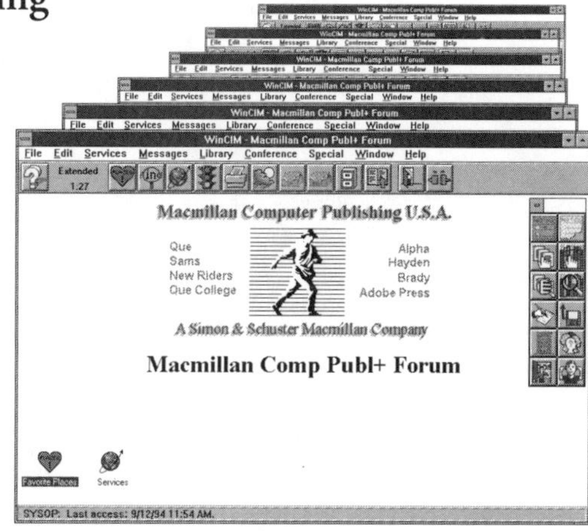

Find the books that are right for you!

A complete online catalog, plus sample chapters and tables of contents give you an in-depth look at all our books. The best way to shop or browse!

- Get fast answers and technical support for MCP books and software
- Join discussion groups on major computer subjects
- Interact with our expert authors via e-mail and conferences
- Download software from our immense library:
  - Source code from books
  - Demos of hot software
  - The best shareware and freeware
  - Graphics files

Join now and get a free CompuServe Starter Kit!

To receive your free CompuServe Introductory Membership, call **1-800-848-8199** and ask for representative #597.

The Starter Kit includes:

- Personal ID number and password
- $15 credit on the system
- Subscription to *CompuServe Magazine*

Once on the CompuServe System, type:

GO MACMILLAN

for the most computer information anywhere!

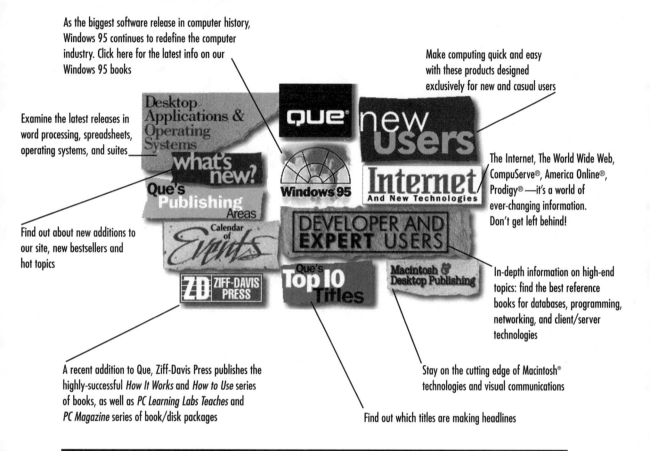

Complete and Return this Card for a *FREE* Computer Book Catalog

Thank you for purchasing this book! You have purchased a superior computer book written expressly for your needs. To continue to provide the kind of up-to-date, pertinent coverage you've come to expect from us, we need to hear from you. Please take a minute to complete and return this self-addressed, postage-paid form. In return, we'll send you a free catalog of all our computer books on topics ranging from word processing to programming and the internet.

‑r. ☐ Mrs. ☐ Ms. ☐ Dr. ☐

‑ame (first) ☐☐☐☐☐☐☐☐☐☐☐ (M.I.) ☐ (last) ☐☐☐☐☐☐☐☐☐☐☐☐☐☐☐

‑ddress ☐☐☐☐☐☐☐☐☐☐☐☐☐☐☐☐☐☐☐☐☐☐☐☐☐☐☐☐☐☐☐☐☐☐☐

☐☐☐☐☐☐☐☐☐☐☐☐☐☐☐☐☐☐☐☐☐☐☐☐☐☐☐☐☐☐☐☐☐☐☐

‑ity ☐☐☐☐☐☐☐☐☐☐☐☐☐☐☐ State ☐☐ Zip ☐☐☐☐☐ ☐☐☐☐

‑hone ☐☐☐ ☐☐☐ ☐☐☐☐ Fax ☐☐☐ ☐☐☐ ☐☐☐☐

‑ompany Name ☐☐☐☐☐☐☐☐☐☐☐☐☐☐☐☐☐☐☐☐☐☐☐☐☐☐☐☐☐☐☐☐☐

‑-mail address ☐☐☐☐☐☐☐☐☐☐☐☐☐☐☐☐☐☐☐☐☐☐☐☐☐☐☐☐☐☐☐☐☐

. Please check at least (3) influencing factors for purchasing this book.

- ‑ront or back cover information on book ☐
- ‑pecial approach to the content ☐
- ‑ompleteness of content ☐
- ‑uthor's reputation ☐
- ‑ublisher's reputation ☐
- ‑ook cover design or layout ☐
- ‑ndex or table of contents of book ☐
- ‑rice of book ☐
- ‑pecial effects, graphics, illustrations ☐
- ‑ther (Please specify): ______________ ☐

. How did you first learn about this book?

- ‑aw in Macmillan Computer Publishing catalog ☐
- ‑ecommended by store personnel ☐
- ‑aw the book on bookshelf at store ☐
- ‑ecommended by a friend ☐
- ‑eceived advertisement in the mail ☐
- ‑aw an advertisement in: ______________ ☐
- ‑ead book review in: ______________ ☐
- ‑ther (Please specify): ______________ ☐

. How many computer books have you purchased in the last six months?

- ‑his book only ☐
- ‑ books ☐
- 3 to 5 books ☐
- More than 5 ☐

4. Where did you purchase this book?

- Bookstore ☐
- Computer Store ☐
- Consumer Electronics Store ☐
- Department Store ☐
- Office Club ☐
- Warehouse Club ☐
- Mail Order ☐
- Direct from Publisher ☐
- Internet site ☐
- Other (Please specify): ______________ ☐

5. How long have you been using a computer?

- ☐ Less than 6 months
- ☐ 6 months to a year
- ☐ 1 to 3 years
- ☐ More than 3 years

6. What is your level of experience with personal computers and with the subject of this book?

	With PCs	With subject of book
New	☐	☐
Casual	☐	☐
Accomplished	☐	☐
Expert	☐	☐

Source Code ISBN: 1-7897-0742-X

7. Which of the following best describes your job title?

- Administrative Assistant ☐
- Coordinator ☐
- Manager/Supervisor ☐
- Director ☐
- Vice President ☐
- President/CEO/COO ☐
- Lawyer/Doctor/Medical Professional ☐
- Teacher/Educator/Trainer ☐
- Engineer/Technician ☐
- Consultant ☐
- Not employed/Student/Retired ☐
- Other (Please specify): ____________ ☐

8. Which of the following best describes the area of the company your job title falls under?

- Accounting ☐
- Engineering ☐
- Manufacturing ☐
- Operations ☐
- Marketing ☐
- Sales ☐
- Other (Please specify): ____________ ☐

9. What is your age?

- Under 20 ☐
- 21-29 ☐
- 30-39 ☐
- 40-49 ☐
- 50-59 ☐
- 60-over ☐

10. Are you:

- Male ☐
- Female ☐

11. Which computer publications do you read regularly? (Please list)

____

Comments: ____________

Fold here and scotch-tape to mail.

NO POSTAGE NECESSARY IF MAILED IN THE UNITED STATES

BUSINESS REPLY MAIL

FIRST-CLASS MAIL PERMIT NO. 9918 INDIANAPOLIS IN

POSTAGE WILL BE PAID BY THE ADDRESSEE

ATTN MARKETING
MACMILLAN COMPUTER PUBLISHING
MACMILLAN PUBLISHING USA
201 W 103RD ST
INDIANAPOLIS IN 46290-9042

InfoMagic
11950 N. Highway 89, Flagstaff AZ 86004

ORDER FORM

1-800-800-6613
Tel: +1-520-526-9565
Fax: +1-520-526-9573
E-Mail: info@infomagic.com
Web: www.infomagic.com

FIRST NAME:	LAST NAME:
ADDRESS	
CITY	STATE
ZIP	COUNTRY
TEL, FAX or E-MAIL:	

CD-ROMS & BOOKS available direct from InfoMagic, Inc.:	PRICE	QTY	AMOUNT
LINUX Developers Resource 5 CD Set - Slackware, RedHat, sources, demos & more! ******QUE SPECIAL OFFER!******	$ 15.00		
LINUX CD-ROM Subscription (includes 6 releases) US/CAN/MEX	$ 150.00		
LINUX CD-ROM Subscription (includes 6 releases) INTERNATIONAL	$ 175.00		
LINUX Installation & Getting Started Guide 250 pg manual by Matt Welsh	$ 12.50		
LINUX Network Administrators Guide 350 pg manual by Olaf Kirch	$ 18.50		
LINUX TOOLBOX - 5 CD Set, 250 pg Install Guide, Internet Guide, more! *see shipping fees below	$ 45.00		
LINUX T-Shirt (circle size) M L XL XXL	$ 15.00		
LINUX Journal Subscription - USA the only monthly magazine for Linux 12 issues!	$ 22.00		
LINUX Journal Subscription - CANADA 12 issues!	$ 27.00		
LINUX Journal Subscription - OVERSEAS 12 issues!	$ 32.00		
MOO-TIFF 2 CD Set for LINUX *100% OSF Motif Compatible* Graphical User Interface for PC's running LINUX	$ 99.00		
BSDISC (NetBSD 1.1 & FreeBSD 2.1) Complete unix-like OS with sources & install scripts	$ 35.00		
MOO-TIFF CD-ROM for FREEBSD 100%OSF Motif Compatible Graphical User Interface for PC's running FREEBSD	$ 99.00		
CICA Windows 4 CD Set - hundreds of Windows programs & shareware ready to "Plug & Play!"	$ 30.00		
GAMES for DAZE 2 CD Set - over 800 games ready to Plug & Play! X2FTP archive	$ 30.00		
HOBBES OS/2 4 CD Set - hundreds of programs & IBM shareware to "Plug & Play"	$ 35.00		
INTERNET TOOLS CD-ROM - networking tools & utilities for Unix & DOS	$ 30.00		
MOTHER OF PERL 2 CD Set - a powerfull utility language for Unix, Windows NT, OS/2, DOS, more!	$ 35.00		
SOURCE CODE CD-ROM - 4.4 BSD Lite2, MACH, JPEG, GNU, Interviews, GIF Sources and more!	$ 30.00		
STANDARDS 2 CD Set - International & Domestic Telecommunications & Data Standards, RFC's, ITU/CCIT docs	$ 30.00		
TCL/TK CD-ROM - general purpose scripting language & toolkit for rapid X-Windows development	$ 35.00		
TeX 2 CD Set - powerful tools for creating professional-quality typesetting, fonts & more!	$ 35.00		
WORLD WIDE CATALOG CD-ROM - See the best of the WEB without being on-line! Most popular sites included!	$ 35.00		
X-FILES CD-ROM - from the X-Consortium! Includes complete source distribution for X11R6 and XFree86	$ 35.00		

SHIPPING: **$5.00 - USA/CAN/MEX** **$10 - OVERSEAS**
(Ship rates are per order up to 5 items)

NOTE: International orders with books or more than 5 items will be charged more for shipping depending on weight of shipment and country of destination

*Linux Toolbox : $5 per copy US/CAN/MEX $20 per copy OVERSEAS
*Linux CD-ROM Subscriptions & Journal Subscription prices include all shipping

Sub-Total	
5.5% Sales Tax (Arizona Residents ONLY)	
Shipping	
TOTAL	

PAYMENT:

☐ MC/VISA ☐ AMEX ☐ **Check or Money Order Enclosed**
Int'l checks MUST be in U.S. funds and drawn on a U.S. Bank

Acct No. ______________________ Exp:

Name of Cardholder ______________________

Signature

First Class
STAMP
HERE

InfoMagic

11950 N. Highway 89
Flagstaff AZ 86004